INTRODUCTION TO
MODERN BUSINESS

INTRODUCTION TO
MODERN

NINTH EDITION

Prentice-Hall, Inc., Englewood Cliffs, New Jersey 07632

BUSINESS

VERNON A. MUSSELMAN
Professor, Business Education, University of Kentucky and Investment Counsellor

JOHN H. JACKSON
Professor, College of Commerce and Industry, University of Wyoming

Library of Congress Cataloging in Publication Data

Musselman, Vernon A.
  Introduction to modern business.

  Bibliography: p.
  Includes index.
  1. Business. 2. Industrial management. I. Jackson,
John Harold. II. Title.
HF5351.M86 1984   658.4   83-13682
ISBN 0-13-488312-8

Editorial/production supervision: Sonia Meyer
Interior and cover design: Jayne Conte
Cover photographs: Greg Pease/Baltimore, Maryland
Page layout: Meryl Poweski
Photo researcher: Christine A. Pullo
Manufacturing buyer: Ed O'Dougherty

9th Edition
Introduction to Modern Business
Vernon A. Musselman ■ John H. Jackson

Printed in the United States of America

10 9 8 7 6 5 4 3 2

ISBN 0-13-488312-8

Prentice-Hall International, Inc., *London*
Prentice-Hall of Australia Pty. Limited, *Sydney*
Editora Prentice-Hall do Brasil, Ltda., *Rio de Janeiro*
Prentice-Hall Canada Inc., *Toronto*
Prentice-Hall of India Private Limited, *New Delhi*
Prentice-Hall of Japan, Inc., *Tokyo*
Prentice-Hall of Southeast Asia Pte. Ltd., *Singapore*
Whitehall Books Limited, *Wellington, New Zealand*

To Eugene H. Hughes
who served so faithfully and unselfishly
as coauthor of the first eight editions

CONTENTS

Preface xv

PART ONE

BUSINESS AND ITS ENVIRONMENT

PART THREE

PEOPLE AND PRODUCTION

PART four

MARKETING

PART five

FINANCE AND RISK MANAGEMENT

PART SIX

INFORMATION MANAGEMENT AND DECISION MAKING

PART SEVEN

GOVERNMENT AND WORLD BUSINESS

Preface

The term *business* refers to a system that involves many groups and organizations. Consumers, employers, workers, institutions, and governments are all involved. It is the interrelationship of these various actors that makes the study of *business* so dynamic. Careful consideration of the rules, procedures, opportunities, and the parties involved in business has characterized eight previous editions of *Introduction to Modern Business*.

Today more than ever before, the changes taking place in the world around us must be considered in the study of business. This ninth edition retains the popular features of previous editions; it reflects a wide range of features of what we call business.

SPECIAL FEATURES   Special features of this book include the following:

Study Objectives.   Study objectives begin each chapter. They are written so that students may know what to expect in the discussion that follows.

In the News.   Each chapter opens with a report of some recent happening from the current business scene. These are items of special interest related to the chapter content.

Biographies.   A brief biographical sketch of a successful businessperson is included in each chapter. These sketches are designed to link the concepts in the text to the real world of people in which we live and work.

Current Issues.   Throughout this edition, the authors relate the chapter material to our current business environment. In this environment there are many issues on which students and instructors may not agree. "Current

Issues" presents the pros and cons of some contemporary issues to challenge and stimulate the reader.

Chapter Questions.   Two types of questions follow each chapter: review questions and discussion questions. The review questions are closely tied to the study objectives at the opening of the chapter. They are specifically answered in the text material. The discussion questions are more analytical and are intended to take the reader beyond the memorization level of learning.

Business-Case Situations.   One of the most popular features of the previous editions was the business cases. In response to requests from users, this edition gives two case situations for each chapter.

A New Co-author.   John H. Jackson, University of Wyoming, has joined the author team. Jackson is the co-author with Morgan of *Organization Theory, 2nd ed.*, Prentice-Hall, 1982; Mathis and Jackson, *Personnel, 3rd ed.*, West Publishing Co., 1982; and Jackson & Keaveny, *Successful Supervision*, Prentice-Hall, 1980.

Glossary.   The glossary has been greatly enlarged to include both primary and secondary terms discussed.

Reading References.   Reading references are grouped by major divisions and appear in the back of the book rather than at the end of each chapter.

SUPPLEMENTS   *The Instructor's Assistant.*   A convenient box at your disposal containing all the supplements to the ninth edition of *Introduction to Modern Business*: Student Learning Guide and Applied Readings: Instructor's Resource Manual; Test Item File; Computerized Testing Service brochure; Transparency Masters. There's additional space in the box for the 60 color transparencies, which are free upon adoption. The Instructor's Assistant is ready to work for you!

Student Learning Guide.   This student aid has been enlarged over the ones in previous editions. Its popular features have all been retained, and an outline of the chapter has been added. This *Learning Guide* includes:

> Chapter Outline
> Principal Ideas in the Chapter
> Answers to Business Terms
> Self-Test Items
> Applied Readings

The section "Self-Test" includes different types of items: true-false, completion, multiple choice, and yes-no items. The answers to the Self-Test exercises are included in the back of the *Learning Guide*.

Instructor's Resource Manual.   The Instructor's Resource Manual has been enlarged and improved. Features retained from the previous editions include chapter outlines and answers to textbook questions and cases. New features include expanded annotated lecture outlines, 20 page film guide, and activities and problems.

Test Item File.   The Test Item File contains approximately 2000 objective questions and answers. Adopters of Musselman and Jackson can avail themselves of the Prentice-Hall **computerized testing service.** Our testing service offers two options to the instructor. One option supplies the adopter with either a spirit or a Xerox master of the instructor's selected questions. The second option is a computer tape data bank of the selected questions.

Transparency Masters.   This is a set of 120 black and white transparency masters, 46 of which are from the text and 74 from other sources.

Color Transparencies.   Free to all adopters is a set of 60 color transparencies, some of which are 4-color.

ACKNOWLEDGMENTS   To the many users of previous editions who submitted suggestions, the authors are grateful. We also express our appreciation to the numerous business firms and organizations that have permitted us to reproduce illustrations about their companies from their publications. Our thanks go to the members of our advisory board for their contributions:

Doris Coy
College of the Canyons
Valencia, California

David De Cenzo
University of Baltimore
Baltimore, Maryland

Z. S. Dickerson
James Madison University
Harrisonburg, Virginia

Robert J. Hehre
Northeastern University
Boston, Massachusetts

Gatton Jones
Sell, Inc.
Cincinnati, Ohio

James E. McConnell
State University of New York
Buffalo, New York

John J. Marsh
Northern New Mexico Community College
Santa Cruz, New Mexico

Catherine A. Melton
Collegiate School
Richmond, Virginia

Donald Musselman
James Madison University
Harrisonburg, Virginia

Sarah Pyles
Ashland Community College
Ashland, Kentucky

Ronald Spahr
The University of Wyoming
Laramie, Wyoming

D. L. Stevenson
Pensacola Junior College
Pensacola, Florida

Philip M. Van Auken
Baylor University
Waco, Texas

Special thanks are in order to George Stilphen and Joan Downham for their assistance.

Our deep appreciation goes also to the cooperative staff of Prentice-Hall, Inc., including Jayne Maerker, for her guidance and direction, and her able assistant, Linda Albelli; to Sonia Meyer, production editor; Jayne Conte, designer; Gert Glassen, coordinator for the supplementary aids that accompany the book; and Rita DeVries, copy editor.

Vernon A. Musselman

John H. Jackson

INTRODUCTION TO
MODERN BUSINESS

BUSINESS AND ITS ENVIRONMENT

PART 1

This prologue introduces a true-to-life story of a business situation. It is continued with a brief case at the beginning of each Part of the book. Together, these short cases trace the business experience of two brothers, from college graduation through their later years in business. The purpose of this ongoing case is to show how the material covered in each Part has relevance to typical successful businesspersons.

Roger and Calvin King were graduated from one of our reputable midwestern universities. Roger majored in production management, with a minor in human-resources management. Calvin majored in accounting, with minors in finance and insurance. Both studied computer science and management information systems.

Roger began his business career with a position as a management trainee. Calvin started as an accountant with a public accounting firm. In four years, Roger had become plant foreman in his company's factory. Calvin worked as an auditor and after five years became a junior partner in his accounting firm.

Eight years after entering the business world, the King brothers decided to organize their own business. They opened a factory to manufacture casual and work clothes. They each invested cash, and they divided responsibilities for running the business. They talked to their friends, some of whom invested money in the business. Roger and Calvin signed notes for this debt and agreed to pay interest on these notes.

The Kings began on a small scale, but their business prospered and grew. As it grew, management problems increased in both number and scope. They enlarged their staff of workers and changed their organization's design. Eventually they became engaged in business overseas.

At the beginning of each Part of the book, specific details of the business will be described. Then, as you read the chapters in that Part, you will see how the principles explained apply in this actual business situation. This prologue also serves to relate each of these discussions to those in the other sections.

The American Business System

study objectives

WHEN YOU HAVE FINISHED READING THIS CHAPTER, YOU SHOULD BE ABLE TO:

1. Explain how our business system works

2. Define the term *economics* and explain why we must have an economic system

3. Discuss the essential components of our private-enterprise economy

4. State some important national goals and show how they conflict with one another

5. Identify the factors of production as they relate to goods and services

1

The best thinking comes out of a free system, where good ideas are rewarded and bad ones are penalized.

G. William Miller,
Chairman, Textron, Inc.

T he business system that exists in the United States today is both dynamic and interesting. The variety of ways that people can exchange goods and services (and make money in the process) is amazing. Such innovation is channeled by laws and customs, and by basic business relationships. The latter is our focus in this chapter.

Some believe that business in the United States moved into a new phase in the 1980s. The steady rise in the standard of living of the 1950s and 1960s changed during the decade of the 1970s. People had to scramble to maintain their living standard against rising inflation. The American people seem to be changing their ideas about the future. As a result, future consumer buying patterns will probably be less predictable than in the past.

To understand how business relates to our economic system, we could begin with inflation, productivity, the way markets work—all current topics. But we need to have a perspective on our subject before going too deeply into complex issues. Let us consider first some basic relationships between business and economics. Then we look at how a private-enterprise economy like ours operates, the economic goals of the United States, and the factors of production. We then turn to the way markets work and what determines business climate.

BUSINESS AND ECONOMICS

We are all involved in business. In the United States, the basic necessities, such as food, shelter, and clothing, are delivered by our business system. Underlying this system is a basic mechanism that determines how products and services of all kinds will be delivered. It is called *economics*.

FIGURE 1-1
We are all involved in business whether we want to be or not. (Photo, Dennis Hallinan, FPG.)

Economics affects all of us, whether we understand it or not. ECO-NOMICS is *a science that deals with the satisfaction of human wants through scarce resources.* Since all resources are limited, there are never enough to give people all they want. The economic system of a country must deal with the problem of allocating these scarce resources among the competing parties who want them, and deciding among the variety of products that might be produced.

FIGURE 1-2
Resources vs. Wants

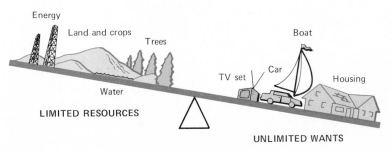

Energy
Land and crops
Trees
Water
LIMITED RESOURCES

Boat
TV set
Car
Housing
UNLIMITED WANTS

The American Business System

5

ECONOMIC SYSTEMS A particular "economic system" results from the way in which people organize natural resources, labor, and management skills to produce and distribute the things they want. In many ways, an economic system makes conflicting demands upon us. It may dictate certain behaviors, such as getting a job to provide income. It may then change the demand for the jobs certain people are trained to perform. Engineers are a good example: Ten years ago, there was little demand for engineers; recently, there has been a strong demand. At some point in the future, we can be sure the demand for engineers will decline again. People must look out for their own interests, yet they may have to join others to make an economic system work.

MOVING NORTH WAS CHEAPER

Economics is a very interesting science. For example: Why did it cost more in 1981 to rent a truck *from* Detroit *to* Houston than *from* Houston *to* Detroit? The distance is obviously the same.

Rental truck and trailer rates vary with supply. In 1981, many people were leaving depressed Michigan looking for work in Texas. And many of them rented trucks or trailers for the trip south. According to U-Haul, a 24-foot truck cost $1,765 going south but only $299 going north. As people discovered that Texas was not awash in jobs either, the rates began to return to a more normal pattern.

CAPITALISM Our Western business system is based on capitalism. It represents a rather drastic change in the way mankind has grappled with economic problems. Even today, most people in the world have little contact with capitalism or private enterprise. Such a system leaves business activities to people who can respond freely to the marketplace. This includes both opportunities and disappointments. So the capitalistic system can be the cause of personal unrest, insecurity, and failure. It can also be the source of progress, innovation, and success. There are costs as well as benefits associated with *any* economic system. Private enterprise is built around the idea of private property. By PRIVATE ENTERPRISE, we mean *the system under which people are free to supply their own capital and operate their own businesses.* Thus, in a private-enterprise economy, individuals own the means of production, including the capital. Such a condition is necessary for capitalism to succeed.

ECONOMICS AND HUMAN BEINGS Human beings are for the most part acquisitive — they like to acquire things. Possessions — or the money to buy them — are important to most people. In fact, it is commonly assumed that people try to gain as much pleasure, wealth, and satisfaction from their business activities as they can. This is called **maximizing** their **utility.**

Economics assumes other things about human beings. These assumptions help us understand a bit about business behavior in a private-enterprise economy. For example, humans are creatures with **unlimited wants.** This suggests that no matter how much people have, they always want a little bit more. Studies confirm this when they show that, regardless of current income, both men and women want about 10 percent more income than they now have. However, we should make it clear that "more" could include things other than money. More leisure, more time for family, or more *something* helps drive and motivate human behavior.

Finally, humans are viewed as **rational.** This means that people choose from among several things those that will bring them the most satisfaction or utility. As rational beings, people choose the ways to do things that give them the most good for the **least cost or effort.**

Economists study ways people get and use their resources because they believe that such knowledge is critical for understanding business behavior. This does not mean that these are the *only* motives that drive business. They are simply the most important. In our system, people are relatively free to do as they wish with their efforts and money. So to understand business, we should study the major motives that govern what people do with those efforts and money.

ADAM SMITH, THE FOUNDER OF FORMAL ECONOMIC STUDY

Although the subject of economics is almost as old as recorded history, formal recognition of economics as a study began in 1776 when Adam Smith published a book called *The Nature and Causes of the Wealth of Nations*. Within six months, the supply of these books was exhausted. At that time, Smith was known as the father of economics, and his *Wealth of Nations,* as it was later called, became the basis of early economic theory.

According to Adam Smith, the best way to run an economy was by relying on the free operation of the "unseen hand" of competition. Competition would ensure that firms offered the best values to consumers, or else consumers would do business with the competitor. This philosophy of economics—the operation of competitive markets—became the basis upon which the economies of the United States and other Western democracies were established.

Adam Smith argued that government control of production was unnecessary. Businesspeople should be permitted to produce the things that would earn them a profit. Smith strongly advocated the principle of *laissez faire* ("to let alone"), which he also applied to foreign trade by recommending free trade. This meant he was opposed to the mercantilists, a school of economic thought that sought to maintain regulation of excess exports over imports.

To a remarkable degree, the policy of free pursuit of self-interest, used as part of other capitalist theories, has had the results Adam Smith predicted. If Adam Smith were alive today, he would probably observe that many of our current economic problems are the same as when he lived. But today, some of the answers have changed.

MAKING ECONOMIC CHOICES

Making a choice requires selecting among alternatives. To make a choice, a business or an individual must have more than a single opportunity from which to choose. Making the best choice means selecting the best alternative for you. The best choice might be different for different people as they try to maximize their utility. **In the making of such choices, economics suggests that for a given degree of satisfaction, people will choose the cheapest alternative.** Or, if costs are the same, people will choose the greatest utility.

To illustrate: A rational businessperson, when selecting among several pieces of equipment of equal cost, will choose the one that affords the greatest

efficiency of operation or the largest output. A government, when selecting among aircraft of comparable performance and capability, will probably choose the cheapest.

During the last recession, the management of Ashland Oil, like those of other companies, had some difficult choices to make. With sales down and costs up, Ashland had to lower its breakeven point to survive. The choice was between adopting more efficient methods and cutting costs by cutting capacity. The decision was a combination of both choices, and in two years, Ashland reduced its breakeven point by 25 percent. The penalty for making a bad decision might have been quite severe, but in this case, the choice was a good one.

THE PRIVATE-ENTERPRISE SYSTEM

There are two basics in a private-enterprise economic system: private ownership of productive resources, and the freedom to make choices. Because the resources to start a business are privately owned, this system is sometimes called **capitalism.** Because citizens can make economic choices on their own as to what they will do, it is also called a **free-enterprise** system. In reality, the American system is a pure form of neither. Productive resources *are* largely privately owned. But the role of government as a regulator is very strong as well. Further, individuals and businesses are not *completely* free to make any possible choice. Therefore, the term **private enterprise** seems to be more appropriate than either **capitalism** or **free enterprise.**

As we have seen, resources needed for production are limited, but people's wants are unlimited. Finding and allocating scarce resources to fulfill people's needs will always be a problem in any country. Deciding how to use the available resources requires answers to some basic questions in any economic system:

? What goods are to be produced?
Who determines what goods are to be produced?

? How are these goods to be produced?
How do we organize our resources to produce them?

? Who will receive the benefits of producing goods and services?
How will these benefits be distributed?

The manner in which these questions are answered includes the relative roles of private and government leadership. As they are answered and implemented, a nation's economic goals become established, and a method of achieving those goals is developed.

In some countries, changes take place over time in the arrangements made to answer the questions above. Hungary and the United States provide two examples:

THE GOVERNMENT SHALL BECOME CAPITALIST AND THE CAPITALIST SHALL BE GOVERNED . . .

In Communist Hungary, two examples of a decidedly capitalistic approach to things have been noted recently. The demand for American jeans has led the government to install a Levi's plant. It is Levi Strauss and Company's first plant behind the Iron Curtain. Hungarian workers for the plant were initially trained in the United States. The Hungarian jeans are basically the same as the American variety and sell at roughly twice the price of those in the United States.

Furthermore, the increasing demand for goods and services in Hungary has led to the establishment of privately owned shops and businesses. A black-market economy based upon private transactions has developed. This second economy takes care of such things as repairing cars, television sets, and homes. It is estimated that two out of three Hungarian workers supplement their income by such private employment. And by caring so well for material needs, Hungary's rulers have quieted political discontent.

In the United States, about 41 percent of all families currently receive some government cash payment, such as Social Security, welfare, or veterans' benefits. These payments are financed by taxing the incomes of individuals and the profits of companies. They are a form of income redistribution in which income is taken from one group and given to another. All of this is done with the approval of the elected representatives of the general public.

SETTING INDIVIDUAL AND COLLECTIVE GOALS

Individual Goals. In the United States, most people are relatively free to run their own economic affairs. To begin with, Americans can choose the type of work they want to do. This assumes, of course, their willingness and ability to prepare and qualify for such work. They may choose to go into business for themselves or to work for someone else. They are free to spend or to save their earnings, according to their own desires. Yet in all of this, each individual is a part of the whole that is society, and people's goals must somehow mesh together. Society's goals reflect this collection of individual goals to an extent.

Society also provides *constraints* on a person's behavior. So do competition, available resources, and other economic realities. Individual goals, then, drive business behavior, but such behavior cannot be entirely free because of society's constraints.

In the United States, consumers exert their influence upon the system by voting in the marketplace with their dollars. So individual goals *do* influence collective goals. It takes an especially flexible system to accommodate both. In the market-oriented private-enterprise system, a business that ignores individual wants does so at its own peril.

Collective Goals. In addition to individual needs, people have a group of collective wants. Examples are education, highways, national defense, and a variety of social benefits. In the United States, we try to maintain high wages and stable prices, provide a high return on investments, and conserve natural resources. At the same time, we try to increase production, protect business from unfair practices, and nurture cooperation between management and labor.

Just as an individual's goals give direction to his or her planning and effort, society's choice of goals gives direction to the national economy. Because society is made up of many individuals, its goals are not completely consistent with one another. Indeed, they may often be in direct conflict. For example, an attempt to maintain stable prices may run contrary to the desire for higher wages and dividends. The desire for increased consumption may conflict with the idea of conserving natural resources. New industry in the local community would provide more jobs for local workers, but it might worsen the quality of the environment by polluting the air or water. Increased technological development may cause, at least temporarily, increased unemployment. And free trade among the industrial nations conflicts with the desire for protection through import duties.

Although we cannot completely reconcile these conflicting national goals, we can agree that **the economic objective of the American people is the desire for a comfortable living standard—subject to conditions that provide for freedom of choice.** All this is also conditional upon maintaining an environment that enables us to live a good life.

ECONOMIC GOALS IN THE UNITED STATES

To understand the American economy, we must consider a number of economic goals that are based on values—values that are widely accepted in this country. These goals can be summarized as follows:

1. *Promote economic growth.* Increase the amount of goods and services available to Americans and at the same time maintain an economy that allows for the distribution of a high level of national income. Promote a high level of stability for prices.
2. *Promote a rising standard of living.* As an increased quantity of goods is produced, a family can live better than before without sacrificing savings.
3. *Maintain full employment.* Useful jobs should be available for all who are willing and able to work.
4. *Encourage price stability.* Stable prices are needed to minimize upswings and downswings in the business cycle and to prevent inflation and deflation in the value of the dollar.
5. *Provide an equitable distribution of income.* This is to be accomplished by maintaining full employment, increasing the productivity of workers, and removing job discrimination.
6. *Ensure economic freedom.* Americans should have the freedom to choose the work they prefer and the right to buy goods freely in the marketplace.
7. *Provide financial security.* People who are disabled, aged, dependent, or otherwise handicapped and unable to care for themselves should be eligible for some type of economic assistance and employment training to qualify for work opportunities.

Some of these goals are interrelated. For example, full employment helps to maintain a high standard of living and give workers financial security. Where goals are in conflict, a system of priorities must be developed. Often, a goal that helps one group is detrimental to others.

THE FACTORS OF PRODUCTION

A major goal of our business system is to produce the goods and services that will satisfy human wants. Some people believe that production simply means turning out radios, cars, clothes, furniture, and other products. This belief is true as far as it goes. But PRODUCTION defined in a broader sense *is the process of transferring inputs from human and physical resources into outputs wanted by consumers.* These outputs may be either goods or services. Production involves four essential elements, which are called the **factors of production:**

1. Natural resources   3. Capital
2. Labor   4. Entrepreneurship

Figure 1-4 suggests that an interlocking relationship exists among these elements. This becomes more obvious when you think about each of the elements.

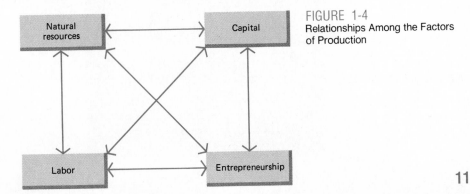

FIGURE 1-4
Relationships Among the Factors of Production

11

NATURAL RESOURCES   Land is one resource that is essential to production. Its most important characteristic is that it is a **fixed resource.** It serves as a location for equipment and buildings. It is also capable of producing crops of all kinds and the minerals used in production. From an economic standpoint, the reward for the use of land is rent, a money return to the owner derived from putting it to profitable use. Such public issues as land zoning and land-use planning are being raised and challenged in the courts to determine who is responsible for issues surrounding the use of land.

On and under the land surface lie our known supplies of timber and minerals. Much has been said about the limited supply of petroleum and natural gas. But all other mineral resources are also in limited supply. Although we have an abundance of coal and an adequate supply of iron ore, we are dependent on imports for many essential minerals. We cannot replace the deposits of mineral resources, and we are consuming them at a rapid pace. Annual consumption of industrial raw materials (fuels, metals, minerals, and building materials) is eighteen tons per capita. The mineral deposits lying on the ocean beds have not yet been explored, and they represent our next area of development.

The rich U.S. land area, together with the mild climate, provides one of our most valuable natural resources. It is the principal source of materials that can be replaced—grains, animals, forests, and fibers.

Historically, there has been plenty of clean, pure water and fresh air. But with worldwide industry developing at the present rate, we are polluting the air, lakes, and rivers at an alarming rate. Ecologists and conservationists have called attention to this situation. And both national and state governments have become concerned. Manufacturing industries are spending billions of dollars annually to protect air and water resources.

FIGURE 1-5
Natural resources: An oil rig. (Courtesy, Shell Oil Co.)

LABOR   **Labor is the second factor of production**—human effort directed toward the creation of goods and services. Unskilled labor is very available, but highly skilled labor is often scarce in areas where it is most needed. Even during times of high unemployment, there are shortages of certain types of skilled labor. Computer skills are currently a good example.

In the United States, we have an adequate supply of labor for both agriculture and manufacturing. There are two major trends in the makeup of our labor force: (1) The number of women entering the labor force has been steadily increasing in recent years, and (2) the percentage of people employed in the production of goods is decreasing while the percentage involved in services is increasing.

The reward for labor is wages. If labor costs (or any costs) force the selling price of the product up and the price becomes too high, the demand for that product will decline. Less demand for the finished product causes changes in the amount of labor employers need.

Wages and fringe benefits are both income to workers. Fringe benefits now constitute over 35 percent of the total cost of wages in the United States. The amount of wages a worker receives constitutes his or her **money income.** *The value of that wage in terms of its purchasing power* is called REAL INCOME. During periods of inflation, workers seek to preserve their real income. During periods of unemployment, they are concerned about the loss of jobs.

The largest single employment area in the United States is trade, about one-fourth of the total. The second largest employment segment is services. Manufacturing is third, employing one-fifth of the total. The percentage of employed workers in nine selected industries is shown in Table 1-1.

FIGURE 1-6
Automobile Production Line.
(Courtesy, General Motors.)

TABLE 1-1
Percentage of Employees in Nine Selected Industries, 1940–1990

INDUSTRY	1940	1950	1960	1970	1980	1990 (PROJECTION)
Manufacturing	25.2	27.5	27.2	25.8	21.6	20.2
Wholesale and retail trade	16.1	17.7	19.4	19.9	22.5	23.4
Government	9.8	11.0	14.1	16.7	15.9	13.9
Services	8.0	9.2	11.1	15.4	20.2	23.1
Agriculture	25.5	18.2	11.8	6.0	2.7	2.0
Transportation and public utilities	7.0	7.2	6.5	6.0	5.3	5.2
Construction	3.0	4.2	4.7	4.5	5.8	5.7
Finance	3.3	3.3	4.1	4.9	5.3	5.7
Mining	2.1	1.7	1.1	0.8	0.7	0.8

CAPITAL

Capital is another major factor of production. The use of the term **capital** is not restricted to money invested in a business enterprise. Business capital includes all the additions of value that require money to purchase or to build. *Machinery, equipment, and supplies used in the production of other goods and services* are called CAPITAL GOODS. A farmer's capital goods would consist of his tractors, cultivators, harvesters, trucks, and all other types of machinery and tools.

The purpose of capital goods is to assist labor in production and increase the amount of goods and services produced. Capital provides the tools and other means for labor to produce. Without capital to purchase machinery, farmers would still be producing by primitive means only enough to feed themselves. The result would be a hungry world. The United States feeds much of the rest of the world because of its capital-intensive farming methods.

THE ENTREPRENEUR

The history of early industrial development and trade in America is largely the history of U.S. entrepreneurs. It describes people with the pioneer spirit, initiative, and inspiration, and a willingness to work and take risks. An ENTREPRENEUR is the *chief initiator or organizer of a business enterprise.* In proprietorships and partnerships, the entrepreneurs take the **risk.** They are the ones who stand to gain or lose from the business operations. In corporations, it is the stockholders who are the risk takers.

Historically, management has been considered to be a right and responsibility of the entrepreneur. However, a distinction should be made between the **owner-manager,** or entrepreneur, and the **professional manager.** The professional manager has a somewhat different set of motives and responsibilities, since he or she is not the sole owner of the enterprise.

Management and labor are seldom in agreement as to the value of the contribution each makes to the success of the enterprise. Labor has been gaining more and more input in decision making in large unionized businesses. Management brings together, coordinates, and directs the various components of the production process. Managers are responsible for manufacturing operations and marketing. Chapters 4 and 5 discuss in detail the theory, principles, and practices of business organization and management.

FIGURE 1-7
Equipment is part of the farmer's capital.
(Courtesy, John Deere.)

CURRENT ISSUE

SHOULD WE MODIFY PRIVATE ENTERPRISE?

The United States is universally recognized as the capital of capitalism, the land of free markets and the home of resourceful entrepreneurs. More than any other country it is known for leaving an entrepreneur free to decide prices for his products and set wages for his workers, free to grow and prosper — and free to go bankrupt if he fails. But, as always, there are those who clamor for increased government participation in business.

With which of the following statements do you agree, and with which do you disagree?

1. The government should own and operate selected basic industries — coal, railroads, and airlines.
2. The government should control radio and television, but leave the newspapers in private hands.
3. The government should prescribe limits for rent and salary increases.
4. The government should regulate prices.
5. The government should stay out of business except to prevent monopolies and regulate utilities and other franchise operations.
6. We need no wholesale changes in our private enterprise free-market system.

If you were to suggest *one change* in the relationships between government and business, what would it be?

JACK NICKLAUS – ENTREPRENEUR

Jack Nicklaus won the Ohio State Junior Golf Championship for the first time at age 13, and the U.S. Amateur title at the age of 19. As a professional, he has won more major tournaments that any other golfer. He was PGA Player of the Year five times.

Nicklaus says, "Before you learn to win, you have to learn to lose." The qualities that made him a winner at golf have also made him a successful businessperson. His ability to concentrate is unusual, as is his willingness to take risks.

Nicklaus has thirty-two successful business ventures and plays an active management role in many of them. Companies in which he has ownership interest employ more than a thousand people. His business interests are concentrated in three areas — real estate, insurance, and oil and gas development. Golden Bear products sell around the world — more in Japan than in the United States. Naturally, golf-course design and landscaping are important parts of his business interests. He has designed almost fifty golf courses around the world.

Jack was born in Columbus, Ohio, in 1940. He is a graduate of Ohio State University. He married the former Barbara Bash in 1960, and they have five children.

HOW MARKETS WORK

We are used to thinking about the market system in which we participate as buyers. We are less familiar with the market as an **allocation mechanism.** By this we mean a way of deciding what and how much will be produced, and to whom it will be distributed.

THE MARKET AND PRODUCTION

The factors of production must somehow be organized so that the things people want can be made. Figure 1-8 shows how the market organizes production. The energy and skills of labor, land, and capital are made available to business for a price. Businesses provide entrepreneurship to convert these factors into products and services that are used and paid for by consumers. In addition to organizing production, the market acts as a distribution device.

THE MARKET AND DISTRIBUTION

With every purchase of a business product, money moves from the consumer. And with every purchase of the services of labor, capital, and land, money moves back to consumers. The form of such payments is this:

Labor — wages, salaries, fees
Capital — interest, profit
Land — rent

The relative payment each receives depends on the demand for that particular service. Scarcity of one or more of the factors *raises* the cost of that factor. Oversupply of one of the factors tends to *lower* the price. For example, when many people need capital, interest rates go up. When there is less demand for capital, interest rates trend down. When rental units are overbuilt in an area, rents go down. (Sometimes this is done through special promotions, such as a month's "free" rent.) When places to live are scarce, rents increase.

The market is a very simple allocation device. Decisions as to where resources will be used are based largely on one consideration: **price.** By

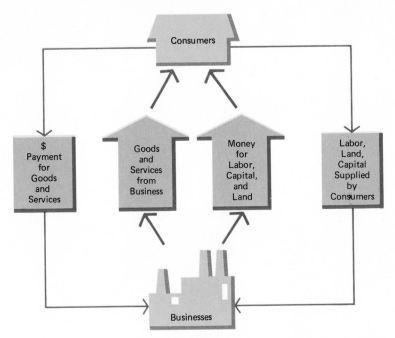

FIGURE 1-8
The Market and Production

watching prices, people can learn what course of action will maximize their income or minimize their expenses.

Gasohol illustrates how consumers operate in the marketplace. It came on strong at first; the supply couldn't meet the demand. It was highlighted in the national news. Then gradually it faded completely and nothing was heard of it. But in the early 1980s most gasoline stations had a special pump for gasohol—only this time it was sold as "super unleaded with ethanol."

THE DEMAND CURVE Why should willingness to buy be related to price? Because people want to maximize but they can use only so much of any commodity. After all, how many Big Macs can you eat? The tenth Big Mac is worth less to you than the first. The demand curve (showing how much a buyer will purchase as the price changes) summarizes this relationship rather well. Figure 1-9 shows a demand curve.

In looking at Figure 1-9, you can see that as the price decreases, we will purchase (or demand) greater amounts of an item. The quantity of a good or

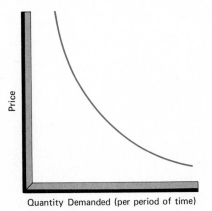

FIGURE 1-9
The Demand Curve

Price

Quantity Demanded (per period of time)

service we want to acquire depends on the price we must pay for an additional unit of it. If it were cheap enough and you were hungry enough, you might purchase a third Big Mac. But most of us would pay almost nothing for a fourth, because we simply can't eat it.

THE SUPPLY CURVE

Sellers are more willing to supply goods and services when they can get more money for them. For example, if you were offered $10 to cut a cord of firewood, would you do it?[1] How about for $80? Would you cut a cord of wood for $400? Obviously, as the price goes up, we become more interested in the project. For this reason, the supply curve (the amount a supplier will provide at a given price) rises as prices increase. Figure 1-10 shows the supply curve.

As prices rise, the number of sellers drawn into the market increases and the quantities of goods and services offered increase. Conversely, when prices fall, the decrease will permit one person after another to buy. This adds to the total number of goods purchased at that lower price. Clearly, these are opposing behaviors for buyers and sellers. Sellers want high prices, but buyers want lower prices. How does the market mechanism resolve this dilemma?

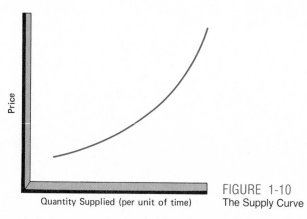

FIGURE 1-10
The Supply Curve

Quantity Supplied (per unit of time)

EQUILIBRIUM PRICES

The interplay of supply and demand results in an equilibrium price, one at which the quantity demanded equals the quantity supplied. This "interplay" works as follows: A supplier makes 30,000 pairs of shoes in response to what he thinks will be a $60 selling price. The shoes don't sell, so eventually, prices must be cut to move them. As the price is cut, more shoes sell, until at some point (let's say $30), all 30,000 pairs are sold.

The equilibrium price of $30 can be shown on a graph (Figure 1-11) that combines the supply and demand curves we have just seen. Note that where the demand and supply curves meet, we have a price where the amount supplied and the amount demanded are equal. That is the **equilibrium price.** At that point, the market is in balance.

Equilibrium prices have two important characteristics:

1. They will be set through the free interplay of supply and demand forces in a free and competitive market.
2. Once established, they will continue until a change in supply or demand occurs.

---

[1] A cord is a stack eight feet long, four feet high, and four feet wide.

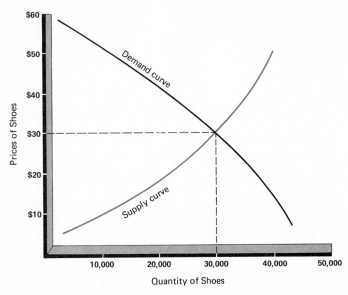

FIGURE 1-11
Equilibrium Price

MARKET FAILURES The market mechanism is a marvelous allocator of goods and resources! But it has some failings that a student of business should know well. Lack of information, "externalities," and market restrictions can be major failings. They must be dealt with if a market system is to function properly.

Lack of Information. Without adequate information on prices, products, and so on, the market does not function well. Which brand is best? Is this product safe? How long will this product last? Will this thing really work? These issues make a market system work *as long as* consumers have good information. A certain amount of ignorance always remains, but with a lot of wrong information, the market will not reach equilibrium prices.

Externalities. "Externalities" are the side effects of production on people other than those who buy or sell the goods. A good example is pollution. Pollution is the production of wastes, dirt, noise, and other things we don't want. We do not know how to produce goods without some waste by-products. But the nature of externalities is such that they *do not* pass through the economic system. A factory may produce harmful pollution without having to pay anyone for the "use" of the air. The market can be an efficient allocator of goods and resources *only* if the costs and benefits of those goods are included in the system. When some of the inputs are not privately owned but belong to everyone, the system does not handle them very well. Some other approach has to be taken in dealing with externalities.

Market Restrictions. The market system works efficiently only when it is free to do so. One major roadblock to efficiency is too little competition in the marketplace.

When only one or a very few firms supply goods, they can control the price charged. They can often control the entry into the industry by more firms as well. Such a situation is referred to as a **monopoly** (one supplier of goods) or **oligopoly** (only a few suppliers). The effect of monopoly and oligopoly is a higher price for consumers.

Such market restrictions reduce market freedom, since consumers cannot really "vote" in the marketplace for a competitor if there is none. For this reason, the United States has an "antitrust" policy designed to encourage competition. How well it works is the subject of some debate, however.

WHAT DO YOU DO WHEN PRICES FALL?

Inflation, the ever-upward spiral of prices, is familiar to us all. We have learned to cope somewhat, by purchasing things *now* before prices go up. We borrow money to buy because we can repay the loan with cheaper dollars later. But how in the world do you cope with *disinflation*? If prices are actually falling, what strategies are best? With inflation, it makes sense to have assets in *things* rather than dollars. With disinflation, the opposite is true. We are better off having assets in dollars or income-producing securities.

MARKET STRENGTHS   The market system has three major strengths. **First,** it encourages people to use a lot of energy and skill, and to take risks in pursuit of their goals. The result is a dynamic, innovative, business system.

Second, the system minimizes the need for the government to plan the economy. However, it is clear that a certain government presence may be required to deal with the market failures mentioned above.

Finally, the market system, when it is working properly, puts the responsibility for making decisions in the hands of consumers. This means that even though a product may be seen by some as silly or useless, if others really want it, it will be produced.

WHAT DETERMINES THE BUSINESS CLIMATE?

There is more to understanding the business system than understanding how markets work. We must look at the national trends and the things that affect the business climate through good times and bad.

Perhaps the most extreme example of the importance of such knowledge for American business is the Great Depression. The depression hit America in 1929 like a tornado, creating total havoc. One-fourth of the workforce lost their jobs, and over a million families lost their homes. Nine million savings accounts were lost when banks went broke. Uncounted businesses went bankrupt, with the owners' life savings and source of livelihood gone forever.

John Maynard Keynes provided us with a view of what was happening that had a profound effect on America's recovery from the depression. Keynes argued that the level of business activity in a capitalist system depended on the willingness of entrepreneurs to invest. He showed that a market system could reach a bad position from which it could not free itself. Keynes' message was that **government spending** might be a major ingredient in recovery.

TEXAS DENTISTS AND COMPETITION

The Federal Trade Commission recently took on the Texas Dental Association. More than 90 percent of the dentists in Texas belong to the association. The FTC got the dentists to agree to stop refusing to let insurers see X rays and other patient records before the companies would pay for expensive nonemergency dental work. This and other policies of the dental association raised insurance premiums and dental-care costs, the FTC contended.

This is the kind of action that causes dentists, doctors, and other professionals to tell Congress that the FTC is too powerful.

What do you think? Is the market for dental services subject to the same failures as other businesses in a market system?

INVESTMENT

Investment is the use of resources to create new capital. Such money may be spent for equipment, construction, and inventories. The money spent on new investment has a large effect on the economy. In fact, the effect is greater than the amount of dollars directly spent on investment. The effect of investment is multiplied. The **multiplier** works like this: If a new plant is built in a community, local suppliers and construction workers have their incomes increased. They save some and spend the rest on additional goods. The people from whom they buy the goods and services also have more income. They spend a part of their increased income, and the suppliers of the goods and services *they* buy have more money too, and so on. The multiplier explains why investment is such a powerful tool for business prosperity.

SAVINGS

The amount that the workers decide to save will determine how strong the multiplier will be. More savings means less spending and a less powerful multiplier. *But* savings is also the source for future capital investment. What is important here is the regularity and reliability with which saving occurs so that the business climate is predictable.

THE GOVERNMENT

The government can be used to manage the business system. The government typically borrows money to finance its operations. This may take the form of borrowing more than it receives. When this happens, a **deficit** is created. Deficit financing may or may not be a problem, depending upon whether it contributes to inflation.

The government, through either "fiscal" or "monetary" policy, can affect business activity. **Fiscal policy** refers to affecting demand by increasing either taxes (reduces demand) or increasing government spending (increases demand). **Monetary policy** is managing the money supply to increase or decrease demand. The use of these two tools to affect the business system has increased since the Great Depression. But it is clear that our understanding of all their effects is not yet too good.

Our business system has boom and bust cycles. Recessions and recovery are a part of doing business. Figure 1-12 shows the major business cycles over the period 1915 to 1980. Government action has an effect on business cycles.

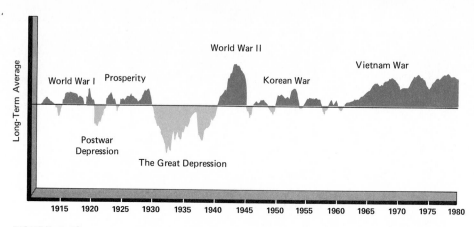

FIGURE 1-12
Business Cycles Since World War I

CURRENT PROBLEMS IN THE BUSINESS SYSTEM

Three issues have earned a lot of press coverage lately, as well they should, since they affect every consumer in our business system. They are inflation, productivity, and unemployment.

INFLATION

The years of high and volatile inflation during and following the Vietnam War put an end to three decades of relative price stability in the United States. INFLATION is a *general increase in the prices of goods and services throughout the economy.*

Economists have long felt that inflation is a self-limiting process. It is caused by a temporary imbalance between the demand and the supply for goods and services. When either the demand drops or the supply increases, inflation should level off. However, the old idea that inflation carries with it the basis for an economic decline no longer seems to hold true.

PRODUCTIVITY

Many experts believe that only by rebuilding America's industrial base and developing new sources of energy can the persistent rise in inflation be stopped.

PRODUCTIVITY is the *output of goods and services per unit of labor.* Productivity in the United States (output per worker) has increased very slowly in recent years. This does not necessarily mean that people are not working as hard, but it does indicate that they could use better tools and machines in their work. But productivity is at least in part a result of investment that has been falling. How can one stimulate productivity? Increased investment, more research and development, and better management techniques appear to be the keys.

UNEMPLOYMENT

At one time, unemployment was viewed as a break in inflation. It was thought that inflation could be cured by accepting some unemployment increase. But the period of 1961 through 1983 shows that this relationship did not hold. Figure 1-13 shows that as unemployment went up, so did inflation.

We have come a long way in understanding the ups and downs of our business system. But as the discussion of inflation, productivity, and unemployment shows, we still have much to learn. There is little agreement on how to best solve these problems.

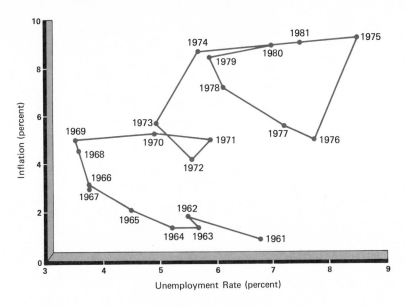

FIGURE 1-13
Recent inflation and unemployment. (Sources: Department of Commerce and Department of Labor.)

MEASURING THE BUSINESS SYSTEM

Two measurements of the business system are commonly referred to in the newspapers and on the TV news. They are the **gross national product** and the **index of leading indicators.**

GROSS NATIONAL PRODUCT

Of the several measures of business growth, the one most commonly used is the gross national product. By GROSS NATIONAL PRODUCT (GNP), we mean *the total value of all finished goods produced and services rendered in an economy for one year.* In a way, the GNP serves as an index of the degree to which our output is growing. It is the most complete measure of what the people in a country produce. Figure 1-14 shows the various components that make up the GNP.

The GNP has its limitations as a measure, despite the fact that it is convenient and widely used. (The GNP does *not* measure the value of *all* the goods and services produced. For example, the food a farmer grows for his own consumption and the services a housewife gives her family are not

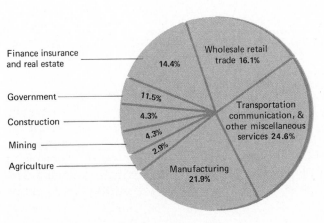

FIGURE 1-14
Composition of Gross National Product, 1981. (Source: U.S. Department of Commerce, Bureau of Economic Analysis, Survey of Current Business, July 1982.)

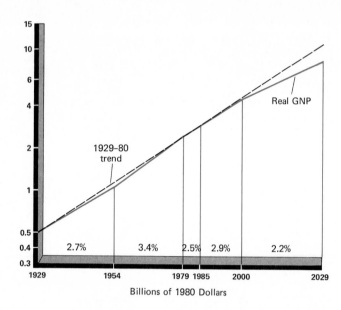

FIGURE 1-15

The American GNP. (Source: Council of Economic Advisers and Bureau of Economic Analysis.)

included.) The GNP is limited (with a few exceptions) to goods and services that are exchanged in markets. The GNP for the United States is shown above in Figure 1-15.

THE LEADING BUSINESS INDICATORS

Information from the U.S. Department of Commerce is important to the business and industrial community. Among the data published regularly is the "Composite Index of Leading Indicators." This index has twelve components, which are appraised monthly. The data for each component are collected monthly and are then combined to form one index. These measures when taken together show how the general business climate will move in the future. Changes during a single month may not be significant. But when the composite index shows continued gains month by month, this is an indication that business will improve. Index movements over short periods may reflect the influence of random events. Examples of such events are unusual or extreme weather patterns, or a prolonged strike by members of a large labor union, such as the teamsters, the dockworkers, or the mine workers.

The components that make up this composite index are shown in Table 1-2.

TABLE 1-2
The Twelve Leaders

1. Average workweek of production workers, manufacturing
2. Layoff rate, manufacturing
3. Value of manufacturers' new orders for consumer goods and materials in constant dollars
4. Index of net business formation
5. Standard & Poor's index of 500 common-stock prices
6. Contracts and orders for plant and equipment in constant dollars
7. Index of new private housing units authorized by local building permits
8. Vendor performance — percentage of companies reporting slower deliveries
9. Net change in inventories on hand and on order in constant dollars
10. Change in sensitive prices of key raw materials — excludes foods, feeds, and fibers
11. Change in total liquid assets — the liquid wealth held by private investors
12. Money supply in constant dollars

SOURCE: U.S. Department of Commerce, *Business Conditions Digest.*

SOME UNANSWERED QUESTIONS

Although our mixed economy has many advantages, it also has its disadvantages. Business, labor, government, and the public must cooperate if our system is to serve the best interests of all the people. The U.S. private-enterprise system has demonstrated its ability to function acceptably, maintain a high living standard, eliminate most poverty, and find ways to reduce unemployment. But many challenging issues still exist, such as:

1. How can we best expand economic growth?
2. Should the government guarantee everyone who is able and willing the opportunity to work?
3. How large should business enterprises and labor unions become? Are big business and powerful labor unions good for the country?
4. Should government funds be used to subsidize economic growth?
5. How should the burden of taxes be determined in order to make it more equitable?
6. How can we determine the long-range social and economic costs and benefits of various government programs?
7. How can we balance production growth with the conservation of natural resources?

These are but a few of the major economic issues facing our nation. Some of them are more complex than others, but all command the attention of those in public and private positions of importance. In the next several chapters, many of these issues are explored in more detail.

SUMMARY OF KEY CONCEPTS

Economics is everyone's concern. It deals with the management of resources in meeting people's wants.

The fundamental economic problem of every society is *wants versus scarcity*. People's wants have no limits, but the resources available are limited.

Individually and collectively, we must make *choices*. The law of economics dictates that for a given degree of satisfaction, one will choose the cheapest alternative. When the costs are the same, one will choose the greatest satisfaction.

The economic goals of our country are:

a. Economic growth
b. Rising standard of living
c. Full employment
d. Price stability
e. Equitable income
f. Economic freedom
g. Financial security

The basic factors of production consist of natural resources, labor, capital, and entrepreneurship.

Supply and demand are major concepts in understanding how the market system works.

Investment, savings, and government spending help explain the business climate.

The multiplier greatly enhances the effect of investment, making it a powerful force for business cycles.

When we measure the success of a business system, some of the criteria used are:

a. Business growth
b. Productivity
c. Rising standard of living
d. Economic stability
e. Index of leading indicators

You should be able to match these business terms with the statements that follow:

a. CAPITAL GOODS
b. CAPITALISM
c. ECONOMICS
d. ENTREPRENEUR
e. EQUILIBRIUM PRICES
f. FACTORS OF PRODUCTION

g. GROSS NATIONAL PRODUCT
h. INFLATION
i. LABOR
j. MARKET SYSTEM
k. PRODUCTIVITY
l. REAL INCOME

1. The science of using scarce resources to satisfy human needs
2. An economic system based on property ownership and the profit motive
3. The essential components that together make up manufacturing
4. Equipment, tools, and machinery used in production
5. Human resources available for production
6. A person who invests time, money, and effort in a business enterprise and assumes the risks involved
7. The selling system in which price is determined by supply and demand
8. The price result of the interplay of supply and demand
9. An increase in the general level of prices
10. The output of goods produced measured in relation to raw materials and labor used
11. The sum total of all goods and services produced in one year
12. Wages stated in terms of their purchasing power

REVIEW QUESTIONS

1. What is the main economic concern of any country?
2. What questions must the people of a nation answer when deciding how to develop an economic scheme?
3. State and define the essential foundations of our private-enterprise economy.
4. What are the chief economic goals in the United States?
5. What are the essential factors of production in any economy?
6. How does investment affect business activity?

DISCUSSION QUESTIONS

1. Sometimes our national goals are in conflict with one another. What criteria should be followed in resolving such conflicts?
2. In what way is the right to own property a basic right in a capitalistic economy?
3. How are economic, political, and social freedoms interrelated?
4. Which of the economic goals of a private-enterprise economy do you think is most important, and why?
5. Which of the factors of production are lacking in most nonindustrialized countries?
6. Select one of the issues mentioned in this chapter, and state your position regarding it.

BUSINESS CASES

BARTER IS BACK, BIGGER THAN EVER

Barter refers to the swapping of goods with little or no money changing hands. It was carried on extensively during the colonial period in America.

Barter is making a comeback, and on a national rather than an individual level. Many nations are being squeezed by the high cost of petroleum. These nations are finding it increasingly difficult to come up with the hard currencies they need to pay for it. So they have resorted to what they call trade agreements—a modern form of barter.

The U.S. Department of Commerce reports that between 10 and 20 percent of the $1.2 trillion annual stream of world commerce is in the form of "countertrade."

One example of countertrade is the building of a plant in Hungary, being supervised by Levi Strauss and Company. It is being paid for through a ten-year "buy-back" agreement. Levi Strauss receives 60 percent of the plant's production.

Another example is the deal whereby Pepsico is supplying soft-drink syrup to the Soviet Union. In addition, it is aiding in the construction of Pepsi-Cola bottling plants there. In exchange, Pepsico received the exclusive U.S. marketing rights to Stolichnaya Vodka.

Trade experts predict that the kind of barter known as countertrade will boom in the 1980s.

1. Is barter subject to the same market constraints as transactions where cash is involved? Why, or why not?
2. Why do you suppose the behavioral assumptions of economics hold for people in communist countries as well as the United States?

1-2 MAKING ECONOMIC CHOICES

James Peterson owns a large cattle ranch in Colorado, which has been in his family for three generations. He is fortunate because a creek of clear water runs through his ranch and supplies drinking water for his cattle. On the back boundary of his ranch, bordering upon the creek and beyond, are fifty acres of forest. Years ago, a sizable deposit of low-sulfur coal was discovered on the opposite side of the ranch.

The Mountain Timber Corporation has approached James about buying his timber. This would yield him a considerable one-payment sum of money. However, he fears that it would denude the land and contaminate the water in the creek. The payment for the timber looms large for the present. But there are important questions about what effect cutting the timber would have on maintaining a watershed for his cattle in future years.

The Western Coal Company has also offered James an attractive contract to strip-mine his land for the coal. This, too, is a tempting offer but would destroy the beauty of that part of his ranch. This coal-deposit area lies under a rolling rugged area, which he views from the front of his home. In fact, it is his favorite view of the countryside.

Although there are no restrictions in the deed to his ranch, James knows that his father constantly resisted opportunities to let the coal be mined. He repeatedly spoke of the beautiful view and vowed to keep it that way for posterity.

Adjacent to the creek is some relatively level and productive ground. But the annual rainfall in this area is insufficient for growing crops. James has wondered about pumping water from the creek to irrigate this portion of his farm. None of his neighbors are irrigating, but if they should all undertake such a practice, there would not be enough water to go around.

The cost of feed has risen recently, and the profit margin on raising cattle has narrowed somewhat. But the economic forecast is for higher beef prices in the future.

So James is faced with making some choices.

1. What choices are available to him?
2. What specific alternative would enable him to have the "best of both worlds"?

Chain-Saw Safety: What Is Responsible Behavior?

Chain saws are popular items. The number of saws in the United States is estimated to be about 16.5 million, up 136 percent from only five years ago. And almost 1½ million saws are being shipped annually. However, with the growth in chain-saw sales and usage, there has been an alarming increase in accidents. The saw, with its sharp teeth revolving at 70 miles per hour, is an awesome and dangerous tool. In a recent year, the Consumer Products Safety Commission estimates, there were 123,000 chain-saw injuries that required medical attention, up 73 percent from five years earlier.

Many of the most severe accidents involve "kickback," which occurs when the chain is pinched or when the tip strikes a hard object. This may cause the saw to jump up and back faster than the user can react to protect himself. Kickback can evidently be eliminated by chain brakes, chain design, or redesigned saw tips. The Quebec Logging Association says that accidents were reduced 83 percent when chain brakes were made mandatory. Sweden noted a 78 percent drop in accidents when safety devices were made mandatory there.

These figures seem to argue for manufacturers to design safety into their saws for the public good. However, some manufacturers say that when they offer chain brakes as optional equipment, they *do not sell*. They contend that the industry has been doing a good job working toward voluntary standards and *does not need* federal standards for the product's safety. In fact, the Chain Saw Manufacturers Association hired a consultant to examine the government's accident figures and concluded, among other things, that a chair is far more dangerous than a chain saw.

The manufacturers' efforts at fighting mandatory safety features on their products seem at times greater than their efforts at developing them. This attitude has led to the departure from the association of at least one large manufacturer, McCulloch Corporation.

Product safety is but one area in the field of social responsibility. How far should a business protect the society in which it operates? Saws could easily be made twice as costly with the addition of safety devices that many people would remove. But still, absolute safety could not be guaranteed. What *is* socially responsible business behavior?

Business and Society

study objectives

WHEN YOU HAVE FINISHED READING THIS CHAPTER, YOU SHOULD BE ABLE TO:

1. Define a "pluralistic" society

2. Explain consumerism

3. Trace what is being done to give minorities and women fair treatment in business

4. Discuss what has caused our physical environment to deteriorate, and offer suggestions for restoring it

5. Describe various actions the government is taking to protect and improve the environment

6. Give specific examples of how business is attempting to meet its responsibility to society

2

[Corporate social responsibility is] slippery in part because it doesn't have an agreed-upon opposite; at least there does not seem to be any leading advocates of corporate social irresponsibility.

Daniel Seligman

Business affects all our lives. And because it does, business has some responsibilities to people's lives and well-being. Today, society asks businesses to accept more such responsibility than ever before. The days of a laissez-faire attitude toward business —letting it do whatever it pleases—are over. Determining how far business *should* go toward social goals that may lead away from economic goals presents a real dilemma.

The term **social responsibility** at one time simply meant financial contributions to the arts or the local community, and perhaps ethical behavior. Today, it comprises much more, including health concerns, consumer information, hiring practices, practicing no discrimination, and care of the physical environment.

BUSINESS ENVIRONMENTS

Business both determines and is the product of environmental influences. The factors that make up the environment are constantly changing. So, in order to survive and prosper, business must also change. By ENVIRONMENT we mean *the sum of all the external forces that influence individuals, businesses, and communities.* It includes ethical-legal, economic, political, social, and physical elements; each overlaps and influences the others, as Figure 2-1 shows.

BUSINESS IN A PLURALISTIC SOCIETY Society today consists of many strong and diverse influences, and these different groups are motivated by self-interest. Business is dependent upon the public to purchase its goods and services, and the public attitude toward

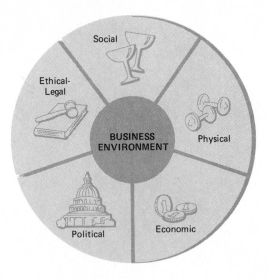

FIGURE 2-1

The Business Firm Interacts with Many Environments

business greatly affects the way in which businesses operate and serve. Business must navigate through the different groups and interests to be successful.

Figure 2-2 (on page 32) depicts the variety of groups that constitute a pluralistic society. A PLURALISTIC SOCIETY is *the combination of diverse groups that influence the business environment.* In a pluralistic society, there are many power centers, each with some but not total independence. Business has a responsibility for achieving acceptable community relations. The multiple groups that influence business and government help diffuse power and prevent it from becoming concentrated in a single segment of society. Progress is made through give and take — by compromise rather than by a clear-cut winner. Pluralism represents the efforts of people to reconcile the needs and interests of a variety of organizations.

THE NEGATIVE IMAGE OF BUSINESS

For the past decade, the institution of business has been battered on many sides. The news has been full of accounts of business scandals, bribery, misrepresentation, price fixing, tax evasion, advertising abuse, and illegal payments. Dozens of individuals and companies have been convicted of such misdemeanors and felonies. Why do such things occur? Is it that certain business leaders become greedy and, in addition to enriching themselves, seek to increase their companies' profits?

Criticism of business has not been restricted to economic, moral, ethical, and political considerations. Business *has* contributed to the deterioration of our physical environment. Chemical and solid wastes have been dumped into lakes and rivers. Dangerous and poisonous waste materials have been buried in abandoned storage and plant sites. Fumes from factories have caused air pollution and acid rain.

The storage of nuclear waste generated by the nuclear-power industry raises the specter of another unfavorable situation like the one that arose at Three Mile Island. Some commercial reactors that have been used to generate consumer electric power face a shutdown if additional temporary storage is not found.

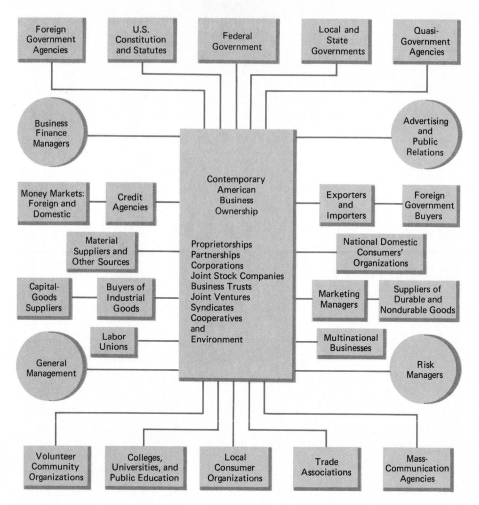

FIGURE 2-2
Business as part of a pluralistic society.
In a pluralistic society, business is a joint venture with other segments of the environment. This venture is not necessarily a conflict for power. Rather, it is an effort to meet the needs of the various groups, including the business firm.

Air pollution has been improving for a decade, thanks to pollution controls, but as Table 2-1 shows, there are still many "unhealthy" days in the cities with major pollution problems.

WHY THE NEGATIVES?   Why has business allowed problems like these to develop? There are several reasons. First, businesspeople are human, and they have the same problems, motives, and failings found in the general population. It seems a bit unrealistic to expect businessmen and businesswomen to be any more (or any less) responsible than the society of which they are a part.

Competition.   But there is a second consideration that we must understand. Competition can sometimes keep businesses from doing what should be done. Henry Ford II once explained why seat belts were not put into automobiles until the government required them. His argument was that even

TABLE 2-1
Number of "Unhealthy" Days
per Year

	UNHEALTHY DAYS
Los Angeles	231
Riverside, Calif.	174
New York City	139
Denver	130
Pittsburgh	119
Houston	104
Chicago	93
St. Louis	89

SOURCE: President's Council on
Environmental Quality.

though there was strong evidence that seat belts saved lives, people would not pay extra for them. They would not buy Ford cars with seat belts when General Motors could sell its cars for less without them. Whether that is entirely true or not, Mr. Ford believed it was and made decisions accordingly.

Economists on the Business Role.   An argument advanced by many economists as to the role business should play in these matters is as follows: The business organization is not the proper vehicle for pursuing social goals. Its legal obligations and competitive pressures limit its ability to engage in social policy making. What business should do is try to produce the highest possible return to stockholders. This enhances investment and increases productivity, innovation, and the amount of goods and services for all consumers. Leave social policy to the government! Business has no expertise or mechanism for representing church, labor, community, welfare, or minority groups. Consumers can vote with their dollars if they don't like the results of those decisions.

OPINION LEADERS' IDEAS: A SURVEY

A survey conducted by the Opinion Research Corporation found that opinion leaders in business, labor, the media, academia, and government do not all agree with the economists' view above. The vast majority in each of these subgroups believed that business *does* have social responsibilities. Labor leaders feel the most strongly that business has social responsibility (97 percent agreed). The others' opinions were similar, if less adamant. Lewis W. Lehr, Chairman of the 3M Company put it this way: "For a company to be especially conscious of its responsibility to the communities in which it operates is more than altruism. It is good business, and good for business," and Raymond A. Hay, Chairman of the LTV Corporation said: " . . . But the corporation's economic responsibilities are so closely related to overall social responsibility that they cannot be ignored." The exception was academic leaders, 23 percent of whom felt that a corporation has solely economic responsibilities.

ANDREW F. BRIMMER

Andrew F. Brimmer is president of Brimmer & Company, Inc., Economic and Financial Consultants. The firm conducts research and advises clients concerning financial matters. Firm members specialize in trends in economic activity and interest rates in money and capital markets. They give special attention to Federal Reserve monetary policy.

Brimmer served as an economist with the Wage Stabilization Board, Seattle, Washington, in 1952. He was an economist with the Federal Reserve Board of New York from 1955 through 1958, and assistant secretary in the U.S. Department of Commerce from 1963 to 1966.

He was a member of the Board of Governors of the Federal Reserve System from 1966 to 1974. He has been in his current position since 1976.

Mr. Brimmer was the recipient of the Alumnus Summa Laude Dignatus for 1972 by the University of Washington Alumni Association; the Government Man of the Year Award by the National Business League in 1963; the Public Affairs Award by the Capital Press Club in 1966; the Horatio Alger Award in 1974; and the Equal Opportunity Award by the National Urban League in 1974.

Andrew Brimmer was born in Newellton, Louisiana, in 1926. He received B.A. and M.B.A. degrees from the University of Washington in 1951, and the Ph.D. degree from Harvard University in 1957. He married Doris Millicent Scott of New York City in 1953. They have one daughter.

Opinion leaders feel that the following are areas of importance for business social responsibility:

Employment	Charities
Job training	Scientific research
Employee Services/benefits	Cultural activities
Support of education	

ATTEMPTS AT IMAGE IMPROVEMENT

In order to improve relations among business, government, and the public, U.S. companies often turn to their public-relations staffs. Company personnel attend congressional hearings and meetings of regulatory agencies. They may attempt to become better informed about the activities of governments. Businesses also listen to consumers and provide more and better information to the public. Public relations must provide for better two-way communication, not merely "propagandizing."

Mobil's Effort to Improve Its Image.   The Mobil Corporation recently spent one-fourth of its public-relations budget in an attempt to improve its corporate image. The company placed ads in leading magazines and newspapers, arguing for mass transit and a national energy policy. Two paragraphs from one of these ads follow:

> In the words of a former chairman of Mobil, "No business is truly safe unless it serves its customers better than they could serve themselves, persuades them that it is doing so, and retains their goodwill in the process. One can't be too sure how long corporations would retain their present opportunities to operate at a profit if making money were their sole contribution to society.

"Mobil tries to be a good employer, a good supplier, a good customer, a good investment, and a socially conscious organization. We try also to be responsive to the aspirations and legitimate needs of minorities and others of the disadvantaged, to environmental problems, and to a host of other concerns. And we would not argue that this is undiluted altruism."

CONSUMERISM

CONSUMERISM is *a movement to inform consumers and protect them from business malpractices.* The consumerism movement focuses on inferior and dangerous merchandise, unfair business practices, and false or misleading advertising. Some consumer groups concentrate on local issues, such as a local business's pricing policies. Other groups concentrate on national issues, such as product safety or truth in lending. Consumerism is a fact of business life today, and the businesspeople who ignore it do so at their peril. The consumer has developed a large constituency and a strong measure of government support.

HISTORY OF CONSUMERISM For many people, the consumerism movement began during the 1960s, because some businesses were not giving the public the kind of products or services it wanted and paid for. But the first major consumer milestone in the United States was reached at the turn of the century. It was then that the Pure Food and Drug Act and the Meat Inspection Act were passed to improve conditions in the food industry. During those years, the idea of self-regulation on the part of business began. This concept led to the movement that eventually resulted in the creation of the Better Business Bureau. BBBs are private organizations that exist in most cities. The BBB listens to complaints from consumers and assists them in protecting their rights. The BBB publishes numerous pamphlets that are available to consumers, such as the following:

Tips on Renting a Car	*Facts on Home Insulation*
Tips on Home Improvements	*Buying on Time*
Facts about Health Insurance	*Home Fire Protection*
Facts on Selecting a Franchise	*Tips on Energy Saving*
Mail Order Profit Mirages	*Truth in Lending*
Multi-Level Selling Plans	*Guarantees & Warranties*
What about Service Calls?	*Read Before You Sign*
Tips on Refunds & Exchanges	*Tips on Sales Contracts*

Rising consumer expectations, along with the increased complexity of products, form part of the base of the consumerism movement. As a result, business managers and the government have developed a keen interest in the rights and values of consumers. The federal and state governments have persons and/or agencies to aid consumers. The U.S. president has a special advisor for consumer affairs.

THE RIGHTS OF CONSUMERS

Consumers, as individuals and as groups, feel entitled to a fair shake in the business world. That includes certain rights:

1. The right to product safety
2. The right to fair and honest dealings in business transactions
3. The right to true and complete data about products they may wish to purchase
4. The right to know the true interest rate they are being charged
5. The right to know details about income, expenses, and profits of businesses whose stock they wish to purchase
6. The right to register complaints about shoddy merchandise and unfair business practices

The consumer has the right to fair and honest dealings in business transactions.
(Photo, Michael Collier, Stock, Boston.)

The expression of these rights has led to fundamental changes in some businesses.

General Motors is quietly testing an idea that would have been unheard of just a few years ago. A program of binding arbitration to settle customer complaints is being run by the Better Business Bureau in a northern state. Under this program, General Motors agrees to let an arbitrator decide disputes between customers and dealers and to abide by that decision.

The program seems to be successful so far. There is evidence that executives in Detroit are concerned that if they do not do a better job of handling consumer complaints, the government will move in. Ford Motor Company is also testing a similar program in another state, and the National Automobile Dealers Association has set up similar plans in forty-four different cities. Indeed, "lemon laws," aimed at helping a buyer of an auto that cannot be fixed, have been passed in several states.

CONSUMER LAWS The federal government has enacted much legislation to aid and protect consumers. The major acts and their chief purposes are enumerated in Table 2-2. Some of these laws protect both consumers and businesses. For example, changes in U.S. law now require that counterfeit merchandise be forfeited. This was becoming a big problem for both consumers and legitimate businesses. Counterfeiters duplicate everything imaginable — from Hennessey brandy and Moët champagne to Dior and Cardin fashions, Puma sports shoes, Dunlop tennis racquets, and Coca-Cola.

It has been estimated that over $100 million annually is involved in counterfeiting schemes. Not only do legitimate businesses lose money, but

TABLE 2-2
Federal Consumer Legislation

LEGISLATION	WHEN ENACTED	PURPOSE
Fair Packaging and Labeling Act	1966	Requires packages and labels to carry identity of article, manufacturer's name and location, and quantity of contents, in legible print.
National Traffic and Motor Safety Act	1966	Requires auto manufacturers to notify buyers of defects discovered after delivery and to remedy these defects.
Consumer Credit Protection Act	1968	Requires seller to disclose terms of sale and give facts of actual interest rate and other charges.
Child Protection and Toy Safety Act	1969	Prohibits manufacture and distribution of toys and other children's articles sold in interstate trade that have electrical or other hazards.
Truth-in-Lending Act	1969	Requires lenders to inform borrowers of all direct, indirect, and true costs of credit. Both the amount of the finance charge and the annual percentage rate must be made clear.
Fair Credit Reporting Act	1970	Requires consumer-credit reporting agencies to adopt procedures for reporting personal information accurately and fairly.
Consumer Product Safety Act	1972	Regulates product standards and creates a Consumer Safety Commission to maintain product safety standards and give more accurate facts about products on labels.
Privacy Act	1974	Prohibits governments at all levels from requiring persons to give their Social Security numbers to receive a driver's license, vote, or exercise other rights. Persons have a right to know what information is maintained by federal agencies about them. Sets up a commission to study problems of consumer privacy.
Real Estate Settlement Procedures Act	1974	Requires lenders to disclose to home buyers all closing costs at least twelve days before closing the sale. Penalties for violations can run up to a year in prison and a $10,000 fine.

SOCIAL RESPONSIBILITY CAN PAY DIVIDENDS

Clairol Inc. accounts for about 75 percent of U.S. hair-dye sales. Recently, however, that achievement was threatened by the actions of federal regulators and an issue of "social responsibility." A substance used in hair colors for sixty years was suspected of causing cancer in humans. Federal regulations would have required Clairol and other manufacturers to post a warning label on their glamorous packages.

L'Oréal, the French cosmetics company, quickly reformulated its hair dyes and succeeded in chipping away at Clairol's share of the market. Nine months later, Clairol, too, removed the suspected cancer-causing ingredient. Reformulation saved the hair-color industry, but attention has been called to the more than 125 suspected cancer-causing chemicals currently being used in cosmetics. For some businesses, these opportunities to be responsible societal citizens will pay off handsomely; for others who misread the consumer or fail to grasp the seriousness of the situation, they will spell real problems.

---

the consumer pays for an item of known quality and receives a cheap imitation. The new law will keep bogus merchandise that comes into the country out of circulation, because the U.S. Customs Department can seize and keep the merchandise.

BUSINESS AND MINORITY GROUPS

Historically, blacks, Hispanics, American Indians, Orientals, and handicapped persons have been discriminated against in hiring and in pay. The government now protects these minority groups, as well as women, against overt discrimination.

The term **minority group** has long been used by sociologists to identify certain subdivisions of a population occupying a definite level within the social system. For purposes of this discussion, we define MINORITY GROUP as a *small division of the population who share a common historical background and cultural patterns from those of other segments of society.*

CHARACTERISTICS OF MINORITY GROUPS

At least three major characteristics are common to various minority groups. First, the group is usually small and therefore plays a lesser role in society than does the majority group. This places the members of such a group at a disadvantage when participating in both political and economic activities.

Second, the group has certain physical characteristics—color, facial structure, hair texture, or something else—that act to physically set members of these groups apart and that may result in automatic exclusion.

Third, minority groups may be accorded fewer social privileges, may be somewhat restricted in their freedom of action, and may be of a lower economic or social status.

FEDERAL CIVIL-RIGHTS LAWS

The principal sources of our rights as American citizens are two documents: the Constitution of the United States and the constitution of each state. The first section of the Fourteenth Amendment to the Constitution provides that "no state shall deny to any person within its jurisdiction the equal protection of the laws." Perhaps more than any other language in the Constitution, the equal-protection clause has been used to establish and broaden civil rights.

Nearly five generations of minority Americans have lived through amendments to the Constitution. More recently, the civil-rights movement has resulted in the passage of several important federal civil-rights laws.

The Civil Rights Act of 1964 launched a major effort to correct discriminating practices. This act made it unlawful for an employer "to refuse to hire, or to discharge any individual, or otherwise discriminate against any individual with respect to his compensation, terms, conditions, or privileges of employment, because of such individual's race, color, religion, sex or national origin. . . ."

The federal government requires businesses and institutions to make provisions for minorities in employment and salary. They must pay women the same salaries as they pay men for identical work categories. Companies doing business with the government must submit reports to show that they are abiding by government laws and regulations. Most businesses, hospitals, and schools fall under some provisions of equal-employment-opportunity legislation.

A summary of federal civil-rights laws is shown below.

SUMMARY OF FEDERAL CIVIL-RIGHTS LAWS

Civil Rights Act of 1866. "All citizens of the United States shall have the same right, in every state and territory, as is enjoyed by white citizens thereof to inherit, purchase, sell, hold and convey real and personal property."

Civil Rights Act of 1957. Enacted to prevent interference with the voting rights of others.

Civil Rights Act of 1960. Strengthens the act of 1957 by requiring stricter enforcement provisions of voting rights. Criminal penalties for bombing and for obstructing federal court orders were imposed.

Equal Pay Act of 1963. Prohibits wage discrimination based on sex. Enforcement is vested in the Wage and Hour Division, Department of Labor. Workers receiving minimum wage under the Fair Labor Standard Act are included.

Civil Rights Act of 1964. Prohibits discrimination based on race, color, sex, and national origin. Prohibits segregation by job classification to deprive employees of equal-employment opportunities. The law also prohibits discrimination in voting, school attendance, hiring, union membership, and the use of public facilities.

Voting Rights Act of 1965. Requires the attorney general to appoint federal examiners to register voters in certain areas.

Age Discrimination Employment Act of 1967. Prohibits age discrimination in employment and encourages hiring older workers based on their ability rather than age. Protects those 40 to 65 years of age from discrimination in employment.

Civil Rights Act of 1968. The act covers 80 percent of all housing for rent or sale. It exempts from its coverage only private individuals owning not more than three houses who sell or rent their houses without the services of a real estate agent and who do not show preference or discrimination in their advertising.

The Voting Rights Act of 1970. Amended the Voting Rights Act of 1965, extending it five more years. Prohibited use of literacy tests for voting and set up uniform residence requirements.

Equal Employment Opportunity Act of 1972. Provides (1) right to employment with companies in interstate commerce having at least fifteen employees, and (2) membership with labor unions that have fifteen or more members. Includes employees hired through a hiring hall or working in an industry engaged in interstate commerce. Opportunities and right to work extended to state and local government employees, including those in public-supported educational institutions.

The Office of Minority Business Enterprise (OMBE) has been established in the Department of Commerce. Its function is to mobilize public and private leadership and resources to support minority-owned business. It coordinates over eighty government programs, which are administered by sixteen different federal agencies. All these agencies affect minority enterprises in some way.

WOMEN AND BUSINESS OPPORTUNITIES

The percentage of women in our labor force continues to increase. Women have been encouraged by changing social values, attitudes, economic considerations, and government action. Higher educational levels, more women as heads of families, the desire for a higher living standard, and inflation are also contributing factors. In 1980, 41 percent of the labor force were women, and this percentage will increase during the 1980s. The growth in the number of women in the civilian labor force since 1950 is shown in Figure 2-3.

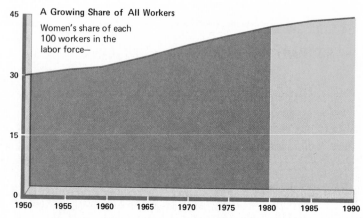

A Growing Share of All Workers

Women's share of each 100 workers in the labor force—

Thus, the nation's work force, which was two-thirds male less than 20 years ago, is fast approaching the day when it will be 50–50, half male and half female.

FIGURE 2-3
Women in the civilian labor force—millions of people 16 years and over.
(Source: The Conference Board.)

OCCUPATIONS AND WOMEN
Occupational opportunities for women continue to improve. Growth rates are fastest in the professional and technical categories. The occupations of employed women are shown in Figure 2-4. However, the median earnings of women continue to be below those of men. This is shown in Figure 2-5.

FIGURE 2-4
Where women are employed.
(Source: The Conference Board.)

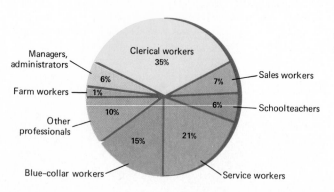

Managers, administrators 6%
Farm workers 1%
Other professionals 10%
Blue-collar workers 15%
Clerical workers 35%
Sales workers 7%
Schoolteachers 6%
Service workers 21%

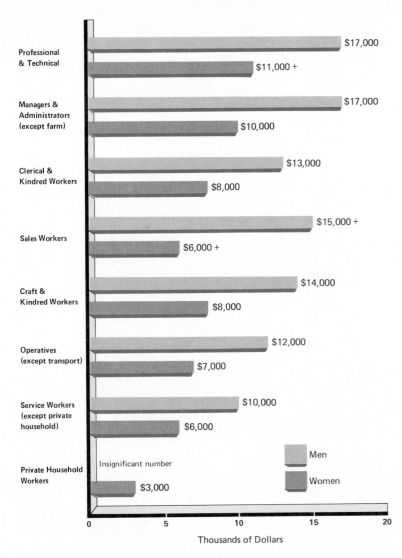

Professional & Technical
$17,000
$11,000 +

Managers & Administrators (except farm)
$17,000
$10,000

Clerical & Kindred Workers
$13,000
$8,000

Sales Workers
$15,000 +
$6,000 +

Craft & Kindred Workers
$14,000
$8,000

Operatives (except transport)
$12,000
$7,000

Service Workers (except private household)
$10,000
$6,000

Private Household Workers
Insignificant number
$3,000

Men
Women

0   5   10   15   20
Thousands of Dollars

FIGURE 2-5
Median earnings of selected occupational groups by sex.
(Source: The Conference Board.)

BARRIERS KEEP FALLING The federal government continues to exert pressure to achieve equal treatment for women and men. The Supreme Court has ruled that:

1. Employers who have underpaid female workers must equalize their wages with those paid male employees.
2. Mandatory maternity leave at a set time in pregnancy violates due process.
3. States may not deny women equal opportunity to serve on juries.
4. The "majority age" for men and women must be the same.
5. Employers cannot differentiate in pension plans on the basis of sex just because women live longer than men.

Efforts are being made by business and government to recruit women for supervisory and management positions.

Positions once reserved for men are now open to women. Women currently hold sales jobs in the steel, aluminum, and lumber industries, which were formerly open only to men. Women are being elected to officer positions in labor unions (one out of every five union members is a woman).

Women serve on the executive boards of the Amalgamated Meat Cutters and Butchers Association, the International Ladies' Garment Workers' Union, and the American Federation of State, County and Municipal Employees Union. Women are also on the board of directors of AT&T.

SOME POSITIVE FACTORS

A decade ago, women were clustered in such fields as nursing and teaching. Today, the young professional woman has much wider opportunities. The proportion of women now preparing for the professions far exceeds the percentage already so employed. For example, whereas women constitute only 11 percent of the nation's physicians, they constitute 24 percent of its medical students. An estimated 10,000 women are studying engineering. This is ten times as many as in 1970. Women constitute 28 percent of all law students. And women constitute 28 percent of all accountants, compared with only 17 percent in 1960. Figure 2-6 shows how women are gaining in the various professions.

FIGURE 2-6
Ten professions where women are gaining.
(Sources: Department of Commerce and Department of Labor.)

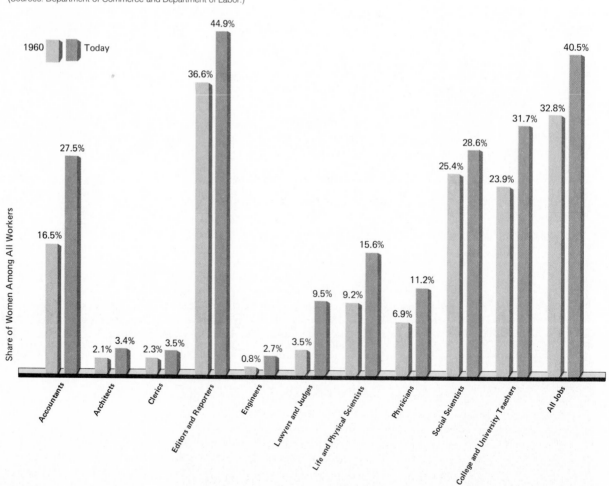

There are many other examples of women who hold top-management positions. Jane Cahill Pfeiffer, a management consultant, was the first woman vice-president of IBM and later served as chairman of the board of directors of the National Broadcasting Company. She also serves on the board of directors of Chesebrough-Pond's and the Bache Group. Marina Whitman, a former member of the president's Council of Economic Advisers, is a board member of Westinghouse, Manufacturers Hanover Trust, and Procter & Gamble. Carol M. Conklin was elected to the position of corporate secretary of General Motors, and Betsy Ancker-Johnson was appointed vice-president of General Motors, in charge of the company's environmental activities.

BUSINESS AND THE PHYSICAL ENVIRONMENT

Of the several economic and social problems facing American business, one of the most costly and difficult to solve is that of improving the physical environment. In the late 1960s, it was discovered that this nation would run out of clean air and water in urban centers unless something was done to improve the environment. Pollutants of all kinds were destroying the quality of our air and water.

The development of nuclear energy as a source of power has brought a new type of pollution. Radioactive contamination in the form of liquid nuclear waste can cause cancer or a number of other serious conditions harmful to human beings. The nuclear-waste disposal problem becomes more imposing because at the present time there is no safe place to dump this atomic-waste material. As former congressman Morris K. Udall, when chairman of the House Environment Subcommittee, observed:

> The harsh truth is that eventually, if civilization is to remain on this planet, we need permanent, renewable, clean, and large-scale energy sources that consume nothing and pollute nothing.

Air pollution across the land.
(Courtesy, United Nations.)

ECOLOGY

ECOLOGY is a science that deals with *the relationships between people and their environments.* The quality of our environment has rapidly deteriorated in the last 40 years. This has resulted chiefly from a combination of three factors:

1. The increasing concentration of the population
2. The development of new technologies
3. The rise in economic affluence

MAJOR FORMS OF POLLUTION

POLLUTION refers to *the deterioration of the natural environment in which we live and work.* Water and air, which were once clean, are now polluted. Each of the three major areas of pollution that follow presents a threat to a healthful environment.

Air Pollution. The average person breathes thirty-five pounds of air each day. This is six times as much as the food and drink normally consumed.

In 1983, over 200 million tons of waste products were being released into the air annually. Slightly over 50 percent of the pollution came from the internal-combustion engines of cars and other motor vehicles. Roughly 22 percent came from fuel burned at stationary sources such as power-generating plants, and another 15 percent was emitted from industrial processes.

Air pollution is associated with respiratory disorders and with diseases of the heart. Illness caused or aggravated by air pollution costs the American people an estimated $4.6 billion annually. This is for medical treatment, lost wages, and reduced productivity.

Air pollution corrodes buildings, damages personal property, and harms forests and crops. It causes $12.3 billion in destruction and decay annually. The pollution in major cities has improved somewhat since the 1970s, owing to the Clean Air Act.

Water Pollution. The sources of water pollution are many. Major sources can be found in almost every variety of industrial, municipal, and agricultural operation throughout the United States. Pollutants present a special threat to ground-water supplies. Because of widespread use of high-nitrate fertilizers and concentrated feedlots, nitrates in both ground and surface waters have increased in recent years. Many of our ground waters now exceed the nitrate limits of drinking-water standards. The significance of this fact is that once an underground water supply becomes contaminated, it is virtually impossible to purify it.

Solid-Waste Pollution. Environmental health cannot be compartmentalized. This is nowhere more evident than in the area of solid-waste management. There are only three repositories for the wastes of society: the earth, its waters, and its atmosphere. The use or misuse of any of these is interrelated with the other two. Restrictions on the use of any one almost invariably lead to increased burdens on the others.

What to do with solid-waste materials has always been a problem. The simple solution of burning garbage is no longer possible in urban areas because of the air-pollution problem it creates.

Solid wastes include an assortment of products that are no longer usable. In this country we produce about 4.6 billion tons of solid wastes each year. Our annual "throwaway" includes 48 billion cans, 26 billion bottles and jars, 4 million tons of plastic, 7.6 million television sets, 7 million cars and trucks, and 30 million tons of paper. It is estimated that waste collection will soon amount to over 340 million tons per year. The cost of this waste collection and disposal exceeds $12 billion per year.

THE ECONOMICS OF RECYCLING

Recycling is vital to our industrial economy. It saves energy, creates jobs, provides a supplemental source of raw material for production, and helps turn the problems of litter and waste into economic opportunities.

For example, recycling saves 95 percent of the energy it takes to make aluminum from ore. In addition, it saves precious raw materials and reduces the amount of investment capital needed. A facility to remelt recycled aluminum can be built for one-tenth the cost of new refining and smelting equipment. Alcoa reported that the recycling of aluminum cans rose from 8 million pounds in 1970 to over 350 million pounds in 1983. There are more than 2,500 recycling centers in the United States, and they have created 15,000 new jobs for workers.

Massive recycling of used aluminum cans is credited with saving energy, conserving resources, and reducing litter.
(Courtesy, ALCOA.)

Reynolds Metals Company reported that in the ten years since its recycling program began, it had paid consumers $100 million for used aluminum. During the most recent year, Reynolds recycled more than half the aluminum cans the company made. During that year, Reynold's recycling of aluminum saved a billion kilowatt-hours of electricity.

COST OF A CLEAN ENVIRONMENT

U.S. businesses were spending more than $16 billion annually in 1982 to prevent pollution, an amount that increases about 12 percent a year. The Council on Environmental Quality estimates that the cost of cleaning up America will be $271 billion over the next decade:

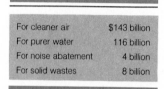

For cleaner air	$143 billion
For purer water	116 billion
For noise abatement	4 billion
For solid wastes	8 billion

Governments—federal, state, and local—will finance about one-fifth of the cost; private business will pay for the remainder.

CURRENT ISSUE

WHO SHOULD PAY FOR CLEANING UP THE ENVIRONMENT?

It is common knowledge that it will require much time and huge sums of money to restore the purity of our air and water, and to clean up our waste dumps. How should this clean-up effort be financed?

With which of the following statements do you agree, and with which do you disagree?

1. Industrial giants caused the pollution; they should pay for it.
2. This cleanup is important to all of us so each person should pay his or her share.
3. The government and business should split the cost on some ratio to be negotiated.
4. Any payments by business would only be passed on to consumers in the form of higher prices. Therefore the government (representing all of us) should pay the bill.
5. Even though business passes these costs on to consumers this is an acceptable way to pay them. (Those who can afford to buy things pay the costs.)
6. Air moves throughout the world. Many nations pollute it. We should not pay to clean it up unless other industrial nations do their share.

What is your idea about cleaning up the air, water, and solid wastes?

The federal government has been very active in enacting laws pertaining to the environment. These laws clearly affect business and what it can do. The first federal law to prohibit pollution of American waters was the Refuse Act of 1899. This act was first enforced in 1970. Since 1965, many laws relating to clean air and water have been enacted. Table 2-3 lists and discusses some of those laws.

TABLE 2-3
Environmental Legislation Affecting Business

Water Resources Planning Act of 1965. This act created a Water Resources Council (WRC) and river-basin commissions. It authorized national air-quality and emission standards for both stationary air-pollution sources and automotive vehicles. The act also requires each state to submit plans for achieving national air-quality standards.

The requirements pertaining to pollution and water quality were strengthened by the **Clean Water Restoration Act** of 1966 and the **Water Quality Improvement Act** of 1970.

Solid Waste Disposal Act of 1965. This act authorizes a program to develop methods of solid-waste disposal, including garbage, paper, and scrap metal. It also provides technical assistance to state and local governments in solid-waste disposal programs.

This act was amended by the **Resource Recovery Act** of 1970 and the **Federal Water Pollution Control Act** of 1972.

Air Quality Act of 1967. This act provides for a systematic effort to deal with air pollution on a regional basis. It establishes coordinated action at various levels of government and segments of industry. The act was amended in 1970 to raise the clean-air standards. Emission standards for automobiles became effective in 1975. These amendments also created the Environmental Protection Agency, which is discussed in the text.

Noise Control Act of 1972. This act requires the EPA administrator to set noise standards for products and equipment that are major sources of noise.

Energy Supply and Environmental Coordination Act of 1974. In order to conserve supplies, the Federal Energy Administration was ordered to require electric-generating plants to use coal where it was practicable to do so.

Resource Conservation and Recovery Act of 1976. This act built upon the foundations of the Solid Waste Disposal Act of 1965 and the Resource Recovery Act of 1970. Its stated objective is to promote the protection of health and the environment to conserve material and energy resources. Among other things, it established the Office of Solid Waste within the EPA to direct the way the law was to be implemented.

THE EPA The U.S. Environmental Protection Agency was established December 2, 1970. Its mission is to integrate and coordinate an attack on environmental problems. Air and water pollution, solid-waste disposal, pesticides, radiation, and noise are all included. Fifteen federal environmental-control programs have been unified into one independent agency. It is a regulatory agency responsible for setting standards and enforcing compliance.

Standard Setting. The EPA must see that the standards it sets will be sufficient to protect the public health and welfare. State and local governments may develop additional controls, but the EPA's direct responsibilities are restricted to protecting health and welfare.

Enforcement Programs. The EPA's philosophy has been to encourage voluntary compliance by private industry and communities. If state and local agencies fail to produce effective plans for pollution abatement or if they do not enforce the programs they develop, the EPA must do so.

Research.   The EPA's research program is authorized under various major congressional acts. This legislation allots more than one-fifth of the agency's operating budget to scientific study.

Financial and Technical Assistance.   By providing financial and technical assistance to state, regional, and local jurisdictions, the EPA serves as a catalyst for environmental-protection efforts. The EPA grants federal funds for the construction and operation of various types of facilities to reduce pollution. It also demonstrates new pollution-control technology.

Since the establishment of the Environmental Protection Agency, the following laws have been enacted by Congress:[1]

Federal Water Pollution Control Act Amendments of 1972
Noise Control Act of 1974
Safe Drinking Water Act of 1974
Energy Supply and Environmental Coordination Act of 1974
Resource Conservation and Recovery Act of 1976
Clean Air Act Amendments of 1977

BUSINESS AND SOCIAL RESPONSIBILITY

If you compared the annual report of any major corporation with a similar report issued ten years ago, you would note the increased amount of financial data included. The report would also discuss what the company is doing and spending to meet its social responsibility to the public. It would be impossible to report in detail what all companies are doing. But we do want to provide sketches to illustrate business's effort to meet its social responsibility.

EXXON   *The Other Dimensions of Business* is a 44-page publication of the Exxon Corporation. The introduction to this publication includes this paragraph:

It has been a long time since corporate leaders held the view that "the business of business is business." As with so many segments of society, the role of business has changed dynamically over the years. In addition to carrying out its traditional economic and commercial functions, business is acutely aware that it must conduct its activities in a responsible and ethical manner. It has regard for the impact of business operations on the physical environment and a sensitivity to the issues affecting the quality of life. Business also helps to support education, health programs, advancement of minorities in employment, community social programs and the arts. Many of the efforts that Exxon and other corporations make in these areas are less known than their familiar products and services. But these efforts form an important, ongoing part of the corporation's daily activities. At Exxon, we feel that it is in the best interest of business to continue to meet public expectations in these areas. We must show through our actions that we believe the prosperity of any business is clearly related to the vitality of the communities in which it functions.

---

[1] All the laws mentioned in this section on federal legislation are discussed fully in the publication *EPA Protecting Our Environment*, published by the U.S. Environmental Protection Agency, Washington, D.C. 20460.

ROCKWELL INTERNATIONAL

A recent annual report of the Rockwell International Corporation highlights the activities of its Social Responsibility Committee. As part of its support for higher education, it established a program to aid in the preparation of minority students as scientists. Through its Product Integrity Committee, the company embarked on a program to reinforce the high quality of its products.

During an eighteen-month period at Rockwell International, the number of minority employees in professional positions increased from 12.0 to 13.5 percent. During the same period, the number of women in professional categories increased from 5.7 to 7.4 percent. The company budgeted $14 million to ensure compliance with required health standards. During a recent year, it placed $29 million in orders for products from minority-owned firms.

3M COMPANY

A few years ago, a chemical engineer from the 3M Company visited the company plant at Cordoba, Illinois, so that he could help in the development of an industrial herbicide. He discovered that the odor from the herbicide production process was most repulsive. As a result of his report, the 3M Company changed the formula to make the chemical almost odor-free. This is one illustration of how the company operates its 3P program ("pollution prevention pays"). Its purpose is to eliminate pollution at its source rather than clean it up later. Through nineteen different projects, 3M reduced the company's annual pollution burden by 500 million gallons of waste water, 73,000 tons of air pollutants, and 2,800 tons of sludge. The results of this program greatly impressed the Environmental Protection Agency, which featured the 3P program of the 3M Company at a two-day conference in Chicago. More than 200 companies were represented at that conference.

XEROX

The Xerox Corporation sponsors a Social Involvement Program, based on certain fundamental beliefs held by the company. Those working for the company may be granted a Social Service Leave for one year, with pay. During that year, instead of working for Xerox, they work on social-service projects of their own choosing, in their respective communities. Xerox provides these leaves of absence, with pay, for highly motivated employees to serve in such projects as rehabilitating the handicapped and giving new hope to those in hospitals and prisons.

The Reverend Jesse Jackson has used the organization he heads, PUSH (People United to Save Humanity), to win gains for blacks. He has done so by using market leverage to get big firms to listen to him.

Jackson's goal has been to get large businesses to deal with small, minority-owned businesses. For example, in 1980, there were only seven black franchises out of 800 Kentucky Fried Chicken restaurants. Only one wholesaler of Coca-Cola fountain syrup out of 4,000 was black. Things have changed now.

Coke has appointed twenty black wholesalers, and Kentucky Fried Chicken will add 105 blacks as franchisees by 1987. Both companies will also provide financing. In addition, Phillip Morris's Seven-Up Company has agreed to set up black fountain wholesalers, hire a black vice-president, and contribute to black colleges.

When talks with Coca-Cola broke down, Jackson urged blacks (who were spending about $300 million a year on Coke's products) not to "choke on Coke." The boycott lasted less than a month before an agreement was reached.

AT&T   Perhaps one of the most important equal-employment cases involves the American Telephone and Telegraph Corporation. The Equal Employment and Opportunity Commission (EEOC) had initiated action against the company on behalf of its women and minority workers. The EEOC was joined in the decree against AT&T by the Departments of Labor and Justice and the Federal Communications Commission. The company paid $18 million to approximately 20,000 workers who were victims of unequal pay practices. It also agreed to wipe out all unequal pay schedules. This cost the company an additional $53 million, resulting from pay increases for a total of 72,000 workers.

Although AT&T was "forced" to improve its pay practices, once it had agreed to do so, it was a model of compliance. In addition to direct payments to employees, the company sustained huge legal, training, and administrative costs. The department responsible for seeing that the terms of the government decree are met requires about 750 full-time employees.[2]

Energy efficiency and conservation is changing our business lifestyle.
(Courtesy, Citicorp.)

---

[2] A full discussion of this case can be found in the January 15, 1979, issue of *Fortune*, pp. 45–57.

In the early stages of America's industrial development, we depended largely on waterpower and coal. However, petroleum was plentiful and cheap during the 1930s and 1940s. So by 1950, oil supplied 40 percent of our energy needs; natural gas, 18 percent; and coal, only 38 percent. Recently, oil supplied 46 percent; natural gas, 28 percent; and coal, only 18 percent.

Following the "oil embargo" of 1973, we began looking to nuclear energy to solve our energy dilemma. But various groups protested the development of nuclear plants. Problems remained unsolved regarding the disposal of nuclear waste, and the Three Mile Island incident set back the nuclear-power industry.

Solar energy offers great promise for the long term, but not much relief in the immediate future. Coal is in plentiful supply, but it pollutes the atmosphere. Periodic labor strikes have slowed the changeover to a greater emphasis on the use of coal.

SOME CONSERVATION EFFORTS OF BUSINESS

The area that offers the greatest opportunity for conversation in the immediate future is energy conservation. Curtailed allocations of natural gas were in effect during the winter months from 1974 through 1979. Industrial plants and large office complexes responded with strong efforts to conserve energy. As the cost of gas increased, homeowners and businesses alike added more insulation and installed energy-saving equipment.

IBM, in a recent annual report, told of its energy saving for one twelve-month period. The energy saved in its major domestic plants, labs, and headquarters amounted to "31 percent for fuel and 22 percent for electricity from pre-conservation levels of consumption."

The Du Pont Company offers energy-conservation consultant services to industry through its Energy Management Services division. One of its studies covering eighteen plants reported an average saving of 22 percent.

The Metropolitan Life Insurance Company of New York, whose offices hold 12,000 people, estimates that it has cut electricity consumption by 25 percent and steam consumption between 40 and 50 percent. It has done so by turning thermostats down to 68 degrees, by removing every other light bulb in the corridors, and by reducing the number of elevators in service.

Representing Du Pont at a meeting sponsored by the Conference Board, CEO Edward G. Jefferson reported that more than 60 percent of Du Pont's energy savings have come from such methods as the following:

1. Tuning controls on steam boilers and furnaces to increase their efficiency
2. Putting steam turbines into plants that need steam for their processes anyway
3. Increasing maintenance to cut down heat waste from steam leaks or poor insulation
4. Recovering heat

The Exxon Corporation reported that in its home-office building, it had, through various conservation measures, reduced the use of electrical energy by 27 percent and gas consumption by 54 percent.

Conservation is a good example of social responsibility that makes economic sense. Perhaps this is an ideal situation, since by such rational/economic decisions to conserve, both the businesses' self-interest and society's interests are served.

Business both determines and is the product of environmental influences.

There are many and diverse interests of business. Some are chiefly self-centered; others are in the public interest. As the social, economic, political, and physical forces change, business must adjust to these changes.

One of the major needs of business today is to build public confidence in business as an institution.

Consumerism developed to enable the public to obtain more information and improved product safety and product quality.

The Civil Rights Act launched a movement to give minorities their due in employment, wages, and promotions.

As a result of the Civil Rights Act and further government action, most businesses now have equal employment opportunity for women and minorities.

The Office of Minority Business Enterprise coordinates the various programs administered by federal government agencies concerned with minority businesses.

To improve the physical environment, we are concerned with air and water pollution, solid-waste disposal, and the conservation of natural resources.

Congress has enacted many laws dealing with air, water, and solid-waste pollution.

Business seems to be making an honest effort to deal with its social responsibility to society. This is a long-term and expensive undertaking.

BUSINESS TERMS

You should be able to match these business terms with the statements that follow:

a. CONSUMERISM   c. ENVIRONMENT   e. PLURALISTIC SOCIETY
b. ECOLOGY   d. MINORITY GROUP f. POLLUTION

1. The sum of all external forces that influence persons and communities
2. The diverse groups in society that combine to influence the business environment
3. A movement to inform and protect people who purchase goods and services
4. A small division of the population whose cultural patterns differ from those of other segments of society
5. A study of the relationships between people and their environments
6. The deterioration of the natural environment

REVIEW QUESTIONS

1. What are the various types of environment in which business functions?
2. What are the "rights" to which consumers feel they are entitled?
3. What is being done to give minorities a fair shake in business and government?
4. What are the major causes of the deterioration of our physical environment?
5. What actions has the federal government taken to restore a clean physical environment?
6. Give some examples of what business is doing to restore a clean environment.

DISCUSSION QUESTIONS

1. What is the meaning of the term *pluralistic society*? What is the basic concern of pluralism?
2. Why has consumerism developed as a force in society?
3. In your opinion, why are there not more women in executive positions in large businesses?
4. How should the cost of cleaning up the environment be divided between business and government?

5. Is the government doing too much, too little, or the right amount in its effort to provide a clean environment? Why do you hold this opinion?

6. Is business as a whole making an honest effort to clean up the environment? Give reasons to support your answer.

BUSINESS CASES

2-1

DOES INSULATION IMPROVE THE HOME?

Bill Jones, a TV producer, has been trying to sell his home for a year. When he finally received an offer on the house, the buyer backed out before the sale, citing health concerns. Bill had insulated his house three years before with urea-formaldehyde foam. The foam has been linked to eye, nose, and throat irritations, and some laboratory rats have developed cancer after breathing heavy doses.

Some 500,000 foam-insulated homes across the nation have faced severe drops in their market value. The owners thought at the time that this was an improvement as well as a conservation effort. Insulation that cost $1,000 to install would in many cases cost $6,000 to $20,000 to remove.

Only half a dozen manufacturers are left, down from thirty at the height of the foam's popularity.

1. Who is "to blame"?
2. Is there an element of social responsibility here?
3. What can be done now?

2-2

A CITIZENS' GROUP PROTESTS

The Hart Petro Corporation has applied for a permit to build an oil-processing plant and ocean dock about forty miles from a city of 80,000 people. This plant would be about four miles from a public beach that was heavily damaged by oil spills a few years ago. At that time, the company was forced to discontinue drilling for oil offshore. The company also requests permission to construct a seven-mile pipeline from its offshore wells to the proposed plant and ocean dock. According to company officials, about seventy-five people would be employed in the plant.

To house its employees, the company seeks a permit to build a fifty-unit high-rise apartment in the area. The high-rise would be located about six miles from the plant. The company would construct a separate sewage-disposal plant for the high-rise and would drill water wells. The energy to operate the entire operation is available from the local public-utility company.

At a meeting of the county government, a complaint was filed by an irate citizens' group residing in the nearby city. This group is asking that the project be rejected because it would be a source of air and water pollution and would destroy local wildlife. In response to the complaint, the company offered to post a bond to cover future environmental damages within reason.

1. What issues are involved in this controversy?
2. What more could the company do to earn approval?
3. Would you vote for approval if you lived in the nearby city? Give reasons to support your answer.

PART 1

CAREERS IN BUSINESS

We have included in this book, at the end of each Part, a short capsule on career opportunities. We discuss career areas that apply to the chapters just concluded. For example, in this section, the chapters were "The American Business System" and "Business and Society." Here, we consider a general overview of careers in business and economics.

Business continues to be the major career field in the United States today. More people go to work for businesses of one sort or another than go into government, or agriculture, or any other type of employment. Preparing for a job in business usually includes education and training in a business field that you find interesting. Education *does* pay off. The U.S. Census Bureau shows that over a lifetime, a person with a four-year college degree can (on the average) expect to earn $370,314 more than someone with only a high school education. Currently, jobs that seem to need trained people most are in accounting, computers and data processing, management and administration, and sales and technical positions.

A college degree does not guarantee anyone a job. In many areas, there are more trained people than there are jobs. Certain college majors provide few job opportunities. Currently, those areas include education, communication, and other liberal-arts areas. However, some people argue that an education should be a broadening experience, not just training for a job. When an education is approached that way, some training or experience usually has to be added later to make a successful career.

BUSINESS AND ECONOMICS

Many people make their living analyzing economic facts so that business managers, business owners, and government officials will be able to make more intelligent predictions and daily decisions. A career as an economist can be an interesting, challenging, and rewarding area of employment.

The economist works largely in three areas: (1) in business enterprises, (2) in government, or (3) in a college or university as a teacher of economics. To a lesser degree, economists are also employed by independent research firms that provide business with analyses of economic data to aid in solving specific problems.

Business Enterprises   Individual firms are the largest employers of economists. These include banks, insurance companies, manufacturing firms, retail distribution chains, transportation companies, construction companies, and farms. Many business decisions depend upon a better understanding of how the economy is working and what action the firm should take to prevent business losses that result from economic fluctuations.

Government   Many economists are employed in the area of government. This includes not only the federal government but also state and local governments. There are also career opportunities in government agencies outside the United States. Much of the government economist's work involves conducting economic studies and collecting and interpreting facts that pertain to the current business scene.

Education   Those who wish to work in economic areas but are not interested in either business or government may have a rewarding career in teaching economics. Most of those who teach at the college level eventually obtain a Ph.D. degree in economics. Some of them work part-time as economic consultants to labor unions, trade associations, and business firms both large and small.

OWNERSHIP, MANAGEMENT, AND ORGANIZATION

When Roger and Calvin organized their manufacturing business they called it King Clothiers. They began as a partnership with each partner having responsibility for different functions in the business. They agreed to share the profits equally.

As the business prospered the Kings decided to open a retail outlet. Juan Perez headed his own store but was thinking about expanding it. You will note in Chapter 3 that he joined King Clothiers as a third partner. His retail store seemed to be just what they needed, and their expertise seemed to be what Juan needed. All went well for a time and then something unusual happened.

Unknown to the Kings, Perez signed a contract for remodeling their retail outlet. Although Roger and Calvin had no part in this action, as partners they were legally responsible along with Juan. Their attorney advised them to change the partnership form of business (with its unlimited liability for each partner) and form a corporation. This they did, and you will see in Chapter 3 why this was a good decision. You will see in Chapter 4 the broad types of functions the Kings performed as managers.

BUSINESS OWNERSHIP FORMS

study objectives

WHEN YOU HAVE FINISHED READING THIS CHAPTER, YOU SHOULD BE
ABLE TO:

1. Name the principal forms of business ownership

2. Identify the strengths and weaknesses of each form

3. Discuss the important provisions of a partnership agreement

4. Explain what corporate stockholders really own

5. Distinguish between a public and a private corporation

6. Identify other legal forms of business ownership

3

When a business firm attempts to mold its whole policy to meet the prices of its competitor, that business is entering a labyrinth the center of which is the chamber of despair. Highest quality never can be given nor obtained at the lowest prices. If a price must be sacrificed, quality must be sacrificed. If quality is sacrificed, society is not truly served.

H. T. Garvey

There are millions of firms doing business in this country. They range in size from the corner drugstore to gigantic manufacturing, trade, and service enterprises. Some are owned and operated by an individual or family, others are owned by a great many people. American Telephone and Telegraph, for example, has more than 3 million owners; General Motors, 1.1 million.

Every person who starts a new business must answer a most crucial question: What is the best form of ownership for my particular business? Each of the legal forms of business ownership has its own special features, advantages, and disadvantages. The success of any business may depend upon choosing the correct form of organization. This chapter examines the different organization patterns, their special features, strengths, and weaknesses.

BUSINESS OWNERSHIP

Juan Perez wanted to start his own men's clothing business, after working for Holbrook Clothing for six years. During this period, Juan had advanced to the position of manager and buyer. He had saved some money, so he decided this was the time to open his own business.

A new shopping center was being developed in the area close to Juan's home, and there were several store spaces available for lease. He had enough capital to begin on a small scale, and three wholesalers gave him enough credit to get started. What form of business organization should Juan use? He could start as a sole proprietorship, a partnership, or a corporation. Juan chose to begin as a sole proprietorship, called Perez Men's Clothing.

OWNERSHIP, MANAGEMENT, AND ORGANIZATION

A Sole Proprietorship

THE SOLE PROPRIETORSHIP

A SOLE PROPRIETORSHIP is *a business owned and operated by one person.* It is the simplest and oldest form of business organization. The single owner assumes all risks, receives all the profits, and sustains all losses. He or she is also the operator and manager.

There are between 10 and 11 million proprietorships in the United States. They constitute 78 percent of all businesses, yet they make only about one-tenth of all sales. Clearly, proprietorships are plentiful but usually small in size. They are found in almost every type of business activity; the local hardware store, bakery, and barbershop are examples. They are usually small because of the limited capital of the owners. About four-fifths of all proprietorships have four or fewer employees.

ADVANTAGES OF THE SOLE PROPRIETORSHIP

In addition to being one's own boss, the proprietorship has these advantages:

1. It is easy to start.
2. The cost of organization is low.
3. The owner has the freedom to manage.
4. Profit incentive is strong.

FIGURE 3-1

Number of businesses by forms of ownership and total annual receipts for firms.
(Source: Statistical abstract of the United States, 1981; p. 534.)

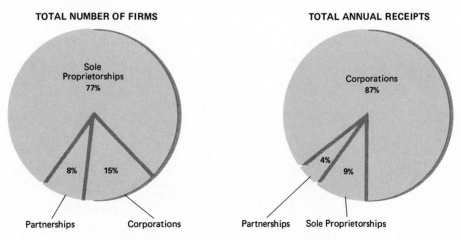

TOTAL NUMBER OF FIRMS

Sole Proprietorships 77%

Partnerships 8%   Corporations 15%

TOTAL ANNUAL RECEIPTS

Corporations 87%

Partnerships 4%   Sole Proprietorships 9%

FINANCIAL
PLANNING

MARKETING

DEVELOPMENT

STRATEGIES
AND TACTICS

How many hats do owner-managers wear?

Ease of Starting.   A proprietorship is easy to start, since there is no need to make a contract with other owners. There is no charter to obtain from the state government. There are few legal restrictions—one may need a license from the local government. The owner is free to choose the name of the new business.

Low Cost of Organization.   Since a proprietorship is not chartered by the state, there is no charter fee to be paid, and the local license fee is small. The main costs of getting started are those for equipment and merchandise. The profits of the business are not taxed—the owner pays income taxes as an individual.

Freedom to Manage.   The sole proprietorship has special appeal as a new firm. The sole owner has the maximum freedom in decision making. There is only one person responsible, and he or she is the boss. Since no one else is involved, the single proprietor can move promptly. There are also fewer government restrictions than for other forms of business.

Strong Profit Incentive.   After expenses are paid, all the profits belong to the owner. They constitute the reward for one's work and for risking one's own capital. Profit serves as a strong incentive and gives the owner maximum satisfaction.

DISADVANTAGES OF THE SOLE PROPRIETORSHIP   Every type of business has its weaknesses as well as its strengths. Those for the sole proprietorship are:

1. Limited size
2. Unlimited liability for debts
3. Limited life
4. Limited management ability

Limited Size.   The size of a sole proprietorship is limited by the amount of capital the owner can raise. This is the sum of money already on hand, plus what may be borrowed.

As the amount of capital needed increases, the owner may find it necessary to change to a partnership. Many small corporations began as proprietorships.

Unlimited Liability for Debts.   The claims of creditors against a business might exceed the value of its assets. **In this case, the *personal property of the owner* may be taken to pay the business debts.** This fact often discourages people from starting their own businesses. It is one of the most serious weaknesses of the proprietorship.

Limited Life.   What happens to a business in case the owner dies or becomes disabled? This is often a real problem for the single-owner firm. If no family member is ready, willing, or able to carry on, it must be sold. If family members are not prepared to manage it, bankruptcy most likely will result. **A sole proprietorship has no legal life beyond that of its founder.**

Limited Management Ability.   Every business has many basic functions that must be performed in order for it to be successful. Among them are buying, selling, advertising, accounting, insurance, credit, and personnel management. Few people are expert in all these areas—the chief cause of most small-business failures. The sole owner is responsible for these things even though he or she is not competent in all areas.

In spite of all this, the sole proprietorship has special appeal for a new firm. Being one's own boss and keeping all the profits are incentives strong enough to motivate many owners to work hard and succeed.

THE PARTNERSHIP

Juan Perez's business grew to the point that he needed more staff. His strength was in merchandising, but paperwork, records, and reports kept piling up. It was at this point that Juan joined the King brothers as a partner, and manager of their retail outlet. His added capital and merchandising experience seemed to be just what the Kings needed. And Calvin's know-how was what Juan needed. Juan was now faced with the necessity of knowing what was involved in forming a partnership.

Like the sole proprietorship, the partnership is a form of ownership that has existed for centuries. In some respects, it is an extension of the proprietorship, but it is designed to include more than one owner.

The Uniform Partnership Act, which has been adopted by most states,[1] defines a PARTNERSHIP as *an association of two or more persons who are the co-owners of the business.* The authority for its creation rests in the common-law "right of voluntary association." So there can be no partnership without the expressed intention of all partners. The legal basis for the partnership is usually a written document called the **Articles of Partnership.**

GENERAL PARTNERSHIPS AND LIMITED PARTNERSHIPS   The law recognizes two distinct types of partnership: general and limited. A GENERAL PARTNERSHIP is *an association of two or more persons with each general partner as co-owner having unlimited legal liability.* The general partners usually take an active role in the business. Unlike the corporation,

---

[1] The following states have *not* adopted the Uniform Partnership Act: Alabama, Florida, Georgia, Hawaii, Iowa, Kansas, Louisiana, Maine, Mississippi, and New Hampshire.

EDWARD F. SHORMA

Edward Shorma almost went broke twice. But in 1982 he was named national Small Business Person of the year. His company makes canvas and vinyl truck covers. It also manufactures high-strength conveyor belts, seats for farm equipment, and wood trim used in construction.

Shorma started in business in 1953 through the purchase of a Wahpeton (North Dakota) shoe-repair business. His first year he grossed $5,600, but now sales run in the millions.

In 1974, Shorma built a new plant to accommodate his growing business, and a year later added a warehouse. In 1979, a patented rollup tarp was well received by the trucking industry. In recent years, the company made great strides in becoming energy self-supportive. The company employs about 40 handicapped and disabled persons in addition to 180 other employees.

Wahpeton is the site of the North Dakota State School of Science. Shorma created a work shift at the plant that employs exclusively the part-time work of college students. He estimates that 250 young people have funded their college educations by working this shift.

Shorma says about his work force, "You have to take time to explain what you want. Then employees can assume more responsibility. I receive great satisfaction charting my own course, pursuing opportunities instead of security."

Edward Shorma and his wife were married in 1953. They have eight children.

the general partnership requires no state charter to operate. Termination of the partnership agreement can occur at any time, depending upon the conditions set forth in the agreement.

A LIMITED PARTNERSHIP is *an association in which one or more (but not all) partners have limited legal liability for the debts of the firm.* Each limited partner is not legally liable for debts beyond the amounts of money he or she invested in the enterprise. It is important to note, however, that limited partners may not participate in managing the business. They are investors rather than participants in the firm's operations. If they do participate in the management, the courts recognize them as general partners, and their liability then becomes unlimited.

Most states have adopted the Uniform Limited Partnership Act, which provides legal sanction and state regulation over limited partnerships. Under this act, a detailed statement about the limited partnership must be filed with the county clerk or some other government official. The kinds of information required varies by states. Most states call the document a **limited partnership certificate.**

Limited partnerships have been popular in recent years as a form of ownership involving speculative business ventures. Common examples are drilling for oil, financing mobile-home parks, and operating cattle-feeding lots. Limited partners have no liability whatever for the debts of the business. They do face the possibility of losing their investment, of course. But their personal assets may not be taken for debts of the firm.

KINDS OF PARTNERS The law recognizes various kinds of partners in a general partnership. An owner who takes an active role but does not want to reveal his or her identity to the public is a **secret partner.** One known to the public as a partner but

FIGURE 3-2
Many professionals, such as
physicians, architects, and
lawyers, conduct their business
as partnerships.
(Photo by Cary Wolinsky, STOCK/Boston)

who takes no active part in the business is a **silent partner.** A **dormant partner** is one who plays no active role and at the same time remains unknown to the public. A **nominal partner** is not actually an owner of the business. But he suggests to others by his actions or words that he is a partner.

A general partner who has been with the partnership for a long time and who owns a large share of the general partnership is a **senior partner.** The title **junior partner** is used to identify someone who has been an owner for a short time and is not assuming substantial responsibility.

A cattle-feeding lot operation might be a
limited partnership.
(Photo U.S. Department of Agriculture)

FORMING A PARTNERSHIP

Basic to all general partnerships is an "agreement of intent." This may be oral, written, or implied by the actions of the partners. It is best that the agreement be in writing to avoid later misunderstanding.

It takes more than a handshake to form a partnership. A written agreement is required.

Partnership Agreement. ***Written or oral provisions agreed to by the partners*** are known as a PARTNERSHIP AGREEMENT or ARTICLES OF PARTNERSHIP. Table 3-1 lists the various elements that constitute common partnership agreements. Some state laws stipulate that a partnership operating under a firm name rather than the partners' names must file such name with a county official, together with a list of the partners and their addresses. Each time a partner withdraws or one is added, this procedure must be repeated. If the written agreement does not show how profits and losses are to be shared, then the law presumes they will be shared equally.

TABLE 3-1
Essential Elements in the Partnership Agreement

1. Name of the partnership
2. Names of partners
3. Location of the business
4. Legal addresses of all partners
5. Nature of the business
6. Intended duration of the partnership
7. Amount of cash or other contributions made by partners
8. Amount of time each partner will devote to business
9. Provisions for salaries or drawing accounts for partners
10. Distribution of profits or losses
11. Duties and responsibilities of each partner
12. Procedure regarding the way in which the books are to be closed upon death or withdrawal of a partner.
13. Special dissolution procedures
14. Methods for resolving disagreements
15. Use of life insurance to purchase protection for surviving partners

Rights and Duties of General Partners. Unless they are waived by the articles of partnership, each partner has certain rights and duties. Some of the more important ones are these:

OWNERSHIP, MANAGEMENT, AND ORGANIZATION

1. The right to participate in the management of the business
2. The right to examine partnership records and financial statements
3. The right to share in the partnership's assets when the agreement is terminated
4. The duty to observe the terms of the agreement
5. The duty to act in good faith when dealing with partners
6. The duty to exercise reasonable care and skill in handling affairs of a partnership involving third parties

ADVANTAGES OF THE PARTNERSHIP

The partnership is similar to the proprietorship, so it has the same characteristics. It does have the advantage of a larger capital. It also has an advantage in management skill, as each partner has special competencies. The idea is to blend them together so that they complement one another.

The partnership has few legal restrictions—no state charter is required, and the owners are taxed as individuals on their profits. Each partner has strong motives to make the business succeed, for business success benefits each of the partners.

DISADVANTAGES OF THE PARTNERSHIP

Although the partnership has some advantages over the single-owner firm, it has some disadvantages as well. Chief among these are:

1. Unlimited liability of partners
2. Possibility of disagreements
3. Lack of continuity
4. Frozen investment

Unlimited Liability of Partners. The chief weakness of the partnership is personal liability of each partner. Suppose, for example, that Partner A enters into a contract that forces the firm into bankruptcy. If Partner A does not have personal assets to meet the loss, the other partners would have to cover it. Each individual partner is liable for the company's debts.

Possibility of Disagreement. Any time there are several owners, disagreements may arise. Even though every person means well, partners do not always see things alike. Sometimes it is interpersonal feelings rather than business decisions that cause serious problems. Division of authority is usually a strength, but it may become a disadvantage.

Lack of Continuity. The death of a partner dissolves the business. Further, the physical or mental disability of one partner may force an end to the business. The acceptance of a new partner to buy the departed one's interest is not always easy. He or she must have management abilities and personal qualities that are acceptable to all partners. This is a very serious weakness of the general partnership.

Frozen Investment. It may be most difficult to withdraw your funds from a going concern. The remaining partners may not have enough money to purchase your share, and a new partner may be difficult to agree upon. Even when other factors are manageable, it may be hard to agree upon a fair price for each partner's share. Before entering a partnership agreement, one must realize that withdrawal of money could become quite difficult.

BUSINESSES ADAPTABLE TO PARTNERSHIPS

There is no clear-cut method of deciding in advance which kinds of business are best for the general or limited partnership. Any small or medium-sized firm could conceivably operate as a partnership.

In some instances, the use of a partnership offers certain advantages. Investment banks and consulting firms are often organized as general partnerships. Such ventures as mobile-home parks and developing shopping centers are adaptable to the general partnership. For many years, several of the larger stock-brokerage firms were general partnerships. Both Montgomery Ward and Procter & Gamble started as general partnerships. Eventually they grew large and became corporations.

JOINT VENTURES

As another unincorporated form of business ownership, the joint venture has become popular. It was first used in Europe during the seventeenth century to carry out trade ventures with merchants in foreign countries.

The JOINT VENTURE is *an association of two or more persons for a limited purpose, without the usual rights and responsibilities of a partnership.* It is actually a temporary partnership arrangement to carry out a single business operation. After the venture is accomplished, it is dissolved. However, long-running exceptions can be noted, such as Japan's Sumitomo Shoji Kaisha Ltd. Sumitomo is an "integrated trading company" that began on the island of Shikoku 350 years ago. It is composed of more than fifty companies and employs more than 250,000 people. Such huge trading companies are joint ventures that are involved in domestic trade and in import, export, and third-country trade. They are credited with playing a major role in the economic recovery of Japan following World War II.

Sumitomo displays an incredible breadth of economic interests. It is involved in financing, warehousing, investments in manufacturing, transportation, petroleum, mining, forest products, real estate, and tourism. All activities are directed toward one end—promoting trade. The huge firm feels that exporting to another country is not enough. To help the balance of trade between Japan and the United States, Sumitomo exports American goods to Japan as well as Japanese-made goods to the United States.

In the eyes of the law, a corporation is a "person." So joint ventures can include partnerships between corporations as well as between individuals. It is common for several oil companies to form a joint venture to explore for oil or natural gas. The Alaskan Pipeline Project is an example. The joint venture is also used for large-scale construction jobs to complete specific projects. When used in the sale of securities, it is called an underwriting syndicate. For example, a group of investment banks may join together temporarily to market a new issue of corporate securities. Such a group can easily be organized, since it does not require a charter.

CORPORATIONS

The business corporation has become the major economic institution in America. Today it is probably impossible for one person to obtain enough capital to start a steel plant, an oil refinery, or an automobile manufacturer.

But by using the corporation as an ownership form, it is possible to obtain large sums from the sale of corporate stocks and bonds. The corporation is found in most fields of business activity.

Despite its complexity, it is the most satisfactory form of ownership for large organizations. In writing about the American corporation, economist John Kenneth Galbraith stated:

> The institution that most changes our lives we least understand or, more correctly, seek most elaborately to misunderstand. That is the modern corporation. . . . The modern corporation lives in suspension between fiction and truth.[2]

Although corporations make up only 14 percent of all U.S. businesses, they account for 86 percent of all sales.

WHAT IS A CORPORATION?

Chief Justice John Marshall of the U.S. Supreme Court defined a CORPORATION as *"an artificial being, invisible, intangible, and existing only in contemplation of the law. . . . "*

More recently, the U.S. Supreme Court called a CORPORATION *"an association of individuals united for some common purpose, and permitted by law to use a common name, and to change its members without dissolution of the association."* You may be surprised to note the life-like characteristics contained in Chief Justice Marshall's definition of a corporation. This definition suggests that it is a "person," as we noted earlier, separate and distinct from the owners. It can sue and be sued. Corporations are separate legal entities from their owners. Likewise, the owners may be separate from the managers.

A corporation is chartered by a state, and its charter may provide for perpetual existence in the certificate of incorporation. Some states have more lenient charter restrictions than others.[3]

Corporations employ many people and control vast sums of economic wealth and physical resources. For example, recently the 500 largest industrial corporations in the United States reported gross revenue of over $1.6 trillion.

TYPES OF CORPORATIONS

Corporations can be classified according to their charter provisions:

1. Private or business corporation
2. Public or government corporation
3. Open or close corporation
4. Domestic, foreign, or alien corporation

Private or Business Corporation. *A business privately operated for profit for the benefit of stockholders* is a PRIVATE CORPORATION. Examples are the Ford Motor Company, General Electric, and Eastman Kodak. Not all corpora-

---

[2] John Kenneth Galbraith, *The Age of Uncertainty* (Boston: Houghton Mifflin, 1977), p. 257.

[3] Arizona, Delaware, Florida, Iowa, Maine, and Nevada are among the states with fewer incorporation requirements. More corporations are chartered by Delaware than by any other state because the laws of Delaware are the least strict. About one-third of the corporations listed on the New York Stock Exchange have Delaware charters.

tions intend to earn a profit. Most states permit the formation of a corporation for charitable, educational, or social purposes.

Public or Government Corporation. *A corporation chartered by the federal government, a state, or a city for a public purpose* is a PUBLIC CORPORATION. The Federal Deposit Insurance Corporation is a well-known public corporation.

Open or Close Corporation. *A profit-making corporation whose stock is sold on the open market* is an OPEN CORPORATION. This type of stock is issued by companies that are listed on various stock exchanges and on local (over-the-counter) markets. *A corporation whose stock is closely held by members of a family or by a relatively few stockholders* is a CLOSE CORPORATION. In recent years, many close corporations, such as the Hughes Tool Company and Ford Motor Company have "gone public" by making their shares available to the public as open corporations.

Domestic, Foreign, or Alien Corporation. *A business chartered under the corporate laws of one state* is regarded as a DOMESTIC CORPORATION of that state. In all other states, it is a **foreign corporation.** A company doing business in the United States but chartered by a foreign government is known in the United States as an **alien corporation.**

ADVANTAGES OF THE CORPORATION

The popularity of the corporate form of business shows that it has some advantages over other forms of ownership. Its chief advantages are these:

1. Limited liability of stockholders
2. Continuity of life
3. Ease of ownership transfer
4. Specialized management
5. Large financial capability

Limited Liability of Stockholders. The owners of corporation stock are not liable for the debts of the business. This means that the risk of each stockholder is limited to the amount he or she has invested.[4] The corporation is a separate legal entity, so it owes the company's debts. That is, creditors of a corporation have a claim against the assets of the firm, but no claim against those of the owners. This gives the corporation one of its greatest advantages over other business forms.

Continuity of Life. Earlier we noted a weakness of the proprietorship and partnership in that an owner's death may end the business. **The corporation stays in business even though an owner or officer dies or retires.**

We might say that a corporation has perpetual existence. Retiring officers may be replaced, and owners may sell their stock to others. A corporation's charter is granted for an indefinite period. Courts may revoke it when it is adversely affecting the best interests of the general public. In practice, however, this seldom happens.

---

[4] There is an exception to this rule in the case of banks. A person's liability may be twice the sum he has invested.

THE TOP TEN INDUSTRIAL CORPORATIONS

We have a tendency to think of "big business" as something that is not subject to change. Yet businesses do change in their relative importance in size, sales, and profitability. For example, of the ten largest industrial corporations in 1917 (measured by total assets), only three—Bethlehem Steel, Exxon, and U.S. Steel—were among the ten largest twelve years later. Of the ten largest corporations in 1966, only seven were in the top ten fifteen years later, in 1981. Since 1917, twenty different companies have appeared on one or more of the listings of the top ten companies in the United States. There were 212 companies that appeared at least once among the largest 100 industrial companies during that time. The relative rankings of the top ten for selected years is shown in Table 3-2.

TABLE 3-2
The Top Ten Industrial Corporations (measured by asset size)

COMPANY	1917	1929	1945	1966	1977	1981
Anaconda Co.[a]	13	8	13	45	—	10
Armour & Co.	4	14	30	99	—	—
Bethlehem Steel	3	5	7	19	28	47
E.I. du pont de Nemours	7	12	5	16	19	12
Exxon	2	2	1	1	1	1
Ford Motor Co.	20	6	10	3	6	6
General Electric	10	11	8	9	9	11
General Motors	30	3	3	2	2	3
Gulf Oil Corporation	49	15	12	5	8	9
IBM	—	—	94	10	5	8
International Harvester	6	17	14	29	45	46
Midvale Steel & Ordinance	8	—	—	—	—	—
Mobil Corporation	—	—	4	8	3	2
Standard Oil (Calif.)	35	10	11	12	7	5
Standard Oil (Ind.)	36	4	6	13	10	7
Standard Oil (N.Y.)	14	7	—	—	—	—
Swift & Company	5	18	29	95	—	—
Texaco	33	9	9	4	4	4
Uniroyal	9	23	46	63	—	—
U.S. Steel	1	1	2	6	14	19

Note: The top ten for each of the years reported constitute those companies included in this table. The relative ranking of each is then shown for each of the years chosen. Where no figures are given, this indicates that the company was not in the top 100 corporations for that year.

[a] Anaconda is now a part of Atlantic-Richfield, which ranked tenth in 1981.

Ease of Ownership Transfer. The stock of an open corporation may be publicly traded and listed on a stock exchange. This makes it easy for people to buy or sell their shares. An owner may make this transfer through an endorsement on the back of the stock certificate. In addition, an owner may transfer shares to another person through the stockholder-relations department of the firm. Most large corporations hire a bank to serve as the transfer agent for their stock certificates. Easy transfer of ownership is a distinct advantage of the corporate form.

Specialized Management.   We noted that corporations are often managed by officers, not by owners. The stockholders elect the board of directors, which hires the company officers. The officers then employ people to manage particular phases of the business. This gives the business expertise in vital areas such as production, finance, purchasing, and marketing.

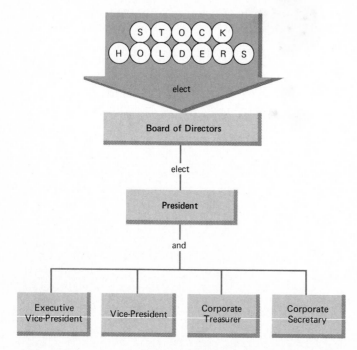

FIGURE 3-4
Management Structure of a Corporation
The governing board of the corporation is its board of directors, elected by the stockholders. The directors, in turn, approve the appointment of the president and other executive officers.

Large Financial Capability.   As a business grows, it must raise additional capital. This is a stumbling block for a single owner or a partnership, but the corporation has more options. It may borrow money for a short period, or it can raise money for the long term by selling bonds or stock. Millions of people are able and willing to invest in businesses through one of these methods. So a successful corporation can usually obtain the funds it needs for expansion. The different types of corporate financing are discussed more fully in Chapter 14, "Business Finance and Investments."

DISADVANTAGES OF THE CORPORATION   Like any other business ownership form, the corporation has weaknesses as well as strengths. The most important among them are these:

1. Cost and difficulty of organization
2. Double taxation of earnings
3. Legal restrictions on activities
4. Separation of ownership and control
5. Lack of personal interest

Cost and Difficulty of Organization.   The sole proprietorship is the easiest to organize, and the corporation is the most difficult. People wishing to incorporate must agree on the company's goals and its plan of operation. A charter must be obtained from the state government. For this process, legal help and advice are important, if not essential. There is more delay to starting a corporation than for either a proprietorship or a partnership. The costs of organizing and being granted a charter may amount to thousands of dollars for a large business.

Double Taxation of Earnings.   Neither the proprietorship nor the partnership pays taxes on its earnings—the owners pay taxes as individuals. The corporation, however, is taxed on its earnings. It is not uncommon for a corporation to pay one-half its net earnings in foreign, federal, and state income taxes.

Most corporations also pay dividends to the owners from earnings. These owners or stockholders then pay state and federal income taxes on the dividends they receive. This amounts to taxing a corporation's earnings twice. This practice is thought to be a hindrance to the capital formation needed to run American business.

Legal Restrictions on Activities.   The corporate charter identifies the kind of activities the business may perform. If the directors of a corporation should decide to engage in a totally unrelated type of operation, technically the charter should be amended to legalize that function. This, of course, requires approval by a state-government agency, and there would be some legal expense.

Formal reports to government agencies are required of corporations that are not required of other forms of business.

Separation of Ownership and Control.   The directors of a corporation are elected by the stockholders and the directors select the company officers. In many cases the directors, as a group, control the election. This is achieved through their own stockholdings and the proxies they solicit. A PROXY is *a power of attorney that transfers to a third party the stockholder's right to vote at the stockholders' annual meeting.* Individual stockholders often have little influence on company policy or operations.

Lack of Personal Interest.   Not all corporations are big businesses, but many are. As any organization grows larger, worker relations become more formal and less personal.

Since the sole proprietor risks his personal funds in the business, he has a very keen interest in it and in worker performance. On the other hand, the personal wealth of the professional corporate manager is not at stake in the company's operation. Officers and directors are not necessarily required to own stock in the companies they manage. This is not to say that professional managers do a poor job, but the motives for what they do are different from those of the owner-manager.

ORGANIZING A CORPORATION   If you know the kind of business you want to start, the next step is to select the state in which to incorporate. If your principal business will be in Illinois, you should probably incorporate in that state. Before you decide, however, you may want to compare one or two other states' requirements. A local attorney would be one source of help to advise you regarding the choice of a state.

After selection of the state, your next step would be to decide upon the information to be provided for the articles of incorporation. Usually the required information for the application is similar to that listed in Table 3-3. The charter contains the scope of business, its duration, and the names of incorporators. They are responsible for preparing the articles of incorporation. These articles are, in effect, an application to the state seeking approval to organize the corporation.

TABLE 3-3
Information for Corporation Charter Application

1. Name, location, and address of proposed corporation.
2. Names and addresses of incorporators.
3. Intended duration of the corporation — stated number of years or perpetual.
4. Nature of business in which corporation is to engage.
5. Names and addresses of directors and officers.
6. Address of principal business office.
7. Amount of capital to be authorized. This is officially known as the authorized capital stock. It is divided into shares, which may range in value from $1 to $1,000, whether common, preferred, or both.
8. Maximum number of shares of authorized stock to be issued, and whether stock will be par or no-par, with or without voting rights.[a] Shares are in the form of stock certificates, numbered and recorded when issued. Each must bear the signature of officers.
9. Name and address of each charter subscriber to stock certificates, and statement showing total number of shares paid for by each subscriber.

[a] A definition of the terms par value and no-par value is given in Chapter 14.

THE CORPORATION CHARTER   When completed, the application is ready to be approved, then you will receive the corporation's charter. Usually a copy is mailed to the clerk of the county in which the company's home office will be located. (This procedure varies slightly in different states.)

CORPORATE OWNERSHIP

Corporate officers have the responsibility for operating the business efficiently. In small corporations, owners may exercise closer control and more influence than in large ones. They may elect themselves to the board of directors and/or appoint themselves to key executive positions. Corporate officers who also serve as directors are known as ***inside directors.***

CORPORATE SHAREHOLDERS   Ownership in a business corporation is shown by stock shares. Common stock generally carries voting rights; preferred stock, as a rule, does not. Common-stockholders receive dividends only after the preferred-stock holders. There are several different kinds of shares, which are discussed in some detail in Chapter 14. For the present, our discussion will deal with only one class of stock — common stock.

What Do Stockholders Really Own?   "Owning a share of stock" is really just what the phrase implies: having a small interest in the total entity called the corporation. But this fractional claim is not for a fixed amount payable at any time. It is worth only what someone else will pay you for it.

FIGURE 3-5
This stock certificate is typical of the kind issued to stockholders of an open corporation.
To sell the shares, it is necessary to endorse certificate on the reverse side.
(Courtesy Tenneco, Inc.)

Ownership in the corporation can easily be transferred from one person to another by selling and buying shares. A common-stock certificate is illustrated in Figure 3-5. To transfer ownership of this certificate, one must sign it on the reverse side.

Rights of the Stockholders.   Stockholders have certain legal rights. For discussion purposes, these can be classified as group rights and individual rights. **Group rights** are rights that stockholders may exercise when assembled at regular and special meetings. **Individual rights** are rights that each stockholder has without other stockholders.

Stockholder group rights consist of the following:

1. Elect directors
2. Adopt and amend the bylaws
3. Change the charter with the consent of the state
4. Sell or otherwise dispose of corporation assets
5. Dissolve the corporation

FIGURE 3-6
A stockholders' meeting.
(Courtesy AT&T, 1981)

In the absence of any state restrictions or restrictions in the corporate charter, each stockholder has at least these individual rights. A stockholder can:

1. Buy and sell stock registered in the owner's name
2. Receive dividends in proportion to the number and class of shares owned, provided the dividend has been duly declared by the directors
3. Share in distribution of assets, as provided in the charter, if the directors decide to dissolve the firm
4. Subscribe to additional stock (usually common, not preferred) before it is offered to the public, unless this right is waived or revoked by a vote of the stockholders
5. Review and inspect company records
6. Sue directors for misuse of power or fraud
7. Vote at stockholders' meetings, annual or special (generally restricted to common-stockholders)

CORPORATION MERGERS

A news release announcing a corporation's plans to merge with another corporation is often welcomed by the stockholders but feared by competitors. Many of today's most successful corporations achieved their large size by joining with other companies. For example, General Foods Corporation has merged with a number of companies so that it now owns and markets more than a dozen branded foods that were formerly owned by smaller companies. Examples are Post cereals and Gaines dog food.

Reasons for a Merger. The reasons for corporate mergers include the following: (1) to take over a going company to expand a market, (2) to achieve tax advantages, (3) to gain new sources of goods, and (4) to acquire cash reserves.

OWNERSHIP, MANAGEMENT, AND ORGANIZATION

The managements of the two companies discuss the advantages and disadvantages of the merger. Laws affecting merger and tax effects are reviewed. There is always the possibility that the merger may require approval of the U.S. attorney general to ensure that there is no violation of the antitrust laws.

Finally, there is a price-per-share proposal by the offering corporation, known as the **tender-price offer.** Each stockholder has a right to accept or refuse to sell his or her shares at the proposed offering price. This tender-offer method is becoming increasingly popular because it is less costly than a long proxy fight. Tender offers are usually made to the target company's stockholders by mail or through newspaper announcements.

Some companies seeking a merger have taken a different approach. This involves buying the company's stock on the open market, paying the market price. That strategy is the gradual buy-in. Among the best-known American corporations to follow this plan are Teledyne, Loew's Corporation (theater owners), and the American Financial Corporation. The idea is to go after a company that would be a good acquisition but to do it at the market price rather than an agreed-upon merger price. By taking control of 5 to 20 percent of the shares, the acquiring corporation can establish a foothold in case it chooses to push for merger later. Ultimately, the stockholders of the two companies may be asked to vote on the issue. Sometimes mergers are very costly owing to legal fees, advertising, and the presenting of arguments to government commissions.

CURRENT ISSUE

SHOULD WE LIMIT THE SIZE OF U.S. CORPORATIONS?

You may have heard of a former officer of General Motors being quoted as saying, "Whatever is good for General Motors is good for the country!" General Motors is one of our largest and most influential companies, furnishing work to 750,000 employees. Certainly when it and other large corporations prosper, American business prospers. On the other hand, we occasionally hear it said about some of our large U.S. corporations that they have become too big and too powerful.

With which of the following statements do you agree, and with which do you disagree?

1. Whatever is good for a company in one of our basic industries is good for the country.
2. A company can become too big and too powerful.
3. Our government regulations keep a large company "in its rightful place."
4. Corporations have too much influence in Congress through their lobbying efforts.
5. Large companies like IBM, General Motors, and AT&T should be broken up into several smaller companies.
6. Organized labor, together with the federal government, keeps corporations from becoming too powerful.

Do you favor limiting the size of U.S. corporations? Why, or why not?

THE CONGLOMERATE   A common result of merger is the CONGLOMERATE — a *collection of unrelated companies producing unrelated products.* A basic purpose of the conglomerate is to achieve quick growth and thereby increase earnings. Gulf & Western Industries became a conglomerate by acquiring more than ninety corporations, and Litton Industries merged with fifty companies.[5]

When will the current merger spree end? Some economists believe it will continue for several more years. By that time, bidding for companies will push stock prices to the point where the return on investments from mergers may be less than the return from starting new plants. Many economists agree that using corporate cash for acquisitions adds little to capital formation or job creation. Thus, mergers should become less popular in future years.

HOLDING COMPANIES   Any corporation that buys sufficient shares in another corporation is called a holding company, and the acquired firm is a **subsidiary.** The owning company is known as the **parent company.** Some holding companies own all the voting stock of their subsidiaries. But even those that own less than half can take advantage of the right to use management-secured proxies. In this way they maintain effective control over the directors of the subsidiary.

U.S. antitrust laws prohibit mergers that "may tend to substantially lessen competition or tend to create a monopoly." A proposed merger combination may be stopped by the U.S. Department of Justice if the intent is to monopolize or restrain trade.

OTHER FORMS OF BUSINESS OWNERSHIP

COOPERATIVES   A COOPERATIVE is *a business owned and operated for the benefit of its members.* Its aim is to give service to its members, rather than to earn a profit. Profits are commonly returned to members in the form of **patronage dividends.** The more business a member does, the larger his or her rebate payment.

A cooperative is in most other respects similar to other types of businesses. It may be incorporated or it may not be. When it is organized as a corporation, a special type of legal charter is issued. Cooperatives usually have these factors in common:

1. The owners are called members. They are also users of the co-op's services.
2. There is a limit to the amount of capital one member may subscribe.
3. Each member has but one vote even though he may own several shares.
4. Patronage dividends paid are in proportion to the amount of goods a member has bought or sold.
5. Directors receive no salary; only managers and employees are paid.
6. Interest on their investments is paid to members.

Most of the large cooperatives are organized by farmers. Two well-known marketing cooperatives are Sunkist Growers, Inc., which markets citrus fruits; and Land-O-Lakes Creameries, which sells dairy products. Southern States Cooperative furnishes its members with materials such as seeds, feeds, and fertilizers.

---

[5] The distinction between **merger** and **acquisition** is not sharp. Acquisition means the outright purchase of assets of a company, or a sufficient interest in it to gain control.

Cooperatives have a tax advantage over corporations. Member rebates are considered a return of part of the purchase price, rather than as dividends on one's investment.

MUTUAL COMPANIES
Mutual companies are similar to cooperatives in that they are owned by those who use their services. **A mutual company is chartered as a corporation, but no stock is issued.** It enjoys most of the advantages of corporations, including limited liability to owner-members. Dividends paid to users are not taxed but are considered to be a partial return to them of premiums paid.

Most mutual companies are either savings banks or life and/or casualty insurance companies. Each person who deposits money in a mutual savings bank is automatically a member. So is each person who buys an insurance policy. These people elect the board of directors who manage the company.

SUMMARY OF KEY CONCEPTS

The sole proprietorship is easy to establish. It gives the owner maximum freedom in management, and all the profits.

The sole proprietorship has two serious weaknesses:

1. Creditors may sue the owner for his or her personal assets.
2. Death of the owner may force an end to the business.

A partnership gives a business increased capital and management expertise. A partner may restrict the amount of his or her activity or liability by being a dormant, secret, or limited partner.

The chief weaknesses of the partnership form of organization are similar to those of the sole proprietorship:

1. Each partner is personally liable for the debts of the business.
2. Death of a partner can cause serious problems in being able to continue the business.

The rights, duties, relationships, and responsibilities among partners are spelled out in the articles of partnership.

In a limited partnership, one or more partners have limited liability. Limited partners are not allowed to exercise managerial authority.

A joint venture is formed by two or more persons for a limited purpose without the usual rights and powers of a partnership. A member may not withdraw until the project is ended.

The corporation overcomes most of the weaknesses of the proprietorship and partnership, in that:

1. It has continuity of existence.
2. Owners are not personally liable for its debts.
3. It is easy to sell one's ownership shares (stock).
4. Specialists may be hired to manage the business.

A cooperative is organized to render specific types of services for its members. It does not operate for the purpose of making a profit.

The mutual company is similar to the cooperative in that it is owned by, and operated for the benefit of, its member users. The mutual company seems most appropriate for insurance companies and savings banks.

BUSINESS TERMS

You should be able to match these business terms with the statements that follow:

a. CONGLOMERATE
b. COOPERATIVE
c. CORPORATION
d. DOMESTIC CORPORATION
e. DORMANT PARTNER
f. GENERAL PARTNERSHIP

g. JOINT VENTURE
h. LIMITED PARTNER
i. OPEN CORPORATION
j. PARTNERSHIP
k. PARTNERSHIP AGREEMENT
l. SOLE PROPRIETORSHIP

1. An organization that is owned and operated by one person
2. A business association in which each general partner has unlimited legal liability
3. An association of two or more persons who are co-owners of the business
4. A partner whose personal liability is limited to the amount invested in the partnership capital
5. An association of two or more persons for a limited purpose without the usual rights and responsibilities of a partnership
6. Written provisions agreed to by the partners
7. An artificial, invisible, and intangible entity existing only in contemplation of the law
8. A profit-making corporation whose stock is sold on the open market
9. A corporation chartered by a state, and doing business in that state
10. A partner who has no active part in the management and remains unknown to the public
11. A collection of unrelated companies producing unrelated products
12. A business owned and operated for the benefit of its members

REVIEW QUESTIONS

1. Why is the sole proprietorship more popular than other forms of business ownership?
2. Give the reasons why so many small firms prefer the proprietorship and large companies prefer the corporation.
3. What purposes are served by special types of partners?
4. What are the weaknesses of a partnership form of business organization?
5. What are the legal rights of corporation stockholders?
6. What are the strengths of the corporate form of organization?

DISCUSSION QUESTIONS

1. Failure rates are highest for sole proprietorships and partnerships and lowest for corporations. In your opinion, what are the causes for such high proprietorship failures?
2. What accounts for the differences in the amount of capital that can be raised by a sole proprietorship and by a corporation?
3. Why is it so important to spell out specifics in a partnership agreement?
4. Do stockholders in General Electric have a voice in the daily operations of that business? Explain.
5. What is double taxation for corporation owners? How could this be eliminated?
6. Explain what we mean by separation of ownership and control in a corporation.

OWNERSHIP, MANAGEMENT, AND ORGANIZATION

3-1   BRANDON AND COWDEN, CONSULTING ENGINEERS

Brandon and Cowden have been in business as mechanical engineers in a city of a half-million people for ten years. During this period, they have rendered consulting services for the construction of more than forty large buildings.

Last year the company made a net profit, after taxes, of $62,000. This was the third consecutive year in which the firm enjoyed a 12 percent growth in total revenue and profits. In fact, the company is now at the stage where it cannot take on any additional projects of any consequence until at least two more engineers are employed. But engineers sometimes hesitate to work for a partnership because it usually does not provide them an opportunity to invest in the company.

A few days ago, one of the largest producers of electrical and mechanical valves and switches used in industrial plants offered Brandon and Cowden an exclusive dealership for the entire state. Cowden estimates that this would require the building of a fireproof warehouse and 4,000 square feet of additional engineering and office space. This would mean spending $400,000 for new buildings and an additional $200,000 in working capital. It would also entail adding at least two engineers immediately. Fortunately, there is no space problem, because the company recently bought a 20-acre tract of land.

The partners will need to find new capital on a long-term basis. Because of this and high interest rates, the local banker suggests they form a corporation. Cowden's attorney says it will cost $2,000 to form and launch the new corporation.

1. Do you see any problem in dissolving the partnership?
2. How would changing the form of legal ownership help Brandon and Cowden?
3. Where might they raise money if they incorporated?

3-2   JOHNSON AND SONS

For the past four decades, Mr. Johnson and his two sons have operated as a general partnership. The firm has established a fine reputation in the area as an industrial construction firm. Mr. Johnson, the founder of the company, retired from the business several years ago. The sons purchased their father's interest and continued the business, which has grown slowly but steadily. Both of the sons would like to retire in the near future. They would like to see the firm continue, but neither wishes to remain active in its management. Should the business continue under its present name, they would like to retain a financial interest in it. They feel that the goodwill they have created will continue to bring new business to the company.

They believe that most of the present employees would remain with the company, and they see this as another plus for retaining a financial interest. Two competent and experienced key managers with the firm and the accountant–office manager have expressed an interest in buying it.

1. Give three reasons why it would seem advisable to retain a financial interest in the company.
2. What forms of organization are feasible options in transferring ownership to the new parties but retaining a financial interest?
3. Under each option, how could the Johnson brothers arrange to retain a financial interest?
4. What type of organization form would you recommend?

In The News

Iacocca's Strong Management Gets Chrysler Going Again

Chrysler Corporation is not out of the woods yet, but it is much more likely to survive than it was a short time ago. The reason is simple: good hard-nosed management by a former Ford Motor Company executive, Lee Iacocca.

It hasn't been easy. Iacocca himself describes what he has come through as "three years of hell." When he talks about Chrysler *before* he arrived, Iacocca refers to it as "they." When talking about the new Chrysler, he uses the word "we." He says, "Fifty percent of their problems were management mistakes."

The mistakes to which he refers were:

1. Too much diversification overseas
2. Poor styling
3. Poor quality
4. Wasteful, worn-out plants
5. Horrible financing

He tackled these problems head on. Peugeot and Volkswagen purchased the overseas operations. A score of obsolete plants were closed or consolidated. The union was persuaded to take a $2.50-per-hour cut, and Iacocca himself reduced his salary to $1 per year. White-collar personnel was reduced by half. He lowered Chrysler's breakeven point to 1.2 million cars from 2.4 million cars.

Styling and quality were tackled by bringing in people from Ford, Volkswagen, and General Motors. These new people helped Chrysler employees to whom earlier management wouldn't listen. The financial situation was improved through federal loan guarantees. These Iacocca was given because he convinced Congress that such aid was a better choice than the 2.7 billion in unemployment benefits that would have to be paid if Chrysler went broke.

In 1979, very few would bet that Chrysler would last out the year, much less be in existence today. The fact that it is, is a pat on the back for the management savvy shown by its top manager, Lee Iacocca.

General Business Management

study objectives

WHEN YOU HAVE FINISHED READING THIS CHAPTER, YOU SHOULD BE ABLE TO:

1. Define management

2. Discuss the contributions made by Frederick W. Taylor

3. Explain how the managerial class movement began in the 1840s and lasted until World War I

4. Contrast the approaches of the classical school, the behavioral school, and the managerial-science school of management theory

5. Indicate why different management functions are of greater importance at the different levels of an organization

6. Discuss the following management skills: technical skills, human skills, and conceptual skills

> . . . without management there would be only a mob rather than an institution.

> *Peter Drucker*
> *Management Consultant*

S uccessful business is good management. But *every* organization, whether it be a government agency, a social club, an athletic team, a church, or a business corporation, needs competent managers. Management is simply getting results. And as with Chrysler, those results are sometimes gained only after drastic changes. Yet more management situations require competent, routine, day-to-day decision activities than need radical surgery.

Good managers can be found in both large and small organizations. The top executive of General Motors makes decisions that affect millions of customers. He is responsible for the well-being of 750,000 employees and the 16,000 dealers who sell and service GM products. The owner of a small business is a manager, too. His or her decisions affect a smaller number of people, but they are just as important for the firm's survival.

This chapter concentrates on the theory and practice of general management activities. Some of the most difficult and challenging management tasks are those that require getting the job done through other people.

THE FIELD OF MANAGEMENT

Since about 1900, scholars and business practitioners have provided a rich and growing written body of management principles and practices. This chapter is an introduction to that field.

WHAT IS MANAGEMENT? The process of MANAGEMENT includes *planning, organizing, directing, and controlling the activities of an enterprise to achieve specific objectives.* Managers perform these functions in varying degrees at different organizational levels.

OWNERSHIP, MANAGEMENT, AND ORGANIZATION

Managers are those who bring together the money, manpower, materials, and machinery necessary to operate a business. They must (1) plan for the future, (2) organize the enterprise, (3) direct the activities of employees, and (4) control the entire business.

Managers are also people who make decisions. In any organization, someone must fill the role of leader. A leader is expected to supply orderly and efficient handling of the affairs of the business. Managers do not themselves produce a finished product or directly sell a product to a customer. Instead, they direct others to do these things. Figure 4-1 shows the "Ms" of management that managers manage.

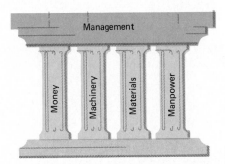

FIGURE 4-1
The "Ms" of Management

Management has been called the art of decision making, since managers spend so much time choosing among alternative solutions to business problems. These problems can occur at all levels. A good example of some major management problems can be found in the college food-catering industry. These are illustrated in the accompanying box.

MANAGEMENT CHALLENGES

Rising food prices annoy everyone, but especially those in the college food-catering business. Providing food for college cafeterias is a big business. Some 11 million students constitute a market worth $2 billion annually.

Greyhound Corporation is a major participant in the market. A study of one Greyhound contract illustates the problems. Greyhound once won from Saga Corporation, another major feeder, the contract to feed 1,500 students at the University of California, Irvine, with a bid of $2.46 per student per day. Within a few months, Greyhound's costs had escalated to more than $3.00 per student, and it was losing $15,000 per month on this operation. It invoked a "pull-out" clause and dropped the contract.

Managing such an operation includes problems besides the rising cost of food. Most contracts contain stipulations that students be provided with specified choices at each meal. There are limitations on how much pasta or poultry can be substituted for meat. Since college business managers set board rates nearly a year in advance, this causes serious problems in estimating costs. Food companies engage in bidding competition with each other, and colleges complain of poor hygiene, quality, and service.

Better management seems to be the key to improving results in this industry. Some companies are trying pay-as-you-go systems and credit cards for meals. Computerized food purchasing has cut costs in some instances, and other companies are employing waste-reduction education programs.

LEVELS OF MANAGEMENT

Large business organizations usually have at least three levels of management. These three levels are (1) top or executive management, (2) middle or administrative management, and (3) operating or supervisory management. These levels are shown in Figure 4-2. As you can see, each level of the pyramid contributes a different amount to major decisions.

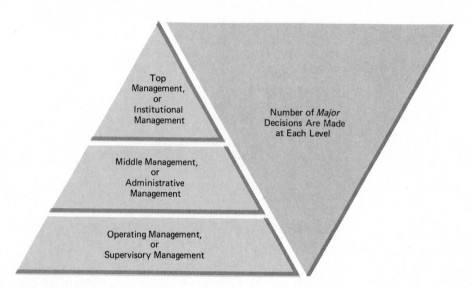

FIGURE 4-2
The Management Pyramid
The three levels of management form the management pyramid.

Top Management.   The highest level is top management, often referred to as senior managers or key executives, who have usually had many years of varied experience. This level is composed of the board of directors, the president or chief executive officer (CEO), and other corporate officers. Top management develops broad plans for the company and makes important decisions about such things as mergers, new products, and stock issues.

Middle Management.   The next level of the management pyramid, known as middle or administrative management, is composed of plant superintendents and/or division managers. These managers have the responsibility for developing the operating plans that implement the broader plans made by top managers.

Operating Management.   This is the lowest level of the management pyramid. It is primarily concerned with putting into action plans devised by middle managers. Operating managers are often referred to as "first-line supervisors," because they are responsible for supervising the workers who perform the day-to-day operations.

IS MANAGEMENT AN ART OR A SCIENCE?

A common debate has to do with whether management is an art (and therefore somewhat difficult to analyze) or a science. Many aspects of management can be (and have been) subjected to very thorough analysis. With

84

improved decision-making aids, management is more scientific than it was many years ago. But many aspects of management are clearly still art. What is the economy going to do? Will this product sell? Who should be promoted? How can we convince them to go along with us? All these questions point at issues that require a "feel" that defies application of scientific principles.

Table 4-1 shows some typical management problems. Which do you feel can be solved with "science" and which with "art"?

TABLE 4-1
Typical Problems Encountered by Managers

PROBLEM	ALTERNATIVE SOLUTIONS
1. Need to raise capital for new project.	a. Borrow from banker. b. Issue bonds. c. Sell more stock in the company.
2. High absenteeism in certain departments.	a. Discuss absenteeism with department manager to find cause. b. Consider changing department managers. c. Talk to employees involved.
3. Trusted employee was caught stealing.	a. Dismiss employee. b. Discipline employee, since this is a first offense.
4. Sharp decline in profits.	a. Review operating costs. b. Raise product prices. c. Increase advertising budget.
5. Dissatisfied executive threatens to resign.	a. Review complaint to see what can be done to keep the executive. b. Encourage the executive to stay. c. Let the executive resign.
6. Union trying to organize employees.	a. Improve conditions that employees complained about. b. Agree to bargain with union. c. Hire an attorney and fight the union.
7. Newspaper article charges firm is polluting the air.	a. Employee public-relations firm to explain the company's side. b. Ignore the article. c. File a lawsuit against the newspaper.

QUESTION: For the problems above, what other alternatives can you suggest?

HISTORICAL BACKGROUND OF MANAGEMENT

Let us look briefly at the historical background that helped to produce the "management boom" in the United States, which began immediately following World War I. The "management boom" refers to a growth in management activity and in information about managing properly.

RISE OF A MANAGERIAL CLASS   When the United States was founded, most of the work being done was farming. Only a few craftsmen were available to make such items as pots and pans, hand tools, and furniture. Most consumer goods were sold by traveling merchants. Shops were almost nonexistent in the towns and in the few cities. By 1820, about 71 percent of those employed were farm workers. There were few factories and almost no machinery.

The first American industrial revolution began in about 1820 and ended in 1850. During this period, Congress enacted high protective tariffs to encourage American business enterprises. The population increased, and many people moved from farms to cities to find employment. New inventions appeared, which caused the growth of new businesses. Eli Whitney introduced the cotton gin, which greatly increased the supply of cotton for the textile industry. Whitney also built a factory to make guns. He believed that his factory could make gun parts using all the same specifications. This made the parts interchangeable and allowed for mass production.

During this period, John Deere and Cyrus McCormick perfected farm equipment. John Studebaker built a factory to make wagon wheels. He later organized a company to make automobiles. The owners of the businesses usually managed them too. Three railroad companies connecting cities in Massachusetts were chartered in 1830. These railroads employed managers using such titles as general agent, passenger agent, freight agent, and claim agent.

The joining of the tracks is a cause for celebration at Promontory Point, Utah (undated). (Courtesy, Denver Public Library, Western History Department.)

The second industrial revolution, which occurred from 1870 to 1900, marked the beginning of large-scale production, business growth, and a decline in farm employment. America symbolized advanced capitalism, great wealth, and large corporations. By 1900, monopolies existed in the oil, tobacco, sugar, steel, and whiskey industries. A national network of rail transportation had been built, which encouraged new businesses and required managers.

It was during the second industrial revolution that some of the largest American family fortunes were founded. By 1879, oil refined into kerosene for use as a source of light and heat made John D. Rockefeller and his associates powerful and rich. The Hill, Gould, Harriman, and Vanderbilt fortunes came from the new railroads. The McCormick fortune was based on farm machinery, and the Carnegie and Frick fortunes on steel. The business tycoons were conspicuous by their great wealth.

Family at work at home. (Photo from Records of the Children's Bureau, by Lewis Hine; undated. Courtesy of National Archives.)

Workers spent long hours on the job, often under poor working conditions, and received low pay. There were no employee retirement plans, sick leave, or paid holidays. Labor unions were just getting started. Workers were often fired if the employer learned about their union membership.

By 1910, businesses employed 1.9 million managers. Figure 4-3 shows the growth in the number of managers projected to 1990.

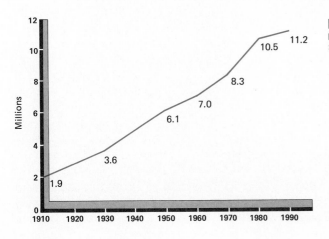

FIGURE 4-3

Managers and administrators (except farmers) employed in the United States 1910–90. (Source: Bureau of Labor Statistics, projected to 1990.)

THE SCIENTIFIC-MANAGEMENT MOVEMENT

Business has always searched to find more efficient ways to manage productivity and at the same time cut production costs. Prior to 1880, managing a business was mostly regarded as common sense, if not an art. But around 1885, Frederick W. Taylor (1856–1915) was one of the first to study work methods, using the ASME (American Society of Mechanical Engineers) as a sounding board for his ideas.

A few years before Taylor, Henri Fayol (1841–1945), was manager of a French coal mine. He also studied management, in search of techniques that would improve the production of coal. Fayol decided that management involved planning, organizing, commanding, coordinating, and controlling. He is generally credited with providing Taylor encouragement to search for more scientific methods.

In this country, Taylor is considered the father of the scientific-management movement. Born of a fairly well-to-do family in Philadelphia, he was urged to study law. His poor eyesight, however, forced him to give up this idea. He went to work as a common laborer in the Midvale Steel Company and eventually became chief engineer. He made numerous experiments to set work standards. In one experiment, he trained a pig-iron worker, who was able to increase his tonnage load from 12.5 to 47.5 tons per day. Taylor also pioneered methods-time-measurement studies. In his opinion, labor-saving machinery or mass production was worthless unless those who managed were able to keep pace with technical improvements.

Steel Foundry
(Photo by Neil Goldstein.)

OWNERSHIP, MANAGEMENT, AND ORGANIZATION

These are among the several principles of scientific management advocated by Taylor:[1]

1. All managers must be trained to use specific principles, replacing the old rule-of-thumb methods for solving problems.
2. Managers should select and train their workers rather than letting them choose their own work habits and procedures.
3. Managers should divide work responsibility as evenly as possible between themselves and their workers.
4. Managers should cooperate with workers to ensure that all work is done in accordance with scientific principles.

A New Development in Management.   John Naisbitt identified **a shift from short-term to long-term as one of the megatrends in America.** Historically, American business managers have been short-term oriented. Emphasis was placed on the current year, even the current quarter of operation. The future of the business was often sacrificed in order that "this year's profits would exceed those of last year." Reginald Jones, former Chief Executive Officer of General Electric said, "Too many managers feel under pressure to concentrate on the short-term in order to satisfy the financial community and the owners of the enterprise, the stockholders."[2]

But management in the United States is changing. As top managers look to the long-term we are seeing many companies diversify into new businesses. Xerox not only began emphasizing the automated office but bought Crum & Forster, one of the leading insurance companies in the country. In General Electric's 1982 Annual Report, CEO John F. Welch, Jr. reported to stockholders that

> The last decade has seen a dramatic shift in our business mix — from the old to the new, from relatively mature businesses to those in their high-growth stages . . . Increasing in relative importance to GE sales and earnings are such high-technology businesses as medical systems, aerospace, plastics and other proprietary materials and such service businesses as General Electric Credit Corporation, General Electric Information Services Company, and construction, engineering and nuclear services.

Aetna Life and Casualty Co., DuPont, Martin Marietta, RCA, and Sears, Roebuck & Co. are other examples of management taking their companies in new directions in order to better insure their long-term future.

SCHOOLS OF MANAGEMENT THOUGHT

As a result of an expanding interest in management education in colleges and universities, a number of theoretical approaches to the study of management have appeared. Such theories have come mainly from managers and educators seeking to discover more about what to teach prospective managers. Of the several theoretical schools of management thought that have emerged,

---

[1] Frederick W. Taylor, *The Principles of Scientific Management* (New York: Harper & Row, 1911), pp. 36–37.

[2] Reginald Jones, interviewed by Judith B. Gardner, *U.S. News and World Report*, Vol. 90, No. 23, June 15, 1981, p. 40.

we will discuss five. This introduction to the subject includes the following: (1) classical school, (2) behavioral school, (3) management-science school, (4) systems analysis, and (5) management by results.

THE CLASSICAL SCHOOL

The classical school began with the formation of large corporations. Much of the early classical literature was written between World Wars I and II. Classical theory defines management in terms of the tasks that managers perform. Advocates of the classical school identified the primary managerial functions of planning, organizing, directing, and controlling—each of which can be divided into subfunctions. The development of managerial skills was directed toward applying these functions.

THE BEHAVIORAL SCHOOL

Variously called the "leadership," "human-relations," or "behavioral-sciences" school of management, the behavioral school became popular in the 1950s. This school concentrates on the human aspect of management and emphasizes the need for managers to understand people. Managers should also know how to motivate the subordinates they supervise and direct. The behavioral school draws from such disciplines as psychology and sociology as part of the manager's educational background.

THE MANAGEMENT-SCIENCE SCHOOL

Unlike the classical school, which identifies management tasks, the management-science school involves mathematics and statistics. Mathematical models are used to solve the operational problems of planning and controlling. A model is a representation of reality. A physical model such as that used in a wind tunnel is one kind of model. Another kind is the mathematical relationships among variables, programmed for computers. Management science is a quantitative approach that has provided valuable tools for solving business problems. The computer has made it possible to study problems that were previously too complex to be solved without it.

SYSTEMS ANALYSIS

Systems analysis offers a means for viewing internal and external operations of a business. The identifying characteristic of systems analysis is that it deals with problems involving all the component parts together. In marketing, for example, making a decision about price requires considering its effect on product image, unit sales, distribution network, and so on.

A SYSTEM is *an entity made up of two or more independent parts that interact to form a functioning organism.* Systems analysis is the method used to solve business problems by identifying the major parts of a problem and their relationships. Types of systems inputs and outputs are shown in Figure 4-4. The computer has made systems analysis a more effective tool of

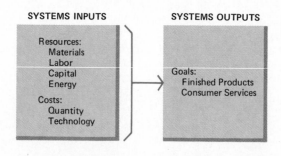

FIGURE 4-4
Systems Analysis: Inputs and Outputs

OWNERSHIP, MANAGEMENT, AND ORGANIZATION

management, since it can handle more information than the human mind can. However, it certainly does not eliminate the need for managers to perform their tasks of management.

RESULTS MANAGEMENT (MBO) Since it was first introduced by Peter Drucker in the early 1950s, results management, or management by objectives (MBO), has grown in popularity. MBO is a program to improve employees' motivation and control. It is also a philosophy of management that recognizes the value of setting performance goals. Figure 4-5 shows the four-step sequence of most MBO programs.

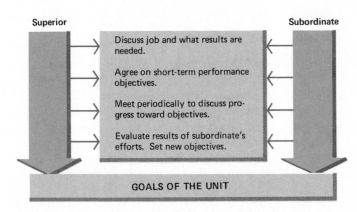

Superior

Discuss job and what results are needed.

Agree on short-term performance objectives.

Meet periodically to discuss progress toward objectives.

Evaluate results of subordinate's efforts. Set new objectives.

Subordinate

GOALS OF THE UNIT

FIGURE 4-5
Results Management, or Management by Objectives

Management by results focuses on results, not the behavior an employee exhibits. It assumes that the results managers or employees produce are the important thing, not how busy they may look.

Those who have used MBO programs believe that they have certain benefits. For example, employees in the program are able to relate their personal performance to the overall organization goals. The program can also improve communications between subordinate and supervisor.

Despite these advantages, there are some disadvantages. For some jobs, it is difficult to set precise objectives. MBO will succeed only where parties are willing to participate. And it is essential that the objectives be reasonable and easily measurable. MBO should not be considered a solution for all managerial problems.

THE MANAGEMENT PROCESS

Management can be viewed as a process consisting of four functions that are interrelated. These functions are planning, organizing, directing, and controlling. Figure 4-6 identifies these functions and indicates their relationships to each other.[3]

---

[3] Management writers differ as to the number of management functions and what they are. Some writers define the functions more narrowly, by including such subfunctions as staffing, motivating, innovating, and communicating. The four basic functions listed in Figure 4-6 are considered to include staffing, motivating, innovating, and communicating as subfunctions.

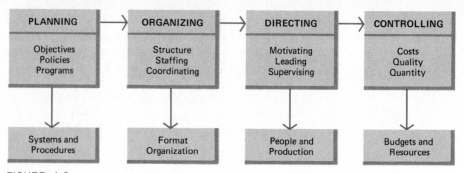

FIGURE 4-6
Functions of Management
Logically, planning seems to be the first function, which is followed by the other three. Some people also regard decision making and policy making as functions. In practice, however, these two activities are more often mingled with one or more management functions.

It can be argued that these functions help separate good managers from poorer managers. For example, controlling is vital to see that things are accomplished as planned. A good manager checks on important areas to see that they are being done properly. A poor manager may simply *assume* they will be done and not check up. Control (as well as planning, organizing, and directing) must be done correctly by successful managers. Let's consider each function in more detail.

PLANNING

Planning involves deciding on a course of action. PLANNING is *deciding what to do, setting company objectives, determining strategy, and selecting alternative courses of action.* It involves the following activities:

1. Determining the firm's short- and long-term objectives
2. Formulating policies, programs, and procedures
3. Considering information from periodic follow-up reviews to determine what changes in plans may be needed.

The record industry is a good example of a unique and difficult planning problem. CBS, RCA, and the other major record-album marketers offer retailers huge discounts on older albums that have not been selling well. The retailers can return unsold merchandise for credit on future purchases. So after Christmas, they send back records by the millions. When the company doesn't have a hit album to generate sales, it is stuck with thousands of dollars' worth of returns. Further, the big recording artists who make the records do not make them at a regular rate. Several artists may bring albums in at the same time. The companies then go through a long period with nothing new to offer. The problem requires some major breakthroughs in planning.

It is as important to plan on a daily basis as it is to plan years in advance. It is also a continuous process, because business conditions are constantly changing. Figure 4-7 illustrates how planning proceeds from general to specific.

ORGANIZING

ORGANIZING is *the way managers divide up the work to be done and the structure they develop to see that it is completed.*

We need organization when a job is too big for one person to do alone. The work must be divided and then reassembled at some point to make a finished product.

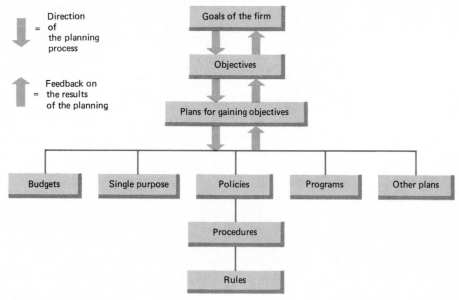

FIGURE 4-7
The Planning Process

For example, consider Sally Jones, making an electronic component in her garage. As sales and demand increase, Sally reaches the point where she cannot do all the work herself, and she hires some employees. As things continue to grow, she moves to a bigger building and hires 100 more workers.

How can she get organized? Simple organizational principles tell us she should:

1. Divide the work to allow specialization
2. Group like or related jobs together
3. Delegate authority to supervisors to run the various subunits
4. Develop coordination mechanisms to see that things run smoothly

Organizing, then, includes making decisions such as, Who handles which jobs and responsibilities? Who reports to whom? How will information be channeled?

Organization charts are pictures of the formal relationships developed from organizing. Figure 4-8 shows a simple organization chart.

FIGURE 4-8
A Simple Organization Chart

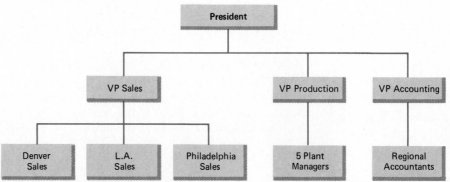

DIRECTING As part of the management process, DIRECTING is *achieving organizational objectives by motivating and guiding subordinates.* It is especially important at the supervisory level, where the largest number of employees are involved. In practice, it is much more than just ordering or commanding things to be done.

Properly directing employees includes understanding a bit about human behavior at work. Communication, motivation, and leadership are important areas for the manager in directing. Let's consider leadership, for example.

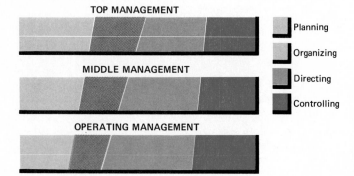

FIGURE 4-9
Proportion of Management Functions Performed at Different Levels
A chart showing the approximate distribution of management effort expended in performing their functions in a medium-size manufacturing business.

What is Leadership? Some people feel that leadership is exactly the same as management. But this is not completely accurate; leaders are found wherever there are groups of people. They may or may not also be managers. LEADERSHIP is *the ability to influence others to behave in a certain way.* In this process, the leader influences members of the group and is responsive to their needs. Leadership is useful in any kind of group or organization. And it can mean the difference between success and failure.

Leadership Styles. Different leadership styles have been found effective in different situations. One style is to make decisions autocratically, without consulting subordinates. Another is to consult with subordinates before

---

[4] "How Executives See Women in Management," *Business Week*, June 28, 1982, p. 10.

making a decision. And still a third is to let the subordinates make the decisions. These three basic styles of leadership are:

1. Autocratic leader
2. Democratic leader
3. Free-rein leader

An **autocratic leader** is one who makes decisions without consulting subordinates. A **democratic leader** encourages the group's participation in making decisions that affect them. A **free-rein leader** allows most decisions to be made by subordinates with a minimum of direction from the leader.

Figure 4-10 illustrates the three leadership styles.

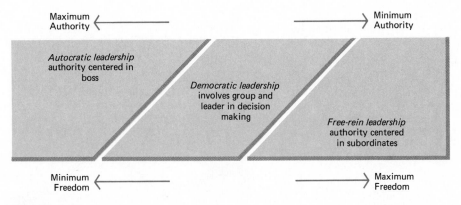

FIGURE 4-10
Patterns of Leadership Behavior
Limits of authority and freedom exercised by managers as leaders vary from authority-centered behavior to free-rein behavior in dealing with subordinates.

Often the question is asked, Which style of leadership is best? The answer depends largely on the specific situation. Some subordinates are too inexperienced to make decisions without consulting their manager. Some problems requiring immediate action must be handled without consultation with subordinates in order to avoid delay. Where time is not a factor, the manager may find it useful to encourage individual or group participation. This is especially true if acceptance of the decision by the group is important.

Are leaders "made" or "born"? Research on this issue is limited. Leadership ability can not be taught in all cases. We see examples of un-taught leaders who seem more successful than those who have been trained in leadership. Between these two extremes there are many who are gifted to a moderate degree. For them, learning about leadership seems improve leadership ability.

CONTROLLING The controlling function is sometimes misunderstood because of the lack of a precise definition. As used here, CONTROLLING is *a procedure for measuring performance against objectives.* It deals with the question, Did what was supposed to happen, really happen? Why, or why not?

The need for control springs from the inherent imperfection of things and people. Things that are planned do not happen *automatically*, without someone controlling to see that they do happen. Generally, the function of controlling includes:

1. Establishing standards from planning
2. Scheduling work
3. Reviewing costs
4. Exercising supervision
5. Taking corrective action

A major mechanism of control is reporting. Managers have recognized for several thousand years that reports on how things are going are critical for control. In fact, writings from the time when the pyramids in Egypt were being built show that reports were required then as control mechanisms.

Good control sets an **expected level** of performance, and the manager wants to be told if the actual results deviate from the expected. This feedback in the form of reports (or some other form) leads to correction and getting the operation back on the proper track. Figure 4-11 illustrates.

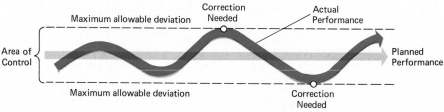

FIGURE 4-11
Control in Action

Budgets.   Budgets are perhaps the most common control mechanism today. Really, they are little more than plans with dollar amounts attached. They can be used to control revenue and expenses, time, space, capital expenditures, cash, and so on. Budgets are based on plans for a period of time — a quarter or a year. The budget allocates amounts of money to various units in the organization based on estimates of needs. If the amount estimated and the amount used begin to differ too much, upper management will want to correct the problem before it gets out of hand. See Figure 4-11.

Good budgets are:

1. Flexible (because they are estimates)
2. Communicated (so people know what they have to work with)
3. Reviewed frequently (so that problems can be corrected early)
4. Treated as a management tool (because they are means to an end, not the end itself)

Other Forms of Control.   Control can take other forms besides budgets — for example, IBM's efforts to control the leaks of its research developments to competitors. These controls are designed to safeguard the more than $1 billion per year the firm spends on R&D. IBM has over 350,000 employees worldwide who could leak information. Recent charges brought against twenty-two Japanese, American, and Iranian businessmen made public some of the giant company's control measures. IBM's attempts at making employees security-conscious, security checks on employees, code names, and the like are all important control devices.

We have identified and discussed the four management functions in the management process. They are common to all levels of management, as was shown in Figure 4-9. But different levels have greater involvement with different functions.

The sequence that these functions follow is not necessarily rigid; they might be performed in another sequence. However, the logic behind their order is that planning must occur first. **Control is the mirror image of planning, in that it is designed to see that what was supposed to happen is happening.**

EXECUTIVE MANAGEMENT SKILLS

You are now familiar with the functions of business management and the areas of an organization in which these functions are performed. Let us turn to the role of the executive, the top manager in a business.

WHAT IS AN "EXECUTIVE"?   What is the typical executive like? What qualities make him or her an executive? What skills does he or she use? The terms **executive** and **administrator,** which are often used interchangeably, had their origin in government. Executives were concerned with the administration and execution of estates, laws, and justice. The terms have since been accepted by business, industry, and other institutions.

An EXECUTIVE is *a top-level management person responsible for the work performed by others under his or her supervision*. Executives originate orders, make decisions, and set company policy. As decision makers, executives use three basic skills, which we will call technical, human, and conceptual. These skills are interrelated, but they can be examined separately.

Technical Skills.   These include the ability to use the methods, equipment, and techniques involved in performing specific tasks. Examples include scheduling, reading a computer printout, analyzing data, and so forth.

Human Skills.   These skills represent the ability to work effectively with others. They require a sense of feeling for others and an appreciation of the rights of others. They are demonstrated by the way the person recognizes subordinates, equals, and superiors.

Conceptual Skills.   These include intelligence, verbal ability, and the ability to see the whole enterprise or organization as a unit of operation. Such skills are critical in decision making. With them, the manager is able to conceive the nature of the problem before attempting to solve it.

ROBERT A. LUTZ

Robert A. Lutz was appointed executive vice-president, Ford International Automotive Operations, in August 1982. He was elected a member of the company's board of directors in September 1982. Prior to that appointment, Mr. Lutz was chairman of the board of Ford of Europe, Incorporated. He brought to Detroit a wide experience in the automotive industry of Europe. He and his associates are credited with achieving much of Ford's success in Europe. Upon assuming the position of executive vice-president, Mr. Lutz said:

> You can save enormous amounts of energy by shaping the car right. So we have decided to go uncompromisingly towards the direction of air-flow management and therefore highly aerodynamic cars. Apart from that we will do a lot to improve the efficiency of the powertrains, and that means advanced manual and automatic transmissions, highly efficient new power plants with extended use of electronics in engine and transmission management.

Mr. Lutz's career in the automotive industry began in 1963, when he joined the planning department of General Motors in New York City. He was assigned to Adam Opel in Germany in 1965. The next year Mr. Lutz was moved to General Motors of France, where he was appointed director of sales in 1968. He returned to Adam Opel in 1969, then joined BMW at the end of 1970.

Born in 1932 in Zurich, Switzerland, Mr. Lutz holds B.S. and M.B.A. degrees from the University of California at Berkeley. He was a captain in the U.S. Marine Corps. from 1954 to 1959. He is married and has four daughters.

The proportion of those skills required differs at various levels, as Figure 4-12 illustrates. For example, supervisors at the operating-management level perform more technical skills than do middle or top managers. Conceptual skills are more important at the executive level. The accompanying sketch of Paul Thayer, who took over LTV Corporation from the legendary J.J. Ling, shows good examples of these skills.

PAUL THAYER

Paul Thayer found LTV in shaky circumstances when he became the CEO. It had become a conglomerate consisting of many partially owned and unrelated companies, and it was coming apart. Creditors were refusing to lend more money until it was fixed. Thayer began, much like Lee Iacocca, by cutting overhead and selling marginal assets. He realized that companies not 100 percent owned are not 100 percent controlled.

Financial maneuvering resulted in the sale of seven subsidiaries, with the proceeds used to buy 100 percent interests in the remaining companies. That led to complete control, which resulted in LTV's returning to a profitable position. Merging LTV with Lykes Corporation required Thayer to personally lead the proposal through the Securities and Exchange Commission.

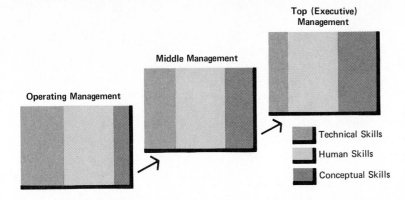

Top (Executive) Management

Middle Management

Operating Management

◼ Technical Skills

◻ Human Skills

◼ Conceptual Skills

FIGURE 4-12

Managerial Skills Needed at Different Levels

As a manager advances from one level to another, different amounts of management skills are required.

SUMMARY OF KEY CONCEPTS

The strength of any enterprise is its management, which bears a heavy responsibility for operating a successful business.

The functional role of managers is to plan, organize, direct, and control what happens in the business.

The levels of management are top management (the highest), middle management (concerned with the carrying out of policies and plans), and operating management (responsible for supervision).

The scientific-management movement was marked by the beginning of the use of scientific principles in managing a business. Frederick W. Taylor was the first American to apply these principles to business.

Advocates of the classical school of management subscribe to the theory that managers are responsible for performing certain functions: planning, organizing, directing, and controlling.

The behavioral school advocates that the training of managers should include instruction on understanding people.

The management-science school makes use of mathematical models and computer science as a tool for decision making.

Management by objectives (MBO) focuses on the results a subordinate achieves rather than the behaviors he or she exhibits.

Managers use three skills in dealing with problems: technical, human, and conceptual. **Technical skills** involve the use of equipment, techniques, and methods in performing management tasks. **Human skills** are used in exercising leadership styles. **Conceptual skills** enable managers to view the entire business as one part relates to another.

The three basic leadership styles are the autocratic style, the democratic style, and the free-rein style. Autocratic leadership is centered in a leader who makes decisions without consulting others. The democratic leader invites the participation of subordinates. Free-rein leadership behavior allows groups to make decisions.

BUSINESS TERMS

You should be able to match these business terms with the statements that follow:

a. AUTOCRATIC LEADER
b. CONTROLLING
c. DEMOCRATIC LEADER
d. DIRECTING
e. FREE-REIN LEADER
f. LEADERSHIP
g. MANAGEMENT
h. ORGANIZING
i. PLANNING
j. SYSTEM

1. The process of planning, organizing, directing, and controlling activities of an enterprise to achieve specific objectives

2. Means by which managers coordinate human and material resources within the formal structure of tasks and authority
3. Preparing a plan of action, setting company objectives, determining strategy, and selecting alternative courses of action
4. An entity made up of two or more independent parts that interact to form a functioning organism
5. The ability to influence others to behave in a certain way
6. Achieving organizational objectives by motivating and guiding subordinates
7. A procedure for measuring performance against objectives
8. A leader who allows most decisions to be made by subordinates, with a minimum of direction from the leader
9. A leader who encourages the group's participation in making decisions that affect them
10. One who makes decisions without consulting subordinates

REVIEW QUESTIONS

1. What is *management*?
2. What factors caused the development of a managerial class in this country?
3. Explain results management.
4. At which level of management does most planning occur? At which level does the least planning occur?
5. What is meant by *management functions*?

DISCUSSION QUESTIONS

1. Why would you be interested in becoming a manager?
2. In your opinion, what major qualifications should a successful manager have?
3. Give some of the reasons why the management-by-objectives approach has been widely accepted.
4. Are there really "schools" of management, or are these just ways to approach a problem in trying to solve it?
5. Do you agree that managers must believe in management theories, since they have nowhere else to turn?
6. In what ways can a business improve the qualifications of its managers?

BUSINESS CASES

CLAYTON, THE SELF-PROCLAIMED MANAGER

Clayton Phillips was a manager. It said so, right on the sign he kept on his desk. Clayton's job was to operate the rock crusher that his father owned as part of his cement ready-mix business. When Clayton got to work in the morning, he started the huge diesels that provided power to the crusher. Then he settled into his front-end loader to spend the day loading the hopper that fed the crusher with material. His day of loading was broken only when the crusher failed to digest a huge rock or gave up and quit on a particularly hard one.

Clayton had studied management in college and went to work for his father with the idea of taking over from the "old man" one day. His dad was glad to have him but knew the young man had a great deal to learn about the business before he was ready for the executive suite.

1. Is Clayton really a manager?

2. Explain what technical skills must be acquired in a small business like this in order to run it successfully.

4-2

WHAT'S WRONG WITH WESTERN TIRES, INC.?

Western Tires, Inc., with headquarters in Arizona, has been manufacturing automobile tires and fan belts for American-made automobiles. These products are marketed under the brand name of Wearwell through tire dealers and service stations as replacement parts. Carl and Lee Busch, brothers, established the company in 1923 and are still the principal shareholders. Carl owns 60 percent of the outstanding common stock, and Lee owns 20 percent. Six employees, including two of the company executives, own the remaining stock.

The company employs 225 men and women, with twenty-three working in the headquarters offices. Carl Busch is president, and Lee Busch is treasurer and is in charge of all accounting, including the payroll department. Lee has been trying to persuade Carl to install a computer. The plant superintendent has also submitted a request to use a computer for quality-control purposes in the plant. The president says a computer costs too much.

Union grievances are frequently filed, but few ever go to arbitration. Usually the president makes the final decision to make a settlement that the union is willing to accept. In general, the company's executives feel that the president lacks leadership qualities and does not know how to get along with others. He is also unwilling to delegate responsibility.

On several occasions, Lee has urged his brother to seek the directors' approval to appoint an executive vice-president. Lee feels that this executive could take over some of the duties now performed by the president.

Last month, the president was ill for twenty-four days because of a stroke. Carl's physician has advised him that he must reduce his workload and delegate more authority to others. During Carl's illness, the company lost a large contract with a fleet owner for 500 replacement tires. When this was discovered, two directors asked the president for an explanation. They wanted to know why he had not authorized his brother, Lee, to negotiate this pending contract.

1. What is wrong with the company organization?
2. What action would you take to solve the company's problems if you were in charge?

In The News
Let's Get (Re)Organized!!

The 3M Company has long been praised as a major source of new-product innovation. But recent problems—a slowdown in growth, and difficulties getting into a new market—stymied the firm.

The answer was dumping the company's 33-year-old organizational plan. One aim of the change was to get more mileage out of research and marketing efforts by grouping products according to the market and technology involved.

3M had been known for its strong divisional organization before the change. Each division had its own research and marketing operations. Unfortunately, the independent divisions were not especially good at cooperating with each other.

In the annual report that followed the reorganization, L.W. Lehr, chairman of the board, wrote, "This will not only strengthen our ability to meet present customer needs, but help us capitalize on the wealth of opportunities that lie ahead." Time will tell if Mr. Lehr was right.

Organizational Behavior and Design

study objectives

WHEN YOU HAVE FINISHED READING THIS CHAPTER, YOU SHOULD BE ABLE TO:

1. Distinguish the meaning of the word *organization* as applied to business from several other meanings

2. Explain why some firms start with one form of organizational structure and eventually change to another

3. Contrast formal organization with informal organization and give examples of each

4. Name six ''principles'' of organization to be considered in formalizing an organizational structure

5. Define the following terms: *authority, responsibility, delegation, accountability*, and *coordination*

6. Explain the difference between the divisional plan and the functional plan of organizational structure

Take my assets — but leave me my organization and in five years I'll have it all back.

Alfred M. Sloan
General Motors Corporation

t is said about Americans in business that they like to get organized.
This is not a new condition. William Allen White (1868–1944), author and newspaper editor, observed that "if four Americans fell out of a balloon they would have a president, vice-president, secretary, and treasurer elected before they landed." Indeed, the highly competitive nature of modern business makes it necessary.

Business firms, like other organizations, did not just "happen that way." Someone must take the lead in designing a planned set of relationships in which people can get the job done.

In this chapter, we examine the behaviors commonly seen in work organizations and the types of organizational structures used in business. Each "plan" for organizing has its strong and weak points. The nature of the business and the way it is managed determine how well a plan for organizing will work.

THE NATURE AND DEVELOPMENT OF ORGANIZATION

There may be differences of opinion as to how a business should be organized. But there is no disputing that proper organization is the backbone of a successful venture. We live in an organizational society. Businesses, governments, unions, athletic teams, hospitals, and educational institutions are all organizations. Human beings need **organization** to do anything that requires more than what one person can accomplish.

THE MEANING OF ORGANIZATION

The term **organization** has two different meanings. The first refers to the organizational "creature" itself—like General Motors, the Pittsburgh Steelers, or the AFL-CIO. The second meaning refers to organizing as a process. The process of organization may include putting people into jobs and grouping jobs together into departments.

In a business organization, someone must decide what each person will do and how much authority each will have. ORGANIZATION can be best defined as ***a structure of relationships to get work done.*** The organizational structure that is developed should help the firm reach its long- and short-term goals and objectives.

Every business has its objectives. These may be for the business as a whole or for divisions or departments, or for individual activities. Ideally, all these objectives when summed up should equal the overall organizational goals. This "hierarchy" or pyramid of goals and objectives is illustrated in Figure 5-1.

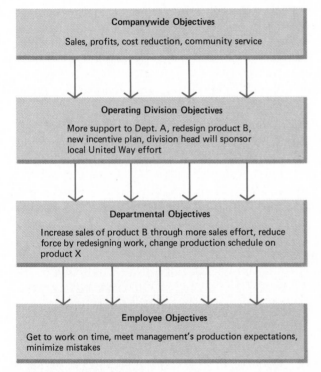

Companywide Objectives

Sales, profits, cost reduction, community service

Operating Division Objectives

More support to Dept. A, redesign product B, new incentive plan, division head will sponsor local United Way effort

Departmental Objectives

Increase sales of product B through more sales effort, reduce force by redesigning work, change production schedule on product X

Employee Objectives

Get to work on time, meet management's production expectations, minimize mistakes

FIGURE 5-1
Hierarchy of Organizational Objectives

Depending upon its nature and size, a business can be organized in several different ways. General Motors is subdivided by **products:** Chevrolet division, Buick division, and so forth. Safeway is organized by **geographical regions.** An oil company, such as Exxon or Mobil, may be divided by **functions:** production, exploration, refining, marketing, and finance.

HOW DOES AN ORGANIZATION DEVELOP? Most business enterprises begin on a small scale. The owner makes the decisions and performs most of the activities. As the firm grows, such activities as production, marketing, and finance may be handled by different people. Different activities become separate departments, with managers and employees. Eventually, a department — finance, for example — may become important enough to be headed by a vice-president. A large company becomes a very complex collection of different activities.

Organizational behavior is concerned not with how organizations behave, but with how people behave in work organizations. People are a primary resource of any firm; understanding how and why they behave as they do helps solve many management problems. Managers can learn much from the behavioral sciences (psychology, sociology, and anthropology) as to what motivates and influences people in their work groups. Important predictors in work organizations include work groups, motivation, job attitudes, and leadership.

WORK GROUPS

Work groups exist in all forms of organizations involving people. But only since 1920 have managers paid special attention to their importance in the workplace. If people work closely with one another and share common interests, they develop a feeling of belonging to the group. As members of a team, workers can provide support to other members by helping one another and coordinating their work.

In a business organization, a WORK GROUP is *a collection of employees who share a common job and view themselves as a group.* In some cases, groups form because workers expect to receive more benefits on the job. In

FIGURE 5-2
Membership in Groups at Work

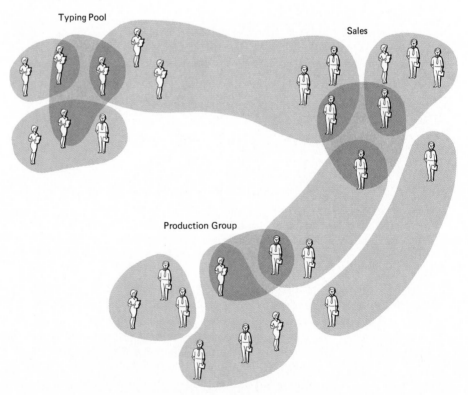

any event, groups persist in organizations because they fill needs for their members. What kind of needs?

1. **For security.** Groups provide social support and protection from threats, real or imagined. Unfortunately, sometimes employees must choose between what the group wants and what the employer expects.

2. **To maintain self-esteem and economic self-interest.** People often develop pride in being associated with a group: "I'm a football player," or "I'm a member of the $1,000,000 Club." Labor unions are usually formed to maintain economic levels, as are such groups as the AMA and the American Bar Association. Unfortunately, in these roles, groups can be quite resistant to change.

3. **To provide communication.** Groups can provide and share information when enough information isn't available through formal channels in the organization. Such information, however, is subject to rumor and other inaccuracies.

Membership in the various groups at work depends on many things—closeness to each other, common interests, common jobs, friendship off the job, and so on. Figure 5-2 shows how work groups can overlap based upon these issues. Work groups are important because they can make management's job much easier or much more difficult.

MOTIVATION   Motivation is the *why* of human behavior. It is an internal drive that causes people to behave as they do. Different people may have very different motives for doing the same thing. Workers may be motivated to join a work group if they feel that their personal needs can be better satisfied by doing so. Needs lead to drives, which in turn lead to behaviors designed to satisfy those needs, as shown in Figure 5-3. Man is a perpetually wanting animal, so fulfillment of a need does not mean that it will not recur.

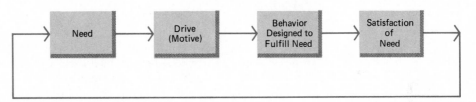

FIGURE 5-3
The Motivation Process

Levels of Employee Needs.   One of the best-known explanations of employee needs and their levels was developed by Abraham H. Maslow, a psychologist, who drew up a list of human needs.[1] Maslow noted that only those needs that have *not* been satisfied can motivate human behavior; furthermore, a satisfied need is no longer a motivator, but it can reemerge as a motivator. For example, because you had a big breakfast, it does not follow that you will not want supper. The hunger need will reemerge.

Maslow's theory of motivation emphasizes two basic ideas:

1. People have many needs, but only those needs not yet satisfied influence human behavior.
2. Human needs are grouped in a hierarchy of importance. When one need is satisfied, another, higher-level need then emerges and seeks satisfaction.

---

[1] Maslow, *Motivation and Personality* (New York: Harper & Brothers, 1954).

Figure 5-4 shows the hierarchy of needs. The basic needs are hunger, thirst, shelter, and rest. These are followed by safety from external-danger needs, such as protection from injury, and job security. Higher-level needs include social needs, self-esteem needs, and self-actualization. Those needs at the top of the hierarchy—such as self-actualization or self-esteem—are more difficult to satisfy.

Maslow's idea does not explain all human motivation at work. His major contribution lies in his hierarchical concept. He was the first to suggest that once a need is satisfied, a higher-level need emerges. Maslow's need theory has had a strong impact on businesses' approach to employee motivation.

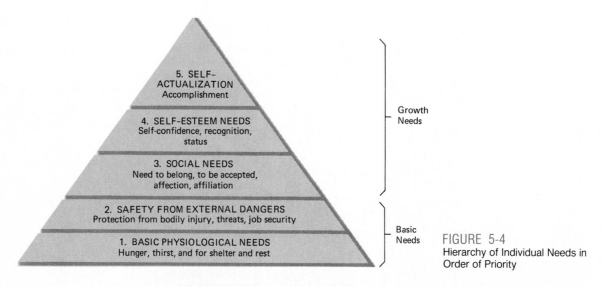

FIGURE 5-4
Hierarchy of Individual Needs in Order of Priority

Work itself can be a powerful motivator and a force in shaping one's identity. Work can be significant and should contribute to one's self-esteem. The question, "Who am I?" often brings a response related to an organization or a job: "I work for IBM," "I am a division manager," or "I am an accountant with Ford Motors."

WORK AND JOB ATTITUDES Major technological advances in recent years have resulted in the greater use of machines and automatic equipment. As a result, workers in plants sometimes complain that their jobs are boring. They may feel that they are not being given sufficient opportunity to use their skills. The trend toward more automation in manufacturing and agriculture has been challenged by labor unions.

Studies have shown that the so-called work ethic is not as strong as it once was in America. The belief that hard work is good in and of itself is part of the work ethic.[2]

Job satisfaction may be the single most studied job attitude in work organizations. It consists of attitudes toward work supervision, pay, co-workers, and promotion. Nationwide studies have shown that between 80

---

[2] Max Weber (1864–1920), the German sociologist, first used the term "Protestant ethic" in 1904 in his book, *Protestant Ethic and the Spirit of Capitalism*. This term has since come to mean competition and the desire to achieve in business.

and 90 percent of employees consistently report that they are satisfied with their jobs. These findings, however, mask the fact that job satisfaction varies from job to job. For example, college professors, lawyers, and journalists tend to score above 80 percent when asked if they would choose the same job again, while auto workers and steel workers score below 40 percent.

Job satisfaction is a useful indicator for management to determine if there are problem areas within the organization's workforce. Job dissatisfaction has been linked to turnover and absenteeism in the workforce.

Morale is the general attitude of the work force in a business toward their jobs. **Job satisfaction** is another term that means much the same thing.

Job Satisfaction Consists of Attitudes toward Work and Working Conditions
(Courtesy of U.S. Census Bureau/Mark Mangold.)

LEADERSHIP The leadership that a manager in a business organization uses to get people to work is an important part of understanding work behavior. Studies have shown that there is no "one best way" to lead employees. It depends on the leader, the employees, and the situation. For example, allowing convicted killers on a chain gang to vote on what they want to do is probably the wrong leadership style for that situation. Likewise, ordering professional research scientists to do something and demanding that they do it is also the wrong style for the situation.

Good managers obtain more work from their subordinates in a business organization by being good leaders. In addition to recognizing the style that is most appropriate in a given situation, they do not rely only on their position as managers to get things done. They have learned to work within the structure effectively.

The kind of leadership style that prevails in a business organization helps to create the "working climate" for employees. For example, at Texas Instruments, the climate that has been created is somewhat different from that found elsewhere. The TI climate is vital to the success of the Dallas company. It stresses a strong work ethic, competition, company loyalty, and rational decision making. The climate is similar to that found in many

Japanese firms—assigning personal responsibility for the quality of the work. As in Japanese companies, there is a strong effort made to align company and personal goals. Other similarities with Japanese management climate exist as well. Eighty-three percent of TI's employees are on "people involvement teams," which search for new ways to improve their productivity. The company looks at its people as being completely interchangeable.

TI feels that it takes five years to train company managers. Those who make it serve in a demanding, no-nonsense climate. And not everyone wants to make it. Some people fit right in, but others bail out quickly. The climate polarizes people—either you fit in or you are rejected.

FORMAL AND INFORMAL ORGANIZATIONS

The history of the business, the technology involved, and the top managers' personalities help determine what a company's formal organization pattern will be. But every organization has an "informal component" as well as the formal one.

FORMAL ORGANIZATION
The FORMAL ORGANIZATION is *the system of jobs, authority relationships, responsibility, and accountability designed by management to get the work done.* The formal structure is created to deal with the work that has to be done. It provides a framework for work behavior. The formal organization offers relatively fixed areas within which people work on their own areas of responsibility. At the same time, of course, the work each person does is part of the larger task the business as a whole is trying to accomplish. The formal organization is the part that shows on the organization charts. The informal organization does not.

FIVE DIVISIONS—MORE OR LESS?

General Motors has five automobile divisions and a problem. How can you differentiate Chevrolets from Buicks from Pontiacs, Oldsmobiles, and Cadillacs if they must share parts for economy? In many cases, there is simply too little visible difference to justify the hefty price differences.

One solution would be to consolidate a division or two. Ford and Chrysler each have only two divisions. Toyota has only one. But to GM insiders, that solution is heresy. The company admits that it has studied the possibility but feels that more divisions mean more sales. Whether this is true is a subject of disagreement.

INFORMAL ORGANIZATION
An "informal organization" exists in every organization. It is not planned. It just happens—based on friendships and contacts both on and off the job. The INFORMAL ORGANIZATION is *a network of personal and social relationships that may have nothing to do with formal authority relationships.*

Informal organizations exist in all businesses because they arise from people's interacting, and people will always interact and form friendships.

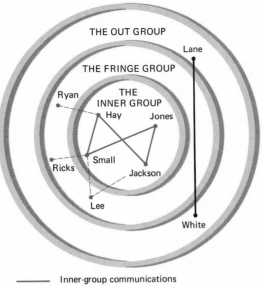

THE OUT GROUP

THE FRINGE GROUP

THE INNER GROUP

Lane

Ryan

Hay   Jones

Small

Ricks   Jackson

Lee

White

——————— Inner-group communications

– – – – – Communication channel with fringe group

FIGURE 5-5
Example of the Informal Organization in
a Work Group

Managers often wish they could do away with the informal organization. It may offer resistance to their formal orders, find unacceptable ways of getting things done, or keep changes from being implemented.

The grapevine is the communication system of the informal organization. Here, communications travel quickly by word of mouth. They may pass on valid information or rumor and untruth. The grapevine can, however, work to assist the formal communication system. A major point about both the informal organization and the grapevine is that they cannot be abolished. They *will occur*, and managers would be well advised to learn to work with them.

An example of an informal organization in one work group is given in Figure 5-5. In the work group are three categories of employees: members of the inner group, those in the fringe group, and those in the out group. Hay, Small, Jones, and Jackson belong to the inner group. They all perform similar work and set the general tone for the total group. Ryan, Ricks, and Lee are part of the fringe group. They have not been completely accepted by the inner group. Lane and White belong to neither group. Even though they work in the same department, they are "loners." Ultimately they may become members of the fringe group.

Informal organizations do not necessarily cause poor job performance. Sometimes the informal organization is the best way to supply information needed for job performance.

UNDERSTANDING FORMAL ORGANIZATIONAL STRUCTURE

Certain fundamentals of organization have evolved over the years as items that must be considered when the formal organization is being designed. These fundamentals include dealing with the following: (1) authority, (2) responsibility, (3) accountability, (4) delegation, and (5) coordination.

KATHARINE GRAHAM

Katharine Graham is the daughter of Eugene Meyer, a California-born financier, who purchased the *Washington Post* at auction in 1933. After graduation from the University of Chicago, she worked as a reporter for the *San Francisco News* and later joined the news staff of the *Washington Post*. She also worked in the Sunday and circulation departments. In 1940, she married Philip L. Graham and then devoted her life to being a homemaker and mother of their four children.

When Eugene Meyer retired as publisher of the *Post,* he turned the reins of the newspaper over to his son-in-law, Philip Graham, who led the *Post* to new heights until his untimely death in 1963.

Mrs. Graham became president of the *Washington Post* in 1963, publisher in 1968, and chairman of the board of the Washington Post Company in 1973. As the newspaper's chief executive officer, she has practiced the principle of delegating full authority to capable persons — and then giving them responsibility commensurate with that authority. She has encouraged and supported the paper's editorial writers and reporters. She has urged them to "seek out the facts and stay with the truth." She is highly respected throughout management circles for her business expertise and success in management. Mrs. Graham believes in sound preparation and successful work experience. She urges young people to "prepare and plan for the future as well as for the present."

Authority.   AUTHORITY is *the power to act and make decisions in carrying out assignments.* In a corporation, the authority comes from stockholders and is delegated to directors. They in turn delegate authority to top executives, who may in turn transmit some authority to lower-level managers. Some people have authority because of their knowledge of a subject; others have authority because they control resources or because they have a charismatic quality.

Responsibility.   RESPONSIBILITY is *a person's obligation to carry out assigned duties.* In delegating (or assigning) activities, the manager assigns to subordinates a responsibility to carry out tasks. Responsibility and authority should be equal. A subordinate should have the power necessary to carry out responsibilities.

Accountability.   ACCOUNTABILITY is *holding a subordinate answerable for the responsibility and authority delegated to him or her.* Accountability is always upward in the organization, because one is accountable to the superior who delegated the task. A person should be held accountable only to the extent that he or she is given responsibility and authority.

Delegation.   DELEGATION is *giving one person the power and obligation to act for another.* Delegation is considered an art of management. It is generally not well practiced. Studies show that a principal reason for managers' failure is that they are not willing or able to delegate authority. As an organization grows, the manager must be willing to assign authority and responsibility to subordinates.

OWNERSHIP, MANAGEMENT, AND ORGANIZATION

Coordination. All parts of a business firm should have a common goal — that is, the success of the venture. To be successful all the various efforts must be coordinated. COORDINATION is *synchronizing all individual efforts toward a common objective.* Its purpose is to make sure things happen at the right time and place, and in the correct order. Although personal contact is the most effective means of achieving coordination, other devices are used. These include forms of written communication — bulletins, letters, and procedure manuals. Group meetings may also be effective.

CENTRALIZATION VS. DECENTRALIZATION

The terms **centralization** and **decentralization** are often used in management. The issue is, How much authority should management delegate throughout the organization?

Centralized Organization. A business that adopts a policy of placing major decision-making authority and control in the hands of a few top-level executives is a centralized management organization. Thus, a CENTRALIZED MANAGEMENT ORGANIZATION is *a system where authority and control are kept in a central area, usually the top.*

Advocates of centralization contend that it permits more effective controls and tends to reduce decision-making time. A further advantage is that it allows all units to follow a uniform plan of action. It is popular in department stores and some food chains. Central headquarters decides on all policies involving buying, advertising, marketing, accounting, personnel, and credit. Sears, Roebuck is an example of centralized management.

The Company Headquarters of Shell Oil Company
(Courtesy, Shell Oil Co.)

Organizational Behavior and Design

A disadvantage of centralized management can emerge when the business grows rapidly and the workload at the top executive level becomes excessive. Delays can occur in making decisions, and this can result in higher operating costs.

A second disadvantage is that centralized organization offers junior managers little experience in making decisions. Virtually all important decisions are made at the company headquarters.

Decentralized Organization. Many large firms have adopted decentralization of management authority. DECENTRALIZED MANAGEMENT is *a systematic effort to delegate to lower levels all authority except that which must be exercised at the highest level.* Decentralization takes place for different reasons. Some companies decentralize decision making because they know that conditions vary from plant to plant. Officials at each plant know their own operations better than centralized personnel do. Therefore, they can make better decisions. Under decentralization, local managers welcome the opportunity to demonstrate their ability.

The organization chart in Figure 5-6 shows how Safeway Stores—one of America's large food chains—has decentralized its entire organization. As indicated in the chart, there are twenty-six separate retail divisions. Each has a vice-president who has the authority and responsibility for operating a specific district. Thus, authority and responsibility are decentralized. Each region is the equivalent of a fairly large retail operation, and each district is a distribution center for warehousing, buying, advertising, and so on.

SHIFT TOWARD DECENTRALIZATION

A strong industrial society requires great centralization of the factors of production—material resources, labor, and capital. The economics of mass production is basic to reducing the unit cost of what is being manufactured. But flexible manufacturing is changing all this. Computers have made production in small batches possible and profitable. Computer chips and semiconductors gave birth to a whole new group of small businesses in Silicon Valley. Such giants as IBM in computers, and AT&T in communications, have reorganized their companies along decentralized lines. Large businesses are delegating increased authority and responsibility to managers at the local level. **An information–service society is a decentralized one.** The shift in the United States from an industrial to an information society is bringing about greater decentralization. In the future we shall probably see this **megatrend from centralization to decentralization** gain momentum.

PRINCIPLES OF SUCCESSFUL ORGANIZATIONAL STRUCTURE

Before we examine the various types of formal organization plans, we should consider some of the principles that underlie a company's organizational structure. These are accepted principles of organization that are often observed.

Every Organization Should Have Objectives. The performance of all parts of the organization should be directed toward the achievement of the same objectives. This is known as **unity of objective.**

A distinction should be made, however, between the organization's objectives and the individual goals of executives, supervisors, and workers. The individual worker's goal is not the same as the organization's objective. For example, individuals may prefer certain ways of doing things that cannot be if the organization is to reach its objective.

We can continue using Safeway as an example with the Safeway corporate objectives listed on page 116. These objectives cover more than the goal of earning a profit and providing a service.

FIGURE 5-6

Organization Chart—Safeway Stores, Incorporated.
The Safeway Stores organization is divided into three groups—supply divisions, retail divisions, and service divisions. Only the retail divisions are shown here. These are grouped by geographical regions, each headed by a vice-president. This figure illustrates a decentralized management organization. Each retail-division vice-president has full power to act within policy guidelines. (Courtesy Safeway Stores, Inc.)

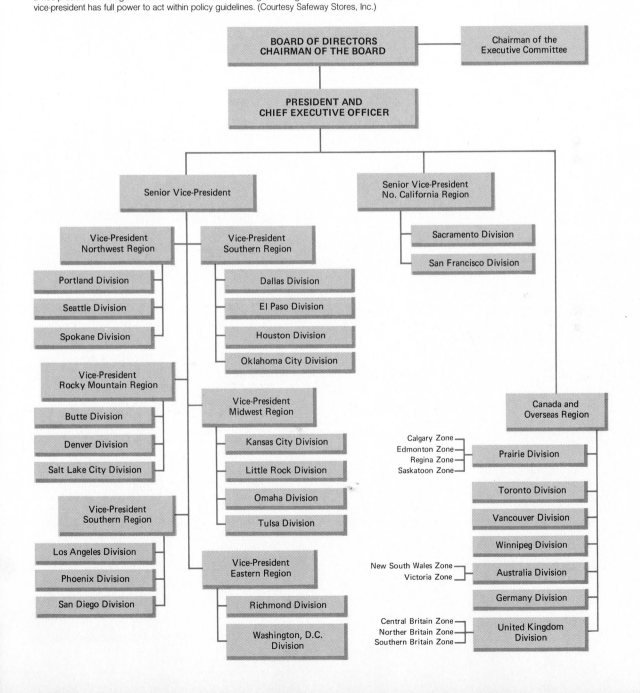

Safeway's Corporate Objectives

1. To make Safeway stock an increasingly profitable investment for our share-holders.
2. To practice responsible citizenship in the conduct of our business and in community and social relations.
3. To satisfy increasing numbers of customers, at a profit sufficient to assure the continuing healthy growth of the company.
4. To provide attractive, convenient stores staffed with courteous employees, and stocked with the products customers want.
5. To be known for superior perishables—meats, produce, dairy products, and baked goods.
6. To operate efficiently at the lowest costs consistent with quality and growth.
7. To be alert to new ideas, opportunities and change.
8. To strengthen our organization by continuous and systematic training and development of employees and managers.
9. To offer our employees responsibility, challenge, and satisfying rewards for accomplishment.[3]

CURRENT ISSUE

SHOULD CORPORATIONS USE MORE INSIDE AND FEWER OUTSIDE DIRECTORS ON THE BOARD OF DIRECTORS?

Most boards of directors have more outside than inside directors. There is growing public opinion that the way to control the number of corporate bribes, payoffs, and other corporation abuses is by replacing a number of inside directors with outside directors.

With which of the following statements do you agree, and with which do you disagree?

1. Inside directors, who are employees, are more knowledgable about the company's business.
2. Management is frequently reluctant to give outside directors confidential facts about the corporation.
3. Outside directors give needed objectivity to executive board deliberations.
4. Outside directors can provide expertise that otherwise is not available from inside directors.
5. Outside directors may be selected because of their special competence, which gives prestige to the company.
6. Since inside directors are employees of the corporation, they are likely to be biased in their opinions on certain issues.

Do you favor requiring corporations to use more outside than inside directors? Why or why not?

---

[3] Courtesy Safeway Stores, Incorporated.

OWNERSHIP, MANAGEMENT, AND ORGANIZATION

Clear Lines of Authority and Responsibility Are Essential in a Good Organizational Structure
(Courtesy, AT&T Photo Center.)

There Must Be Clear Lines of Authority and Accompanying Responsibility, Beginning at the Top and Descending to the Lowest Level. A good organizational structure provides for delegation of authority from, let us say, the president to the vice-president, to the general manager, to the supervisor, and finally to the workers. Thus, authority stems from the highest executive level and is delegated downward. The president of the firm may, for example, assign to the manufacturing vice-president the responsibility for buying raw materials and new equipment. At the same time, the vice-president must have the authority to determine what prices should be paid for these items.

The Number of Levels of Authority Should Be Held to a Minimum. Each time a new management level is created, another link is introduced into the chain of command. And the longer the chain, the more time it takes for instructions to pass downward and for information to travel upward. The number of levels depends upon whether the firm is centralized or decentralized. Where there are too many levels, authority is splintered. In such a case, a problem cannot be solved or a decision made without pooling the authority of two or more managers. In many day-to-day operations, there are cases of splintered authority; most managerial conferences are probably held because of the need to pool authority before making a decision.

No One in the Organization Should Have More than One Supervisor. This is the unity-of-command principle. This principle is useful in clearing authority-responsibility relationships. Whenever a manager lacks total ability to hold his or her subordinates responsible, the manager's position becomes one of confusion and frustration.

Organizational Behavior and Design

SPAN OF CONTROL is *the number of positions one person should supervise directly.* This principle is an important concept in developing the organizational structure. It places some limit on the number of persons who can satisfactorily be managed by a single executive. The span of control depends on many things—the nature of the job, the personalities of the manager and subordinates, and how far apart they are geographically. It is possible for top-level executives to supervise more people when operations are decentralized.

The Organizational Structure Should Be Flexible Enough to Permit Changes with a Minimum of Disruption. Since change is inevitable in any business, the ideal organizational structure is one that permits an executive to make changes without interrupting the continuity of the business. Good organizational structure must not be a straitjacket.

TYPES OF AUTHORITY RELATIONSHIPS

Jobs or positions in business are classified according to the nature of their authority in the organization. These may be **line, staff, functional,** or **project-management** authority relationships. Such relationships are not confined to a particular kind of business. Some of each type can be found in every field of business.

Line Relationships. A line relationship exists where there is direct authority between each superior and subordinate. This means that each manager exercises undivided authority over his or her subordinate, who reports only to that manager. In Figure 5-7, the application of line authority is shown in the first illustration. The flow of authority is direct and unobstructed.

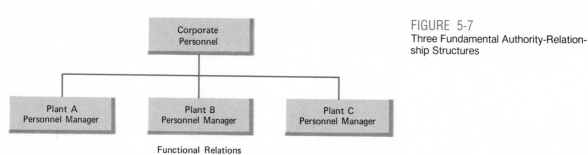

FIGURE 5-7
Three Fundamental Authority-Relationship Structures

Staff Relationships. Figure 5-7 also shows the line-and-staff structure. Notice that the flow of authority is represented by the solid lines and staff relations by the dashed lines. Staff managers furnish special service and advice to line executives.

Since **staff** refers to those in the organization who offer technical and special advice, staff members must be specialists. Their recommendations are made to their superiors, who then decide whether or not they should be adopted. Examples of staff specialists include legal counsel, research director, engineer, and economist.

Functional Relations. Some businesses use a third type of authority relationship, known as functional relations, which is not restricted to managers or departments. This type provides for specialists for each specific major function (hence the name, **functional structure**) no matter where in the business the function is performed. For example, a personnel manager exercises functional authority over all people involved in personnel relations, wherever they are found in the organization. Later in this chapter we will discuss how the functional organization form works.

Project-Management Relations.   Project-management or "matrix" organizational authority relations violate the unity-of-command principle. A manager may have a regular line role in the organization but may also be in charge of a group of people working on a special project. He or she has an immediate superior in the line organization and reports to a project director as well, resulting in two bosses. The matrix organization is becoming increasingly popular but is limited to certain situations. We discuss the use of each of these authority relationships as it applies to a specific organizational form.

ORGANIZATIONAL FORMS

Four types of organizational forms are generally found in modern business: divisional, line-and-staff, functional, and matrix (or project) form. Each of these has its advantages and disadvantages.

DIVISIONAL ORGANIZATION FORM   In the divisional form, the organization is divided into several fairly independent units. Each unit has the resources to operate independently of the other units. The divisions may be based on geography (as Safeway's was) or on product or on market. Figure 5-8 shows an organizational structure based on

FIGURE 5-8
A Divisionalized Organization Form (Product)

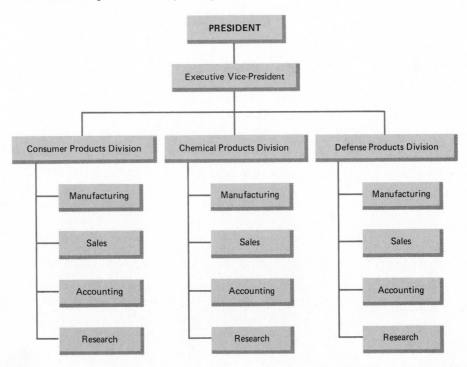

product. Among the largest business firms, the divisional form seems to be the most widely used.

Central corporate offices often exist in this form to help the president with his or her job and to help the divisions. (Figure 5-8 does not show the staff positions that usually make up the headquarters staff.) As with any organizational form, there are advantages and disadvantages to the division-alized form.

ADVANTAGES	DISADVANTAGES
1. Emphasis is on the division's product, and results are clear.	1. Coordination of projects that must cross division lines is often difficult.
2. Control and appraisal are straightforward. If each division is judged as a "profit center," the division manager's results should be apparent.	2. Economy may be a problem, since many functions (marketing, personnel, etc.) are duplicated in each division.
3. Good development ground for managers. Feedback, completeness, and autonomy go with this organizational form.	3. Managers may have difficulty getting exposure outside their own division. The companywide "big picture" may be hard to get.

LINE-AND-STAFF ORGANIZATION FORM

Whenever an organization becomes large, the tendency is to add staff specialists, as shown in Figure 5-9. As an example, when a line executive is confronted with a legal problem, he or she may call on the legal department

FIGURE 5-9
Line-and-Staff Organization Form.
The line-and-staff organization structure plan provides for a combination of line departments and for staff specialists who are advisors to line executives.

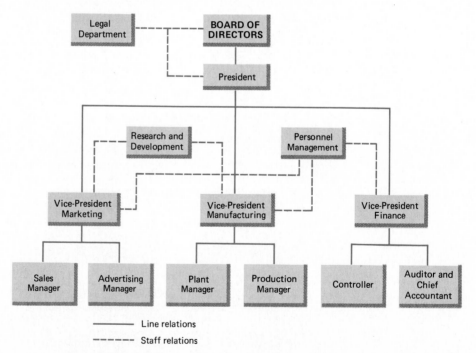

for advice. In Figure 5-9, both research-and-development specialists and members of the personnel-management department provide staff service to various line executives.

Line executives do the work required to carry on the operations of the firm. Staff people are specialists who serve line executives. Dashed lines are sometimes used in an organization chart to show the flow of advice and communications between staff and line units. The key in determining which members are line and which are staff is the nature of the work performed. Normally, executives in staff departments do not have authority over people in line positions. They, of course, exercise authority over employees in their own department or group.

Here is a comparison of the advantages and disadvantages of the line-and-staff form.

ADVANTAGES	DISADVANTAGES
1. The plan gives line executives authority to make all major decisions and issue directives to subordinates.	1. Staff specialists tend to overstep by asserting authority of line personnel, causing friction and misunderstanding.
2. It allows qualified technical specialists to advise line executives on the more complex problems of large companies.	2. The use of staff specialists tends to increase company overhead.
3. No matter in which department an employee works, he or she rarely reports to more than one supervisor or superior.	3. Decisions may be slowed by line executives who wait for technical and research findings by staff specialists before making a decision.

FUNCTIONAL ORGANIZATION FORM

It is possible to assign authority and responsibility in a pattern different from the divisional or line-and-staff form. This may be accomplished by giving a manager authority over specified processes or functions. Each functional manager will concentrate on his or her own special function. In Figure 5-10, you can see that similar and related occupations are grouped together. The functional form is common. Following are its advantages and disadvantages.

FIGURE 5-10

A Functional Organization Form of a Manufacturing Business.
In this functional organization chart, each employee is responsible to five supervisors.

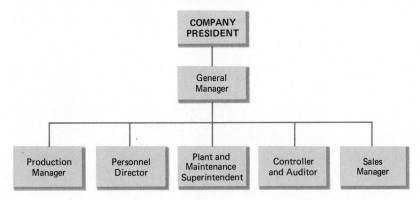

ADVANTAGES	DISADVANTAGES
1. Each manager works exclusively in his or her specialty. The manager can grow with the firm.	1. It can lead to too much specialization.
2. Business activities are divided into functions and assigned to specialists. Each specialist performs only one set of duties.	2. Each department focuses on a *part* of the responsibility for the product; no one is responsible for pulling it all together (except at the top).
3. Each employee can use the advice of various specialists when a problem arises.	3. Coordination can be very difficult.

MATRIX ORGANIZATION FORM

The matrix organization is used when a project structure is added to another structure. It results in bringing specialists from several different parts of the organization together to work on a particular project. The group is led by a project manager who has responsibility for the entire project. When it is completed, the group is dissolved and its members return to their respective departments.

The matrix organization disregards the unity-of-command principle. Further, this plan does not agree with the usual line-and-staff concepts. Yet it works! Some critics of the plan indicate that it discourages informal groups and the traditional supervisor-subordinate relations. On the other hand, the matrix organization allows for maximum use of specialized knowledge, which gives flexibility in the use of knowledgeable persons for difficult assignments. An organization chart for a matrix organization is illustrated in Figure 5-11. The flow of authority is shown by the arrows in the chart.

FIGURE 5-11

Matrix or Project Organization Form.

The matrix organization form sets up special projects, and specialists are assigned to the projects as needed. Centralized functional managers exercise authority that flows vertically. Flow of authority exercised by specialists is horizontal, as shown by the arrow. When a project is completed, the matrix personnel return to their home departments.

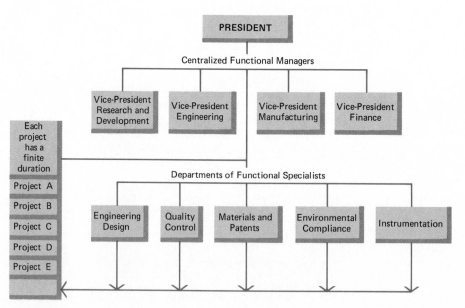

The project or matrix manager must be extremely competent. This manager functions with two bosses and without the clear authority that is usually thought necessary. Many project managers are engineers. Until recently, however, engineering students have rarely been offered management courses especially tailored to their needs. Now engineering schools, in cooperation with the big companies that hire their graduates, are beginning to offer degrees in engineering management.

More than forty schools now offer degrees in engineering management. The term used to identify such graduates is *matrix manager.* That is where the technical and business aspects of a project blend together.

These programs include required courses in such areas as management decision making in engineering, statistics, behavioral systems engineering, engineering law, and venture management. Most of these programs are offered at night so that engineers who want the training but must work during the day can take advantage of them.

ORGANIZATION CHARTS

A common cause of internal conflict in a business organization is the absence of clear responsibilities and authority. Some employees do not understand their assignments and to whom they report. This problem can be aided by the proper use of organization charts.

In discussing the formal organization forms, we presented a chart illustrating each form to indicate how the parts of the organization are related. An ORGANIZATION CHART is *the blueprint of the company's internal structure.*

Organizations use charts for various reasons. In addition to showing specific areas of responsibility and authority, charts can improve communication channels. They can identify the difference between line and staff executives. They also help in planning, budgeting, and controlling operations.

MAKING ORGANIZATION CHARTS

One way to prepare a chart is to begin with the highest position. A single rectangular-shaped box at the top of the organization represents the position occupied by the person who holds the responsibility for final decision making. This is often the president or the chairman of the board of directors.

In Figure 5-12, the office of president is the highest position. It is followed by the sales manager and the finance manager.

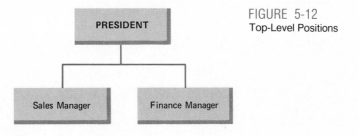

FIGURE 5-12
Top-Level Positions

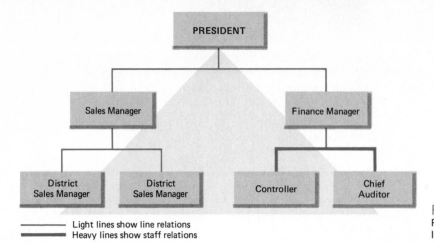

FIGURE 5-13
Partial Organization Expanded to
Include Another Level of Management

If two district sales managers, a controller, and a chief auditor are added, the chart will be expanded as shown in Figure 5-13. Now the chart resembles the shape of a pyramid; hence the name, pyramid chart. The chart will continue to expand as more positions are added. This situation is further illustrated by Figure 5-14, which shows the office of general counsel (a staff position) and four additional staff members. All these officials report to the president.

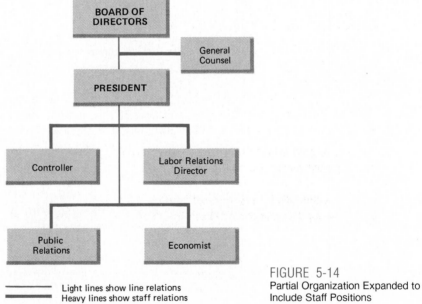

FIGURE 5-14
Partial Organization Expanded to
Include Staff Positions

Types of Organization Charts.   Companies create organization charts to suit their requirements. There are three main types of organization charts:

1. The vertical chart—Figure 5-10
2. The pyramid chart—Figure 5-13
3. The horizontal chart—Figure 5-15

Lack of clarity as to who does what is cited as being a major disadvantage of organization charts. But when job descriptions accompany charts, they give a more complete picture. Charts in themselves do not reflect the actual responsibilities of a given position.

For many, the horizontal chart shown in Figure 5-15 is more difficult to understand than the vertical chart. The horizontal chart does not portray a large and complex organization as clearly as does the vertical chart.

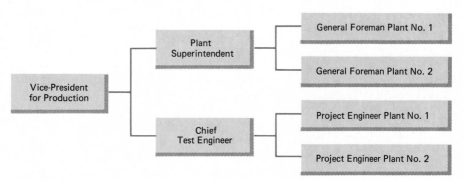

FIGURE 5-15
Horizontal Organization Chart

SUMMARY OF KEY CONCEPTS

Organization is the internal structure in which people interact in accomplishing the business's objectives. It is an essential tool of management in operating the business.

People are the primary resource of an organization. Managers need to understand how these people behave in dealing with each other.

Every business—small or large—needs some kind of planned organization that will enable the group to work effectively under a central authority.

The formal organization is a creation of management. The informal organization is the result of social and communications relationships, which may exist at both managerial and employee levels.

In planning a formal organization, it is essential to provide for the delegation of authority and responsibility. For each employee, responsibility increases with his or her rank and work assignment.

Employees are part of work groups. As individuals, they are motivated by certain wants and needs. Work attitudes, especially job satisfaction, have been associated with turnover and absenteeism.

Four major types of organization plans have been developed. Each can be shown by an organization chart. This chart is a pictorial representation of what employees do and how they relate to each other in performing their work.

The divisional form bases units on product or geography. The result is several "mini-companies."

The line-and-staff organization form, as its name implies, combines line and staff functions. Line executives exercise formal authority over others. Staff specialists serve line managers by acting as advisors in special fields.

In the functional organization form, work is organized by departments on functional lines, such as production, finance, and marketing. There is a direct flow of authority for each function.

The project or matrix organization form is based on the project concept. Specialists are temporarily assigned to the project. When the project is completed, the members of the group return to their respective departments.

Organization charts and manuals are useful management tools. The chart is a blueprint of the organization, showing lines of authority. Staff relations are likewise shown.

BUSINESS TERMS

You should be able to match these business terms with the statements that follow.

a. ACCOUNTABILITY
b. COORDINATION
c. DECENTRALIZED MANAGEMENT
d. DELEGATION
e. DIVISIONAL ORGANIZATION
f. FORMAL ORGANIZATION

g. INFORMAL ORGANIZATION
h. ORGANIZATION
i. ORGANIZATION CHART
j. RESPONSIBILITY
k. SPAN OF CONTROL
l. WORK GROUP

1. A process for providing a structure of relationships to get work done
2. A collection of employees who share a common job and view themselves as a group
3. A system of jobs, authority relationships, responsibility, and accountability, designed by management
4. A network of personal and social relationships that may have nothing to do with formal authority relationships
5. An organizational form in which the units have a lot of autonomy
6. An individual's obligation to carry out assigned duties
7. Holding a subordinate answerable for the responsibility and authority delegated to him or her
8. The giving to one person of the power and obligation to act for another
9. Synchronizing individual efforts toward a common objective
10. A systematic effort to delegate to lower levels all authority except that which must be exercised at the highest organizational level
11. A limit to the number of positions one person should supervise directly
12. A blueprint of a company's internal structure

REVIEW QUESTIONS

1. What are some of the different meanings of the term *organization*?
2. Why does a business change from one form of organizational structure to another?
3. What is the main difference between a *formal* and an *informal* organization?
4. Is there any difference in the authority exercised by a line executive and a staff executive?
5. Why are so many large businesses set up to follow the line-and-staff form of organization plan?
6. Which organizational form is used by most large business organizations?

DISCUSSION QUESTIONS

1. Make an analogy between a business that earns above-average profit and a football team that wins most of its games each season.
2. What are some of the causes of job dissatisfaction among factory workers?
3. If a person is responsible for supervising several employees, why must that person have authority?
4. What is the difference between *delegation* of authority and *decentralization* of authority?
5. Why do some companies prefer to have a strong centralized managerial structure rather than a decentralized management structure?
6. What are some of the advantages and disadvantages of an organization chart?

5-1

THE FRIENDLY DIVISION MANAGER

"I'm division financial manager for the Texas Company. I've been on the job here for six months, and I have a big problem—my boss, Fred Kares, who has been division manager for about fifteen years. Fred loves his job and he loves people. He knows all 300 employees in the division by name, and he spends a great deal of time wandering about, listening to people's problems and helping supervisors out of trouble. He's even pitched in on the job when we've had a tight schedule.

"All this if fine—except for two things. He spends so much time talking to individual employees and to first-line supervisors that he is seldom in his office. He never has time for the long-range problems, and his whole approach makes my job—keeping my end of the division going—much harder. I never know what he has told the employees, so in a way, he's more on top of my job than I am. I'd like to do a good job here, but his attitude makes it hard, even though he's always been friendly and personally helpful to me. The other people on my level all have the same troubles I have, although they've been here longer and are used to it.

"What should I do?"

1. What organizational problems do we see here?
2. Is Fred a good or poor manager?

5-2

BAKER BROS. FURNITURE COMPANY

Baker Bros., a Georgia corporation, operates plants in Georgia that manufacture a line of home and office furniture, sold in the southern states. The company headquarters is located in Atlanta.

The managerial policy of the company has been one of decentralization of management in its plants. With the increase in inflation and competition, the company has experienced difficulty in maintaining this policy. After an extended period of discussion, it was decided that this practice would be abandoned.

The directors voted to reorganize the company under a centralized management. Plant managers would no longer exercise direct supervision at the plants. Instead, each plant would be directly under an operating vice-president at headquarters. The title of "plant manager" was changed to "plant superintendent." Plant-personnel response to this change was one of contempt and protest. The union staged a three-day walkout, making it necessary to close each plant. Two of the managers resigned. The union immediately demanded a greater input in the management decision at the plant level. The company replied that it was the right of management to reorganize the business. Meanwhile, each plant remained closed.

1. What were the issues in this case?
2. What is your recommendation to the directors?

Entrepreneurship and Small-Business Management

study objectives

WHEN YOU HAVE FINISHED READING THIS CHAPTER, YOU SHOULD BE
ABLE TO:

1. Explain who may be classified as an entrepreneur

2. Identify the factors that determine whether a business is ''small''

3. Explain the importance of small businesses in the total business picture

4. Discuss the advantages and disadvantages of operating a small business

5. Name the factors that contribute to the success of small businesses

6. Illustrate the importance of franchising in the retail business picture

6

The small business community constitutes the single most important segment of our free enterprise system. It accounts for forty-eight percent of our gross national product, more than half of the American labor force, and continues to be the major source of inventions and new jobs. Small business is truly the backbone of the American economy.

Jimmy Carter
President, U.S.A.

When this country began, all businesses were small, but the Industrial Revolution brought on "big business." So today, when business is mentioned, most people think of such companies as General Electric, Sears Roebuck, IBM, or Procter & Gamble. They are large companies, but they all started small.

Small independent businesses are everywhere and in every type of work. In the United States, the business climate encourages people to go into business for themselves. In fact the history of business in America is a history of entrepreneurship and small business.

Every year, thousands of new businesses are formed: many of them fail, and their effort and money are lost. But the desire to be one's own boss pushes these people to become entrepreneurs.

This chapter is concerned with the small-business entrepreneur. As you read it, you will see something of the scope of small business and its problems. Why does one business succeed and another fail? Franchising as a special type of small business is also discussed.

ENTREPRENEURSHIP

When thinking of entrepreneurship, you might recall some American business pioneer, such as J.C. Penney, Thomas J. Watson, or Donald Douglas. Or the name of some inventor, such as Cyrus McCormick, Alexander Graham Bell, or Thomas A. Edison may come to mind. They were all entrepreneurs, and successful ones. But how about the person who risked all of his or her money to open the local hardware store? This person is an entrepreneur too. ENTREPRENEURSHIP is *the investing and risking of time, money, and effort to start a business and make it successful.* Certainly an entrepreneur hopes and plans to make a profit from his or her business. But a true entrepreneur also receives satisfaction and reward from serving the needs of others.

WHO ARE ENTREPRENEURS?

Not everyone has the personal qualities needed to be a successful entrepreneur. Those who do not possess them would do well to let others take the risks of business. The behavioral profile that studies have shown to be associated with good entrepreneurs is presented in Table 6-1.

TABLE 6-1
Behavior Characteristics of Entrepreneurs

1. Strong desire to be independent
2. Willingness to assume risks
3. Ability to learn from experience
4. Self-motivation
5. Competitive spirit
6. Orientation toward hard work
7. Self-confidence
8. Achievement drive
9. High energy level
10. Assertiveness
11. Belief in self

MR. MELLON IS AN ENTREPRENEUR

Virtually all railroads have lost money operating in the northeast United States. But Timothy Mellon, a descendant of the Mellon family of Pittsburgh, thinks he can operate there profitably. He is willing to risk his time and money to prove it. Mr. Mellon owns Guilford Transportation Industries, Inc., of Durham, Connecticut.

Guilford acquired the Maine Central Railroad in 1981. Then in April 1982, the Interstate Commerce Commission authorized its purchase of the bankrupt Boston and Main Railroad. On July 29, 1982, the ICC approved Guilford's purchase of the 1,700-mile Delaware and Hudson Railway. This latest decision clears the way for Mr. Mellon to establish a 3,830-mile railway system stretching from Delson, Canada (new Montreal), south to Washington, D.C.

Mr. Mellon and David Fink, vice-president of Guilford, believe they can overcome the problems that have plagued other railroads. Mr. Fink says, "The reduction in costs by running three carriers with one management, the diversion of traffic from Canada, and imaginative marketing will make it successful." Mr. Mellon foresees an economic recovery for the Northeast. He says, "It's a risk; it's a challenge; it's an opportunity."

A strong small-business community is essential in a private-enterprise society. This was again shown by the former board chairman of the Minnesota Mining and Manufacturing Company, R.H. Herzog, when he said:

> It is the individual entrepreneur, the person with the innovative idea—or the small business—that we should be concerned about. The large growth company isn't and never has been enough for this economy. What the large companies contribute in the way of products, jobs, taxes, and dividends must be augmented by smaller companies.

The United States has more than 10 million small businesses, and this number increases each year. Small businesses are found in manufacturing, distribution, retailing, and finance. They provide goods and services for Americans and for export as well. In addition, there are 2.7 million farmers whose operation is considered to be "small."

Of the more than 11 million business firms in this country, 99½ percent have fewer than 2,500 employees. Two-thirds of the manufacturing firms employ fewer than twenty workers. The White House Conference on Small Business[1] reported that small-business firms provided 85 percent of the new jobs created during the 1970s.

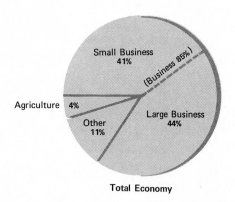

Total Economy

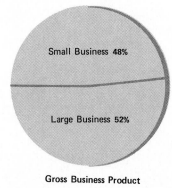

Gross Business Product

FIGURE 6-1
Small Business in the U.S. Economy.
[Source: *Statistical Abstract of the United States: 1979* (Washington, D.C.: U.S. Bureau of the Census, 1979), pp. 435–45; and "Facts about Small Business and the U.S. Small Business Administration" (Washington, D.C.: Small Business Administration, 1979), pp. 2–3.]

SMALL-BUSINESS FACTS (excludes farms)

The total number of businesses in the United States is 11.2 million.

Approximately a quarter of a million new businesses are started each year.

Nearly 80 percent of all U.S. businesses employ fewer than ten people.

Small businesses provide more than half of all business employment.

Small businesses account for 70 percent of all sales in the wholesale and retail trade.

One-third of all small businesses are in the service field.

About 90 percent of all corporations are small businesses.

Of the businesses that fail, 56 percent do so during their first five years of operation.[2]

---

[1] Held in Washington, D.C., in January 1980.

[2] U.S. Department of Commerce, Small Business Administration.

A FIRST START IN BUSINESS

There are three ways to enter business on your own. One is to buy a business that is **already established.** A second is to start a **new business.** In either case, you need some prior business experience or knowledge before launching your own enterprise. A third way is to buy a **franchise.**

Buying a Going Concern.   There are a number of advantages in buying an established business. These should be carefully considered before starting a new one. One of the major advantages is that the location has been proved. With a new business, research must first measure pedestrian traffic at a given point. Small firms depend largely on drop-in trade rather than telephone orders. Research is often done to determine such things as automobile traffic and whether adequate parking is available.

Second, a going concern can be evaluated with reasonable accuracy. The actual operating records can be studied. The seller's books may help to determine how well the business has performed during the past several years.

Third, much of the time, effort, and costs related to starting a new firm can be eliminated. The seller has already accumulated an inventory of stock and has assembled the needed personnel. If competent, they can become an immediate help to the new owner. Furthermore, it is possible to begin with a nucleus of customers and to begin operation immediately, without waiting for stock or equipment.

Fourth, the seller might be eager to retire and willing to make a quick sale by lowering the price. Or the price may be reduced in order to settle an estate.

A Watchmaker making final adjustments on a watch. His business is small and depends on reputation as well as drop-in trade.
(Courtesy of Timothy Eagan, Woodfin Camp & Associates)

Starting a New Business. For various reasons, some people prefer to start a completely new enterprise. Some of the advantages of doing this should be noted.

First, starting from scratch allows the owner to choose his or her own location, employees, brand of merchandise, and kind of equipment. And a loyal clientele can be cultivated without inheriting any ill will that an existing business may have fostered.

Second, one may find that because of the inefficient management of concerns that are for sale, the market has not adequately been served. Thus, there is a need for a new and efficient firm.

Buying a Franchise. Franchising has an advantage in that the franchisor provides some help to the franchisee. This is discussed in some detail later in this chapter.

Disadvantages of Business Ownership. Attractive as being an entrepreneur might seem, there are disadvantages:

1. Your business income may be less regular than your paycheck as a salaried person. It takes a while before a firm earns a profit.
2. The owner has no one with whom to share the responsibilities. There is a heavy burden of responsibility for meeting payrolls and other expenses. Some owners eventually grow weary of this responsibility.

Advantages of Working for Someone Else. Being a salaried employee offers certain advantages; here are some:

1. You bear little financial responsibility for your employer's losses.
2. Working hours are regular and often shorter than those of the owner. (This advantage may not be so significant if you are a top executive.)
3. Employees often have such benefits as overtime pay, paid vacations, medical care, hospitalization, unemployment compensation, and sick leave.

WHEN IS A BUSINESS SMALL? As a rule, most people apply the term *small business* to the local camera shop, service station, or barbershop. This concept may be accurate enough for general use, for most small firms operate on this scale. Public Law 85-536, an amendment to the Small Business Administration Act, states that "a SMALL BUSINESS concern shall be deemed to be ***one which is independently owned and operated and which is not dominant in its field of operation.***"

E.T. DOLLS

The small, family-owned company of Kamar International was chosen to make "E.T." dolls. Why was Kamar given the licensing rights instead of some large company?

MCA Inc. is the parent company of Universal Pictures, maker of the movie "E.T., the Extra-Terrestrial." MCA's vice-president for merchandising is Steve Adler. His 8-year-old son and 11-year-old daughter played a major role in the decision. He took them to some toy stores and asked them to select the plush toys they liked best. They chose Monkey-Do, which is made by Kamar. So Kamar was chosen to make and merchandise the "E.T." dolls.

Wyoming is the most fertile state for small businesses. It has one business for every thirty-five persons. Michigan has the least, only one for every sixty residents. Thinly settled states have more small businesses per capita than thickly settled ones. The states shaded have the most small businesses per capita. (The average for all fifty states is one small business for each fifty residents.)

FIGURE 6-2
Where small business are formed. (Data furnished by the National Federation of Independent Business.)

In general, a small business has few employees, limited capital investment, and low sales. To be eligible for SBA loans and other assistance, a business must meet a size standard set by the agency. For many years, this standard has been based on annual receipts, assets, net worth, and/or number of employees. The SBA has now proposed a new and simpler standard. It is based solely on total number of employees per firm. The number-of-employees standard would vary by industry.

The Committee for Economic Development (CED) offers a slightly different idea for defining small business. The CED considers a company a small business when at least two of the following criteria are present:

1. *Management is independent.* Usually, the managers are the owners.
2. *Capital is furnished by an individual owner or a small group.*
3. *The area of operation is local.* Employees and owners reside in one home community. (Markets served need not be local.)
4. *Size within the industry is relatively small.* The business is small when compared with the biggest units in its field. (The size of the top bracket varies widely, so that what might seem large in one field would be small in another.)

As we can see from the CED criteria, a small business is self-initiated, largely self-financed, and closely self-managed. It is of relatively small size when considered as part of the industry. Most scholars think that the fourth criterion, relative size, is the most important one.

It must be remembered that many small businesses serve big business. Hundreds of mass-produced consumer goods, although produced by giant corporations, are distributed and serviced largely by thousands of small stores. Only one out of four working Americans is employed by a business that has more than 200 employees.

CHARACTERISTICS OF THE SMALL BUSINESS

Apart from the matter of size, small businesses usually have three distinguishing characteristics: management, capital requirements, and local operation.

Management. Since the managers of small businesses are the owners, they are in a position to make their own decisions. As a small operator, the owner is both investor and employer. This gives him or her complete freedom of action.

Capital Requirements. The amount of capital required is relatively small compared with that required by most corporations. It is supplied by one person or at most by a few people.

Local Operation. For most small firms, the area of operation is local. The employer and employees live in the community in which the business is located. This does not mean, however, that all small firms serve only local markets. Small importing and exporting firms and canning and packing plants sometimes operate nationwide.

The main characteristics of the small business and big business are compared here:

Small Business	Big Business
Generally owner-managed	Usually non-owner-managed
Simple organizational structure	Complex organizational structure
Owner knows his or her employees	Owners know few employees
High percentage of business failures	Low percentage of business failures
Lacks specialized managers	Management specialists common
Long-term capital difficult to obtain	Long-term capital usually relatively easy to obtain

Scope of Operation. According to the SBA, approximately 75 percent of all nonfarm business establishments in the United States are small businesses. These provide jobs for 58 percent of all private nonfarm workers in the United States. During the past decade, about 80 percent of the new jobs created in the private business sector were in companies that employed fifty or fewer people. Big business overshadows the small firms in manufacturing. Nonetheless, there are thousands of small enterprises engaged in manufacturing. These include toy factories, machine shops, soft-drink bottling works, cabinet shops, sawmills, and bookbinding plants.

YOU'RE NEVER TOO YOUNG

Noah Flesher of Langhorne, Pennsylvania, started in business at the early age of 8. While puttering around in his father's leather-goods factory, he took a piece of leather, punched holes in it, and made a fob for a key ring.

It looked like Swiss cheese with the holes punched in the leather.

Noah drafted a letter to the Hickory Farms cheese people to see if they might like to buy some fobs. He thought they would make good items for use as sales incentives. Noah enclosed some samples.

As luck would have it, Hickory Farms sent Noah an order. This led to repeat orders, and Noah soon found himself in business.

FIGURE 6-3
Noah Flesher at his workbench.
(Photo by Mary L. Tuthill.)

STRENGTHS OF BEING SMALL

The owner-manager of a small business enjoys freedom of action, flexibility, and a place right on the firing line.

FREEDOM OF ACTION

Change is characteristic of business as it is carried on today. There are always new products, more modern machines, and new technology. The small-business owner is in a position to act quickly to meet changing conditions. This is especially important in meeting relatively small market demands. The large company cannot adapt so quickly. And the large company is not geared up to meet a small-market demand. The small retailer can order goods on a short lead time. The large firm orders large amounts of goods and therefore may place orders well in advance.

ADAPTING TO LOCAL NEEDS

Most small-business owners are long-time residents of the communities they serve. So they are in the best position to assess local needs. The local merchant has a close contact with customers and employees and can cater to these local needs and wants. The volume of business is small, so he or she can sell profitably in the small market.

TAKING PART WHERE THE ACTION IS

The small business gives the owner (or owners) a chance to participate in management. Often a valued employee's services can be retained by offering him or her an opportunity to become part owner.

DISADVANTAGES OF BEING SMALL

The individual owner faces some handicaps in managing a business and seeing that it succeeds. The owner must be good at everything, so that he or she can raise needed capital and compete with larger companies for qualified employees.

LACK OF SPECIALIZATION

Business today is very specialized. The individual owner does not have specialized skills in all areas of management. He or she is responsible for personnel, purchasing, finance, advertising, and daily operation. This puts the owner at a management disadvantage. A single owner may be inclined to overdo in his or her strong areas and neglect weak areas.

RAISING NEEDED CAPITAL

Since the owner or only a few people furnish the capital, it is quite limited. Unlike the giant corporation, the small independent merchant cannot raise large sums. Cash flow may be sufficient for day-to-day operations. But when a major expansion is at hand, finding needed capital may be difficult.

ATTRACTING QUALIFIED EMPLOYEES

The small business may pay good wages, but it cannot offer the job security provided by large firms. Small businesses usually do not have formal training programs. They offer employees fewer fringe benefits, and promotion opportunities are limited. All this puts them at a disadvantage in attracting the best-qualified workers. The higher the level of work to be done, the greater the disadvantage. College graduates, for example, prefer to work where there is good opportunity for advancement. The large companies have many more positions, and this makes promotions more likely.

Most people who decide to become entrepreneurs have worked for others, and they have a pretty good idea of the type of business they want to establish. They must decide if they have the necessary qualities, and they must develop a business plan. They must assess their competence in management and their ability to meet capital needs, and they must decide on the best form of business organization. The small businessperson must be well organized. Alan Cadan operates a small business from his home in Connecticut. He said, "The only way to run a business by yourself is to be organized. You have to be on top of things."

DEVELOPING A BUSINESS PLAN

There are three major areas to deal with when developing a business plan: a personal profile, a business profile, and the financial package. The specifics of these areas are presented in Table 6-2.

TABLE 6-2
Elements of the Business Plan

Personal profile:
  Credit rating, references
  Detailed résumé highlighting business experience
  Personal references
Business profile:
  History
  Analysis of competitors and market
  Discussion of competitive strategy and operating plans
  Profit plan and forecast
  Cash-flow plan
  Breakeven analysis
Loan package:
  Amount requested
  Type of loan requested
  Justification
  Repayment provisions and schedule

SOURCE: From Donald L. Sexton and Philip M. Van Auken, Entrepreneurship and Small Business Management. *Reprinted by permission of Prentice-Hall, Inc.*

MANAGEMENT COMPETENCE

In the preceding chapter, you learned about the management of a business organization. Specifically, we identified what management does and discussed certain qualities of leadership. Managing a small business requires the same process as managing a large business. A person must decide if he or she has the competence to manage in all the areas concerned:

Personnel	Merchandising
Physical facilities	Selling
Accounting	Advertising
Finance	Risk
Purchasing	Day-to-day operations

A person who lacks expertise in certain areas must plan on hiring qualified people to fill those needs.

ALLAN ROY THIEME

What Allan Roy Thieme started as a labor of love became a successful business operation. After his wife was stricken with multiple sclerosis, he designed a motorized wheelchair for her. Now he manufactures and sells the Amigo wheelchair.

To get started in business, Thieme applied for assistance to the Small Business Administration. The SBA offered advice but no loan. So the Thiemes mortgaged their home and borrowed money from friends and relatives. His business success led to his being selected by the SBA as the Small Business National Person of the Year in 1981.

Mr. Thieme says the purpose of Amigo is to make it possible for people with walking disabilities to participate more fully in life and living. He says that the small-business owner must "educate himself every day."

Most medical supplies are sold through special-equipment retail stores. But Thieme uses satisfied Amigo owners to sell his vehicle. Four out of five members of his sales force are Amigo owners or relatives of owners.

Allan Roy Thieme was born in Bridgeport, Michigan, and is a product of the Bridgeport and Saginaw school systems. He took classes in the evening and by correspondence to improve his educational preparation. In addition to the SBA award, he was given the Distinguished Service Award in 1970 by the Saginaw Jaycees; the President's "E" Award in 1981 for outstanding contributions to the U.S. export market; and was recognized in 1981 as the Michigan Small Business Person of the year. He also received the U.S. Chamber of Commerce 'Special Salute' at their 1982 meeting; and *Sales & Marketing Management* Magazine's Special Citation Award for outstanding achievement in 1981.

MEETING CAPITAL NEEDS

Studies show that inadequate capital is a major cause of small-business failures. The smaller the percentage of owner capital in a business, the greater the risk of failure. Capital includes both money used to start the firm and trade credit from manufacturers, wholesalers, and others. A general rule is that the owner furnishes at least two-thirds of the capital. No more than one-third should come from such other sources as trade credit or loans.

In the estimation of capital requirements, a common mistake is to underestimate funds needed for the first year of operation. Most new businesses are not profitable during the early years. One must plan on operating at a loss for a while. During this period, the business operates out of capital, not profits. Even after it becomes profitable, a given amount of what is called working capital must be available. WORKING CAPITAL consists of *money on hand or in banks, goods on hand, and accounts receivable.*

Fixed capital is funds invested in land, buildings, and equipment. Some or all of the fixed capital needed may be obtained through loans. The role of the Small Business Administration in obtaining fixed capital is discussed later in this chapter. Money available for goods, supplies, and wages must come from *working capital.*

Money invested in the business by owners is called EQUITY CAPITAL. Money acquired by loan is **debt capital.** The borrower must pay interest on the debt capital. It is also expected that the principal will be returned at a later date.[3]

---

[3] Equity and debt capital are discussed in Chapter 14. The legal meaning of equity is given in Chapter 19.

Venture Capitalists. VENTURE CAPITALISTS are *individuals, groups, or businesses that invest in promising young businesses.* They are usually investment specialists that hope to receive a good return on their investment. In some cases, they plan to sell their equity at a later date at a good profit.

Venture capital is not a loan to a business, it is an investment. Venture capitalists usually receive stock in return for their investment. **Venture capital** is risk money invested in small businesses that are likely to experience rapid growth.

Small-Business Investment Companies. There are more than 400 small-business investment companies in the United States. They are made up of groups of people who invest in high-risk companies of great potential. They usually invest in companies that are successful and appear to have great promise for rapid future growth. In 1981, $1.3 billion was added to the venture-capital pool of funds.

CHOOSING THE FORM OF OWNERSHIP

In Chapter 3, we discussed several forms of business ownership designed to meet the needs of all kinds of business enterprises. The three forms — proprietorship, partnership, and corporation — were discussed in detail. What was said there applies to both large and small businesses.

The simplicity of the sole proprietorship makes this form well suited to small firms. But under certain conditions, the partnership and corporate forms are also satisfactory for small-scale ventures. It is important to decide as early as possible which form to use.

Sole Proprietorship   Partnership   Corporation

FIGURE 6-4
Choosing the Organization Form.

Subchapter S. Many small businesses are organized as corporations under Subchapter S tax laws. There is a single owner-officer, which gives the limited-liability advantage of a corporation. But for tax purposes, a Subchapter S business is taxed as a proprietorship.

The Subchapter S Revision Act, enacted in 1982, greatly changed Subchapter S rules. It simplified the rules to make Subchapter S taxation more nearly resemble partnership taxation. Among other changes, the act:

1. Increased the number of eligible shareholders to thirty-five
2. Imposed new requirements for making, revoking, and terminating Subchapter S elections
3. Requires that all *new* Subchapter S corporations are to be on a calendar-year basis

Thriving communities are continually expanding. As new suburban areas grow, shopping centers soon develop. A small business must have some special features in order to prosper. Some of the factors that give an entrepreneur a competitive advantage over other businesses are these:

1. Satisfaction of an unmet consumer need
2. Superior service
3. Better merchandise display
4. Higher quality at the same price
5. Lower price for the same quality
6. Greater product safety
7. Personalized customer service
8. Better product information
9. More convenience in store layout
10. More complete information in advertising
11. More attractive packaging

PROBLEM AREAS FOR SMALL BUSINESSES

What are the problems that irk the small business person the most? The national Federation of Independent Business surveyed its members to find out. The most pressing problems are listed in Table 6-3.

TABLE 6-3
Problem Areas for Small Businesses

1. Interest rates	14. Control of inventory
2. Cost of insurance	15. Ability to advertise cost-effectively
3. Cost of utility bills	16. Employee turnover
4. Cost of labor	17. Obtaining of needed loans
5. Local tax rates	18. Cost of rent
6. Location of qualified employees	19. Losing of skilled employees to large firms
7. Cost of supplies and inventory	20. Local inspectors and inspections
8. Cash flow	21. Obtaining of licenses and permits
9. Low profits	22. Employee relations and/or unions
10. Crime rate	23. Unfavorable business location
11. Competition from large firms	24. Access to highways, roads, parking, public transportation
12. Workers' compensation	
13. Insufficient sales	

FAILURES AMONG SMALL FIRMS

In every size business — small, medium, or large — risks are involved. Unfortunately, too many businesspeople are unprepared to acknowledge risk as an important factor. They overestimate their own qualifications and assume they will succeed where others failed. Small firms are vulnerable to economic conditions, competition, and a poor location. As we examine the following reasons, it becomes apparent that there are also other causes of small-business failure.

CAUSES OF FAILURE   Nationwide statistics involving business failures, gathered by the credit-reporting firm of Dun & Bradstreet, show that **lack of management experience is a major cause of small-business failure.** Poor management shows up in several ways:

1. Inability to manage and direct others
2. Lack of capital — often an indication of poor financial management
3. Lack of ability in sales promotion
4. Inability to collect bad debts and to curtail unwise credit policies

A detailed list of causes of business failure follows. Several of these causes overlap. Some are closely identified with the owner's lack of experience and of general ability.

Specific Causes of Small-Business Failure

Insufficient Capital Structure:
Lack of capital to buy adequate stock and equipment
Insufficient capital to take advantage of special merchandise "deals"
Lack of capital to enable one to take merchandise discounts

Use of Obsolete Business Methods and Equipment:
Failure to maintain stock-inventory controls
Lack of credit controls
Inadequate financial and tax records

Absence of Business Planning:
Inability to detect and understand market changes
Failure to understand changing economic conditions
Failure to maintain plans for emergencies
Failure to anticipate and plan financial needs

Personal Qualifications:
Insufficient knowledge of the business
Unwillingness to work long hours when necessary
Failure to delegate responsibility and assign duties
Inability to maintain customer relations
Lack of tact in dealing with employees

SIGNS OF BUSINESS FAILURE   How can a proprietor tell in advance that the business is showing signs of failure? Early signs include the following:

1. Declining sales over several accounting periods
2. Progressively higher debt ratios
3. Increased operating costs
4. Reduction in working capital
5. Reduction in profits (or increasing losses)

As these signs begin to come together, the threat of failure grows, and it becomes more evident that corrective action is necessary. Some positive steps include:

1. Reducing operating expenses
2. Striving to improve sales, possibly through increasing advertising
3. Reviewing credit losses to eliminate poor risks
4. Reexamining stock inventories to determine whether they are excessive

BUSINESS FAILURES   In every kind of business, risk is present. But the probability of failing is significantly greater for small firms as a group. Not all concerns that go out of business actually fail. About half just stop operating, mostly for such reasons as the retirement or death of the owner. Other firms have filed either a voluntary or an involuntary petition for bankruptcy.

Number and Rate of Failures.   Statistics on the number and rate of failures tend to fluctuate from year to year. The failure rate among new businesses is greater than for those that have been established for some time. Figure 6-5 shows that 55.7 percent of business failures occur during the first five years of existence. Only 21.9 percent of business failures occur among firms that have been operating for at least ten years.

Certain kinds of businesses are more vulnerable to failure than others. For example, small furniture-manufacturing companies have a very high failure rate. Small machine shops have a low failure rate. In retailing, where small firms predominate, camera and photographic-supply shops and menswear stores have a high failure rate. Retail stores selling appliances, radios, and television sets tend to have a low failure rate.

FIGURE 6-5
Business failures by age of Firm.

SERVICE BUSINESSES

More than a million business enterprises in the United States are classified as part of the "service trades." Service is an area of business in which small firms are the backbone of the industry. A SERVICE BUSINESS is *one that is basically labor-oriented and provides services rather than goods.* The chief areas for small businesses are shown below. In addition, there are many other kinds of "service trades," such as telephone-answering services, interior decorators, locksmiths, and accountants.

Service-Type Establishments

1. *Communication services* — telephone companies and TV and radio stations
2. *Entertainment* — casinos, theaters, and sports
3. *Lodging services* — motels and hotels
4. *Personal services* — barber and beauty shops, dry-cleaning shops, photography studios, laundries, and funeral homes
5. *Real estate and insurance* — firms selling property and all forms of insurance
6. *Repair shops* — servicing appliances, radios, TVs, watches, furniture, and automobiles
7. *Restaurants* — cafeterias, coffee shops, and dining rooms
8. *Special business services* — bookkeeping and accounting, collection agencies, credit bureaus, and tax services
9. *Transportation* — automobile agencies, taxicab companies, household movers, and storage
10. *Rentals* — specialized home furnishings, lawn and garden equipment, and medical equipment
11. *Professionals* — attorneys, physicians, and technicians

The service sector is growing faster than other sectors of the economy. More than one-third of all business concerns sell services rather than products. The percentage of the consumer dollar spent for services is increasing.

We do not often think of spectator sports as a service business. But look at the thousands of people, enjoying this football game.
(Courtesy; Arrowhead Stadium, Kansas City, Missouri.)

NATURE OF SERVICE BUSINESSES Service businesses possess characteristics not common to businesses that produce goods. To begin with, they serve limited markets and, as a result, have small trade areas. For example, beauticians operate mainly in beauty shops catering primarily to people residing in the local area.

Few service businesses maintain much merchandise inventory, so the amount of space needed is reduced. In most cases, the sale of goods is incidental to the service function.

The level of skill required to provide a service is the dominant factor in determining its cost. Some services, such as renting equipment, do not require a high degree of skill. This type of service is relatively cheap. Others, such as making lenses for glasses or making dentures, require considerable skill. This type of service is relatively costly. A service business can start small and add personnel as business volume grows.

The basic charge for the service often includes more than just the direct service rendered. Take, for example, electricians, plumbers, collection agencies, and household movers. The hourly labor charge assessed includes the cost of investment in trucks and other equipment used. It also includes an overhead percentage for operating the business office — rent, utilities, secretarial and accounting services, and, of course, a profit for the owner.

THE SMALL BUSINESS ADMINISTRATION

The federal government has been very active in supervising the affairs of small businesses. In 1953, Congress passed the Small Business Act that created the Small Business Administration (SBA). The three major areas of SBA assistance to small businesses are:

1. Loans
2. Management and technical assistance
3. Assistance in processing government contracts

SBA LOANS According to the Small Business Act, the Small Business Administration may:

> make loans to enable small-business concerns to finance plant construction, conversion, or expansion, including the acquisition of land, . . . equipment, facilities, machinery, supplies, or materials; or to supply such concerns with working capital to be used in the manufacture of articles, equipment, supplies, or materials for war, defense, or civilian production or as may be necessary to insure a well-balanced national economy.

The SBA offers a variety of loan programs to eligible small-business concerns. There are two basic types of regular business loans:

1. Direct loans from the SBA
2. Guaranty loans, whereby the SBA guarantees up to 90 percent of a loan made by some private lender.

Under the law, the SBA cannot make a direct loan unless a private lender refuses to make it. The maximum on direct business loans is $150,000. The funds the SBA has for direct loans are limited so most business loans are of

146

the guaranteed type. On the guaranteed loans, the maximum is $500,000. Maturity may be up to twenty-five years.

The average size of an SBA business loan is $85,000, and the average maturity is nine years.

MANAGEMENT AND TECHNICAL ASSISTANCE

Each SBA field office is staffed with specialists in different areas of management. Their services are available to people in established businesses as well as new business enterprises.

The SBA works with colleges and universities in setting up seminars and short courses. These deal with organizing, planning, staffing, directing, financing, and controlling in small businesses.

The Small Business Administration sponsors a group called SCORE (Service Corps of Retired Executives). This group consists of former business executives and owners who make their skills available to small-business owners. Their services are on a part-time and voluntary basis; there is no charge for their services. SCORE volunteers call the attention of management to company weaknesses and offer suggestions on how to correct them.

In addition to these personal services, the SBA has published booklets dealing with almost every aspect of operating a small business.

HELP IN SECURING GOVERNMENT CONTRACTS

Under a "set aside" program, certain procurement orders may be earmarked for bidding by only small businesses. Under what is called the "production pool" arrangement, small firms may combine their bids where the order is too large for a single business.

CURRENT ISSUE

SHOULD THE GOVERNMENT SUBSIDIZE NEW BUSINESSES?

Because of large federal deficits, the White House was urged to reduce government aid to small businesses. But some legislators are champions of more government help. Obviously, we cannot move in both directions at the same time.

With which of the following statements do you agree, and with which do you disagree?

1. Small businesses are so important to the U.S. economy that the government should do more to help them.
2. The government should help businesses only when they begin; that is, during their first five years.
3. Successful businesses should be given loans for longer than fifteen years.
4. The maximum amount that a new business can borrow should be reduced.
5. Minorities and women should be given preference by the SBA.
6. Every new business should stand or fall on its own merit.
7. The government should not subsidize small businesses.

Do you favor government subsidies for small businesses? Why or why not?

The SBA works with other government agencies with regard to subcontractors. Such agencies as the Defense Department and the Space Agency have regulations that apply to prime contractors. They must give small firms an opportunity to bid on subcontracts.

The Small Business Administration works closely with the Office of Minority Business Enterprise (OMBE).[4] Lists of such businesses that might bid on subcontracts are supplied to prime contractors.

FIGURE 6-6
Small Business Speaks, Government Listens.
Small business people are heard by law makers and administrators. Here, U.S. Commerce Secretary Malcolm Baldridge gets an earful. (Courtesy Jed DeKalb, State of Tennessee.)

FRANCHISING

Franchising has been a fast-growing segment of retail business. It accounts for more than one-third of all retail sales and is growing at the rate of 12 percent per year. Franchising accounts for one-eighth of the gross national product. It is a way for people with limited capital to have their own businesses. The best-known examples of franchising are in the fast-food industry. McDonald's, Kentucky Fried Chicken, and Wendy's are franchise operations. Most car dealers operate under franchise contracts. This is also true of gasoline service-station operators. Franchising is also popular among

---

[4] The OMBE is discussed in Chapter 2.

OWNERSHIP, MANAGEMENT, AND ORGANIZATION

motels, drugstores, car rentals, and auto-parts suppliers. The fastest-growing franchise areas are listed in Table 6-4.

TABLE 6-4
The Fastest Growing U.S. Franchises in 1982

TYPE OF FRANCHISE	PERCENT OF INCREASE
Recreation, entertainment, travel	+34.1%
Miscellaneous business services	+30.7%
Accounting, credit, collection agencies, general business services	+21.9%
Printing, copying services	+20.8%
Soft-drink bottlers	+19.4%
Business aids, services	+19.1%
Employment services	+18.5%

SOURCE: U.S. Department of Commerce estimates.

HOW FRANCHISING WORKS

The FRANCHISE is *a legal licensing agreement between a manufacturer (or operating company) and a dealer for conducting business.* The licensing company is called the **franchisor,** and the dealer is called the **franchisee.** The Small Business Administration defines **franchising** as a system of distribution under which an individually owned business is operated as though it were part of a large chain, complete with product name, trademark, and standardized operating procedures.

The parent company (franchisor) permits the dealer to use its name and product or service. The franchisor gives the local dealer an exclusive territory, counseling, new-employee training, and continuing supervision. National advertising, supplies, and materials are also furnished.

Start-up support may include any or all of the following:

1. Site selection
2. Building plans
3. Equipment purchases
4. Work-flow pattern
5. Employee selection
6. Advertising
7. Graphics
8. Grand-opening help

Continuing supervision would include such factors as:

1. Records and accounting
2. Consultation
3. Inspection and standards
4. Promotion
5. Quality control
6. Legal advice
7. Research
8. Materials sources

The franchisee provides the management at the local level. The International Franchise Association regards franchising as "a continuing relationship between the franchisor and franchisee. The sum total of the franchisor's knowledge, image, success, manufacturing, and marketing techniques are supplied to the franchisee for a consideration."

McDonald's hamburger franchises are a good example of a successful franchise operation. Key to McDonald's success has been very careful control over the quality of the franchisee's operation. Inspectors from the franchisor check periodically to see that all operations are up to standard. McDonald's developed a school for training managers in "the McDonald's way" of doing everything from cleaning the floors to making shakes. This operation is referred to as Hamburger University.

THE CONTRACT AGREEMENT

In a franchise, the legal basis of operation is the contract between the two parties. However, the parent company may cancel the franchise if the franchisee violates the terms of the agreement. The National Association of Franchised Businessmen compiles complaints from franchisees and publishes a list of tips for making franchising contracts. The exact terms of the franchise contracts differ, but in general, they include the following provisions:

The Franchisor Agrees to:	The Franchisee Agrees to:
1. Assign an exclusive sales territory to the franchisee	1. Operate the business according to the rules and procedures offered by the franchisor
2. Provide a stipulated amount of management training and assistance	2. Invest a stipulated minimum amount in the business
3. Furnish merchandise to the franchisee at a price competitive with the market	3. Pay the franchisor a certain amount (usually as a royalty on a fixed percentage)
4. Advise the franchisee on location of business and design of building	4. Construct or otherwise provide a business facility as approved by the franchisor
5. Offer certain financial assistance or financial advice to the franchisee	5. Buy supplies and other standard materials from the franchisor or an approved supplier

SOME PROS AND CONS OF FRANCHISING

Like any business, franchising has both advantages and disadvantages. It does not guarantee success. Like any other business, its success depends on the effort and skills of the manager. Let us look at some specific points regarding this type of retail operation.

Advantages. One of the major advantages is the training and direction provided by the franchisor. The initial training is followed by continuing supervision. A second advantage is the franchisor's financial help. Start-up costs are high, and the entrepreneur's sources of capital are often limited. If the prospect is considered a good risk, the franchisor often provides the franchisee with financial backing. This is particularly true of such franchises as automobile dealerships. It is usually not true of fast-food and other small-investment companies. In addition, the franchisee has the benefit of using a recognized trade name, product, or brand title. Such names as

Wendy's, Walgreen Agency, Dairy Queen, Holiday Inn, and NAPA are widely recognized. Since most small-business failures are attributed to lack of business know-how, this advantage of a good franchise is obvious.

Disadvantages. The training program that some franchisors promise leaves much to be desired. The day-to-day details of operating the business are often omitted. At the other extreme, some franchise agreements allow the franchisees very little freedom to exercise their own ingenuity. They may find themselves tied into a contract forbidding them to buy either equipment or provisions elsewhere. A franchisee seldom has the right to sell the business to a third party without first offering it to the franchisor at the same price. Most contracts allow the franchisee to leave it to a member of his or her family with approval of the franchisor. However, this family member must have the qualifications to be a franchisee and must agree to the franchise contract.

BASKIN-ROBBINS

Baskin-Robbins Ice Cream Company is America's oldest and largest ice-cream franchise operation. It was started in the late 1940s by Burton Baskin and Irvine Robbins. Today it has over 2,500 outlets. It is expanding aggressively in the United States, Canada, Great Britain, and Japan. Baskin-Robbins offers more than 500 flavors as a rotating lineup of 31 choices.

In addition to franchising retail outlets, Baskin-Robbins also franchises its factories. Retail franchisees pay $75,000 to $100,000, which includes the cost of leasehold improvements and equipment.

31 flavors at the oldest ice-cream franchise operation in America.
(Courtesy Baskin-Robbins Ice Cream.)

The federal government has in recent years shown a keen interest in small businesses. Three milestone laws aiding small business were enacted in 1980. They are known as the "Regflex," Equal Access, and Patent Policy laws.

THE REGULATORY FLEXIBILITY ACT

This act initiates a two-tier regulatory plan for small businesses. It requires federal agencies to tailor regulations to the ability of small firms to comply. Government agencies are now required to:

1. Publish an agenda of upcoming regulation proposals
2. Weigh the effect of proposed rules on small business
3. Explain the need for each proposed rule
4. Review all rules within ten years to see which ones are not needed

THE EQUAL ACCESS TO JUSTICE ACT

This act gives small businesses an opportunity to have their court costs and legal fees paid if they win in suits against a government agency. To be eligible to recover fees, a business must have a net worth of less than $5 million or fewer than 500 employees. There are five key provisions of the Equal Access law:

1. It makes no difference whether the government or the taxpayer started the legal action.
2. Proof of bad faith by the agency is not required.
3. The agency must show that its actions were "substantially justified."
4. It is not necessary to prevail on all issues to receive an award.
5. There is no dollar limit on awards.

GOVERNMENT PATENT POLICY ACT

This act allows small businesses to obtain exclusive rights to inventions developed under government contracts. (The government would still hold the rights to the patent.) Its purpose is to encourage the development of products that otherwise would not be profitable to market.

TABLE 6-5

Comparative Revenues: Company vs. Franchisee Units; Average Sales Per Establishment, 1981 (estimated)

	COMPANY OWNED	FRANCHISEE-OWNED	DIFFERENCE	% DIFFERENCE
Laundry and drycleaning services	$553,000	$102,000	$451,000	442%
Automotive products and services	$534,000	$125,000	$409,000	327%
Equipment-rental services	$502,000	$140,000	$362,000	259%
Hotels and motels	$2,467,000	$1,134,000	$1,333,000	118%
Retailing (nonfood)	$348,000	$233,000	$115,000	49%
Restaurants (all types)	$523	$435	$88	20%

SOURCE: Department of Commerce

Entrepreneurs risk their capital to start and manage small businesses.

The history of business in America is the history of the small-business enterprise.

A business is considered to be "small" when it is independently owned and operated and not dominant in its field of operation.

Small firms account for 58 percent of all business employment.

Small businesses are characterized by independent management, relatively small capital requirements, and service to a small geographical area.

Although small businesses are most common in retailing, they play a major role in manufacturing and wholesaling.

Small businesses enjoy an advantage over large businesses in freedom of action in management and flexibility in adapting to local needs and conditions.

Small firms are at a disadvantage in competing with large firms for capital, management specialization, and qualified employees.

Successful businesses must have a business plan, sufficient working capital, and managerial competence.

A competitive edge may be gained through such factors as superior service, high quality, low prices, attractive packaging, and greater product safety.

Business failures are caused by absence of planning, poor management, insufficient capital, and weakness in sales promotion.

Many businesses sell services rather than products. A service business does not require capital investment for merchandise inventory. So small businesses are found in a wide variety of service, labor-dominated enterprises.

The federal government has taken specific action to help small businesses. The Small Business Administration makes business and disaster loans, provides management and technical assistance, and aids in the procurement of government contracts. It also makes small loans to minority businesses.

Franchising is a major part of retail merchandising. The franchisor supplies important training, management know-how, and supervision to franchisees.

BUSINESS TERMS

You should be able to match these business terms with the statements that follow:

a. ENTREPRENEURSHIP
b. EQUITY CAPITAL
c. FRANCHISE
d. FRANCHISEE
e. FRANCHISOR
f. SERVICE BUSINESS
g. SMALL BUSINESS
h. SMALL BUSINESS ADMINISTRATION
i. SUBCHAPTER S
j. VENTURE CAPITAL
k. WORKING CAPITAL

1. The investing and risking of effort and money to start a business
2. A business that is independently owned and operated and not dominant in its field
3. Funds available to purchase supplies and materials, and pay salaries
4. Risk money that is invested in businesses likely to experience rapid growth
5. Money invested in the business by the owners
6. A business organized as a corporation but taxed as a proprietorship
7. A business that is basically labor-oriented and serves a local community
8. An agency created by the federal government to aid small-business firms
9. A licensing agreement between an operating company and a dealer
10. The business that grants the license in a franchise agreement

1. What criteria must a business meet if it is to be classified as "small"?
2. How would you describe or characterize a small business?
3. What strengths are characteristic of small businesses?
4. What weaknesses are characteristic of small businesses?
5. In what chief areas does the SBA assist business enterprises?
6. What are the general provisions of the franchise agreement?

**DISCUSSION
QUESTIONS**

1. If you wished to start a small business, how would you go about it?
2. What do you consider to be the chief advantage of a business's being small?
3. If you were starting your own business, what type of business would you organize, and why?
4. What factors make for success in managing a small business?
5. Why are small firms so common in service-type businesses?
6. Why is franchising so popular in fast-foods retailing?

BUSINESS CASES

THE FUTURE OF HART'S GROCERY

Daniel Hart and his mother have just inherited his father's business. They have received a cash offer for their store building and the adjoining parking lot. They could invest that money and receive a good monthly income without working for it. But what about Daniel's ten years' experience in his father's grocery business? And what about the history, tradition, and reputation of Hart's Grocery?

Daniel's grandfather, Harry Hart, established the business fifty years ago. Harry had clerks to take telephone orders and counter clerks to put the orders together. He granted credit and delivered customers' orders to their homes. Harry Hart gave good service, and his clerks were efficient and friendly. At that time, almost every family bought its food at an independent grocery. There were some chain grocery stores, but they were small and very much like the independent groceries.

Harry changed with the times and tried hard to keep up to date. He joined a wholesale grocery cooperative. He stopped granting credit except to a few special customers. He rearranged his layout to accommodate self-service by his customers. After thirty-five years of operation, Harry left a going and profitable business to his son Wallace.

Wallace had worked in his father's store for several years. So he carried on much as Harry had taught him. He kept his meat department as it always had been. The butcher catered to each customer's personal needs. Later, Wallace changed to a cash-and-carry mode of operation, and moved to a new location. He had been losing customers because there was no place for them to park. So he bought a larger building with an adjoining lot, with parking for as many as twenty cars. He started the practice of giving trading stamps to bolster sales. Two years after he moved to this larger building, the street in front of the store was widened. It now has four traffic lanes, two going in each direction. The faster-moving traffic means that fewer people stop off at Hart's on their way home from work. Sales volume has decreased from $75,000 to $60,000 per week.

Wallace's early death left the business in the hands of his wife Mary and his son Daniel, who had worked for his father for the past ten years. Most of the other independent groceries in the community are gone. The chain stores and large independents operate as supermarkets. Is there a future for Hart's Grocery in this community of 150,000 people?

1. Do you think there is a future for the independent grocery per se?
2. Can Daniel operate Hart's Grocery profitably in today's environment?
3. What advice would you give Daniel?

6-2 BUY AN EXISTING FIRM OR START A NEW ONE?

Helen and James Worth have four children, the oldest of whom has just been graduated from high school. They have been in the retail florist business in Winchester for twenty-five years. Their business has been profitable, but this seems to be a good time to move to a college town. Recently the Worths received an offer from an entrepreneur who wishes to buy their business — Main Street Florists.

Helen did some scouting in Cleveland, about 100 miles east of Winchester. There is a private four-year college and a community (junior) college in Cleveland, a city of 80,000 population. There are four shopping malls, each one located in the suburbs. There are florist shops in three of the malls but none on the east side of the city. Helen has proposed to James that they open a new florist business in this eastern shopping mall. James is somewhat reluctant to pioneer another new business. He has suggested that, instead, they consider buying one of the three established florist shops.

As you know, there are advantages and disadvantages to each plan. What do you see as the chief factors that would determine which procedure they should follow?

PART 2

CAREERS IN MANAGEMENT

A manager holds a challenging and important position! Whether you are managing your own small business or managing for someone else, the responsibilities and the salary can be important.

Management requires experience. For that reason, people are seldom put right into a management job upon graduation from college. Various management trainee positions usually provide entry-level experience for new graduates. The best then move into management positions.

Management trainee is a broad term used for a starting place in all areas of business. The American business system uses college graduates in many different management areas. These graduates begin in sales, banking, accounting, production, personnel administration, or distribution. And there are all kinds of opportunities related to the production and operation of a business. These positions include supervisors in product manufacturing, factory managers, and so forth.

Management careers may be in line jobs or as staff specialists. Staff managers may include the fact-finding specialists, whose services support the managers who make decisions. Labor-relations specialists deal with unions as interpreters of union–management labor contracts. People with management training can work as representatives of such organizations as the AFL-CIO, the country's largest labor organization.

GROWING NEED FOR MANAGERS

The work of the manager as a decision maker is not limited to a given industry. Managers are needed wherever there are people working together toward a specific goal. This includes areas of government, as well as hospitals, chambers of commerce, trade associations, and educational foundations.

A recent study conducted by Haskell and Stern Associates, a New York executive-search firm, found that "general management" positions will be the hardest to fill in the 1980s. The study surveyed personnel executives and discovered that most companies will need management "generalists" to run their operations in the next decade. But, because many lower-management positions have become so specialized, the supply of "generalists" is scarce. Also tough to find in the 1980s will be computer specialists and engineers. The easiest jobs to fill will be in the legal, sales, and financial areas. A partial list of management positions would include the following:

Manufacturing supervisor	Hospital director
Traffic manager	Accounting supervisor
Grocery-store manager	Plant manager
Food supervisor	Design supervisor
Hotel manager	Company president
Construction superintendent	Purchasing supervisor

OWNERSHIP, MANAGEMENT, AND ORGANIZATION

PEOPLE AND PRODUCTION

It was Roger King who was in charge of the personnel function for King Clothiers. Fortunately, there was an adequate local labor supply when the firm was started. But other businesses also found Centerville a good place to locate. New people being interviewed increasingly asked about the fringe benefits that were being offered by the company. It was clear that to be competitive, King Clothiers had to start providing its workers with some fringe benefits. But which ones should be offered?

As the business grew, it became a target for union organizers. When plant workers began talking about forming a union, at first the managers resisted. But later they decided it would be to their advantage to have a formal agreement with the workers. What items should be included in this collective agreement?

The Kings ran into two other major problems. Their building was too small. When they started in business, they had not foreseen the need for so much more space. There was no satisfactory way to enlarge the present building. This meant they had to move to a new location or have two plants. What was the best management solution to this problem? Related to this was the need to conserve energy. Energy cost more than it had when they began operations. And the present building was not modern. In addition to providing more space, a new building would also be more energy-efficient.

PART

3

HUMAN-RESOURCES MANAGEMENT

study objectives

WHEN YOU HAVE FINISHED READING THIS CHAPTER, YOU SHOULD BE ABLE TO:

1. Explain what personnel managers do

2. Discuss the relationships among job analysis, job description, and job specification

3. Identify the different aspects of employee staffing

4. Distinguish between a promotion and a transfer

5. Describe the issue surrounding ''comparable worth''

6. List the different components of a sound staff-maintenance plan

We shall have "better business" when everyone realizes that while it pays to invest money in their industries and develop natural resources, it pays still higher dividends to improve mankind and develop human resources.

H. E. Steiner

n any business organization, it is people who make it successful. When a single proprietor goes into business, he or she coordinates and directs the work of a few employees. The owner has a close association with them and knows their abilities, needs, problems, and ambitions. However, as a business grows in size, top management can personally know only a small part of the workforce. One person can no longer manage all the details of the many employer–employee relationships.

So a large business must make special provisions to direct and coordinate personnel matters and keep employees satisfied and productive. People do not automatically become productive employees. They must be recruited, hired, matched with the proper jobs, trained, appraised as to performance, and paid acceptable wages. Employees' working conditions must be monitored for safety, their activities coordinated, and records maintained on their performance. If these things are done properly, most people are satisfied with their jobs.

Early human-resources management was primarily record keeping, planning the company picnic, and maintaining the retirement records. But the upper levels of management soon saw the importance of a motivated, competent work force. This has changed the role of personnel management in most companies.

Further, the federal government has passed laws dealing with every phase of human-resources management. Hiring, test validation, compensation, child-labor laws, health and safety, and pension funding are all subject to federal law. There are severe penalties associated with failure to live within the laws that govern these personnel activities. Managers have found it necessary to upgrade and professionalize their methods of managing human resources.

The box that follows shows an example of the extent to which some companies will go to accommodate people. With the high cost of moving, high mortgage rates for new homes, and working spouses, many employees do not want to move, and extraordinary measures may be required to transfer them.

Alcoa decided that it wanted to move a compensation analyst from Knoxville to Pittsburgh. But he refused to go unless his wife had a job in Pittsburgh too. Alcoa arranged an interview for his wife. It also gave the analyst an interest-free loan to buy a home, as well as an allowance to ease the difference between the old and new mortgage rates. And it paid all moving expenses.

Eastman Kodak and Atlantic Richfield both make an effort to line up jobs for spouses. Moving employees often means helping spouses find new jobs. A recent Merrill Lynch Relocation management survey showed that 30 percent of the companies surveyed help spouses continue their careers.

Many companies pay cost-of-living adjustments for people being transferred to high-cost areas. State Farm pays managers an extra 37 percent in Anchorage, 27 percent in Honolulu, 26 percent in New York, 24 percent in Boston, 9 percent in San Francisco, 6 percent in Buffalo, and 5 percent in Washington, D.C. United Airlines pays 10 percent extra for employees in Hawaii, and J.C. Penney pays 20 percent extra in New York.

WHAT DO PERSONNEL MANAGERS DO?

Personnel or human-resource managers are responsible for a wide variety of items related to people at work. Figure 7-1 shows major activities engaged in by personnel managers.

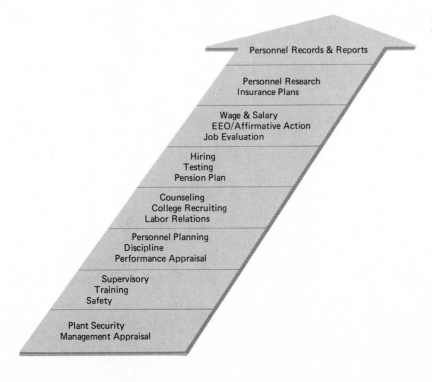

FIGURE 7-1
What Do Personnel Managers Do?

Personnel Records & Reports

Personnel Research
Insurance Plans

Wage & Salary
EEO/Affirmative Action
Job Evaluation

Hiring
Testing
Pension Plan

Counseling
College Recruiting
Labor Relations

Personnel Planning
Discipline
Performance Appraisal

Supervisory
Training
Safety

Plant Security
Management Appraisal

Notice in the figure that "equal employment opportunity/affirmative action" is a major responsibility of personnel departments. That item was of little concern to business twenty years ago. Changes in federal laws have now made it a top-priority item.

THE ORGANIZATION AND PERSONNEL MANAGEMENT

The personnel function is handled differently in different organizations. In some businesses, all managers are to some extent responsible for the "people-oriented" activities. In others, major personnel activities are centralized in a personnel department. Studies show that as organizations expand, the personnel function becomes a major time requirement for managers. When this happens, the personnel function is usually centralized. Figure 7-2 shows how the personnel department may be given equal status with other departments in the organization.

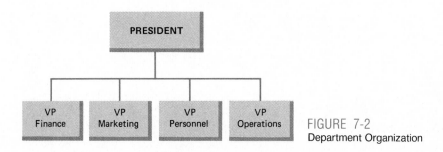

FIGURE 7-2
Department Organization

The personnel department is usually a staff function rather than a line function. The personnel manager has advisory authority rather than direct authority.

In its staff capacity, the personnel department assists other departments in hiring and training employees and in serving the needs of those employees. But final decisions on personnel matters are made by the department heads.

Sometimes the personnel department is given line authority. In this capacity, it does not simply assist or serve other departments. Its staff makes the final decision in hiring, conducts specialized training, and decides who is to be promoted.

Regardless of the organization pattern used, the basic personnel activities must be done by someone.

CRITICAL PERSONNEL ACTIVITIES

In every business organization, certain personnel activities must be carried on to keep the workforce productive and morale high. These activities are:

Work analysis and design
Staffing
Training and development
Appraisal
Compensation
Maintenance

Let's examine each of these activities to see why they are basic in every business organization.

Department Heads in Conference

WORK ANALYSIS AND DESIGN

Before people can be recruited and hired for jobs, management must know what work is to be done. The way the work is to be divided and assigned to different jobs is the place to start.

A JOB is *an organizational unit of work.* A **job** is made up of a collection of tasks, assignments, duties, and responsibilities. A **position** is a specific work station occupied by the employee. Each employee occupies a particular position. Several positions may involve the same types of duties that make up any one job. The components that make up any job are shown in Figure 7-3.

Job analysis is the place to start a personnel examination, because it focuses on what people do. The U.S. Employment Service defines JOB ANALYSIS as *determining, by observation and study, pertinent information about the nature of a specific job.* The specific tasks that constitute the job, along with the skills, knowledge, and abilities that are required of the worker, make one job different from all others. **Job analysis includes not only a study of the work itself but also an analysis of the conditions and environment in which the work is performed.**

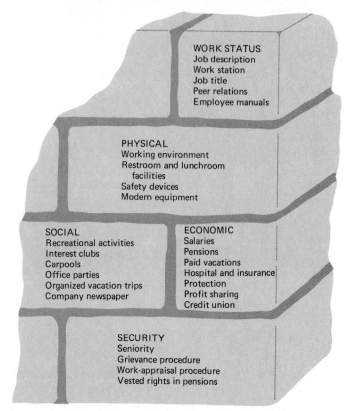

FIGURE 7-3
Job Components

From the standpoint of the personnel department, job analyses are made in order to:

1. Evaluate the work station to see how it relates to other positions
2. Identify activities to be performed
3. Determine the requirements for measuring employee performance
4. Identify potential safety hazards
5. Identify basic information on operational procedures
6. Clarify lines of authority and responsibility
7. Provide the data needed for developing a job-classification system
8. Make sure there is compliance with such legal regulations as those of the Fair Labor Standards Act

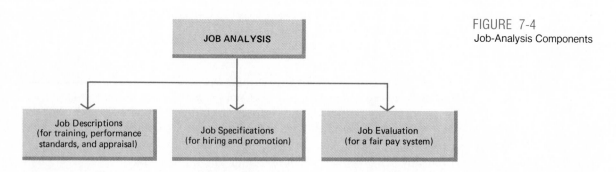

FIGURE 7-4
Job-Analysis Components

Data for making job analyses are obtained by interview and observation. Asking questions can help one get a true picture of the qualifications the worker needs to perform his or her tasks effectively. The information obtained from job analysis is used in one of three ways: for job descriptions, for job specifications, and/or for job evaluations. (See Figure 7-4.)

JOB DESCRIPTION The JOB DESCRIPTION is *a written description of what an employee is to do on a particular job.* Below is an illustration of a job description for a bookkeeper. You can see that it includes:

1. The job title
2. Its distinctive characteristics
3. Specific tasks to be performed
4. The job's relation to other jobs
5. The skills, tools and equipment used, and how they are to be used
6. The materials and supplies used
7. The physical and mental skills required
8. Specific duties and responsibilities assigned to the job

JOB DESCRIPTION FOR BOOKKEEPER

Position _____

Incumbent: ___Patricia Johnson___ Hours _____

Salary _____ Date Job Analyzed: ___April 28___ Date Employed _____

Position Summary

Incumbent is under the supervision of Office Manager. Maintains accounting records for income from patient billings, and income payments by Medicare, Medical, and insurance companies; reviews and ages individual delinquent accounts and determines means for collecting payment. Prepares forms submitted to Medicare, Medical, and insurance companies for claims assigned by patients. Reviews accounts receivable preparatory to determining appropriate action for collecting delinquent accounts. Opens all incoming mail and deposits payments in the bank. Maintains daily cash receipts. Explains to patients the nature of the charges made if there is a question. Assists patients' preparation of Medicare, Medical, and insurance forms. Compiles information for submission to an outside agency for computerization of patients' account billings.

Skills: Uses calculating machine, typewriter, copy machine, and transcriber. Also has ability to relate to patient's anxieties and, where appropriate, refer case to the Social Worker. Knowledge of and experience in accounting essential. Understanding of Medicare, Medical rules valuable.

Specific Job Duties

BOOKKEEPING DUTIES:

1. Maintain proper records to record income from billings and health-care agencies
2. Perform daily posting to accounts-receivable accounts
3. Maintain a control account to verify patient billings
4. Submit billings for patient accounts; provide data for use in computerized billing
5. Compile and analyze list of delinquent accounts
6. Submit assigned claims to Medicare, Medical, and insurance companies

RELATED DUTIES:

1. Refer delinquent accounts to collection agency
2. Compile daily records for medical doctors showing names of patients admitted and discharged that day
3. Explain the nature of the charges to patients who have complaints
4. Assist patients in completing their claim forms to health agencies
5. Refer special cases who may benefit from help from Social Worker regarding social problems

The description serves management as the basis for job placement and for training, appraising, and transferring employees.

JOB SPECIFICATION

A **job specification** describes the **qualifications of the person** and is used for hiring requirements, whereas the job description describes the job the person is to do. Here is a job specification for an elevator operator's job:

1. *Physical Requirements:*
   Good health.
2. *Education—Knowledge—Proficiencies:*
   Must have minimum of eighth-grade education.
3. *Work Experience:*
   No previous work experience necessary; however, a history of work performed in any capacity would be desirable.
4. *Aptitudes:*
   Should have the ability to learn and retain instructions.
5. *Personal Characteristics:*
   Should be emotionally stable and have the ability to adapt self to varying conditions and work harmoniously with others.

JOB EVALUATION

A **job evaluation** compares a particular job with others to make sure that it is being fairly priced. Job evaluation can be done in different ways. But the most popular way is to break a job down into identifiable parts and then assign points or weights to each part. Then each job in the company is evaluated in terms of those components. Factors that are often assigned points are skill, responsibility, effort, and working environment.

STAFFING

When it is clear what jobs have to be filled and what those jobs entail, the personnel manager can begin to fill them. Staffing consists of two parts: recruiting and selecting people.

RECRUITMENT

RECRUITING is *the process of forming a pool of qualified applicants.* If the recruiting process provides only as many applicants as there are jobs, there is no selection. The company must either take what is available or leave the jobs unfilled.

There are several sources for recruiting new employees:

Friends of employees	Vocational schools
Former employees	Employment agencies
Former applicants	Labor unions
Colleges and universities	

Recruiting can be done through personal contacts, newspapers, magazines, TV, or radio ads. When a sufficiently large pool of applicants exists, selection can take place. Studies have shown that newspaper ads are most effective on Sundays, evidently because more potential applicants read them on that day.

Applicants for a job at a car frame company busily filling out application forms, 1983. (Photo, United Press International.)

SELECTION AND PLACEMENT

We have seen that job analysis is the first step in the wise selection of workers. By making use of information from the analysis, the personnel department can carry out the important task of selecting new workers and placing them in the jobs for which they are best qualified. So the next step might be called **applicant analysis.** Employees must be selected without regard to race, sex, religion, or age; business must comply with equal-employment-opportunity laws.

Application forms.   Almost every business uses some type of application form to obtain information for the applicant's personal file (see Figure 7-5). Such information as name, education, age, address, and telephone number is always included.

The would-be employee's history of work experience is probably the most important information provided by the application form. This record indicates more than the type and extent of the applicant's experience. It also shows whether the applicant sticks with a job or changes jobs frequently.

Application forms and interviews could be used to discriminate against protected classes of people. Therefore, all questions must be job-related. People who have been discriminated against include those in the 40-to-70 age bracket, and members of minority groups.

Name | HAVE YOU EVER USED OR BEEN KNOWN BY ANOTHER NAME(S)? | IF YES, BY WHAT?

Present Address: Street City County State Zip

Permanent Address: Street City County State Zip

PERSONAL

Date of Birth Mo Day Yr | THE AGE DISCRIMINATION IN EMPLOYMENT ACT OF 1967, PROHIBITS DISCRIMINATION ON THE BASIS OF AGE WITH RESPECT TO INDIVIDUALS WHO ARE AT LEAST FORTY (40) BUT LESS THAN SEVENTY (70) YEARS OF AGE

Telephone (Include Area Code) | Position Applied for | Date Available | Salary Required

Are you currently scheduled for an interview and/or being considered for any position here other than the position covered by this application? | Write Yes or No

Would you work any shift? | Write Yes or No | If no indicate which shift you prefer __1st (Day) __2nd (Evening) __3rd (Night)

Whom should we notify in case of emergency? Name | Address | Telephone No.

PHYSICAL

AN APPLICANT WILL NOT BE DENIED EMPLOYMENT DUE TO A PHYSICAL OR MENTAL HANDICAP WHERE REASONABLE ACCOMMODATION CAN BE MADE FOR SUCH HANDICAP

Do you have a record of a mental or physical handicap? | Write Yes or No | If Yes, explain

MILITARY

Branch | Date Entered Mo Yr | Date Separated Mo Yr | Type of Discharge | Final Rank

Primary Duties | Reason for Separation (Give Details)

EDUCATION

SCHOOL	NAME OF SCHOOL	LOCATION CITY & STATE	LAST DATE ATTENDED	GRADE POINT AVERAGE	DEGREE/ MAJOR
High School					
College or University					
Other					
Other					

EMPLOYMENT

ACCOUNT FOR ALL FULL-TIME OR PART-TIME EMPLOYMENT AND PERIODS OF UNEMPLOYMENT FOR PAST 5 YEARS EVEN IF RESUME IS INCLUDED. IF NECESSARY, ATTACH ADDITIONAL SHEET.

EMPLOYER | YOUR POSITION AND DUTIES | START END Month Year

Street City & State Zip | __Full-time __ Part-time

Supervisor | Reason for Leaving

FIGURE 7-5
Job Application Form

People are living longer in our society, and the average age of the workforce is increasing. Table 7-1 lists the life-expectancy figures for men and women who are 50 years of age and older.

As people's life expectancy increases, they will choose to work longer. Therefore, companies have had to change their former ways of viewing this valuable group of employees. Nearly 25 million Americans are over 65, and that number will increase in the future.

TABLE 7-1
Life Expectancy for Men and Women

PRESENT AGE	MEN	WOMEN
50	24.5 years	30.4 years
55	20.6	26.2
60	17.0	22.1
65	13.9	18.3
70	11.1	14.7
75	8.7	11.6
80	6.9	9.0
85	5.5	6.9

Life expectancy is the average number of years of life remaining for persons of a given age. Women at age 50 live almost six years longer than men, but at age 85 they are expecteo to live slightly more than one year longer.

For many years, race and sex discrimination cases overshadowed age discrimination. However, the Standard Oil Corporation recently agreed to a $2 million settlement for 160 older workers who were laid off just because they were older. The potential for more age discrimination cases in the courts has increased with the passage in 1978 of the Age Discrimination Act.

THE EMPLOYMENT INTERVIEW

Very often the next step in the selection process is to interview the applicant. **The chief purpose of the interview is to gather additional information about the applicant to validate answers to any or all questions on the application form.** The interviewer attempts to discover how the applicant might fit into the organization and what his or her attitude would be toward the job. The interviewer also explores the applicant's attitude toward work in former jobs and ability to express himself or herself clearly. In order to match the right person with the right job, the interviewer tries to pick the kind of job that would suit the personality and competence of each applicant.

The interview is intended to achieve yet another important function — it supplies the applicant with information about the firm, such as its policy on salaries and promotions, working conditions, and skills required.

A selection interview with a job applicant. (Photo by Bob David. © 1978. All rights reserved.)

The usual practice is to conduct a preliminary interview and later a follow-up interview. The purpose of the preliminary interview is to size up the applicants in a general way and to eliminate those who obviously would not fit into the company. The follow-up interview may take place just before the worker is finally accepted or rejected. For this interview, specific items may be covered to ensure that critical questions are not overlooked.

Here are ten questions that help interviewers organize their thinking and reinforce their decisions when hiring new workers:

1. What is the applicant's real reason for changing jobs?
2. Does the previous work record show stability?
3. Is the level of ambition compatible with the job requirements?
4. What has the applicant accomplished on his or her own?
5. Is the applicant's attitude toward former employers positive?
6. Is the applicant's experience favorable?
7. Does the applicant leave a positive or a negative impression?
8. Are there any outward signs of physical limitations—excessive weight, nervousness, chain smoking?
9. How much does the applicant know about his or her own abilities?
10. Are interview impressions consistent with the applicant's work-history record?

TESTS IN SELECTION Selection tests can be of two types, aptitude and ability. An APTITUDE TEST *checks on the potential a person has for a certain kind of work.* Aptitude tests and other indirect tests, such as IQ or personality tests, must be **validated.** That is, the firm must be able to demonstrate that a high score on such a test is related to good performance on the job. Invalid selection tests not

FIGURE 7-6
Selection and Employment Procedure

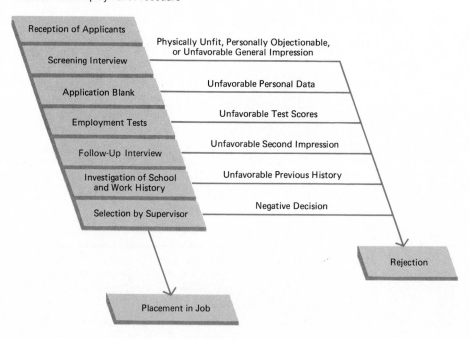

- Reception of Applicants
- Screening Interview — Physically Unfit, Personally Objectionable, or Unfavorable General Impression
- Application Blank — Unfavorable Personal Data
- Employment Tests — Unfavorable Test Scores
- Follow-Up Interview — Unfavorable Second Impression
- Investigation of School and Work History — Unfavorable Previous History
- Selection by Supervisor — Negative Decision

Placement in Job

Rejection

only are useless but may discriminate against certain minority groups, and therefore they are illegal. An ABILITY TEST *determines what one can do— not what one's potential might be.* A good example of an ability test is a typing test. These tests must be related to job skills. Establishing validity for ability tests is easier than for aptitude tests.

The physical examination. The company must know whether a potential employee is physically able to perform the work called for in the job assignment. The job might require constant standing, manipulative skills, or keen eyesight.

The physical examination is used primarily to discover any problems that might prevent satisfactory performance on the job. This would include not only the job for which a person is applying but also those to which he or she might be promoted or transferred.

The steps in the employment procedure are illustrated in Figure 7-6.

TRAINING AND DEVELOPMENT

Most managers strongly support employee development. The lower the job level, the greater the available labor supply. Positions that demand special skills often go unfilled for lack of available applicants.

Orientation sessions are one way to familiarize new employees with company policies and procedures. As a part of the orientation, a person is trained to perform the basic operations essential to the job. The most common types of training are on-the-job training, conference or discussion, and job rotation.

SUPERVISORY TRAINING

Supervisors must have special preparation for their work too. **Supervisory training is basically leadership training** in orientation, administration, human behavior, technical knowledge, and instruction. Employees who rank high in desirable personal qualities, who get along well with others, and who exert leadership in group situations are those most often promoted to supervisory positions. Supervisory personnel may be given released time to attend classes, or such classes may be held after the regular workday. In some instances, companies pay tuition and book costs at local colleges or universities.

EXECUTIVE DEVELOPMENT

As supervisors gain experience, learn the business, and earn promotions, they find themselves a part of company management. Their preparation may include a period of apprenticeship in one or more junior-management positions. This is usually supplemented by formal courses. Universities offer seminars and workshops for people who are newly appointed to top executive positions.

ASSESSING TRAINING NEEDS

It is often accepted as true that if some training and education is good, more training and education is better. However, this is most true when training efforts have been tailored to each person's needs. This is done through a careful assessment of an employee's needs and potential. One good way to assess training needs is to compare performance on the job with the stan-

JOAN MANLEY

Joan Manley became the publisher of Time-Life Books not by accident, but by design. She graduated from the University of California in 1954 with a degree in English. Even then she knew that her career goal was focused on book publishing.

Mrs. Manley had the foresight to develop her secretarial skills as an entry into the job market. Although her first job title was that of secretary for Doubleday, she worked in book sales. Her outstanding work in that area soon caught the attention of her superiors. In 1960, one of them, Jerome Hardy, started a new program — Time-Life Books, for Time Inc. — and he offered her a position as his assistant. By 1970, her talents for increasing sales earned her the title of publisher. In 1971, she became the first woman to serve as a vice-president of Time Inc. Mrs. Manley is now group vice-president and director for books and is also responsible for overseeing the Book-of-the-Month Club, Little, Brown and Company, and the New York Graphic Society, which are owned by Time Inc. She also chairs the board of Time-Life Books.

Joan Manley knows that it takes more than just hard work to succeed in management. She says that "a chief executive's problem is always in the future, not in the present." This requires planning for the future, but adjusting and correcting those plans as new developments dictate. This also points up the importance of choosing key personnel correctly. In training her associates, she believes in "maximizing their individual assets — give them maximum freedom but with direction." Mrs. Manley was eager to "serve time" in the various positions she has occupied. She believes in preparing oneself well before accepting new responsibilities.

dards outlined in the job description. The manager can then pinpoint areas for improvement and can develop programs to help people improve their performance.

APPRAISAL

One of the most important personnel activities consists of evaluating employees' performance. If employees do not know how their performance compares with what is expected of them, how can they improve? Yet this is also one of the most neglected personnel activities. It is common to hear managers say, "They know how they are doing, why should I have to tell them?" Many studies, however, have shown that employees *do not know* how they are doing unless they are told regularly.

Managers resist giving performance appraisals because they can be unpleasant. It is no fun to tell employees they are doing poorly. But it "comes with the territory" and is an important part of managers' work. The personnel department usually helps devise the appraisal system that will be used in the firm. The employee's immediate supervisor is usually responsible for making the appraisal.

RATING DIFFICULTIES

There is considerable evidence that ratings made by peers differ greatly from those made by superiors. Similarly, there are differences between self-ratings and those made by superiors. Self-ratings seem to overrate the ability to get along well with others. Ratings by superiors give more weight to such qualities as initiative, loyalty, and knowledge of one's work.

172

Performance appraisal is often poorly done. This is because many managers are not trained in doing it properly. And often, those that *are* trained put it off because a negative performance appraisal is an unpleasant task. Performance appraisal is *important*. How can employees be expected to improve their performance if they don't know where they need to improve? Employees must be told how they are doing, especially in service jobs that typically have less obvious production standards. The growth in information-service jobs is shown in Figure 7-7.

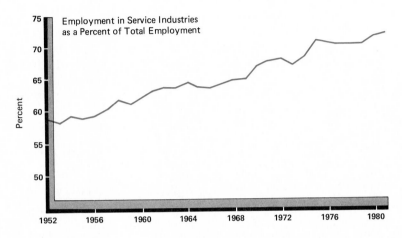

FIGURE 7-7
The Growth in Information-Service Jobs

PROMOTION   The term PROMOTION refers to *the shifting of an employee to a new position in which both the status and responsibilities are increased.* Promotions are good for the firm as well as the employee. Management knows that when deserving employees are placed where they can produce the most, both productivity and morale increase. An employee should not be given a promotion when it has not been earned or when others are better qualified or more deserving. When two employees are equal in ability and performance, the promotion usually goes to the person who has been with the company longer. This person is said to have **seniority.** An advancement in pay that does not involve a move into a new job classification is called a *horizontal promotion.* An advancement that moves an employee into a job with a higher rank or classification is called a *vertical promotion.*

If management is to avoid labor unrest and turnover, it must develop a systematic policy for promotions. Qualified employees become dissatisfied and leave if few opportunities for advancement exist or if promotions are not based on merit.

TRANSFER   The term TRANSFER refers to *the shifting of an employee from one position to another without increasing his or her duties, responsibilities, or pay.* Every business finds it necessary to transfer workers. If workers have been assigned to a job on which their work is unsatisfactory, they may be shifted to another. There are times, too, when the workload is heavier in some departments than in others, or when it is desirable to rotate workers into and out of dangerous positions.

Employee rewards are of two types—financial and nonfinancial. Salary payments are financial rewards and include insurance coverage, profit sharing, and pensions. Nonfinancial rewards include good working conditions, recognition for achievement, and other types of job benefits. In this section we focus on types of monetary payments. If workers are underpaid, they become dissatisfied. If they are overpaid, a company's products may be overpriced in a competitive market.

EQUITY

An important issue in a pay or compensation system is equity. EQUITY refers to *the extent to which employees think a pay system is fair.* If a pay system is viewed as unfair (a lazy or poor worker getting the same raises as better workers, for example), it usually results in a reduction of effort on the job.

SALARY AND WAGES

Most workers in the United States today are paid either a salary, hourly wages, or piece wages. A **salary** is usually expressed in annual terms and does not depend on the number of hours worked. **Hourly wages** are based on the number of hours spent working. **Piece wages** are based on the number of units produced.

Most management and many other white-collar jobs are salaried jobs. Salaried work rather than hourly wages is something of a status symbol. However, salaried people may be required to work overtime without additional pay.

For some types of work, it is more practical to base pay on the nature of an employee's responsibilities rather than on his or her productivity. In fact, it is often impossible to measure an employee's output objectively. When quality rather than quantity is important, or where the employee is continually interrupted, hourly wages are appropriate. Hourly wages have one disadvantage—they may encourage employees to do less than a "full day's work."

Under the piece-rate payment plan, a certain sum is paid for each unit a worker produces. The unit payment may be based on the output of an individual worker, or it may apply to the work of a group or even an entire department.

LEGISLATION AFFECTING COMPENSATION

Several major laws can affect the compensation systems a business firm may choose. They are:

The Fair Labor Standards Act
The Equal Pay Act
The Walsh-Healey Act
The Davis-Bacon Act
State laws

The Fair Labor Standards Act set a **minimum wage** to be paid to a broad spectrum of employees. Executive, professional, and administrative employees are **exempt** from the act. Government employees are also exempt. The FLSA also contains overtime-pay requirements. Generally, pay at 1½ times the hourly rate is required for time worked over forty hours in any one week.

The *Equal Pay Act* is an attempt to prohibit wage discrimination based on sex. According to the act, "men and women performing equal work in the same establishment under similar conditions must receive the same pay if their jobs require equal skill, equal effort, and equal responsibility." Corning Glass recently had to pay $1 million in back wages to women under the Equal Pay Act, and AT&T paid over $30 million for violation of this act.

The issue of "comparable worth" is currently in the news. This theory holds that jobs that are in some sense comparable in their value to the employer should be equally paid. The theory is being advanced to secure more pay for women in jobs that are "comparable" but not necessarily identical to higher-paid "men's" jobs.

> Since the early 1980s, nurses and city workers in San Jose, California, secretaries in Minnesota, and clerks in Pennsylvania have struck over "equal pay." A dozen states and several cities have done job evaluations under the pressure of "comparable worth." Unions have shown a good deal of interest in the issue, motivated by a desire to sign up more women members. Only about 16 percent of the nation's female workforce belongs to labor organizations.

The *Walsh-Healey Act* requires federal supply contractors to pay a minimum wage. Its formula for calculating overtime differs slightly from that of the FLSA.

The *Davis-Bacon Act* affects federal construction projects. It requires firms engaged in federal construction to pay the **prevailing wage rate** in the local community. That rate is frequently defined as the average union rate for the local area where the construction is taking place.

State laws tend to cover workers who are not covered by federal laws, especially those in intrastate commerce. A recent survey showed that thirty-nine states and the District of Columbia have their own minimum-wage laws.

INCENTIVE PLANS **Some firms have set up wage-payment plans designed to reward the worker with added compensation for exceptional performance.** Known as wage-incentive plans, they are based on the piece-rate method of making wage payments.

Incentive plans are especially appropriate (1) when labor costs are heavy in a cost-competitive market, and (2) when production technology is not well advanced.

In 1895, Frederick W. Taylor developed the first wage-incentive plan, now known as the *Taylor Differential Piece-Rate Plan*. Here is how it works. First, a careful scientific study is made of each worker's operations. Then a standard rate of output is established that is within the reach of the average worker. Two rates prevail—one for the worker who fails to reach the standard, and a higher rate for the worker who exceeds it. For example, if the standard output is 100 units per day, a worker who produces fewer than 100 units might receive $0.60 per unit. A worker who exceeds 100 units might receive $0.63 per unit. The worker who produced 98 units would receive $58.80 for a day's work, whereas the worker who produced 105 units would earn $66.15.

A Detroit Assembly Line. (Photo by Chuck Ternes/General Motor Assembly Division.)

A good wage-incentive plan will include the following objectives:

For management:
1. Lowered costs resulting from increased productivity
2. Improved cost control, leading to production that is more consistent, more uniform, and less variable in actual cost
3. Improved utilization of facilities
4. Improved worker morale, as earnings become proportionate to individual effort

For employees:
1. An opportunity to earn money in excess of the base rate and in proportion to individual effort
2. An opportunity for individual recognition
3. An opportunity for a healthful competitive spirit among employees
4. An opportunity for employees to control (at least partially) the level of their standard of living by their own initiative

Employee profit sharing.   PROFIT SHARING refers to *wage-payment plans that provide pay beyond basic pay schedules.* These extra payments go to all employees, and the amounts are tied directly to the profits earned.

The basic philosophy of profit sharing is to create a "partner relationship" among employees. It draws labor and management closer together and develops a working relationship and atmosphere favorable to efficient workmanship. Those who advocate profit sharing claim that it creates high employee morale, reduces the number and extent of employees' grievances, reduces labor turnover, provides greater security for workers, and improves public relations.

176

There is, of course, a wide variety of practices in profit-sharing programs. Some plans provide for cash payments. Others provide for deferred payments, which may be tied to the issuance of stock. Some of the factors entering into the structure of a profit-sharing plan are these:

1. Whether the percentage to be paid is a fixed or a sliding rate
2. Whether the percentage is to be applied to profits before or after taxes
3. The amount of the profits to be shared

Eastman Kodak's profit-sharing plan is determined by the amount of the cash dividend paid on the common stock. Employee bonuses are paid on the basis of individual yearly earnings.

One of the best-known profit-sharing plans is that of the Lincoln Electric Company of Cleveland, Ohio, which the company inaugurated in 1934. Under this system, "each job is evaluated to establish its importance to the company's operations, and a pay rate is established for it. . . . The workers are rated twice a year and they are graded on the quality and quantity of their work, their skill, and their attitudes." These ratings determine the amount of bonus each worker is to receive in relation to his or her base salary. According to the company president, productivity has increased on the average about 15 percent each year, as compared to the national average of slightly over 3 percent. Employees leave the company at a rate of 6 percent per year, as compared to a rate for other manufacturing plants of 36 percent. Last year, the average worker earned $44,000. The employees work hard and do not enjoy many of the fringe benefits others do. But Lincoln's success has run GE out of the welding business and has giant Westinghouse confined to a small market share.

Production-sharing plans.   PRODUCTION SHARING is similar to profit sharing, for such programs use the cooperative efforts of management and labor. *Rather than shared profits, they represent a sharing of savings that result from reducing production costs.* One of the best-known production-sharing plans is the *Scanlon Plan*. This plan emphasizes the sharing of production savings with *all workers*. It was developed in 1937 by Joseph Scanlon to reduce costs in a steel mill where Scanlon was a union representative. The plan has two basic features:

1. The use of departmental committees to determine the amount of cost savings
2. A direct payment to the workers as a reward for increased efficiency

The basic philosophy of the Scanlon Plan is that more efficient plant operation rests on cooperation from the entire team of company employees.

Actually, production sharing is more than a way of giving monetary compensation to workers. It represents labor–management cooperation. In some cases, such as under the Scanlon Plan, the awards for suggestions that improve production efficiency are paid to the group rather than to the individual who submits the suggestions. The emphasis is on teamwork for the benefit of all. With teamwork, production increases of as much as 50 percent have been achieved.

Mitchell Fein, an industrial engineer, in the 1970s developed an approach called *Improshare*. Under Improshare the workers receive bonuses based directly on increased output. The U.S. General Accounting Office study of this subject, reported in March 1981, "The results of productivity sharing plans suggest that these plans offer a viable method of enhancing productivity at the firm level.''

A 1982 survey of U.S. manufacturing companies with 500 or more employees found that 15 percent of them have some kind of gain-sharing plan.

FRINGE BENEFITS The practice of awarding fringe benefits to employees has grown tremendously during the past two decades. New types of benefits are added each year, and collective-bargaining contracts with unions deal as much with benefits as with direct wage payments.

The earliest benefits to be provided were payments for holidays and vacation periods. Then came hospitalization, legal aid, life insurance, income-tax counseling, subsidized lunches, education payments, sick leave, supplemental unemployment payments, and retirement plans.

Benefits equal more than one-third of payroll dollars, and they are increasing faster than wages. From 1971 to 1981, benefits rose 161 percent. During this same period, wages increased 115 percent (inflation as measured by the Consumer Price Index). A breakdown showing the components of the weekly benefits package is shown in Table 7-2.

Cafeteria-type benefits offer employees the opportunity to choose their individual fringe benefits. The company usually provides a minimum "core" of life and health insurance, vacations, and pensions. The employee buys additional benefits to fit his or her needs with credits earned.

CURRENT ISSUE

SHOULD FRINGE BENEFITS BE CURTAILED?

The recent history of employee benefits in business has been *more! more!* and *more!* Has the time come to move in the other direction?

With which of the following statements do you agree, and with which do you disagree?

1. Business should reduce the amount of the employee benefits package and pay more in cash.
2. Fringe benefits add too much to the cost of production and are helping to make American industry noncompetitive.
3. Business should reduce the cost of employee benefits but add any saving to workers' wages.
4. Most employee benefits are not taxable to the employee, so an even larger percentage of workers' wages should be paid in the form of "benefits."
5. Employee benefits are really a part of labor costs. Thus, they should be taxed just as wages are taxed.
6. Employee benefits should be given on a sliding scale, with the lowest-paid workers receiving the most benefits.

If you were in charge of administering the benefits package for a company, would you favor reducing their cost in relation to wages, or increasing it?

TABLE 7-2
Weekly Employee Benefits, per Employee

	1971	1981	PERCENT CHANGE
Old-age, survivors, disability and health insurance (FICA taxes)	$7.15	$21.60	+202%
Insurance (life, hospital, surgical, medical, etc.)	7.10	20.63	+191
Pensions (nongovernment)	7.73	17.88	+131
Paid vacations	7.69	16.96	+121
Paid holidays	4.69	11.48	+145
Paid rest periods, coffee breaks, lunch periods, etc.	5.38	11.46	+113
Workers' compensation	1.58	4.94	+213
Paid sick leave	1.56	4.60	+195
Unemployment compensation taxes	1.15	4.25	+270
Profit-sharing payments	1.65	3.69	+124
Dental insurance	N.A.	1.29	N.A.
Short-term disability	N.A.	1.23	N.A.
Thrift plans	0.31	1.23	+297
Christmas or other special bonuses, suggestion awards, etc.	0.67	1.17	+75
Salary continuation or long-term disability	N.A.	0.79	N.A.
Employee education expenditures	0.15	0.77	+413
Employee meals furnished free	0.25	0.58	+132
Discounts on goods and services purchased from company by employees	0.23	0.48	+109
Other employee benefits	1.63	2.41	+48
Total employee benefits	$48.92	$127.44	+161
Average weekly earnings	$158.85	$342.04	+115

N.A. Data not available.
SOURCE: U.S. Chamber of Commerce.

Conoco, in Greenwich, Connecticut, has been testing a cafeteria benefits plan among its 731 salaried employees. Ultimately this plan will be offered to all 48,000 employees. The core coverage includes 80 percent of covered medical expenses, $20,000 to $50,000 of life insurance (based on salary), accident insurance, one to five weeks' vacation, and disability benefits.

Employees can then "spend" credits based on their annual salary for more fringes. Most employees choose additional medical coverage, higher life insurance coverage, and hearing, vision, and general health insurance options. Other options could be prepaid legal insurance, group auto insurance, homeowners' insurance, or day care for children. Employees who do not want these options do not have to buy them.

Cafeteria plans have not yet been widely adopted, because they are expensive and complicated to administer. One study found that while 70 percent of the executives surveyed liked the idea, only 18 percent considered them desirable for their own situations. In many industries during the early 1980s, fringe benefits were reduced. The auto and steel industries are notable examples. Allis-Chalmers in Milwaukee cut vacation time by 20 percent and reduced holidays from twelve to ten. Corning Glass, Republic Airlines, John Deere, and many others cut benefits as a result of tight profit pictures.

MANAGEMENT COMPENSATION

Wage-incentive plans for managers are very popular. Research shows that for managers, pay is a strong incentive for exceptional service when it is directly related to effective performance. A study of 500 managers at all levels, covering a wide variety of organizations, showed that the majority are concerned with how their salary is divided between cash and fringe benefits. These fringe benefits are usually not taxed. So the more the manager gets in benefits rather than wages, the less tax he or she pays.

The STOCK-OPTION PLAN is popular today as a device for rewarding top management. Under this plan, *management personnel are permitted to buy company stock at some future time at the market price of the stock on the date the option was granted.* This plan is viewed as a means by which a company can induce valuable officers to remain with the company.

But a single type of benefit does not always suit all those in top-management positions in the company. To meet the needs of a group of managers, the so-called cafeteria wage-payment plan is sometimes used. Under this system, several different types of benefits are made available, and each manager is allowed to select the type that would be of the most value to him or her.

EMPLOYEE MAINTENANCE

Employee maintenance refers to several different activities required to maintain personnel at a high level of efficiency. We discuss here health, safety, morale, absenteeism, and turnover.

HEALTH

An employee who does not feel well is often unproductive. Some companies maintain extensive health services on the premises. It often makes economic sense for management to be interested in employees' physical well-being.

A complete health program provides for first aid, dental services, optical needs, mass X rays and inoculations, periodic physical examinations, and even psychological and psychiatric counseling. Attention is also given to sanitation and lighting, adequate heat and ventilation, safety, and industrial hygiene. Illness is responsible for the loss of 2 percent of a worker's productive time and 8 percent of all separations from the labor force. Thus, the argument for an adequate health program appears to be a sound one.

Currently, the biggest health problems facing workers are reported to be alcoholism and drug abuse. It has been estimated that these problems cost American industry over $10 billion a year. Many companies provide counseling services for employees who have such problems. General Motor's program is something of a model. In nine years, it treated 52,000 employees and has given the company a $2 to $3 return on each $1 invested in the program. GM found that 96 percent of its absenteeism is caused by 13 percent of its workforce. This 13 percent have alcohol, drug, or emotional problems. So far, about 70 percent of those entering treatment stay on the road to recovery. Drugs cause accidents, damage to machines, loss of imagination, and a casual attitude toward getting work done. Theft is also a problem — a hospital discovered, for example, $200,000 worth of linens missing. An undercover agent found that six employees were stealing linens and selling them for drugs.

SAFETY   A poor safety record in any organization is extremely costly. Accidents may result in physical injury to employees or in damage to machines and supplies, to the physical plant, and to raw materials and finished products. Injuries sometimes cause lost time by other employees as well as by the injured worker.

It has been said that the true costs of an accident are like an iceberg. Most of them are hidden below the surface and are discovered and measured only through extensive study. Examples of such hidden costs are time spent by management in compiling information and reporting the accident, and loss of productive efficiency. Other examples are work that spoils because of lost production time, and costs of training new workers. Approximately 2 million work injuries occur every year, of which one in twenty results in permanent total disability, and one in twenty-three in permanent partial disability. The annual cost of industrial accidents is in excess of $5 billion annually.

Research has been done to determine the causes of industrial accidents. The purpose has been to work out preventive procedures. The factors found to contribute to industrial accidents include:

1. The personal characteristics and attitudes of workers
2. The impersonal factors—technical deficiencies in the work environment

Personal deficiencies include lack of worker knowledge, improper attitudes, physical defects, indifference to danger, and so forth. Technical deficiencies include inadequate lighting and ventilation, poor design of equipment, improper materials-handling techniques, ineffective safeguards on machinery,

Airline machinists testing an evacuation slide with the help of flight attendants. (Photo, AFL-CIO News.)

and others. However, it is significant to personnel management that four out of every five accidents are caused by personal rather than technical deficiencies.

The techniques used by modern firms in safety education and enforcement include records of injuries, posters, the plant magazine, individual and group conferences, films, training in the use of fire equipment, and manuals that contain safety rules and penalties for infractions.

The federal government's Occupational Safety and Health Administration (OSHA) became effective in 1971. This agency has three major purposes:

1. To develop health and safety standards for workers
2. To inspect businesses to see that they comply with the standards
3. To set up record-keeping systems for recording occupational injuries, accidents, and fatalities

Employee Rights. **One of the great trends in this country is from representative to participatory democracy.** One area where this is occurring rapidly is in that of workers' rights. Worker participation in management through quality circles has been widely publicized. But due process in dismissal actions, access to personnel files, equal pay for comparable work, the right to self-expression, and privacy, have gained recognition in many companies.

We have become a rights-conscious society. In the past decade employee rights have been recognized as never before. This is an important area illustrating the trend toward participatory democracy.

MORALE   Morale can affect efficiency of operation, and it is of great importance to management, especially to those involved in the personnel function. Research shows that absenteeism and turnover are more sharply influenced by the morale of the workforce than by any other environmental factor.

MORALE is *the feeling that individuals or groups have toward their jobs, their associates, and the company.* It is affected by those factors that make up the working environment, including the extent to which one's needs are satisfied in a particular job and as a member of the company's team.

If employees feel that they are being treated fairly, that their salaries are adequate, and that working conditions are good, they are apt to have high morale. **Employee attitude** is similar to morale. Some employee attitudes that indicate high morale are these:

1. Low employee turnover rate
2. Few grievances or strike threats
3. High level of compliance with rules and policies
4. Appreciation of working conditions and facilities
5. High production level, with few deliberate work stoppages
6. Evidences of cooperation from employees (union)

Attitudes or performance contrary to these would, of course, indicate low employee morale.

Morale is the result of a combination of many complex attitudes: workers' personal feelings and biases, their values, economic and cultural environment, degree of security, physical health, emotional stability, realization of job expectations, and the flow of communication between management and the workers.

ABSENTEEISM   ABSENTEEISM is *the failure (whether voluntary or involuntary) of a worker to be present at work as scheduled.* According to this widely accepted definition, **tardiness** is also a form of absenteeism. Studies show that there is a close relationship between absenteeism and morale. Excessive absenteeism is an indication of low morale.

Management sometimes uses the rate of absenteeism as an indication of the level of morale. If an employee who is eligible to work twenty-five days during a month fails to work on three of these days, the absentee rate would be 3/25, or 12 percent. By using this same method, the rate of absenteeism for a department or an entire firm could be computed. Rates are sometimes computed for various groups of employees according to age, sex, level of job, and so on. Such analyses make it much easier to determine the causes of absenteeism.

Recent studies of absenteeism seem to show that:

1. Absences are most common on Mondays and on days before and after a holiday.
2. Women have fewer absences than men.
3. Older workers have fewer absences than young workers.
4. Supervisors have fewer absences than hourly paid workers.
5. Paid-sick-leave policies do not increase absences when there is a one- or two-day waiting period before the sick pay begins.

TURNOVER   **High turnover, like absenteeism, is an indicator of low job satisfaction or morale. People leave when the job is not satisfying to them.** A certain amount of turnover is acceptable and even good, as it allows for new employees and new ideas. But excessive turnover results in untrained persons' holding important jobs, and high selection and training costs. It also distracts managers from other important duties.

SUMMARY OF KEY CONCEPTS

Human-resources management is usually a staff function. The personnel manager *advises* rather than directs the heads of other departments.

Critical personnel activities include

Work analysis and design	Appraisal
Staffing	Compensation
Training and development	Maintenance

The personnel function of a business attempts to select the right employees, place them in appropriate positions, and keep them as satisfied company members.

Before workers are hired, jobs must be analyzed and job specifications and descriptions must be prepared.

Employee training and development is important, for it provides a company with more valuable workers.

A fair and feasible salary compensation plan rates a high priority in human-resource management. This includes an adequate package of fringe benefits.

Wage-incentive plans are less popular today with workers than formerly. But pay incentives are very important to managers.

Employee maintenance helps reduce absenteeism and turnover. Employee morale is a maintenance concern in personnel management.

Considerable attention is given to an appropriate working environment. This includes the health and safety of workers.

The federal government has enacted several laws for the protection of workers. The Occupational Safety and Health Administration (OSHA) is quite active in enforcing their provisions.

Employee morale is essential to efficient production. When workers feel that they are being treated fairly and their working conditions are good, morale is high.

Low absenteeism and low turnover are usually indications that worker morale is good.

BUSINESS TERMS

You should be able to match these business terms with the statements that follow:

a. ABILITY TEST	h. MORALE
b. ABSENTEEISM	i. PRODUCTION SHARING
c. APTITUDE TEST	j. PROFIT SHARING
d. JOB	k. PROMOTION
e. JOB ANALYSIS	l. RECRUITING
f. JOB DESCRIPTION	m. STOCK OPTION
g. JOB SPECIFICATION	n. TRANSFER

1. An organizational unit of work
2. Determining pertinent information about the nature of a specific job
3. A written statement of what an employee is to do on a particular job
4. The process of generating a pool of qualified applicants
5. A test that checks on the potential a person has for a certain kind of work
6. Moving an employee to a new position with increased status and responsibility
7. The shifting of a worker to a new position without increasing his or her duties or responsibility
8. Wage-payment plans that provide compensation beyond basic pay schedules
9. Extra compensation based on savings that result from reduced production costs
10. The right of managers to buy company stock in the future at today's market price
11. The feeling that individuals or groups have toward their jobs, their colleagues, and the company
12. The failure of an employee to report for work

REVIEW QUESTIONS

1. What critical personnel activities are of concern to management?
2. How do *job analysis*, *job description*, and *job specification* differ?
3. What are the various aspects of personnel recruitment?
4. What is meant by *equity* in a compensation system?
5. What specific things are indicative of high morale among workers?

DISCUSSION QUESTIONS

1. How would you summarize the function of the personnel department in one sentence?
2. Which of the steps in the employment procedure do you consider the most important?
3. Compare and contrast *job transfer* and *job promotion*.
4. How do *profit sharing* and *production sharing* differ?
5. What are the most important aspects of employee maintenance?
6. How are *morale*, *absenteeism*, and *job turnover* related?

7-1

VOLUNTARY SEVERANCE PAY

The Instant Camera Corporation found it was facing increasingly sophisticated competition that was carving up its market. The company had to shrink its workforce deeply to reduce costs. As much as 25 percent of the workforce would have to be laid off. As a result of collective bargaining with the union, the company could lay off only workers with less than ten years' experience. That would mean that three out of four jobs might change hands, since more-senior workers could "bump" less-senior workers from their jobs. It looked as though chaos would result!

However, a new idea appeared to offer some promise. Perhaps a voluntary program offering incentives for long-term employees to leave the company would work. At the low end, a $10,000 per year employee with ten years' service would get a $5,000 payment to leave. For a top-level senior hourly worker, the payment could amount to $40,000, and for an executive, as much as $175,000.

1. What do you think of the idea?
2. What are the major problems and unknowns?
3. Will it work? Why, or why not?

7-2

EMPLOYEE RIGHTS AND ATTITUDES

ADCO Corporation manufactures television sets. When it moved from the Boston area to New Hampshire because of the latter's lower taxes and cheaper labor, it left its workers behind.

ADCO's move caused a great deal of bitterness. The company tried to keep its plans secret until a week before it shut down its Salem factory. All the Salem workers were refused jobs at the new plant. Since then, several of the company's former workers have been driving to Portsmouth, New Hampshire, to tell the company's new employees what they think of ADCO.

The company felt the move was an economic necessity in the light of the challenge by foreign firms. ADCO had lost $1.5 million in the previous year. The cost of production in its former Salem location was simply too high.

Workers did not accept the economic argument. They were angry and wanted answers. The move was made anyway, and ADCO management reports that the company is saving $4 million a year in operating costs. The company president knows that the former employees say that ADCO is a terrible employer. The present employees are considering forming a union. These things do not seem to bother management.

1. In moving from the Boston area to New Hampshire, what could the company have done differently to minimize labor problems?
2. What are the possible long-term effects of this situation for ADCO?

J.P. Stevens and Company, the big textile firm, fought a sixteen-year war against the Amalgamated Clothing and Textile Workers' Union. The company used a variety of tactics, some of questionable legality, to keep the union out of its southern textile plants.

In a classic ruling, however, the National Labor Relations Board declared the union the bargaining agent for about 1,000 workers at the company's plants and warehouses in Wallace, North Carolina. But the board went further. It ordered the company to pay the cost of the union's organizing campaign. The board said that its order was based on the company's illegal actions during the campaign, which had "poisoned" the electoral atmosphere. The board also ordered Stevens to reimburse with interest the Labor Relations Board for the costs of investigating, preparing, presenting, and conducting the case.

These extreme measures seem to be a result of frustration with Stevens's apparent philosophy: It is cheaper to pay the fines than to allow the union in. Stevens had lost a representation election once before in court, and it then closed the plant in which the union had won.

One federal appeals court has branded the company "the most notorious recidivist in the field of labor law." The board in the current decision said that "employee rights have been threatened over the years by the efforts of Stevens to destroy the union through persistent violations of the law."

J.P. Stevens will no doubt remain a target for union-organizing attempts in the future.

Labor-Management Relations

study objectives

WHEN YOU HAVE FINISHED READING THIS CHAPTER, YOU SHOULD BE ABLE TO:

1. Explain what employees expect to receive from union membership
2. Report on the historical development of labor unionism in the United States
3. Identify the largest unions and those industries where unionism is strongest
4. Distinguish among the union shop, open shop, and closed shop
5. Explain how collective bargaining between management and labor takes place
6. Describe the different ways that disputes between labor and management are settled

8

It is not the employer who pays wages — he only handles the money. It is the customer who pays wages.

Henry Ford

T he early history of labor–management relations in the United States was primarily one of conflict. Managers resented the idea that an "outsider" could come in and organize their employees. Employees who wanted a union were viewed as being ungrateful and often treated accordingly.

However, the labor policy of the United States is designed to foster and promote free collective bargaining between employers and employees. This collective bargaining generally applies to wages, hours, and conditions of employment. Today, management often has a rather different perspective of labor unions from what it had as recently as a decade ago.

In this chapter, we look at the reasons employees organize, the history of unions, and the legal background for labor relations in the United States. We also consider collective bargaining and how it works, and administration of the labor contract. Finally, this chapter considers methods for resolving labor disputes.

WHY EMPLOYEES JOIN UNIONS

Several factors can prompt people to band together in a union. Perhaps the most important ones in our country are (1) the **added strength** that comes from an effective organization of large numbers working together, and (2) the advantages of having **qualified negotiators** when bargaining with employers.

Regional AFL-CIO Conference.
(Photo, AFL-CIO News.)

Some insight can be gained from reading the following paragraph from the preamble to the constitution of the Cigar Makers' International Union of America, organized in 1864.[1]

> Past experience teaches us that labor has so far been unable to arrest the encroachments of capital, neither has it been able to obtain justice from lawmaking power. This is due to a lack of practical organization and unity of action. "In union there is strength." Organization and united action are the only means by which the laboring classes can gain any advantage for themselves. Good and strong labor organizations are enabled to defend and preserve the interests of the working people.

Much progress has been made since 1864, and this preamble would, of course, be written differently today. It does, however, point out quite clearly one of the advantages of union membership—strength in numbers.

LEGAL RATIONALE FOR UNIONS Why is the right to join a union supported by law in the United States? The Norris-LaGuardia Act puts it this way: " . . . the individual unorganized worker is commonly helpless to exercise actual liberty of contract and to protect his freedom of labor, and thereby obtain acceptable terms and conditions of employment. . . ."

---

[1] *Third Annual Report of the Bureau of Statistics of Labor of the State of New York, for the Year 1885* (Albany, 1886), pp. 544–45.

The National Labor Relations Act says, "The inequality of bargaining power between employees who do not possess full freedom of association . . . and employers who are organized . . . substantially burdens and affects the flow of commerce, and tends to aggravate recurrent business depressions by depressing wage rates. . . ."

THE PSYCHOLOGY OF JOINING A UNION

Several recent strikes have focused on the personal reasons why people choose to join unions. Two groups of factors seem to be of major importance, as shown in Figure 8-1.

The first group of factors can be labeled *job dissatisfaction*. This includes dissatisfaction with job security, type of work, the amount of influence over the job, and supervision. The second group of factors is the belief an employee has about the union's ability to really change anything. If employees feel that the union *can be* instrumental in changing a bad situation, they are likely to vote for the union. Dissatisfied workers will look for a way to solve the problems. Satisfied workers usually will not.

Perhaps to better understand why labor–management relations are the way they are, we should look briefly at the history of American labor–management relations.

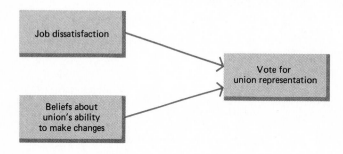

FIGURE 8-1
Factors in Workers' Decisions to Organize

HISTORY OF AMERICAN LABOR UNIONISM

The history of the American labor movement, which dates from the beginning of this country, is colorful and at times marked by violence. Even before the Declaration of Independence, skilled artisans in handicraft industries joined together in benevolent societies. Their primary purpose was to provide members and their families with financial assistance in the event of serious illness, debt, or the death of the wage earner. Although these early associations had little resemblance to present-day labor unions, they did bring workers together to consider problems of mutual concern and their solutions.

EARLY UNIONISM

In the late 1700s, printers in New York City combined to get an increase in wages. Philadelphia printers engaged in the earliest documented strike, for a minimum wage of $6 per week. Philadelphia carpenters struck for a ten-hour day (unsuccessfully), and shoemakers and printers formed unions that lasted for only short periods of time. The shoemakers (cordwainers) were found guilty of criminal conspiracy after a strike.

During the 1820s, despite several economic slumps, the unions continued to grow. Most unions were small locals, since progress in rapid communication had not been great. But the isolated locals soon learned that by pooling their resources and cooperating with one another, they could more effectively deal with employers. At the same time they can give help and support to locals in distress.

In 1852, the typographical union joined locals together as part of a permanent national organization. Molders and printers also organized unions. By the end of the Civil War, at least thirty-two national unions had been formed. Some of them still exist today, such as those of the carpenters, bricklayers, and painters. The purpose of these unions has always been the same: to influence wages, obtain better working conditions, and achieve more satisfactory work rules throughout their trade.

National unions (or international unions, as they are called because many have Canadian members) have certain advantages. Among these are:

1. Full-time staff
2. Specialists
3. More power in some cases

The relative size of the ten largest international unions today is shown in Figure 8-2.

FIGURE 8-2
The Ten Largest Unions.
(Source: U.S. Bureau of Labor Statistics.)

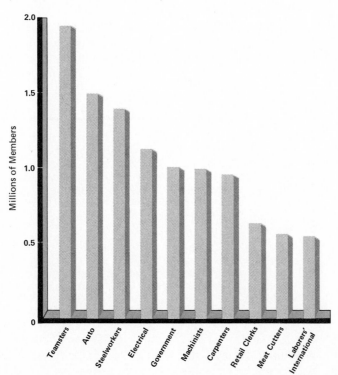

THE KNIGHTS OF LABOR

The first federation of unions to have any success was the Noble Order of the Knights of Labor. It was founded as a local union of garment workers in Philadelphia in 1869. Seventeen years later, this union claimed more than 700,000 members throughout the United States. But internal conflict developed between those who favored the process of collective bargaining and those committed to political action and social change. This weakened the Knights of Labor and led to the formation of the American Federation of Labor.

THE AMERICAN FEDERATION OF LABOR

The Federation of Organized Trades and Labor Unions was established in 1881 through the combination of a number of craft unions. In 1886, another group of unions, which had previously been affiliated with the Knights of Labor, broke away from that group and joined with the unions in the federation. At that time, the organization adopted the name American Federation of Labor (A.F. of L.). It was designed to have little direct power over its sovereign units, but it did have the power to expel a union or a group of unions from membership.

Historically, the A.F. of L. was predominantly craft unions, although a very few industrial unions were affiliated with it. The affiliated unions found that by joining together into one organization, they commanded greater strength in securing favorable congressional legislation.

Under the leadership of its first president, Samuel Gompers, the A.F. of L. grew and prospered. Previously, unions had been chiefly concerned with social objectives. Samuel Gompers led the A.F. of L. to emphasize the economic aspects of unions—what is known as **business unionism,** or "bread-and-butter unionism." This is a concentration on wages, hours, and conditions of employment.

For many years, the A.F. of L. followed a policy of neutrality in political activity. In addition to business unionism and nonparticipation in politics, Gompers strongly advocated the autonomy of each craft. He felt that this principle was inherent in forming a strong foundation for successful union growth and influence.

Having a union president on a company's board of directors is not a new idea in Europe but has been little tried in the United States.

When the Chrysler Corporation reluctantly put UAW President Douglas Fraser on its board, there were many concerns. But the arrangement has worked quite well. The company has nothing but praise for Mr. Fraser's contributions. He not only fought to keep plants open and save jobs, but persuaded Chrysler workers to give up hundreds of millions of dollars in wages and benefits.

Other board members were amazed at how well he fit in. He acted like any other board member and did not give the feeling he was there only as a labor advocate. Lee Iacocca said, "He has stimulated our board to think." Union officials are confident that his presence on the board has not compromised his effectiveness in their behalf. "He didn't give anything away," as one rank-and-file member put it.

THE CONGRESS OF INDUSTRIAL ORGANIZATIONS

The A.F. of L.'s policy of a single union for each craft led to the formation of a new labor organization, the Congress of Industrial Organizations (C.I.O.). As American industry became more mechanized, there were increasing numbers of workers operating machines rather than following a trade or craft.

LANE KIRKLAND

Lane Kirkland became president of the AFL-CIO in November 1979, succeeding the late George Meany. Kirkland was born in Camden, South Carolina, in 1922 and was graduated from Georgetown University in 1948.

Kirkland is a licensed master mariner and sailed as deck officer aboard several merchant ships. He held various posts with the AFL-CIO between 1948 and 1958. He was director of research and education, International Union of Operating Engineers, from 1958 to 1960 and rejoined the AFL in 1960. He served as secretary-treasurer of the AFL-CIO from 1969 to November 19, 1979, when he became president.

Kirkland has served on the National Commission on Productivity, the Presidential Commission on Financial Structure and Regulation, the President's Maritime Advisory Committee, and the Committee on Selection of Federal Judicial Officers, among other important services to government. He has also served on the board of directors of the American Arbitration Association, the Rockefeller Foundation, the Council on Foreign Relations, the Brookings Institution, and the National Planning Association.

Understandably, these workers could not qualify for membership in the "trade" unions. So in 1935, the presidents of eight of the A.F. of L. unions formed what was called the Committee for Industrial Organization.

This new group wanted to organize large industries (such as rubber, steel, and automotive) along the lines of industrial unionism. The feeling became so intense that, in 1936, the unions that had associated themselves with the Committee for Industrial Organization were suspended from membership in the A.F. of L. This move resulted in the group's formation as a rival labor organization, which in 1938 adopted the name "Congress of Industrial Organizations." During the next decade, by advocating the organizing of workers in many fields that had not previously been organized, the C.I.O. grew in power. It soon began to compete seriously with the A.F. of L.

MERGER OF A.F. OF L. AND C.I.O. In the early 1950s, the leaders of these two rivals realized that the cause of organized labor would be greatly strengthened if they could join forces. So in December 1955, the A.F. of L. and the C.I.O. unified the two federations into the AFL-CIO. Now four out of five labor unions are affiliated with the AFL-CIO.

The AFL-CIO is a voluntary federation of 121 national and international labor unions, which are in turn made up of 60,000 local unions. **The AFL-CIO itself does no bargaining; it is not a union, but a federation of unions. The bargaining is done by representatives of individual unions or a collaboration of several unions.** The AFL-CIO serves its constituent unions by:

1. Speaking for the whole labor movement before Congress and other branches of government
2. Representing American labor in world affairs through its participation in the International Labor Organization — a United Nations specialized agency — and through direct contact with the central labor organizations of free nations throughout the world

3. Helping to organize workers
4. Coordinating such activities as community services, political action, and voter registration

Each member union affiliated with the AFL-CIO remains autonomous, conducting its own affairs, with its own officers and its own headquarters. It is free to withdraw at any time, but as long as it is affiliated, it must observe the items stipulated in the AFL-CIO constitution.

GROWTH IN UNION MEMBERSHIP

The economic prosperity that followed World War I and the protective pro-union legislation during the 1920s and 1930s brought about rapid growth in union membership. A great push for union growth was the passage of the Wagner Act in 1935. From 1935 to 1945, union membership increased fourfold, from fewer than 4 million to almost 15 million. However, union membership has been decreasing in recent years as a percentage of the labor force, as shown in Figure 8-3. And according to the latest figures available when this book was written, there has been a decrease also in the absolute number of union members.

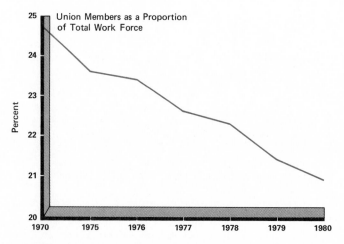

FIGURE 8-3

The Big Slippage in Union Membership.
As more and more workers have moved out of the industrial sector and into service and white-collar jobs, labor has found it increasingly difficult to gain new recruits. With this trend likely to accelerate, organized labor will probably represent an even smaller percentage of the labor force in the years ahead. (Source: U.S. Department of Labor.)

The degree to which American workers are organized varies greatly throughout different regions and industrial groups. The most highly unionized industries are those that have been long established, such as transportation. Unions in transportation include the Teamsters, the railway unions, and the public-transit unions. Construction, in which the workers are organized on a craft basis, has signed up almost all of those who belong to the construction trades. Table 8-1 lists the most heavily unionized industries.

194

TABLE 8-1
Union Membership by Industry

INDUSTRY	PERCENT OF EMPLOYEES WHO ARE UNION MEMBERS
Construction Electrical machinery Ordnance Paper Transportation Transportation equipment	75 percent or more
Apparel Federal government Food Manufacturing Metal fabricating Mining Petroleum Primary metals Telephone Tobacco manufacturers	50 to 75 percent
Chemicals Furniture Leather Lumber Publishing, printing	25 to 50 percent
Agriculture and fishing Government Finance Service Textile mills Trade	Less than 25 percent

SOURCE: Bureau of Labor Statistics, Directory of National Unions and Employees Associations.

The largest single union in the United States today is the International Brotherhood of Teamsters, which has more than 2.2 million members. It is not affiliated with the AFL-CIO. The second largest is the United Automobile Workers, with 1.6 million members.

Trends Within the Figures.   We saw in Figure 8-3 that the overall trend in union membership is down. But one of the areas in which labor unions are making progress in organizing workers is among government employees. This group includes office employees, teachers, firefighters, police officers, hospital workers, and sanitation workers.

Early unionization was primarily in the mining, construction, and transportation industries. These industries have either plateaued or declined. The big increases in employment have come in different industries:

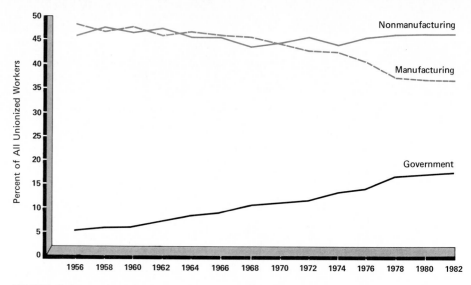

FIGURE 8-4
Union Membership by Sector.
(Source: U.S. Bureau of Labor Statistics.)

wholesale and retail trade, finance and insurance, service industries, and government jobs. Many employers in these industries have relatively smaller businesses, and this makes for a smaller organizing payoff for unions. However, in government employment, where large concentrations of employees exist, unionization has been increasing. See Figure 8-4.

The occupational pattern has also changed over time. Major employment increases have been in the clerical and professional occupations. There has been a decline in the less-skilled blue-collar jobs that produced union members in the past.

TABLE 8-2
Total Employment; Projected 1990 Requirements in Thousands

OCCUPATION GROUP	PROJECTED 1990		CHANGE 1978–90		AVERAGE ANNUAL RATE OF CHANGE, 1978–90[a]
	NUMBER	PERCENT DISTRIBUTION	NUMBER	PERCENT	
Total employment	114,000	100.0	19,627	20.8	1.6
Professional and technical workers	16,900	14.8	2,655	18.3	1.4
Managers and administrators, except farm	12,200	10.7	2,095	20.8	1.6
Sales workers	7,600	6.7	1,649	27.7	2.1
Clerical workers	21,700	19.0	4,796	28.4	2.1
Craft and kindred workers	14,900	13.1	2,514	20.0	1.5
Operatives	16,600	14.6	2,184	15.3	1.2
Nonfarm laborers	5,100	4.5	371	8.1	.6
Service workers	16,700	14.6	3,861	29.9	2.2
Farmers and farm laborers	2,400	2.1	−398	−15.9	−1.2

[a] Annual compound rate of change, calculated from unrounded figures.

SOURCE: U.S. Department of Labor, Employment and Training Report of the President (Washington, D.C.: U.S. Government Printing Office, 1980), p. 345.

Department of Labor projections are for increases in the areas that have traditionally *not* been strongly union in the past. As Table 8-2 shows, major increases are expected among professional and technical workers, managers and administrators, and sales, service, craft, and clerical occupations.

> John T. Dunlop, former Secretary of Labor and then a Harvard professor, says unions not only will survive their current problems, but will prosper.
>
> "Union membership remains high," he notes. "Historically, the membership ebbs and grows, depending on the times." For example, over the last 100 years, membership grew in about twenty years and was steady or in decline for eighty. Dunlop puts little weight on the givebacks and concession bargaining that took place during the 1981–82 recession.

LEGAL BACKGROUND FOR LABOR RELATIONS

The laws that govern labor and labor relations in this country form the basis for the relationship between business and labor unions.

Two distinct types of legislation affecting labor and employers have been enacted. The first pertains to working hours, safety regulations, and health. This group of laws will be referred to as **work legislation.** The second concerns the rights and responsibilities of labor unions and employers. These will be referred to as **labor laws.**

WORK LEGISLATION The earliest control over working hours was applied specifically to women and children. In 1924, Congress unsuccessfully proposed a constitutional amendment granting itself power to regulate the labor of persons under 18 years of age. All states, however, have laws of one kind or another governing the length of the working day and the use of child labor. Many states have legislation restricting the hours women can work in certain employment. Also, many states regulate the minimum wages that may be paid to workers.

The Fair Labor Standards Act of 1938. The major piece of legislation in this area, the Fair Labor Standards Act, was passed in 1938. It contains provisions related to both wages and hours in industries engaged in interstate commerce. In effect since October 24, 1940, this act originally stated that workers should be compensated at a rate 1½ times their standard rate of pay for working more than forty hours per week.

This act also sets a floor under minimum wages. The first minimum wage was set at 25 cents an hour and was increased to 40 cents on October 24, 1945. This "floor," or minimum, has repeatedly been raised, until it reached $3.35 per hour in 1981.

The law specifies that any time an employee is "permitted to work" must be counted as working time. All time spent in physical or mental exertion, that is "controlled or required" by the employer and pursued for the benefit of the employer is to be counted as working time. Thus, the work not requested but nonetheless permitted is working time. If work is permitted away from the premises or even at the employee's home, it is counted as working time.

The law says that an employer may not discriminate on the basis of sex by paying employees of one sex at rates lower than those paid the opposite sex. This applies to equal work on jobs requiring equal skill, effort, and responsibility and performed under similar working conditions. The federal Fair Labor Standards Act is administered by the Wage and Hour Division of the U.S. Department of Labor.

Other work legislation includes *equal-employment-opportunity laws*, *Occupational Safety and Health legislation*, and *child-labor laws*, which are discussed elsewhere in this book.

THE NATIONAL LABOR POLICY The policy of the U.S. government toward labor is a product of three major pieces of legislation. They, together with their amendments and administrative and court rulings, have defined what labor and management may and may not do. The main pieces of legislation are the Norris-LaGuardia Act (1932), the Wagner Act (1935), the Taft-Hartley Act (1947), and the Landrum-Griffin Act (1959). Two other laws, the Civil Service Reform Act (1978) and the Railway Labor Act (1926), affect the government and the rail and air carrier industries exclusively.

The Norris-LaGuardia Act. The Norris-LaGuardia Act was the first piece of legislation written to protect the rights of unions and workers to engage in union activity. The act has two main purposes:

1. It forbids federal courts to issue injunctions against a variety of union activities.
2. It forbids employers to require the signing of "yellow-dog contracts." These were contracts that workers had to sign to get a job initially. The contract made workers swear they would not join a union, or else they could be fired.

The Norris-LaGuardia Act did not require management to bargain with workers. But it did provide labor with some leverage in the form of strikes, boycotts, and so forth without fear of federal injunction.

The Wagner Act. **The Wagner Act of 1935, otherwise known as the National Labor Relations Act, is clearly a workers' law, for its regulations are designed to control the actions of employers.** In general, it guarantees workers the right to organize. This was achieved by making it unlawful for employers to:

1. Refuse to bargain collectively with representatives chosen by employees
2. Interfere with the employees' right to bargain collectively
3. Dictate in any way to labor officials about their administrative procedures
4. Discriminate against union members in either hiring or firing
5. Discriminate against employees who take advantage of their rights under the law

The law established the National Labor Relations Board to administer the provisions of this act in settling disputes. It also serves as a sort of court in protecting workers against unfair practices. One chief function is to prevent or correct the five illegal practices enumerated above. Another is to establish proper bargaining units and organizations to represent the workers. In substance, the Wagner Act has provided an orderly process of democratic elections by workers. It replaces the former tactic of striking to force the employer to recognize the union as the employees' rightful bargaining agent.

> Louisville, Kentucky, may be the strike capital of the country. Over the past ten years this city has had one of the worst strike records in the nation. Louisville's average of 9.6 days lost per worker compares unfavorably with the national average of 4.4. Not surprisingly, management blames the unions and vice versa.
>
> Louisville's manufacturing jobs have slumped from more than 130,000 to about 90,000 in the last decade. It appears that some of the cuts have come as a result of decisions to get away from high labor costs and uncertainty associated with worker militancy.

The Taft-Hartley Act. Throughout the history of the labor movement, no single federal law has incurred stronger opposition from unions than the Taft-Hartley Act of 1947. Its true title is the Labor Management Relations Act. After a bitter battle in Congress, the Taft-Hartley Act was passed over the veto of President Truman. By this time, the political climate had shifted in favor of management, largely because of the advantages given to unions under the Wagner Act. **The main objectives of the Taft-Hartley Act are to equalize the rights and privileges of management and labor and to recognize the public interest.** Although the act gives management no new rights, it achieves a balance of power by withholding some of the rights that had previously been extended to unions.

The act holds that it is an unfair labor practice for an employer to:

1. Refuse to bargain collectively with employees
2. Encourage or discourage membership in any labor organization
3. Contribute financial or other support to any labor organization
4. Interfere with the organization or administration of any labor organization
5. Discriminate against an employee because of testimony the employee gives under the act

Under the act, unions may not:

1. Refuse to bargain collectively with employers
2. Restrain nonstrikers from crossing a picket line or threaten violence to nonstrikers
3. Cause an employer to discriminate against any employee in order to encourage or discourage union membership
4. Force the employer to pay for services not performed (often called "featherbedding")
5. Engage in secondary boycotts
6. Stop work over a jurisdictional or interunion dispute
7. Charge the members excessive or discriminatory initiation fees

Employers as well as workers are permitted to appeal to the National Labor Relations Board against unions in connection with such practices. Certain practices may be subject to court action and lawsuits for damages. Restrictions on the use of injunctions are eased. The Taft-Hartley Act provisions are administered by the National Labor Relations Board.

Special rules were written into the Taft-Hartley Act for handling certain controversies or strikes. These are the ones which, in the judgment of the president, create or threaten emergencies by impeding the national health or safety. In any such dispute or strike, the president is authorized to appoint a board of inquiry to investigate the facts. After that, a court injunction can be obtained forbidding the occurrence or continuance of a stoppage for a period of eighty days.

During this **cooling-off** or waiting period, efforts are to be made to settle the dispute. If no voluntary agreement can be arranged within sixty days, the employees are polled by secret ballot on whether they will accept the employer's final offer. After all these steps have been taken, however, the injunction must be dissolved whether or not the dispute is settled.

The Landrum-Griffin Act. Working under some of the most intense public pressure in years, Congress passed, on September 4, 1959, the first major labor-reform amendments to the Taft-Hartley Act. This act was the Labor Management Reporting and Disclosure Act, commonly called the Landrum-Griffin Act. It is quite correctly titled, for the major portion of the law requires a series of reports to be made to the secretary of labor. It is designed to regulate internal union affairs by requiring:

CURRENT ISSUE

SHOULD PUBLIC EMPLOYEES HAVE THE RIGHT TO STRIKE?

The number and length of strikes among teachers and sanitation workers in several major cities have frequently made the newspaper headlines. Because of these events, many people believe that government workers should be denied the right to strike. This has reached the stage of becoming an issue; it is difficult to distinguish between their rights and those of other workers.

Traditionally in our society, public employees did not have the right to strike. It was reasoned that the public cannot strike against itself.

With which of the following statements do you agree, and with which do you disagree?

1. In order for society to be free, there must be certain abridgements of freedom upon some persons (or groups) within that society.
2. Every worker has the inalienable right to withhold his or her services. This includes those who work in the public sector.
3. Prohibiting strikes in public employment would be fair. People would know when they accepted public employment that they were giving up that right and privilege.
4. The idea of the right and power of the people to set up governments assumes it is every person's duty to obey the established government.
5. Public employees should not be denied the rights given other workers.
6. Public employees should have the right to strike but they should not organize into unions.

What do you see as the most forceful argument in each case:

a. Supporting strikes by public employees?
b. Prohibiting strikes by public employees?

1. Reports of the constitution and bylaws of union organizations
2. Reports of union administrative policies pertaining to initiation fees, union dues, and other financial assessments; the calling of union meetings, qualifications for membership in the union; and the ratification of contracts
3. Annual financial reports by the unions, showing the amounts of assets, liabilities, and cash receipts; salaries of officers; and loans to members, union officials, or businesses
4. Reports of personal financial transactions on the part of union officials that might in any way conflict with the best interests of the union
5. Reports by employers of any expenditures made in order to prevent their employees from organizing; for example, workers hired to sabotage efforts at organizing by union representatives

This law gives employers and union members new protection from union racketeers and unscrupulous labor leaders. Members have more voice in their local union affairs. Local officers must be elected by secret ballot at least once every three years, and national officers every five years. Union members can sue in federal courts if justice is not provided.

The National Labor Relations Board. The National Labor Relations Board was created by Congress in 1935 to guarantee labor the right to organize and bargain collectively. The board consists of five members appointed by the president of the United States. Each member serves for five years.

There are two types of labor hearings. The first conducts an investigation of employers who are accused of *unfair labor practices*. The Labor Management Relations Act of 1947 assigned responsibility for this type of case to a general counsel. If the employer is found guilty, the company is ordered to stop interfering with the workers' right to organize. If necessary, the federal courts may be called on to enforce the counsel's rulings.

The second type deals with *representation*. This type comes under the direct jurisdiction of the labor board. It provides election machinery to determine the workers' preferences on how they want to be represented in collective bargaining.

According to the policy of the board, the workers have the exclusive right, without any interference from the employer, to decide whether they want to be represented by any union. If they do, the workers decide which union they want. The union that receives a majority of the votes is selected as the workers' official representative. (Figure 8-5 shows the results of these certification elections in recent years.) The board also initiates procedures for orderly collective bargaining between the chosen union and the employer.

Several states have conciliation boards to serve in disputes that do not fall under the jurisdiction of the National Labor Relations Board. Several larger cities also have mediation boards.

STATE "RIGHT-TO-WORK" LAWS

Under Section 14-b of the Taft-Hartley Act, individual states are permitted to outlaw any form of compulsory unionism, including the union shop. This was a change from the original interpretation of the National Labor Relations Act of 1935 (Wagner Act). It allowed the unions the right to negotiate compulsory union-membership agreements. It also prevented a state or municipality from nullifying the unions' right in this respect.

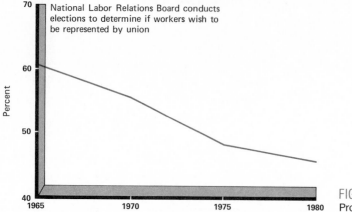

FIGURE 8-5
Proportion of Representation Election Won by Unions

Florida enacted the first "right-to-work" law by constitutional amendment in 1944. Right-to-work laws dealing largely with agricultural labor have been passed by twenty states, as shown in Figure 8-6. In all, twenty-five states have enacted such legislation, but five have subsequently repealed it.

FIGURE 8-6
States with "Right-to-Work" Laws, 1980

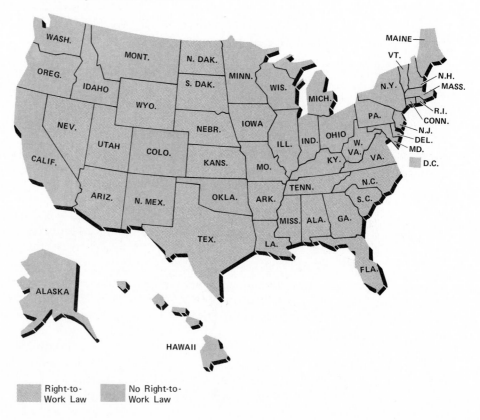

UNION SECURITY   The union usually wants some degree of security in its operations to make sure it continues to represent the workers. Three main levels of union security are often negotiated.

The Closed Shop.   Under this agreement, any new employee had to be a member of the union before being hired. In this way, the union was the only source of employment available to the employer. But the closed shop was declared illegal by the Taft-Hartley Act, passed in 1947.

Although the closed shop is now illegal, management and labor may agree to a clause offering the union the opportunity to fill vacanies.

The Union Shop.   The union shop is the type of union security most commonly found. **It recognizes the compulsory union membership of all employees.** Management may employ anyone it desires, but he or she will be required to join the union within a stated period of time. The Taft-Hartley Act provides a minimum of thirty days as the grace period before compulsory membership.

The Open Shop.   An open shop is not unionized and there is no effort on the part of management either to promote or to prevent a union. Employees are free to choose whether or not to organize. In many such situations, some employees are already members of a union. This makes the open shop an attractive target for union organizers.

COLLECTIVE BARGAINING

The method by which the management of a firm and the union come to agreement on a contract through negotiations is called COLLECTIVE BARGAINING. It is called collective bargaining because workers act collectively — as a group — in bargaining with management.

Employees engage in collective bargaining because they feel they can gain something as a group that they cannot as individuals. Economic issues are very basic to collective-bargaining objectives. Several studies show that wages and fringe benefits are high on the list of factors members use to judge their union's performance. Two other collective-bargaining issues that appear frequently are grievance handling and job security.

In a sense, collective bargaining is a form of decision making. It is a method for making decisions about the terms and conditions of employment in a company. The individual exercises his or her voice in the bargaining process through the union representatives. **Workers share with other workers and with the employer the responsibility for agreeing on orderly, established bargaining procedures.** Procedures such as determining working conditions, practices to be used in promotions and layoffs, and penalties for violation of the work rules are established.

CERTIFICATION ELECTIONS   A union becomes the bargaining agent for a group of workers when it is certified as representing the majority of them. Most commonly, this is determined by a secret vote conducted by the National Labor Relations

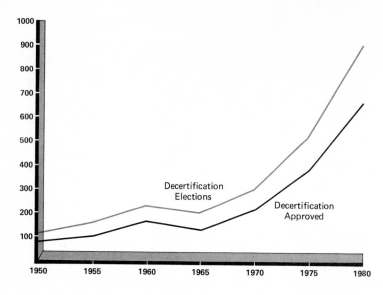

FIGURE 8-7
Decertification Election Trend, 1950–1980.
(Source: National Labor Relations Board.)

Board. If a clear majority of the workers involved indicate a desire to be represented by the union, then that union is "certified" as the exclusive bargaining agent for the employees.

Certification elections are held to determine which union (if any) *will represent* the employees. Decertification elections are held to *remove* the union as bargaining agent. If a majority of employees want the union decertified, that union is removed. Figure 8-7 shows the recent trend in decertification elections and their results.

HOW COLLECTIVE BARGAINING WORKS

After certification, representatives of the union and of management meet at the bargaining table and try to reach agreement on a contract. Rarely are the two sides in agreement when they begin their meetings, and rarely is the final product of their deliberations precisely what either side originally wanted.

The first meeting between the negotiation teams usually establishes rules, policies, and schedules for future meetings. Sometimes at this first meeting, the representatives of labor formally present their specific proposals for changes in the existing labor agreement. At later meetings, management submits counterproposals. Both groups seek opportunities to suggest compromise solutions in their favor until an agreement is reached.

Collective bargaining is a matter of give and take, with labor and management gradually moving closer together. Figure 8-8 shows the typical movement on an issue by union and management through collective bargaining. (It could be wages, working conditions, or anything else.) The introduction of other issues can lead to a "tradeoff" kind of bargaining. When this happens, one issue may be traded for another. For example, management offers a 20-cents-an-hour wage increase and no additional fringe benefits, while the union wants 22 cents in wages and a new dental-care insurance plan. The ultimate resolution after bargaining might be a 17-cent pay raise plus the dental plan.

When union and management representatives have finally agreed on a contract, the union representatives take the contract back to their members.

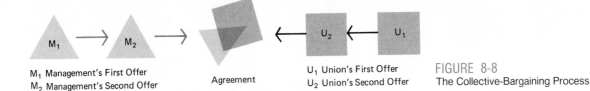

M₁ Management's First Offer
M₂ Management's Second Offer

Agreement

U₁ Union's First Offer
U₂ Union's Second Offer

FIGURE 8-8
The Collective-Bargaining Process

If it does not satisfy the members, they may send their representatives back to continue the bargaining process, or they may decide to reinforce their demands by going on strike.

If labor and management find it impossible to come to an agreement, a third party may be brought in from the outside. This might be a mediator or mediation team.

Once the contract has been ratified by the union and management, it becomes the guiding principle of labor–management relations for the duration of the agreement. All collective agreements run for a specific period of time, usually from one to three years. Months before an agreement is to terminate, representatives of both management and labor sit down together to negotiate terms for a new contract.

There are now more than 150,000 collective agreements in force in the United States. On the average, 300 such agreements are concluded every day.

COLLECTIVE-BARGAINING PATTERNS

The precise form or pattern of collective bargaining varies considerably, depending largely upon the nature of the industry.

Local-market Bargaining. As its name implies, this pattern occurs mainly locally. The building-construction industry is an example, for building contractors operate essentially in a local market. The work must be done where it is needed, unlike the kinds of manufacturing that can easily be moved from one city to another. Since their product is not transportable, building contractors compete only in the local-market area.

Bargaining takes place between various local unions of construction workers and the local trade association of contractors. These local unions have great autonomy in bargaining, and no attempt is made by their international unions to impose a uniform pattern of wages or working conditions.

Retail food stores and newspaper publishers are similarly competitive in a local market only, and therefore collective bargaining is customarily done at the local level.

Industrywide Bargaining. The women's-apparel industry is a good example of one in which manufacturers compete over a nationwide market. Most of the companies are small-scale producers requiring relatively little capital investment. Labor accounts for a major part of the cost of the finished product.

In this industry, the negotiations take place for all employees represented by the union throughout the industry. A standard contract will probably exist for all employees in the industry, with certain local adjustments. The garment manufacturer knows that competitors will be providing wages and benefits to their employees similar to what he or she is providing.

Coalition Bargaining. In coalition bargaining, several different unions within a given industry will collaborate in bargaining with an employer. Organized labor favors coalition bargaining because it tends to strengthen bargaining lines where they are weakest—among small and weak unions.

An outstanding example of success in coalition bargaining is the experience of several unions negotiating with General Electric. The General Electric Company had historically insisted on bargaining separately with individual unions. However, eventually several electrical unions — all affiliated with the AFL-CIO — formed an alliance, cutting across union jurisdictions, to bargain as a group with GE. The largest and strongest of the eleven unions, the International Union of Electric Workers, took the lead in the negotiations. The AFL-CIO backed the negotiation team by pledging a sum of $8 million to carry out the negotiation effort. It employed a nationwide network of teletype stations in strategic cities to keep union members informed and in line. Although the GE management at first resisted the idea of coalition bargaining, in the end it settled with the coalition group.

THE BARGAINING AGREEMENT

The written labor agreement as we know it today is a peculiarly American phenomenon. It first appeared in the late 1930s, during the time when unions in such industries as rubber, steel, and automobile manufacturing were organized. Before then, labor agreements, which existed principally in the railroad and printing industries, were abbreviated, generalized agreements that left working rules to informal arrangements. Under such generalized agreements, neither party was inclined to curtail its flexibility by agreeing to detailed clauses. Management most wanted the freedom to manage and operate without hindrance from the union. The union wanted to be free to seize any opportunity to make gains for its members.

COLLECTIVE BARGAINING AS DECISION MAKING

In one sense, collective bargaining is a decision-making process. Unions and employers interact in a complex legal framework. Between them, they set the "rules" that govern the employer/employee relationship for that unit, during the agreement period. Collective bargaining helps management and workers reach decisions through compromise.

No bargaining agreement (or contract) can spell out *all* situations that might arise during the life of the contract. In an effort to reduce the "grey" areas left unclear, contracts have become longer over the years and more "understandings" have been reduced to writing.

In the United States, "workers and management are seen to have diametrically opposed interests," writes sociologist Robert E. Cole. In Japan, workers view the corporation as "the sustaining force" of their lives and therefore eagerly cooperate with management. But in the United States, "management writes off worker cooperation because it is seen as either irrelevant or impossible to achieve." These differences in management's and workers' attitudes toward their relationship explain in part differences in productivity and quality in the two countries.

PURPOSE OF THE BARGAINING AGREEMENT

Today, the trend is for both parties to spell out every possible detail, so that any dispute that may arise is covered by the contract. Negotiating an agreement now often takes many months of give-and-take negotiation. Because agreements are all-inclusive contracts, they generally cover a wide range of topics and conditions, and they range from a few pages in length to a hundred or more. Labor agreements are expected to:

1. Indicate clearly the classification of workers to be included and those to be excluded under the terms
2. Spell out detailed rights and duties of the parties concerning working hours, wage rates, overtime, promotions, layoffs, transfers, management prerogatives, and work scheduling
3. Provide procedures for settling grievances and arbitration
4. Define procedures for renewing the agreement

Most contracts stipulate work assignments to avoid jurisdictional disputes. These occur when there is a question about whether certain work should be performed by employees in one bargaining unit or by those in another. Such issues as the subcontracting of work outside the union and the automation of mechanical processes are highly controversial subjects that require lengthy negotiations.

Wage increases are a complex issue, occasionally resolved only after a strike. And there are always many questions apart from wages, such as these:

1. Should the employer contribute toward the health plan, or should he or she put the money into improving the retirement plan?
2. Should seniority lists be made up by departments or by job classifications, or should they be plantwide?

The factors that are generally included in labor agreements are summarized here.

Wage rates and wage-payment policies

Normal workday or workweek

How overtime is to be calculated

Time to be taken for meals, regulations for making up lost time

Working conditions — rest periods, restroom facilities, safety rules and devices, medical care to be furnished

Vacations, leaves of absence, holidays, paid holidays; when vacations are to be taken; how the length of vacations varies with length of service

Selection, promotion, and layoff procedures

Production standards

Seniority — the degree it is to be recognized and how it is to be determined

Transfer of workers to new job assignments

Employment practices for using temporary workers

Welfare of workers

Grievance procedures

Strikes and lockouts

Length of the agreement and when it is to terminate

To choose just one of these items for illustration, let us consider the holidays with pay that are given to employees. Table 8-3 shows the holidays and the percentage of union contracts that give each day off with pay.

TABLE 8-3
Holidays Included in Union Contracts

Thanksgiving	98	New Year's Eve	27
Labor Day	98	Employee's Birthday	22
Christmas	98	Veteran's Day	20
July Fourth	97	Floating Day	14
New Year's Day	97	Columbus Day	9
Memorial Day	96	Election Day	8
Good Friday	50	Christmas–New Year's Week	8
Day after Thanksgiving	49	Lincoln's Birthday	5
Christmas Eve	47	Martin Luther King's	
Washington's Birthday	36	Birthday	3

Based on an analysis of 400 union contracts selected from the national file of over 5,000 cases.
SOURCE: Basic Patterns in Union Contracts, Bureau of National Affairs.

DISPUTE RESOLUTION

Unions and managements have different interests and goals. At times agreement cannot be reached using ordinary bargaining methods. When the parties are unable to move further toward settlement of their differences in a contract, an *impasse* has occurred.

IMPASSE Most negotiations do *not* result in an impasse. In the last decade, only about .2 percent of total worktime available was lost to strikes. The strike is the final and most publicized step in an impasse. However, many impasses are resolved before strikes become necessary. Procedures are used that allow opening of communications, position readjustment, or face saving.

Bringing in a third party is a common way of trying to resolve an impasse. Three kinds of third-party involvement are mediation, fact-finding, and arbitration. **Mediation** is a process in which a neutral person tries to help the parties toward agreement. Techniques are aimed at keeping communications open and pointing out potential for settlement that the others have missed. **Fact-finding** involves a neutral third party who studies the issues in a dispute and makes a public recommendation as to what a reasonable solution should be. The third party in effect acts for the public and counts on public pressure for resolution. **Arbitration** is different from both these methods, in that the arbitrator is given the power to impose a settlement on the parties.

GRIEVANCES AND GRIEVANCE PROCEDURES Once a collective-bargaining contract is signed, that document governs the union–management relationship. The typical contract specifies what management can and cannot do and what the union's responsibilities are. The contract identifies areas in which management has agreed to share decision making. Anything not addressed in the contract is a management prerogative.

The contract focuses on employee and employer rights. When an employee feels that his or her rights have been violated, he or she can file a grievance. A GRIEVANCE is *a specific, formal dissatisfaction expressed through an identified procedure.* A **complaint,** on the other hand, is a dissatisfaction that is not expressed through the formal grievance procedure. Formal grievance procedures vary, depending upon the terms of the contract. Figure 8-9 illustrates a typical grievance procedure.

As you will note in Figure 8-9, the process can be quite a lengthy one involving many persons. Some grievance procedures include only steps 1, 3, and 5. The supervisor is the key to successful settlement of grievances with a minimum of difficulty. When supervisors are doing a good job, it is at this level that most grievances are settled.

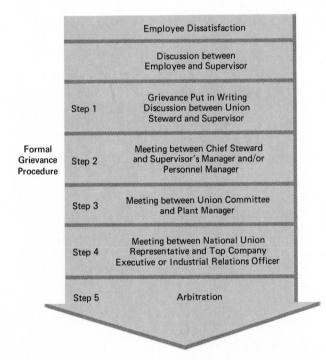

FIGURE 8-9
A Typical Grievance Procedure

Arbitration. The final step in the grievance procedure, arbitration, is of special interest. An ARBITRATOR is *an impartial labor expert who hears and settles grievances.* Usually the company and union each pay half of the arbitrator's fee, and the decision is binding.

"Interest" arbitration, used to reach agreement on the contract itself, is seldom used. But "rights" arbitration, arising out of interpretation of an existing contract, is used frequently in settling grievances. Arbitration has an important place in settling grievances, and the supply of arbitrators is quite limited. When both parties to the dispute agree to arbitration, the process is known as **voluntary arbitration.** If the union and the company are required by law to submit their dispute to a third party for a decision, the process is known as **compulsory arbitration.** Arbitration is commonly used in labor and industrial disputes when it is provided for in the contract.[2]

Many collective-bargaining agreements provide that specific disputes must be submitted to voluntary arbitration. A study of 1,254 labor agreements in fourteen industries was completed by the Bureau of Labor Statistics. Three-fourths of these agreements provide for arbitration as the terminal point in the grievance machinery. Of the total number of workers covered by the arbitration provision, 28 percent were subject to permanently established arbitration machinery. The remaining 72 percent were subject to procedures calling for the selection of arbitrators whenever the need arose.

Of all the arbitration agreements, 93 percent (covering 91 percent of the workers) provided for **automatic** arbitration, or arbitration at the request of either party. **Under this procedure, arbitration must be carried out if either party requests it.** Both parties have agreed in advance to accept the decision as final and binding. Discharge disputes are the most frequent reason for labor arbitration, the American Arbitration Association says. The second most popular cause is disciplinary issues.

Several private organizations have been established to serve management and labor in settling their disputes. The Council on Industrial Relations for the Electrical Contracting Industry, for example, was established in 1920 for the purpose of serving the entire industry. Any segment of the electrical industry in which contractual relations exist between employers and the International Brotherhood of Electrical Workers may make use of the council's arbitration machinery.

Federal Mediation and Conciliation Service.   As an independent federal agency, this service assists business and unions by providing a staff without charge to act as mediators and conciliators in labor disputes. The agency also maintains a roster of qualified labor arbitrators. The service, in addition to its central office in Washington, D.C., maintains regional offices in seven metropolitan areas and field offices in more than seventy smaller cities. The agency arranges for general educational seminars for labor and management and workshops on labor arbitration.

When the parties to a dispute decide to use arbitration, they make a request to the service for a roster of arbitrators. From it they select an arbitrator who hears the dispute and writes the decision. The arbitrator is paid a fee for the service and is reimbursed for expenses. **The decision (award) is binding upon the parties, for they have agreed to this in the bargaining agreement.**

American Arbitration Association.   The American Arbitration Association (AAA) is a public-service, nonprofit organization. It is dedicated to resolving disputes of all kinds, chiefly through arbitration. The five most common

---

[2] In all, thirty states have enacted arbitration statutes modeled more or less along the lines of the Uniform Arbitration Act. Naturally, the statutes in some states are more comprehensive than in others, but they usually cover at least two of the three primary forms of arbitration practice in the United States — commercial, labor–management, and accident claims.

forms of arbitration are commercial, accident claims, labor, international, and inter-American. The AAA has a list of some 26,000 men and women who are especially skilled in resolving disputes.

In the field of labor arbitration, the AAA makes available to industry and labor a roster of qualified labor arbitrators. Persons may be selected from this list by the parties to a dispute. The arbitrators chosen hear both sides of the issue and write the award.

The association publishes a number of pamphlets, bulletins, and research studies dealing with arbitration. It also conducts educational seminars about arbitration and labor relations.

NATIONAL-EMERGENCY DISPUTES

Industrial disputes have long been the concern of the federal government. Whenever a strike jeopardizes the public welfare, the government usually steps in and works for an immediate settlement of the controversy. A national-emergency dispute may be simply defined as a strike that jeopardizes the health or safety of the general public.

What *exactly* constitutes an emergency that threatens the public is not entirely clear. Coal and steel strikes, at times, have been called national emergencies. Whether a strike is an emergency and not merely an inconvenience is a political decision. The Taft-Hartley Act provides that the president of the United States makes the decision.

A board is assembled to investigate the dispute, and submits a report to the president. After the report is received, the president may intervene or petition the court for an injunction preventing a strike or lockout for a period of eighty days.

During the eighty days, the parties are required to continue bargaining. Toward the end of the injunction period, the National Labor Relations Board polls the employees to see if they will accept management's total offer. If the dispute is not settled, a strike can begin after the end of the 80-day period.

The Railway Labor Act provides a set of procedures somewhat different for resolving national emergency disputes with railroad and airline companies.

INDUSTRIAL RELATIONS TODAY

The last few years have seen some interesting changes in industrial relations. One trend, perhaps related to economic conditions, may be only temporary in nature: concession bargaining.

CONCESSION BARGAINING

During the 1981–82 recession, a phenomenon appeared that had not been seen much in U.S. labor negotiations. **Concession bargaining** stands in sharp contrast to union leader Samuel Gompers's simple slogan, "More." Companies increasingly asked that workers give back some things and settle for less.

The airlines industry, for example, won an almost universal 10 percent wage cut from employees. Ford, Chrysler, and GM extracted concessions from employees in exchange for reducing layoffs. The same was true for many other industries. Attitudes initially among the rank-and-file workers toward givebacks were negative. However, as it became clearer that without concessions there would be layoffs, concessions became a regular occurrence. Part of the reason for the need for concession bargaining comes from the international competitive position of U.S. companies.

INTERNATIONAL COMPETITION

Major shifts are taking place in the worldwide division of labor between the developed and developing nations. Developing nations are experiencing rapid expansion of their industrial workforces. New centers of production are springing up in the Third World. Meanwhile, the cost of labor has risen sharply in the industrialized nations. (See Table 8-4.)

The differences in labor and other costs abroad are translated into lower total cost to manufacture products in developing countries. As a result, products from those countries are cheaper and more competitive. Further, U.S. companies may subcontract some production to foreign companies or move plants overseas to take advantage of the lower costs. The net result is fewer jobs in the United States.

TABLE 8-4
How the Pattern of Compensation Shifted Around the World

	HOURLY COMPENSATION (IN U.S. DOLLARS)			PERCENT RISE IN REAL TERMS (AND IN LOCAL CURRENCY)
	1975	1978	1980	
Industrial Countries				
United States	$6.36	$8.33	$9.09	5.8%
Canada	6.14	7.52	7.97	8.2
Japan	3.05	5.47	5.58	5.6
Australia	5.20	6.29	N.A.	0.5
Belgium	6.44	9.88	11.30	10.0
Britain	3.27	4.19	5.46	5.0
France	4.63	6.70	8.17	21.5
Germany	6.24	9.48	11.33	16.1
Ireland	2.82	3.99	N.A.	13.5
Italy	4.65	6.18	7.38	16.2
Netherlands	6.57	9.77	11.31	9.3
Newly industrializing countries				
Greece	$1.40	$2.37	N.A.	34.3
Portugal	1.58	1.63	N.A.	−3.9
Spain	2.70	3.83	5.62	22.5
Brazil	1.13	1.67	1.80	21.7
Mexico	1.89	2.00	2.31	9.0
Hong Kong	0.71	1.13	1.25	20.9
South Korea	0.37	0.85	1.14	78.5
Taiwan	0.48	0.80	1.01	31.7

SOURCE: U.S. Bureau of Labor Statistics.

Early attempts at organizing the labor force were largely ineffective. However, with the formation of the American Federation of Labor in 1886, a definite shift occurred, both in purpose and growth. Under the leadership of A.F. of L. President Samuel Gompers, business unionism was the order of the day, with economic benefits for union members being the chief objective.

The era of most rapid growth occurred during the ten-year period following the passage of the Wagner Act in 1935, when union membership increased fourfold. Then, in the early 1950s, the A.F. of L. and the C.I.O. merged. This strengthened labor considerably, and union membership jumped to 18 million by 1956.

Organized labor has become a way of life in America. The chief objectives of organized labor have been increased pay (including additional economic fringe benefits), improved working conditions, and strengthening of the unions themselves.

Labor and management are bound together by common interests and common goals. When they are able to work together to prevent a work stoppage, everyone gains— management, labor, the public, and government.

Bargaining today is done collectively, with labor acting as a unit through its representatives. Some bargaining is done at the local level, but more often it is done on an industrywide or national level.

The labor agreement covers a wide variety of factors: wage rates, methods of wage payments, working conditions, seniority rights, vacations and holidays, dismissal policies, and the handling of grievances.

There are private organizations whose sole function is to help management and labor reach agreement. The federal government is also very active in this field, through the Federal Mediation and Conciliation Service and the National Labor Relations Board.

The public, acting through the federal government, has established the policy of the self-determination of workers in deciding who their representatives should be in negotiations with their employers. When it is possible for disputes to be settled without a strike, the general public benefits, as well as management and labor.

Current issues in management/union relations include concession bargaining and competition from abroad.

BUSINESS TERMS

You should be able to match these business terms with the statements that follow:

a. ARBITRATION
b. BARGAINING AGREEMENT
c. COALITION BARGAINING
d. COLLECTIVE BARGAINING
e. GRIEVANCE
f. MEDIATION
g. OPEN SHOP
h. RIGHT-TO-WORK LAW
i. UNION SHOP

1. An agreement made between labor and management outlining the terms and conditions of work
2. A situation in which there is no effort on the part of management to promote or prevent a union
3. A state law banning the formation of union-shop agreements
4. The process by which management and labor agree on a contract
5. A situation in which several different unions collaborate in bargaining with an employer
6. A worker's written statement of some element of dissatisfaction about his or her work situation
7. The settling of a dispute where labor and management agree beforehand to accept the decision of a "go-between"

1. What are the chief reasons that employees join labor unions?
2. In which industries are workers most highly organized?
3. Describe the procedure normally followed in collective bargaining.
4. Enumerate the principal items usually covered in a labor contract.
5. What is the difference between an *open shop* and a *union shop*?
6. What is concession bargaining?

1. How does the presence of labor unions in a business help workers who are not union members?
2. How are workers' complaints handled before they reach the arbitration stage?
3. Why are so-called right-to-work laws so strongly opposed by unions?
4. Why is there such conflict between management and labor over the issue of participation in decision making?
5. What, in your opinion, is the number-one issue between organized labor and management?

BUSINESS CASES

8-1

CONCESSION BARGAINING

Taylor Electric Parts, Inc., manufactures electrical components for use in the automobile industry. In recent years, parts made in Mexico and Taiwan have entered the U.S. market at prices much lower than those offered by Taylor. Taylor management has stated that because of this foreign competition it wants to renegotiate the labor agreement it has with its union. A new, lower-cost contract must be negotiated so that Taylor can compete more effectively with foreign-made products. Management has also said that it expects the new agreement to have lower wage rates, fewer fringe benefits, and less restrictive work rules. Otherwise, workers will be laid off because of the company's inability to compete successfully with imported products.

1. What are the tradeoffs in this case?
2. Why would a union give back benefits it obtained in previous years?
3. Is it reasonable for the company to expect the union to make concessions when workers usually expect their unions to get them improved wages, benefits, and working conditions?
4. In this case, foreign competition created pressure on management to seek concessions from the union. What other factors might also lead to concession bargaining?

8-2

TRADE-OFF

Sam Jackson has a difficult decision to make. He is vice-president of labor relations for a large public utility. Currently a grievance is on his desk and he must decide how to handle it. He is soon to meet with the union vice-president. If they cannot resolve the problem the next step is arbitration, which could be costly.

The case involves an employee who took time off to attend the funeral of a third cousin and wants pay for it. The contract only authorizes payment of wages for employees to attend funerals of immediate family members (usually thought to be spouse, son, daughter, father, mother). However, the employee was very close to this cousin, since they had grown up together. The company's position has been no pay. The company has been concerned that this case could set a precedent that would open the door to paid time off for many funerals.

1. What are the trade-offs in this case?
2. What would you do if you were Mr. Jackson?

Production, Logistics, and Research

study objectives

WHEN YOU HAVE FINISHED READING THIS CHAPTER, YOU SHOULD BE ABLE TO:

1. Distinguish between production and manufacturing

2. Discuss the contributions that agriculture, mining, and manufacturing make to the U.S. business system

3. Define the term *logistics* and explain what activities it includes

4. Explain the difference between production and productivity

5. Show why this country is becoming predominantly a service economy

Creativity and innovation are hallmarks of America's success. It is in part the responsibility of business to provide the environment and the stimulus to keep this process vital.

David T. Kearns,
Xerox Corporation

H ave you ever wondered how difficult it might be to make a hand calculator? Or why a disposable razor is so cheap? Where do all these items in a store come from, anyway?

Except for fresh fruits, vegetables, and meats, the things we buy have been manufactured. Manufactured goods are made by combining raw materials, labor, and energy. The raw materials and energy come from the earth and oceans. The process of raising crops, removing materials from the forests, mines, and oceans, and combining such things is called **production.** The term *production* also includes the manufacturing processes; manufacturing converts raw materials into finished products.

Our discussion in this chapter covers farming, mining, and manufacturing. We also consider productivity, research, and development in industry. Further note is made of the shift in emphasis toward the service sector of our business system.

AGRICULTURE PRODUCES BASIC RESOURCES

We begin with agriculture because it provides basic resources, and because it is *business.* Any way you measure it, agriculture is *big* business. Agriculture-related employment by 1982 had reached 23 million people.[1] U.S. farm sales amount to $170 billion annually, and farm debt stands at $195 billion. Exports of agricultural products exceeded imports by $23 billion for the 1980

---

[1] *1981 Yearbook of Agriculture,* p. 18.

year. Most family-scale commercial farms now utilize capital resources of $500,000 or more. And a resource base of $2 to $3 million for a single operation is not unusual. As an industry, agriculture-related jobs account for one-fifth of our gross national product.

AGRICULTURE IS CAPITAL-INTENSIVE At the beginning of World War II, labor accounted for 41 percent of the total farm input; capital amounted to 41 percent and real estate 18 percent. But by 1976, labor had declined to 16 percent of total input, real estate had increased to 22 percent, and capital had jumped to 62 percent. Over the last century, agricultural production shifted from being labor-intensive to becoming capital-intensive.

As a result of this shift, agriculture has taken on many of the characteristics of other "value-added" economic sectors. In addition to long-term investments, large capital sums are needed for short-term expenses as well (such items as fuel, fertilizer, and chemicals). Farmers are now concerned with the same type of problems as are other businesspeople. They share with the others the uncertainties of the marketplace. In addition, they are exposed to the risks and uncertainties of disease, insects, droughts, hailstorms, and so forth. To survive, farmers must have a high level of financial-management skills.

Aerial view of farmhouse, barns, grain silos, and cattle feeding in their feedlots. (Courtesy of the U.S. Department of Agriculture.)

TABLE 9-1
Farm Income Data

	1978	1979	1980	1981
Realized gross income ($ bil.)	126.0	151.3	150.6	166.8
Cash receipts ($ bil.)	112.5	131.7	139.5	143.5
Production expenses ($ bil.)	100.6	118.7	130.5	141.6
Net income of operators, including inventory changes ($ bil.)	25.4	32.4	20.1	25.1
Net income per farm (actual dollars)	10,427	13,333	8,278	10,304
Net income per farm (1977 dollars)	9,566	10,666	5,913	6,869
Farm operator income from nonfarm sources ($ bil.)	28.7	33.8	36.6	39.3

SOURCE: U.S. Dept of Agriculture

**AGRICULTURAL
PRODUCTIVITY
IS HIGH**

Productive agriculture has one of the best records for productivity. This has resulted from increased crop yields and the use of machinery. The farm sector posted an annual productivity increase of 3 percent over the last decade, compared to 2.1 percent for manufacturing. Each American farmer now produces enough food and fiber to support seventy-eight people; twice the number of ten years ago. (See Figure 9-1.)

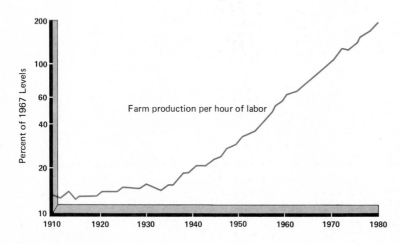

FIGURE 9-1
Farm Production per Hour of Labor

PRODUCTION OF OTHER RESOURCES

Forestry, mining, and fishing are important producers of basic resources. Combined, they employ about 5 percent of our labor force. Like agriculture, they provide materials that feed our factories and stores. The United States produces large quantities of aluminum, iron ore, coal, copper, and petroleum. But it is short on many important minerals, which it must import.

In recent years, the production of energy resources has been particularly important. Neither agriculture nor manufacturing can be carried on without energy. Like any other commodity, it must be produced, distributed, and managed. And like other commodities, it is not naturally available in the right quantities when and where it is needed.

The next frontier area for mineral development will most likely be the ocean floor. Experiments have been carried out preparatory to large-scale

PEOPLE AND PRODUCTION

mineral recovery efforts. As of now, the commercial recovery of mineral deposits from the seabed is a future development. It awaits a solution to the legal-political battle over a treaty dealing with the ocean floor. The United Nations Conference on the Law of the Sea has been trying to negotiate such a treaty since 1974.

WATER In the past, we had an abundance of fresh air and clean water. But this is no longer true.

Yesterday, our most pressing industrial problem was energy. Tomorrow, it most likely will be water. "The allocation of water supply in a nation not only affects the quality of life, but also affects the economic dynamics of the country," according to U.S. Congressman Robert Roe, when chairman of the House Public Works Subcommittee on Water Resources. Water shortage, we are told, has become a problem of the 1980s that may even exceed in political importance the energy crisis of the 1970s.

Undeniably, water supply has emerged as a problem in the United States and elsewhere. The giant Ogallala Aquifer, which provides irrigation water for the farmers of half a dozen states, is dropping at a rate of three feet per year in parts of west Texas. Ranchers and energy-company officials in Wyoming and surrounding coal-rich states argue endlessly over supplies of water. The energy people want their share in order to transport coal by liquid slurry. But the ranchers and other citizens want to preserve the water to which they have gained rights over the decades. In a number of communities, householders buy bottled water at their supermarkets because their well water has been contaminated.

Some economists have suggested that water may well become Canada's most vital export to the United States.

TABLE 9-2
Water Sources and Uses

DAILY PRECIPITATION*	WATER SOURCES	WATER USES
66% Evaporates	75% Withdrawn from rivers and lakes	47% Agriculture
31% Disperses to rivers and lakes	25% Withdrawn from ground water	44% Industry
3% Drains underground		9% Urban and residential

SOURCE: U.S. Water Resources Council
* On a typical day, about 4.2 trillion gallons of precipitation fall on the lower 48 states of the United States.

MANUFACTURING ADDS VALUE TO RAW MATERIALS

MANUFACTURING is defined as *the process of using materials, labor, and machinery to create finished products that satisfy human needs or wants.* We saw earlier that materials, people, machines, and money are frequently called the means of production. Converting them into useful finished goods creates **form utility.**

The lesson of how to produce goods on a mass scale came to us from England. There, in the middle of the eighteenth century, the Industrial

Revolution was booming. As thousands of laborers and enterprising businesspeople migrated to America from England and Western Europe, manufacturing developed here.

EARLY AMERICAN MANUFACTURING

In early colonial days, very little was done to encourage manufacturing industries in America. But it soon became apparent to some leaders that if this country was to grow and gain economic independence from Britain, factories must be established.

Alexander Hamilton was one of the first to see the importance of manufacturing. He had visions of this country's becoming a strong industrial power. In 1790, as secretary of the treasury, he issued a "Report on Manufacturers." He advocated protective tariffs (to give American goods a price advantage), restrictions on imports, and prohibition against exporting raw materials that were essential for manufacturing. Even before Congress could officially act on his report, Hamilton helped to organize the Society for Establishing Useful Manufactures. This was a private organization intended to encourage the production of cotton and linen goods, paper, printing, and public works.

Soon American ingenuity produced sewing machines, flour mills, and shoe factories. Then in 1793, Eli Whitney invented the cotton gin, and cotton cloth soon became the cheapest and most popular woven material in America.

The cotton gin revolutionized early American manufacturing. (Courtesy, Smithsonian Institution.)

The development of the woolen textiles followed that of cotton. John and Arthur Scholfield came to Massachusetts from England and erected a woolen mill at Byfield. Others followed them in the industry, and by 1810 there were two dozen woolen mills in operation. A half century later, woolen mills had been established not only in New England but also in Texas, California, and Oregon. By 1860, there were more than 1,700 such mills, employing 60,000 machine operators.

PEOPLE AND PRODUCTION

The total number of workers in the manufacturing and construction industries more than doubled between 1820 and 1840. Thus, more goods were being made in the factories than in the homes and small shops. By 1850, manufacturing accounted for one-eighth of the total national income. The value of goods manufactured in that year reached $1 billion.

CURRENT MANUFACTURING

Manufacturing still provides employment for more people than any other segment of business except trade.

Manufacturing not only employs millions of workers directly but also supports additional workers in other fields of employment. The Industrial Bureau of the Atlanta Chamber of Commerce reports that the payroll of a factory employing 150 people supports, on an average, 383 occupied homes, 24 professionals, 6,000 acres of farm products, 18 teachers, and 33 retail stores. All this accounts for $500,000 in annual retail sales, 320 automobiles and the services needed for them, and $2.5 million in property valuation.

Manufacturing can truly be called the cornerstone of our American business system. Its economic contribution lies in three areas: (1) It provides employment for millions of workers, (2) it changes the form of raw materials into useful products, and (3) it adds to the value of raw materials.

When you read about manufacturing in the United States, data are often reported by geographical regions. Figure 9-2 shows what areas are included in the different regional divisions.

The Middle Atlantic and East North Central regions together account for approximately one-half the country's total manufacturing in terms of number of people employed and in dollar value added by manufacturing.

FIGURE 9-2
Manufacturing Regions of the United States.
(Source: Department of Commerce, Bureau of the Census.)

NEW-PRODUCT DEVELOPMENT

The United States has a long history of innovation and ingenuity in manufacturing. RCA, Du Pont, and Minnesota Mining have strong reputations for developing new products. A product is said to be A NEW PRODUCT when *it serves an entirely new function or makes a major improvement in a present function.*

A very important Du Pont development is Kevlar. It may be Du Pont's most important new product since nylon. Pound for pound, it is five times stronger than steel. When first introduced, it was quickly employed as belt material for radial tires. It is valuable as a reinforcing fiber in plastics and is used in jet-aircraft parts and hulls for boats. Kevlar has greater impact resistance than graphite. And when a crack starts in a panel hole or notch, Kevlar can stop it.

FIGURE 9-3

Harrier II is in reality a *new product.*
New technology has given it a 100 percent payload improvement at a 50 percent cost saving. (Courtesy McDonnell Douglas Corporation.)

Kodak shipped more than eight million disc cameras the year it was introduced. This was twice the number of pocket cameras shipped the year the pocket cameras were introduced ten years earlier. The disc camera was truly a new product, combining electronics, optics, and chemistry. John Robertson, assistant general manager for marketing at Kodak, stated, "we wanted a camera so simple to use that there would be no concerns." One half of those surveyed who bought disc cameras said they would not have bought a camera if the disc system had not been available.

PROPELLERS COME FULL CIRCLE

Within the next decade, aircraft may again use propellers, as they did before the internal turbojet engine. Such designs are a step forward, not back. Called propfans, these propellers would be outside the plane cowling. But they would be driven by an advanced-design turbojet engine. Actually, propfans might be thought of as enlarged turbofans that have burst their engine cowlings.

The advantage of the propfan is fuel efficiency. A large external fan can generate more thrust than a small internal fan. More thrust means less fuel. NASA estimates that propfan jets could save as much as one-fourth of the fuel now used on commercial flights and one-third for military missions.

A NEW EMPHASIS ON QUALITY

There is a new emphasis on quality in American manufacturing. For more than a year, the Ford Motor Company emphasized the theme, "Quality is Job Number One." Motorola ran a series of advocacy advertisements telling about its use of quality circles in manufacturing. L.W. Lehr, president of the 3M Company, wrote a special letter to company stockholders on July 30, 1982, entitled, "A New Approach to Quality." In his letter, he detailed several items that are typical of this new emphasis on quality. Here are excerpts from that message:

A New Approach to Quality

As part of our quality effort, we have formed a corporate quality team, composed of the executive vice presidents of our four major business sectors, as well as myself and other members of management.

Recently, we put in writing a formal statement on quality, which says:

"3M will develop, produce and deliver on time, products and services that conform to requirements. These products and services must be useful, safe, reliable, environmentally safe and represented truthfully in advertising, packaging and sales promotion."

Throughout the company, we are establishing quality improvement teams, composed of people from research, manufacturing, marketing and other disciplines.

These teams are formulating comprehensive quality improvement programs, which emphasize that first-class quality is a cornerstone to continued 3M success.

Among other things, these quality improvement teams will be working to reduce the cost of quality. That is, the cost of scrap, rework, inspection and other things associated with quality problems. As a company, our aim is to reduce the cost of quality by 50 percent by 1987.

One of the keys to quality improvement, of course, is active participation by individual employees, that is, the people who are closest to a job and often in the best position to suggest how to do it better.

Among several ways our people are participating is through quality circles, where small groups of workers meet voluntarily to help solve various job-related problems.

The emphasis on quality has been brought about by a perception on the part of consumers that American products have become inferior to some foreign products. American producers have accepted the challenge and seem to be giving a new emphasis to quality control.

DIVERSIFICATION IN PRODUCTION

Diversification is a chief characteristic of today's production activity. It is not restricted to manufacturing operations, for companies engaged in services are also diversifying. In fact, companies that once produced only goods are now offering services as well. DIVERSIFICATION refers to *the making or offering of several different kinds of products and/or services.* Diversification gives a business stability through more regularity in company operations.

BORG-WARNER EXPANDS INTO SERVICES

Borg-Warner was a manufacturer catering to two large market sectors — automotive and housing. Both sectors were greatly depressed in the mid- to late 1970s.

Borg-Warner's production was very much an up-and-down affair.

In the 1974–75 depression, company earnings dropped 40 percent from their 1973 high. So in 1976, company chairman James F. Bere steered his company into services.

The company added armored-car transport and retail inventory financing to its offerings. The result: During 1981's troubled economy, Borg-Warner earned a record $172 million on sales of $2.7 billion. Chairman Bere says, "We have come a long way in reducing our vulnerability to big swings in our traditional manufacturing business."

OTHER EXAMPLES OF DIVERSIFICATION

U.S. News and World Report, Inc., is diversifying away from magazine publishing. It is expanding its computer-based publishing services and its satellite transmission network.

The packaging industry had been in the doldrums. So Ball Corporation diversified into aerospace, making satellites and infrared instrumentation. It is also emphasizing its plastics and zinc-casting products. These are machine-intensive rather than labor-intensive product lines.

Quaker Oats historically has been a food-processing company. But it has launched into direct selling to consumers. The company president predicts that by the late 1980s, Quaker's direct-to-consumer business will account for 20 percent of company sales. In addition to the mail-order business, Quaker is now in retail selling. It has added Jos. A. Bank Clothiers, Inc., Herrschners, Inc. (a needlepoint company), and Brookstone Co. (high-quality tools) to its company operations.

THE ROBOT REVOLUTION

For a decade, America has been making a small start toward total automation. But low-cost, high-quality imports have slowed the pace toward automation. Today things are different. James S. Albus, head of the robotics research lab at the U.S. National Bureau of Standards, said:

> The human race is now poised on the brink of a new industrial revolution that will at least equal, if not far exceed, the first Industrial Revolution in its impact on mankind.

PEOPLE AND PRODUCTION

The first major use of robots in U.S. manufacture was for painting and welding jobs. But it has been forecast that robots will be used in all major hostile environments. Examples are in repairing underground and undersea cables, on satellites, and in mining operations. Alan M. Christman, general manager for manufacturing industry marketing at Control Data Corporation, said, "Top executives . . . realize that to remain in business in the 1990s, they will have to automate."

Predicasts, a market research firm in Cleveland, predicts that U.S. manufactured robotic sales will increase from $600 million in 1985 to $4 billion in 1995. A robot is basically an arm with claw fingers. It is operated by a computer that feeds instructions by electrical impulses to the arm. The Robot Institute of America is an industrial trade group. Its definition of ROBOT is:

> A reprogrammable, multifunctional manipulator designed to move material, parts, tools, or specialized devices through variable programmed motions for the performance of a variety of tasks.

The key words here are *reprogrammable* and *multifunctional*. A machine that puts caps on bottles, for example, is automated. But the "thing" that picks up chocolates and puts them in a box is a robot. The pick-and-place type is the simplest version of robot. It is governed by an electromechanical control system. It accounts for about one-third of all robots used in U.S. industry today.

Many U.S. companies are making major commitments to the use of industrial robots. At the St. Louis McDonnel Douglas plant, a million-dollar robot controls a laser beam. It is used to cut out sheets of graphite used in brake assemblies for jet aircraft. This robot also cuts parts of tail sections and wings that are welded by another robot. With the help of robots, two people at the McDonnell plant now do work that once required thirty workers.

FIGURE 9-4
Robot arms search out and weld critical areas of car bodies.
(Courtesy Chrysler Corporation.)

Perhaps the most ambitious robot program has been launched by the General Electric Company. Its program may in time replace nearly half its assembly-line workers with robots. Some automation experts say that "smart" robots (that see, feel, and "think") could replace two-thirds or more of today's factory workforce.

In addition to the use of robots, manufacturers are making other changes to reduce costs. General Motors Corporation spent $200 million to build a new, modern Buick plant (Buick City) in Michigan. Patterned after Toyota City in Japan, parts plants are clustered around the assembly plant. The idea is to eliminate the need for maintaining parts inventories at the assembly plant. It was thought that this most modern plant would reduce manufacturing costs by several hundred dollars per car.

Flexible Manufacturing Systems. FMS is the acronym for today's process of factory automation. First we had numerically controlled machine tools that performed their operations automatically according to coded instructions on tape. Then came computer-aided design and computer-aided manufacturing (CAD/CAM). This replaced the drafting board with the CRT (cathode ray tube) screen and the numerical control tape with the computer.

Flexible automation's greatest potential lies in its capacity to make goods cheaply in *small* volumes. Since the time of Henry Ford, the unchallenged low-cost production system has been Detroit-style "hard" automation that stamps out look-alike parts in large volume. But such mass production is of less importance compared with "batch production" in lots of anywhere from one to several thousand.

Seventy-five percent of all machine parts today are produced in batches of fifty or fewer. Many assembled products too, ranging from airplanes and tractors to office desks and large computers, are made in batches. Flexible manufacturing brings a degree of diversity to the plant not previously available. Different products can be made on the same line at will. General Electric, for example, uses flexible automation to make 2,000 different versions of its electric meter at its Somersworth, New Hampshire, plant with total output of more than one million meters a year. FMS can be reprogrammed for design changes or new parts.

LOGISTICS

Much time, labor, money, and energy is used to produce goods to satisfy people's needs and wants. It all starts on our farms and in our forest areas, or in the mines, lakes, and oceans. Raw materials are located just about everywhere. Bringing them together in the right places, at the right times, and in the right quantities requires expert management. Both raw materials and completed goods must be protected while in use and in storage.

The term LOGISTICS refers to *the management process for providing an orderly flow of materials to the firm and of finished goods to the marketplace.* It embraces the details of supply, product handling, and transportation activities. The logistics operations of a manufacturing enterprise have a dual purpose. First, there must be assembled a wide assortment of raw materials and supplies in the right quantities, at the right time, and at an

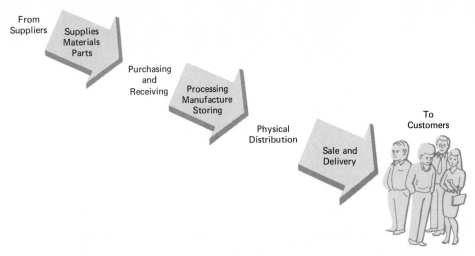

FIGURE 9-5
A Logistics System

acceptable price. Second, the logistics plan must deliver the finished products to customers in a manner satisfactory to them. **Logistics operations give time and place utility to goods.**

The first logistics concern of management, then, deals with the details of materials management — purchasing, storing, and handling all types of unfinished goods. This aspect of logistics is discussed here. The physical distribution of *finished goods* is discussed in Chapter 13. The various components of logistical operations account for about one-fifth of the gross national product.

PRODUCT PROCUREMENT AND MANAGEMENT

Raw materials, supplies, and capital goods (machinery and equipment) must be available before production can begin, and all these must be replaced continually. They must be ordered, received, stored, controlled, and dispersed repeatedly.

Normally, a purchasing manager is placed in charge of procuring all types of needed materials and equipment. The agent and his or her top assistants develop needed purchasing policies. These policies cover quality standards, requisition and buying procedures, and inventory maintenance and control.

In recent years, the materials-management function in some businesses has been extended to include the purchase of energy. At Du Pont, for example, the Department of Energy and Materials buys raw materials, supplies, and equipment. In addition it also procures energy, conducts explorations for minerals, and plans alternate energy resources.

Inventory Control. *The management of goods and supplies on hand* is known as INVENTORY CONTROL. There are two aspects of inventory, or product, control: one relates to flow and the other to security. One common practice in inventory control is to issue raw materials and supplies only upon written request. Each requisition should be prenumbered, dated, and signed and should show exactly what was issued, to whom, and for what purpose.

Standardizing materials when practicable and establishing limits within which the inventory should be maintained are also helpful control procedures. Some of the factors that must be considered, in deciding how much inventory to maintain, are:

1. Availability:
   a. Number of suppliers
   b. Reliability of suppliers
   c. Efficiency of transport facilities
2. Storage space available
3. Efficiency of handling techniques
4. Rate of consumption
5. Stability of market prices

A new technique in inventory management is called **material requirements planning,** or MRP. Instead of having large inventories on hand, the idea is to have materials arrive as needed. To be successful, this requires

FIGURE 9-6
Automated Distribution Center.
This automated distribution center is part of the IBM plant at Raleigh, N.C. Products and parts are moved by the latest in materials-handling equipment. Up to 30,000 pallets and 300,000 small-parts locations are controlled by an IBM system/370 Model 169 Computer (Courtesy International Business Machines Corporation.)

PEOPLE AND PRODUCTION

close coordination between purchasing and production. It also requires self-discipline to feed accurate information into the system. And even this will work only when the system's output information is observed. In a recent year, the average U.S. manufacturing company turned over its materials inventory seven times. American firms in recent years have shown a 20 percent annual increase in materials-inventory turnover.

MATERIALS-CONTROL CONSULTANTS

A number of consultants are helping managers apply computers in controlling inventories. One of these is Oliver W. Wight, who lives in rural New Hampshire. He simplifies the pattern for those he is teaching by asking these questions:

What are you going to make?
What does it take to make it?
What materials do you have on hand?
What more is needed?

Mr. Wight offers software packages as a service evaluation. These are helpful to companies without the resources to develop their own inventory-control systems. He says, "The small companies are doing better than the giants."

DECISIONS ON INVENTORY

You can think of inventories as reservoirs of goods being held available for filling orders. At intervals, products are added to the reservoir as they come off the production lines. Goods are withdrawn from the reservoir as sales are made.

The decision that management faces is at what level goods should be allowed to accumulate, and to what level they should be permitted to fall — setting the upper and lower limits. These control limits are partially determined by the forecast sales volume. The more accurate the sales forecast, the more economical the management of the inventory.

This demonstrates again the importance of having all components of the business work together. The question of how much inventory to maintain is closely related to the regular flow of finished goods. It is also conditioned by promptness in handling goods by transportation agents, the time required to process orders, and the sales forecast. Inventory maintenance must be determined by types of products, not by total volume of sales.

Cost Considerations. There are three major categories of inventory cost factors: holding costs, costs due to shortages, and replenishment costs.

Holding costs include warehousing expenses, finance costs arising from capital investment in inventories, and losses resulting from capital invested in inventories. It also includes losses resulting from price changes due to market conditions, insurance on inventory, and losses resulting from spoilage or obsolescence. **Shortage costs** arise from failure to have sufficient goods on hand to fill orders at the time they are received. They include special clerical and handling costs, loss of income because of losing the sale, and, in extreme cases, loss of customers. **Replenishment costs** are usually tied closely to production costs — overtime required to make up shortages, loss of production time caused by equipment breakdowns, and so forth.

PRODUCTIVITY IN INDUSTRY

Production gives us the big picture—the total amount of goods and services being produced, and the resources needed to produce. *When we consider output in terms of inputs, we are talking about* PRODUCTIVITY—the efficiency of production:

$$\frac{\text{Output}}{\text{Inputs}} = \text{Productivity}$$

Productivity growth is a basic source of improvement in our standard of living. An increase in the efficiency of production results in more goods and services from the same input of production resources. This translates into a gain in national real income.

Advances in productivity depend in large measure on finding better ways to produce. Output per worker increased at an average rate of 3.2 percent a year from 1948 to 1966. For the next seven years, it increased at 2.3 percent per year. And from 1973 to 1981, it increased only 0.7 percent a year on the average. But *Fortune* magazine's research department estimates that for the decade of the 1980s, the annual growth rate should be about 2.3 percent.[2] Notice in Figure 9-7 the big increase in productivity from 1975 to 1977 following the 1974 recession. There was a drop in 1980 but an improvement since then.

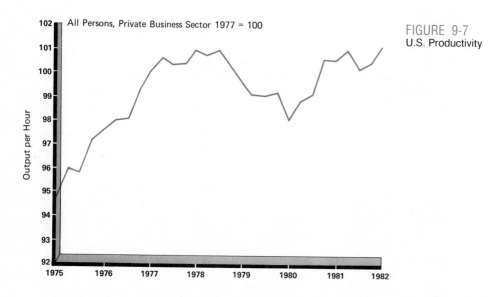

All Persons, Private Business Sector 1977 = 100

FIGURE 9-7
U.S. Productivity

Philip Caldwell, chairman of the Ford Motor Company, has emphasized the importance of productivity. He stated that increased productivity is one of the key factors in the future success of the auto industry in the United States.

___

[2] *Fortune,* June 28, 1982, p. 25.

TOTAL-FACTOR PRODUCTIVITY

We are most familiar with labor productivity—measured as the output per worker per hour. But to see the total view of how well the company is moving, we must consider total-factor productivity. This means we must consider the capital input as well as labor.

Total-factor productivity in the United States has risen constantly since World War II. However, the rate of increase has recently slowed down. The causes for this are complex, but some probable explanations include:

1. The increase in the amount of capital needed for better safety and pollution abatement
2. Less-than-full-employment conditions during the past decade
3. A shift in the labor-force mix, with a higher percentage of women, who, on the average, have less experience than their male counterparts
4. Failure of the capital-formation process that allows business to invest in new plants and equipment

From 1948 to 1980, total-factor productivity increased by an average 2.3 percent per year. Labor productivity increased by an average of 3.0 percent, but capital productivity increased by an average of only 1.0 percent per year. (See Figure 9-8.)

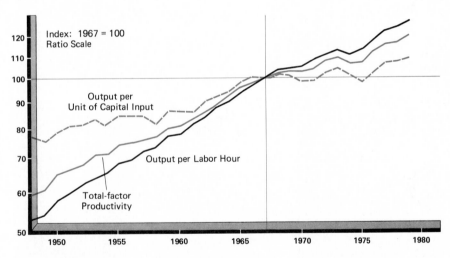

FIGURE 9-8

Productivity in the private domestic business economy.
(Source: The Conference Board.)

PRODUCTIVITY IN THE SERVICES AREA

More attention is currently being given to increasing productivity in the service area. Much of this is related to the use of computers. Hundreds of computers (and thousands of people) now work together. Files can be exchanged with simple computer codes. This gives executives access to "electronic mailboxes," news wires, stock quotations, calendars, and other types of business data. Electronic mail services have made possible the sending of electronic mail to ten locations more cheaply than sending a telegram to a single site.

Other industrialized nations are now improving their productivity more than is the United States. The progress they have made during the past two decades is shown in Figure 9-9.

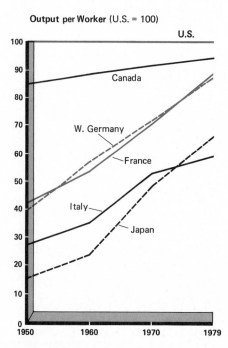

Output per Worker (U.S. = 100)

FIGURE 9-9

Output of selected industrialized nations.

Although America continues to produce more goods and services per employed worker than any other nation, other countries are steadily narrowing the gap. (Source: U.S. Department of Labor.)

RESEARCH AND DEVELOPMENT

Many of America's heroes have been inventors. Technical change accounts for more than half of the U.S. economic growth. Industry's R&D was about $44 billion in 1983[3]; the federal government spent about $40 billion on R&D that year. Total expenditures for R&D are expected to exceed $85 billion in 1985.

---

[3] This figure includes $20 billion supplied by the federal government.

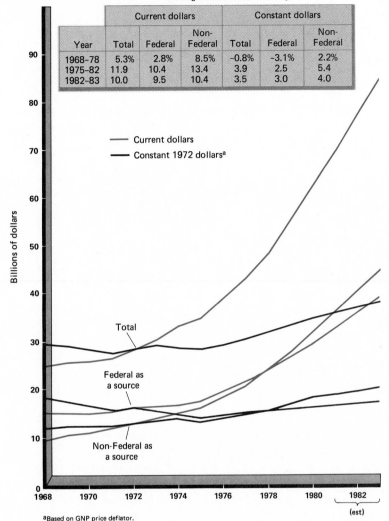

Average annual rates of change

	Current dollars			Constant dollars		
Year	Total	Federal	Non-Federal	Total	Federal	Non-Federal
1968–78	5.3%	2.8%	8.5%	–0.8%	–3.1%	2.2%
1975–82	11.9	10.4	13.4	3.9	2.5	5.4
1982–83	10.0	9.5	10.4	3.5	3.0	4.0

— Current dollars
— Constant 1972 dollars[a]

Billions of dollars

Total

Federal as a source

Non-Federal as a source

aBased on GNP price deflator.

1968 1970 1972 1974 1976 1978 1980 1982
(est)

FIGURE 9-10
National Research and Development
Expenditures.
(Source: National Science Foundation.)

In the past, government research expenditures were devoted largely to defense efforts. But in recent years, there has been a shift toward creating marketable products for civilians. It is thought by many that whereas the private sector doesn't spend enough for commercial R&D, the government sector doesn't handle R&D well.

Most of the increase in productivity comes either directly or indirectly from research. RESEARCH is defined by the National Science Foundation as *original investigation aimed at discovering new scientific knowledge.* **Basic research** is research aimed at increasing knowledge. **Applied research** is research aimed at finding a practical use for an idea.

DEVELOPMENT is *the attempt to use new knowledge in the production of useful devices or processes.*

About one-tenth of research and development spending is for **basic research,** and about one-fourth is for **applied research.** Almost two-thirds is spent for **development.** More than one-half the money spent for R&D is

EDWARD GRAHAM JEFFERSON

During Edward G. Jefferson's 30-year Du Pont career, he has worked at plants to improve products and processes; in research to translate new discoveries to commercial reality; and in divisional, departmental, and corporate management to help lead and build the business.

"I think people who take themselves too seriously tend not to take others seriously enough," says Jefferson. "A sense of humor is essential if you are to overcome setbacks."

Mr. Jefferson joined Du Pont in 1951 at the Belle Works, West Virginia. He served in supervisory positions at Belle and at the Washington Works, Parkersburg, West Virginia, before transfer to Wilmington in 1958. In 1973, he was appointed a director, senior vice-president, and member of the executive committee. He was named president and chief operating officer on January 1, 1980, and became chairman and chief executive officer on May 1, 1981.

Mr. Jefferson was born in 1921 in London. He holds a doctor's degree from King's College, University of London, where he was awarded the Samuel Smiles Prize for Chemistry. He is a member of the Policy Committee of the Business Roundtable, the Conference Board, the Business Council, the American Institute of Chemical Engineers, and a member of the Directors of Industrial Research.

Mr. Jefferson is a member of the boards of The Seagram Co. Ltd., Chemical Bank, the Diamond State Telephone Company, and the National Action Council for Minorities in Engineering.

He is married to the former Naomi Nale Love of Charleston, West Virginia, and they have three sons.

supplied by the federal government. Most R&D is performed by university staffs and by scientists and engineers in private industry. The way in which government research funds are distributed is shown in Figure 9-11.

R&D is vital in the science- and technology-oriented industries, such as drugs, chemicals, electronics, and aerospace. Intensive competition often forces consumer-goods companies, such as food packagers, soap makers, and toy manufacturers, to create a flow of new products that rely on discoveries in the other industries. At the opposite pole, retailers largely depend on their suppliers to develop new products.

The dollar amounts spent for research and development have increased. But recently research efforts in the United States have lagged behind

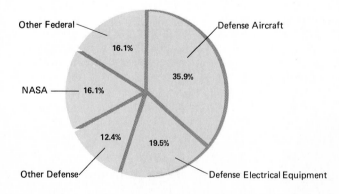

FIGURE 9-11
Federal Funding of Research and Development.
(Source: The Conference Board.)

the work being done in other countries. The number of patents has leveled off at about 100,000 a year and the percentage granted to people in foreign nations has increased. In a recent year, for example, 37 percent of the U.S. patents granted went to applicants in other countries. And the percentage of GNP being spent for R&D has dropped significantly. See Figure 9-12.

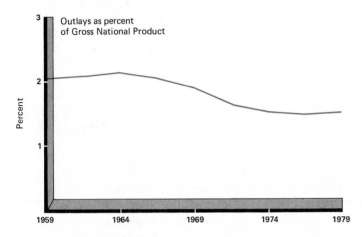

FIGURE 9-12
U.S. Industrial Research and Development Spending.
(Source: National Science Foundation.)

PRODUCT RESEARCH Product research is largely concerned with the improvement of present products and the development of new ones. It is for the most part experimental research carried on in research laboratories. Most large businesses maintain research labs devoted to the discovery, development, and testing of new materials and products.

A considerable proportion of the funds supplied by the federal government has been channeled into research concerned with the military and space programs. The government contributes heavily to experimentation in the biological and physical sciences and in aeronautics, in both state and private universities. It also subsidizes most of the research and development done by private businesses in the aircraft and electronics industries.

Some of the results of research that have increased the productivity of industry are these:

1. The visual phone system now in use in many large cities. Meetings and conferences are conducted by picturephone—directors' meetings, sales presentations, job interviews.
2. Fiber optics enable 2,700 computers to talk to each other at the same time. Hairlike glass fibers carry messages on a beam of light. A single optical fiber can carry 150 million bits a second in one direction. Fiber optics will undoubtedly be the dominant cable system for telecommunications by the year 2000.[4]
3. Tiny electronic chips in computers. A small chip that can be held in one's fingertips can hold thousands of pieces of information.
4. General Electric has developed energy-saving controllers for AC electric motors. As a result, controllers that once cost several hundred dollars today cost $100 or less.

---

[4] Fiber optics may very well be one of the next growth industries. The market for fiber optics systems in the U.S. was only $10 million in 1977. It is estimated by Predicasts, Inc., that this market will soon reach $150 million and will be $1 billion by 1990.

A packaging innovation is paper bottles that don't need refrigeration. The aseptic container is being used as a replacement for beverage cans and bottles. It is a foil-lined paperboard carton, which is less costly than glass and aluminum. Called Tetra Pak, it was developed in Sweden. Beverages packaged in it keep up to six months without refrigeration. And Kraft has been packaging its A La Carte line of food products in its "retort" pouch for three years. Products packed in retort bags are said to equal frozen goods in freshness and taste.

BUSINESS USES THE SPACE SHUTTLE

For American business, the space shuttle is very significant. There is a long waiting list of would-be users. As of March 1982, business firms had already purchased all available commercial cargo space through 1987.

The first commercial use of the shuttle was for launching satellites for use in long-range communication. NASA predicts that as many as 100 communication satellites will be needed by the year 2000. They would carry a million voice circuits or 1,000 TV channels.

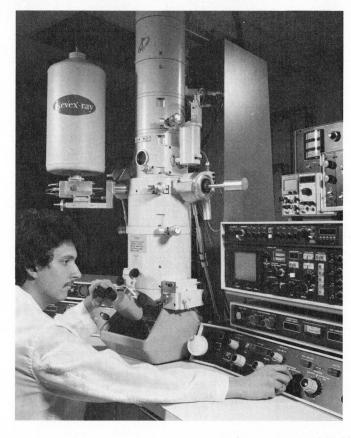

FIGURE 9-13
This analytical electron microscope at Eastman Kodak Company tells scientists not only what a particle looks like, but also what it is made of. (Courtesy, Eastman Kodak Company.)

A second important orbital business is the production and processing of high-purity chemicals and alloys. Materials that are impossible to produce on earth may be manufactured in the zero-gravity environment. Other uses of the space industry include:

Space stations that may be used for research and engineering development, or for making repairs to satellites
Solar-power stations to produce electricity
Monitoring of weather conditions

All this will stimulate construction projects here on earth to produce and maintain space equipment. NASA estimates that 550 workers would be needed to build a solar satellite. Each satellite would require 100,000 tons of materials. It has been estimated that by the year 2000, business in space could reach the sum of $30 billion.

SHIFT TO AN INFORMATION – SERVICE ECONOMY

Much is written in current periodicals about agriculture, manufacturing, and energy. Much less is written about the information and service businesses. However, in terms of jobs and the gross national product, the United States has become an information–service economy. By 1956, more people were employed in white-collar jobs than in blue-collar jobs. Since then, manufacturing employment has levelled off while employment in the information and service sectors has increased.

John Naisbitt, a social forecaster, says that the United States has become an information society. This promises major changes for basic industries, growth areas, and trade. He says that currently information accounts for 62 percent of the workforce. This includes people who create information, process information, or distribute it, that is, programmers, secretaries, accountants, lawyers, brokers, and people in insurance, banks, education, and government.

It is estimated that 3 million of the 3.6 million increase in total manufacturing jobs from 1948 to 1978 were nonproduction workers. The chairman of American Express, defines services so as to include financial institutions, hotels, restaurants, airlines, railroads, stockbrokers, lawyers, doctors, advertising, real estate, engineering, retailing, education, and all levels of government. He also includes the exploding information industries: data processing,

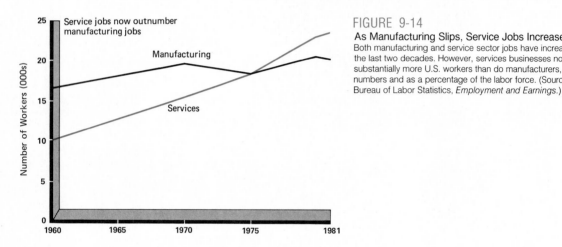

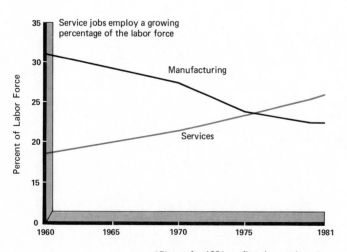

FIGURE 9-14

As Manufacturing Slips, Service Jobs Increase.
Both manufacturing and service sector jobs have increased over the last two decades. However, services businesses now employ substantially more U.S. workers than do manufacturers, both in real numbers and as a percentage of the labor force. (Source: U.S. Bureau of Labor Statistics, *Employment and Earnings*.)

*Figures for 1981 are first six months only

software development, news gathering, publishing, broadcasting, and communications. Using this broad definition means that seven out of ten Americans have jobs in services.

As a nation, we have been slow to adjust to this transition to being an information-service economy. **But the shift is real and represents one of the megatrends in America today.**

SUMMARY OF KEY CONCEPTS

Agriculture is big business. It is most basic to the American economy.

The productivity rate for agricultural production is high when compared to manufacturing.

Forestry, mining, and fishing also provide basic resources for manufacturing.

Manufacturing provides employment for more people than any other segment of the U.S. business system except trade.

Diversification is an important characteristic of American business. Diversification helps to overcome cyclical fluctuations for manufacturing operations. It gives stability to overall company operations.

Robots hold the key to low-cost manufacturing operations. It is anticipated that robots will in time replace from one-half to two-thirds of the present factory workforce.

Logistics operations give *time and place utility* to goods. An orderly flow of materials is essential for efficient production.

The current trend in inventory management is material-requirements planning. The idea is not to maintain large stocks in storage but to have materials arrive as needed.

Advances in productivity depend largely on finding better ways to produce. The best index of productivity considers the capital input as well as labor. This is called *total-factor productivity*.

The U.S. economy is rapidly becoming a service economy. Services provide employment for many more people than does manufacturing.

BUSINESS TERMS

You should be able to match these business terms with the statements that follow:

a. DEVELOPMENT
b. DIVERSIFICATION
c. FORM UTILITY
d. HOLDING COSTS
e. INVENTORY CONTROL
f. LOGISTICS
g. MANUFACTURING
h. NEW PRODUCT
i. PRODUCTIVITY
j. RESEARCH
k. ROBOT
l. SHORTAGE COSTS

1. The process of using raw materials, labor, and machinery to produce finished products
2. What is given to materials by converting them into useful products
3. A product that makes a major improvement in a present function
4. The making or offering of several different kinds of products or services
5. A reprogrammable, multifunctional, manipulative machine
6. A management plan for providing an orderly flow of materials and finished goods
7. Managing goods and supplies on hand
8. Inventory costs resulting from storage and warehouse expenses
9. Output measured in terms of input
10. Original investigation aimed at discovering new scientific knowledge
11. The attempt to use new knowledge in the production of useful devices

1. What do we mean when we say that manufacturing *adds value* to raw materials?
2. When is a product considered to be a "new" product? Why are new products so important in production?
3. Why the new emphasis on total-factor productivity?
4. Which comes first, research or development? How are they related?
5. What do we mean when we say that the United States has become a service economy?

1. Why is agriculture so important to American production?
2. Why is manufacturing so important to American business? (Consider more than the goods produced and people employed.)
3. Why has diversification become so important in U.S. industry?
4. The availability of good-quality imports at a fair price held back the robot revolution in this country. Why did American business change and finally decide to "join them," so to speak?
5. How are research and productivity related?

BUSINESS CASES

9-1

PROBLEMS IN LOGISTICS

The Hartford Company operates a large public distribution center. During the past twelve months, a number of problems have become serious and resulted in reduced productivity. Area heads blame the workers and one another. The workers complain of a lack of coordination and inadequate supervision. They say that merchandise is unnecessarily being moved to new locations. They are not always sure to which "boss" they are accountable. The superintendent seems to have lost control over the area heads. Morale is low, and employees who have been with the company for many years are threatening to quit. The absentee owners, Elton and Everett Hartford, are considering several alternatives:

a. Appoint a committee of three area heads to make an analysis of the situation and recommend changes.
b. Hire a new superintendent and give him full control but keep the present area heads.
c. Employ an outside consultant.

What do you see as the strengths and/or weaknesses of each plan?

9-2

CONTROL IN RECEIVING DEPARTMENT

The Sisk Company assembles hi-fi record players, radios, and television sets for "private-brand" retailers. An audit of the company books revealed that payment had been made for several dozen expensive cabinets that apparently had never been received.

There were three men who worked for Sisk in purchasing and receiving, and their functions overlapped and duplicated one another. Each man initiated purchasing requisitions and checked receiving reports, approving them for payment. It was discovered that one of these men had been working with an outside accomplice, ordering cabinets and okaying payment for them when they had never been received by the Sisk Company.

1. How could you determine which of the three men was the guilty party?
2. How could the purchasing and receiving procedures be reorganized to eliminate and make impossible the described practice?

PART 3

CAREERS IN PERSONNEL/INDUSTRIAL RELATIONS AND PRODUCTION/OPERATIONS MANAGEMENT

PAIR Personnel and Industrial Relations (PAIR) is an area that has emerged as a professional career field only in the last ten years. Previously, many personnel jobs were filled by people who "liked people" or who were in the way but too young to retire.

Government regulation and a growing understanding of how much employees *really* cost have increased the importance and visibility of those professionals who deal with the "people problems" in organizations.

Personnel specialists will be in demand during the 1980s, yet personnel is often not an entry-level position. That leaves the person who wants a career in personnel/industrial relations with the problem of where to get experience.

Courses that provide the kind of educational background necessary for a career in personnel include these:

General Education: English, Math, Statistics, Psychology, Social Sciences

Business Core: Accounting, Finance, Computer Science, Marketing, Economics, Business Law

Specialization Courses: Personnel, Labor Law, Collective Bargaining, Organizational Behavior, Wage and Salary, Personnel Planning, Selection and Placement, Training and Development, Industrial Psychology, Testing and Test Validation

The following are illustrative job areas in PAIR:

Personnel Director	Safety Coordinator
Director of Industrial Relations	Employee Relations Counselor
Employment Manager	Corporate Ombudsman
Compensation Analyst	EEO Compliance Manager
Benefits Coordinator	Training Director
Job Analyst	Manager of Organization Development
Personnel Interviewer	Pension Analyst
Personnel Research Analyst	Employee Services Coordinator
Labor Relations Specialist	Testing Consultant

POM Production/Operations Management (POM) is another career field with great potential as an occupation. POM people, if in a line management job, are usually directly involved in getting production out. They work with materials, labor, costs, equipment, information, and time.

Training for such positions includes many courses offered in business schools and, in some cases, even engineering courses:

General Education: Math, Statistics, Computer Science, Physics, Chemistry, English

Business Core: Accounting, Finance, Management, Marketing, Economics

Specialization Courses: Cost Accounting, Production/Operations Management, Computer Systems, Management Information Systems, Simulation, Inventory Control, Production Planning, Materials Management, Purchasing, Work Measurement, Logistics, Management Science

Jobs in the POM area include the following:

Materials Manager	Project Manager
Purchasing Manager	Scheduler/Expediter
Systems Analyst	MRP Manager
Production Control Manager	Inventory Planning Manager
Vice-President, Manufacturing	Industrial Engineer
Production Superintendent	Productivity Manager

MARKETING

Neither of the King brothers had special expertise in marketing. This was one of the major reasons for bringing Juan Perez in as the third partner. His suggestion was to use his retail store as a mall outlet location to sell factory rejects. This proved to be a good idea, but other marketing problems soon surfaced.

At first, King Clothiers sold its entire production to one wholesaler, Michael Cohen. Cohen operated a group of retail stores in the Midwest. But as business slumped, his orders fell off, and King Clothiers had to close for three weeks. All employees were asked to take their vacations at the same time. Obviously, the need was for more than one customer. Cohen urged them to find other buyers and this they did.

Production and marketing are greatly interrelated, as you will see. Do you market what you produce, or do you produce what you can market? You do both, and these interrelationships are discussed in the chapters that follow.

PART

4

In The News
Sun-Diamond — A Market Co-op Prospers

Sun-Diamond Growers of California is a marketing cooperative with 6,000 members. Members grow Sun-Maid raisins, Diamond walnuts, Valley figs, and Sunsweet prunes, and the co-op markets them. Sunsweet and Diamond became aligned in 1974, and the other growers joined in 1980. Since the four have been aligned together, proceeds to members have increased by 5 percent. And this has occurred while world markets have been depressed during a recession. Sun-Diamond's strategy is to place the emphasis on marketing by creating brand identity. It is capitalizing on the fact that its brand names are well known throughout the country. It plans to test-market pure fruit-juice blends to compete with artificially flavored drinks. Sun-Diamond is exploring a new direction by licensing its brand names. It has joined with several bakeries to produce Sun-Maid raisin bread and English muffins. It is licensing dairies to produce Sun-Maid raisin and Diamond walnut ice cream. It hopes also to complete similar arrangements for Sunsweet prune yogurt. Sun-Diamond's domestic market accounts for 70 percent of sales, and overseas markets for 30 percent. Sun-Diamond's management feels that marketing is the key to the future of cooperatives.

The Marketing Process

study objectives

WHEN YOU HAVE FINISHED READING THIS CHAPTER, YOU SHOULD BE ABLE TO:

1. Show how marketing gives *utility* to goods and services
2. Describe the way marketing contributes to the U.S. economy
3. Distinguish between marketing activities and marketing functions
4. Identify the four ingredients that make up the *marketing mix*
5. Explain how public policy values affect the marketing system
6. Justify the role of research in marketing

10

Marketing is so basic that it cannot be considered a separate function.

Peter Drucker
Management Consultant

R ed Motley made famous the statement, "Nothing happens until somebody sells something." There is much truth to that. We could also turn that idea around—there is no demand for a product until someone buys something.

How are consumer needs for goods satisfied? The marketing process distributes and sells new products. They are brought to your attention through another phase of marketing—advertising. And you, together with others, create the demand for these goods. Producers learn about what you want through still another phase of marketing—research. And product engineers design goods to satisfy people's wants. When we buy a good, we vote in the marketplace for that good.

This chapter introduces the role of marketing in our economy. Emphasis is given to marketing functions that involve a variety of activities. The directing and integrating of these functions and activities are done by marketing managers.

MARKETING IN OUR ECONOMY

Marketing activity is all around us. Goods flow from forests, farms, and factories to marketing units. You are perhaps most familiar with retail outlets such as the grocery or department store. But behind them are the wholesalers, agents, brokers, warehouses, advertisers, and transporters. Goods are continually on the move to meet people's needs and wants. Marketing is an important and integral part of our economic system.

DEFINITION OF MARKETING

The term MARKETING is defined by the American Marketing Association as *the performance of business activities that direct the flow of goods and services from producer to consumer or user.* This definition shows marketing as encompassing such activities as merchandising, promotion, pricing, selling, and transportation (see Figure 10-1).

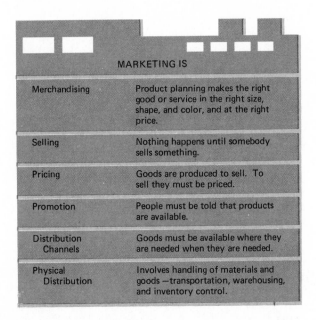

MARKETING IS	
Merchandising	Product planning makes the right good or service in the right size, shape, and color, and at the right price.
Selling	Nothing happens until somebody sells something.
Pricing	Goods are produced to sell. To sell they must be priced.
Promotion	People must be told that products are available.
Distribution Channels	Goods must be available where they are needed when they are needed.
Physical Distribution	Involves handling of materials and goods —transportation, warehousing, and inventory control.

FIGURE 10-1
Marketing

To have a **market,** there must be a buyer and a seller, a product or service, an agreed-upon price, and an exchange. To the economist, the market for a specific good is the sum of all transactions between buyers and sellers of that good at any given time.

Buyer

$725

Sound-Stereo equipment

Seller

FIGURE 10-2
What Constitutes a Market?

What has been labeled "the marketing concept" has changed over the years. In the early days of business in America, it was **product-oriented.** The idea was to produce as many goods as possible, because the market was limitless.

Following the Civil War, many businesses became very large. The modern era of mass production developed around the turn of the twentieth century and situations of excess supply developed. So some firms turned to increased advertising, more personal selling, and broader distribution. The marketing philosophy shifted from a product orientation to a **sales orientation.** It brings the marketing manager in at the beginning of the production cycle.

After World War II, business in the United States prospered. Managers began to see the need to work with their customers, and a new marketing concept developed. This new **MARKETING CONCEPT** has three components:

1. A customer orientation
2. A profit orientation
3. Coordination and integration of marketing activities

CUSTOMER ORIENTATION

When buying a car, why are we able to choose from so many models and colors? Because the producer is trying to give customers what they want and will buy. Why did the U.S. car makers shift their production emphasis during the late 1970s to smaller cars? Because customer demand was for smaller cars that used less gasoline. **Customer orientation** means letting customers' wants guide the firm's production activities. For example, consider "convenience foods." With both husband and wife working in so many families, convenience foods is a growth industry. Most fast-food outlets have broadened their offerings in response to customer wants. McDonald's added fish, then chicken to the menu. Kentucky Fried Chicken added fish and hamburgers. Wendy's added the taco salad, a salad bar, and chicken.

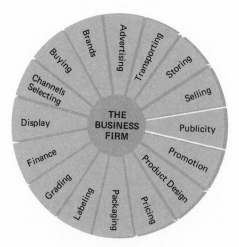

FIGURE 10-3
Marketing Activities

EDWIN TAYLOR

It's not easy to build a successful small business, but Ed Taylor and his wife, Fran (the former Frances McLaurin of Electric Mills, Miss.), have done it in just 20 years. They've solved a lot of problems and helped a lot of people along the way.

When Ed decided to go out on his own after some experience with business products, he started by selling supplies from his home. Fran kept the books and answered the telephone. Now they own — with their children — Taylor Office Supply in Baton Rouge, La., with two buildings, 25 employees, and a reputation for being responsive to customer needs.

Ed says:

> If you tell a customer you're going to do something, you better *do* it. Free enterprise is what makes this country work. We had opportunities to view the system in China and Russia — long lines for meager food supplies and goods, and someone else making all the decisions. We are thankful to have been born in America. The opportunity we had in 1963 is still available to anyone who is willing to work hard and make some sacrifices.

The same vitality and energy that Ed brings to his business he brings to community activities and personal interests. He works with the Baton Rouge Little Theatre, Kiwanis, and the Chamber of Commerce.

Fran and Ed share an avid interest in travel. They have been in every state of the Union, Europe, China, and Russia.

PROFIT ORIENTATION The chief goal of most business concerns is to make a profit. Profits enable a firm to grow and to increase the dividend return to owners. But if a firm is to make a profit, it must also meet the needs of society. It must provide a quality product and a safe product. Profit is at least in part a reward for being customer-oriented.

INTEGRATION OF MARKETING ACTIVITIES There are many types of marketing activities. You are familiar with advertising, packaging, display, and selling. But there are many more, as enumerated in Figure 10-3. These activities must be woven together if a company is to be successful with its marketing.

THE CONSUMER AND MARKETING

Our earlier definition of marketing emphasized the role of the consumer. The saying, "The customer is king," suggests that the consumer is the starting place in the marketing process. The Food Marketing Institute is on record as stating that "business tries to strike a fair balance between profits and the interests of the public."

The Bureau of Labor Statistics predicts an increase in total consumer spending of 48 percent between 1980 and 1990. Spending for durables will increase by 64 percent, for nondurables by 37 percent, and for services by 51 percent. The predicted percentage of growth during the decade for selected items is shown in Table 10-1.

TABLE 10-1
Growth in Consumer Spending in the 1980s (in constant dollars)

	PERCENTAGE GROWTH DURING THE DECADE
Personal Consumption Expenditures:	48
Durables	64
Nondurables	37
Services	51
Selected Expenditures:	
Food	28
Clothing	47
Housing	49
Motor vehicles/parts	56
Furniture & household equipment	70
Drugs	55
Insurance	50
Air transportation	70
Jewelry & silverware	63
Photographic equipment & supplies	76

SOURCE: Bureau of Labor Statistics.

CONSUMERISM Consumerism became a force in the 1960s and today is an important factor for most marketers. It seeks to increase the rights of consumers in relation to sellers. Consumerism's primary goals are:

1. To obtain complete truth in advertising
2. To ensure that products perform as advertised, are safe, and do not harm the physical environment
3. To inform and protect consumers from business malpractice

President John F. Kennedy, in a special message to Congress, asked for strong action to assist consumers. He listed four rights of consumers that he believed needed protection: the right to safety, the right to a choice, the right to know, and the right to be heard. These rights were later supported by Presidents Lyndon Johnson and Richard Nixon. A fifth right, the right to full value, might very well be added. Thus, a consumer bill of rights would contain the following:

1. *The Right to Safety:* The consumer has a right to be protected from dangerous products that might cause injury or illness, as well as from the thoughtless actions of other consumers.
2. *The Right to a Choice:* The consumer has the right to be able to select products from a range of alternatives offered by competing firms.

3. *The Right to Know:* The consumer must have access to readily available, relevant, and accurate information to use in making purchase decisions.
4. *The Right to Be Heard:* The consumer must be able to obtain redress for injuries or damages suffered and have someone respond to legitimate complaints about abuses taking place in the market.
5. *The Right to Value:* The consumer has a right to expect a product to perform as advertised and meet the expectations that were created so that the consumer is getting full value for the money spent.

Consumerism is an example of the **major trend in this country from representative democracy to participatory democracy.** It illustrates the principle that power should flow from the people upward, rather than from the government downward. Consumerism holds that business is responsible for providing quality goods and observing fair business practices.

PRODUCT UTILITY   The term UTILITY *refers to the want-fulfillment power of a good or service.* We saw earlier that the manufacturer gives "form" utility to raw materials. Marketing gives "time" and "place" utility to finished goods.

TIME UTILITY means *a product is available when the consumer wants it.* For example, Detroit initially did *not* make small cars when consumers wanted fuel economy. The Japanese did, and the foreign-car share of the American market jumped to more than 30 percent. It is through research that marketers learn about future consumer needs and wants. PLACE UTILITY is created by *having a product where it is wanted, when it is wanted.* For example, when the demand for oil-drilling rigs is in Western Wyoming but most of the available rigs are in Oklahoma, there is little place utility.

CLASSIFICATION OF CONSUMER GOODS   Products may be classified according to consumer perception and behavior. Consumer goods are usually classified as convenience, shopping, and specialty goods. **It is the consumers' willingness to shop, not the good itself, that determines its classification.**

CONVENIENCE GOODS are *low-priced and easily available.* They can be readily purchased in nearby retail stores. Groceries, drugs, soft drinks, and cigarettes are classed as convenience goods. SHOPPING GOODS *are bought only after comparisons of price, quality, and style*—in other words, after shopping for them. Clothing, jewelry, and furniture are examples of shopping goods. SPECIALTY GOODS *are specific items that one wants.* If people are willing to spend considerable time and money in order to find a particular brand or style, it can be considered a specialty good. Cars, boots, designer dresses, stereo systems, and fine cameras are examples of specialty goods. (See Figure 10-4.)

Stereo systems for cars have blossomed into a lucrative market. Amplifiers, tape decks, speakers, and FM receivers to replace factory-installed units are all in great demand. Both teenagers and those in the 25- to 44-age group are heavy buyers. These expensive specialty systems, often $300 to $1,500, are expected to increase in sales volume, and the cost may come down as the technology improves. They are classified as specialty items because many of the customers know exactly what they want in a stereo system and are willing to pay whatever it takes to obtain it.

FIGURE 10-4
Consumers will shop carefully for a fine camera. (Photo by Larry Mulvehill, Photo Researchers, Inc.)

The lower the family income, the larger the percentage of income that is spent on necessities. The higher the family income, the larger the percentage that can be spent for specialty goods, leisure activities, vacations, and education. The amount of this "discretionary income" available helps determine what kinds of goods and services will be chosen.

WHY GIVE GOOD SERVICE TO CUSTOMERS?

Customers bring to the merchandiser needs and wants. We are paid to serve them.

Customers' goodwill is our most valuable asset. It must be earned or deserved.

Customers' impressions of us and our businesses are determined by our attitudes and the quality of service we give.

Customers' satisfaction is the source of repeat business, the source of future profits.

Customers pay the bills. If they are not satisfied, where are our paychecks coming from?

Customers' concerns make of us better employees.

Anonymous

THE MARKETING OF BUSINESS AND INDUSTRIAL GOODS

In addition to consumer goods, there is a large market for business and industrial goods. Industrial goods make up a very broad group of products. When one buys a computer for *home use*, this is part of the consumer market. But when a person buys a computer for *store or factory use*, this is part of the industrial market.

INDUSTRIAL GOODS are *materials or products bought for use in making other goods or for resale.* The number of industrial buyers, excluding the government, exceeds 12 million. Their annual purchases are far greater than the consumer market. The industrial market includes all types of tools, machinery, and equipment as well as raw materials. Also, goods are often included in another product and resold many times.

Raw materials are industrial goods. Cotton boll; textiles; textile warehouse. (Photos by Andree Abecassis, Gary Gladstone, and Michael Melford, all of the Image Bank.)

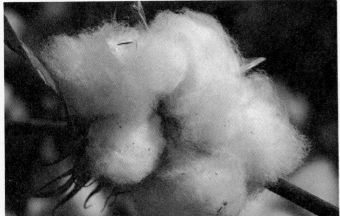

CLASSIFICATION OF INDUSTRIAL GOODS

All types of businesses buy industrial goods. Factories, farmers, construction contractors, and mining companies buy a wide assortment of industrial goods. Industrial goods include:

1. Raw materials
2. Industrial equipment and machinery
3. Industrial supplies
4. Tools and other equipment
5. Processed materials
6. Parts and subassemblies

Because there is such a wide variety of industrial goods, they are marketed in many different ways. The principal distribution channels used are described in Chapter 13.[1]

THE ECONOMIC CONTRIBUTIONS OF MARKETING

Beginning in 1981, wholesale and retail trade combined provided employment for more people than any other segment of business. With constant changes in society, it is not surprising that marketing has changed considerably over time. We discuss the most important changes.

THE INCENTIVE TO BUY

Marketing is really a twentieth-century development. During the nineteenth century, many of the goods manufactured were made to order. Marketing consisted of little more than delivering the goods produced. But as manufacturing capabilities increased, more goods were produced *before* there were definite orders for them. Eventually, the quantity of manufactured goods being produced exceeded the demand for them. Mass-production techniques were forcing the development of mass-marketing procedures. This required advertising to sell the goods. Ours is still generally an economy of abundance, needing a marketing system that motivates people to become buyers.

IMPORTANCE OF SERVICES

Marketing is often viewed in connection with physical products rather than selling services. However, today services account for more than half the consumer dollar. So marketing is applied to intangibles such as services as well as to products.

Holiday Inns, for example, have combined a standardized offering with locations on heavily traveled routes and has become a giant international firm based on services. At the same time, Motel 6 and Days Inn have emphasized economy prices to achieve a profitable share of the motel market. Manpower temporary-help agencies are successful service companies because of distinctive marketing programs. Effective marketing of services involves everything that product marketing involves.

THE VALUE-ADDED CONCEPT

More than half the sales price of a product or service pays for the marketing activities required to provide the customer with a finished offering. This was once referred to as the **cost of marketing.** The current approach is to consider this as the VALUE ADDED to the offering *by performing marketing activities.*

---

[1] Marketing channels for both industrial goods and consumer goods are illustrated in Chapter 13.

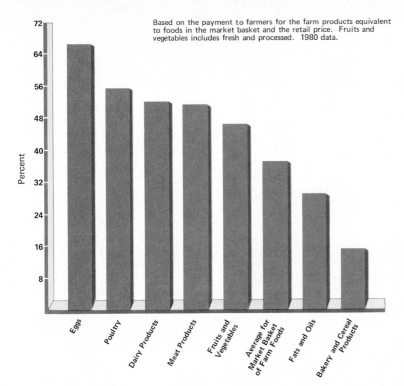

Based on the payment to farmers for the farm products equivalent to foods in the market basket and the retail price. Fruits and vegetables includes fresh and processed. 1980 data.

FIGURE 10-5
Farm Share of Retail Food Prices

We have already seen that raw materials are enhanced in value by being processed. But a finished product or service has little value until it is in the possession of the person who can use it. Thus, the money spent in marketing goods adds to their value.

The "cost of marketing" varies with the product or service involved. For example, of the farm-food dollar, about 60 cents is for marketing. But cost varies within a given product group. As shown in Figure 10-5, about 60 cents is the farmer's share for poultry and eggs, and only about 15 cents for grains (bakery and cereal products). This same variation occurs in other categories of consumer products. The different components of the cost of marketing farm-food products is shown in Figure 10-6.

FIGURE 10-6
Components of the Farm-Food Marketing Bill

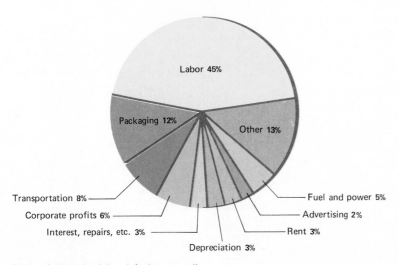

Based on foods marketed through foodstores as well as away-from-home eating places. Other includes promotions, professional services, property taxes, local hired transportation, and insurance. Preliminary 1980 data.

Teenagers are an impressive buying power. (Photo by Bob Rashid, CLICK/Chicago.)

TEEN-AGE MARKETS

The number of teens is expected to number 23 million in 1990. As a group, they have impressive buying power. Three out of five have either part-time or full-time work. The Simmons Market Research Bureau estimates the weekly earnings of U.S. teens to be $600 million. In addition, four out of ten receive allowances, amounting to $80 million a week. This means that teens' market clout totals $35 billion a year. And most of this money is disposable income.

MARKETING FUNCTIONS

Six "universal marketing functions" together make up marketing:

1. Market analysis
2. Marketing communication
3. Market segmentation
4. Product differentiation
5. The valuation function
6. The exchange function

The role and relationships of these marketing functions in the movement of goods are shown in Figure 10-7. Each function is discussed in the paragraphs that follow.

MARKET ANALYSIS How does the law of supply and demand apply to marketing? Producers must know what consumers want. Consumers want producers to know what they want. This is what market analysis is all about: both buyers and sellers are participants. In MARKET ANALYSIS, *participants learn about the supply of, and demand for, a given product.*

Potential Market
Separations

Resolved Through
Marketing Functions

Become

Space
Time
Perception
Values
Ownership

Market Analysis
Marketing Communication
Product Differentiation
Market Segmentation
Valuation
Exchange

Mutually
Satisfying
Marketing
Relationships

FIGURE 10-7
Role of Marketing Functions. (From *Marketing Principles,* by William G. Nickels, 1978. Reprinted by permission of Prentice-Hall, Inc.)

It is through market analysis that sellers learn who and where their potential customers are. After locating them, sellers gather information about these potential customers that is pertinent to marketing their products. And buyers, through the shopping process, learn about potential sellers. They find out about the cost and quality of their goods. The total of all potential exchanges between buyers and sellers of a particular good or service, at any given time, makes up the **market** for it.

MARKETING COMMUNICATION

Communication is the adhesive that binds market forces together. Through market research, buyers can communicate their wants and what will satisfy those wants to sellers. Sellers then produce products that meet these expressed wants. Then, through advertising, sellers communicate back to potential buyers. COMMUNICATION refers to *the flow of information back and forth between buyers and sellers.* Without communication, the market system does not work very well to control prices. A good example of what can happen with better communication is the removal of the ban on advertising as it applies to lawyers.

Since information is the key to correct decision making, this makes communication a very important marketing function. The specific activities that help sellers carry out the communication function are advertising, sales promotion, personal selling, publicity, and research. The product itself communicates through its design and the attractiveness of its packaging.

MARKET SEGMENTATION

Can you think of any one product or service that would satisfy all customers? Probably not. Even a basic commodity such as salt requires different package sizes to satisfy various needs. No company has sufficient resources to satisfy all customers, manufacturers, wholesalers, retailers, and so forth. So a firm must select the specific market or markets on which it will concentrate its efforts. The term **market** is used here to refer to a group of people or organizations with unsatisfied needs or wants who have sufficient buying power.

To arrive at markets of a manageable size, a business firm must engage in MARKET SEGMENTATION. *This involves taking a total market and then dividing it into submarkets (or segments) that have similar characteristics.* The individuals or organizations within each segment are similar to one another in terms of their wants, buying power, and shopping patterns.

Common bases for market segmentation include geographical location and such personal factors as income, age, education, and family size. Rates of

The Marketing Process

259

usage and personality differences have also been tried as segmentation bases with some success. Some entrepreneurs have even segmented the consumer market into right-handed and left-handed people and have opened shops featuring specially designed left-handed products.

Makers of jogging or running shoes have really practiced market segmentation. The magazine *Runner's World* recently featured no fewer than 103 different kinds of training and racing shoes. For years, Adidas was the front-runner in the U.S. market, but U.S. manufacturers like Nike and New Balance have seen sales take off. Converse, which had two-thirds of the basketball market, decided that running was more than a fad and entered the market.

Nike has introduced a shoe that rides on a cushion of air chambers. The shoe took three years and more than a thousand designs to develop. It had to eliminate the problems of going flat and a pogo-stick effect before becoming successful. Further market segmentation is evident as American manufacturers turn to the European market, casual shoes with "the jogger look," and the whole geriatic market.

After market segmentation and an appraisal of the potential and competition within various segments, a company then selects one or more **target markets.** A market with one or more custom-tailored components is necessary for each target market. The four major marketing-mix components will be discussed at length in the chapters that follow.

Buyers also segment their markets. They select the few stores they wish to patronize. And they select the professional persons from whom they wish to purchase professional services.

PRODUCT DIFFERENTIATION

Producers want to make products that best meet the wants of buyers so that they can sell more. They want their goods to be different from those produced by others. Changes may be made in the product itself—design, quality, or appearance. Or they may be made in the packaging, pricing, or labeling. In time the buyers, too, may change what they are willing to pay to receive exactly what they want.

PRODUCT DIFFERENTIATION includes *all the ways that buyers and sellers adjust product offers.* This is done in order to bring about a product exchange. Product differentiation enables a seller to offer goods that differ from other goods so that they will be preferred over the others. Take instant coffee as an example. The Nestlé company positioned its TV advertising to establish the distinctive qualities of its freeze-dried Taster's Choice coffee. Procter & Gamble attempted to differentiate Folger's coffee crystals from those of other competing brands. The idea, in each case, was to emphasize those features that made each product different from competing products.

Proctor & Gamble says that it will market *a new product* only if it is superior in some important respect to competitive products already on the market. Unless a product has some point of superiority that appeals to the public, the company feels that it will be difficult for it to carve out a position in an established market.

THE VALUATION FUNCTION

Valuation occurs when buyers and sellers decide whether the benefits of an exchange are worth its costs. VALUATION refers to this *cost – benefit analysis of the marketing exchange.* It is a continual process, occurring both before the exchange and after. *Is that new car worth $15,000 to me?* Pricing a product is a part of valuation.

A major emphasis in marketing is to see that the benefits exceed the costs. (**Costs** here include such factors as time and effort as well as money.) **Values may be changed by either increasing the benefits or lowering the costs.**

From society's point of view, the value of the public's satisfaction should exceed both monetary and environmental costs. If the costs of an exchange appear to exceed the benefits, probably no exchange will occur.

THE EXCHANGE FUNCTION

The goal of all the marketing activity described above is the EXCHANGE— *a cash–benefits tradeoff.* The exchange function may include financing, storage, delivery, installation, and/or servicing. The exchange does not end the marketing process. Valuation and communication continue, and market analysis may be started again.

MANAGEMENT'S ROLE IN MARKETING

The task of marketing management is to design a "mix" of the marketing functions that is compatible with the buying environment. To do this, marketing people must plan their market strategies carefully.

MARKETING DECISION MAKING

Those in management who make basic marketing decisions are influenced by two groups of forces. The first group consists of forces within the business. They can be controlled to some extent. The second group consists of forces outside the business and beyond the influence of management. These two groups can be summarized as follows:

Inside, Controllable Forces	Outside Forces
Advertising programs	Competition from other firms
Brands management	Economic changes
Distribution channels	Government controls
Internal organization	Local legal regulations
Pricing	Sociological forces
Product patterns	Technological innovations
Shipping media	Variations in the business cycle

Kroger management gives us an example of marketing decision making. In 1983 Kroger surpassed Safeway to become number one in supermarket sales. What was the strategy that brought this to pass?

Every chain has a certain percentage of any given market. Whether this is 12 percent or 30 percent, it must advertise its products. It must also supply its stores from a warehouse. The higher the market share the lower these costs per customer. Kroger management had decided earlier to concentrate on areas where market share could be raised. The company abandoned areas where they were weak and strengthened areas where they were already strong. Kroger maintains a large fleet of trucks that delivers goods to retail outlets with great efficiency. Kroger also surveys 250,000 customers a year to learn what they want.

DETERMINING THE MARKETING MIX A profitable marketing program depends largely on the marketing mix. Choosing the marketing mix involves a combination of four strategies. The MARKETING MIX is defined as *a blending of strategies involving four ingredients: product, distribution channels, promotion, and price.* The offering

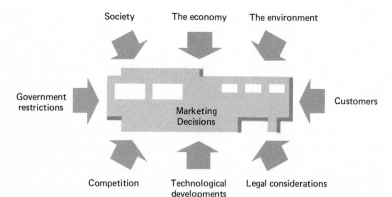

FIGURE 10-8
Uncontrollable Forces and Marketing Decisions

may consist of a product(s) or service(s), or both. (For example, Goodyear, Firestone, Sears, Wards, and K mart sell batteries and tires as well as automotive maintenance and repairs.) The four strategies in the marketing mix are illustrated in Figure 10-9.

A business may have more than one marketing mix to satisfy distinct groups of customers. Texas Instruments, for example, has one set of calculators and distribution arrangements for commercial customers and another for consumers. Also, a firm will periodically change its marketing mix because of changes in customers' needs or competition. **Marketing management is the process of adjusting each of these four factors to sell the product.**

FIGURE 10-9
Decision Strategies in the Marketing Mix

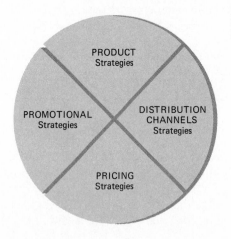

GOVERNMENT REGULATION OF MARKETING

Actions of the federal, state, and local governments all affect marketing operations, often very dramatically. For example, Congress repealed the "fair trade" laws in 1975. For almost forty years, these laws had permitted manufacturers to set minimum retail prices for their products under certain conditions. Detailed below are facts about one agency and law that in many ways typify the aggressive posture government bodies have assumed in their relations with marketers.

In 1914, Congress passed the Federal Trade Commission Act. The act states that "unfair methods of competition in commerce are unlawful." It also established a five-member commission with broad investigative and regulatory powers.

Since about 1965, the FTC has stepped up its investigations and regulatory activities. Some FTC activities are intended to maintain competition in industry. Others are intended to protect consumers in their dealings with marketers. Recently the FTC has been particularly concerned about deceptive advertising.

FTC actions have been directed at a wide range of industries and companies, including the cereal, automotive-repair, and funeral industries, as well as grocery retailers and automobile manufacturers. The commission has some "bite" to go with its "bark." It can issue quasi-legal trade regulations related to certain business practices. It issues cease-and-desist orders requiring that an offending activity be halted. It can also enter into consent orders with businesses, under which a firm agrees to halt a disputed practice. The role of the FTC is discussed further in Chapters 12 and 20.

CURRENT ISSUE

THE GOVERNMENT, THE CONSUMER, AND THE PRODUCER!

In our capitalistic economy, consumers, producers, and government all play important roles. Government encourages producers, but it also protects consumers against unfair practices by producers. Consumers want products of good quality that are safe to use. Confrontations occur between producers and consumers, and between producers and the government.

With which of the following statements do you agree, and with which do you disagree?

1. Safety is more important than high quality.
2. Government policy seems to favor producers over consumers.
3. Consumers must continually battle producers in order to protect their rights.
4. Government regulations favor consumers over producers.
5. Consumers need to work together to enhance their best interests.
6. Were it not for the government, producers would take advantage of consumers.

How can government best serve the interests of both consumers and producers?

The Robinson-Patman Act was passed in 1936. According to the act, it is illegal for manufacturers and wholesalers to grant different prices to different purchasers of goods of like quantity and quality if such discrimination would lessen competition to the seller's and buyer's benefit.

An interesting provision in the act is that the buyer, as well as the seller, can be found guilty if he or she *knowingly* accepts the discriminatory lower prices. However, the act does permit price differences resulting from attempts to meet competitors' prices, from fluctuating market prices, or the threatened obsolescence of a perishable product. As you can see, the Robinson-Patman Act is exceedingly complex. This has made compliance by businesses and consistent application by courts very difficult.

MARKET RESEARCH

What to produce is always a question facing manufacturing concerns. We have already learned that the consumer votes in the marketplace. If articles are not purchased, they are no longer made. How does a company decide what to produce? This decision is made through market research.

In past years, companies have been known better for product research than for market research. The Edsel was apparently as well made as other Ford Motor Company products. But the public did not accept it. Ford management failed to correctly assess the market before going into production with the Edsel. The Chrysler Corporation has long been known for the high quality of its engineering. But it has lagged in marketing knowhow. In fact, in the late 1970s, the entire U.S. auto industry failed to research adequately the public demand for smaller cars. Market research must be done before production is begun. This is being done today as never before in American manufacturing. Marketing research must precede and be coordinated with early product planning and development.

FIGURE 10-10
Sources of Marketing Information

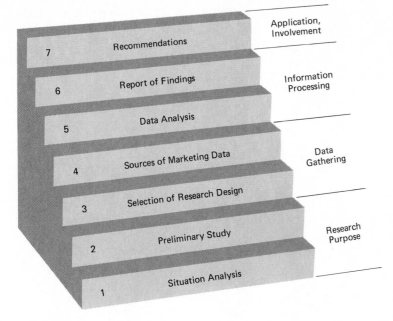

FIGURE 10-11
Steps in the Marketing-Research Process

STEPS IN MARKET RESEARCH

Market research begins with questions about what the market manager wants to know. It includes all the data desired and determines how these data should be used. Market research follows basically the same steps as other types of research. The sequence of steps, shown in Figure 10-11, is as follows:

1. *Situation analysis.* This first step consists of surveying all available information related to the company objective. The purpose is to reach an understanding of the problems involved.
2. *Preliminary study.* The second step of the research process includes a representative coverage of the field. The market analyst might interview consumers, wholesalers, and retailers.
3. *Selection of research design.* Based on step 2, the formal plan of attack is devised. The methods and procedures to be used are indicated. Often they are tried out and modified.
4. *Sources of marketing data.* Here the analyst details the data sources to be consulted. A set of guidelines is developed. Quite often, both primary and secondary sources of data are used.
5. *Data analysis.* The data collected are tabulated, examined, and interpreted.
6. *Report of findings.* This is the written report to be submitted to company management.
7. *Recommendations.* This last step includes the specific recommendations of the researcher. They must be supported by the data collected.

EXPENDITURES FOR MARKET RESEARCH

Company expenditures for market research vary considerably. One recent study of 250 companies showed that nine-tenths of them spend less than 1 percent of their annual sales on market research. This is quite a contrast with expenditures for product research and development, which often amount to 10 percent and more.

Certain factors exert an influence on expenditures for market research: company size, nature of the business, and desire for market leadership. In general, the larger the firm and the more complex its operations, the greater its market-research budget. Also, where a company strives for market leadership in its field, its expenses are greater for market research.

MARKETING IN THE FUTURE

Successful marketers have long-range plans for their marketing programs. These plans must include items that will influence marketing in the days ahead. These include ecology and energy, world trade, the service sector, and computers.

ECOLOGY AND ENERGY
Until recently, marketers catered to the convenience of customers by providing throwaway packaging. However, recycling has become popular. Recycling means much more than collecting glass bottles and aluminum cans. It includes all types of reusable materials: iron and steel scrap, nonferrous metals, paper, and so forth. The Fort Howard Paper Company, for instance, makes most of its products from recycled paper. We may be approaching the time when scrap materials will become our major resources — the unmined supply of our backup resource. To conserve our natural resources, goods must be made more durable and easier to repair.

In the United States, we have become accustomed to an abundance of materials and energy. Now both must be conserved. The use of energy has in the past increased more rapidly than population, productivity, and gross national product. During the 1970s, petroleum became increasingly scarce and expensive. During the early 1980s, petroleum and natural gas were readily available. Until solar energy becomes practicable, we will have to trade off between energy development and the environment.

WORLD TRADE
No country is self-sufficient. All countries depend upon others for important basic resources. But tariffs and other legal barriers hinder trade among nations. Free trade among nations is given lip service everywhere. But in practice, many countries have legal restrictions against "foreign business firms." The European Economic Community, called the Common Market, has shown how countries can benefit from working together in marketing their products. After five years of painstaking negotiations, the major trading nations signed a world trade pact in April 1979. This agreement reduces tariffs by about one-third over a period of eight to ten years. This will undoubtedly help to increase and improve international trade. International trade is discussed more fully in Chapter 21.

THE SERVICE SECTOR
We saw earlier in this chapter that more of the consumer dollar is spent for services than for goods. And the service sector is growing much more rapidly than the manufacture of goods. Health care and communications are two of the leading growth areas. Personal selling may decline in importance in the communications area as advertising increases its role in the promotion of communications. Cable TV and two-way cable TV offer great promise, as people can order goods without leaving home. Doctors may make analyses and order prescriptions from their offices while the patients are still at home. It is more economical to move information than people.

USE OF COMPUTERS The use of computers in managing information is discussed in some detail in Chapter 18. Although the emphasis there is not on marketing, computers are becoming increasingly important in marketing. Gathering, analyzing, interpreting, and applying data constitute the heart of marketing research. And this is what computers do best. Product design is an important part of an integrated marketing procedure, and computers play a major role in product design. Everything from tire tread to training programs can be "modeled" on a computer to test performance *before* the product is produced. Today's marketing concept means that computers will be an integral part of future marketing practices.

SUMMARY OF KEY CONCEPTS

Marketing is a useful and necessary function for virtually all businesses. It includes those business activities designed to price, promote, and distribute want-satisfying products and services to customers.

For a **market** to exist, there must be a buyer and a seller, a good or service, a price, and an exchange.

Marketing is a twentieth-century development. Effective marketing is necessary to motivate individuals and organizations to become buyers.

The marketing concept has three basic elements: customer orientation, profit incentive, and integration of marketing activities.

Product utility refers to want satisfaction. Marketing gives time and place utility to raw materials and goods.

Consumer goods are classed as convenience, shopping, and specialty goods.

The annual sales of industrial goods exceed those of consumer goods.

Marketing contributes to the good of the economy by

a. Creating the incentive to buy
b. Adding to the value of goods

There are six different marketing functions. These functions are all interrelated and must be coordinated with the production function.

To arrive at markets of manageable scope, a company must divide a total market into submarkets. This is called market segmentation. A company selects one or more segments as its target markets and develops a marketing mix for each target.

Management's role in marketing is to plan and implement one or more offerings, distribution channels, prices, and promotional methods to satisfy selected customers.

Market research is essential in today's economy. But most firms spend much less for market research than for product research.

BUSINESS TERMS

You should be able to match these business terms with the statements that follow:

a. CONVENIENCE GOODS
b. INDUSTRIAL GOODS
c. MARKET
d. MARKET ANALYSIS
e. MARKET SEGMENTATION
f. MARKETING
g. MARKETING CONCEPT
h. MARKETING MIX
i. SHOPPING GOODS
j. TIME UTILITY
k. VALUATION
l. VALUE ADDED

1. A buyer and seller, a product or service, an exchange, and an agreed-upon price
2. Business activities that design, price, promote, and distribute want-satisfying products and services to customers
3. A philosophy of doing business, emphasizing customer orientation, profit seeking, and integration of all marketing activities
4. Making goods available to people when they want them
5. Low-priced goods that are readily available
6. Goods that are purchased to use in making other goods
7. Goods that are bought only after comparing price, quality, and style
8. The process by which buyers and sellers learn about the supply of, and demand for, a given product
9. Dividing a total market into submarkets
10. The cost–benefit analysis of the marketing exchange
11. An increase in the value of goods or services because of market activities
12. A combination of products, distribution channels, prices, and promotion used to satisfy selected customers

1. What is the meaning of the term *marketing?*
2. How does marketing give utility to goods?
3. How does a shopping good differ from a specialty good?
4. What are the six universal marketing functions?
5. What major components make up the marketing mix?
6. How does marketing add to the value of goods?

1. What do you consider the most important marketing activities?
2. Consumers account for much more of the GNP than do industrial users. Yet the total sales of industrial goods exceed those for consumer goods. How do you explain this?
3. Why is *value added* a better term than *cost of marketing* for the cost of marketing activities?
4. What is involved in market segmentation? Why would sellers want to segment the market for their products or services?
5. Which of the four elements of the marketing mix occurs first? last?
6. Why does market research occur both before a product is made and after it is sold?

BUSINESS CASES

TRADING STAMPS, SALES, AND PROFITS

Harvey Hagan is an independent grocer. Last year he made a profit of 3.8 percent of his gross sales, which were $350,000. He adopted a trading-stamp plan for a six-month trial period to try to increase sales. The cost of the stamps to him was $1.80 per $100 of sales. After a period of six months, he analyzed the results of his experience, which were as follows: His sales increased by 20 percent; his profit (before deducting for trading stamps) increased to 4.2 percent. He found that since some customers did not take stamps, stamps were issued on only 80 percent of his sales. He must now decide whether or not to continue giving trading stamps.

1. What did it cost to give stamps for six months?
2. What is your recommendation about continuing to give stamps, and why?

10-2 GIVE DOUBLE ON DISCOUNT COUPONS?

George Slusher operates three grocery supermarkets in a community of 100,000 population. His normal gross margin of profit is 20 percent, and his normal weekly sales volume is $124,000 per store. To increase sales and attract some new customers, he gave double value for manufacturers' discount coupons. The average sales increase for the week for each of the three stores was 22 percent. The average value per coupon was 18 cents. George's costs because of accepting and processing coupons include delay time of the checker, delay time of the bagger, in-house sorting and processing, cost of transferring coupons to the clearinghouse, and investment in coupons until reimbursed from the clearinghouse.

1. What was the gross profit per store on his increased sales for the week?
2. Considering the "costs of couponing," did George make or lose money on this project?
3. Assuming that he lost money by giving double value, how could he afford to do so?

In The News

A New Product, the Octopus

It can tell time, play music to wake you up, and take your picture. It weighs less than sixteen ounces and will fit in your coat pocket.

It's the Octopus, a new product, the ultimate in economy and convenience. It combines a flash camera, an AM-FM radio, a stop watch, a flashlight, a digital clock, an alarm buzzer, and a space for coins or keys. It is truly the gadget to end all gadgets.

The idea for the Octopus came to the inventors while they were vacationing at the beach. They saw a woman carrying a radio, camera, and umbrella. Keys were hanging from a long chain around her neck. While watching her struggle along the beach, Connie and Dalton Hendren of Harrodsburg, Kentucky, gave birth to the concept of the Octopus.

(Photo by Dalton Hentren.)

Product Development and Pricing

study objectives

WHEN YOU HAVE FINISHED READING THIS CHAPTER, YOU SHOULD BE ABLE TO:

1. Identify those attributes that combine to make a *product,* and explain when an item is considered to be a *new product*

2. Indicate the stages a product goes through from the time it is introduced until it is withdrawn from the market

3. Show how a trademark differs from a brand name

4. Explain how supply and demand determine pricing

5. Distinguish between cost-plus and demand-oriented pricing

6. Explain how a company might determine that point in pricing when its product will become profitable

11

You cannot do away with the competitive system so long as trademarks remain to distinguish one product from another. You cannot cut out large-scale manufacture so long as there are established brands which breed consumer confidence and thus make mass production not only possible and profitable, but also economical.

Philip Salisbury

A company may have several successful products, but it still works to produce new ones. New products mature, and declining products present somewhat different problems for businesses. A price must be set for every new product, and prices must be changed from time to time.

This chapter illustrates the stages a product moves through from its creation to maturity. We describe different methods of pricing a product and the factors that enter into pricing decisions. How to determine the price at which a product becomes profitable and the way that competition affects pricing are explained.

THE PRODUCT

What do consumers purchase when they buy goods? In most instances, they purchase more than simply a product. They also buy the personal satisfaction that comes from the use of that product. Quite often, they buy a particular product because of the reputation of the company that makes it.

A PRODUCT is *a combination of attributes that creates customer appeal: style, design, utility, packaging, color, size, and prestige.* It is these differences in qualities that make a Cadillac cost more than a Chevrolet. Mennen's shave cream, Rise, became three products when the company created Rise with lanolin and Rise with menthol, in addition to the regular Rise. Any new combination of attributes can create a new product. Products are not the same thing to everyone, either. For example, a PRODUCT OFFER is *what the seller perceives a product to be.* A product is what the users perceive it to be. The two may be quite different.

Want satisfaction can be had from tangible and/or intangible qualities. When you buy a car, your choice of make and model depends on a number of *tangible* physical qualities. These include seating room, number of doors, and perhaps the sound system, as well as the car's color, styling, and design. But there are also the quiet ride, ease of handling, comfort, and how you feel the car will affect your social standing. These *intangible* factors may be either real or imaginary. Your final choice is also influenced by certain social, psychological, or emotional attributes.

According to Thomas A. Murphy, former chairman of the board of General Motors:

> One chief problem facing business today is gaining customer acceptance of products tailored to meet government regulations. Customer satisfaction, as always, remains a primary concern. Business must satisfy the traditional demands of individual customers in the marketplace, and also meet the broader demands of society, as such demands are expressed by government.

WHAT IS A "NEW" PRODUCT?

A great deal of advertising claims "newness" or improvement for the product being offered. In a strict sense, a NEW PRODUCT is *one that serves an entirely new function or represents a major improvement in an existing function.* Rubik's Cube, home computers, videotapes, all-cotton Permapress shirts, and instant cameras are examples of products that were new when they were first introduced. The real test of newness is what the product does for the ultimate user.

COKE VERSUS PEPSI

In early 1982, the country's top two soft-drink makers launched major new products. PepsiCo. Inc. started testing Pepsi Free, a caffein-free soft drink. The Coca-Cola Co. started marketing Diet Coke for the first time.

These two leaders together account for 60 percent of all U.S. soft-drink sales. Each company budgeted more than $100 million in 1982 to introduce these new products.

We have become accustomed to seeing new products. Some companies, such as 3M and Du Pont, have a strong reputation for innovation, research, and new-product development. But whether a product is new depends on its reception in the marketplace. Do buyers perceive an item to be significantly different from its competitive products? This difference might be in design, appearance, or performance. Dancer Fitzgerald Sample Inc., a New York advertising agency, said it counted 1,510 new products sold through food outlets and drugstores last year, up 15 percent from 1,317 items for the previous year. That total was the highest in the 19 years that the agency has been tracking introductions.

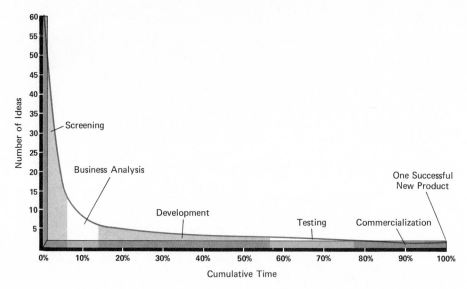

FIGURE 11-1

One successful product is the end result of many ideas. Of approximately fifty-eight ideas introduced, about forty-six fail the initial screening for technical feasibility. Of the remaining twelve, five are eliminated for lack of profit potential, four do not survive the product-development stage, and two more drop out during test marketing. The one idea left is the new product to be introduced on the market. (Source: *Adapted from Management of New Products,* 4th ed. (New York: Booz, Allen, and Hamilton, 1968), p. 9, and *Marketing,* 2nd ed., (Englewood Cliffs, N.J.: Prentice-Hall, Inc., 1981), p. 260. By permission.

GENERAL ELECTRIC'S $10 LIGHT BULB

General Electric placed on the market a new two-way light bulb. It is an energy-efficient bulb with an expected life span of five years. How would you price such a bulb? You won't sell a replacement for it for five more years. It is a good product for demand-oriented pricing. Obviously, this item must be priced for the long term. GE offered it at $10 a bulb.

What is the potential for this bulb? There are more than a billion sockets in homes and businesses where bulbs must be replaced. The company estimates that the buyer will save $5 over the bulb's life span in reduced energy use. But how do you convince the public to pay $10 for an item usually bought for less than $2?

Quite often, an old product is made into a new product. An excellent example is the Holiday Inn roadside sign. In 1982, that hotel chain began to replace its old signs with a simpler, sleeker one. The replacement process will take three years and cost $40 million.

The original sign with its many colors was to attract people who were driving by. Those people once made up more than 90 percent of Holiday Inn's clients. Today, fewer than 3 percent stop in without a reservation.

Each new sign uses one-third of the electricity used by the old sign. And maintenance costs are about half as much as for the old one. These savings will pay for each new sign in five years.

SERVICES
Services are similar to products. Providing a service is often the only "product" a business offers. Repair and maintenance people, broadcasters, sports figures, beauticians, consultants—all deal in services. They play a major role in consumer want satisfaction.

More than half the consumer dollar is spent for services, and this percentage is increasing. Sums spent for medical services, leisure activities, and education are increasing continually. Today, services are the fastest-growing segment of business in this country.

GENERIC TERMS, BRAND NAMES, AND GENERIC PRODUCTS

A BRAND is *a word or phrase that identifies a particular product or a class of products.* Producers do not want you to buy "a soap" or "a detergent" to wash dishes. They advertise a brand name, such as Cascade, All, Electrasol, or Calgonite. Companies spend large sums to promote their brand names. Procter & Gamble is the leading television advertiser, and it advertises its *brands* rather than the company. In fact, its brands often compete with one another. Brands become symbols of quality, and this attracts buyers and leads to repeat purchases.

Sometimes constant advertising causes a trademark* to become a "generic" term. As such, it becomes synonymous with an entire product or service class. For example, *Scotch tape* is used by most of us for any type of transparent tape, and *Xerox* to many people means photocopier. But they are company trademarks. A TRADEMARK is *a distinctive symbol, title, or design that gives legal identity to a company or its product.* Some companies, such as Xerox and Coca-Cola, spend large sums to protect their trademarks. This is done in order to prevent them from becoming generic terms. Words that companies once owned but lost as generic terms include *thermos, cellophane, shredded wheat,* and *lite.*

Coca-Cola has gone to great lengths to keep *Coke* from meaning any cola-flavored soft drink. The company has paid "checkers" to go to restaurants and order "a Coke." If the person is served Pepsi or some other soft drink as a Coke, action is threatened against the proprietor. Miller Brewing Company fought hard to use "Lite" as a trademark for its beer. It lost when it was decided that *lite* was considered a generic term.

Most supermarkets today carry generic products. A generic product does not carry either a manufacturer's or a private-brand label. It is merely labeled as to contents. Sometimes the word *generic* appears on the label. These products are lower in price than the same items sold under well-known brand names

Texaco launched a modernization program for its stations. It changed its graphics design—the star. It started redesigning its stations using distinctive red, black, white, and gray colors. It also changed the product names on its gasoline pumps. Instead of such names as Fire Chief and Sky Chief, Texaco used the generic names of *regular leaded, lead-free, super lead-free,* and *diesel.*

---

* Trademarks from American Telephone and Telegraph Company, General Electric Company, and the Coca-Cola Company are reproduced here by their permission.

Manufacturers' versus Private Brands.   The brand name is usually the principal method by which the consumer identifies a product. When shopping for a breakfast cereal, a person may think of Corn Flakes, Total, or Wheaties. This brand identification is one way the average consumer has of coping with the many brands on the shelves. Most network television commercials feature manufacturers' brands—the products and services of large companies. For example, regular viewers of sports events can usually name the various makes of cars produced by the Ford Motor Company.

Brands may be manufacturers' brands (such as Ford or GE), or "private" or "dealer" brands, such as Ann Page (A&P), Hyde-Park (Malone & Hyde), Riverside (Montgomery Ward), and Kenmore (Sears). The products themselves are often made by the same companies that make the manufacturers' brands. But private brands are owned by middlemen rather than manufacturers. **The market strategy behind private-brands is pricing goods slightly lower than manufacturers' brands of equal quality.** This is done without attaching the lower price stigma to the manufacturer's brand.

PRODUCT LINE AND PRODUCT MIX

Specialization is a characteristic of both production and distribution. A wholesaler might handle only groceries and other closely related lines. Another wholesaler might deal in pharmaceuticals, and still another might sell hardware or dry goods. Most retailers likewise stay with related product or service lines. In the service area, a business may sell insurance or banking

FIGURE 11-2
Components of a Product

services, operate a small-loan operation, run a dry-cleaning plant, or provide some other specialized type of service. But we do not see a bank doing dry cleaning.

A firm's product mix consists of one or more product (or service) lines. A basic question is, How many competing brands or lines should be handled? Another is, What is the best product mix for those lines? Both wholesalers and retailers must decide to what degree they will carry related and unrelated product lines. A final question is, How "deep" should each product line be? The *depth* of product lines refers to the number of different products in a particular line. An example of depth in a particular line is the laundry detergents produced by Procter & Gamble. The company makes Tide, Bold, Gain, Bonus, Dash, Cheer, Oxydol, and Duz.

PRODUCT LIFE CYCLE

The product-management process is not complete when a product or service first hits the market. A product or service moves through five stages during its life. Each stage requires different strategies. The stages are:

1. Introduction
2. Market growth
3. Market maturity
4. Saturation
5. Market decline

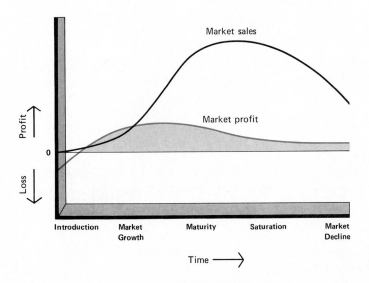

FIGURE 11-3
Product Life Cycle

These stages are illustrated in Figure 11-3 and discussed briefly here.

PRODUCT-INTRODUCTION STAGE The product-introduction stage is the period during which a company first presents a new product or service class to the market. Since start-up costs are large and sales are initially small, a product usually incurs a loss during the introduction stage. Because the product is new and competition is scarce, the product sells for a relatively high price. Customers must be made to want the product. They must be told what the product is, what it will do, and how to use it. Wholesalers must be found to distribute it. Promotion costs are

high in order to convince the public to buy it and try it. Some new products are test-marketed in a restricted area to assess their acceptance by the public.

For example, nylon, the first wholly synthetic fiber, was perfected in the 1940s. Within a decade, nylon had completely displaced silk in women's hosiery. As nylon reached its peak, new fibers—polyester and acrylics—were introduced. Today, a single polyester-fiber factory located on 300 acres of land can produce as much polyester fiber as the amount of cotton grown on 600,000 acres.

MARKET-MATURITY STAGE

As the product becomes well known, sales continue to increase but at a reduced rate of growth. As competition stiffens, the company must decide whether to reduce prices further or increase promotional efforts. If both steps are taken, the profit margin is reduced to the lowest acceptable level for the producer. Some competitors may leave the market while seeking more viable goods to produce or sell.

Segmentation and product differentiation[1] are frequently used to move a product back into the growth stage. Kodak's new disc camera represents an attempt to move cheap, small cameras out of the maturity stage and back into the growth stage.

SATURATION STAGE

In the saturation stage, the market peaks and levels off, and it may start to decline. Few if any new customers buy the good, and repeat orders become smaller. A reduction in total sales is inevitable unless the good is improved or new uses for it are discovered or developed. The profit margin declines still further.

---

[1] These are discussed in Chapter 10.

MARKET-DECLINE STAGE During the final stage of the product life cycle, sales decline rather rapidly. New products replace the sales of older articles. For example, color TV sets replaced black-and-white sets. When a company deserts a certain product, competitors absorb that market. Thus, for the few producers that remain, there is sufficient market for that product to be produced at a profit. Eventually the product is abandoned because of the small demand for it. For example, rayon was forced off the market by new fibers—nylon, acrylics, and polyesters.

HOW TO REVITALIZE OLD PRODUCTS

Here are some examples of how goods were moved out of the maturity or declining stage back into new growth:

Ivory soap sales were increased when Procter & Gamble promoted it for adults as well as babies.

Hanes increased sales of L'eggs pantyhose by marketing them in supermarkets—a radical idea at the time.

Sales of Arm & Hammer baking soda increased when it was advertised for freshening refrigerators and cat litter boxes.

MARKET STRATEGY A **product line is a "class" of product or service** (such as microwave ovens, cars, or clothing). Hence, it consists of various brands. Marketing strategy over the product's life cycle is concerned with:

1. The timing of a sales-promotion effort
2. Research aimed at product improvement or new uses
3. The study of new, competing products
4. Decisions about possible abandonment

Early in the development stage, advertising is planned for a new product. At first, the advertising promotes the whole product class; later, it focuses on a particular brand. Decisions on price must be made from time to time over the product's life cycle. There has been a trend away from the brand-management concept toward managing product lines. So the entire marketing mix is adjusted to reflect the stage of the life cycle.

New products are often test-marketed in selected areas. Free samples and/or coupons may be distributed. When the product is accepted by the public in the test-market area, the market area is expanded. Many nationally advertised brands were at first marketed in selected regions only.

PRODUCT MANAGEMENT

Today, the need for a product is carefully explored before it is produced on a large scale. People may be assigned as "product managers" and given responsibility for coordinating product development and marketing.

NEW-PRODUCT PLANNING AND MARKETING

What happens when management plans to produce an item to meet a market demand? The scope of such planning includes answers to the following decision questions:

1. What attributes should the product have that customers want?
2. In what ways will it differ from competing products?
3. What new uses can this product offer?
4. Can any current company product be modified to meet these requirements?
5. How should it be priced in relation to other, similar articles?
6. In what quantity should we make it?
7. What would be effective and efficient distribution arrangements for this offering?
8. When should we launch our advertising campaign?
9. What types of advertising media should we use?

When a product is developed to meet a market demand, attention must be given to competition and to possible changes in customers' wants.

STAGES IN PLANNING

There are seven stages in new-product planning (see Figure 11-4). Although they normally follow one another, some steps can be performed at the same time:

1. The first step is *idea generation and screening*. Suggestions for possible new products are explored. Any new suggestion must be compared with company objectives.
2. The next step is the *market forecast*. This estimates the size and type of product to introduce. It assesses the overall market potential for the product as such, not for the specific type that might be produced by a particular company.
3. The *product concept* is established, concerned with the specific qualities of the proposed product. This must be kept in constant review during all remaining stages.
4. This is followed by an *evaluation* or feasibility study, which is done by the engineering staff. It answers the question of whether the product will perform the functions planned for it.
5. *Consumer reaction* is needed at this point, to prevent the waste that would result from proceeding too far in the wrong direction. This is a preliminary sounding of consumer acceptance, often involving in-home consumer-use tests.
6. The planned product is then *tested* in the laboratory and in a limited geographic market.
7. If the test results are favorable, the product then goes into full-scale production and distribution in the *commercial market*. This is the final execution of the total plan.

WITHDRAWING A PRODUCT

Sometimes a company must withdraw a product, either because it does not sell or because it is unsafe for users. One outstanding example of the former is Corfam,[2] a synthetic leather product developed by Du Pont. The product was not acceptable to the public and was unprofitable to the company. So it was eventually abandoned, after many years and an expenditure of millions of

---

[2] Corfam was later picked up by a company in Poland where it is now being produced.

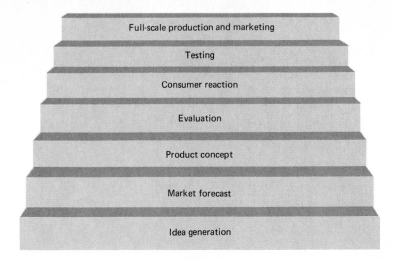

FIGURE 11-4
Stages in New-Product Planning

dollars. Many products containing asbestos have recently been withdrawn or reformulated.

Planned Product Obsolescence.   When management people plan a new product, they may also be planning to drop some of their current products. **Smart management does not wait for one of its products to die. Dropping a product is integrated with the introduction, growth, and maturing of new ones.**

CURRENT ISSUE

IS PLANNED OBSOLESCENCE DETRIMENTAL TO CONSUMERS?

Planned product obsolescence is a marketing strategy used by companies whose products have reached saturation. By frequent changes in the design or contents of the model or product, sales are stimulated for producers and middlemen.

With which of the following statements do you agree, and with which do you disagree?

1. Planned obsolescence wastes resources and is therefore contrary to the public's best interest.
2. New model changes increase the cost of machine tooling and production shutdown time.
3. Product obsolescence creates problems of liquidating older, obsolete models.
4. Planned obsolescence creates employment.
5. Planned obsolescence is necessary to support a high-level economy.
6. Companies whose products have reached the maturity stage would be forced to close if this strategy were not used.
7. Consumers want frequent new models as evidence that they are up to date.

Should planned obsolescence be restricted only to those goods requiring resources that are not in short supply?

When a product moves into the declining stage of its life cycle, it becomes expensive to maintain. It must remain available to customers, but it is produced in smaller quantities at a higher unit cost. Because of slow sales, it remains in inventory for a longer period of time—and this is costly. Furthermore, it may require more time and attention of the sales force than active products do. It may also taint the company image because it does not compare favorably with newer products.

Sometimes the product does not become obsolete, but its design, size, or physical appearance does. In this country, consumers are accustomed to changes in styles and fashions. Company management usually leads the way by introducing new styles. The annual automobile body-style changes of the 1950s and 1960s are a good example.

PRICE AND PRICING OBJECTIVES

PRICE is *the exchange value of a product or service.* It is the amount a buyer is willing to pay for a good or service. It can also be the value a seller is asking for items offered for sale. Price is a major factor in competing for sales of both industrial and consumer goods.

As a general rule, the point at which supply and demand curves intersect determines the price for a specific good. For example, consider the price of a plastic toy. At $1.19, there might be a large demand for it. But at $3.00, the demand would decline sharply. Perhaps no manufacturer could afford to make the article and sell it for $1.19. But at $3.00, several producers would be willing to enter the market. According to economic theory, the price finally established for the toy occurs where a curve representing demand, and a curve representing supply, intersect. This is illustrated in Figure 11-5.

It is difficult for a producer to establish the "correct" price. When people buy goods in a department store, do they pay cash, or do they want credit? Do they take the goods with them, or do they want them delivered? Do they want the things they buy gift-wrapped? All these extra services cost money

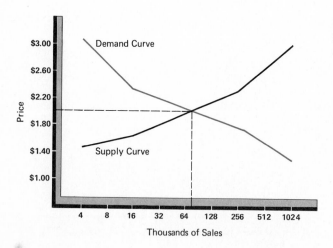

FIGURE 11-5
Demand and Supply Determine the Price

and must be reflected in the price. What is the one correct price that a firm can offer to all potential buyers? Is it feasible to offer goods at two prices — cash and credit prices? Gasoline sales are currently being priced at "credit-card" and "cash" levels at some stations.

PRICING OBJECTIVES

Businesses price goods in order to accomplish certain objectives. A company with a broad line of products may price various goods to achieve different objectives. One article may be priced to maximize profit on that item. Another may be priced relatively low in order to increase its share of the market. Three chief objectives govern pricing practices:

1. Increasing market share
2. Maintaining market share
3. Profitability

Volume Objectives. **Increasing and maintaining market share are both volume objectives.** The profit margin is set at a low level in order to attract business. The objective is to sell more items to raise the total profit — both company image and product line are promoted. Discount coupons are but one device that can be used to increase sales of individual products.

Profitability. **Profitability is the "bottom line" in pricing.** Management knows that both the quantity sold and the profit margin determine profit. An increase in the current price would limit sales. An increase in the price that exceeds the decline in sales would be profitable. If the sales decline exceeds the price increase, it would be unprofitable. For example, let us assume a price increase of 10 percent. If that percentage should cause sales volume to decline by only 7 percent, it would be profitable. But if it resulted in a decline of 12 percent, it would be unprofitable. Management must set its goals before adopting a pricing policy.

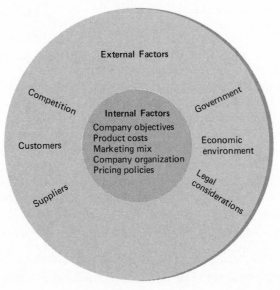

FIGURE 11-6
Factors Affecting Pricing Decisions

The first step in launching a pricing strategy is to establish a basic price.

A pricing system must consider material and labor costs, overhead expenses, profit margins, and competitors' prices. There are three basic approaches to pricing: cost-oriented, to meet competition, and demand-oriented. These different approaches to pricing meet different needs.

THE COST APPROACH

There can be no profit until a firm has recovered its costs. Therefore, most companies use some type of cost approach in pricing. The three chief cost-pricing schemes are the cost-plus approach, target rate of return, and break-even analysis.

Cost-Plus Pricing.   Some types of business must base their pricing on costs plus a profit. This is especially true where goods are produced to customer specifications. Construction contractors and utilities use this approach. Many wholesalers and retailers also use it.

The usual procedure here is to add a stated percentage of the cost as company profit. The formulas used are these:

$$\text{Direct costs} + \text{Overhead costs} = \text{Total cost}$$

$$\text{Total cost} + \text{Profit margin} = \text{Price}$$

This is illustrated in Figure 11-7. The profit margin in this case is 16⅔ percent of cost.

| Direct Costs $60 | Overhead Costs $30 | Profit $15 | = | Price $105 |

FIGURE 11-7
Cost-Plus Pricing

By using a fair profit standard, cost-plus pricing provides security in an uncertain market, for the seller is relatively safe from price-cutting competition. (This assumes that competitors are satisfied with their present market share.) Competitors are not likely to reduce their profit margins in order to gain a larger market share.

Many services are priced on a cost-plus approach, as pricing is related to labor costs. Cost-plus is also used in producing goods where one cannot determine ahead of time what the costs may be. The development of a new product for the government illustrates this type of good.

When a business firm is both a buyer and a seller of finished goods, retail prices may be set by adding a certain sum to their cost. This is called **markup pricing.** MARKUP is *the difference between a middleman's cost and selling price.* Hence, if a product cost the middleman $40 and is marked to sell for $60, the markup is $20. This represents a markup of 33⅓ percent. **Markup is generally expressed in terms of percentage of selling price.**

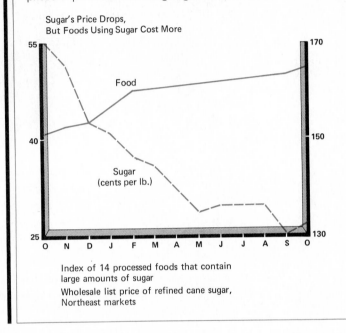
The following steps give the percentage of markup when both cost and selling price are known:

$$\text{Selling price} - \text{Cost} = \text{Dollar markup}$$

$$\$60 - \$40 = \$20$$

$$\frac{\text{Dollar markup}}{\text{Selling price}} = \text{Percentage of markup}$$

$$\frac{\$20}{\$60} = 33\tfrac{1}{3}\%$$

Target Rate of Return. This approach is used when the pricing policy is to earn a specified rate of profit on the amount invested. This varies from the cost-plus approach, since the markup is determined by the rate of return desired. This target rate of return may be what is normal in the market. Or it may be what management considers to be a fair return on investment. The desired rate of return may not be maintained constantly. During some periods, it may be more or less than the set rate. But over a period of time, it should average the set rate.

Target-rate-of-return pricing may be difficult where a company has a wide range of product lines or competes in a variety of markets. The problem results from the difficulty involved in estimating direct costs and overhead.

Breakeven Analysis. Breakeven analysis puts more emphasis on sales volume than the cost-plus approach does. For a new product, one would expect to sustain a loss up to a certain point in sales. Management wants to know at what point cost and income would be equal. The breakeven analysis hinges on variable costs. Administrative costs and overhead are usually *fixed*. But the price of labor and material varies with the volume produced.

The breakeven point is calculated by this formula:

$$\frac{\text{Fixed costs}}{\text{Price} - \text{Variable cost per unit}} = \text{Breakeven point}$$

The breakeven point is the price at which the revenue received equals the total cost of a product. Suppose, for example, that the fixed costs for a small manufacturer are $60,000 for the year. These include basically the cost of keeping the plant open whether anything is produced or not. The costs for raw materials, energy, and labor (variable costs) are $9 per unit produced, and the sales price is $15 per unit:

$$\frac{\$60,000}{\$15 - \$9} = 10,000 \text{ units, the breakeven point}$$

This is illustrated in Figure 11-8. The company must sell 10,000 units to break even and does not begin to make a profit until after that point.

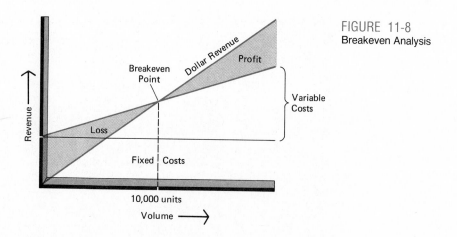

FIGURE 11-8
Breakeven Analysis

PRICING RELATIVE TO COMPETITION In some markets, competition is chiefly on a price basis. (Gasoline retailers rediscovered this truth as people learned to pump their own gas.) In this case, a company prices its products in relation to those of its competitors. A price might be established to meet competitive prices, or it might be set above or below that of the competition.

At the Prevailing Price. When pricing at the prevailing price, one does not attempt to meet every competitor's price. Rather, one meets the price of firms whose competition is most severe. This would include those in the same area that might be luring one's customers away.

Pricing Above the Competition. Many people think that price is an indication of quality. They feel that the more an item costs, the better its quality. So some producers price above the prevailing market price to suggest a higher quality. This can best be done where it is difficult to judge the quality of the goods being purchased.

Carnation Instant Breakfast is a good example. The company brought the product out and it sold very poorly in test markets. But when the

The price paid to the farmer is determined by competitive bidding. (Photo by David Hiser, The Image Bank.)

company almost doubled the price, sales took off. People equated the higher price with a high-quality product and bought it.

Pricing Below the Competition.   You might question how a producer could price below the competition and still make a profit. One way would be to produce goods of lower quality than those on the market. If a plant is in a labor-surplus region, costs of production might be lower. Another way would be to use low prices as the chief promotional effort; advertising costs would be kept to a minimum.

PRICE COMPETITION means that *the strategy is to sell goods below the going market price.* Below-the-market pricing is possible only when there is evidence that customers will be attracted to a cost savings. In general, prices below the market mean that choice or selection is limited and that extra services are held to a minimum.

AIRLINE DECONTROL SHIFTS PRICING FROM COST TO COMPETITION

Today, airlines are free to set their fares. When they were regulated, pricing was based on cost. Now that airlines are no longer regulated, pricing is based on competition.

Under regulation, airlines had to file proposed fare changes with the Civil Aeronautics Board. These requests had to be filed 30 days in advance. The CAB limited an increase to 5 percent and a decrease to 50 percent. Based on rising costs, most airlines filed for a modest 1 or 2 percent increase every month or two.

Costs still influence but no longer determine airline fares. To meet competition and fill empty seats, airlines cut fares on the popular routes they fly.

Deregulation enhanced the growth of low-cost carriers. They were attracted first to those routes patronized by large numbers of passengers. Their competition forced the trunk lines to lower their fares on these routes. It is currently a supply-and-demand situation, where price is the incentive.

DEMAND-ORIENTED PRICING

Demand-oriented pricing is based on an estimate of what the sales revenue will be at different prices. When these estimates are complete, they are compared to costs at these different prices. The basic idea is to set a high price when the demand is high, and set lower prices when the demand is low. The chief consideration is how the consumer values the product. Cost becomes a factor when consumers' value for the product is so low that one cannot sell the product at a profit.

Management must project estimated demand over a period of time. The question to be answered is, How many customers will buy at the different price levels? These formulas show how price, quantity, and total revenue are related under demand-oriented pricing:

$$P \times Q = TR$$

where: P = Price
          Q = Quantity
          TR = Total revenue

The **law of diminishing demand** is:

P↑ Q↓   As price goes up, quantity demanded goes down.

P↓ Q↑   As price goes down, quantity demanded goes up.

Demand elasticity is the relative responsiveness of the quantity demanded to changes in price. Demand may be elastic or inelastic. It is elastic if a decline in price of 1 percent increases the amount demanded by more than 1 percent. It is inelastic if a 1 percent decline in price increases the total demanded by less than 1 percent.

$$\text{Elastic demand is:} \quad P\uparrow \times Q\downarrow = TR\downarrow$$
$$P\downarrow \times Q\uparrow = TR\uparrow$$
$$\text{Inelastic demand is:} \quad P\uparrow \times Q\downarrow = TR\uparrow$$
$$P\downarrow \times Q\uparrow = TR\downarrow$$

The difference is the amount of TR's response to changes in price (P).

Product-Line Pricing. Seldom does a company produce and sell a single product. Rather, it sells a complete line of related products. **The pricing strategy for each item in the line must work for the other items also.** In addition, products must be placed in the market in such a way as to maximize profits for the entire line of products.

Price-cross elasticity refers to the effect that a price change on one product has on other related products in the line. A positive price-cross effect results when a price increase in one product causes a sales increase of another product in the line. For example, an increase in the price of the economy model of an instant camera may cause customers to buy more of the deluxe model.

PRICING PRACTICES

Management decisions on pricing are much more involved than the mere placing of a price tag on items offered for sale. Among the things that must be considered in pricing are the following:

1. How to establish different prices for different geographical areas or different customers
2. Whether to set a price and maintain it, or start high and gradually come down
3. Whether to supply suggested retail prices
4. How to differentiate prices offered to distributors from those given to retailers

The pricing strategy used by 7-Eleven illustrates the complexity of selecting an effective pricing practice. Nearly everything you buy at a 7-Eleven store can be bought cheaper at a nearby supermarket. The selection is usually very limited; most items include only one brand. The customers are small spenders, spending on the average less than $3 on each visit. But 7-Eleven stores are a huge retailing success because they sell **convenience.** Pricing is of secondary importance to people who go into a 7-Eleven store.

PRICING OF NEW PRODUCTS The pricing of a new product is determined partially by how different it is from existing products. When a product is so different that it cannot be compared with any other product, pricing is difficult. In the past, some new products have been priced by adding a given markup to the unit cost. Now

Home computers lead into a new way of life. (Courtesy Apple Computers Inc.)

more companies seem to use a demand-oriented pricing system. The monopoly during a product's early stages supports an initial high price.

In order to secure maximum profit, management must project potential demand at varying price levels. A high starting price will help retrieve the cost of research and development. A low initial price would tend to hold off the competition for a longer period.

The Skimming Approach.   A popular approach to the pricing of new products is called **skimming.** Under SKIMMING, the producer sets *a high price relative to similar products during the introductory phase. Then the price is gradually lowered during later phases.* This strategy is usually used when price is the basis for segmenting the market. It enables the producer to recover development costs quickly. Home computers illustrate well the practice of skimming. The high price first charged attracted much competition. It wasn't long until dozens of companies were offering home computers, producers had to lower their prices.

The Penetration Approach.   This is the opposite of the skimming approach. PENETRATION PRICING is *introducing the new product at a price that is low compared to similar products.* The producer plans to retrieve development costs through large sales generated by the low pricing. Whereas skimming encourages competition, penetration pricing discourages it. The penetration strategy anticipates both market demand and potential competition.

Pricing policies are modified as a product moves through its life cycle. As an article approaches the end of the market stage and enters the maturing stage, its price is usually lowered. If management decides to increase penetration of the market (that is, obtain as many customers as soon as possible), a low price will be set when a new product is introduced. On the other hand, if management wishes to "skim" the market (that is, obtain large profits per unit), a relatively high initial price will be established. Pricing strategies are not always apparent from the prices asked.

DISCOUNTS AND ALLOWANCES

Discounts are reductions from the published prices of the manufacturer. Discounts are available to both wholesalers and retailers. Some of the most commonly used discounts are trade, cash, quantity, and seasonal.

Trade Discounts. **Trade discounts are a means of adjusting catalog prices to reflect the cost of a service that the wholesaler or jobber must perform.** For example, a full-service wholesaler would be given a trade discount from the price that a limited wholesaler would pay. This would compensate the wholesaler for credit, handling, and transporting costs.

Cash Discounts. Probably the most common type of discount offered to buyers to induce them to pay promptly is the cash discount. A **cash discount** is a reduction in the invoice price because one is paying for purchases before the final payment is due. A typical cash discount is 2/10 net 30. An invoice for $100 dated April 1, with terms 2/10 net 30, allows the buyer to take a discount of 2 percent ($2) from the invoice price of $100 if the bill is paid before April 10. If not, the full amount of $100 is due at the end of thirty days.

Quantity Discounts. Another pricing policy is the **quantity discount.** This is offered to the buyer for purchases of large quantities, such as a discount of 10 percent for the purchase of 100 or more units.

The Robinson-Patman Act of 1936 (an amendment to Section 2 of the Clayton Act) prohibits varying pricing policies that will place small firms at too great a disadvantage. It prevents sellers from granting special pricing allowances unless these concessions are open to all purchasers on "proportionately equal terms."

Seasonal Discounts. Many products have peak seasons when demand is much greater than at other times during the year. Merchants who are willing to purchase and store goods during the off season might be given a discount from the regular price charged. Off-season discounts enable a manufacturer to even out production schedules and make better use of plant facilities.

From a buyer's point of view, the discount must more than compensate for tying up the buyer's additional funds. When delivery of the goods is also accepted, an even greater discount must be received to pay for storage costs.

Promotional Allowances. Manufacturers sometimes give middlemen discounts to compensate them for advertising or other promotional expenses. These discounts are usually given for local advertising of national-brand merchandise. Local advertising rates are usually lower than national rates and capitalize on the reputation of the local business.

SUMMARY OF KEY CONCEPTS

Two important components of the marketing mix discussed in this chapter are *product* and *pricing.*

A **product** is a good or service produced to satisfy the wants of the ultimate user. For a product to have maximum value, it must be distributed to the place where it is in demand.

A product is considered to be "new" if it serves a new function or makes a significant improvement in an existing function.

There are five phases in the life cycle of any marketable product: introduction, growth, maturity, saturation, and decline.

New products are planned to be put on the market. But the deletion of older products from the market is also planned.

There are seven stages in new-product planning.

Pricing is a basic means of competing with other businesses. The **price** of an item is its exchange value—the amount acceptable to buyer and seller.

The two chief pricing objectives are volume sales and profitability.

The chief **pricing policies** are the cost approach and demand pricing.

The skimming approach and the penetration approach are both important **pricing practices.**

Practices that make price differentials possible are various types of discounts: trade, cash, quantity, seasonal, and promotional allowances.

BUSINESS TERMS

You should be able to match these business terms with the statements that follow:

a. BRAND
b. BREAKEVEN POINT
c. COST-PLUS PRICING
d. DEMAND-ORIENTED PRICING
e. MARKUP
f. NEW PRODUCT
g. PENETRATION APPROACH

h. PRICE
i. PRICE COMPETITION
j. PRODUCT
k. PRODUCT OFFER
l. SKIMMING APPROACH
m. TRADE DISCOUNT
n. TRADEMARK

1. A combination of attributes that gives an item customer appeal
2. An article that serves a new function or represents a major improvement in an existing function
3. What the seller perceives a product to be
4. A word or phrase that identifies a particular product
5. A distinctive symbol, title, or design that gives legal identity to a company or its product
6. The exchange value of a product or service
7. Adding a percentage of the cost as company profit
8. The difference between the cost and selling price
9. The price at which the revenue equals the total cost of a product
10. The strategy of selling goods below the going market price
11. Pricing based on a comparison of estimated sales revenue and costs at different price levels
12. Setting a high price during the introductory stage, then gradually lowering it later
13. Introducing a new product at a price that is low compared to similar products
14. A means of adjusting catalog prices to reflect the cost of a service rendered

REVIEW QUESTIONS

1. What are some of the attributes that combine to make a product?
2. When is a product considered to be a "new" product?
3. What factors are important when setting up a pricing system?
4. Which of these factors are internal and which are external: competition, government, marketing mix, legal aspects, pricing policies?
5. What is the basic strategy in price competition below the market price?

1. Which stage in the life of a product is the most important?
2. What is the chief difference between a brand and a trademark?
3. Why are generic products and private brands so popular with people who trade in discount houses?
4. Explain how a company might determine the point in pricing at which a product would become profitable.
5. How do supply and demand work together to affect product pricing?

BUSINESS CASES

11-1

HARGIS & SON NEEDS A NEW PRODUCT

Hargis & Son is located in the Toledo, Ohio, industrial area. The company has had a long and successful history making parts for automobiles. When the auto industry hit the skids, Hargis broadened its product line. The company started making parts for home-appliance manufacturers. But that industry is on a plateau and Hargis needs another new product.

The company has a sound cash position and a good line of credit with local banks. Management is undecided whether to broaden its manufacturing operations or launch a services arm. Some of the alternatives being considered are:

a. Start making electronic toys
b. Buy a toy-making company
c. Establish a new trucking company serving companies in Ohio
d. Start a consulting service in the area of personnel development

In the light of today's economic development in your area, which of these appear to be viable choices? Support your answer.

11-2

PRICING A NEW PRODUCT

A leading manufacturer of office equipment recently announced that it had "almost" perfected the talking typewriter. This typewriter allows the user to talk into its mike and a voice decoder translates the spoken word into typed text. So instead of typing, the user merely talks to the typewriter.

This is a unique product that is not expected to be easily duplicated by competitors. Considering its uniqueness and the heavy anticipated demand, which of the following pricing strategies should this office-products company use to introduce its talking typewriter to the market?

a. Breakeven pricing
b. Cost-plus pricing
c. Competition-based pricing
d. Skimming
e. Quantity discounts

When competition enters the market, which of the pricing strategies above would be most appropriate?

PROMOTIONAL ASPECTS of MARKETING

study objectives

WHEN YOU HAVE FINISHED READING THIS CHAPTER, YOU SHOULD BE
ABLE TO:

1. Define promotion and explain what aspects of marketing it includes
2. Outline the various steps in the personal-selling process
3. Name some of the components of success in selling
4. Discuss the economic aspects of advertising
5. Compare the different advertising media as to their relative importance
6. Explain what is included in sales-promotion activities

12

If you think advertising doesn't pay — there are 25 mountains in Colorado higher than Pike's Peak; name one.

The American Salesman

Promotion is the third element in the marketing mix. In the preceding chapter, we studied product development and pricing. In this chapter, we consider promotion. The fourth element in the mix, distribution, is discussed in Chapter 13.

A company may well have a fine product or service offering and it may be priced correctly. It may also have an adequate distribution system tailored to its target market. But it must reach that market. **Promotion** refers to efforts to reach the customers in that market and persuade them to act.

In this chapter, we look at four different aspects of promotion. The first two are personal selling and advertising. Then we turn to sales promotion and public relations. Together, these four factors make up the **promotion blend.**

NATURE AND TYPES OF PROMOTION

As a marketing term, PROMOTION is *a firm's efforts to influence customers to buy.* Promotion includes the elements of giving information and influencing customer behavior. Its purpose is to enhance the firm's image or increase the sales of the firm's products.

Promotion includes all selling activities. The most important of these are personal selling, advertising, sales promotion, and public relations. The

Personal Selling	Advertising	Sales Promotion	Public Relations

FIGURE 12-1
The Promotion Blend

way in which these activities are combined make up a company's "promotion blend." The way the different components of the promotion blend are put together depends upon the firm's marketing objectives. Promotional strategy is designed to achieve those objectives. Promotion's role depends on the other elements in the marketing mix. For example, if a company chooses to use a high-pricing strategy, promotion assumes a major role.

Developing a promotional effort consists of choosing communication media and blending them into an effective program. Seldom does a company rely on a single type of promotional activity—a combination of methods is used to communicate with customers.

PROMOTION IS COMMUNICATION

Promotion is communication, since the marketer is the sender of a sales message, and the customer is the receiver. Promotion includes all the methods used to get the message through clearly.

The first purpose of the message is to inform. But its real objective is a response from the potential buyer. Marketers send promotional messages through sales manuals, news releases, artwork, displays, samples, prizes, and personal sales presentations. These make up the communication channel. Personal selling uses personal contacts, the telephone, and the mail. Advertising uses mostly the mass media—newspapers, radio, and television. Sales promotion uses displays, exhibits, sampling, and so on. Public relations encompasses all of these. These activities share the common objective of getting feedback in the form of a purchase.

The Communication Flow

| The Marketer (Sender) | Promotion (Messages) | Customer (Receiver) |

FIGURE 12-2
Promotion as Communication

PERSONAL SELLING AS PROMOTION

A simplified definition of SELLING would be *"the art of personal persuasion employed to induce others to buy."* Personal selling is the oldest method of selling. This method is unique, for it involves a two-way exchange of ideas between buyer and seller. In our treatment of personal selling, we discuss:

1. The behavioral approach in selling
2. The selling process
3. Successful personal selling
4. Sales management

BEHAVIORAL APPROACH IN SELLING

In recent years, marketing executives have received valuable information from behavioral scientists regarding human behavior in the marketplace. The study of behavior starts with an understanding of motivation. MOTIVATION is *an inner force that moves people toward satisfying a need.* Motivation involves a three-stage cycle consisting of a need or want, a drive, and a goal. The drive may be physical, such as the need for water, food, or sleep. Or it may be psychological, such as the need for recognition or security. The drive is the stimulation to act, which is created by the need or want. The third stage, reaching the goal that satisfies the need, is the result of the drive.

For some years now, psychologists have recognized that human behavior is motivated by both environmental conditions and individual characteristics.

Abraham H. Maslow formulated a theory of motivation, which received considerable attention in marketing. He brought together the viewpoints of several schools of psychological thought. Maslow identified a hierarchy of five levels of needs, which he arranged in the order he felt people seek to satisfy them.

These needs are significant to marketers. The physiological needs relate to what a product does — automobiles transport people. Safety needs relate to people's security — homes provide safe and comfortable living quarters. The belongingness needs relate to products that make one personally attractive or acceptable, and so on.

THE PERSONAL-SELLING PROCESS

The successful personal-selling process involves five basic steps. They are the same whether the sale is conducted in one presentation or over a period of time. They cannot always be precisely timed or sharply distinguished from one another. These steps are shown in Figure 12-3.

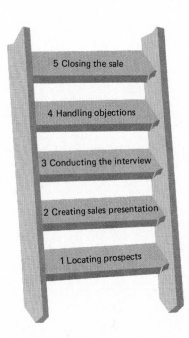

FIGURE 12-3
Basic Steps in the Personal-Selling Process

Locating the Prospective Customer. **Prospects** are potential customers. In some businesses, salespeople are supplied with a list of prospects. In others, potential customers must be discovered by the salesperson. Such customers can be found among one's acquaintances, through inquiries of friends and business associates, through social contacts, and through advertising.

Creating a Sales Presentation.   The presentation may be informal or tightly structured. Many presentations use visual materials, charts, graphs, slides, or filmstrips. The presentation should be flexible so that it may be adapted to suit the situation.

Conducting the Sales Interview.   The third step in the selling process is conducting the interview. One useful approach is the **"AIDA"** persuasion process. This process involves four stages through which the purchaser passes mentally—*attention, interest, desire, and action.* After gaining the prospect's attention, the presentation must develop the buyer's interest. Product samples, models, or a special price discount are effective in doing this. Moving into the desire and action stages sometimes requires more than one interview. A salesperson must know when to stop the presentation to avoid "overselling."

Handling Objections.   The progress of the sales interview may hinge on the effectiveness of the salesperson's handling of objections. Seldom do interviews follow the script, for the customer raises questions. The customer may want time to think the idea over, or may not like the price. Or the item's quality may be questioned. The salesperson must learn how to answer questions and objections, and move the interview toward completion.

Closing the Sale.   At some point, the customer reaches a decision to buy or not to buy. If the presentation is successful, the sale will be made. Sales are not always closed at the end of the initial presentation. If more meetings are required, a date should be established for the first follow-up interview.

At some point, the customer reaches a decision to buy or not to buy. (Photo by Ann McQueen, STOCK/Boston.)

A successful salesperson studies the prospect carefully and discovers which technique will be most effective in closing the sale. For example, the salesperson determines how the customer wishes to pay for the article, and then moves along smoothly to the right closing technique without offending the customer.

One sales manual of instructions says this about closing a sale:

1. When your prospect begins to pause in making the final decision, this is the time to step in and close.
2. Watch your prospect's facial expression. If the prospect indicates by a smile or a twinkle of the eye that he or she is pleased with the article, then get out your order book.
3. Listen to the prospect's voice; if there is a slight inflection or a raising or lowering tone, this is your tip to make your closing remarks.

Follow-up Contacts. Sometimes a follow-up visit is needed to close a sale. But follow-up contacts should be made in many cases even though they are not needed. The follow-up contact is an important complement to the selling process. How well is the customer satisfied with the product or service? What postsale servicing is needed? Is needed servicing being provided promptly and pleasantly? And, of course, is another sale in order?

SUCCESSFUL PERSONAL SELLING

Every salesperson wishes to be successful; the professional salesperson works consciously to become more effective. **To progress in successful selling, one must want to succeed, exercise self-discipline, and develop good selling techniques.** Purpose, planning, enthusiasm, confidence, and drive are all ingredients in selling success. Sales personnel may be directed by management, but self-motivation is most important.

SUCCESS IN SELLING

Success in selling employs a variety of techniques. Here are a few that are often mentioned by successful salespeople:

1. Find out what your customers' real wants and needs are. Listen as they tell you what they are interested in.
2. Know all about your product and what it can do for your customer. Product knowledge is a "must" in personal selling because it creates customer confidence, builds enthusiasm, and gives a professional touch to the situation. Stress the unique advantage of your product over others.
3. Present a positive rather than a negative approach. The sales presentation is more effective when the salesperson says, "May I help you?" than when he or she says, "You wouldn't like to see our new model, would you?" A negative approach calls for a negative answer.
4. Prepare yourself to handle objections. If the prospect says the price is too high, you might reply, "Yes, the price may be a little higher than you planned. However, in the long run you'll save money because of the superior quality of this product." In any event, don't argue with your prospect about whether a price is too high.
5. Use praise judiciously.

Psychologist Donald Moine said that the best salespeople use indirect hypnosis in selling without even knowing it. By changes in their rate of speech, its volume, or its tone, certain phrases have the effect of commands. After a customer's confidence is won, the sales pitch begins. Fact is linked with suggestion, just as a hypnotist does it. For example, "You have a wife and three children, and we think you need $80,000 protection for them."

Personal selling is a two-way flow of communication. It should concentrate on need satisfaction, not on the hard sell.

WORDS THAT SELL Closing a sale is an agent's ultimate goal. Both a reputation and income are determined by the sales record. Therefore, a successful sales representative pays special attention to the words he or she uses. Some words encourage a sale's closing, and others produce a negative reaction. In the comparison below, words that help to sell are matched against words that don't.

Words That Sell	Words That Don't
Agreement	Contract
Analysis	Estimate
Certify	Claim
Economic value	Low price
Inexpensive	Cheap
Investment	Cost
Negotiate	Bargain
Offer	Give
OK it, please!	Sign it!
Opportunity	Deal
Own	Buy
Quality	Expensive
Service	Sell
Specialist	Expert

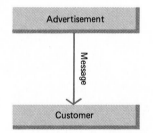

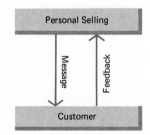

FIGURE 12-4
Personal Selling Is Two-Way Communication

SALES MANAGEMENT Frederick E. Webster, Jr., interviewed the chief executive and operating officers in thirty major corporations. He found that they believe that marketing is the most important management function in their businesses. They also see it becoming even more important in the future.[1]

---

[1] Frederick E. Webster, Jr., "Top Management's Concerns about Marketing: Issues for the 1980's," *Journal of Marketing*, Vol. 45 (Summer 1981), 16.

As a major part of marketing, sales management differs very little from management in other areas of a business firm. Much of the discussion in Chapters 4 and 5, although aimed at management in general, applies in sales management as well.

The main task in sales management consists of coordinating the selling efforts of individuals. This is a very personal thing and requires administrative ability, tact, and diplomacy. Various aspects of sales management include the following:

1. Establishing sales-force objectives
2. Planning an organizational structure
3. Recruiting, selecting, and training
4. Directing the sales force—motivation, supervision, compensation
5. Evaluating and then determining promotions and rewards

The sales-management process is illustrated in Figure 12-5.

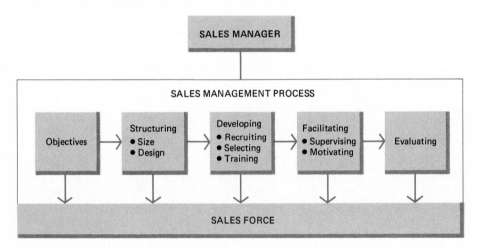

FIGURE 12-5
The Sales-Management Process

ADVERTISING AS PROMOTION

Most companies use a blend of personal and nonpersonal means of selling. More money is spent for advertising than for other types of nonpersonal promotion. The parallel relationship of personal selling to advertising in promoting the flow of goods is shown in Figure 12-6.

To the homemaker, advertising may mean the grocery ad in Wednesday's local newspaper. To the sales manager, advertising is a method of communicating with the public to make the selling job easier. To the accountant, advertising is one of the costs of doing business; and to the economist, it is an integral part of today's business system.

All of us have been influenced to buy certain things because of some form of advertising. It is universally recognized that advertising conveys selling messages better than other techniques in certain situations.

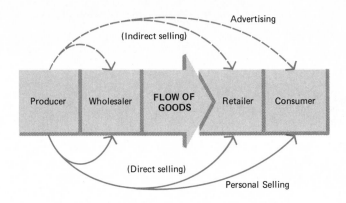

FIGURE 12-6
Personal Selling and Advertising in Marketing

WHAT IS ADVERTISING? The Definitions Committee of the American Marketing Association defines ADVERTISING as *any paid form of nonpersonal presentation and promotion of ideas, goods, or services by an identified sponsor."* Two things are important in this definition: payment for the advertisement, and a sponsor who pays for it. At times it is possible to communicate without cost to the sponsor—for example, through editorial comments by newspapers or magazines about a firm or a product. This type of information is considered publicity rather than advertising. Usually public relations is more concerned with developing a favorable image with the public than with directly promoting the sale of products.

PURPOSES OF ADVERTISING **The overall purpose of advertising is to influence the level of product sales and thereby increase the advertiser's profits.** Sometimes a firm is forced to advertise because of the actions of competitors or government. In such instances, the opportunity to increase profits may be slim. Yet failure to advertise could result in either reduced sales and less profit or legal action.

As a tool of marketing, advertising generally serves the following purposes (sometimes called "the three Rs of advertising"):

1. *Retain "loyal" customers:* Persuade present customers to increase their buying. An example is Eastman Kodak's appeal in its advertising that reads, "Don't forget to feed your camera this weekend."
2. *Retrieve "lost" customers:* Slow down the flow of present customers away from the preferred brand. The Florida Citrus Commission changed strategy when it started advertising, "It isn't just for breakfast any more."
3. *Recruit "new" customers:* Increase the flow of customers toward the advertised product. Replace those lost to competitors. Widen the total market. Johnson & Johnson appealed to adults to use the shampoo they had earlier pushed for babies. They featured Fran Tarkenton shampooing his hair and saying, "Everyone knows about no more tears."

Most companies think all this is very important—in fact, vital—to their sales. How important? Well, consider this: Of the 192 pages in a recent issue of *Business Week,* 128 pages were advertising. (Sixty percent of the advertisements were in color.)

MEASURING THE RESULTS OF ADVERTISING **For a determination of the effectiveness of advertising, its results should be evaluated. And they must be evaluated in relation to its objectives.** A practical way to measure its effctiveness is through increased sales volume.

VICTOR K. KIAM II

Victor K. Kiam stars in his own commercials. You may have seen him on television. He has appeared using a Remington Shaver, telling you it will shave as close as a blade or he'll give you your money back.

Kiam graduated from Yale with a B.S. degree in 1947 and a B.A. in 1948, and received a master's degree in Business Administration from Harvard in 1951. He was with Lever Brothers from 1951 to 1955, the International Latex Corporation from 1955 to 1968, and the Benrus Corporation from 1968 to 1977. He was chairman and CEO of Benrus from 1971 to 1977. Since 1979, he has been chairman and president of Remington Products, Inc.

Remington once ranked first in electric shavers, but its market share declined and it was losing money. Kiam bought the company in 1979. He trimmed overhead, lowered prices, and stepped up advertising. He turned the company into a profit maker. He believes that in addition to producing a quality product, you have to let people know about it.

Victor Kiam is a ranked tennis player, the holder of several U.S. patents, and an internationally recognized speaker. He is the founder of the School of Entrepreneurial Studies at the University of Bridgeport. He is a member of the World Business Council, a Fellow of the Institute of Directors in London, and a trustee of the University of Bridgeport.

Kiam is married to the former Ellen Lipscher of New York City, and they have three children. They make their home in Stamford, Connecticut.

Sales for a period of time following an advertising campaign can be compared with those for a prior period. A second way is to determine how well the advertising message is received. As with product-test markets, advertising-test markets are often used before a nationwide campaign is launched.

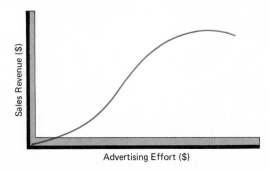

FIGURE 12-7
The Sales Response Function

TYPES OF ADVERTISING   Advertising can be classified into certain types, depending upon its use and purpose.

Product Advertising.   This type of advertising is designed to sell one or more definite and identified products or services. It usually describes and praises their features and good qualities and may even emphasize their prices. Product advertising is used to sell both consumer and industrial goods. Consumer and industrial goods have different marketing characteristics. They are sold in different trade channels, to different markets, under different pricing policies, and by different selling methods. Edward G. Harness,

304

former board chairman of Procter & Gamble, had this to say about advertising as it relates to products:

> Advertising has no life of its own. It has no unique power to persuade. It is not a separate and distinct force in our society. It should not be praised or criticized for its own sake. It is simply a part of a total marketing process which, to be successful, must be based on a worthwhile product.

CASHING IN ON A NAME

Sophia Loren receives a 5 percent commission on each vial of Sophia perfume sold. John McEnroe received $500,000 for endorsing Dunlop tennis rackets, plus a small commission on each sale above that amount.

Institutional Advertising. This type tries to create a favorable attitude toward the company offering to sell a good. It tries to build goodwill that will generate long-run rather than immediate sales. For example, a manufacturer may run an institutional advertisement to tell the public about the firm's efforts to reduce air pollution. Large corporations can afford to spend money on institutional Advertising.

National Advertising. This type is used to sell nationally distributed brands by using a medium with nationwide circulation. It is generally associated with advertising by the manufacturer rather than by a retailer or local advertiser. Moreover, national advertising refers only to the *level of the advertiser*. It has no relation at all to geographic coverage. If such a manufacturer places an advertisement in only one city, it is still called national advertising.

Local Advertising. Local (or retail) advertising is placed by a local merchant. It usually differs from national advertising by being more specific in terms of price, quality, and quantity. In national advertising, the purpose is to build a general demand for a product that may be sold in many stores. In local advertising, the stress is on the store where the product is sold.

Corrective Advertising. Corrective advertising takes place to correct specific false or misleading claims that might have been made in previous advertising. Classic examples of corrective advertising include the following: STP's corrective ads to clarify the claim that STP oil treatment will stop cars from burning oil; Anacin's $24 million worth of corrective advertising disclosing that Anacin is not a tension reliever; Listerine's correcting an earlier claim that it "fights colds." These and other corrective ads have been ordered by courts to rectify earlier misleading advertisements.

Advocacy Advertising. Many companies carry on advertising programs devoted to public-service themes. The Warner-Swazey Company features this type of message regularly in its advertising. The Mobil Oil Corporation ran a series of such ads during the energy crisis. Motorola and Pfizer had such series in the early 1980s. Companies use advocacy advertising when, in their opinion, the news media are not presenting both sides of an issue. Advocacy advertising is similar to the editorials that appear in business magazines and newspapers. Stephen A. Kliment defines advocacy advertising as:

> . . . any kind of paid public communication or message from an identified source and in a conventional medium of public advertising, which presents information or a point of view bearing on a publicly recognized controversial issue.[2]

Bradley Graham, in his article, "The Corporate Voice," published in *The Washington Post*, March 25, 1979, said: "Weyerhauser in its ads doesn't sell paper, it preaches conservation. Kellogg doesn't peddle cereal, it promotes nutrition. Bethlehem Steel argues the fine points of U.S. Trade policy."

FIGURE 12-8

Example of an Advocacy Ad. (Courtesy of Pfizer Company.)

THE PFIZER HEALTHCARE SERIES

A pain in the stomach that comes from the heart.

You feel a sense of fullness. Of pressure. A sharp pain in the chest. A heaviness. Maybe you're short of breath. Symptoms we innocently mistake for indigestion may also be symptoms of a heart condition called angina pectoris. More typically, you may have an unusual sensation in your left arm. A pain in your left shoulder or neck. Even a pain in your jaw or teeth.

The right diagnosis can be life-saving if your heart is warning that it is not getting enough blood and is short in oxygen and nutrients.

Who can diagnose angina?
You cannot. Your doctor can.
Diagnosis of angina is usually simple and straightforward. Treatment depends upon the type of angina you have.
Angina occurs:

1. When there is coronary vessel spasm.
2. When blood flow is limited by vessel wall thickening.
3. When a combination of vessel spasm and wall thickening reduces blood, oxygen and nutrients to the heart.

You can reduce the workload on your heart by reduction of weight, smoking, tension and stress, and also by recreation and rest. Moderate exercise helps, too. Medicines can increase blood flow in the vessels of your heart. And if your angina is related to high blood pressure, your doctor may prescribe medicines to help bring it down.

Obviously, you cannot be your own doctor. You need a support system. We call it...

Partners in Healthcare
You are the most important partner.
Only you can spot the warning signs and report them to your physician. And it's you who must decide to accept the guidance and counseling of your physician and pharmacist. When medicines are prescribed, only you can take them as directed.

Your doctor interprets the warning signs, orders your tests, and makes the diagnosis.
He also prescribes the best medication for you among those available—considering each drug's characteristics—and monitors your progress.

All those who discover, develop and distribute medicines complete the partnership.
Pfizer's ongoing research brings you essential medicines for a wide range of diseases. Through our development of these and many other medications, we are fulfilling our responsibility as one of your partners in healthcare.

 **Pfizer** PHARMACEUTICALS • A PARTNER IN HEALTHCARE

2 Stephen A. Kliment, "Advocacy Advertising by U.S. Corporations: Can Money Buy Friends?" *Madison Avenue*, February 1981, p. 29.

ADVERTISING SLOGANS

Amtrak launched an ad campaign to convince leisure travelers of the uniqueness of the train experience. The ads took advantage of what nature supplied Amtrak at no extra charge for four-color: beautiful, exciting scenery right outside its own picture windows. The copy line was, "See America at see level." The results: For six months seats and/or sleeping accommodations were completely sold out on 733 of its trains. Amtrak had 17 percent of its ad budget in magazine advertising.

If you had your preference, would you ruther go to Druthers? Or wouldn't you rather have a Buick? And sooner or later you'll own Generals!

Slogans do help sell merchandise. Many American businesses use slogans to identify their products. One of the best known uses of slogans relates to Coke. The Coca-Cola Company has used slogans for years. You can recall several, but you probably don't realize how often the slogan has changed. Here is a review of some of the Coke slogans:

Some of Coca-Cola's Ad Themes Through the Years

1886 Drink Coca-Cola
1905 Coca-Cola revives and sustains
1906 The Great National Temperance Beverage
1922 Thirst knows no season
1925 Six million a day
1927 Around the corner from everywhere
1929 The pause that refreshes
1938 The best friend thirst ever had
1948 Where there's Coke there's hospitality
1949 Along the highway to anywhere
1952 What you want is a Coke
1956 Makes good things taste better
1957 Sign of good taste
1958 The cold, crisp taste of Coke
1963 Things go better with Coke
1970 It's the real thing
1971 I'd like to buy the world a Coke
1975 Look up, America
1976 Coke adds life
1979 Have a Coke and a smile
1982 Coke is It

Logos sell merchandise too. Companies use logos at their places of business and in their advertising. Do you have an alligator, a fox, or a hound on any of your clothing? The Izod-Lacoste alligator is one of the best-known logos. Since General Mills bought David Crystal, the alligator logo has really been popularized. It appears on dresses, shirts, jeans, jackets, sweaters, swimwear, socks, pajamas, and what have you. More than 30 million Izod alligator items are sold every year.

The marketing of shampoo products is a good illustration of competition through advertising. This is a billion dollar market, and one where brand loyalty is weak. A company can spend millions in launching a new product only to see market share fade in a couple of years. Gillette Company spent $45 million to launch "Silkience"; Helene Curtis spent $35 million in a promotion blitz; and Procter & Gamble spent $50 million to bring out "Pert."

If a competitor advertises a product similar to yours, you return the favor. In a single issue of *Business Week* magazine, fourteen different computer companies advertised their products. Here are some examples of their attention-catching captions:

Sticklers for accuracy are sold on T.I. computers.

Texas Instruments

Making a *quick* decision isn't enough. You've got to make the right one. And with HP 125, you can do both.

Hewlett-Packard

E.F. Hutton simplifies life with Apples.

Apple Computer

Don't let a microcomputer that only performs solo get your goat.

Get an i Bex

Business Week itself advertised as follows:

Join the 800,000 plus subscribers whom *Business Week* is guiding more smoothly through 1982. With our "focused information for management" you're ready for opportunities, turning points, crises. You're perking with new ideas, techniques, solutions.

Shortly thereafter, *Forbes* responded with:

Do you know anybody who is somebody in business who does not read *Forbes* Magazine?

Companies not only compete for business by advertising; they also compete *in* their advertising. For example, Savin Corporation used a full-page ad in *The Wall Street Journal* to take a jab at the Xerox Corporation. The top half of the page said, in letters an inch and a half high:

We created a new way of copying, more revolutionary than xerography.

And Xerox advertised as follows:

Our New Typewriter Has More Memory Than What's Their Name's.

Soon after Avis advertised offering to rent "Cadillacs at the Cutlass price" and said, "Trying Harder makes Avis Second to None," Hertz used a full-page ad in *The Wall Street Journal* to say:

Now Avis claims to be second to none. That should read "Second to no. one."

ADVERTISING AND THE PUBLIC

Advertising alone will not persuade consumers to pay what they feel is an unreasonable price. Yet consumers often believe that a nationally advertised brand is worth a higher price than an unadvertised brand. For example, customers are willing to pay a little more for Armour's canned ham than for an unknown brand. Their experience leads them to think that it will taste better. The consumer may determine this added value by prior use, or may accept the claims of the advertiser. However, if the advertised brand has no important differences, its price may be no higher than that of unadvertised competitors.

Is advertising an economic waste? Critics question the social value of advertising. For one thing, they claim that advertising fails to create new demands and merely results in switching brands. For such consumer goods as toothpaste, cosmetics, detergents, and gasoline—where advertising is highly competitive—the total per capita consumption has risen steadily over the years. To say that all advertising is purely competitive and therefore wasteful suggests that competition itself is wasteful. From the advertiser's standpoint, the potential dollar sales should produce enough gross-margin dollars—the excess of sales over cost of goods sold—to pay the advertising costs. Advertising is expected to pay for itself in added sales. Evidence shows that mass advertising is essential to maintain both mass consumption and mass production.

Truth in Advertising. There are, of course, dishonest advertisers. As the watchdog for the American public, the Federal Trade Commission (FTC) is constantly battling with companies about their alleged exaggerations or untruths. What do we mean by "tell the truth"? Is the advertisement expected to tell the literal truth, or merely to give a reasonably accurate impression? On this subject, the Supreme Court has made these statements:

> Advertising as a whole must not create a misleading impression even though every statement separately considered is literally truthful.
>
> Advertising must not obscure or conceal material facts.
>
> Advertising must not be artfully contrived to distract and divert readers' attention from the true nature of the terms and conditions of an offer.

The FTC embarked on a strong truth-in-advertising campaign in the early 1970s. It demanded that advertisers be prepared to substantiate their claims. An FTC resolution states that advertisers are not voluntarily meeting the public's needs for more objective information about their claims. The resolution adds:

> Public disclosure can enhance competition by encouraging competitors to challenge advertised claims which have no basis in fact. . . .

In another area of concern, the FTC is seeking to prevent deceptive price advertising. Typical practices that the commission warns advertisers to avoid are contained in its publication, "Guides against Deceptive Pricing." This publication is available to businesses in cooperation with Better Business Bureaus.

A recent study published by the *Harvard Business Review* gives some business executives' views regarding advertising:

1. Only one out of three believes that advertisements really give a true picture of the product.
2. Two out of five believe that the general public's faith in advertising is at an all-time low.
3. Nine out of ten feel that advertisers should be required to prove their claims.

Much advertising can be considered truthful. Still, there are too many unscrupulous advertisers who make misleading or half-true statements about their products. Exaggerated claims for killing germs, curing colds, and inducing sleep have been challenged by government agencies.

In 1938, Congress passed the Wheeler-Lea Act, amending the Federal Trade Commission Act of 1914. The act gives the FTC power over "unfair or deceptive acts or practices." Several statutes aimed at specific industries grant the FTC authority to act on matters related to labeling and advertising.

ADVERTISING MEDIA

If an advertising message is to reach its audience, some type of carrier must be chosen. In the field of advertising, these carriers are called **MEDIA.** (A specific advertising medium is sometimes called a **vehicle.**) The success of advertising depends upon both the message and the medium selected. The media most commonly used for advertising purposes are these:

Newspapers	Outdoor advertising
Magazines	Transportation advertising
Direct mail	Point-of-purchase displays
Radio	Speciality
Television	

KINDS OF MEDIA Some large companies use almost all the media listed above. But small companies, for financial reasons, may use only one or two. Many factors must be evaluated in selecting the proper media. These include the cost, extent of coverage (circulation), size of the selection from which to choose, degree of flexibility, timeliness, and nature of coverage (geography).

Newspapers. There are approximately 1,800 daily newspapers in the United States, with a combined circulation of 62 million; and there are about 700 daily newspapers with Sunday editions, with a combined circulation of over 55 million. There are 8,000 weekly newspapers.[3] In terms of spending, the newspaper is the leading medium. It accounts for 28.5 percent of the total advertising dollar. This vehicle is very effective when a business is seeking to cover a single metropolitan area. Copy can be prepared and submitted only a few hours before press time, although most newspapers specify that copy be turned in several days in advance. However, the short life of each newspaper edition and the poor reproductive quality of illustrations are two limiting

---

[3] *Editor and Publisher Yearbook*, 1981.

factors. Studies show that the average length of time a person reads a newspaper is only twenty minutes. **The newspaper advertisement is used when the appeal attempts to reach the general public, not a select group.**

The Campbell Kids are slimming down to fit a new weight-conscious image emphasizing nutrition and athletics. (Courtesy Campbell Soup Company.)

Television.   Television is a mass medium. It can be used either on a nation-wide or on a regional basis, or it can be concentrated on the local market. As with radio, television has the advantage of immediate reception, providing timeliness to an even greater extent than newspapers. A magazine or newspaper may be in print several hours or days before it is read by the subscriber, but the TV message is received by the listener at once. Television's greatest advantage is that it combines sight, sound, motion, and demonstration. And for many viewers, it does all this in color—a unique combination for advertising. On the other hand, its message is short-lived, and production costs are high. Expenditures for TV advertising are the second largest. TV claims one-fourth of all advertising dollars.

Ninety-five percent of all American households have television sets, and 80 percent of all adults (18 years of age and older) view television daily. It is mass medium that appeals to all age groups.

Most prime time is given to the national networks. Because of its broad coverage at prime time, advertising on the national network is expensive. Nabisco paid CBS and NBC $4.5 million to sponsor the Rose Parade on both networks on January 1, 1983. This was thought to be the first time that one company had 4½ hours of *exclusive* sponsorship on two networks—a total of seventy-six commercials. A 30-second commercial in prime time for the 1984 Olympics cost about $250,000. The ten companies that spent the most for network TV advertising during a recent year, in order of the amount spent, are shown in Table 12-1.

Complaints about the frequency of TV advertisements are causing the networks to consider carefully how many ads are "enough." Affiliated stations have been unhappy because the increase in the number of national network commercials reduces the number of advertising minutes they can sell locally.

TABLE 12-1
Big Advertisers on TV (in order of amount spent)

RANK	NAME OF COMPANY	INCREASE OR DECREASE OF EXPENDITURE OVER PREVIOUS YEAR
1	Procter & Gamble Co.	+15%
2	General Foods Corp.	+1
3	American Home Products	+2
4	Ford Motor Co.	+28
5	PepsiCo	+22
6	General Motors Corp.	+0.2
7	General Mills	−4
8	Bristol-Myers	−8
9	McDonald's	−5
10	Philip Morris	+20

Direct-Mail Advertising.   Direct-mail advertising ranks third behind newspapers and television in the amount of money spent. More than 10,000 companies currently use mail-order advertising. Direct-mail advertising averages over $10 billion. It is estimated that 85 percent of third-class mail and between 10 and 15 percent of first-class mail are direct-mail advertising.[4]

The chief advantage of direct-mail advertising is that the advertiser can select precisely the audience to be reached, which is not possible with other media. Segmentation makes it possible to have inquiry lists by product class, dollar amount, merchandise class, recentness of purchase, method of ordering, or method of payment. Direct-mail advertising is the most flexible, for it may serve a local, regional, or national market. Also, it offers an opportunity to make one's message personal. It provides great flexibility in production design and accurate timing in its scheduling. Direct-mail advertising does not require the purchase of time or space, as the other media do. The cost of direct-mail advertising is for printing, securing mailing lists, and postage.

Magazines.   In contrast to newspaper ads, magazine advertising reaches a more selective group. People buy magazines intended for them as members of special groups, such as teachers, doctors, engineers, farmers — and, yes, even advertising personnel. Magazines are generally printed on high-quality paper that enhances creative designs and the use of color. Copy must be

---

[4] Direct Mail Advertising Association.

FIGURE 12-10
Magazine ads are highly creative and attractive.
(Reprinted with the permission of Land O'Lakes, Inc. All
rights reserved.)

submitted weeks in advance of the publication date. People keep magazines much longer than newspapers and thumb through them again and again. Magazines provide a wide range of prospects, reaching people with many and special interests.

The W.R. Simmons Company reported that 90 percent of the nation's adult population (18 years of age and older) are magazine readers. The Daniel Starch research organization reported a study covering 12 million inquiries. This organization found that 54 percent of all inquiries to any single magazine ad are received within one week after its publication. Another 25 percent are received during the second week. By the end of the sixth week, 95 percent of the return is in.

Advertising rates are based on circulation. The cost of reaching customers can be determined in this way:

$$\frac{\text{Page rate} \times 1,000}{\text{Circulation}} = \text{Cost per thousand readers}$$

The twelve companies that spent the largest sums for magazine advertising in a recent year, in order of the amount spent, are listed in Table 12-2.

TABLE 12-2
Top 12 Magazine Advertisers, 1981

RANK	COMPANY	AD DOLLARS IN MAGAZINES
1	Philip Morris Inc.	$102,834,866
2	Reynolds, R J Industries, Inc.	89,264,693
3	Seagram, Co. Ltd.	67,517,826
4	General Motors Corp.	65,503,848
5	BAT Industries, Ltd.	61,166,983
6	Sears Roebuck & Co.	58,911,949
7	Ford Motor Co.	55,078,100
8	General Foods Corp.	37,165,667
9	Loews Corp.	36,486,469
10	Time Inc.	36,455,029
11	Procter & Gamble Co.	35,737,289
12	American Tel. & Tel. Co.	35,167,071

SOURCE: Magazine Publishers Association.

Radio. Radio as an advertising medium is considerably different from what it was before television. Some people thought that television would destroy radio advertising. To the contrary, it has increased greatly. In total, the more than 4,000 AM stations and more than 2,000 FM stations reach 80 percent of the population on any given day. Whereas there may be only one or two daily newspapers in a specific market, there are several radio stations. Radio messages are designed for special audiences, such as homemakers, farmers, and youth groups.

Spot advertising on the radio gives individual market selection. The advertiser can therefore tailor the message to the market coverage selected. Spot advertising enables a business firm to present its message at the most favorable time in an individual market. It provides the greatest flexibility in time, wording, station, and market.

IN A RECESSION, CUT ADVERTISING FIRST?

When sales and profits drop during a recession, management looks for ways to cut expenses. One of the most tempting areas is advertising costs. But is it one of the wisest? Here is what happened during the five most recent recessions:

According to the American Business Press, companies that maintained or increased advertising expenditures posted greater sales and profits than companies that cut theirs.

What happened during the 1974–75 recession is of particular interest. Companies that did not cut their ad budgets in either year had higher sales and income during those two years than companies that cut in either or both years.

EXPENDITURES FOR ADVERTISING

The total spent for advertising exceeds $54.8 billion annually. When taken as a whole, the amount of money that American corporations spend for advertising equals the amount they pay to their stockholders in dividends. A study completed by the Association of National Advertisers shows that for most companies dealing in consumer goods, advertising is among the three largest expenditures. For retailers, advertising ranks as the number-two expenditure, exceeded only by salaries.

The percentages spent by the various media are shown in Figure 12-11.

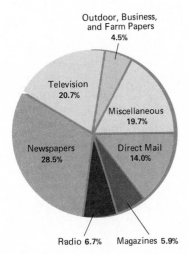

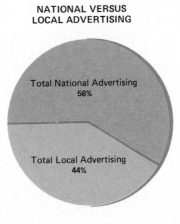

FIGURE 12-11

Advertising Expenditures by Medium, 1980. (Graph based on data published in *Advertising Age,* January 5, 1981.)

FREEZE FREEZES FLORIDA FRUIT ADS

Florida had a severe freeze in citrus land in the winter of 1982. It damaged 84 percent of the state's citrus crop. The Florida Citrus Commission placed a 10-day embargo on the shipment of fresh fruit. It also cut $1 million from its $20 million advertising budget for the year.

SALES PROMOTION

Sales promotion is basically a motivational activity. It is neither personal selling nor advertising, yet it has some of the characteristics of both. Advertising relies on outside media to broadcast messages about companies and their products. **The basic means used in sales promotion are internally created and distributed.**

Sales promotions are special functions and should be tied to personal selling or advertising. More money is spent on sales promotion than on advertising. It is estimated that in 1982, almost 60 percent of the promotional dollar went for sales promotion.

Sales promotion is aimed largely at three groups: company sales personnel, middlemen, and consumers. Devices aimed at company people and intermediaries are sales manuals, training films, exhibits, catalogs, and demonstrations. The major types of sales-promotion activities that are directed toward consumers are point-of-purchase displays, sampling, coupons, premiums, and contests.

POINT-OF-PURCHASE DISPLAYS

The POINT-OF-PURCHASE DISPLAY is *a device by which a product is displayed to stimulate an immediate purchase.* It consists of displays inside stores, close to the place where the goods are stacked. These displays are intended to stimulate impulse buying—decisions made on the spot without prior planning to buy. Supermarkets make space available for representatives to set up a display and perhaps cook sausage, hot dogs, and the like.

PRODUCT SAMPLING

Distributing a small sample of a product is a good way to promote it. Sampling puts into practice the axiom that "a good product promotes itself." To be most effective, sampling programs should be coordinated with advertising efforts. The samples should be distributed soon after the product is advertised. Samples are distributed largely by mail and through house-to-house delivery.

COUPONING

Cashing in a coupon is a quick and easy way to get a bargain. Quite often the consumer knows little more than that about the coupon process. But couponing has become a $1.3 billion business operation.[5]

The cents-off coupon goes directly to the consumer. This ensures that the ultimate user receives the saving. The rest of the process is carried out in one of several ways. Perhaps the manufacturer gives the wholesaler a discount on the purchase. The agreement might be that the wholesaler would pass the saving along to the retailer. The retailer would then lower the price and give the saving to the consumer.

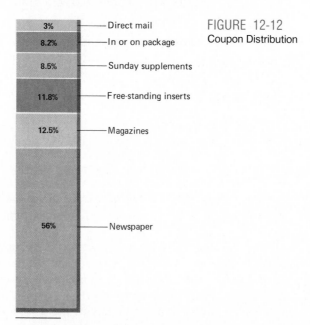

3%	Direct mail
8.2%	In or on package
8.5%	Sunday supplements
11.8%	Free-standing inserts
12.5%	Magazines
56%	Newspaper

FIGURE 12-12
Coupon Distribution

[5] According to estimates, this consists of $604 million in production, distribution, and handling costs, and $740 million in redemption costs.

In a recent year, 90 billion coupons were issued, but customers redeemed only a little over 4 billion. A.C. Nielsen estimates that 76 percent of all U.S. households used coupons. Nielsen's research arm reported that newspapers print and distribute the bulk of these. The percentage of coupons distributed by different methods is shown in Figure 12-12.

Cash refunds are sometimes used in lieu of the cents-off coupon. The cash refund or rebate specifics are usually printed right on the package; thus they do not cost much to distribute.

PREMIUMS A premium is offered the consumer as a reason for buying a specific good. If the purchase is made, the premium is received as a gift. Toys and other gimmicks are returned to buyers in exchange for box tops, universal product codes, or bottle caps. Premiums are seldom related to the product being sold. The premium leads the buyer into thinking that he or she is receiving "something for nothing."

Some premiums cost the manufacturer very little. In addition to the box top, the consumer must send in a certain amount of money. This sum comes close to paying the producer's net cost of the premium. The seller must pay,

CURRENT ISSUE

IS COUPONING A GOOD PRACTICE ECONOMICALLY?

Not everyone is agreed that the use of coupons is a good practice. Certainly the consumer who redeems coupons receives an immediate saving. But who pays for this? Does the producer, wholesaler, retailer, or the consumers who do not redeem coupons?

With which of the following statements do you agree, and with which do you disagree?

1. The cost of couponing does not justify its use.
2. Producers simply pass the cost of coupons on to others in the form of higher prices.
3. Wholesalers and retailers absorb the cost of couponing.
4. The savings made by consumers who use coupons justify their continued use.
5. The use of cents-off coupons is a good inflation fighter.
6. It is the consumers who do not redeem coupons who pay for the system.
7. Instead of issuing coupons, the seller should reduce the price of the goods.
8. If businesses did not spend money on couponing, they would spend it in other types of sales promotion.
9. Compared to the sums spent on advertising, the amount spent on coupons is minimal.
10. Consumers like coupons, and that alone justifies their use.

1. Are non–coupon users being discriminated against in pricing?
2. If couponing were discontinued, would consumer prices be lower?

Mary Jane Hayes, "The Coupon Queen" of Englishtown, N.J. (Photo by Susan McCartney, Photo Researchers, Inc.)

of course, the promotion and handling costs. The buyer still saves money, since the item usually costs less than its price in local stores.

For several years, Texaco offered a toy fire engine and gasoline truck as a premium at a price well under $5. More than a million of these premiums were distributed annually. And it has been estimated that Texaco gained more than 100,000 new customers each year the company used this premium. Premiums such as recipe booklets, packets of flower seeds, or plastic toys cost less than the average cents-off coupon.

Trading stamps represent a different form of premium. Their use is a long-term promotional effort. Trading stamps may be strong for a few years and then wane in popularity. But some retailers prefer trading stamps to other forms of promotion.

CONTESTS One popular form of contest asks the consumer to write a jingle, a limerick, or a slogan. Another favorite is a bake-off using the manufacturer's product. Items submitted are judged and a reward given.

Another form is the sweepstakes. Here, the entrant's name is placed in a pool of names, and the winner's name is drawn out of the pool. Every person entering has an equal chance to win. One's chances of winning in a typical sweepstake event are small, since millions of names are usually sent in. Pepsi offered prizes ranging from $1 to $50. Kraft offered a "family reunion vaca-

318

tion." Publisher's Clearinghouse offers a new home. Sweepstakes may or may not require one to purchase a company's product.

Sweepstakes enhance a product's image and generate a high level of consumer interest. They offer a ready-made reason for setting up a point-of-purchase display. Most sweepstakes appeal to people of middle age who have children.

PUBLIC RELATIONS AS PROMOTION

Only recently has public relations been considered a part of the marketing mix. It is concerned with publicity and new-product developments.

The American Marketing Association defines PUBLICITY as *"any form of nonpaid commercially significant news or editorial comment about ideas, products, or institutions."* Publicity consists primarily of news stories and personal appearances. When a new firm is opening for business, publicity appears in the local newspaper. When a business is remodeling, building an addition, or moving to a new location, these also form the basis of stories in the local news media.

Authors, athletes, and other public figures are usually willing and available to make public appearances at department stores and other businesses to promote their activities. Publicity implies third-party endorsement.

Word-of-mouth publicity from satisfied customers is invaluable. Extra effort to give top-quality merchandise, fair treatment, and personal service will cause this publicity to be positive and will result in additional sales.

A company's public-relations department is usually not a part of its marketing organization. So public-relations activities related to marketing must be coordinated with other facets of public relations. Promotional efforts must be in line with the company's overall public-relations policy.

SUMMARY OF KEY CONCEPTS

Promotion refers to a company's efforts to influence people to buy.

Promotion is basically communication. Advertising is a one-way flow of communication. Personal selling is a two-way flow.

Personal selling usually involves an oral presentation by the seller to a prospective buyer.

There are five important stages in the personal-selling process.

Advertising attempts to reach large numbers through nonpersonal means.

As a tool of marketing, advertising serves to retain loyal customers, retrieve lost customers, and recruit new ones. As a social force, it has altered our living habits and has helped to raise living standards.

Economically, advertising has promoted the growth of industry, lowered unit costs, and served to identify families of products under one name or brand.

The more popular advertising media are newspapers, radio and television, magazines, and direct mail.

Sales promotion is basically a motivation activity. It is aimed at company personnel, intermediaries, and consumers.

Sales-promotion activities aimed at consumers include point-of-purchase displays, sampling, couponing, premiums, and contests.

Public relations is the fourth component of promotion. It includes some aspects of the other three.

You should be able to match these business terms with the statements that follow:

a. ADVERTISING
b. AIDA PROCESS
c. EVALUATION
d. FOLLOW-UP
e. INSTITUTIONAL ADVERTISING
f. LOCATING PROSPECTS

g. MEDIA
h. MOTIVATION
i. PERSONAL SELLING
j. PROMOTION
k. PROMOTION BLEND
l. PUBLICITY

1. A company's efforts to influence customers to buy
2. Combination of communication methods used in promotion
3. An inner force that causes people to act to satisfy a need
4. Selling activities that involve personal contacts between buyer and seller
5. The first step in the selling process
6. Attention, interest, desire, action
7. A customer contact after a sale is closed
8. The final stage in the sales-management process
9. Paid forms of nonpersonal promotion by an identified sponsor
10. The means used by an advertiser to communicate to the buying public
11. Advertising that aims to create a favorable attitude toward a company
12. Nonpaid news about ideas, products, or institutions

1. What do we mean when we say that promotion is communication?
2. Identify the steps in the selling process.
3. What are some of the selling techniques used by successful salespeople?
4. What purpose is advertising designed to serve?
5. How do the various advertising media compare in the amount of money spent for them?
6. Why should sales-promotion activities be tied to personal selling and/or advertising efforts?

1. Which promotional activity do you consider to be of greatest importance? Why?
2. What is most important in successful personal selling?
3. Why do we say that advertising is a one-way flow of communication?
4. Do you think couponing is here to stay? Why, or why not?
5. What promotional activities in a men's retail clothing store do you consider of most importance?

BUSINESS CASES

12-1

ADVERTISING A NEW SERVICE

Commercial banks are faced with increasing competition from savings and loans, credit unions, brokerage firms, and even retailers (such as Sears), which are all offering "bank-type" services. As a result of this increased competition, many banks are scrambling to offer new innovative services in order to retain their current customers and gain new accounts.

The local, home-owned bank, First National Bank of Laramie, Wyoming, wishes to compete head-to-head with the larger, multistate banks entering its market. In order to be competitive, it is introducing the "2001" account. This is a special account in which any deposit balance over $2,000 is "swept" into a money-market account that pays a high rate of interest. Consumers do not have to manage their money for the highest possible returns. The bank will perform this service for them.

In order to introduce this new service to the local community of 25,000 people, First National has budgeted $6,000 for three months of introductory advertising.

Which of the following media are most appropriate for the bank's campaign? Why?

a. National television
b. Magazines
c. Newspapers
d. Radio
e. Direct mail (statement stuffers)

Is there a role for any of the other elements of the promotional blend (personal selling, sales promotion, publicity) in introducing this service? Why, or why not?

12-2   ADVERTISING A NEW PRODUCT

The Sturgill Company produces a complete line of assorted jams, jellies, and canned fruits. It has been successful and has experienced an acceptable growth in company sales and profits for the past twenty years. Eighteen months ago, it introduced a Star brand of peanut butter, which is packaged in 12-, 16-, and 20-ounce jars.

The Sturgill plant is located in Louisiana, and its products are sold in twelve southern and southwestern states. Its complete line of products is sold through six wholesale grocery companies and three large food brokers. The food brokers serve the Memphis, Dallas, and Oklahoma City areas.

In eight of the twelve states, Sturgill products are stocked in 80 percent of all independent food stores and voluntary chains. In the remaining four states, distribution ranges from 60 to 75 percent of the food stores. Star brand peanut butter, however, is handled by only half the retail outlets that sell Sturgill's other products.

The Sturgill management team has decided that it should do something to push its peanut butter. The six regional sales supervisors have recommended that the advertising budget be increased by $300,000. This budget increase has been approved. However, there was a division of opinion among the company executives. Should they spend this money advertising Star brand peanut butter, or all Sturgill products, with some emphasis on the Star brand? The choice of advertising media was left to the promotion committee.

1. What types of promotion do you think are feasible in this situation?
2. Which type of promotion would you single out as the one on which the largest amount of money should be spent?

Marketing Channels and Physical Distribution

13

study objectives

WHEN YOU HAVE FINISHED READING THIS CHAPTER, YOU SHOULD BE ABLE TO:

1. Describe the most common distribution channels used when marketing consumer goods
2. Discuss the main functions performed by wholesalers and other types of middlemen
3. Outline the ways retailers help both the wholesalers and the consumers
4. Name some of the trends in current marketing practices
5. Name the major components of logistics
6. Describe the role of warehousing in an efficient distribution system

The middleman is not a link in a chain forged by a manufacturer, but rather an independent market, the focus of a large group of customers for whom he buys. . . .

Philip McVey

arketing gives time and place utility to goods. A product serves the greatest good only when it is delivered to the place it is needed. Since most goods today are produced for sale to others, they must be distributed through marketing channels. Decisions about distribution involve many issues, including:

1. The number of middlemen to use
2. How to maintain communication channels between the different levels of middlemen
3. The selection of specific middlemen
4. The geographical placement of inventory stock
5. The location of distribution centers

This chapter discusses establishing marketing channels, the functions of wholesalers, retailing, warehousing, and the physical movement of goods.

THE NATURE OF DISTRIBUTION CHANNELS

For any particular product or service, one or more CHANNELS OF DISTRIBUTION *must be developed. This channel is the route taken by products and title to them as they move from original producer to ultimate user.* This product flow includes a number of institutions involved with the passing of the title to the goods.

INSTITUTIONS IN MARKETING CHANNELS

A marketing channel includes a number of marketing institutions and supporting agencies. Together they transfer title and deliver goods from the point of production through to the final sale.

We have already learned about the roles of producers and consumers. All others who play roles in the marketing channel are classified as *middlemen*. These include wholesalers, agents, brokers, commission merchants, jobbers, and retailers.

The Committee on Definitions of the American Marketing Association defines **MIDDLEMAN** as follows:

> A business concern that specializes in performing operations or rendering services directly involved in the purchase and/or sale of goods in the process of their flow from producer to consumer.

Some middlemen handle the goods physically; others do not; only some of them take title to the goods. The different types of wholesalers and the role of retailers as middlemen are discussed more fully later in this chapter.

ESTABLISHING DISTRIBUTION CHANNELS

When a company has identified its "market," it must next decide how to get the product to the market. Such decisions involve channel design—company objectives and customer desires are important in the design. Is it desirable to have company-owned stores? to employ salespersons who represent the company exclusively? to use existing middlemen, such as agents, brokers, or wholesalers? Sherwin-Williams uses company-owned stores; Purina Mills employs salespeople who represent them exclusively; and General Foods uses brokers who also represent other companies.

When existing middlemen are used, the movement of goods through them often must conform to their existing practices. Product attributes also influence channel design. For example, perishable produce must use channels that entail few middlemen, to avoid unnecessary handling and delays. If the product is large or heavy, the channel must minimize product handling as the product moves from one transporter to another.

INTENSITY OF DISTRIBUTION

Distribution can be intensive, selective, or exclusive. **If INTENSIVE, many wholesale and retail middlemen are used.** This is often used **to saturate a market with the product.** Under intensive distribution, the chief responsibility for advertising falls on the producer. Retailers are not interested in spending money to advertise goods that others also sell.

If the distribution is **SELECTIVE, a few wholesalers and a limited number of retailers will be used.** The geographical area to be covered may be restricted. Strategy then is concerned with specialized methods of distribution rather than maximum coverage.

In **EXCLUSIVE DISTRIBUTION, only one retailer in any given community handles the product.** The dealer selected can afford to push the product aggressively, because he or she will reap the benefits of these efforts.

Exclusive
One Retailer

Selective
Limited Number of Retailers

Intensive
Many Retailers

FIGURE 13-1
Intensity of Distribution

In exclusive distribution, the producer might exercise some control over pricing and promotion. In intensive distribution, the producer would be able to exercise little or no control.

Designer dresses may be sold exclusively by only one retailer in a community—a ladies' dress shop. But inexpensive dresses or copies of designer dresses could be found in several different stores—intensive distribution.

SELECTING SPECIFIC DISTRIBUTORS

After the channel is designed and the intensity of distribution decided, individual middlemen must be chosen. Middlemen specialize just as producers do. Some concentrate on a few customers and earn good commissions by making large sales. Some give a wide variety of services; others offer only a few. Some cover wide geographical areas; others operate reasonably close to home base.

The specific services wanted by the producer must be matched with those offered by the middlemen available in the territory to be served. Middlemen are interested in representing good companies that make good products, just as manufacturers are anxious to have reputable middlemen representing them.

Six principal factors can affect the choice of middlemen:

1. Reputation of the company's management team
2. Middleman's access to the desired market
3. Location of the business
4. Product policies and product lines of the middleman
5. Breadth of services to be given to the customer
6. Promotion policies of the firm

TYPICAL DISTRIBUTION CHANNELS

Different goods follow different marketing channels to the final user. Sometimes even the same good may follow different channels. Let us consider the most common distribution channels.

FROM PRODUCER DIRECTLY TO CONSUMER

The most direct channel for distributing consumer goods is from the producer to the consumer. However, only a few types of goods have been successfully marketed in this manner. The local dairy still delivers milk to homes, although with improved refrigeration. Farmers still make limited use of the direct channel to sell small quantities of fruits and vegetables.

From Producer Directly to Consumer.
A farmers' market. (Photo by Murray Lemmon, USDA.)

Most manufacturers using this direct-selling channel ordinarily employ one or more of these methods: **manufacturer-owned retail stores, house-to-house selling, or direct mail.** Melville Corporation (shoes) markets its goods through company stores. Avon, Tupperware, and Fuller Brush use house-to-house selling. Ambassador (leather goods), Columbia House (records), and New Process Company (clothing) sell by direct mail.

FROM MANUFACTURER TO RETAILER TO CONSUMER

A second channel is direct from manufacturer to retailer to consumer. Many kinds of goods, such as automobiles, furniture, appliances, and shoes, are commonly sold this way. This enables the producers to influence the training of salespeople and the way in which the retailer promotes the product. If speed is important in the marketing of an item (fashion goods, for instance), buyers for retail stores may place their orders at the sales offices of the manufacturer.

To expedite their dealings with retail buyers, several manufacturers will join together to display their samples and take orders at a show or fair. An example is the semiannual furniture shows at Chicago, Dallas, and Hickory, North Carolina.

Manufacturers who distribute their goods over a wide area sometimes establish branch warehouses. In them they maintain a stock of goods to meet

From Manufacturer to Retailer to Consumer.
A discount shoe store does a brisk business in children's shoes and sneakers. (Photo by Gabor Demjen, STOCK/Boston.)

regional demands. By shipping orders directly to retail stores, they render much the same service as the ordinary wholesaler.

A growing variation of this channel is "direct marketing." Mail solicitation through major mailers, such as credit-card companies and oil companies, has been used to reduce the cost of billing customers. Everything from wallets to motorcycles is offered in shiny brochures included with customers' bills. Companies called syndicators work with the giant mailers. They pay for selecting merchandise to be offered, preparing brochures, and processing orders. In return, the mailers pocket commissions that help offset the cost of computerized credit-card systems. In this format, the syndicators never really take possession of the merchandise. They act only as intermediaries between manufacturer (or retailer) and customer.

FROM MANUFACTURER TO WHOLESALER TO RETAILER TO CONSUMER

Most convenience goods, such as drugs, hardware, and groceries, move along the route from manufacturer to wholesaler to retailer, and then to the consumer.

Wholesalers purchase goods in large quantities from numerous manufacturers. From their wide variety and types of goods, they supply the needs

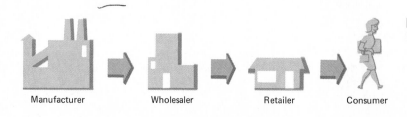

Manufacturer   Wholesaler   Retailer   Consumer

FIGURE 13-2
Distribution Channels

MARKETING

of retailers. The wholesaler reduces the number of accounts that the manufacturer deals with, and the manufacturer saves the expense of servicing thousands of individual businesses.

The wholesaler likewise saves the retailer money and time. An independent grocery or hardware merchant normally stocks the shelves with thousands of different items. Instead of contacting hundreds of manufacturers, the merchant can do business with just a few wholesalers.

CHANNEL MANAGEMENT When the channels have been chosen and the middlemen selected, the channels must be *managed*. The job of channel management is to see that products move smoothly through the whole channel. Ideally, the distribution channel is viewed as a **total system.** In practice, however, most channel members operate rather independently of other members. Each channel member has individual objectives, and these may vary from those of other members.

MARKETING INDUSTRIAL GOODS

Industrial goods, you will recall, are products bought for use in making other goods. There is no single market for industrial goods—rather there are several markets. Industrial goods are sold to farmers, miners, lumberers, fisheries, contruction contractors, factories, governments, institutions, wholesalers, and retailers. Some industrial marketers specialize, dealing with only one type of market. Others cover several different types.

The distribution channels through which industrial goods travel are markedly different from those followed by consumer goods. No retailers are needed, and fewer middlemen are used. Consequently, the distribution of industrial goods is usually a simpler process. The most commonly used channels are these:

1. Direct from factory to industrial user, sometimes by way of a factory sales branch
2. From factory to agents (or brokers) to industrial user
3. From factory to wholesale distributor to industrial user

Some types of goods are sold directly to the ultimate users by the manufacturers. Approximately 12 to 15 percent of industrial goods are sold this way through the sales branches of manufacturers. This short distribution

FIGURE 13-3
Channels of Distribution for Industrial Goods

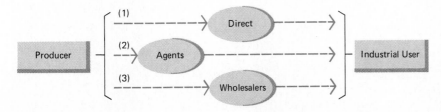

channel is appropriate for goods such as computers and machine tools. These require expert installation and maintenance service. The best way for the purchaser to be sure of getting this service is through face-to-face dealings with the manufacturer. Also, when most of a manufacturer's customers are concentrated in a small geographic area, there is simply no reason to work through a middleman. Finally, many orders for industrial goods are so large that the unit cost of direct negotiations between manufacturer and buyer is negligible.

MARKETING AGRICULTURAL PRODUCTS

Most farm products are really neither consumer goods nor industrial goods, and they are marketed differently from both types of products. Farm operations are carried on in every state, with most farmers producing on a relatively small scale. And in most instances an individual farm operator raises more than a single type of product. Thus, farm products must be assembled and concentrated in order to make them available to manufacturers, processors, and consumers.

To do this job, in the United States there are approximately 14,000 individuals or companies that assemble farm products. Some of them are small operators with a minimum amount of invested capital and little in the way of specialized equipment. Others own and control a whole chain of elevators, warehouses, or packing plants.

Fruits, vegetables, milk, and eggs are ready for consumers with little or no processing, but they must be distributed quickly. Grains, cotton, wool, and livestock must be processed or manufactured into products before being sold to consumers.

There are three basic types of middlemen engaged in marketing farm products: **wholesalers, brokers, and commission merchants.**

Loading Grain, Iowa.
(Photo by Elizabeth Hamlin, STOCK/Boston.)

MARKETING GRAINS   Although the value of the corn produced in the United States is about twice that of wheat, much of it is fed to livestock right on the farms and in feed lots. So more wheat than corn is marketed, transported, and processed into manufactured goods. It requires some 7,000 elevators in this country to handle wheat and other grains. In earlier years, most grains were moved by rail, but currently, trucks and water carriers are being used on an ever-increasing scale.

MARKETING LIVESTOCK   Farmers and ranchers currently sell approximately one-third of their livestock on consignment to commission merchants in central markets. They sell about one-fourth through local auction markets, about one-sixth to local buyers, and one-sixth to packers at their processing plants. The remaining twelfth is sold to other farmers. Animals are purchased at more than 700 concentration yards, most of them owned and operated by the meat packers. Today, most livestock is transported by trucks.

MARKETING FRUITS AND VEGETABLES   Because of the perishable nature of fresh fruits and vegetables, they are usually moved by truck to nearby canneries and processing plants. A small amount is sold directly to retail stores, again delivered by truck. Also, some is sold to truck jobbers who sell to nearby markets. Trucks provide much faster delivery than rail and are much more versatile.

Farmers in California, Florida, and south Texas ship fresh produce the year around. They use refrigerated trucks or refrigerated rail cars if the market is some distance away.

Farmers may join together in cooperatives to sell fruits and vegetables. The produce from such an organization is usually sold to wholesalers or chain-store buyers. It may be shipped either by truck or by refrigerated railroad cars.

The 1980 census reported that there are almost 1,000 brokers who sell fruits and vegetables, and slightly more than 2,200 businesses that assemble fruits and vegetables, approximately half of which are packers.

COOPERATIVES   As we saw in Chapter 3, a **cooperative** is a business enterprise owned and operated by a group of people to serve their marketing needs. Each member has an equal voice in the control of the firm, which is generally operated without profit. If profits do accrue, they are distributed to members in proportion to their patronage. Two distinct functions served by cooperatives are marketing and purchasing.

Agricultural Marketing Cooperatives.   Agricultural marketing cooperatives are associations operated by the growers or producers of a single product or a group of closely related products. Sunkist Growers, Inc., is a familiar example, marketing oranges and lemons; and Land-O-Lakes Creameries, Inc., markets dairy and poultry products. Such middlemen are important agencies in the marketing of several kinds of farm products. They market the grain, dairy products, fruits, vegetables, nuts, and livestock of more than 4 million producers. In addition to actual selling, these associations have several other purposes: (1) to improve merchandising practices; (2) to create demand through the use of brand names and advertising; (3) to promote more orderly marketing; (4) to extend financial assistance to members; and (5) to encourage the growing of higher-quality products.

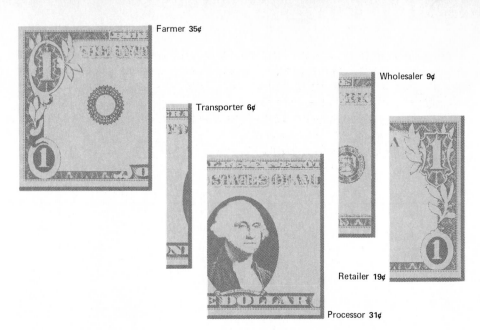

Farmer 35¢

Transporter 6¢

Wholesaler 9¢

Retailer 19¢

Processor 31¢

FIGURE 13-4
Who Gets the Food Dollar?
(Source: U.S. Department of Agriculture.)

Agricultural Purchasing Cooperatives.   A second type of cooperative association that serves farmers is the **agricultural purchasing cooperative.** These associations purchase and resell to members and nonmembers alike such commodities as fertilizer, seeds, gasoline, feeds, and farm machinery. Many of them also stock household appliances, but they do not attempt to handle most kinds of consumer goods.

The principal objective of these associations has been to enable their members to obtain their farm needs at lower prices. Their business has increased with the trend toward farm practices that require many kinds of equipment, seeds, and supplies. Membership is open to any farmer willing to buy one or more shares of stock in the association. Dividends, in cash or stock, are distributed on the basis of the patronage of members. Each member has a voice in controlling the affairs of the association.

WHOLESALERS' FUNCTION IN MARKETING

WHOLESALERS are *middlemen who buy merchandise for resale, primarily to other business firms rather than to consumers.* Their main function is one of assembly and dispersion. They are different from agents, for they buy, take title to, and take possession of the products they handle. Full-service wholesalers provide credit, market information, and pricing suggestions to their customers. In some instances, they help with store layout, accounting systems, and other facets of store operation.

The wholesaler is the most important source of supply to many retailers. The small retailer could scarcely operate without a wholesaler's services. The importance of wholesalers in our marketing system can best be understood by investigating how they serve the manufacturer and the retailer.

HOW THE WHOLESALER SERVES OTHERS

An effective wholesaler serves as a selling agency for manufacturers and a buying agency for retailers. *For manufacturers,* a wholesaler:

1. Informs the manufacturer about such matters as desirable package styling, advertising appeals, and product features. The wholesaler gains this knowledge through close contact with retailers.
2. Provides the manufacturer with thorough coverage of nearly every retailer who might be interested in stocking its product. This is an especially valuable service for manufacturers whose products need wide distribution.
3. Enables the manufacturer to minimize selling cost per unit. The manufacturer of food products, for example, would otherwise have to maintain enough salespeople to call on thousands of retail stores and restaurants.

For retailers, a wholesaler:

1. Saves much time in the buying process. Suppose that every hardware store had to buy directly from the thousands of manufacturers whose goods it stocks. If only half these manufacturers sent representatives to call on the retailer once every three months, the retailer would be visited by more than 400 salespeople daily!
2. Carries a complete line of goods from which the retailer can replenish stock easily and swiftly. So the retailer need not keep a huge supply of goods on hand or tie up large amounts of capital in inventory.
3. Serves as a valuable source of information and advice. For example, wholesalers may give suggestions on display and sales promotion of the goods they sell, as well as ideas on new items available.

The Wholesaler...

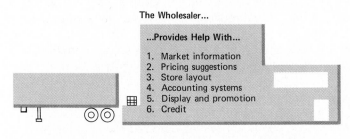

...Provides Help With...

1. Market information
2. Pricing suggestions
3. Store layout
4. Accounting systems
5. Display and promotion
6. Credit

...To Retailer

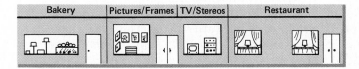

FIGURE 13-5
The Wholesaler's Functions

TYPES OF WHOLESALERS

The main distinctions among wholesalers, aside from the kinds of products they distribute, involve:

1. Whether they take title or possession of the goods
2. The number of functions they perform
3. The type of commission, fee, or regular income they receive.

| MERCHANT WHOLESALERS | **Merchant wholesalers** — sometimes simply called wholesalers or jobbers — perform more functions than do the other types of wholesalers. They take title to goods; store, deliver, and assemble them; and maintain a regular place of business. Their income comes from selling goods for an amount greater than their cost, rather than from commissions or fees. *Merchant wholesalers who provide a wide variety of services, such as granting credit, making deliveries, and giving out current trade information, are appropriately called* SERVICE WHOLESALERS. |

MERCHANT WHOLESALERS

Merchant wholesalers — sometimes simply called wholesalers or jobbers — perform more functions than do the other types of wholesalers. They take title to goods; store, deliver, and assemble them; and maintain a regular place of business. Their income comes from selling goods for an amount greater than their cost, rather than from commissions or fees. *Merchant wholesalers who provide a wide variety of services, such as granting credit, making deliveries, and giving out current trade information, are appropriately called* SERVICE WHOLESALERS.

LIMITED-FUNCTION WHOLESALERS

As their name implies, LIMITED-FUNCTION WHOLESALERS *render fewer marketing activities than merchant wholesalers. They do not take title to the goods they handle.* For example, the **truck wholesaler** combines the marketing functions of selling and delivery. The truck wholesaler does not grant credit but collects for each sale. The **drop shipper** sells merchandise that is delivered directly from the manufacturer to the customer. The delivery is called a drop shipment. Examples are coal, lumber, and building materials that are sold in carload lots.

AGENT MIDDLEMAN

AGENT MIDDLEMEN are a third category of wholesalers. They do not take title to the goods they sell, and they provide relatively few services. Their *main function is to make a sale for the manufacturer or distributor.* They are usually paid a commission based on volume of sales. Brokers, selling agents, and manufacturer's agents are classed as agent middlemen.

    Commission merchants, unlike other agents, actually take possession of the goods they market. They usually arrange for the shipment of goods, store them temporarily, sell them, and deliver them to the buyer. At times, they grant credit to the buyer. For all these services, they charge their clients a commission — a percentage of the sales price. Sometimes they include their expenses in handling and storing the goods. The majority of commission merchants deal in agricultural products.

RETAILERS' FUNCTION IN MARKETING

Most people are quite familiar with retailing. Sears, K mart, the local druggist, and Safeway are all retailers. The retailer is another middleman, serving both the consumer and the producer. *Retailers* are business firms that buy goods from wholesalers (and manufacturers) and sell them to consumers. RETAILING includes *all the activities related to the sale of goods and services for final consumption.* Retail stores vary greatly in size, kinds of goods and services offered, prices, and organization patterns. Some retail firms have individual owners; others are partnerships, corporations, or cooperatives. Retailing provides employment for about 12 million people.

RETAILING AND THE MANUFACTURER

The nearly 2 million retail stores in the United States cover the nation. They provide producers with a means of reaching the entire population. The manufacturer usually chooses to build the plant in a location near the source of raw materials or where labor is plentiful. Modern means of materials handling and distribution enable the manufacturer to sell goods everywhere through retailers. A single plant will sell goods through many retailers, and one retailer will sell goods made in many plants.

    The largest retailers in this country are listed in Table 13-1.

TABLE 13-1
The Largest Retailing Companies (Ranked by Sales)

COMPANY	SALES[a] (IN MILLIONS)	EMPLOYEES[a]
Sears, Roebuck	$27,357	337,400
Safeway Stores	16,580	157,411
K mart	16,527	280,000
JC Penney	11,860	187,000
Kroger Company	11,266	127,271
F.W. Woolworth	7,223	139,800
Lucky Stores	7,201	66,000
American Stores	7,096	64,000
Federated Department Stores	7,067	120,800
Great Atlantic & Pacific Tea Co.	6,989	60,000
Winn-Dixie Stores	6,200	63,000
Montgomery Ward	5,742	95,900

[a]For the year 1981.

TYPES OF RETAILERS

There is a wide variety of retail stores trying to meet consumers' needs. Most of them are probably familiar.

THE DEPARTMENT STORE

John Wanamaker made the "department store" famous, even though his was not the first to be established. Others of which you have no doubt heard are Macy's and Gimbel's of New York City. The JC Penney stores are widely scattered throughout the United States. JC Penney, which has a large mail-order component in small communities, has become a true department store in large communities. The chief strength of the department store has been the wide variety of items offered for sale.

THE SUPERMARKET

The most dramatic change in supermarkets during the last few years has been the addition of nonfood items.

How many shops and stores do you think you would have to visit to buy oil for your car; make a deposit to your checking account; purchase home-owners' insurance; buy Mexican foods, imported cheeses, and exotic fruits; and buy underwear, a hammer and nails, a top-10 record, and a book?

A few years ago, you might have had to make many stops to finish your shopping. Today, however, these errands can be accomplished with one stop—at the local supermarket.

MOVE TO SUBURBIA

Downtown Detroit no longer has a major department store. J.L. Hudson, the last one to serve the area, closed its flagship store after the 1982 Christmas-shopping season. The facility was no longer profitable, and management decided that the sales no longer justified staying open as a service to downtown customers. P. Gerald Mills, Hudson's chairman, explained that consumers have changed their shopping habits: "They prefer a multifaceted shopping environment."

Supermarkets have historically been large grocery stores selling canned and dry food items, meats, and vegetables. But today's supermarket has added drugs, toiletries, and hardware items because the profit margins are higher on these. The food segment of a supermarket's inventory yields profits of only a penny on the dollar.

Most large supermarkets also have bakery departments and delicatessens. In addition, supermarkets are handling items not formerly available. Frozen foods used to be packaged only in aluminum foil; today, many items are prepared ready to go right into the microwave.

In 1982, the Kroger Company started offering consumer financial services at its Grove City, Ohio, store. Kroger's financial centers are managed by Capital Holding Corporation, an insurance company based in Louisville, Kentucky. These centers offer the opportunity to buy money-market and mutual-fund shares as well as life and property insurance. No doubt there is a Safeway, Winn-Dixie, A&P, Kroger, or Food Fair in your community.

THE CONVENIENCE STORE

The corner drugstore, the independent grocer, and the five-and-dime store were early examples of the convenience store. Today, the convenience store is a small grocery and delicatessen. It stays open long hours and caters to emergency needs. The 7-Eleven store is probably the most widely distributed convenience store in America.

Open for Business.
(Courtesy, 7-Eleven Stores.)

THE CONVENIENCE STORE

Where do you go for ice cream at midnight, or a sweet roll and coffee on your way to work at 6:00 in the morning? There are more than 7,000 7-Eleven stores in North America helping meet such consumer needs and wants. When this chain was started over 50 years ago, the stores were open from 7 A.M. to 11 P.M., as the name implies. But as the idea caught on, many stores remained open 24 hours a day.

The typical customer is in and out in just two minutes. He or she spends on the average less than $3. 7-Eleven stores sell a wide choice of items: basic groceries, drugs, soft drinks, beer, cosmetics, fast foods, and magazines.

SAM M. WALTON

Sam Walton opened his first Wal-Mart Discount City store in Rogers, Arkansas, in 1962. Today, the company is recognized as a leader in the retail discount department-store industry, with more than 500 stores in a thirteen-state area. Mr. Walton has received many honors during his career; however, in 1978, he was doubly honored by his colleagues in the retail industry when they voted him the Discounter of the Year and the Retail Man of the Year. This was the first time in the history of retailing that one person had received both honors. In March 1980, he was selected in Financial World's "Annual Competition to Honor America's Top Executives" as the most outstanding chief executive officer in the retail industry by a panel of fifty leading securities analysts.

For the sixth consecutive year, Forbes magazine in its "Annual Report on American Industry" has ranked Wal-Mart Stores, Inc., number one in the general-merchandise chain-store division in every category — return on equity, return on total capital, sales growth, and earnings per share.

Mr. Walton is chairman and CEO of Wal-Mart Stores, Inc., with headquarters in Bentonville, Arkansas. He was graduated from the University of Missouri in 1940 with a degree in economics. After serving in World War II, he was discharged in August 1945 with the rank of captain.

Mr. Walton serves on numerous corporate boards of directors. He is president of three banks and past president of the Chamber of Commerce of both Bentonville and Newport, Arkansas. He believes in giving the customer good service and quality products at a fair price. Most companies establish their retail stores and then build warehouses to serve them. Walton works the other way — he builds a warehouse and then places his stores in small towns around it.

Sam Walton is married to the former Helen Robson of Claremore, Oklahoma. They have four children and make their home in Bentonville, Arkansas.

THE DISCOUNT HOUSE Discount houses have been in existence for a long time. However, the nature of the discount operation has changed significantly. The first discount house was small, and:

1. It stocked only a limited number of items.
2. It specialized in some type of goods where the markup margin was high, such as furniture, jewelry, luggage, or small appliances.
3. It did a significant amount of its selling through catalog ordering.

Today, the discount retail store occupies thousands of square feet, handles a wide variety of items, displays its merchandise, and operates on a small profit margin. K mart, Gold Circle, and Treasure Island stores are widely known.

As prices continue to rise and shopping time and gasoline costs rise, the discount store that brings everything together in one location seems destined to prosper. However, the trend is for discount stores to add more expensive products to their product lines. At the same time, the traditional department stores are giving more emphasis to cheaper lines of goods. As the discount stores and the department stores continue to adopt each other's points of strength, discounting may lose some of its visibility. Price competition may give way to forms of nonprice promotional activities: quality, service, convenience of location, and standard forms of advertising.

SPECIALTY STORES There are many specialty stores in any shopping mall. Common examples are jewelry, shoe, toy, candy, men's clothing, ladies' clothing, bakery, sporting-goods, and gift shops. Their marketing strategy is one of offering a broad selection of goods in a rather narrow range. Specialty stores are a good example of retail-market segmentation, which was discussed in Chapter 10.

L.L. BEAN'S SPECIALTY STORE

L.L. Bean is to camping what Kellogg's is to cereal. It is located in Freeport, Maine, a small Atlantic-coast town (population 5,863). In a single year, 2.5 million people visit Freeport to buy parkas, boots, canoes, and hunting, fishing, and camping gear. L.L. Bean's store is open 24 hours a day, 365 days a year. In addition to its store, L.L. Bean sells merchandise by mail order.

NONSTORE RETAILING In addition to retail stores, a large volume of goods is sold through mail-order catalogs, vending machines, and on a door-to-door basis. Most people are familiar with the Montgomery Ward, Sears, and Spiegel catalogs. But Finger-hut, Alden's, Swiss Colony, and Miles Kimball also distribute their specialty-goods catalogs throughout the country. More than 72 million adults—45 percent of the adult population—ordered goods through the mail in 1983. More than $100 billion worth of business is generated each year through the mail. Mail-order selling is growing at twice the rate of store retailing. It makes shopping convenient, and often at reduced prices.

Canteens in schools and factories supply snacks and fast lunches. (Photo by Hugh Rogers, Monkmeyer.)

Vending machines are now found in most public buildings and in many factories, warehouses, and stores. This kind of retail merchandising has grown considerably in recent years, having more than doubled during the last decade. Vending sales involve multiple activities: buying the equipment, finding the locations, purchasing the goods, stocking the machines, and maintaining the equipment.

Route sales of newspapers and dairy products are examples of another form of nonstore retailing. And the Avon lady and the Tupperware representative sell their products to individuals or groups gathered in homes.

The Newspaper Advertising Bureau predicts that by 1990, half of all consumer buying will be through nonstore means.

SPIEGEL—FROM MASS TO CLASS

Spiegel, Inc., is the nation's fourth-largest direct-mail marketer. In the past, it has made a mass appeal to low-income shoppers. Its competition has come from Sears Roebuck, JC Penney, and discount houses.

But today, Spiegel's pitch is to upper-level working women who make good salaries. They have more money to spend and like the convenience of shopping by mail. Its full-color fashion books offer designer apparel. Spiegel's new competition is the full-line department store.

PHYSICAL DISTRIBUTION

Setting up distribution channels involves the selection of middlemen — wholesalers and retailers. Physical distribution is concerned with the handling of goods. In Chapter 9, we saw that logistics is concerned with materials handling and control. It also entails the handling and distribution of finished products. Business management wants to minimize the amount of capital tied up in unsold finished goods.

The total system of physical distribution includes purchasing, inventory management, storage, materials handling, protective packaging, and transportation. According to the National Council of Physical Distribution Management, physical distribution includes:

> . . . the broad range of activities concerned with efficient movement of finished products from the end of the production line to the consumer, and in some cases includes the movement of raw materials from the source of supply to the beginning of the production line. These activities include freight transportation, warehousing, material handling, protective packaging, inventory control, plant and warehouse site selection, order processing, market forecasting, and customer service.[1]

---

[1] Definition by the National Council of Physical Distribution Management, Executive Offices, Chicago.

For a short definition, we cay say that PHYSICAL DISTRIBUTION refers to *the movement of goods between producers and users.*

One way in which many firms have established control over physical distribution is to centralize the most basic components of physical distribution yet leave product schedules and inventory control in the production department.

A second arrangement establishes physical distribution as a line-and-staff function on the same level with production, finance, and marketing. Under this arrangement, physical distribution is responsible for materials flow, inventory control, warehousing, customer service, order processing, packing, and shipping.

The centralization of the various aspects of physical distribution can best be done when a firm's operational activities are similar among its different product lines. When the production processes, the materials handling, the marketing channels, and the modes of transportation are similar, overall control is much easier.

Sometimes this similarity exists for either the raw materials or the finished goods but not for both. Then the logistics pattern may consist of two different schemes—one for inbound materials and another for outbound finished goods.

The distribution system is usually adapted to the product rather than the product to the distribution plan. Some of the factors that affect the level of customer service are the degree of concentration of customers, the size of a typical order, and the frequency with which orders are received and processed. Another factor is the extent to which the manufacturer must provide storage, compared with the assistance the manufacturer might have received from others in the distribution channel.

Warehouse and Distribution Center for Stop and Shop Stores.
(Photo by Gabor Demjen, STOCK/Boston.)

WAREHOUSING AND DISTRIBUTION

Warehousing is an essential part of physical distribution, for most goods are not consumed as soon as they are produced. Orange juice and fresh vegetables are ready for processing only during the harvesting season, yet they are in demand the entire year. Warehousing enables producers to store and move these goods to markets as they are in demand. It also allows manufacturers to gear their production to meet peak seasonal demands without the added cost of overtime or around-the-clock operations. And the proper use of transportation services in conjunction with warehousing helps the manufacturer adjust the operation to fit the time, place, and rate of consumer demand.

TYPES OF WAREHOUSES

There are essentially two types of warehouse operations: private and public. PRIVATE WAREHOUSES are owned or leased and *are operated by individual enterprises*—manufacturers, wholesalers, and retailers—*for their own use.* They may maintain storage and distribution centers near their plants, or they may maintain branch operations at other locations.

PUBLIC WAREHOUSES *make their storage and handling facilities available to any business wishing to use them.* Patrons of public warehousing facilities pay for the services they receive on the basis of space and time requirements. Some warehouses store all types of general merchandise; others store only special commodities, such as farm produce or frozen foods. Public warehouses are in operation in all principal market areas in the United States.

SHARED SERVICES IN WAREHOUSING

Distribution costs, like most other costs, are increasing because of a number of factors. These include increasing capital investments in land, buildings, and equipment. Also, expanding inventories caused by a greater variety of products, and an increase in the number of small (less-than-carload) shipments are factors. These costs in combination have given impetus to sharing warehousing services.

Public warehousing currently operates some 25,000 facilities, and this number is being increased at the rate of 12 percent annually. As they move from strictly local operations to national networks, they are able to offer a wider variety of services and increase their efficiency of operation.

One of the services now being shared among warehouses, and by companies utilizing the same facilities, is data processing. This includes invoicing, billing, credit checking, inventory control, accounting, storage, and retrieval. Sharing of services can help the pooling of shipments to constitute full-car or -truck loads. This can effect a considerable saving, for the shipping rate per hundred pounds for a partial load is usually about twice that for a full-car or -truck load. Motor carriers report that small shipments make up 70 percent of their total volume of business. Shared services in warehousing may very well be the idea that will receive the next big push in distribution.

DISTRIBUTION CENTERS

In discussing a logistics system in the past, we have talked largely in terms of warehousing. But unfortunately, "warehousing" has taken on the idea of depositing goods for an extended period of time. Since this suggests a lack of movement, a newer term, **distribution center,** was coined. A DISTRIBUTION

CENTER *includes storage, product handling, and preparing goods for ship-ment.* It puts the emphasis on movement of goods. It expresses better than *warehousing* the concept of prompt and efficient service to customers. The current trend is toward large regional distribution centers rather than small warehouses scattered all over the country.

CHOOSING TRANSPORTATION MODES

Both costs and the acceptable level of customer service are important in establishing distribution centers. The types of transportation modes available is very important and often is a limiting factor. Transportation makes its chief contribution to the economy by:

1. Widening the market area
2. Giving time and place utility to goods
3. Enhancing specialization in production
4. Reducing the need for maintaining large inventories

Today, it is possible to reach a third of the U.S. consumer market within one day, using only five distribution centers. However, to reach four-fifths of the total consumer market in one day would require five times as many distribution points. Thus, management can combine the available options in many different ways. Management might choose, for example, to serve one-third of the market through five distribution centers and reach some fraction of the remaining market by a number of centers above five but fewer than the total of twenty-five. The best choice of number and location of distribution centers would be determined by the relation of costs to revenues and profit margins.

AIRPORTS ARE A BIG BUSINESS

Airports play an important role in physical distribution. Chicago-O'Hare has 1,700 flights a day, moving 100,000 passengers and 250,000 pieces of luggage. In addition, it handles hundreds of tons of freight daily. It provides work for 35,000 people, operates three fire stations, a 170-person police force, a post office, and a large hotel. Its heating-and-cooling plant is adequate to serve a city of 50,000 population.

It has the same problems that one finds in any small city: sewage treatment and disposal, road building and grounds maintenance, snow removal, and fire and police protection.

Choosing the kind of transportation cannot be done strictly on the basis of comparative costs. Shipping costs constitute only one of the factors in the physical-distribution mix. The saving in freight costs might very easily be offset by costlier packaging, storage costs, or handling expenses. The right mode of transportation is the one that maximizes efficiency in the total physical-distribution scheme. For example, air freight may be the best choice when time is especially important. For other goods, the greatly reduced rates for water transport may be the best choice. Railroads transport more tons of products more miles, but they haul largely coal, ores, grains, autos, and heavy machinery. Trucks deliver a wider variety of products and reach many more communities.

747 Container Trip to London.
Cargo containers are loaded aboard to begin their trip from Kennedy Airport, New York City. (Courtesy, Pan American.)

TYPES OF CARRIERS   Transportation firms are classified by law as common carriers, contract carriers, and private carriers.

A **common carrier** offers its services to the general public to transport property for a stated rate and according to standard rules. It is expected to give the same service and charge the same rate to all shippers. Examples of common carriers are railroads, bus lines, intercity freight motor lines, some air-freight lines, most airlines, most domestic water carriers, all freight-forwarding companies, and REA Express. Common carriers are subject to various kinds of state and federal regulations, which are discussed later in this chapter.

A **contract carrier** sells its transport services on the basis of individual agreements or contracts that define the carrier's liability. Some contract carriers specialize, transporting only certain types of goods. Automobile trucking companies, household moving vans, and chartered buses and planes are examples of contract carriers.

A **private carrier** transports its own goods. Manufacturers, wholesalers, and retailers who make their own deliveries in their own trucks are classed as private carriers. Since they are usually small companies operating in small geographical areas, they are subject primarily to local and state regulations.

TABLE 13-2
Share of Market (Ton-Miles)

	RAIL	TRUCKS	WATERWAYS	AIR	PIPELINES
1939	62.3	9.7	17.7	0	10.3
1978	35.2	24.4	16.6	.27	23.8
1979	36.1	23.7	16.5	.17	23.7
1980	37.5	22.5	16.5	.17	23.3
1981	37.7	23.0	16.5	.19	22.5

After years of decline, the railroad share-of-market is starting to climb.

SOURCE: Transportation Association of America.

THE TRAFFIC MANAGER

The traffic manager often heads a "traffic department." Most of the traffic manager's routine work consists of collecting accurate, up-to-date information about tariff rates; selecting common carriers to be used in transporting foods; preparing claims of overcharge, damage, or loss; and auditing freight bills. He or she is also expected to trace lost shipments, supervise the actual handling of freight, and maintain control over back orders.

In addition, the traffic manager:

1. Helps consolidate small orders into carload shipments
2. Arranges systematic warehouse-distribution points for less-than-carload lots
3. Studies and perfects ways of reducing losses in shipments caused by improper packaging and handling
4. Selects the most advantageous or strategic destination points for shipments

The traffic manager must know when to use rail, water, truck, or air to transport goods. It is also his or her responsibility to seek adjustments on overcharges caused by discriminatory rates, by preparing such cases and presenting them before commissions and other government bodies.

The transportation manager's role is no longer one of merely tracing shipments and checking freight rates. Charles S. Davis is transportation manager at General Electric's Appliance Park in Louisville, Kentucky. A variety of household appliances are made there. The annual expenditures for cartage come to $150 million.

Mr. Davis reports that representatives from freight-hauling companies visit his office continually, seeking a share of this shipping business. Since 1980, government regulation of freight hauling has decreased considerably. The Motor Carrier Act of 1980 gives carriers greater flexibility and freedom in setting rates and providing services. All this has increased competition for the freight-hauling business.

Through negotiation, Mr. Davis can secure bids for GE's freight business. Many carriers are willing to grant discounts from their posted rates. For example, bids for shipping a truckload of washing machines from Louisville to Chicago in 1981 ranged from $359 to $780. With this much difference in freight costs, transportation savings increase company profits.

THE TOTAL COST OF DISTRIBUTION

We have seen that there are two main components to physical distribution. The level of service given and the total cost of distribution work against each other. The level of service must be maximized to satisfy all channel members. But as service is increased or improved, the costs increase. **Management has the problem of maximizing service while keeping costs low.**

It is much easier to measure costs than it is to evaluate the quality and level of service. Storage costs may be "traded off" against quantity and time savings in financing and/or transportation. However, the total costs include packaging, handling, and the like. A slower method of shipping may increase inventory or packaging costs. Only by consideration of all aspects of the distribution system can the goal of the lowest cost be achieved.

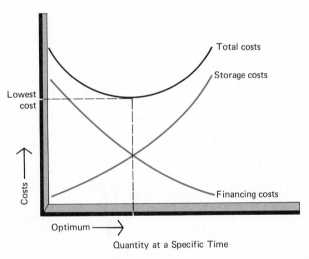

FIGURE 13-6
Tradeoff in Distribution Costs

REGULATION OF TRANSPORTATION

Because transport companies operate in specific territories by government franchise, they are subject to special government regulations. These relate to routes, rate structures, and services. In many instances, regulations are needed to protect the general public and the best interests of transport companies as well.

Most states have commissions that regulate **intrastate transportation** operations—those that occur entirely within the state. These commissions were first concerned with railroads, then later with motor carriers; now airport facilities are included.

Most transport companies cross state lines, and a state regulatory body has jurisdiction only within its own state. Therefore, the federal government

TABLE 13-3
Recent Laws That Shape the Transportation Industry

Year	Law	Description
1958	Transportation Act	ICC prohibited from holding up rates of one mode to protect another. Commission given authority to order abandonment of passenger service.
1966	Department of Transportation Act	Cabinet-level department established.
1970	Rail Passenger Service Act	Created National Railroad Passenger Corporation (Amtrak).
1973	Regional Rail Reorganization Act	U.S. Railway Association created to develop reorganization of bankrupt Northeast carriers.
1973	Federal Highway Act	Permits limited use of Highway Trust Fund for mass transit.
1976	Railroad Revitalization and Regulatory Reform Act	Government-financed Conrail established. Greater freedom in railroad rate making.
1977	Air Cargo Act	Deregulation of air-cargo industry.
1978	Air Carrier Regulatory Reform Act	Deregulation of domestic air-passenger operations on a graduated basis.
1980	Motor Carrier Act	Relaxed rules on opening new lines and expanding present ones; also relaxed pricing methods.
1980	Staggers Rail Act	Provides railroads with flexibility in pricing.
1980	International Air Travel Act	Establishes new guidelines that stress maximum competition. Eases entry for foreign routes.

is responsible for the rules governing **interstate transportation** operations. The passage of the Interstate Commerce Act in 1887 was to provide railroad regulation. This act created the Interstate Commerce Commission, which dealt with rate discrimination. The act stipulated that the tariffs or rates to be charged were to be reasonable and just. It also stipulated that railroads could not charge a higher rate for a short haul than for a long haul under similar circumstances.

Both transportation traffic and the types of transport companies have continuously increased since 1887. So there have been several laws passed broadening the jurisdiction and responsibilities of the Interstate Commerce Commission (see Table 13-3). The commission was given jurisdiction over interstate pipeline shipments in 1906 and over water transportation in 1940. Now it not only has jurisdiction over the tariff schedules of railroads but is concerned with the appraisal of the value of properties, and with methods of accounting, curtailment of services, financing, and consolidations.

SUMMARY OF KEY CONCEPTS

The distribution of materials and goods to the places where they are needed is very complex.

The channel a product takes may be a short or a long and complex one.

Middlemen include agents, brokers, and jobbers as well as wholesalers and retailers.

The wholesaler and the retailer work together as a team. The wholesaler performs many services for the retailer. In return, the retailer simplifies the distribution process for the wholesaler. The retailer greatly reduces the number of customers the wholesaler must contact to sell goods.

Retailers are classified according to the mix of merchandise handled and their organizational structure, pricing strategy, and services offered.

Whereas manufacturing gives goods *form utility*, distribution gives them *time and place utility*.

Warehousing and shipping form the heart and center of distribution. Efficiency in materials handling and control are important aspects of warehousing.

The traffic manager is responsible for the choice of carriers and control over packaging and shipments.

You should be able to match these business terms with the statements that follow:

a. COMMISSION MERCHANT
b. CONTRACT CARRIER
c. DISTRIBUTION CENTER
d. DISTRIBUTION CHANNEL
e. EXCLUSIVE DISTRIBUTION
f. INTENSIVE DISTRIBUTION
g. MERCHANT WHOLESALER

h. MIDDLEMAN
i. PHYSICAL DISTRIBUTION
j. PRIVATE WAREHOUSE
k. PUBLIC WAREHOUSE
l. RETAILER
m. WHOLESALER

1. The route taken by a product as it moves from producer to consumer
2. A business or individual who performs marketing functions between the producer and the consumer
3. Marketing goods through a single retailer in any given community
4. Using many middlemen in order to saturate the market
5. A middleman who purchases goods from producers and sells them primarily to retail firms
6. A wholesaler who provides a full set of marketing services to other businesses
7. An agent middleman who takes title to goods
8. A middleman who buys goods from producers or wholesalers and sells them to consumers
9. A warehouse owned by a firm for its own use
10. The movement of materials and/or products between producers and users
11. A warehouse that makes its storage and handling facilities available to any and all businesses
12. A facility that provides storage, product handling, and preparation of goods for shipment
13. A shipper that sells transport services on the basis of individual agreements

1. What is a **distribution channel,** and why is it important?
2. What are the main functions of wholesalers?
3. What is the chief service that the wholesaler renders for retailers?
4. What is the chief service that retailers render wholesalers?
5. What idea does the term *distribution center* convey that *warehousing* does not?

1. What are the main considerations when selecting middlemen?
2. What types of products are best suited to exclusive distribution?
3. Explain how the various types of wholesalers differ from one another.
4. How does the chief role of the retailer differ from that of the wholesaler?
5. What, in your opinion, is the future of nonstore selling?

BUSINESS CASES

13-1

WHOLESALE OR RETAIL?

Curtis Jewelers has operated as a wholesale company in a midwestern community for thirty years. The company has supplied retail stores in the state with a wide variety of jewely and related items.

For the past twelve weeks, however, Curtis has been issuing "membership cards" to individuals. Cardholders may purchase goods on a cash-and-carry basis at wholesale prices.

The owners of the retail stores Curtis has supplied have protested this new operation. They view it as unfair competition. In fact, they issued this warning: "You need to decide whether you are going to operate as a wholesale or retail business. Unless you discontinue this 'membership card' retail operation, we may be forced to cease patronizing your firm with our wholesale purchases."

The management team of Curtis has told the retail jewelers, "How we operate is our business." They have done this even though they recognize that by doing so, they might well lose this group of customers. This group has made up the hard core of their regular sales volume.

1. Do you feel that this business can ethically run both wholesale and retail operations without making any differential in the prices charged the two groups of customers?
2. Has the time come to decide whether to operate at wholesale or retail?
3. Is there a third alternative open to Curtis Jewelers? If so, what is it?

13-2   A BROKER'S DECISION TO EXPAND

Henry Knowlton is an established food broker who lives in one of the northeastern states. He represents Corporation B, one of the leading processors of canned fruits and vegetables. He also represents a dog-food company, a honey processor, a charcoal producer, and a sugar refiner. He considers his company to be a specialist in canned foods.

Henry employs four salespersons who call on "the trade." This is made up of sixteen wholesale grocery houses located in the central and eastern half of the state. He and his representatives are extremely busy and do well if they can manage to contact each wholesale customer once every two weeks. His office staff of three have all they can do typing orders, handling correspondence, and filing reports.

Corporation B launched a frozen-fruit and -vegetable line, which is growing rapidly. The marketing manager of Corporation B has approached Henry about taking on the frozen-food line in his territory. A nearby processor of jams and jellies recently asked Henry to represent that company in the territory he serves.

Three of the wholesalers served by the Knowlton Company have warehouses in the city where Henry lives. One of these wholesalers has been growing very rapidly and is expanding his operation. In fact, he now serves ten retail stores in two adjoining states and plans to add eight more stores.

A food broker not only sells merchandise for the principals he represents but also helps his wholesalers sell their products in retail stores. When a new store opens, Henry's people spend considerable time making sure that this new store stocks a complete line of products that the Knowlton Company represents. They also see that the merchandise is displayed properly on the shelves of the retail store.

Henry's problem consists of meeting these new demands with an already overloaded staff. If he takes on additional lines, he will need another salesperson. He feels that to do this might damage his reputation for efficient and personal service. In addition, he might be forced to stop traveling the territory himself.

Henry built his business through personal contacts with his customers. So he is not sure what effect this step would have on future business. He is not sure he wants to accept a full-time administrative role.

He knows his commissions would increase significantly if he could add either or both of the new lines. Also, he knows that any increase in sales would mean hiring additional clerical help. Adding another salesperson and a fourth office person would require larger office space, and this would increase his overhead.

1. What alternatives are open to Henry?
2. What factors would influence your course of action if you had his problem?

PART 4

CAREERS IN MARKETING

Probably no field of business enterprise offers more varied job opportunities than does marketing. Some areas require special training, such as research, product engineering, art, or copywriting. The chief job areas in marketing are these:

Personal selling	Buying
Advertising	Transportation
Marketing research	Product management
Wholesaling	Product testing
Retailing	

Personal selling and advertising are examined in the following section. The other job areas are discussed briefly here.

MARKETING RESEARCH

Marketing research is an important area that has developed rather recently. Most of the business firms that are members of the American Marketing Association have formal marketing-research divisions or departments. Like researchers in any other area, marketing researchers should have a knowledge of mathematics, statistics, computer applications, and consumer behavior.

WHOLESALING AND RETAILING

There are almost 2 million retail stores in the United States, and 300,000 wholesale firms. Every store must have a manager. A retail manager can run his or her own firm or work for someone else. Twelve million people work in retailing, and the retailing of services is growing most rapidly. Large department stores need department managers, personnel directors, credit personnel, and general merchandise managers. Wholesale businesses need buyers, sales representatives, promotion people, and traffic managers.

BUYING

Every type of business must have buyers or purchasing agents. Many of these people visit the firms that supply their goods. Others travel to central markets where goods are displayed. Industrial firms and government agencies usually use purchasing agents. Such people should have a knowledge of shipping, credit, and finance.

TRANSPORTATION

Shipping costs vary with different modes of transportation. These costs are always paid by the buyer or the seller. All kinds of firms need people with a knowledge of transportation. In addition to industrial firms, wholesalers, and retailers, the airlines and trucking firms offer marketing job opportunities. Industrial companies and wholesalers need people who are knowledgeable in traffic management, materials handling, and physical distribution.

PRODUCT MANAGEMENT

We saw in Chapter 11 that product development is an integral part of marketing. Product managers are found in companies that sell both industrial and consumer goods. Product-management positions are among the most challenging, most competitive, and most interesting of all the jobs in marketing.

PRODUCT TESTING

We noted earlier the current emphasis being given product safety and consumer protection. Both businesses and governments employ people for product testing. Some business organizations have advisors who speak on behalf of consumers regarding marketing needs and procedures. People in product testing must know something about consumer market behavior and consumer proctection laws.

CAREERS IN SELLING AND ADVERTISING

More people are employed in selling than in any other type of marketing activity. Jobs selling to wholesalers and industrial markets involve travel and expenses when away from home. In many instances, a car is furnished this type of salesperson.

In advertising, millions of business firms need someone to handle their advertising. And there are some 7,500 advertising agencies that employ specialized personnel. Advertisers and media employ more people than do the agencies. It has been estimated that there are 100,000 people employed in professional advertising positions. And almost 10,000 positions must be filled annually. The field is growing, and vacancies occur owing to deaths, retirements, and promotions.

Careers in promotion include preparing floor and window displays in retail stores, as well as preparing all types of advertising copy for in-house displays and local newspapers. Important attributes for advertising personnel include the ability to write, visualize, create, and innovate. Advertising personnel must be flexible in viewpoint and must be able to adapt to new situations.

The president of the National Association of Advertisers stated that business needs ten different types of professionals in advertising:

1. Writers	6. Psychologists
2. Artists	7. Statisticians
3. Dramatists	8. Media analysts
4. Salespeople	9. Financial managers
5. Marketers	10. People managers

The major types of specialists and their functions are these:

1. *Media director* — This person selects the media that best achieve a client's objectives. He or she coordinates the use of several types of media into a feasible plan.

2. *Production specialist* — This person must have a knowledge of printing processes and broadcasting technicalities. The production person's primary job is to keep the project — pamphlet, booklet, or ad — moving through the various processes. (These positions are also needed in publishing firms, printing firms, and company advertising departments.)

3. *Art-and-layout director* — This person, who must possess talent and skill as an artist, is responsible for the quality of the artwork. The director confers with the client, the account executive, and others in the agency to determine the best possible layout and art for the ad.

4. *Account executive* — This person occupies one of the most important and "sensitive" positions in an agency. He or she is responsible for keeping the client satisfied with the agency's work. Besides being creative and a good salesperson, the account executive must be familiar with business practices and have an understanding of marketing, merchandising, and advertising.

5. *Copywriter* — Often called the "idea person," the copywriter prepares the copy — the message the advertiser wishes to present. In the final stages of the copy, the copywriter works with various specialists, including the art-and-layout director and the account executive.

FINANCE AND RISK MANAGEMENT

How does one finance a business enterprise? Roger and Calvin King used their savings to get started. They also borrowed from their friends, later paying them back with interest. After the business became a corporation, they issued stock. Most of their friends agreed to accept stock in exchange for notes they held.

The King management had to decide whether to issue common or preferred stock. Most of their friends wanted preferred stock, so this is what they sold. (The Kings and Perez owned the common stock, which had voting rights. In this way, they maintained control of the company.)

The Kings used stock for their long-term financing, and loans from their bank for short-term financing. Their legal advisor suggested they consider selling long-term bonds. You will see in these chapters the difference between bonds and stocks as ways to finance a business enterprise.

Calvin King was responsible for financial and risk management. There are many types of risk in any business. Protection against some types may be provided through insurance, but not all types. In this section, ways to cover risks by means other than insurance are explained.

PART

5

BUSINESS FINANCE AND INVESTMENTS

study objectives

WHEN YOU HAVE FINISHED READING THIS CHAPTER, YOU SHOULD BE
ABLE TO:

1. Describe financial management

2. Distinguish between equity financing and debt financing, working capital
   and fixed capital

3. Compare the advantages and disadvantages of stocks and bonds as
   sources of long-term financing

4. Explain the difference between income stocks, growth stocks, and investment with speculation

5. Discuss the purpose of securities markets and the stockbroker's role in
   serving a client

14

Finance is, in a real sense, the cornerstone of the enterprise system.

Eugene F. Brigham

T he financial management of a firm is somewhat similar to your own personal money management, but in some ways, it is quite different. You may have multiple sources and uses for funds just as a business does. And the way you manage your finances may determine whether you have the money to do the things you want to do. But for most of us, the level of financial planning, tax management, and controls we need is much less than what a business firm requires.

A business firm is, from one perspective, a pool of funds. The funds may *come from* several places, including people who buy company stock, creditors who lend the business money, and past earnings kept in the business. The funds *are used for* several purposes: for buying fixed assets such as machinery and buildings, for merchandise, accounts receivable, and to pay bills.

Regardless of its source or use, a continuous supply of capital is required to run the business. The flow of capital funds in the firm is what **financial management** is all about.

Management of capital is a task usually assigned to a financial officer — the treasurer or controller. The financial manager usually has the responsibility for the following:

1. Evaluating sources of funds and their costs
2. Deciding where funds will come from
3. Determining how the funds are to be used

In this chapter, we look at some important basic concepts in finance.

Then we consider long-term financing and look at the stock market and how it operates. In the next chapter, we look at the related issues of short-term financing, the credit system, and banking.

IT'S NOT ALL CAREFUL ANALYSIS

The world of high finance has the feel of rationality associated with it. But even this most careful and rational aspect of business has its moments. For example: A group led by Salomon Brothers, Inc., submitted the best bid for $200 million of revenue bonds auctioned by the California Department of Water Resources. But the bid came in thirty seconds late, and the bonds were awarded to another company.

A spokesman for Salomon Brothers explained that "the computer run took longer than expected." Oh, well—win some, lose some!

BASIC CONCEPTS IN FINANCE

BALANCE SHEET ITEMS
The report that accounts for changes in funds is called a **balance sheet.** We look at balance sheets in more detail in Chapter 17, dealing with accounting. But to illustrate basic ideas of finance, we present the balance sheet here.

Table 14-1 shows the categories in a balance sheet or **statement of financial position.** This serves a financial manager as a starting point in checking a firm's financing.

TABLE 14-1
Balance Sheet or Financial Position

Current Assets:	Current Liabilities:
Cash	Money owed by the firm
Money owed to the firm	Taxes owed by the firm
Inventory	Wages owed by the firm
Fixed Assets:	Short-term debt
Buildings and equipment	Long-Term Liabilities:
Land	Bonds outstanding
	Long-term loans
	Shareholders' Equity:
	Common stock
	Paid-in capital

The total of all items on the left side of the balance sheet equals the total of the items on the right. That is why the term *balance* is used. Notice that assets (things the firm *owns*) and liabilities (what the firm *owes*) may be either long-term or short-term. Let's look at each item in more detail.

Current Assets. Current assets are those things the firm owns that can be quickly converted to cash (usually within one year). Examples are cash itself, money that is owed to the firm, and an inventory of goods to be sold. Other current assets might include marketable securities, bank accounts, or any quickly salable item the firm owns.

Fixed Assets.   Fixed assets are needed for long periods of time. Examples are buildings and land. FIXED CAPITAL is ***money invested in fixed assets to be used over a long period of time.*** Since fixed assets are of a permanent nature, they become part of the permanent capital structure. Figure 14-1 illustrates the various kinds of fixed assets used in a business.

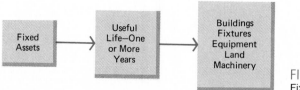

FIGURE 14-1
Fixed Capital/Assets

The amount of fixed assets required depends on several factors. For one thing, large firms require more fixed capital than small ones. Service-type firms can be started with less fixed capital than can manufacturing establishments. Changes in consumer preferences, new competition, and population trends are other factors. All these factors require planning in advance in order to avoid making errors in fixed-asset acquisitions. For most firms, fixed assets are the largest investment in the business.

Current Liabilities.   Current liabilities are money that the firm owes that must be repaid within one year. Perhaps the most common example is money that has been borrowed from a bank. Other current liabilities might include wages owed to employees, and insurance premiums, rent, utilities, and taxes owed.

Long-Term Liabilities.   Long-term liabilities are called *funded debt.* These may include bonds and long-term loans. Sources of term loans are often banks, insurance companies, or pension funds. Bonds are debts owed by contract to the bondholders who purchased them.

Shareholders' Equity.   **Equity,** or **net worth,** is the stockholders' ownership of the business. It is the amount that is left when debts are all paid. There are three components:

1. Stock sold to investors
2. Money paid in by the founder
3. Retained earnings

SOURCES AND USES OF FUNDS   An extremely important concept is the distinction between *sources* and *uses* of funds in the firm.

The movement of funds in a firm is a continuous flow. For every use of funds, there must be a *source*, or the flow stops. Assets represent a net use of funds, and shareholders' equity and liabilities represent a net source. Figure

14-2 shows a funds-flow cycle for a typical business. You can see that at any given time, *sources* of cash are sales of stocks, loans, sale of assets, or accounts receivable. Cash is *spent* on dividends, loan payments, material, labor, and asset purchases.

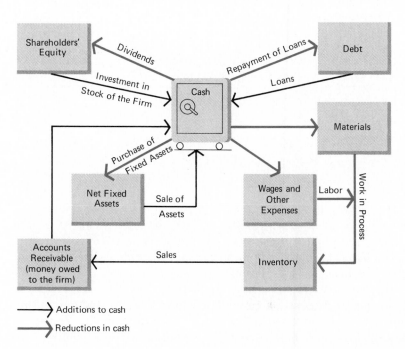

FIGURE 14-2
Funds Flow in a Typical Business

Cash Flow.   The analysis of the flow of cash through a firm gives a good picture of that firm's ability to pay its bills, and the timing of cash needs. This analysis is called **cash-flow analysis.**

WORKING CAPITAL   Working capital is much the same as cash flow, but it includes items in addition to cash. Accountants define **net working capital** as the excess of current assets over current liabilities. For purposes of this discussion, WORKING CAPITAL is *the value of the assets that can readily be turned into cash for current use in operating the firm.*

As we have seen, *current assets* are those that can be turned into cash quickly. The machinery in a factory, however, is a *fixed asset*. It cannot be quickly converted into cash. Without enough working capital to pay bills, in the short run, a business cannot operate. If, for example, you owned a factory worth $1 million but did not have the cash on hand to meet your payroll, you would probably be out of business unless you could borrow. For that reason, *cash flow* and *working capital* are two important basic financial ideas.

ONE HOT JOB

Managing cash for big corporations has taken on a high degree of sophistication. "Cash managers" move millions of dollars with the finesse of a short-order cook. A million dollars can earn more than $100,000 a year if it is not left idle but is invested in short-term money-market instruments.

Computers help these modern money managers to know daily the amount of cash available. Five years ago, about half the cash managers (or asset managers) were about to retire, recalls T.W. Thompson, vice-president of New York's Chemical Bank. Now 80 percent are sharp young M.B.A.s.

At the Monsanto Company, Robert Westoby watches tens of millions of dollars flow daily through the company's many bank accounts. He runs a portfolio of investments ranging from $150 million to $350 million, depending on the time of year. He squeezes every dollar he can out of idle funds by investing them quickly in Treasury bills, certificates of deposit, banker's acceptances, and so forth. Some cash may be invested for only a very few days, but the net result is additional cash for Monsanto.

CAPITAL INSTRUMENTS

Business firms, like individuals, occasionally need to raise money. Suppose Great Western Power Company forecasts an increased demand for electricity in its service area and clearly needs a new power plant. Where is it going to get the $950 million necessary to build the plant? In such a case, a company must find other firms or individuals with extra funds it can use. Great Western can either borrow funds or sell stock.

If the company borrows, it can borrow short-term or long-term. Since short-term borrowing must be paid back quickly, it is probably not the best way to finance a project with a 40-year life. For this reason, the company will probably choose to issue bonds. But typically, the firm must put up some of the money itself as well. This may come from retained earnings or from the sale of stock.

The capital that comes from each of these sources belongs to someone else. The bonds will be sold to individuals or pension funds that choose to invest money in bonds. The stock will be sold to individuals who want to invest in stocks. Even money that comes from retained earnings is money that might have been paid out to stockholders as dividends.

LONG-TERM EQUITY FINANCING

Long-term **equity** financing, as we have seen, comes from three sources:

Common stock
Preferred stock
Retained earnings

PROS AND CONS OF EQUITY FINANCING

EQUITY is *the ownership claim to the resources of the firm.* Ownership can be (1) the initial funds or services contributed by the owner, (2) the additional money contributed later, and/or (3) the reinvested profits earned by the business. In most companies, shareholders' equity consists to a large extent of common stock held by stockholders.

The use of equity financing in general offers the following advantages:

1. There are no interest charges to be paid the owner.
2. A firm financed by equity capital is financially stronger and better able to withstand a business recession than is one that uses debt.
3. Assuming that the firm is well financed in the beginning, the owner's ability to obtain borrowed capital is improved.

The disadvantages, however, cannot be ignored. One disadvantage is that equity financing is not always a dependable and available source of money. Then, too, the owner may find it difficult to obtain more funds in sufficient quantities to meet various needs. Adding a partner does not always prove satisfactory.

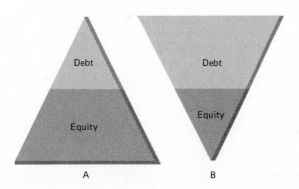

FIGURE 14-3
Equity Financing
Sound financing would resemble A. Inflation sometimes inverts the pyramid to look like B.

Stock financing generally attracts more capital than can be obtained by other forms of ownership. Corporations can issue more than one kind of stock to satisfy investors. Some investors choose to invest in preferred stocks or bonds rather than in common stock. The major advantages of stocks as a source of funds are as follows:

1. Issuing stock is adding to direct ownership.
2. Dividends are distributed from profits—they do not have to be paid unless declared by the directors.
3. Stocks carry no maturity date, and there is no obligation to repay the owner his or her investment.

COMMON STOCK

Common stock is issued either as par value or no-par value. *The value printed on the stock certificate* is the PAR VALUE. Some states use the par value as a basis for taxing the corporation. When common stock is sold originally for more than par, the difference is called **paid-in surplus.** When no stated value is on the stock certificate, it is known as **no-par-value** stock.

Common stock has other values in addition to par and no-par value. Two values commonly used are **book value** and **market value.** Book value is found by dividing the number of common shares outstanding into the total assets minus all debt and minus the preferred-stock value. Book value provides stockholders with some idea of the amount that has been invested in the corporation common stock. The market value is easily determined by referring to daily stock-market prices on the financial page of the daily newspaper.

During the late 1970s, businesses were pushing corporate takeovers, mergers, and stock repurchases. The single most important reason for the binge of acquisitions and stock repurchases was the replacement value of corporate assets, according to Leon Cooperman, partner in Goldman, Sachs & Co. "It's cheaper to buy than to build," he says.

Cooperman concludes that during that period companies reduced the amount of stock on the market by about $7.4 billion, through the purchasing of their own stock and the stock of others.

Stock Option Plans. A STOCK OPTION PLAN is *a fringe benefit given to key executives to purchase company stock under certain conditions of price and time.* For example, a company allows its executives to buy 5,000 shares each of common stock within a certain time period at $25 a share, the current market price. The plan must be approved by the Internal Revenue Service. Later, if the market price advances to $60 a share, those executives will have a realized profit of $175,000 by selling their stock. This plan is often used to provide a long-term incentive. It is different from a stock warrant in that it is a fringe-benefit plan for officers of the firm, not a plan for general stockholders.

Stock Splits. A STOCK SPLIT is *a division of common stock outstanding into additional units.* If you owned thirty shares and received a two-for-one stock split, your thirty shares would increase to sixty. Each new share would

FINANCE AND RISK MANAGEMENT

now be worth half the value of the original share. The usual reason for a stock split is to bring the market price down into the trading range of more investors. If a stock selling for $200 a share has a four-for-one split, the new price "when issued" (w.i.) would be set at $50 a share.

A stockholder owning 100 shares of General Electric common during the mid-1920s would by now have a total of 4,800 shares, mostly because of stock splits. If there had been no splits but the stock continued to rise in price, as it did, GE stock would now be quoted at about $5,000 per share.

"CREATIVE FINANCING" ON THE FARM

Farmers are *buying* space for their grain in local grain elevators. This isn't the way the grain-storage business worked in the past, but it is a way to provide financing for the additional grain-storage space needed in the United States.

The grain-elevator owners are squeezed for money by high interest rates and low farm income. So they have become partners with farmers by selling the space to them rather than renting it as in the past. That allows them to pay off the loans they received to build the elevators.

Stock Dividends.   A STOCK DIVIDEND is *a distribution of earnings or capital paid in stock.* Sometimes it is paid on a percentage basis. A 10 percent stock dividend means that one new share will be issued for each ten shares you may hold. So, if you owned twelve shares at the time the 10 percent stock dividend was declared, you would be entitled to receive 1⅕ (1.2) new shares for each ten you owned. Since fractional shares are not issued, you would be able to buy on the market enough fractional shares to equal one full share. A stock dividend does not increase the value of investor's stock but increases the number of shares.

PREFERRED STOCK   **In addition to issuing common stock, many corporations raise additional capital by selling preferred stock.** This is stock that carries certain preferences over common stock. These are stated on the preferred-stock certificate and in the corporation charter. Here are some of the special features of preferred stock (although these are not necessarily found in all preferred stock):

1. Preference as to assets
2. Preference as to dividends
3. Guaranteed dividends
4. Convertibility
5. Cumulative and noncumulative forms
6. Preference in liquidation
7. Participating form

The board of directors cannot omit dividends on preferred stock while declaring a dividend only to common-stock holders. Preferred-stock holders know at the time they buy the stock what the dividend rate will be. Thus, if an investor owns 100 shares of 7 percent preferred stock with a $100 par value, the maximum return is $700 in any one year. If the corporation assets are liquidated, holders of preferred stock have a preference over common-share holders when funds from the sale of assets are distributed. As a rule, however, preferred stock does not give the holder voting privileges, whereas common stock does.

The use of *convertible preferred stock* in planning corporate mergers has become popular. Such preferred stock is convertible into some other form of securities, often common stock. Usually, conversion is at the option of the stockholder. This is permitted when the common stock reaches a certain price. If the common stock should reach a high price, holders of convertible preferred would be allowed to exchange their preferred for common in hopes that the common would go higher.

Participating preferred stock participates in dividends on common stock when the dividends on the common exceed some predetermined level.

Preferred Stock Certificate.
(Courtesy A.T. & T. Co. Photo/Graphics Center.)

RETAINED EARNINGS

Profit retained in the business is another source of business financing. **Retained earnings** are profits of the firm that have not been paid as dividends to stockholders. As such, retained earnings are a major source of money for future growth. The typical American corporation retains between 35 and 60 percent of its earnings each year and pays the rest as dividends on common stocks. Usually, a corporation's financial management tries to maintain a balance between retaining earnings and paying dividends to stockholders. Some corporations have been known to retain all earnings and declare stock dividends. These dividends are not taxable to the stockholders until the shares are sold.

An obvious problem in financing with retained earnings arises when a firm's opportunity to invest increases faster than its retained earnings. Then, other methods must be used as well. Management often decides to retain earnings rather than paying them out as dividends. A firm should earn as much on retained earnings as stockholders could earn with alternative investments of comparable risk.

WILLIAM M. BATTEN

William M. Batten is now the chairman of the New York Stock Exchange.

Batten led an active college life, majoring in economics at Ohio State. He was president of the study body, and a member of Beta Gamma Sigma and Phi Kappa Psi fraternities.

He started his career as a salesman with J.C. Penney and worked his way up to assistant manager in Lansing, Michigan. He spent time in personnel before becoming assistant to the president, then vice-president, president, and finally, chairman of the board.

He retired from Penney's in 1974 and became chairman of the New York Stock Exchange in 1976.

Mr. Batten served in the military during World War II and has led a very active civic and professional life in addition to his work. He currently resides on Long Island, New York.

LONG-TERM DEBT FINANCING

The use of debt rather than equity capital is one way that financial management can increase the rate of return on equity. Some companies choose to borrow when in need of funds. Others find that to retain earnings is a better

Bond Certificate.
(Courtesy New York Stock Exchange.)

way to obtain funds. In general, it is considered wise to borrow if more can be earned on borrowed funds than the funds cost. For example, to borrow at 10 percent and earn 15 percent is profitable financing. This principle is known as financial leverage.

FINANCIAL LEVERAGE Leverage may work in reverse. If business conditions worsen and earnings fall below 10 percent, the leverage factor is no longer favorable. The bankruptcy of several companies during the recession in the early 1980s resulted from their inability to earn enough to pay the interest on their debts.

LEASE-A-JET

Financially strained American Airlines and order-hungry McDonnell Douglas, aircraft manufacturer, worked out an innovative solution to both companies' problems: Lease-a-Jet.

American ran into a debt ceiling imposed by creditors, so it could not purchase the twenty DC-9s it needed. So American rented the planes from McDonnell Douglas. That keeps their borrowing capacity free and keeps the manufacturer in operation as well. A sign of the times, perhaps?

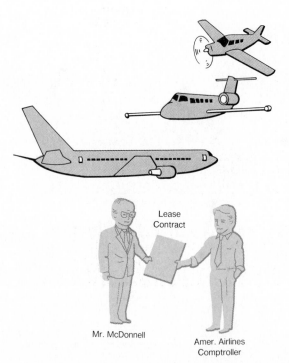

Mr. McDonnell

Amer. Airlines Comptroller

A Leasing Contract

The sale of bonds is widely used by corporations to obtain long-term financing. A BOND is a *certificate of indebtedness owed to the bondholder by the corporation.* It is a *debt*, maturing at a stated future date, on which interest is paid annually or semiannually.

ADVANTAGES AND DISADVANTAGES OF BOND FINANCING

Financing by bonds offers several advantages:

1. The sale of bonds may not affect management control. Unlike stockholders, bondholders have no voting rights.
2. Bond interest is a deductible expense from corporate income.
3. Borrowing does not dilute the shareholders' equity, because no additional shares are issued.

There are some disadvantages, of course:

1. The debt must be repaid with interest.
2. The fixed interest charges may become a financial burden during periods of low earnings.
3. Bondholders may foreclose if interest is in default.

CLASSES OF BONDS

There are several classes of bonds. Most corporation bonds are sold in $1,000 denominations. The type of bond used is usually tailored to meet the needs of the individual corporation issuing it. Table 14-2 lists the various kinds of corporate bonds commonly used as a source of long-term debt financing.

TABLE 14-2
Kinds of Corporation Bonds

NAME OF BOND	DESCRIPTION
Convertible bonds	Bonds convertible into other securities, such as common stock, are known as convertible bonds. The conversion privilege appeals to the speculative impulses of some investors.
Coupon bonds	A coupon bond is payable to the bearer, with title passing by delivery without endorsement.
Debenture bonds	A debenture bond is not secured by a specific lien on the property but is issued against the reputation of the corporation to support the bond. Such bonds often carry a slightly higher interest rate, because they include a higher degree of risk.
Equipment trust bonds (certificates)	This type of secured bond is classified as a chattel mortgage, because the security consists of movable goods instead of immovable real estate. These bonds are issued by railroads to buy locomotives or other kinds of rolling stock. The bonds may be sold to a bank or insurance company, with a trustee named who carries out the provisions of the trust.
Mortgage bonds	Bonds that are secured by a conditional lien on part or all of a corporation's property are mortgage bonds. The issuing corporation uses the property, but title rests with the bond trustee.
Registered bonds	A registered bond has the owner's name written on the face of the instrument and on the records of the issuing corporation. A registered bond must be endorsed in order to be sold.
Serial bonds	Bonds of a single issue, but with various dates of maturity, are known as serial bonds.

BOND RETIREMENT

As part of the bond issue, the issuing corporation is required to include one or more plans for retiring the bonds. This information informs the prospective investor when the bond is scheduled to be retired or paid off. Three plans are used: the serial-bond plan, the sinking-fund plan, and the call-option plan.

Serial-Bond Plan. This plan states that a certain number of bonds will be retired annually. A twenty-year serial bond of $20 million, for example, is really forty different bond issues of $500,000 each. The maturity dates range from six months to twenty years. The shorter maturities of serial bonds usually have lower yields than the longer maturities.

Sinking-Fund Plan.   Bonds that provide for a sinking fund call for periodic deposits with the trustee of a stated amount of money. These deposits will provide enough money to retire the bonds when they are due. This is similar to installment financing.

Call-Option Plan.   This plan allows the corporation the right to call or buy back the bond at a stated price prior to the time the bond matures. Calling a bond before it matures is usually done to take advantage of lower interest rates in the money market. The bonds are usually called at a higher price than the par (stated) value. This is a way to pay the investor for the risk of reinvesting in new securities.

BOND RATINGS   Most investors and certain government agencies rely on "ratings" given bonds and preferred stocks by qualified independent organizations. Two organizations, Standard & Poor's and Moody's, are widely quoted. A rating by either organization is considered reliable. Table 14-3 lists the bond ratings made by these two organizations. Generally speaking, most investors buying for income should consider nothing lower then BBB-rated or Baa-rated bonds.

TABLE 14-3
Risk-Rating Scales for Bonds

STANDARD & POOR'S	RATING	MOODY'S INVESTORS SERVICE
AAA	Highest quality	Aaa
AA	High quality	Aa
A	Good quality	A
BBB	Medium grade, some speculative risk	Baa
BB, B	Speculative with defensive qualities	Ba
CCC, CC	Very speculative	B
C	Bonds with no interest being paid; may be in default	Caa
D	Lowest rating	C

STOCK EXCHANGES AND SECURITIES MARKETS

So far, we have dealt with the problems of determining long-term capital needs, the sources of funds, and the types of securities — stocks and bonds — that are used. There is a widespread interest in stocks and bonds by individual investors, as well as by business firms seeking capital. In fact, more than a dozen large and small securities markets, referred to as stock exchanges, have been organized in the United States. These markets are meeting places where people seeking capital can negotiate with those who have capital to invest.

FIGURE 14-4
An exterior view of the New York Stock Exchange. (Photo by Irene Springer.)

The organized exchanges are actually auction markets where traders and investors, through brokers, negotiate by setting "asking" prices and making "bids" on securities.

THE NEW YORK STOCK EXCHANGE Often called the "Big Board," the New York Stock Exchange is a corporation of about 1,366 members. Each member has purchased a "seat" on the exchange. This membership gives its holder the privilege of trading on the exchange floor. Members include member-firm corporations, registered traders, floor brokers, and specialists. Member firms are the brokerage houses that deal with the public. Their seats belong to the firm owners. Registered *traders* buy and sell stocks for their own personal accounts. *Floor brokers* help commission brokers to expedite orders. *Specialists* are exchange members assigned to certain stocks for which they will make a market. They may also buy and sell for their own accounts.

More than 2,100 stocks of almost 1,800 companies are listed and traded on the New York Exchange. The price of exchange seats has ranged from a low of $17,000 to a high of $625,000. The New York Exchange was 192 years old in 1984.

THE AMERICAN STOCK EXCHANGE Also located in New York City, the American Stock Exchange was started in the 1850s and is the second largest stock exchange. It was known as the New York Curb Exchange until 1953. It has a full membership of approximately 500 seats and 400 associate members. More than 1,200 companies are listed and traded on the American Exchange. Its listing requirements are less stringent than those of the New York Exchange.

REGIONAL AND LOCAL STOCK EXCHANGES

The principal regional exchanges are the Midwest Stock Exchange in Chicago, the Pacific Stock Exchange, and the Philadelphia Stock Exchange. Other regional exchanges are located in Boston, Cincinnati, Honolulu, Chicago (the Board of Trade), Salt Lake City (Intermountain), and Spokane.

In addition to these regional exchanges, there is a huge local over-the-counter (OTC) market where unlisted stocks are sold. This market is not in a particular location. Rather, it is a method of doing business, in which some 55,000 unlisted securities are bought and sold by a large group of brokers and dealers. As agents, they make a market for those who want to invest or sell. This market is known as the "third market." It is patronized by large institutional investors, including mutual funds and insurance companies. Prices of OTC securities are supplied by the National Association of Securities Dealers to newspapers through NASDAQ, its automated system for reporting quotations.

FOREIGN STOCK EXCHANGES

One of the oldest stock exchanges in the world is the London Stock Exchange. It lists and trades about seven times the number of issues listed on the New York Stock Exchange. The Paris Stock Exchange (Bourse) is an active market. Exchanges in Switzerland include those in Zurich, Geneva, Basel, and Lausanne. The Toronto Stock Exchange has more than 1,000 listed securities. There are nine exchanges in Japan, the largest being in Tokyo.

COMING: A CENTRALIZED SECURITIES MARKET

The long-awaited formation of a central market for securities has finally become possible. Congress, by enactment of the Securities Acts Amendments, provided the Securities and Exchange Commission (SEC) with authority to implement such a market. The general objective is to enable all investors to have their orders executed in the specific market that offers the best price for a specific stock.

A nationwide system linking all existing markets electronically would be required. Stockbrokers and dealers could route orders to all markets trading the stock in order to obtain the most favorable execution. A central file would establish storage of all limit orders. The Intermarket Trading System, linking all the regional exchanges and the New York and the American exchanges with the National Association of Securities Dealers, would create a central market. So far, however, total market reform as mandated by Congress has been a slow process and has not yet been accomplished.

FUNCTION OF THE SECURITIES MARKETS

Within our economic system, securities exchanges operate as marketplaces where buyers meet sellers through authorized agents. It is possible for two persons in widely separated areas of the United States, through their brokers, to trade with each other without personal contact. You may wonder why you cannot buy a stock directly from a corporation listed on the exchange, just as you buy an automobile from your dealer. The reason is that a corporation has only so many shares outstanding. If you want to buy ten, twenty-five, 100, or 1,000 shares, you must usually buy from someone who already owns (or a combination of several who own) that number of shares. You must buy from a broker who is the agent for each party.

There are certain facts worth keeping in mind about buying or selling stock on an exchange:

1. When you buy stock, you buy from another person through a broker.
2. When you sell stock, you sell to another person through a broker.
3. The exchange provides the marketplace for the sale.
4. The exchange neither buys, sells, nor sets the price of your stock.
5. Through their daily operations, the exchanges provide a continuous market with a constant release of market information.

Stock Quotations. Many newspapers publish daily stock quotations of listed securities on a national, regional, or local market. Figure 14-5 shows a partial list of stocks, with explanations given in the margins. For example, sales recorded in lots of 100 shares are **round lots.** Orders for less than 100 shares are **odd-lot** sales. Price quotations are in dollars and fractions ranging from ⅛ to ⅞. A quotation of 25⅝ indicates that the price of the stock is $25.625 per share.

The symbol *P/E* means "price-earnings ratio." This is an analytical ratio of earnings divided into the price of the stock. A stock selling at $30 with annual earnings per share of $2 has a P/E ratio of 15. The P/E ratio is a highly regarded measure of stock value, because it gives an indication of corporate success measured against the current stock price. For instance, if a stock has a very high ratio ranging from 25 to 40, this does not necessarily

FIGURE 14-5

The meaning of daily newspaper stock-market quotations.

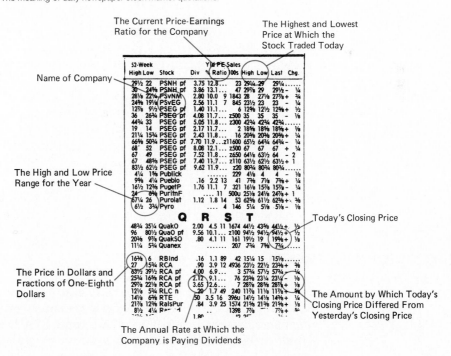

indicate high quality. Rather, it may mean that earnings are currently low, with future earnings expected to be higher. Generally, speculative investment stocks sell at either extremely low or extremely high P/E ratios. Companies with outstanding growth potential tend to have higher P/E ratios than income stocks.

Bond Quotations.   Corporate bonds are quoted daily in many newspapers, but in a different manner than stocks. Stocks are quoted at the exact price for which they are being bought or sold. Most bonds are quoted in denominations of $100, although the face value is $1,000. For example, a bond quoted at 97 in your newspaper means that the trading price is $970 on that date. It is selling for 97 percent of par—the price of its denomination. Bonds are grouped into several categories, such as domestic corporate bonds, U.S. government bonds, and foreign bonds.

The point around which the bond yield varies is the interest rate. It is fixed for the life of the bond. As a rule, the bond yield is stated as a percentage of the face value of the bond. Thus, a bond paying 7 percent interest on $1,000 yields the investor $70 per year (.07 × $1,000). If the market price drops to $900, the yield goes up. But if the market price increases, the yield declines.

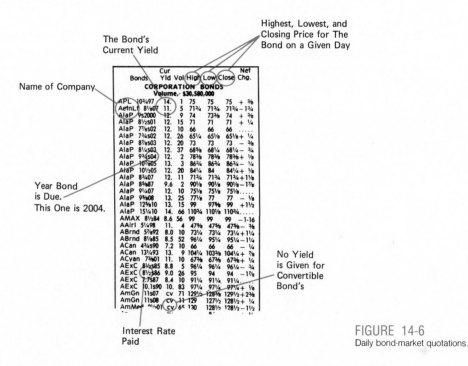

FIGURE 14-6
Daily bond-market quotations.

SECURITIES INVESTMENTS

Investing in common stocks is a convenient and affordable way to participate directly in the private-enterprise system. A corporation offers its shares of common stocks in order to obtain capital for the business. Once these stocks are sold to the public, they become investment securities for the owners.

The floor of the New York Stock Exchange during trading. (Photo by Edward C. Topple, New York Stock Exchange.)

INVESTMENT VS.
SPECULATION

Definitions. The term INVESTMENT identifies *the purchase of securities that offer safety of principal and satisfactory yield equal to the risks.* SPECULATION is *the assumption of above-average risks for which there is anticipation of a higher financial return.* The stock trader who speculates tends to deemphasize dividends and is willing to accept more risk, hoping that large profits can be made in a short time. A PORTFOLIO is *a collection of investment securities owned by the investor.*

It is often suggested that before investing in any stock, one should have enough money in a savings account to meet an emergency and a reasonable amount of life insurance for protection. Assuming your reserve funds are adequate, what is your first step in beginning an investment program?

Choosing Your Investment Objective. In contrast to the speculator, the investor determines his or her investment objective by considering one or more of the following:

1. Safety of principal
2. Growth in the value of the asset
3. Income from dividends

Table 14-4 shows investment objectives for selected types of securities.

TABLE 14-4
Portfolio Investment Objectives

SECURITIES	SAFETY	GROWTH	INCOME
Common stocks	Least	Best	Varies
Preferred stocks	High	Varies	Steady
Bonds	Highest	Very little	Very steady

In arriving at investment decisions, it is critical that investors be informed about changes occurring in the financial markets. Two of the most complete security services are *Moody's Investors' Service* and Standard & Poor's *Industry Surveys*. Standard & Poor's also offers *Dividend Records, Called Bond Record*, and the *Outlook*, available by subscription. The securities services sold on a subscription basis include, among others, the following:

1. *United Business Service*, 210 Newbury St., Boston, Mass.
2. *Value Line Investment Service*, 5 East 44th St., New York, N.Y.
3. *Stock Picture*, a composite of 1,700 charts, published by M.C. Horsey & Company, Salisbury, Md.

THE DOW JONES AVERAGE'S SHORTCOMINGS

Some people argue that the much-reported Dow Jones Average is much ado about nothing. Critics contend that it is too "smokestack"-oriented, containing too many older, heavy-manufacturing companies whose day is gone; that the average does not adequately consider service-oriented industries, where the growth is. Be that as it may, look at the evening news on TV tonight and see which index is reported!!

Stock Averages. Two widely used statistical averages concerning daily stock-market quotations are the Dow Jones (DJ) and the *New York Times* market index. The DJ averages, published by *The Wall Street Journal*, consist of four groups of stocks and five bond-price indexes. The DJ industrial average, which is the granddaddy of stock-market averages, consists of the thirty industrial companies shown in Table 14-5. Other DJ stock averages include twenty transportation companies, previously known as the "railroad" average, fifteen utility stocks, and a DJ composite average of sixty-five stocks. The *New York Times* stock average consists of twenty-five industrial companies, twenty-five rail stocks, and a fifty-stock composite average.

TABLE 14-5
The 30 Stocks in the DJ Average

Allied Corporation	IBM
Alcoa	International Harvester
American Brands	International Paper
American Can	Merck
American Express	Minnesota Mining
AT&T	Owens-Illinois
Bethlehem Steel	Procter & Gamble
Du Pont	Sears, Roebuck
Eastman Kodak	Standard Oil of Calif.
Exxon	Texaco
General Electric	Union Carbide
General Foods	U.S. Steel
General Motors	United Technologies
Goodyear	Westinghouse Electric
Inco	F.W. Woolworth

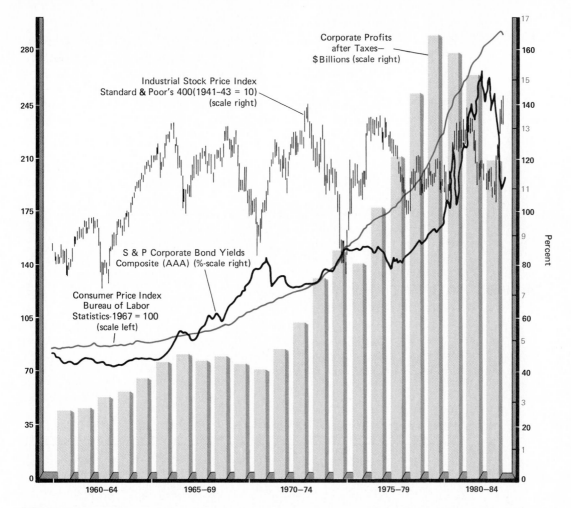

FIGURE 14-7
Trends of Stocks, Bonds, Profits, and Business.
(Adapted from *United Business & Investment Report,* February 28, 1983, United Business Service. By permission.)

Standard & Poor's 500 Stock Price Index is widely used. It is composed of 400 industrials, forty utilities, twenty transportation, and forty finance companies (banks, investment, and life insurance). The New York Stock Exchange publishes a common-stock index reflecting the price changes of *all* common stocks on the Big Board. The American Stock Exchange index covers stocks on that exchange.

OTHER LONG-TERM-FINANCING SOURCES

We have already noted that large sums of capital for long-term use are obtained from the sale of stocks and bonds and retained earnings. Other financial institutions, such as life insurance companies, mutual funds, pension funds, and savings and loan associations, also supply long-term business financing. These institutions provide long-term funds by buying stocks and bonds and by making long-term loans.

LIFE INSURANCE COMPANIES

The assets of life insurance companies have now reached more then $350 billion. Much of this is invested in corporate stocks and bonds, real estate, and mortgages on real estate. Life insurance companies finance the construction of commercial buildings, shopping centers, and apartments.

MUTUAL FUNDS

Mutual fund is a name coined to identify investment trusts and companies created for the investment of funds contributed by many people. Technically, a mutual fund is a corporation whose assets are shares of stock owned by the fund shareholders. The corporation is managed by professional investment managers, who select the fund's investment portfolio.

Mutual funds are especially attractive to people with money to invest but lacking the skill or the time to make investment decisions. These funds are chartered by the state to sell their own stock to investors seeking the advantages of diversification and professional management. Investors may make monthly or one-time purchases, or even quarterly investments in varying amounts. Profits are distributed in cash or are reinvested in the fund.

PENSION FUNDS

Many companies and labor unions provide funds for employee pensions. These funds invest large sums in common and preferred stocks and in real estate. Today, the pension funds are valued at more than $160 billion. These funds are regulated by the U.S. Department of Labor, the Pension Benefit Guaranty Corporation, and the Internal Revenue Service, as provided for in the Employee Retirement Income Security Act of 1974.

TABLE 14-6
Federal Regulations of Securities Markets and Sales

LEGISLATION	PURPOSE
Securities Act of 1933	Known as the "truth-in-securities law," this act requires that full disclosure of new securities be given in a registration statement and prospectus.
Securities Act of 1934	This law authorizes the SEC to administer market securities. All brokers and dealers engaged in interstate trade must register with the SEC and comply with SEC rules. The SEC and Federal Reserve Board jointly set margin requirements. The act prohibits transactions regarded as trading abuses involving over-the-counter markets.
Maloney Act of 1938	Serving as an amendment to the Securities Act of 1934, this act allows investment bankers to form associations for self-regulation. The National Association of Securities Dealers was created to regulate OTC securities.
Investment Advisors Act of 1940	All persons serving as security advisers must register with the SEC. Although registration is intended to guard against fraud, it does not indicate any degree of expertise or favorable results.
Investment Company Act of 1940	This law created the framework for the mutual-fund industry by requiring investment trust companies to register with the SEC. The term *mutual funds* is another name for what are technically known as investment companies.
Securities Act Amendments of 1964	The Securities Acts of 1933 and 1934 were amended in 1964 to cover securities sold over the counter, which were assigned to the SEC. Dealers and brokers selling OTC stocks must register with the SEC.
Securities Investor Protection Act of 1970	This act created a nonprofit corporation—the Securities Investor Protection Corporation (SIPC, pronounced *sip-ic*)—to protect individual accounts with brokers. If a member broker or dealer is insolvent, the SIPC protects brokerage accounts up to $100,000, of which $40,000 covers cash in accounts. The SIPC does not protect customers against market losses from price declines. Some brokers carry $500,000 extra protection per client. Funding for the SIPC comes from assessments made on member firms.

| DEPOSITORY INSTITUTIONS | Banks and savings and loan associations accept time deposits from savers. These funds are sometimes sources of long-term financing for firms, but more often are short-term. |

REGULATION OF SECURITIES MARKETS

Control over the securities markets is now a responsibility of both the states and the federal government. But it was not until the stock-market crash of 1929 that federal laws were passed to prosecute market manipulators and swindlers. Subsequently, statutes have been enacted by states and the federal government.

| STATE LAWS | All states have various kinds of laws controlling securities sales. These are dubbed "blue-sky laws," because they represent an attempt to stop the sale of the "blue sky" to unwary investors. Such laws seek to protect the public against fraudulent stock offers. In most states, the securities commissioners enforce these laws. |

| FEDERAL LAWS | The first federal statute dealing with the sale of stocks and bonds was enacted in 1933. The principal securities laws enacted since then are summarized in Table 14-6. |

SUMMARY OF KEY CONCEPTS

All businesses require capital. The largest single investment by an owner or owners is in fixed assets, which include land, equipment, and buildings:

The primary objectives of financial management are to:

1. Obtain an adequate supply of capital and credit
2. Evaluate alternative sources of funds and their costs
3. Manage the financial resources of the business wisely

Business uses long-term financing for continuing operation and acquiring fixed-capital assets. The two main sources of long-term financing are equity (owner) capital and debt capital.

Equity capital is supplied by owners and partners of small firms and by stockholders of corporations. Other sources of capital are profits retained and reinvested and lease financing.

If a business is able to earn more than the cost of interest on borrowed money, it is advantageous to obtain debt capital.

Bonds do not affect management control, since bondholders have no voting rights in the affairs of a business. Bonds do not dilute the stockholders' equity.

There are certain financial disadvantages to bonds as a source of funds. They are a debt that eventually must be paid. Fixed interest charges on bonds can become a financial burden during the time when earnings are declining.

Common stock is a popular source of long-term capital. There is no fixed dividend rate stated or guaranteed. While common-stock holders assume the greatest amount of risk, they stand to make maximum gains when profits are high.

Corporations issue preferred stocks. Dividends on preferred stocks take priority over those on common stocks. Preferred-stock dividends often exceed bond interest.

Stock exchanges are marketplaces where securities are bought and sold. The sale of securities is used for starting new firms and for expanding old firms.

Securities bought by investors should be acquired in accordance with an investment objective. The three major investment objectives are (1) safety of principal, (2) dividend income, and (3) growth of capital (growth stocks).

Bonds and preferred stocks are forms of investment with a high safety-of-principal factor. Stocks of corporations whose sales and earnings are expanding more rapidly than the general economy and more rapidly than the average growth in that industry are growth stocks. Stability and regularity of income are two characteristics of income stocks.

BUSINESS TERMS

You should be able to match these business terms with the statements that follow:

a. ASSETS
b. BOND
c. EQUITY
d. FIXED CAPITAL
e. INVESTMENTS
f. PORTFOLIO
g. SPECULATION
h. STOCK DIVIDEND
i. STOCK OPTION
j. STOCK SPLIT
k. WORKING CAPITAL

1. Assets that can readily be turned into cash for current use in operating the firm
2. Items of monetary value owned by a business
3. Money invested in fixed assets to be used for a long period of time
4. The ownership claim to the resources of the firm
5. The purchase of securities that offer safety of principal and satisfactory yield equal to the risk
6. A privilege of key executives to purchase company stock under certain conditions of price and time
7. A division of outstanding common stock into additional units
8. A distribution of profits or capital paid to stockholders
9. A certificate of indebtedness indicating debt that is owed the bondholder by the corporation
10. The assumption of above-average risk for which there is anticipation of commensuratively higher financial return
11. A collection of securities owned by an investor

REVIEW QUESTIONS

1. What is *working capital,* and how is it used in a business?
2. What major factors determine the amount of required fixed capital?
3. What are four sources of long-term capital financing?
4. Describe the difference between *book value, market value, par value,* and *no-par value* in common stock.
5. From the investor's viewpoint, what are the main features of preferred stock?

DISCUSSION QUESTIONS

1. From the owner's viewpoint, what advantages does equity financing offer?
2. A corporation may prefer to sell bonds rather than issue more common stock. Why?
3. From the corporation's viewpoint, why pay dividends in stock rather than cash?
4. How does a stock split help anyone?
5. What is the main purpose of the Securities Investor Protection Corporation, and who benefits?

14-1

SHOULD THE DECKER COMPANY EXPAND?

The Decker Appliance Company, which produces a line of home appliances, has an excellent reputation for high-quality merchandise. The company sells its appliances to two chain stores under separate private-label brands. The two chains buy virtually the entire output of Decker products each year. Both companies have contracts that will expire in another ten months. Each chain has informed the Decker management that it would like to sign a new three-year contract that would result in a substantial increase in the company's annual production. To do this, the company would have to expand its plant by adding new and more modern equipment.

Tentative estimates indicate that a proposed production expansion would involve the need for new financing amounting to $1 million.

The Decker Company, a close corporation owned by four members of the Decker family, is capitalized at $5 million, with 100,000 shares of common stock outstanding, with a par value of $50. The company recently retired its preferred stock. There are no bonds. Its credit is the highest rating available, according to Dun & Bradstreet.

The stock is sold over the counter, but transactions seldom occur, since there are only about 500 shares held outside the Decker family. The last quoted price was $40 per share. The dividend last year was $2.80 per share, with annual earnings of $500,000. As an investment, the stock yields 7 percent.

At a meeting of the stockholders and the board of directors, various proposals were discussed. One plan consisted of financing the expansion from earnings and leasing. A second plan was to amend the charter and increase the number of shares of authorized common stock from 100,000 to 200,000. The company would then sell 25,000 shares of common at $40 per share. This would produce $1 million.

1. If you were a stockholder of the Decker Company, how would you feel about expanding the plant's production?
2. Which plan for financing the expansion do you prefer?
3. What risks do you see in increasing production?

14-2

MARTINI AND HOFFNESTER WINERY

S.A. Martini and J.R. Hoffnester recently purchased a winery in the Napa Valley in California. Since the winery has not been in business for a number of years, it will be two or three years before the new enterprise, a corporation, will show any positive cash flows. It is estimated that it will be one year before the winery is in operation. One or two additional years are needed for the first batch of wine to reach an age at which it can be sold. During these first two or three years, however, the firm will experience considerable cash outflows for working capital, fixed capital expansion, and operating expenses. Since Martini and Hoffnester have used all their available finances to acquire the winery, they need advice on how to acquire additional capital to carry them through the next three years.

1. For these circumstances, what are the advantages and disadvantages of common stock, preferred stock, bonds, a term loan, and lease financing as sources of financing for the winery?
2. What is your advice to Martini and Hoffnester on the best form of financing?

CREDIT AND THE BANKING SYSTEM

study objectives

WHEN YOU HAVE FINISHED READING THIS CHAPTER, YOU SHOULD BE ABLE TO:

1. Explain the purpose of credit and how it is used in business
2. Identify the various kinds of credit instruments and their uses
3. Distinguish between money and credit
4. Understand the operations and purposes of the Federal Reserve System
5. Discuss how the Federal Reserve controls the supply of money and credit
6. Contrast the kinds of services provided by commercial banks with other sources of short-term and intermediate-term financing

The biggest problem facing commercial banking today is not the new competition, but the old regulations.

Walter B. Wriston

This second chapter dealing with finance focuses on money, short-term credit, and our banking system. Business, when you get down to the basics, *is money*. Not only do businesses need money to operate, but our economy needs a steady, predictable flow of money. Credit *is* money, in a sense. You can buy things with credit just as you can with greenbacks. Yet credit and its proper use continue to be a lesson that many people (and businesses) have trouble learning.

Banks provide money to individuals and businesses. They are in the "money-service" business. As federal regulations change, banks are expanding their services to include almost everything in the financial area. But their primary business is to lend money when a person or company runs short. It is this function of banking that supplies much of the short-term financing businesses need.

The nation's "central bank," the Federal Reserve System, is charged with controlling money and interest rates in this country. It and other federal agencies try to provide some order and stability to the entire money and banking system.

In this chapter, we consider these related topics and explain the essentials of this interesting area.

MONEY AND ITS FUNCTIONS

For more than 2,000 years, money has been a desirable commodity. Such items as seashells, salt, tobacco, and pieces of metal have sometimes served as money. Today we know much about how to control the value of money without changing the quantity. Money is essential in a market economy, where most output is bought and sold rather than used by the producer.

MONEY is *anything generally accepted in exchange for goods and services.* In this sense, money serves as a medium of exchange.

OUR MONEY SUPPLY

Our money supply in the United States is composed of three kinds of money: (1) coins, (2) currency (paper money), and (3) bank deposits (demand deposits).

Bank deposits include the following different kinds of demand deposit:

1. Negotiable Order of Withdrawal (NOW) and Automatic Transfer Service (ATS) acounts at banks and thrift institutions
2. Credit-union share-draft accounts
3. Demand deposits at mutual savings banks

It became apparent in the 1960s and 1970s that the amount of money in the hands of the public had an influence on business activity and the economy. This was especially true when there was a bulge in the supply of money without a similar bulge in the supply of things to buy. People were apt to use the extra money to bid up prices. The symbol M_1 is used to represent the money supply. M_1 consists of cash plus demand deposits (checking accounts) on deposit in commercial banks. This is money readily available for spending.

A second symbol, M_2, includes M_1 plus time deposits (savings accounts held by all depository institutions and money-market mutual funds), but it does not include large certificates of deposit. The symbol M_3 includes M_2 plus large deposits in all depository institutions.

Money does three major things. It acts: (1) as a medium of exchange, (2) as a standard of value, and (3) as a store of value.

Medium of Exchange. As a medium of exchange, money is the means by which goods are bought and sold. An employee works in order to be paid in money, which is used to buy the things he or she wants. Likewise, the seller offers goods on the market for money.

Standard of Value. Money is a standard of value in that it is the unit by which all values are measured. In a society where specialization and exchange prevail, there is a need for a simple standard of value in the form of money.

Store of Value. People with money may use it in many ways. They may spend it, hold it in a checking or savings account, or in some other form. When it is used as a store of value, money is saved and not spent. The fact that money can be accumulated makes it acceptable to sellers who want to use it as a store of value.

QUALITIES OF MONEY

For anything to work as money, it must be acceptable in trade as a convenient medium of exchange. It must possess certain qualities. Even though governments may declare money to be "legal tender" (acceptable in payment of a debt), it must be acceptable to those using it. A store owner would rather close the shop than surrender goods for money that he or she regards as worthless. For money to be acceptable, it must possess divisibility, durability, portability, and stability, and it must be difficult to counterfeit. Table 15-1 lists and explains these attributes.

TABLE 15-1
Attributes of Money

Types of Quality	Explanation
Divisibility	For money to be acceptable, it must be readily divisible into units of value to facilitate making change. Paper money and coins satisfy this quality. Bank deposits are even better because they can be withdrawn in the amounts desired.
Difficulty in counterfeiting	People have long been tempted to make their own money. Governments take elaborate precautions to reduce counterfeiting as much as possible. Special paper and ink help to make it more difficult to counterfeit.
Durability	The quality of durability is essential. Money should not deteriorate rapidly with frequent handling. Currency and checks may not always pass the durability test to perfection, but they are preferred to apples or bushels of wheat.
Portability	Money must be easy and convenient to transfer. This implies relatively high value per unit of size and weight. People prefer paper money to silver dollars because paper money is light in weight.
Stability	Money is considered to have stability when its purchasing power (the value of goods a dollar will buy) is fairly constant. When prices in general are increasing, the value of money is decreasing. When prices are decreasing, the value of money is increasing. Thus far, gold has approached the quality of stability more than any other commodity.

CREDIT AND CREDIT INSTRUMENTS

Credit touches the lives of almost everyone, and in different ways. It is such an important part of business that our economic system is often characterized as a "credit economy." An understanding of credit, therefore, is essential for personal use as well as for business activities.

MEANING OF CREDIT The word **credit** comes from the Latin word **credere** meaning "to trust." When related to business, CREDIT is *the ability to secure goods or services in exchange for a promise to pay later.* Credit is regarded as a function of management. Management must deal with such matters as approving credit transactions, investigating credit risks, and collecting accounts.

Credit involves two characteristics: First, there is the element of *faith* on the part of the creditor in the willingness and ability of the debtor to fulfill the promise to pay. When such faith is present, the creditor is willing to give goods, services, or money. The second element of credit is *futurity*: In every credit transaction, the lender accepts some risk over a period of time. Credit instruments always involve a *time* during which the creditor's confidence is placed in the debtor's promise to pay. And until payment is made, there is always a risk that it will not be made. Because of these characteristics, *credit instruments* are different from other commercial documents.

FUNCTIONS OF CREDIT   Credit serves business in several ways: First, it makes capital available that would otherwise be idle. It works like this: In exchange for payment of interest, people entrust their personal savings to banks and other financing institutions. The banks, in turn, lend these savings to businesses.

Second, like money, credit also serves as a medium of exchange. Through its use, transactions can be completed quickly, with a minimum of work, and without the exchange of money. Without credit, the high level of economic activity characteristic of the U.S. economy would be curtailed.

Third, credit is a tool that helps a business match capital to its varying needs. By borrowing additional capital, a business can increase production during peak business activity. By extending credit, a business can induce customers to buy, thus gaining a competitive advantage over the firm that does not give credit. For example, during a sales slump, General Motors, Ford, and Chrysler compete on the basis of interest rates they will allow on credit.

TRADE CREDIT   Trade credit differs radically from other forms of short-term credit, because it does not come from a financial institution. An example is the "put-it-on-my-tab" arrangements many rural general stores used years ago. Such an arrangement is called an open-book account. This has become the most common source of working capital. In accounting language, it is accounts receivable for the seller, and accounts payable for the buyer. Often, except for the invoice, no formal instrument is involved.

Orchard Street, New York City on a Sunday afternoon, 1982. (Photo by Jan Lukas, Photo Researchers, Inc.)

Credit and the Banking System

Reasons for Trade Credit.   A firm may be willing to grant credit to increase sales. A firm may be able to increase sales without large expenditures for new production equipment. It may then be possible to spread the fixed costs over a large number of units and reduce the cost per unit.

From the debtor's viewpoint, the use of trade credit is a convenience. For example, a distributor may make many deliveries to a customer during a month. If payment is not made for each delivery, trade credit is the result. In some cases, it may come about because acceptable credit is not available elsewhere. Commercial banks are either unable or unwilling to assume the costs or the risk inherent in many trade-credit sales. Many firms would find it difficult to maintain suitable inventories in the absence of trade credit.

Credit managers estimate that open-book accounts constitute about 85 percent of the retail and wholesale trade in the United States. The seller enters into no formal written agreement, but relies on the buyer to pay for the goods at the appropriate time. However, the seller's record alone is not the best legal evidence of debt in the event of a dispute, so it is common practice to support these credit transactions with sales slips or delivery receipts.

SWANK BANKING

As competition heats up for the public's deposit dollars and loan business, some banks are going to great lengths to distinguish themselves from the herd.

BancOhio National Bank in Akron offers a service called "Private Banking." People who make $50,000 per year or who have a net worth of $150,000 have access to a plush private room where tellers will cash their personal checks, exchange foreign currency, and help them buy gold, Treasury bills, and so on. Bank officers can authorize up to a $25,000 line of credit, help with tax shelters, and so forth.

Such services in most cities are available only to those with a six-figure annual income or $1 million net worth. BancOhio officers hope their approach to banking will move the bank to a number one rank in the Akron area.

CREDIT INSTRUMENTS   In addition to the use of open-account or trade credit, working capital may also be obtained through the use of credit instruments for short periods. These instruments can be divided into two broad groups: **promises to pay** and **orders to pay.** The first group comprises promissory notes. The second includes drafts of all kinds and trade acceptances.

Negotiable Promissory Note (Promise to Pay).   This is the legal instrument in the promise-to-pay category used by commercial banks and business firms. The borrower signs a note stating the terms of the loan, its length, and the interest rate to be charged.

In Figure 15-1, which shows a negotiable promissory note, Joseph Doe, Jr. (the maker), agrees to pay the East End State Bank (the payee) $100, with interest at 9 percent, sixty days from the date of the note. A promissory note has an advantage over open-book accounts in that it represents evidence of the debt. When the promissory note is signed by the debtor, it acknowledges the accuracy of the debt at the time he or she agreed to it.

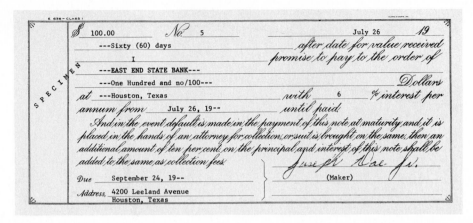

FIGURE 15-1

A negotiable promissory note. (Courtesy East End State Bank, Houston, Texas.)

The note may be written so that the interest is paid at maturity or at specified intervals during the period of debt. Or it may be discounted, in which case the interest is deducted from the principal at the time the note is made. For example, Tom Jensen elects to borrow $1,500 from his bank at 10 percent interest for sixty days. When he signs the note, the bank accepts it and pays him the money. If he used a discounted note, the bank would subtract $25 (interest for two months) from the amount of the note and pay him $1,475. Tom would repay the full amount of $1,500 at the end of sixty days. *Interest deducted in advance* is a BANK DISCOUNT.

Banks or other lenders may ask the borrower to obtain the signature of a third party as a cosigner of a promissory note. Thus the cosigner becomes an accommodation endorser, equally liable for the debt. Common examples are young people buying their first automobiles. Often parents are asked to cosign such a note.

Draft or Bill of Exchange (Order to Pay). A DRAFT is *an unconditional written order made by the drawer, addressed to the drawee, ordering the drawee to pay a specific sum to a third party (payee).* A draft differs from a promissory note in that it is drawn by a creditor and not a borrower. It is also an order to pay, not a promise to pay. *A draft payable on demand* is a SIGHT DRAFT. *A draft payable at a fixed future date* is a TIME DRAFT. Another form of draft used by a bank is a bank draft. It may be drawn upon an out-of-town bank in which the bank maintains deposits.

Figure 15-2 illustrates a sight draft in which Richard B. Brown is the drawer of the draft. It is payable on demand to Joseph Doe, Jr. (payee), from Brown's account in the First City National Bank (drawee). This draft is issued to Brown through the courtesy of the East End State Bank as a service.

Trade Acceptance. A TRADE ACCEPTANCE is another form of trade credit in addition to the open account and promissory note. *It is a draft drawn by a seller of merchandise ordering the buyer to pay the amount of the purchase*

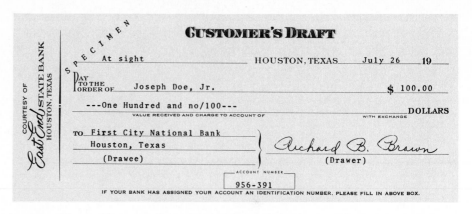

FIGURE 15-2
A sight draft, payable upon presentation. (Courtesy East End State Bank, Houston, Texas.)

at a fixed date. The buyer expecting to honor the draft accepts it by writing "Accepted" on the face of the draft and adding his or her signature and the date. The buyer also designates the bank at which the draft will be paid when due. It should be noted that the seller is both the drawer and the payee. The buyer is the drawee and the acceptor.

When a trade-acceptance draft drawn by the seller on a named bank is accepted, it is a bank acceptance. The bank's responsibility is then substituted for the buyer's. Bank acceptances are especially used in foreign-trade transactions where the parties may not know each other.

If the buyer's credit is good enough for a trade acceptance to be marketable, the seller may elect to sell the draft before it is due. The seller is able to receive immediate payment by doing so.

FIGURE 15-3
A cashier's check—a check drawn by a bank against itself. This type of check may be purchased from a bank for remittance purposes. (Courtesy Crocker National Bank, San Francisco.)

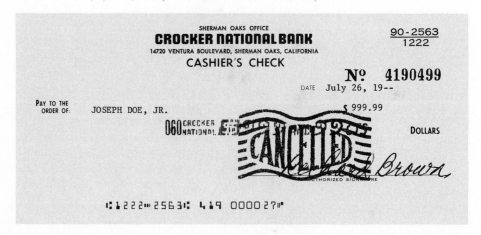

Cashier's Check.   ***A check drawn by a bank against its own funds*** is a CASHIER'S CHECK. Banks issue cashier's checks to pay their obligations or to transfer funds. A bank customer can obtain a cashier's check to make a payment for goods. Payment is guaranteed by the issuing bank.

Figure 15-3 illustrates a cashier's check. Notice that it differs from a regular check in that it is signed by the bank's cashier and drawn on the bank's funds, not on a correspondent bank. ***A bank that maintains an account relationship with another bank or engages in an exchange of services*** is a CORRESPONDENT BANK. Banks in large cities act as correspondents for banks in smaller cities.

Among the services that a correspondent bank performs for other banks are the following.

1. Collecting checks, drafts, and other credit instruments
2. Accepting letters of credit and traveler's checks
3. Making credit investigations of firms

Certified Check.   If a bank's customer wishes to make payment to a person who would otherwise refuse to accept a personal check, he or she can obtain a certified check. ***A check that is guaranteed by the bank both as to signature and as to payment*** is a CERTIFIED CHECK. An officer of the bank certifies the check by writing "accepted" or "certified" on the face of the check and then signing it. The amount of the check is immediately withdrawn from the depositor's account and is held by the bank pending the cashing of the check. Certified checks are used mainly in real estate and securities transactions in which payment in cash or by check is required. The drawer of a certified check cannot stop payment on it. The drawer should redeposit the check if it is still in his or her possession, rather than destroying it.

Figure 15-4 illustrates a certified check. Joe D. Smith is the drawer of the check, Jennie Smith is the payee, and Crocker National Bank is the drawee bank. Jennie Smith will be paid $100 from the account of Joe D. Smith.

FIGURE 15-4

A certified check is safer because the bank guarantees payment. (Courtesy Crocker National Bank, San Francisco.)

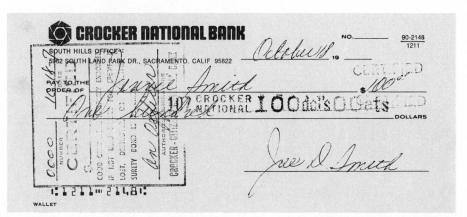

An efficient and safe banking system is a primary requirement for providing the financial needs of business. Businesses rely heavily on banks for capital funds, some of which come from personal savings held by banks for depositors. These funds are made available for short-term and intermediate-term loans.

DUAL BANKING SYSTEM

A unique characteristic of our banking system is its dual nature, involving both state and federal regulations and examinations. Banks are the financial institutions through which the monetary policy of the federal government is carried out. The economy must have a responsible system of banks capable of maintaining the confidence of the public.

In each state, a banking department or division supervises banks and enforces the state regulations covering various aspects of banking in that state.

Much of the stability of our banking system is due to the Federal Reserve Bank. Federal Reserve Banks are called "bankers' banks," because they provide financial services to financial institutions.

COMMERCIAL BANKS

We have in the United States about 14,700 commercial banks. About one-third of these are national banks, and the other two-thirds are state banks.

Commercial banks chartered by the state are STATE BANKS. Each state has an agency that reviews bank charter applications issued by the state in which the bank is to operate. State banks that qualify may become members

The Federal Reserve Building, Washington, D.C.

of the Federal Reserve System. These banks may also have depositors' accounts insured by the Federal Deposit Insurance Corporation (FDIC). Most of the large state banks are members of the Federal Reserve, but many small ones are not.

Commercial banks chartered by the federal government are NATIONAL BANKS. These banks tend to be large in size. All national banks are approved by the Comptroller of the Currency, an arm of the U.S. Treasury Department. All national banks must be members of the Federal Reserve and are subject to regulation by the Fed. Regulations affecting state and national banks may vary in practice, but from the individual depositor's or borrower's viewpoint, there is very little difference.

In addition to supplying the largest part of the total money supply, commercial banks perform two important financial functions:

1. They accept deposits from business firms and individuals in the form of checking (demand-deposit) or savings (time-deposit) accounts.
2. They use these deposits to make loans to businesses and individuals. The making of such loans is the bank's main source of income.

Commercial banks also provide numerous services, such as the following:

1. Collect notes, drafts, and bond coupons
2. Prepare and mail dividend checks for corporations
3. Administer trust funds and estates
4. Prepare foreign-trade documents
5. Furnish commercial letters of credit
6. Provide payroll service to businesses
7. Rent safe-deposit boxes
8. Supply financial advice to firms and individuals

Table 15-2 lists the ten largest commercial banks in the United States. BankAmerica in California is the nation's largest bank, with deposits in excess of $121 billion.

TABLE 15-2
America's Ten Largest Banking Companies Ranked by Deposits

RANK	BANK NAME AND LOCATION	DEPOSITS IN MILLIONS OF DOLLARS	NUMBER OF EMPLOYEES
1	BankAmerica (San Francisco)	$121,000	87,500
2	Citicorp (New York)	119,000	58,200
3	Chase Manhattan (New York)	78,000	34,150
4	Manufacturers Hanover Corporation (New York)	59,000	26,200
5	J. P. Morgan & Co. (New York)	54,000	12,062
6	Continental Illinois Corporation (New York)	46,000	12,700
7	Chemical New York Corporation (New York)	45,000	19,700
8	First Interstate Bankcorp (Los Angeles)	37,000	31,200
9	Bankers Trust New York Corporation (New York)	34,000	12,400
10	First Chicago Corporation (Chicago)	34,000	11,100

SOURCE: Annual corporate reports for 1981.

MUTUAL SAVINGS BANKS

Mutual savings banks are the oldest type of savings institution in this country. The first ones were organized in 1816 in Boston and Philadelphia. There are at present about 467 savings banks located in eighteen states and the Commonwealth of Puerto Rico.[1]

These banks were organized to promote savings. Since early commercial banks did not provide savings accounts, mutual savings banks were formed for this purpose. These savings deposits are invested by the bank in real estate mortgages, bonds, and other investments. The difference between the income from loans and investments and the interest paid to depositors is the gross profits of the banks. Mutual savings banks are chartered by the state and are entitled to membership in the Federal Deposit Insurance Corporation. Accounts are insured up to $100,000 in any one bank. Commercial banks accept savings deposits in those states that do not charter mutual savings banks.

Under Public Law 96-221, mutual savings banks can now be federally chartered. This law allows them to lend up to 5 percent of their assets in commercial and business loans.

SAVINGS AND LOAN ASSOCIATIONS

As with mutual savings banks, savings and loan associations receive deposits and invest them. However, savings and loans primarily invest their deposits in home mortgages. During the early 1980s, savings and loans fell on very hard times as home-mortgage rates went over 20 percent and their primary source of income dried up. For example, the industry lost $3.3 billion in the *first half* of 1982. As a result, changes were made in regulations affecting savings and loans to make them more competitive and flexible. The S&Ls are now in a position to become more competitive with banks and other depository institutions.

CREDIT UNIONS

Credit unions have been in existence since 1908, when parishioners of the Roman Catholic Church of St. Mary started one in Manchester, New Hampshire. But credit unions grew slowly until after World War II.

A CREDIT UNION is *an organization formed by individuals on a cooperative basis to make loans to its members and encourage them to save.* Systematic savings are promoted through the purchase of credit-union

---

[1] The following eighteen states charter savings banks: Alaska, Connecticut, Delaware, Indiana, Maine, Maryland, Massachusetts, Minnesota, New Hampshire, New Jersey, New York, Ohio, Oregon, Pennsylvania, Rhode Island, Vermont, Washington, and Wisconsin.

shares as an investment. Loans are made to members for any "productive" purpose.

Under Public Law 96-221, credit unions now compete more directly with banks. They have permanent authority to issue share drafts. These are check-like drafts members can write to withdraw funds on deposit. Credit unions may set their rates on loans as high as 15 percent. They may make loans to individuals for cooperative housing units. Insurance coverage has been raised from $40,000 to $100,000 per account under the National Credit Union Share Insurance Fund (NCUSIF).

Credit unions are nonprofit but must be self-supporting. The interest paid on deposits and charges for loans depends on the earnings of the loan portfolio of the credit union. Interest on loans must be enough to pay administrative expenses and interest on the deposits of the members.

PAY A BANK TO STOP PAYMENT ON A CHECK (AND *MAYBE* IT WILL)

Citibank, like most banks, offers a service whereby you can stop payment on a check you have written. This is especially handy for checks you wish you hadn't written.

One man gave the owner of a used car a check for $100 as "earnest money" while he had a mechanic examine the car. The mechanic said the car was a bad one, and the potential purchaser said "no deal." The owner promised to tear up the check, but the buyer stopped payment on the check just to be sure.

When his statement came from the bank, not only had the check been cashed, but he had been charged a $6 fee from the bank for the stop-payment order. A bank spokesman said whoever made the decision thought it was a different check and simply did not stop payment. The bank did give the man back his $6, but he was out $100.

HISTORICAL BACKGROUND OF AMERICAN BANKING

Banking is a very old business. Long before the Constitution gave Congress the power to create money and control its value, groups of private citizens had established banks. The first was the so-called Massachusetts Bank, founded in 1681. Borrowers pledged their land as collateral in the form of notes, which banks held as security. The First Bank of the United States was chartered for twenty years — from 1791 to 1811. A Second Bank of the United States was also chartered for twenty years — from 1816 to 1836. From 1836 to 1863, there were no national banks, and wildcat banking was at its peak. Almost anyone could start a bank. Since banks were considered the "patent medicine" for the ills of business, they were used to try to cure everything that was wrong. Many early investors in banks lost their money because of bank failures.

In 1862, the National Currency Act was passed to charter national banks. It required the founders of a bank to pledge $50,000 in capital. By 1890, most banks (80 percent) were under a national charter — few banks were authorized by state governments.

Following the money panic of 1907, Congress decided it was time for more federal regulation. In 1908, Congress appointed a National Monetary

The Bank of Arizona in Prescott, about 1897, a forerunner of today's First National Bank of Arizona. (Courtesy New York Public Library Picture Collection.)

Commission to study banking reforms. The Glass-Owen Act of 1913 created the Federal Reserve System, which is still America's central bank.

The stock-market crash in October 1929 led to a complete collapse of the economy. So the Banking Act of 1933 was passed to stabilize our banks. The Federal Reserve Board was authorized to regulate interest on savings accounts and to control bank reserves in order to stimulate the economy.

THE FEDERAL RESERVE SYSTEM

At present, the Federal Reserve System is composed of 5,668 member banks, twelve Federal Reserve Banks, and twenty-four branch banks. In addition, there are three important related groups: a Board of Governors, the Federal Open-Market Committee, and the Federal Advisory Council, as shown in Figure 15-5.

The Board of Governors is appointed by the president of the United States with approval of the Senate. Each of the seven members is appointed for a fourteen-year term unless the appointee is replacing a member whose term has not expired. Every second year, the term of one member expires and that member is replaced. Anyone serving a fourteen-year term is not eligible for reappointment. This board is regarded as autonomous and nonpolitical, in that it is free from control by any executive branch of the federal government.

PAUL A. VOLCKER

Paul A. Volcker became a member of the Federal Reserve Board on August 6, 1979. He was designated as chairman of the board for a four-year term.

Volcker was born on September 5, 1927, at Cape May, New Jersey. He received a B.A. degree from Princeton University in 1949 and an M.A. degree in political economy and government from the Harvard University Graduate School of Public Administration in 1951. He attended the London School of Economics in 1951–52. Volcker's first association with the Federal Reserve System was as a summer employee at the Federal Reserve Bank of New York in 1949 and 1950. He returned to the New York Bank in 1952 as a full-time economist and remained with the Federal Reserve until 1957, when he became a financial economist at Chase Manhattan Bank. In 1962, Volcker joined the United States Treasury as director of financial analysis, and in 1963, he became deputy undersecretary of the Treasury for monetary affairs. From 1965 to 1969, he was a vice-president of Chase Manhattan Bank. In 1969, he was appointed undersecretary of the Treasury for monetary affairs, where he remained until 1974. During this time, Volcker was the principal U.S. negotiator in the development and installation of a new international monetary system departing from the fixed-exchange-rate system installed following World War II. He spent the 1974–75 academic year at Princeton University as a senior fellow in the Woodrow Wilson School of Public and International Affairs.

Volcker became president and chief executive officer of the Federal Reserve Bank of New York on August 1, 1975. He continued in that office until he became chairman of the Federal Reserve Board. As president of the Federal Reserve Bank of New York, Volcker was a continuing member of the Federal Reserve System's principal monetary policy-making body, the Federal Open Market Committee. He was elected vice-chairman of the FOMC on August 19, 1975. As chairman of the Federal Reserve Board, Volcker is also chairman of the FOMC.

FIGURE 15-5
Structure of the Federal Reserve System.
(Source: The Federal Reserve System.)

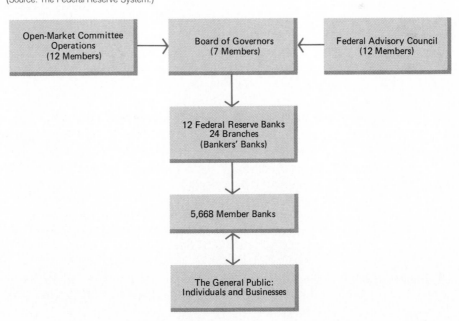

FIGURE 15-6
The Federal Reserve districts and their branch territories. (Courtesy Board of Governors, Federal Reserve System.)

MAJOR FUNCTIONS The Federal Reserve System performs two major functions. One is to supply certain basic banking services, such as acting as a clearinghouse for checks, serving as a fiscal agent for the government by distributing currency and coins, and supervising the operations of the member banks. The second function is a dual one: to maintain a sound credit policy for all member banks and at the same time to promote a high level of consumer buying. This is important because it serves the entire economy. (The methods by which credit and the circulation of money are regulated are described later in this chapter.)

FEDERAL RESERVE BANKS The United States is divided into twelve Federal Reserve districts (see Figure 15-6), each with is own Federal Reserve district bank.

Federal Reserve District Banks.   Each of the twelve Federal Reserve district banks is a separate corporation, with its own nine-member board of directors. Class A and Class B directors are elected by member banks from each district. The Board of Governors appoints three Class C directors. They cannot hold stock of a member bank but may be employees or officers of the bank.

Branch Banks.   Within the twelve districts, there are also twenty-four branch banks in addition to the twelve district banks. For example, in district 12, the Reserve district bank is in San Francisco. Branch banks are in Los Angeles, Portland, Salt Lake City, and Seattle. These four branch banks, together with the Federal Reserve district bank in San Francisco, serve all the member banks in district 12.

Contributions of the Federal Reserve System to the Economy.   Federal Reserve Banks play a vital role in helping to maintain a sound banking system and a stable economy. The Federal Reserve System is only one of several forces affecting business conditions. However, it has managed to eliminate many of the banking evils that existed before enactment of the Federal Reserve Act. Over the years, the system has provided a second line of defense against bank runs by enabling the member banks to discount commercial paper. The Federal Reserve System and the Federal Deposit Insurance Corporation have made banks much safer for depositors.

Chemical Bank card cashing machine, New York City, 1982. (Photo, Teri Leigh Stratford.)

Member Banks.   While national banks are required to be members of the Federal Reserve System, state banks may become members if they can meet the requirements. Table 15-3 lists the number of national and state banks that are members of the Federal Reserve.

TABLE 15-3
Kinds and Number of Banks

KIND OF BANK	NUMBERS
Federal Reserve member banks	5,668
Nonmember commercial banks	9,039
Total commercial banks	14,707
Classes of member banks:	
National banks	4,654
State banks	1,014
Total	5,668
Classes of nonmember banks:	
Commercial banks	9,039
	14,707
Mutual savings banks	467
Total all banks	15,174

SOURCE: Federal Reserve System.

Among the advantages of membership are the following:

1. Member banks can borrow from the Federal Reserve.
2. Membership adds financial stability to the member bank.
3. Currency can be obtained immediately from a Federal Reserve district bank.
4. Eligible commercial paper can be discounted and advances obtained from the Federal Reserve.
5. Member banks are audited by Federal Reserve auditors.
6. Deposits up to $100,000 for each depositor are insured in each member bank by the Federal Deposit Insurance Corporation (FDIC).
7. Member banks participate in the clearing of checks.

OPERATIONAL AND CREDIT FUNCTIONS   The Federal Reserve's primary function is to control the economy's credit and supply of money. It performs this function by using three important tools:

1. Reserve requirements
2. The discount rate
3. Open-market operations

Reserve Requirements.   The Federal Reserve has for years required member banks to keep on deposit in Federal Reserve banks a reserve account. The amount of each reserve has varied with the size of each member bank's deposits. Control of these reserves has enabled the Fed to increase or decrease the money in circulation.

Effective September 1, 1980, under Public Law 96-221, reserve requirements were expanded. All depository institutions that accept deposits from the public are required to keep a reserve account in the nearest district bank. This now gives the Fed more direct control in regulating the supply of money. These reserve funds are noninterest-bearing. Although the reserve requirement is mandatory for all banks and savings institutions, not all must become members of the Federal Reserve System. In the past, about 60 percent of the nation's banks were exempt from these reserve requirements.

Table 15-4 shows how the multiplying effect works to accumulate reserve deposits in order to increase the supply of money. Let us assume that the prevailing member-bank reserve requirement set by the Federal Reserve is 20 percent.

TABLE 15-4
Multiplying Capacity of Reserve Money Through New Deposits[a]

TRANSACTIONS	DEPOSITED IN CHECKING ACCOUNTS	MONEY LENT	SET ASIDE AS RESERVES
Bank 1	$100.00	$ 80.00	$ 20.00
2	80.00	64.00	16.00
3	64.00	51.20	12.80
4	51.20	40.96	10.24
5	40.96	32.77	8.19
6	32.77	26.22	6.55
7	26.22	20.98	5.24
8	20.98	16.78	4.20
9	16.78	13.42	3.36
10	13.42	10.74	2.68
Total for 10 banks	446.33	357.07	89.26
Additional banks	53.67	42.93[b]	10.74[b]
Grand total, all banks	500.00	400.00	100.00

[a] Based on an average member-bank reserve requirement of 20 percent of demand deposits.
[b] Adjusted to offset rounding in preceding figures.

Bank No. 1 accepts a $100 deposit, withholds $20 for its reserve, and is allowed to lend or invest $80. This meets the 20 percent reserve requirement.

The $80 is lent to another depositor and becomes a credit to his or her account. That depositor writes a check for $80, giving it to a new recipient who deposits it in bank No. 2, which now has $80 in demand deposits. Bank No. 2 withholds $16, or 20 percent, as required reserve and immediately lends $64, the remainder, to one of its customers.

This same process continues until $500 becomes the grand total. The total amount of money lent is $400. The total reserve is $100. The $100 deposit has now increased to $500, which is added to the total money supply.

The Discount Rate.   *The interest rate charged by Federal Reserve district banks on loans to member banks* is called the DISCOUNT RATE. There are times when a member bank needs money for a short period. A member bank can borrow from a Federal Reserve Bank in two ways: It can sell or rediscount promissory notes or other commercial paper, which is called **rediscounting.** Or it can borrow on its own secured notes in much the same way as a business borrows from a commercial bank. This latter transaction is known as obtaining an **advance.** Under the law, each Federal Reserve Bank sets the rediscount rate and the rate on advances that apply to member banks of that district. The rates are subject to review by the Board of Governors.

The Federal Reserve Board may raise or lower the discount rate. By a raise in the rate, borrowing is reduced because borrowers must pay higher interest rates. Or the board may lower the discount rate to stimulate the economy by encouraging borrowing.

Open-Market Operations.   A more common way to control the money supply is through the Open-Market Committee. Open-market operations consist of the purchase and sale of government securities on the "open market" rather than by direct dealings with the Treasury. (See Figure 15-7.)

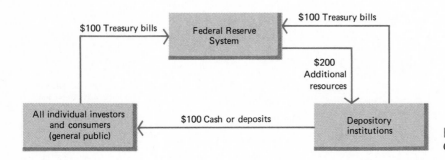

FIGURE 15-7
Open-Market Operations.

When the Board of Governors decides it is time to increase the nation's money supply, the Open Market Committee buys Treasury bills or long-term bonds. This action increases bank reserves.

Referring to Figure 15-7, suppose that the Federal Reserve buys $200 worth of Treasury bills, $100 from individuals and $100 from depository institutions. To pay for these bills, the Federal Reserve will increase depository institutions' reserves held by the Federal Reserve System. An individual may take the $100 out of the depository institution and spend it, or leave the $100 on deposit. The depository institution will use the additional $100 of reserves to make more loans. So the purchase of securities by the Federal Reserve System will increase the availability of credit in the banking system and place cash in individual hands to stimulate consumption. This action of the Open Market Committee would be taken when the economy is in a state of recession, to stimulate the economy. If the goal is to slow the economy down, the Open Market Committee will reverse the process and sell securities.

Clearing Bank Checks.   Americans write billions of checks annually to pay for goods and services. The process of returning these checks to the banks on which they are drawn is performed with amazing speed and accuracy. This procedure is called the **clearing process.**

Commercial banks in large cities operate a "clearinghouse association," which is not directly part of the Federal Reserve System. Commercial banks in a given city send their representatives to exchange checks drawn on other banks in that city. The cost of operating the clearinghouse is paid by the local commercial banks that participate.

Out-of-town checks are sent to the Federal Reserve Bank. These checks are separated by Reserve districts and exchanged. This is known as the **transit process.** Figure 15-8 illustrates the transit process step by step-check clearance involving banks located in two Federal Reserve districts. In this case, firm A draws a check to pay firm B in a different Federal Reserve district. If both parties involved have checking accounts in the same bank, check clearing becomes a simple matter of increasing the checking account of firm B and decreasing the checking account of firm A. Actually,the parties involved live in different cities. The Federal Reserve System becomes involved in the check clearance, as illustrated in Figure 15-8.

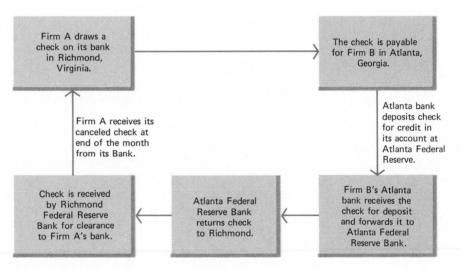

FIGURE 15-8
Step-by-step journey of a bank check through the Federal Reserve System.

ELECTRONIC BANKING SERVICES

A broad range of banking services are performed electronically, without the use of paper. This process is known as EFT, an acronym for Electronic Funds Transfer.

The most obvious of these electronic instruments is the automated teller machine (ATM). It makes deposits, withdrawals, and account transfers.

It is easily activated by a "debit card" and a secret security code. ATMs furnish customers ready access to their bank accounts twenty-four hours a day, seven days a week. In a similar system, department stores and super-markets use electronic terminals instead of cash registers at their sales counters.

ELECTRONIC BANKING THREATENS VISA AND MASTERCARD

Both VISA and MasterCard have achieved strong brand recognition throughout the world, building huge bases of cardholders. But they are so popular that banks issuing them no longer have a competitive advantage. Banks seem to want their own brand identity as they move toward electronic banking—and that means their own cards. As a result, banks have been very slow to adopt the VISA and MasterCard "debit card." Most banks have chosen not to issue the cards that were to be the entree of those organizations into the ATM (automated teller networks). The long-run effect of this trend on the vitality of the two plastic giants will be negative unless they can change things.

The shift from money to electronics may prove to be as important as the shift from barter to money.

MAJOR SOURCES OF CONSUMER CREDIT

Large-scale consumer credit is essentially an innovation of the twentieth century. CONSUMER CREDIT is *credit granted to consumers to promote personal consumption.* The loans are usually repaid on an installment basis. The availability of consumer credit and its rapid growth have made major changes in consumer buying habits and decisions. At first, consumer credit was used largely to buy durable goods such as home appliances, automobiles, and furniture. Now, nearly all kinds of goods are bought on consumer credit plans providing for installment payments. Who supplies consumer install-ment credit? As shown in Figure 15-9, most installment credit is furnished by commercial banks, finance companies, and credit unions.

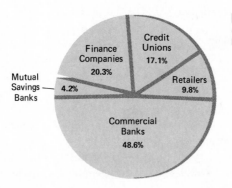

FIGURE 15-9
Chief sources of consumer installment credit. (Source: Federal Reserve Board.)

FINANCE COMPANIES   Although finance companies perform a diversity of services for consumers, their main purpose is to supply short-term credit financing. Two types of commercial finance companies have developed: (1) consumer finance companies, and (2) sales finance companies.

Consumer Finance Companies.   Sometimes known as "small-loan companies," consumer finance companies specialize in short-term loans, mostly under $1,000. These loans are used for financing business inventories, for making small personal loans, and sometimes for providing short-term working capital for small firms. The loans are repaid in installments and usually carry a high rate of interest.

HOW "TRUNCATION" IS USED IN FINANCIAL INSTITUTIONS

A technique called *truncation* is being used to reduce paper flow and cut operating costs in banks and other financial institutions.

Truncation, as the term is used in the banking industry, refers to the nonreturn of canceled checks to customers after payment has been made. Instead of returning your canceled checks, your bank microfilms each canceled check. Meanwhile, your checks are held a few months and then destroyed, which saves filing space. Approximately 40,000 checks can be stored chronologically on a microfilm tape four inches wide. A copy of any check can be retrieved in a matter of seconds if you have a need to see it.

For many years, the public has been sold on the value of having checks returned with the monthly statements. Proponents of truncation are suggesting that the bank is doing you a favor by not returning your canceled checks. "The world is drowning in paper," as one banker puts it.

Indeed, the American Bankers Association estimates that as many as 44 billion checks will be processed annually by the end of the decade. If banks could shorten the processing of half of those, it would save them $1 billion per year.

But some consumer activists argue that without canceled checks, consumers will be more vulnerable to errors by banks and will find it more difficult to settle disputes with merchants. The problem is a loss of information and a loss of accountability by the bank to the consumer, they say.

CREDIT CARDS — PLASTIC MONEY   The growing credit-card craze has made this the age of plastic money for those credit-card users who say, "Charge it." With a credit card, you can buy almost anything on credit. American Express, Diners Club, and Carte Blanche are the main travel-entertainment cards used by executives because of their convenience and because of the tax records they offer. Other charge cards are issued by oil companies, car-rentals, airlines, and department stores.

The big struggle for supremacy is between two giants—VISA and MasterCard. VISA is owned by Visa U.S.A., a for-profit corporation owned by the issuing banks. The sponsor of MasterCard is the Interbank Card Association, a nonprofit organization whose member banks share operating revenues and costs. Both organizations charge cardholders interest on the unpaid balance beyond a certain number of days. Goods and services at many stores that honor credit cards are priced higher to cover the service-charge fee collected by credit-card companies. These fees range from 3 to 9 percent per sale. VISA and MasterCard do a combined business of about $40 billion annually. Approximately 18 million families own three or more cards, and do credit business of $50 billion a year.

EXXON (AND OTHERS) CHARGE LESS FOR CASH

Following a test in four "pilot" markets, EXXON launched a program that encourages its dealers to pay a discount to customers who pay cash. EXXON, like other gasoline retailers, was suffering sales losses at the hands of "discount" gasoline dealers. But credit cards have been profitable for most companies, because they feel that having a credit card brings customers to the station. So they did not want to do away with them altogether. EXXON reduced the dealers' cost of gasoline and is now charging dealers a fee on the credit-card portion of their business. It is the individual dealer's decision as to how much of a discount will be passed along to customers who pay cash.

REGULATION OF FINANCIAL INSTITUTIONS

In concluding our discussion of banks and other financial institutions, we will summarize the regulatory role of government.

REGULATORY MEASURES   Congressional authority to regulate money and credit is chiefly based on Section 8 of Article I of the U.S. Constitution. Under this provision, Congress has certain rights, which include the following: borrowing money, coining money, paying debts, and regulating commerce.

The Federal Reserve Act.   Under this legislation enacted in 1913, the Federal Reserve Board has the power to examine and control commercial-bank reserves and the supply of bank credit. Reserve Board Regulation Q sets maximum interest rates on time deposits. Regulation Z was adopted, effective 1969, by the Board of Governors to implement general provisions of the Consumer Credit Protection Act (Truth-in-Lending Act).

Federal Deposit Insurance Corporation.   The FDIC is another government agency charged with bank regulation. Few people now worry about safety of their bank deposits, because the FDIC offers deposit protection to participant banks.

Under the provisions of Public Law 96-221, deposits in banks are insured by the FDIC. In 1980, the maximum coverage for each account was raised from $40,000 to $100,000. The FDIC also makes periodic inspection of insured banks.

Truth-in-Lending Act.   Otherwise known as the Consumer Credit Protection Act, this legislation became effective July 1, 1969. It ensures accurate and complete disclosure of credit terms to consumers. Loan companies, banks, retailers, and other businesses engaged in installment consumer selling must supply complete facts about the cost of consumer loans.

Fair Credit Reporting Act.   This act, which became effective in April 1971, gives people access to their credit-information files. Any incorrect facts on file about a person's credit must be changed. Those who can prove that credit-bureau reports deliberately wronged them can sue for court costs and actual damages.

Depository Institutions Deregulation and Monetary Act of 1980.   Acclaimed as the Magna Carta for thrift and savings institutions, Public Law 96-221 became law March 28, 1980. (See Figure 15-10.)

    This law calls for a gradual deregulation of Regulation Q during the six years following passage. Regulation Q was issued by the Federal Reserve to set maximum interest rates on time and savings deposits. The idea behind Public Law 96-221 is to place thrift institutions on a more equal basis with banks in order to promote competition. As a result, S&Ls may offer checking accounts that pay interest. All financial institutions are required to keep

CURRENT ISSUE

SHOULD CREDIT PURCHASERS PAY HIGHER PRICES?

An ever-increasing amount of consumer goods is being sold on credit. Department stores issue their own company credit cards. National credit cards such as VISA and MasterCard continue to increase in popularity. Stores that recognize these national credit cards must pay from 3 to 9 percent for that service. Is it right to charge cash customers the same as those who buy on credit?

With which of the following statements do you agree, and with which do you disagree?

1. The cash customer subsidizes those who buy on credit.
2. Whether one pays cash or buys on credit is a matter of personal customer choice.
3. The easy availability of credit cards to most families encourages the use of credit. This in turn makes goods cost more.
4. The use of customer credit increases sales volume, and this in turn tends to lower prices.
5. Since retailers save the cost of credit when customers pay cash, the cash customer should be given a discount off the price equal to the cost of credit.

1. Is the cash customer being discriminated against?
2. Should buying on credit be prohibited? Why, or why not?

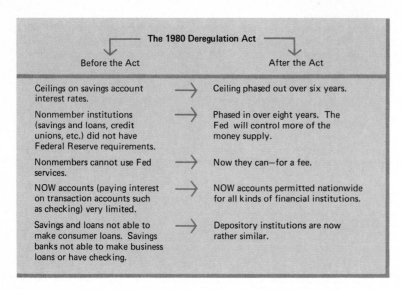

FIGURE 15-10
The 1980 Deregulation Act.

funds on deposit with the Federal Reserve in order to strengthen the Federal Reserve's control of the nation's money supply. This is a key element used by the Fed to fight inflation. Earlier in this chapter, other provisions of this law were explained in the discussions dealing with banks, S&Ls, credit unions, and mutual savings banks.

SUMMARY OF KEY CONCEPTS

Every business uses a variety of credit for short-term and intermediate financing. Credit is the basis of all loans.

Credit instruments are based on either promise-to-pay or order-to-pay negotiable instruments. The open-book account and the promissory note are promise-to-pay documents. Drafts and trade acceptances are order-to-pay documents.

Short-term credit is available through such credit arrangements as bank loans, installment credit, and loans granted by finance companies. Security for short-term business loans may be corporate stock, order bills of lading, or warehouse or trust receipts.

Commercial banks are the principal sources of short-term business loans. These banks also supply a variety of financing services. They accept demand and time deposits, discount negotiable instruments, serve as trustees of funds, supply financial advice, and issue bank drafts.

Commercial banks are either state or national banks. State banks are chartered by the state government. National banks receive their charters from the federal government.

All national banks must be members of the Federal Reserve System and subscribe to the Federal Deposit Insurance Corporation. State banks may be members if they meet the requirements.

The broad objective of the Federal Reserve System is to control the supply of money and credit to promote price stability, encourage economic growth, and help maintain high employment.

During periods of inflation or deflation, the Federal Reserve is responsible for determining monetary policy. Three devices—regulation of bank reserves, regulation of the discount rate, and open-market operations—are used.

In addition to regulation of commercial banks by the Federal Reserve, loan companies, finance companies, and credit unions are also subject to federal controls.

The Consumer Credit Protection Act requires finance companies and others engaged in installment consumer selling to publish, at the time of the credit sale, the cost of finance charges and terms of annual interest.

The Fair Credit Reporting Act, a federal law, permits people to see information about them on file in retail credit bureaus. If the credit bureau is unable to verify the facts, it must delete them from the records.

BUSINESS TERMS

You should be able to match these business terms with the statements that follow:

a. BANK DISCOUNT
b. CASHIER'S CHECK
c. CERTIFIED CHECK
d. CONSUMER CREDIT
e. CORRESPONDENT BANK
f. CREDIT
g. DISCOUNT RATE

h. DRAFT
i. MONEY
j. NATIONAL BANKS
k. SIGHT DRAFT
l. STATE BANKS
m. TIME DRAFT
n. TRADE ACCEPTANCE

1. Anything generally accepted in exchange for goods or services
2. A draft payable on demand
3. A check drawn by a bank against its own funds
4. A draft drawn by the seller of merchandise ordering the buyer to pay the amount of the purchase on a fixed date
5. Interest deducted in advance
6. Commercial banks chartered by the federal government
7. A draft payable on a fixed date
8. Credit granted to consumers to promote personal consumption
9. Interest rate charged by the Federal Reserve district bank on loans to member banks
10. Commercial banks chartered by the state
11. A bank that maintains an account relationship with another bank or engages in an exchange of services
12. An unconditional written order made by the drawer addressed to the second party (drawee) that orders the drawee to pay a specific sum to a third party (payee)
13. A check guaranteed by the bank both as to signature and as to payment
14. The ability to secure goods and services in exchange for a promise to pay later

REVIEW QUESTIONS

1. What are some of the reasons for the use of trade credit?
2. What is the difference between a *promise-to-pay* instrument and an *order-to-pay* instrument?
3. What is the difference between a *cashier's* check and a *certified* check?
4. Give several examples of the kinds of service that commercial banks perform for business.
5. Who owns the Federal Reserve System? Is the Federal Reserve subject to control by Congress?

1. Should bank membership in the Federal Reserve be optional?
2. Is the federal government exercising too much, too little, or the right amount of power in supervising consumer credit?
3. Should all banks be required to participate in the Federal Deposit Insurance program?
4. Do you believe credit unions should be allowed to offer demand-deposit checking accounts to compete with banks? Explain.
5. Why do consumer finance companies generally charge higher interest rates than commercial banks on short-term loans?
6. What is the main reason for the growth of credit unions?

BUSINESS CASES

15-1

K & A TOOL COMPANY

Much of the financing of K & A Tool Company, Inc., is currently in the form of trade credit, commercial paper, and bank borrowing. K & A officers have been hoping that interest rates will decline in the future. They wish to raise additional needed capital through the sale of long-term debt (corporate bonds) and new common stock.

Mr. Allen, the firm's comptroller, has been observing recent Federal Reserve action on monetary policy. He is trying to predict whether interest rates will rise or fall in the near future. If it is apparent that interest rates will fall, the firm should currently be concerned with the issuing of both new bonds and stock.

The Federal Reserve discount rate has been lowered twice during the last month, and reserve requirements were reduced once. The net open-market operations of the Fed have been to buy securities; but Mr. Allen needs help in interpreting the Federal Reserve's action.

1. Will the action of the Federal Reserve tend to cause credit to be more available, or less? If more credit is available, obviously, interest rates will decline, and vice versa.
2. Is this a good time for K & A Tool Company to be replacing some of its short-term credit with long-term financing?

15-2

ALAMO PUMP CORPORATION HAS GROWING PAINS

The Alamo Pump Corporation was organized in 1969 to manufacture water pumps for irrigation systems and industrial plants. The corporation owns three important patents related to water and steam valves. Its products are sold mainly through farm-implement dealers. Alamo's general office is in San Antonio, Texas. Its stock is locally owned.

Last year the corporation earned 5 percent on sales of $1 million and paid a dividend of 50 cents per quarter on 12,000 shares of common stock. During peak production periods, usually during the summer months, Alamo often experiences a shortage of working capital, which requires one or more short-term bank loans. However, the new treasurer, a stockholder, is critical of this practice of borrowing. He contends that the corporation should plan to avoid peak production periods. Following is a recent simplified balance sheet:

Alamo Pump Corporation

ASSETS		LIABILITIES	
Cash	$ 50,000	Notes payable	$ 10,000
Accounts receivable	800,000	Accounts payable	300,000
Merchandise inventory	70,000	Common stock (20,000	
Machinery	100,000	shares, $3 per share par	
Land and buildings	100,000	value)	60,000
		Surplus	750,000
Total assets	$1,120,000	Total liabilities and capital	$1,120,000

1. Do you agree with Alamo's treasurer?
2. What is Alamo's main problem, and how can it be solved?
3. What other sources of short-term credit can you suggest?

Risk Management and Insurance

study objectives

WHEN YOU HAVE FINISHED READING THIS CHAPTER, YOU SHOULD BE
ABLE TO:

1. Define *risk* and identify those types of risk that can be covered by insurance

2. Understand the term *insurable interest* and state who may or may not have
   an insurable interest in property or another's life

3. Identify the types of risk that businesses face and show how businesses
   can protect themselves

4. Visualize the components of a risk-management program

5. Describe how potential losses can be avoided, reduced, or transferred by
   methods other than insurance

6. Illustrate how the risk of price changes can be transferred to others through
   hedging

16

> Practically nothing happens without risk . . . and risk is almost never taken without a good chance of reward.
>
> *R.H. Herzog, 3M Company*

Almost nothing happens without risk. Illness, accidents, investments, a person's job — all are subject to risk. Risk lurks everywhere every day!

Risk is one of the hazards of doing business. The chance that some loss will occur is always present. Some risk losses can be reduced, but they cannot all be avoided. Some can be pooled or shared with others through insurance.

Business managers must determine the risks a business faces. Then ways can be developed to guard against them. How to deal with possible losses is what risk management is all about.

This chapter shows how risk can be shared with others through insurance. It also describes how the burden of business risks may be distributed.

THE NATURE OF RISK

RISK is *the uncertainty associated with an exposure to loss.* It is caused by some unfavorable or undesirable event. Property is always subject to destruction or damage by fire, water, wind, vandalism, or earthquake. There is also the possibility of riots, robbery, dishonesty, negligence, and injuries to employees or customers, resulting in some form of loss. Risk also involves such possibilities as loss of life, illness, or physical disability. Such events are called *perils* or *hazards.*

A **peril** may be defined as the cause of loss. Fires, tornadoes, and heart attacks are examples. A **hazard** is a condition that leads to a loss or makes it more severe. The storing of gasoline or turpentine in the basement or garage

A 7-alarm fire in a North Philadelphia manufacturing company engulfed a neighboring plant and threatened a dozen other businesses. (Photo, United Press International.)

is a hazard. The storing of gasoline doesn't cause a loss, but its presence will make any fire loss that occurs more severe.

The key word in that definition of risk is *uncertainty*. Property owners are uncertain as to whether they will have to pay for such losses as those mentioned above. The uncertainty arises because it is impossible to know in advance whether the losses will occur.

A second definition often given for RISK is the *variability in possible outcomes of an event based on chance.* This means that the larger the number of likely outcomes that might occur, the greater the risk. This definition focuses attention on the **degree of risk.** The degree of risk depends on how accurately the results of a chance event can be predicted. The more accurate the prediction, the lower the degree of risk.

TYPES OF RISK

There are two broad types of risk: **speculative** and **pure.** A distinction should be made, because only one of these types is insurable.

SPECULATIVE RISK refers to *exposures that may result in a possible gain or a loss.* Betting on a horse race is an example of a speculative risk, because in a wager, you may either win or lose. Business is a speculation. The proprietor may lose the investment through competition, new inventions, or inefficient management. Or the proprietor may make a profit. The buyer of wheat may sell it at a loss or a gain, depending on the circumstances. Certain types of speculative risks can be shifted by hedging, a subject we will examine in this chapter.

insurable

PURE RISK *involves only a chance of loss.* **Here, an uncertainty exists about whether destruction will occur.** Some examples of pure risk are loss of property or well-being through fire, flood, windstorm, total disability, or accident. If the destruction never occurs, there will be no loss. Pure risks are insurable, whereas speculative risks are not. Figure 16-1 identifies the various kinds of pure risks that directly relate to individuals and businesses.

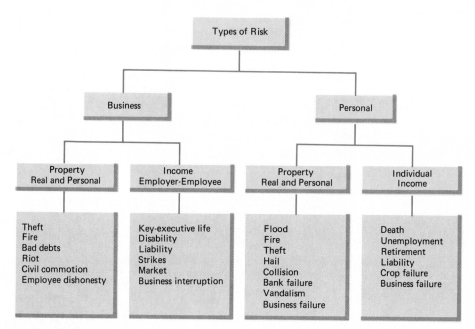

FIGURE 16-1
Insurable Pure Risks.

PRINCIPLES OF INSURANCE

INSURANCE is *a financial arrangement that redistributes the cost of unexpected losses.* It is a plan for sharing losses with others. A loss in a particular situation is unexpected, but for a group of people (or pieces of property), losses can be predicted more accurately. If an insurance system is to function, being able to predict losses accurately is a basic necessity. An insurance program does not do away with losses. Rather, it redistributes their costs by collecting payments from all participants in the group. When many people (or businesses) are exposed to a specific kind of risk, their total losses are predictable and can be spread throughout the group. Everyone pays a small amount of the cost (premium). As a result, no one sustains a large share of loss.

From a legal point of view, insurance is based on a contract. An INSURANCE CONTRACT is *a written agreement whereby one party agrees to pay another party for losses.* The terms of an insurance contract are listed in

The burden of loss falls on the unfortunate homeowner where there is no insurance system.

Cost to homeowner
Total loss = $30,000

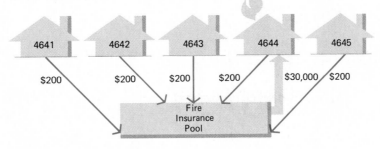

The burden of loss redistributed to all homeowners when an insurance system operates.

Cost to each homeowner = $200
Total loss = $30,000

FIGURE 16-2

Insurance redistributes the costs of losses. (From Mark S. Dorfman, *Introduction to Insurance*, 1978. Reprinted by permission of Prentice-Hall, Inc.)

the **policy.** The party agreeing to pay for the losses is the **insurer,** and the one who will receive payment for the loss is the **insured.** The payment made by the insured is called a **premium.** By means of the policy contract, you transfer the risk of loss to the insurer, and the cost of the loss is shared with others.

ELEMENTS OF AN INSURANCE CONTRACT

1. Parties The *insured* is the person whose life or property is protected; the *insurer* is the company giving the insurance coverage.
2. Policy Agreement between the contracting parties — contains the provisions and limits of coverage.
3. Premium Regular money payment made to the company by the insured.
4. Beneficiary Person to whom damage payment is to be made.
5. Claim Evidence of loss submitted to the company by the insured.
6. Settlement Payment agreed upon in case of loss.
7. Proceeds Amount of money paid to the beneficiary.

DONALD T. REGAN

Donald T. Regan was sworn in on January 22, 1981, as the sixty-sixth secretary of the Treasury. Prior to that time, he was chairman and CEO of Merrill Lynch & Co., Inc.

Secretary Regan serves as chairman pro tempore of the Cabinet Council on Economic Affairs and as the administration's chief economic spokesman. The Cabinet Council on Economic Affairs has primary responsibility for advising the president on developing and implementing domestic and international economic policies.

As secretary of the Treasury, Mr. Regan administers the work of the Treasury Department, which collects the nation's taxes, pays its bills, prints and mints its currency and coins, manages the nation's accounts and debts, and has extensive law-enforcement responsibilities. He holds membership on numerous national and international financial, trade, and economic bodies. He is the U.S. Governor of the International Monetary Fund and the International Bank for Reconstruction and Development.

Secretary Regan has served as a member of the Policy Committee of the Business Roundtable, a trustee of the Committee for Economic Development, and a member of the Council on Foreign Relations.

Mr. Regan joined Merrill Lynch in 1946 as an account-executive trainee and worked as an account executive in Washington, D.C. Early in 1952, he was named manager of the Trading Department in New York, and he became a general partner in the firm in 1954.

Regan's innovative leadership of Merrill Lynch was recognized by the board of editors of *Fortune* magazine with the Hall of Fame for Business Leadership Award in March, 1981. He is the author of *A View from the Street,* an analysis of the events on Wall Street during the crisis years of 1969 and 1970.

Mr. Regan was born in Cambridge, Massachusetts, and was graduated from Harvard with a B.A. in 1940. He and his wife, the former Ann Buchanan of Washington, D.C., have four children.

INSURABLE INTEREST   A basic principle underlying insurance contracts is the principle of INSURABLE INTEREST. *This simply means that the policyholder must demonstrate a financial loss to himself or herself* in order to collect. Without the use of this principle, a person could insure the life of any other person and then take his or her life in order to collect the insurance benefits.

An insurable interest is always said to exist when people insure their own lives or property. A person has an insurable interest in his or her spouse and other members of the family, or in business partners. The insurable interest must exist at the inception of the policy, but not necessarily at the time of death of the insured. A secured creditor, such as a mortgagee, has an insurable interest in property on which money has been loaned. A business has an insurable interest in the return expected from an investment in property. Therefore, a proprietor can insure the property owned by the business.

INSURABLE RISK   A second basic principle of insurance is the principle of **insurable risk.** This states the conditions under which a risk can be economically insured. *If the requisites of insurability are not met, the risk is not economically insurable.*

From the standpoint of the insurer, the following must be the case if a risk is to be insurable:

1. *The loss should be purely accidental and not merely unintentional.* If such losses are not accidental, there is no uncertainty involved, and insurance serves no useful purpose, since insurance is used to reduce risk.
2. *The nature of the loss must be determinable and measurable.* The loss must be capable of calculation and be predictable, such as by the use of mortality tables for life insurance.
3. *The loss should not be in the nature of a catastrophic hazard.* Perils such as those caused by a nuclear-energy explosion are difficult to insure initially because possible losses from such a hazard are unpredictable.
4. *The risk must be spread over a sufficient number of cases.* In computing fire losses for rate-making purposes, it would be improper to group commercial buildings with private residences. The hazards facing these classes of buildings are different.

FIGURE 16-3
How many different kinds of risk are present in this department store situation? (Photo, Mike Mazzaschi, STOCK/Boston.)

LAW OF LARGE NUMBERS

Have you ever questioned how an insurance company can afford to assume a $50,000 risk for an annual premium of $1,000?

The explanation lies in the application of the law of large numbers, often referred to as the **law of averages.** According to this mathematical law, out of a very large number of similar risks, only a certain number of losses will occur. For example, from the number of fire losses in 25,000 similar types of buildings over a three-year period, it is possible to predict how many of these structures will be destroyed by fire during a given year. The important factor in predicting losses by this principle is the use of large numbers of cases.

The law of large numbers, therefore, can be stated as follows: **The larger the number of cases used, the more nearly will the actual experience approximate the probable outcome.** This law uses the application of probability to past experience. Consequently, when past experience reveals the total losses, the share to be assigned to each individual insured during the next period can be equitably calculated by "actuarial" methods. This is the basis of all mortality-table calculations used by life insurance companies. In a similar manner, fire insurance companies study fire losses, using large numbers of cases to predict losses.

RULE OF INDEMNITY

The rule of indemnity states that **a person may not collect more than the actual cash loss in the event of damage caused by an insured peril.** Thus, a person may insure property in excess of its actual value but cannot collect damages for more than that person's actual loss. There is no opportunity for gain in a pure risk, only losses. As a general rule, only contracts for property and liability insurance are subject to the indemnity principle. Contracts for life insurance and most health insurance are not indemnity contracts.

HISTORY OF INSURANCE, 5,000 YEARS OLD

The insurance business is at least as old as recorded history.

There was a form of marine insurance in Babylon 5,000 years ago. In these contracts, shipping merchants got loans from rich merchants and the loans were not repaid if shipments were lost at sea. Presumably, interest on the loans was at extra-high rates to compensate the lenders for the extra risk.

Fire insurance also goes far back, but it did not receive much impetus until after the Great Fire of London in 1666. Two British companies — the London Assurance Corporation and the Royal Exchange Corporation — were formed more than 250 years ago and are still in business.

Modern property, fire, and liability insurance are largely British inventions.

Lloyd's of London started in 1689 in a coffeehouse owned by Edward Lloyd. He gathered marine information along the docks and passed it on to his customers in the form of Lloyd's Lists. These lists are still being published. His customers consisted of captains and shippers, and other businesspeople.

The first American insurance company was formed by Benjamin Franklin in 1752. It was known as the Philadelphia Contributionship. The first American life insurance firm was the Presbyterian Ministers' Fund, which was started in 1759. The company is still in business in Philadelphia.

Kerry S. Clem, director of risk management for Esmark, Inc., stated:

> The risk manager's role is becoming that of a "retail broker" of services, figuratively speaking. In essence, a risk manager acts as general manager of a variety of suppliers and in turn provides these risk-related services to operating divisions within the corporation.

Risk management is concerned with protecting against perils that would result in financial losses. Insurance is the most common method, and it is discussed more fully later. But it is only one method for dealing with potential losses and the uncertainty they cause. Success in business requires that one consider exposures to loss and make plans to deal with them. *The planning to deal with potential losses before they occur* is known as RISK MANAGEMENT. A sound risk-management program involves:

1. Identifying exposures to loss
2. Making plans for dealing with potential losses
3. Updating risk programs regularly

IDENTIFYING EXPOSURES TO LOSS

The recognition that a problem exists is the first step in solving it. With regard to exposures to loss, the starting point is to identify them. The pure risks, which can be managed once they have been identified, are of four main types:

1. Direct losses to property
2. Indirect losses to income
3. Liability losses
4. Loss of key personnel

Price fluctuations in commodities are a special type of risk that can be managed; they are discussed later in this chapter.

Direct Losses.   Most property is subject to possible direct losses. The question is, How great might the loss be? Replacement costs are usually larger than historical costs. The risk manager will probably want to cover the larger value.

Indirect Losses.   Every direct property loss has the potential for causing an indirect loss of income. If property is damaged to such an extent that it is taken out of production, there is no income from it while it is being repaired or replaced. The risk manager must estimate how much income would be lost owing to such downtime of productive facilities.

Liability Losses.   The company must be protected against possible claims brought in lawsuits. Product liability insurance is generally available to manufacturers. But rates have gone up sharply over the past few years, and coverages have been greatly reduced. The insurance now issued usually provides for relatively high deductibles. Thus, more of the risk is shifted to the producer. In addition, there has been a trend toward policies covering the current year only, excluding all claims not made during that year. This also adds to a company's risk. Virtually all manufacturers have been affected by product liability difficulties.

Personnel Losses.　　Key company employees may exert influence in many different areas. Those whose absence would be most costly are usually the executives of the company. Part of identifying potential risk is estimating the cost of qualified replacements. Key-employee life insurance provides protection against loss from death.

MAKING PLANS FOR DEALING WITH POTENTIAL LOSSES

The risk manager makes plans for dealing with losses *before they occur* (see Figure 16-4). There are four ways in which this can be done:

1. Risk avoidance
2. Risk transfer
3. Risk assumption
4. Loss reduction

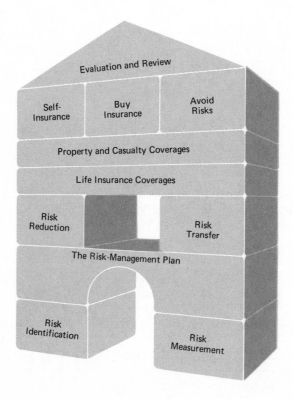

FIGURE 16-4
The Risk-Management Program.

Risk Avoidance.　　An effective way to meet certain kinds of business risks is to practice certain good managerial techniques. For example, recognize product obsolescence early, before losses result. Many companies maintain a research department to study economic trends. It is the job of the risk manager to see that management practices help avoid risks.

One way to avoid risk would be not to introduce a proposed new product. An example would be an insufficiently tested new drug. The decision would be to delay it until some uncertain factors became known. Another way would be to locate a new plant in a known, stable community rather than taking a chance on an unknown location.

In every category of risk today, loss control is becoming a professional discipline. In addition to occupational safety and health, it is being applied with success to all kinds of property risks and to liability exposures in general.

A successful loss-control program is usually made up of thousands of details. Each one by itself may not seem to be significant: Is the control valve on the water pipe for the sprinkler system kept open? Are the warning lights on a lift truck in operation? Has a new employee had a hearing examination? Should a guardrail be installed around a conveyor belt?

If such details are to be of concern to people in an organization, the program must start with top management. The necessary item in successful loss control, specialists agree, is management commitment.

Most loss-control programs start with a review of operations and the listing of actual and potential hazards. Then goals are set up and counteraction measures are begun and monitored. Data are collected on all losses incurred, and the results are compared with earlier experience. Most safety programs operate in this way.

Risk Transfer. Risk transfer is done largely through insurance and hedging. The most common method is through insurance. Insurance transfers the risk to professional risk bearers, such as insurance companies. Consumers as well as businesses transfer risk to others. One type of risk transfer that is becoming increasingly popular is the risk associated with buying a home. Home warranties (either a type of insurance or a service contract) are very popular in some areas of the United States. Home warranties are often sold through real estate brokers. They allow the real estate company the opportunity to offer a risk transfer that makes homes easier to sell.

Most home warranties offer a one-year breakdown protection not only on the house but on the plumbing, electrical, heating, and air-conditioning systems. The cost is around $250, plus a $50 deductible for each repair call. In this way, homeowners can transfer some of the risk of buying a home to the insurance company. Many are choosing to do so.

Hedging is a way of managing risks caused by price changes. Businesses may hedge in order to protect against:

1. A decline in inventory investment
2. A rise in the price of raw materials
3. A future drop in the price of finished goods

Hedging is a means of protecting profits from the peril of price risks. It is the mechanism for minimizing price risks, and the "futures market" is the

FIGURE 16-5
The floor of the New York Mercantile Exchange. (Photo by Jan Lukas, Photo Researchers, Inc.)

method used. Trading is in standardized contracts. These contracts specify the commodity to be traded; the quantity, quality, and place of delivery; and the time. The only variable is the price. Futures markets do not themselves buy or sell commodities.[1] Rather, they provide a meeting place for buyers and sellers and establish the rules for trading.

How Hedging Works.　　HEDGING provides price insurance by the taking of ***equal but opposite positions in the cash and futures markets.*** Insurance is based on the principle of risk *sharing*, but hedging is based on the principle of risk *shifting*. The risk of harmful price changes is shifted to another. This is achieved through the purchase or sale of futures contracts.

Let us consider an example of protecting against an increase in the price of raw materials.

Suppose you are a flour miller in Illinois and have accepted an order from a large bakery in Chicago for several tons of flour, to be delivered at two-month intervals starting in four months. You had to give the bakery a fixed price for the flour. You figure that you will need 100,000 bushels of wheat to mill the required amount of flour to fill this order, but you cannot afford to buy all the wheat now. In fact, you have enough space to store only 25,000 bushels at one time. So you must buy wheat several times before you mill the complete order.

As an experienced miller, you know that you cannot predict the price of wheat accurately during the next four months. But you have agreed to a fixed price to charge for the flour. By hedging, you can minimize your risk so that you make your normal trade profit from milling flour.

---

[1] The term *commodity* is generally used to refer to raw produce such as grains, fibers, and minerals, in contrast to finished goods. *Spot* transactions on the commodity market are purchases or sales of commodities for cash, requiring immediate delivery. *Futures* transactions are purchases for future delivery.

FINANCE AND RISK MANAGEMENT

If wheat advances 10 cents a bushel on an average over the next four months, you stand to lose $10,000. So you hedge by telling your commodity broker to buy you 100,000 bushels of July wheat (futures contract), which at the moment is 10 cents a bushel cheaper than cash wheat. Regardless of what the price is—it would make no difference if July were up or down—you would still hedge.

When you buy your futures contract, you pay in cash for only a small part. This is known as buying on margin. Your commodities broker will arrange for the transaction. You now have a contract for 100,000 bushels of wheat for July delivery. However, you know that you will sell this contract before the delivery date.

The day you are ready to mill the first part of the wheat to make delivery of so much flour, you place an order with your broker for 25,000 bushels of spot wheat. At the same time, you order a sale of 25,000 bushels of July futures wheat at the market price. Now you have engaged in a hedging process. But there is still the matter of price. Assume that the spot or current wheat prices have advanced 10 cents a bushel, as you feared they might. For the 25,000 bushels of spot, you lose $2,500 because you had to pay more for them. But since spot and future prices almost always advance or drop together, the price of July wheat will go up 10 cents, too. So, although you paid more for the spot wheat, you made the same amount as profit on the sale of futures wheat, and you came out even. This is illustrated in Figure 16-6.

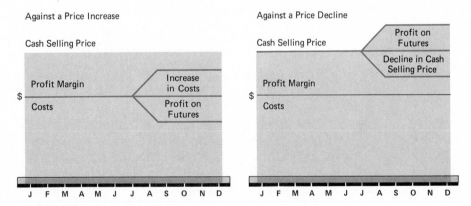

FIGURE 16-6

Hedging.
The increase in costs that occurs in July is offset by a futures profit. In July there is a decline in selling price. This reduced profit margin is offset by a profit from futures transactions.

Each time you need another 25,000 bushels of spot wheat, you simply repeat this hedging operation, until you have filled the full order of flour. When you quoted the bakery a fixed price on flour per hundredweight, you included all your expenses—broker's commission, storage, margin of profit, and so on. Without hedging, you could not afford to take this risk. It is possible to hedge against either a declining or a rising market.

Risk Assumption. A self-insurance reserve fund assumes that it is more profitable for a business to accept potential risks than to insure them with an insurance carrier. To set up such a fund, it is necessary to set aside a certain sum annually as a reserve to be used if property is destroyed. Self-insurance is rather simple and easy to administer. However, it is not a practical method for most businesses. The plan requires the business to carry an excessive amount of risk during the early years of the plan, because during this time, the fund is low.

This method is often more successful when used by a large company with widely scattered operations. The chance of a severe loss to property at several locations during any one year is remote. And if each unit in the company contributes to the fund, the total amount will ordinarily be adequate to pay for any loss.

Insurance coverage in recent years has climbed to new heights. It is a nearly universal method used to transfer risk to professional risk bearers. Moreover, some portions of a company's risk may have become uninsurable at any cost. At this point, the start of company self-insurance is the only choice.

There has been some measure of relief from the tight insurance markets of the early 1970s. Primary insurance for business, however, is not likely to be as easily available and inexpensive in the future as it was a decade ago. Inflation, broader concepts of corporate liability, and high jury awards have raised the demand for insurance beyond the supply. To fully protect a company's assets, the risk manager must retain large portions of many risks, rather than transferring them to commercial insurers.

Which risks? By and large, those exposures can be self-insured that predictably result in a large volume of small claims and that are not subject to huge losses. The two principal ways of retaining risks are by means of high deductibles and by establishing a formal-funded self-insurance program. For a corporation, this can mean retaining as much as the first $1 million or more of the company's risks. In short, the risk manager is tending more and more to assume the risk for potential losses.

Loss Reduction. It is possible to reduce or remove the chance of loss by taking preventive or protective measures. Examples are designing buildings to withstand shocks from earthquakes, installing safety equipment, or using fireproof materials. Installing an automatic spinkler system is another protective measure. Safety campaigns among workers tend to decrease accidents. Regular inspections of equipment and premises will help to avoid injuries. These measures are valuable even though they do not entirely eliminate the chance of loss.

UPDATING RISK PROGRAMS REGULARLY Like any other program, one of risk management must be reviewed periodically. New assets may have been acquired or old ones discarded. New production processes may have introduced new hazards or eliminated old ones. New laws, new personnel, or new products may require changes in the risk program. So a careful review is necessary to keep risks within acceptable limits.

For example, in a tight market, a risk manager may buy insurance coverage with large deductibles. Or he or she might dispense with some coverages entirely — say, collision coverage on a fleet of automobiles.

FUTURE DEVELOPMENTS IN RISK MANAGEMENT

1. Increased use of computers for loss-simulation models
2. Increased use of automated records to help pinpoint hazards—accident and injury causes
3. Increased use of self-insurance features as part of risk-management programs
4. Increased use of large deductibles in insurance programs
5. Use of basket-type deductibles that apply overall to separate property and liability policies
6. Groups of companies forming their own subsidiary insurance companies or risk-sharing pools

---

BUSINESS USES OF INSURANCE

There are many types of insurance, and no business uses them all. A large business, however, will use many different types. Of the many forms of insurance protection available, there are two basic kinds: (1) property and casualty insurance, and (2) life insurance.

PROPERTY AND CASUALTY INSURANCE

Every business that owns property must protect it against damage or loss. Most people are familiar with auto and fire insurance, but a business must also cover other types of losses. There are eight major types of potential property and casualty losses:

1. Fire and extended coverage
2. Automobile insurance
3. Burglary, robbery, theft, and larceny insurance[2]
4. Fidelity, surety, credit, and title insurance[3]
5. Marine insurance[4]
6. Accident and health protection
7. Public liability
8. Workers' compensation protection[5]

Much publicity has been given to the high cost of medical malpractice insurance. One might think that this would play a dominant role in the total insurance picture. Table 16-1 shows that it is the least important in terms of total premiums paid.

---

[2] *Burglary* is the unlawful taking of another's property by force. *Robbery* includes the taking of possessions either inside or outside the premises. *Theft* is a general term that covers any form of stealing. *Larceny* is the fraudulent taking of property.

[3] A *fidelity bond* protects a business against the taking of funds by employees. A *surety bond* protects against loss for not performing a contract.

[4] *Marine insurance* protects against loss of goods in transit, on land, on sea, or in the air. It is the *oldest type of insurance*, dating back 5,000 years.

[5] All fifty states and the federal government have enacted laws requiring workers' compensation protection.

TABLE 16-1

Premiums Paid in 1981, by Property and Casualty Lines (in millions)

TYPE	AMOUNT	PERCENT
Automobile	$33,783	42
Workers' compensation	14,539	15
Homeowners'	11,405	11
Commercial multiperil	6,817	7
General liability	5,980	6
Fire	3,107	3
Inland marine	2,414	2
Allied lines	1,597	2
Medical malpractice	1,310	1
All other	10,906	11

Let us use a retail department store as an illustration of how a business would use insurance. To start with, both the building and its contents would be insured for fire and related losses. **Extended coverage** includes such perils as windstorm, tornado, lightning, smoke damage, water damage, and falling objects. In addition, protection against possible boiler explosion and a faulty sprinkler system might be included. Burglary, robbery, and theft insurance would in all likelihood be carried.

The business would need accident protection and workers' compensation for employees and liability insurance for the public. Life insurance might well be carried on key executives. It could also be a part of the benefits package for employees. Marine insurance would cover losses to goods delivered to customers. A fidelity bond would be used to cover all employees who handle large sums of money. A selected number of perils and how they would be covered by insurance are listed in Table 16-2.

For the nation as a whole, the cost of compensating for job-related injuries, illnesses, and deaths has been rising at the rate of about 12 percent a year. This rate of increase is greater than the rate of inflation. Including

TABLE 16-2

Business Risks and Their Coverage Through Insurance

BUSINESS RISK	TYPE OF COVERAGE
Merchandise damage caused by water and smoke	Fire with extended coverage
Death of company president	Key-person life insurance
Loss of income while closed as the result of a fire	Business-interruption insurance
Employee absence due to hospital illness	Blue Cross
Lawsuit because of customer injury	Liability insurance
Employee embezzlement	Fidelity bond
Loss of roof owing to storm	Extended coverage
Goods damaged during shipment	Marine insurance
Medical expenses of employee injured on the job	Workers' compensation
Holdup of cashier	Robbery or theft insurance

Shoplifting has become a high risk. (Photo by Bob Combs, Rapho/Photo Researchers, Inc.)

insurance premiums and benefit payments, the cost now totals about $12 billion a year.

One cause of the upward spiral is that medical costs are going up more rapidly than prices generally. But another major factor is that almost every state has liberalized benefits. Thirteen states, for example, now have cost-of-living escalators (as cost of living goes up, so do benefits). In addition, state compensation boards and the courts are accepting more and more disabilities as job-related.

The major trend is certainly toward self-insurance, with excess coverage being written by outside carriers for protection against large, unpredictable claims. In several states, a third or more of all employees who are covered by workers' compensation now work for companies with self-insurance programs.

LIFE INSURANCE Unlike any other form of insurance we have studied in this chapter, life insurance is designed to cover the loss of future income as a result of death. People buy life insurance for various reasons, but the main one is to obtain financial protection for the insured's family.

Life insurance is also used by businesses to accomplish several purposes. It can furnish funds to replace invaluable employees or partners (key executives) who have been lost by death. Or it can be used to furnish pension funds. An increasing number of businesses use life insurance for the financial security of the employees or to insure the owners, managers, or employees against the loss of life. Uses of insurance include the following:

1. Group life insurance
2. Credit life insurance
3. Key executive or owner's insurance
4. Pension plans

TABLE 16-3
The Largest Life Insurance Companies

COMPANY	ASSETS[a] (IN MILLIONS)	EMPLOYEES[a]
1. Prudential	62,498	62,817
2. Metropolitan	51,757	44,000
3. Equitable Life Assurance	36,758	26,485
4. Aetna Life	25,158	16,690
5. New York Life	21,041	18,755
6. John Hancock Mutual	19,936	20,424
7. Connecticut General Life	15,103	14,909
8. Travelers	14,803	41,234
9. Northwestern Mutual	12,154	6,798
10. Teachers Insurance & Annuity	11,439	1,897

[a] For the year 1981.

The largest life insurance companies in the United States are listed in Table 16-3.

Group Life Insurance.   Group life insurance is a master policy covering each employee of a business. As a rule, no medical examination is required, and each year an employee is on the payroll, the policy is automatically renewed. Employers often pay at least part of the premium along with the group health plan. Group purchase of insurance has some advantages. The cost is lower because of a saving to the insurance company in marketing and administrative expense. All employees are eligible, whereas on an individual policy, some might be turned down. The employer's payment — whether part or all of the total premium — is not taxed as income for employees.

Credit Life Insurance.   The wide use of installment credit has increased the use of credit life insurance. Its purpose is to guarantee the repayment of amounts due on installment contracts or personal loans. It is written on a one-year basis and is used by banks, credit unions, finance companies, and some mortgage lenders. If the borrower were to die during the period of the loan, the amount of the policy would be used to pay the debt. Credit life insurance is different from credit insurance. The latter mainly covers possible losses from the extension of credit on open-book accounts.

Key-Executive or Owner's Insurance.   The prosperity and growth of a business depend very much on the chief executive. Many firms buy life insurance on the owner or manager — the top executive. This is called "key-person insurance." The company pays the premium and is the beneficiary. If a sole proprietor dies without such insurance, the survivors must pay any existing debts. By having insurance on the owner, it is possible to pay the debts and sell what is left for the benefit of the owner's family or survivors.

In the case of a partnership, a policy payable to the surviving partner can provide funds with which to buy the deceased's interest in the firm. Partners should execute a buy-and-sell agreement when the policy is purchased. In this agreement, the authority to use life insurance funds to buy the partnership interest is spelled out.

Premiums on partnership or key-executive insurance are not tax-deductible as a business expense. When key-person insurance is paid for by a corporation, the proceeds can be used to hire and train an adequate replacement upon the death of the key executive.

Retirement and Pension Plans. As we learned in Chapter 8, many companies provide retirement programs involving a pension plan. This is in addition to federal Social Security. Such a plan may be based on life insurance for employees. The most common plan is the **deposit administration plan.** It involves establishing a fund with an insurance company for all employees. When an employee retires, money is withdrawn from the fund to buy the retiree an annuity policy.

An **annuity** is a contract (usually with a life insurance company) by which the company agrees to pay a person (the annuitant) a sum of money monthly or annually starting at a certain age and ending upon death. In the case of a company pension, funds for annuities are contributed by the employee and employer for the purpose of providing the employee a pension at retirement.

Professional Athletes. Professional sports is a big business. The franchise for a professional football, baseball, or basketball team sells for millions of dollars. A player may be so valuable to his team that he is referred to as "the franchise." These players carry life and accident insurance on themselves.

Minnesota Twins' Bombo Rivera is carried off the field after a leg injury, 1980. (United Press International.)

Team management carries insurance on team members individually and as a unit. The management of the Philadelphia Phillies, for example, insures the team as a whole for $24 million. The amounts carried on individual players vary according to their value to the organization. The individual players would carry personal insurance, in addition, for health, accident, and life.

UNINSURABLE RISKS

Juries and judges in many states are awarding extremely large liability claims, which insurance companies are required to pay. On top of payments for loss of earning power and medical expenses, they are awarding large sums for pain and suffering and punitive damages. This situation is found in product-liability and workers' compensation as well as medical-malpractice suits.

Unless this trend is halted, large categories of risk may become uninsurable by private companies. Should this happen, the federal government will have to come to the rescue or these perils will go uncovered.

Payments can be made only from premiums collected and the interest earned on them. There is no magical bottomless pool of money from which claims may be paid.

PRIVATE INSURING ORGANIZATIONS

Insurance protection is available from several insuring organizations that offer a variety of policies. Those needing insurance can buy from private organizations or, in some instances, from a government agency. As we have seen, **insurance is a cooperative plan for sharing risks with a group.**

TYPES OF PRIVATE INSURANCE COMPANIES

On the basis of ownership, insurance companies are classified as **stock companies** or **mutual companies.** Both stock and mutual insurance companies invest their reserve assets (funds set aside to meet future obligations) in several ways to earn money.

Stock Companies.   A STOCK COMPANY is *a profit-making corporation organized to sell certain types of insurance.* It is chartered by the state. The corporation is operated by a board of directors elected by the stockholders, similar to other profit-making corporations. Stock companies never issue assessable policies—those in which the insured can be assessed an additional premium if the company's loss experience is excessive. Instead, the stockholders are expected to bear any losses, and they also reap profits from the operation. Some stock companies may pay dividends to policyholders on certain types of insurance policies. The initial capital subscribed by the stockholders becomes the working capital, and the company's income is earned from premiums paid by policyholders.

Mutual Companies.   Mutual companies are associations of people organized under the state insurance code. They are nonprofit corporations, owned by policyholders. Since each policyholder is legally an owner of the company, he or she is in theory both an insurer and an insured. There are no profits as such, since any excess income goes to the policyholder as a dividend that may be used to reduce premiums. The policyholders elect a board of directors, who manage the company.

The bylaws of a mutual company may permit additional assessments to policyholders in case funds are insufficient to meet losses and expenses. In most mutuals, however, assessments are not permitted once the company has attained a certain size. In very small mutuals, assessments are limited to one additional annual premium.

According to the American Council of Life Insurance, mutual life insurance companies account for slightly over one-half the total life insurance in force in the United States.

LLOYD'S OF LONDON

Lloyd's of London, one of the oldest insurance associations in the world, is a third type of private insuring company. Lloyd's, whose main business is marine insurance, began in 1689. It is actually not an insurance company but an association of insurers. It is operated as a corporation composed of members, much the same as the New York Stock Exchange. There are more than 400 different syndicates that Lloyd's comprises.

Insurance contracts are written by individual member underwriters. If any single risk is too great for a member to carry alone, one or more of the other members share the contract. One of Lloyd's largest losses resulted from cancellation of computer-lease contracts when IBM introduced a new computer model.

Lloyd's transacts business in all parts of the world and insures extremely varied risks, such as the birth of triplets or changes in the weather. Lloyd's of America is organized like Lloyd's of London, but it has no connection with the English company. Lloyd's is well known for insuring such things as the life or health of movie stars and outstanding athletes. When the United States failed to participate in the 1980 Olympic games, Lloyd's had a $40 million loss.

Fraternal Societies and Class Mutuals. Fraternal societies often issue life insurance as an inducement to obtain members. These societies are usually lodges with a ritual form of initiation. As charitable and benevolent institutions, they are usually exempt from taxation. But as life insurance carriers, these insurance societies are subject to the code that regulates other life insurance companies. Originally, these societies began as pure assessment operations, charging no advance premium but assessing each member periodically for losses to be paid. Class mutuals are also insurance companies serving specific types of businesses, including lumber mills, farms, and factories.

Blue Cross and Blue Shield. Blue Cross and Blue Shield give consumers a form of health insurance. In return for a regular premium, Blue Cross agrees to pay a member's hospital costs. Blue Shield covers doctor's services. They function similarly to insurance companies in that members pay regular premiums. They are not truly insurance companies, for they do not maintain reserves. Also, Blue Cross payments usually go to hospitals rather than the insured.

Social insurance was developed in response to the socialist political point of view. The movement of workers into urban areas resulted from the Industrial Revolution in Europe. They were no longer self-sufficient as they had been in rural life.

Chancellor Bismarck of Germany led in creating a social insurance system. The law, enacted in 1889, provided for benefits for (1) medical treatment, (2) accident compensation, (3) unemployment insurance, and (4) old-age and disability pensions. The rest of Europe soon followed Bismarck's lead. By the start of the twentieth century, social insurance programs were common in industrialized European countries.

In the United States, our most serious economic experience has been labeled the Great Depression. It grew out of the 1929 stock-market crash, and it was deepened by drought in the Southwest in the early 1930s.

A part of President Franklin D. Roosevelt's "New Deal" program was the Social Security Act of 1935. Today, the program is known as the *Old Age, Survivors, Disability, and Health Insurance Program*. It is not a *private* insurance program; it is a federal government-administered insurance program. In 1965, Congress passed what is now known as the Medicare program. It is a supplement to the earlier Social Security insurance program.

UNEMPLOYMENT AND WORKERS' COMPENSATION

Unemployment insurance provides income to workers who lose their jobs. This program originated as a part of the Social Security Act of 1935. Today, it is a federal–state program financed by taxes paid by employers. An unemployed worker receives a percentage of his regular wage for a designated number of weeks. The amounts received vary greatly among the various states.

The question has been raised as to who actually pays for this program. In all probability, three groups contribute: (1) the employer who pays the tax; (2) the employee, indirectly through lower wages; and (3) the consumer, through higher prices.

GOVERNMENT REGULATION OF INSURANCE

Government has always exercised various controls over enterprises, and insurance is no exception. The U.S. Supreme Court in 1868 (*Paul* v. *Virginia*) held that insurance is not interstate commerce, and therefore the federal government should have no regulatory power over insurance companies. This decision was upheld repeatedly until 1944, when it was reversed by the U.S. Supreme Court in the *South-Eastern Underwriters Association* case. Despite this reversal, Congress has left the regulation of insurance companies pretty much to the states.

Congress, however, did pass the McCarran-Ferguson Act (Public Law 15) in 1945. The intent of this act is to make certain that no state law relating to insurance should be affected by any federal laws unless such law is directed specifically at the business of insurance. The law also reaffirms that the part of the Sherman Act relating to boycotts, coercion, and intimidation shall remain applicable to insurance.

NEED FOR REGULATION There are several reasons why insurance needs to be regulated. First, it is a commodity that is bought long before benefits are received. Government has the responsibility to see that there are rules to guarantee the benefits. Second, laws are needed to approve new policy contracts and reserve requirements, and to protect the insured against unfair practices. It is necessary to have some controls over pricing policies.

GOVERNMENT-SPONSORED INSURANCE PROGRAMS

Federal Deposit Insurance Corporation
  Insures each depositor's account in banks
Federal Savings & Loan Insurance Corporation
  Insures each depositor's account in savings and loan associations
Social Security Administration
  Provides for pensions, disability benefits, unemployment benefits, and medical payments for workers
Civil Service
  Provides for pensions for retired federal employees
Workers' Compensation[6]
  Provides medical payments and income payments for workers injured on the job

---

CURRENT ISSUE

WELFARE OR WORKFARE—WHICH IS BETTER?

Many welfare recipients don't mind being required to work in order to receive welfare benefits. But some prefer handouts to work. What should be the policy when unemployment insurance payments run out?

With which of the following statements do you agree, and with which do you disagree?
  1. Recipients should be on their own.
  2. The length of time to receive payments should be extended indefinitely.
  3. Welfare recipients should be required to work at public institutions.
  4. To require recipients to work causes them to lose their self-respect.
  5. The work requirement enables recipients to keep their self-respect.

What is your opinion regarding workfare versus welfare?

---

[6] Both unemployment benefits and workers' compensation are administered by state governments, but the basic legislation was enacted by the federal government.

State Regulation.   Insurance companies have traditionally been state-regulated. Each state has its own insurance department, with an insurance commissioner or superintendent in charge. Its purpose is to protect the interests of both the public and the insurance companies against unfair competition. State regulatory bodies are committed to ensure the continued solvency of each company so that it is ready to discharge its obligations to policyholders.

The use of a standard fire policy or a modified version is required by law. Most states demand a standard workers' compensation policy. The rising clamor for a better way to deal with automobile-accident and health claims, and the demand to stop the skyrocketing of premiums and long delays in claims, are some of the problems still unresolved.

SUMMARY OF KEY CONCEPTS

Risk is the chance of uncertainty associated with an exposure to loss. Generally, risk involves an event that may cause economic loss. Since risks impose an economic burden, it becomes important to business to find a way to protect against risk losses.

Risk can be speculative or pure risk. In a speculative risk, there may be either a gain or a loss. In a pure risk, there is only the chance of loss.

Pure risks can be covered by insurance. Insurance provides a way of sharing potential risk losses. It does this by spreading consequences of loss among a large number of businesses subject to similar risk.

Only those who have an *insurable interest* in property or another's life may buy insurance. In order to have an insurable interest, one must suffer a financial loss should property be damaged or a person die.

To be insurable, a risk must meet the following conditions:

1. The loss must be accidental.
2. The nature and extent of the loss must be determinable.
3. The loss cannot be a catastrophic hazard.
4. The risk must be spread over a large number of cases.

The principle of *indemnity* means that a person or business cannot collect more for damages to property than the actual cash loss suffered.

A risk-management program has three major components:

1. Identifying exposures to loss
2. Making plans for dealing with potential losses
3. Updating risk programs regularly

Hedging is a means of protecting against future price changes by transferring risks to others. These changes may be either a rise or a decline in raw-material prices or of finished goods.

Stock insurance companies are owned by stockholders, who need not be policyholders. Mutual companies are owned by the policyholders—there are no stockholders. Mutual companies pay dividends to policyholders if the amount collected is in excess of what is required to operate the company.

The two main types of insurance protection used by business management are:

1. Property and casualty insurance
2. Life insurance

Casualty insurance protects against such perils as damage to an automobile, fire, burglary, robbery, public liability, accidents, and illness.

BUSINESS TERMS

You should be able to match these business terms with the statements that follow:

a. ACTUARY   h. MUTUAL COMPANY
b. BURGLARY   i. POLICY
c. FIDELITY BOND   j. PREMIUM
d. HEDGING   k. PURE RISK
e. INSURABLE INTEREST   l. RISK
f. INSURANCE   m. RISK MANAGEMENT
g. MARINE INSURANCE   n. SPECULATIVE RISK

1. The uncertainty associated with an exposure to loss
2. A risk that may result in either a gain or a loss
3. A financial arrangement that redistributes the costs of unexpected losses
4. A contract made with an insurance company
5. A payment made by the insured for his or her insurance protection
6. The right to insure property because one may suffer a financial loss
7. Planning by a businessperson to deal with potential losses before they occur
8. Protecting against price changes by taking equal but opposite positions in cash and futures markets
9. An insurance company that is owned by the policyholders
10. An agreement with a bonding company that protects a business against misappropriation of funds
11. The unlawful taking of another's property by force
12. Insurance that protects against loss to goods while they are in transit

REVIEW QUESTIONS

1. What is the difference between a *pure risk* and a *speculative risk*? Which one is insurable?
2. What four requisites make a risk insurable?
3. What is meant by the term *insurable interest*? Why is an insurable interest necessary in order for a person to buy insurance?
4. What are the major components of a risk-management program?
5. What is the rule of indemnity?
6. What types of price changes can be protected against through hedging?

DISCUSSION QUESTIONS

1. Explain and illustrate the concept of risk.
2. What do we mean when we say that insurance does not eliminate risk?
3. What is the first procedure in risk management?
4. Explain how hedging enables a manager to transfer the company's risk to others.
5. How can a risk manager protect against losses caused by employees?
6. How does Lloyd's of London differ from a typical insurance company?

16-1

RISK MANAGEMENT THROUGH INSURANCE

Harper's is an independent department store located in a city of 600,000 population. It is incorporated, although it was started as a partnership. It handles low- and medium-priced goods. Last year's sales were $4,650,000, with a net profit after income taxes of $325,400. The company occupies a four-story fireproof structure that was built in 1968. The top floor is used for handling and pricing goods as they arrive, and temporary storage. A sprinkler system was installed throughout the building. The value of the building is $820,000, not including the land. For tax purposes, the building has been depreciated 2 percent per year.

The insurance coverage is handled by the company vice-president. He has been carrying fire, public liability, business interruption, and group life and hospitalization on all employees. Workers' compensation is carried, since it is required by state law.

The company treasurer wants to buy other types of insurance protection. He wants extended coverage added to the fire policy, and elevator liability insurance. The company secretary wants sprinkler leakage, theft coverage, and key-person life insurance.

1. What do you consider the most important needs of this company?
2. What action should management take to determine what its complete needs are?
3. Which company officer should be responsible for administering the insurance program? Why?

16-2

PROTECTION THROUGH HEDGING

On September 20, Mr. Benedict, a flour miller, bought 10,000 bushels of wheat for $3.85 per bushel. As a hedge against a price decline, he sold the same amount of December wheat on the futures market for $3.87. One month later, he sold 10,000 bushels of milled wheat (flour) from his warehouse to a baking company. The cash price for wheat on that day was $3.91. The amount he received for his flour was $3.91 plus 12 cents a bushel for milling and overhead costs. On the same day, he bought 10,000 bushels of December wheat on the futures market for $3.93, thinking this was necessary to complete the hedge.

1. Did Benedict have a loss or a gain on the hedge?
2. What purpose did hedging serve for Mr. Benedict?

PART 5

CAREERS IN FINANCE AND INSURANCE

FINANCE Careers in finance are very diverse. They range from bank teller to stockbroker to vice-president/finance. People in finance share one common denominator, however. They work with money and with figures representing money. Their concerns may include investment and alternative sources and uses of funds.

Educational preparation for careers in finance and insurance include the following:

General Education: Math, Statistics, English, Computer Science.

Business Core: Accounting, Management, Business Law, Management Accounting.

Specialization Courses: Managerial Finance, Investments, Capital Budgeting, Working Capital Management, Financial Markets and Institutions, Bank Management, Real Estate Finance, Risk, Principles of Insurance, Life Insurance.

Jobs in finance might include:

Treasurer	Insurance Sales
Controller	Secondary-Market Manager
Vice-President/Finance	Financial Planner
Loan Officer	Treasury-Management Consultant
Bank Teller	Cash Manager
Stockbroker	Underwriter
Bond Analyst	Trust Manager
Financial Analyst	Portfolio Manager

RISK AND INSURANCE Many large companies, and some small ones with sizable real estate holdings, employ specialized risk managers to handle their insurance problems. These people have become important members of the top-management team in many companies.

At one time, companies paid little attention to insuring pure risks—insurance protection was purchased on a rather haphazard basis. This resulted in duplication of coverage on the one hand, and gaps in coverage on the other. Little, if any, control was exercised over the cost of losses. And to save money, some risks were assumed when they should have been insured, and vice versa.

Today's risk managers evaluate and review plans for shifting the company's risks involving various forms of coverage. They are expected to be qualified in all areas of insurance. In addition, they must be familiar with other methods to protect company property.

Risk managers must understand insurance contracts, including terms and restrictions contained in policies. They work very closely with the accounting department, which can furnish the risk manager with property values based on company records. They must also be concerned with ways to prevent accidents involving company workers employed in production.

Insurance is a major industry in the area of financial management. It ranks in importance right alongside banking, real estate, communications, and transportation. Insurance companies in the United States employ almost 2 million people, and insurance exerts a powerful influence on the national economy.

SPECIAL PREPARATION FOR A CAREER IN INSURANCE

Selling insurance is a highly personalized business. As an agent, you must be able to explain insurance policies and advise your client on the most desirable forms of coverage. Most life insurance companies conduct special courses for new salespeople before they allow them to represent the company.

During the past few years, increasing emphasis has been placed on more advanced training for field agents in both the life and the casualty field. In 1927, the American College of Life Underwriters was created to provide higher educational standards in life insurance training. The college cooperates with other universities and colleges by encouraging educational programs and by providing study outlines and textbook recommendations. The college annually conducts a series of nationwide examinations. Candidates who pass these examinations and meet other requirements are awarded the coveted Chartered Life Underwriter (CLU) designation.

The success of the American College of Life Underwriters prompted the organization, in 1942, of the American Institute of Property and Liability Underwriters to promote courses. The designation CPCU (Chartered Property Casualty Underwriter) is awarded to those who meet the general requirements and pass examinations in all insurance except life.

Earning either of these two designations is regarded as a mark of distinction and professional achievement. Insurance companies agree that their employees are better qualified as a result of this professional training.

Underwriters. Underwriters specialize in different types of risk. They are used in life, fire, casualty, liability, marine, and automobile insurance. They study applications for coverage and decide whether the company should accept the applicant for a policy. They study the nature of the risks involved in each application. In life insurance, for example, they review the medical examination of each applicant. They review all new types of policies and their probable uses.

Actuaries. One of the most complex and indispensable home-office occupations is that of the actuary. He or she collects, compiles, and analyzes mortality statistics. The actuary uses the mortality tables, together with various mathematical formulas, to determine premium rates on new policies. Mathematics and writing skills are important tools of the trade, as are finance, economics, and accounting. Actuaries must pass a series of written examinations to qualify for membership in the Society of Actuaries. The society conducts these examinations periodically, and only those who pass the examinations are considered fully qualified actuaries.

Field Agents. By far the largest number of people in the field offices are agents (salespersons). As a rule, an agent represents only one life insurance company. This is known as the "American Agency System." However, some life insurance agents share or broker their business with other companies, mainly because some applicants are not a good enough risk to be accepted by the field agent's company. Brokerage is not as common in life insurance as it is in other lines, especially in automobile, fire, and property insurance. Some field agents are paid on a commission basis, and some are on a salary.

Brokers. For other forms of insurance—particularly fire, casualty, automobile, and marine—insurance brokers are the salespeople. Generally, they own their own firms or work for local brokerage firms. Actually, a broker solicits business from prospects just as any agent might do, but the broker serves as the insured's agent when placing the business with a particular company. A broker is not as important in life insurance as in other forms. Insurance brokers are paid a commission or receive a combination salary and commision.

INFORMATION MANAGEMENT AND DECISION MAKING

The Kings made many decisions in moving their business forward. Like all businesspeople, they found that the amount and quality of the information they had available was reflected in the quality of the decisions that were made. For example, if you had to choose among notes and interest, bonds and interest, stocks and dividends — would you know the difference? Notes are for the short term and are *current liabilities.* Both bonds and stocks are for the long term and are *fixed liabilities.* Interest is an expense and reduces profits; dividends are a distribution of profits. How this is handled makes a big difference in accounting. Interest is paid before taxes on profits; dividends are paid after taxes on profits. It was very important whether the Kings used notes, bonds, or stocks to finance their business operations.

Then there is the question, when do you buy a computer? At first, the Kings had little need for one. Later they found it useful to share time on a computer. When microcomputers became available, the Kings bought one. They were able to develop a management information system using the computer. This provided information on the business in a timely and useful manner.

Every business must abide by certain legal rules. The Kings started with a partnership agreement; later they prepared a corporation charter. In both buying and selling, they had to observe laws regarding property, negotiable instruments, and the law of sales. Not having any special legal competence, the managers contracted for the services of a firm of attorneys.

THE ACCOUNTING FUNCTION

study objectives

WHEN YOU HAVE FINISHED READING THIS CHAPTER, YOU SHOULD BE ABLE TO:

1. Describe the purpose of accounting in a business organization

2. Identify the groups outside the business who are interested in accounting reports

3. Name the main financial reports prepared by accounting departments and explain how they aid management

4. State what a balance sheet shows about the financial condition of a business

5. Outline the principal means used in interpreting financial reports

6. Explain how budgets are prepared and how they help in financial planning

17

. . . There is no doubt that measurement standards have an impact on behavior. The way you keep score determines in part the way you play the game.

John C. Burton

To be successful, any business enterprise must have accurate information to use in making decisions. And today, accounting is the most important source of numerical information needed by business managers. The computer has given managers more data faster than ever before, and this has improved the accounting function.

Accounting is the means of communicating facts about the financial condition of a business. The recording of business transactions and their organization into usable form is the heart of the **accounting system.** The analysis and interpretation of these data is done by accountants. This chapter discusses some of the basic elements of accounting and their uses. The two basic financial statements—balance sheet and income statement—are explained. The ways in which accounting data are used to appraise operational results are presented.

GROUPS SERVED BY ACCOUNTING DATA

ACCOUNTING is *the process of recording and reporting financial information about a business.* It includes the activities of recording, classifying, interpreting, and reporting financial data. These data are very important to managers, owners, creditors, the government, and labor unions.

MANAGERS Accounting provides the basis for measuring the business performance and progress. Manufacturers need to know their production costs as well as their sales results. Retailers need data from which to calculate sales, cost of sales, operational costs, and income. Inventory records are needed for control purposes. Financial reports and budgets enable management personnel to estimate how much a business will sell and, therefore, how much to buy.

Accounting reports are necessary for planning in an organization. If a company is manufacturing several products, cost accounting can supply important data on each product. These would include the relative cost of production and distribution for each product and the amount each will contribute to earnings. These data are used in deciding which products to push, where to cut costs, and which to discontinue.

OWNERS/INVESTORS   In a corporation, the stockholders need to know about the firm's financial position. Investors who own corporate stock receive periodic financial reports from management. Such a report often includes a letter to the stockholders from the company president. It explains the trends in company sales and profits and the outlook for the future. The letter is usually followed by abbreviated data on earnings, expenses, and profits. An annual report is also sent, containing a detailed balance sheet and an operating statement. Together, these show the financial condition of the business, the amount of profit or loss, the dividends being paid, and the amount of earnings being reinvested in the business.

A recent study on the uses of the annual report found that it rates as the most important source of investment information for investors. All respondents rated financial statements as the most important part, and the pictures and president's letter as the least important.

The study also found that investors who place the highest importance on the annual report have had some special preparation in accounting, finance, or management.

CREDITORS   Accounting reports normally prepared at the close of the business year are the most reliable source of information on the financial condition of any business. If a business wants credit with a bank, the loan department of the bank analyzes the firm's financial statements in considering whether or not to grant the loan.

How does a creditor (a person to whom the business owes money) measure a firm's ability to pay? The creditor can use any or all of the "three C's" of credit—character, capacity, or capital—but chances are he or she will look closely at the firm's capital as revealed in its accounting reports. Financial reports reveal a firm's capacity as well as its capital, but creditors have more confidence in an actual statement of capital. Credit losses are usually high in cases where adequate accounting data are not available.

Financial statements also serve as the basis for a firm's financial "rating" by firms such as Dun & Bradstreet and banks making loans to the business. People who invest in stocks and bonds almost invariably review a firm's rating and financial reports when they are considering purchasing its securities.

GOVERNMENT AGENCIES   Various government agencies have an interest in the accounting records of a business enterprise. For tax purposes, both federal and state laws require business entities to file financial statements.

The government is quite specific as to how tax data must be reported. In one case, the IRS attempted to dictate to a chicken-raising unit of the Rocco Company how it must report its income:

> The chicken and turkey unit lost money the first year. Using the cash-basis accounting method, Rocco filed a consolidated tax return with a $2.4 million loss. However, the IRS perceived that if the company had used the accrual-basis method of accounting, it would have had a profit.
>
> The IRS argued that it could force Rocco to use accrual accounting and make Rocco pay $455,000 in income tax. The case went to tax court, and the court decided the use of cash-basis accounting was acceptable and the IRS could not "pluck" this taxpayer.

In this case, the government lost, but often taxpayers must conform to IRS approaches to accounting for tax purposes.

Contributions made by business to the Federal Old Age and Survivors Insurance Program and to the state and federal unemployment compensation programs are based on a firm's payroll records. Computation of state sales taxes and federal excise taxes also requires accurate accounting records.

Accounting records such as time cards and payroll analyses enable the government to determine whether a business is complying with minimum-wage laws. All corporations whose stock is listed on a nationwide stock exchange are required to file reports of their financial operations with the Securities and Exchange Commission quarterly. When the federal government is purchasing goods on a cost-plus contract, it requires detailed accounting reports from the seller.

LABOR UNIONS Financial information about a firm's income and expenses is the basis for demands made by labor during collective-bargaining sessions. Demands for wage increases and added fringe benefits are usually accompanied by arguments and data based on the firm's profits. Labor unions give more attention to a company's financial statements today than ever before. Union officials often know as much about the factors that affect a firm's profits as does the firm's management. Increases in rates of productivity, reductions in unit costs, and trends in profits are among the factors that union leaders study carefully.

> President Jimmy Carter attempted to end a labor strike against the Rock Island Railroad which was severely disrupting Midwest grain traffic during the 1979 harvest season. The president sought to show that the Rock Island was without enough money to continue operations so that other railroads could take over its grain-hauling business until the strike ended. However, a federal judge reviewed the company's accounting records and rejected the government argument that the railroad was out of cash. He found that the railroad would show a profit for the month even though the strike continued.

Both in making wage and benefit demands and in deciding whether or not to strike, unions may consider company financial statements.

WILLIAM E. SIMON

William E. Simon has had long experience in public service and finance. His financial career began in 1952 with Union Securities in New York, after which he became associated with Weeden and Company. In 1964, he joined Salomon Brothers, where he headed the government and municipal securities departments.

In January 1973, Mr. Simon was appointed deputy secretary of the Treasury. As such, he supervised the administration's program to improve and restructure U.S. financial institutions. Later that year, he was named administrator of the Federal Energy Office and assumed the overall responsibility for the government's energy policy during the oil embargo. Given his broad experience in energy and finance, Mr. Simon was appointed the sixty-third secretary of the Treasury in 1974.

Mr. Simon is the author of the bestseller, *A Time for Truth,* published by Reader's Digest Press/McGraw-Hill Book Company in the spring of 1978. A second book, *A Time for Action,* was published by the same company in 1980.

Deeply committed to the American free-enterprise system, Mr. Simon assumed a number of new responsibilities in the business community upon leaving the cabinet in 1977.

He is a member of the board of directors of Citibank/Citicorp, Dart & Kraft, Inc., Halliburton Company, United Technologies Corporation, and the Xerox Corporation.

He has also served as chairman of President Reagan's Productivity Commission, as a member of President Reagan's Economic Advisory Board, as cochairman of the board for the Institute for Educational Affairs, and as a member of the board of trustees of both the Hudson Institute and the George C. Marshall Research Foundation.

ACCOUNTING PROCEDURES AND METHODS

We have noted that one of the things accountants do is to determine the record system best suited to a particular business. Without good records data would lack uniformity and usefulness.

THE ACCOUNTING PROCESS The flow chart in Figure 17-1 shows the kind of details involved in the accounting process. Its purpose is to provide people inside and outside the business with specific financial data. The process starts with the question of what entry is needed and ends with the final preparation of reports to serve several different users.

Recording Transactions. The first step in the process of recording data is making entries in the appropriate journals. Here, all entries are entered in order and an explanation is given for each. The journals (books of original entry) most commonly used are the cash receipts and payments journal, sales journal, purchases journal, and a general journal for miscellaneous entries. The sources of these entries are the various business papers that result from business transactions. There should be some sort of written record as the authority for each transaction entered in the journals. The journal entries are periodically summarized in various financial statements and reports.

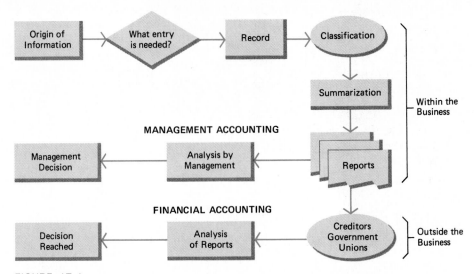

FIGURE 17-1
The Accounting Process.

Interpretation of Summary Statements. **The final and most important step is drawing conclusions from the financial statements. They reveal many aspects of a firm's financial condition, and their analysis requires precise knowledge of accounting.** An accountant is able to determine whether a business can pay its current obligations and whether a company's debts are excessive. These facts may serve as control factors and are used by management to formulate financial policy to meet changing conditions. Budgets for the next accounting period may be prepared by examining a firm's financial reports.

Reporting Financial Data. A business may need any special type of report at any time. However, the two major reports prepared regularly are the **balance sheet** and the **income statement.** These are generally referred to as **financial statements.** They are both discussed fully in this chapter.

TABLE 17-1
The "Big 8" of Accounting

NAME	NUMBER OF OFFICES	NUMBER OF EMPLOYEES
Coopers & Lybrand	405	27,700
Touche Ross	389	20,200
Arthur Young	386	21,500
Deloitte, Haskins & Sells	330	24,000
Price Waterhouse	300	23,577
Ernst & Whinney	300	20,000
Peat, Marwick, Mitchell	295	23,100
Arthur Anderson	157	22,626

THE ACCOUNTING PERIOD

Profits and losses are computed for a given period of time, whether for one month, six months, or one year. *This time period* is known as *the* ACCOUNTING PERIOD, *or fiscal period.* For tax purposes, the accounting period is one year. But a business may elect to use either a calendar year or a fiscal year. Most sole proprietorships and partnerships try to avoid ending the fiscal year on or about April 15, which is the date that annual income-tax returns are due.

THE ACCOUNTING EQUATION

There are two types of equities in a business: equity of the creditors, and equity of the owners.

The total value of the assets must equal the total equities. This is shown in the form of what is called the BASIC ACCOUNTING EQUATION:

$$\text{Assets} = \text{Liabilities} + \text{Owners' Equity}$$

You will see shortly that the balance sheet is an enlargement of the accounting equation.

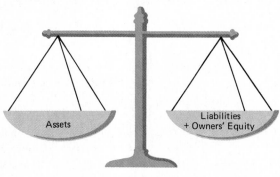

Assets = Liabilities + Owners' Equity

FIGURE 17-2
The Accounting Equation.
This must always balance.

FINANCIAL STATEMENTS

We have already seen that the two most important financial statements that come from the accounting process are the balance sheet and the income statement. Both statements are produced to give a financial picture of the business. Here, we examine the contents of each and observe various methods of interpreting the data in each.

THE BALANCE SHEET

The BALANCE SHEET is *a statement of the financial condition of a business or institution on a specific date.* It is sometimes referred to as the *position statement.* It is like a physician's report of a person's physical condition. It is true at the moment it is put together, but the picture will change when new transactions occur.

The balance sheet is a statement of assets, liabilities, and owners' equity.

Assets. ASSETS *include all items owned by the business that have value.* Examples are cash, merchandise, accounts receivable, land, buildings, and equipment. **Current assets** include cash and other items, such as merchan-

FIGURE 17-3
Fixed Assets Include Operating Equipment.
Here, a Boston firm nearly doubles production through Wassell scheduling, without adding either equipment or employees. Manpower and order control are scheduled and tracked. (Courtesy Wassell Organizations, Inc.)

dise and accounts receivable, that can be converted into cash within a period of one year. **Fixed assets** are those whose life extends longer than one year. Fixed assets normally include items needed to operate a business, such as buildings and equipment. Fixed assets are to be used rather than bought and sold for a profit. A classification of **intangible assets** is also sometimes shown. This refers to such assets as patents, copyrights, and goodwill.

COLLECTION OF RECEIVABLES

How long does it take to collect accounts receivable (the money others owe you)? Here are some examples of the average collection period for several industries:

Meat packers	15 days
Confectionery	22 days
Food	22 days
Lumber	25 days
Textiles	42 days
Scientific instruments	50 days
Alcoholic beverages	51 days
Agricultural chemicals	62 days
Footwear	66 days
Tires	86 days

Liabilities.   LIABILITIES are *a firm's debts.* This is the "equity" the creditors have in a business. Examples include accounts payable, notes payable, taxes payable, mortgages payable, and bonds payable. Like assets, liabilities are classified as current and long-term, depending on whether or not they will fall due within one year. Notice the examples of current and long-term liabilities in the balance sheet of the Holbrook Company (Table 17-2).

TABLE 17-2
Balance Sheet for Holbrook Clothiers December 31, 19_____

ASSETS

Current assets:		
Cash	$148,075	
Accounts and notes receivable	310,800	
Merchandise inventory	151,020	
Total current assets		$609,895
Fixed assets:		
Buildings and equipment	250,575	
Less allowance for depreciation	190,430	
Total fixed assets		60,145
Total assets		$670,040

LIABILITIES AND OWNERS' EQUITY

Current liabilities:		
Accounts and notes payable	$143,700	
Taxes payable	7,050	
Total current liabilities		$150,750
Long-term liabilities:		
Mortgage payable		243,830
Total liabilities		394,580
Owners' equity:		
James Holbrook, capital		275,460
Total liabilities and capital		$670,040

Owners' Equity.   Owners' equity is also called *capital*. It is the difference between the total assets and the total indebtedness:

$$\text{Assets} - \text{Liabilities} = \text{Owners' equity}$$

In a corporation, the money paid in (invested) by the owners is called **capital stock.** The profit earned over the years and reinvested by the business is called **retained earnings** (or earned surplus). The total of capital stock and retained earnings constitutes the equity of the owners. Note that in Table 17-2, the capital of Holbrook represents the equity of the sole proprietor. This would be the original investment plus the profits of all prior years (reduced by prior losses and personal withdrawals).

THE INCOME STATEMENT   Not all the essential facts about a firm's financial condition that are needed for decisions are provided in the balance sheet. It reveals only facts about the firm's assets, liabilities, and ownership. No mention is made of the income and expenses and of whether the business earned a profit or sustained a loss.

We can regard the balance sheet as a snapshot of time—in other words, the financial position at a given date and time—whereas the income statement is a movement statement; it covers the business activities over a period of time:

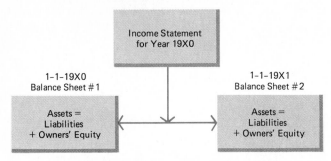

The continuum of time between balance sheets #1 and #2 is accounted for by the income statement for the year 19X0 and will reflect the amount of change from balance sheet #1 to balance sheet #2 unless there was a major change in long-term debt, or owners' equity was increased or decreased by withdrawals, or investments or assets that were not consumed were acquired by current debt.

FIGURE 17-4
The Balance Sheet as a Snapshot.

The INCOME STATEMENT *shows the firm's operations and reflects its profit or loss status.* Whereas the balance sheet shows a firm's financial condition on a given date, the income statement shows the results of operations over a period of time.

Income. The chief purpose of a privately owned business is to earn a profit. This is achieved by selling products at prices higher than their cost. This produces *income,* which increases the owners' equity in the business.

In a retail establishment, the income must exceed the cost of goods purchased and the operating expenses of the business. NET INCOME is *the amount left after subtracting all costs and expenses.* To have a net income, a manufacturing enterprise must sell its products at a price that exceeds the combined cost of raw materials, labor, overhead, and selling and shipping costs. It is now required that a corporation report both net income before federal income taxes and net income after taxes. Income earned from the normal course of business operations—the manufacture and/or sale of goods—is sometimes shown under the caption *operating income.* Income from interest earned or discounts taken on bills payable is shown as nonoperating or *financial income.*

Cost of Goods Sold. A wholesale or retail business buys its goods to resell. So their cost plus transportation charges constitutes the cost of goods sold. For a manufacturing firm, this cost includes raw materials, transportation expense, and labor, in addition to manufacturing operating expenses generally lumped together as overhead.

Expenses. *When payments are made for services received, they result in a direct decrease in the owners' equity.* These decreases are called EXPENSES and are frequently classified as administrative, operating, or selling expenses. Administrative expenses include management costs and various office expenses. Operating expenses include the depreciation of equipment and machinery, factory labor, and utility expenses. Selling expenses include salaries and travel expenses for salespeople, advertising costs, and shipping expenses.

APPRAISING OPERATIONAL RESULTS

Regardless of how complete summary statements are, the value of most accounting data lies in the way these data are analyzed and interpreted. In a small business, the bookkeeper prepares the financial statements and the owner interprets them. In a large business, accountants prepare the statements and the chief accountant and the administrative officers interpret them.

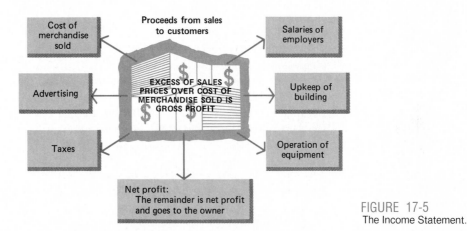

FIGURE 17-5
The Income Statement.

FINANCIAL ANALYSIS THROUGH COMPARISONS

Financial analysis takes many forms. Here, we want to consider various comparisons of different types of data.

Comparison with Past Performance. Probably the most frequently used comparison shows a relationship between current performance and that of the preceding period (year, quarter, or month). For such a comparison to be valid, the data for both periods must be recorded and analyzed in the same manner. This type of comparison, in which pertinent figures are listed side by side, shows the trend in business operations.

For example, Nordman Corporation of Amherst, Ohio, a manufacturer of equipment for applying paints, adhesives, and coatings, records material prices daily, monthly, quarterly, and annually. These material prices can then be compared with past prices, and the increase in costs can be carefully plotted. This plotting permits accurate forecasts for future material costs.

Comparison with Planned Goals. Comparing actual results with the performance that was earlier planned for is important. To what degree were the objectives set earlier achieved or exceeded? In addition, one must seek an answer to the question, What was responsible for the difference? That is, did the trend in the entire industry shift? Were there changes in the overall economy? Were the changes peculiar to our situation?

This type of comparison focuses on problems and new opportunities. Management can then decide whether more vigorous efforts are needed to achieve objectives or whether the goals and objectives should be modified.

Comparison with Competitors' Achievements. Data showing industry averages are provided for most types of businesses. A special accomplishment or significant deviation compared with one's competitors would show up as being above or below the averages.

In addition to broad categories of data published in government documents, valuable data are often supplied by trade associations. These associations make periodic reports to their member companies. Comparative data are usually available on costs and profit ratios, and sometimes on prices or pricing policies.

Use of Percentages. Another statistical tool that management uses is percentages. For example, various items in the income statement, such as cost of goods sold, administrative expenses, and selling expenses, are shown both in dollar figures and in percentages of income from sales. The income statement for Holbrook Clothiers (Table 17-3) shows these percentages in the column on the right. An examination of that statement shows that the cost price of the goods sold was 61.5 percent of the selling price, making the gross profit 38.5 percent of the selling price. Both the dollar amounts and the percentages of the administrative and selling expenses are shown. The net income of $26,857 represents a rate of 3.4 percent of sales.

Sometimes the income statement is broken down according to departments in the business. In this way, management can see at a glance how the various departments compare with one another in total sales, costs, and profits.

TABLE 17-3
Income Statement of the Holbrook Clothiers for the Year Ending December 31, 19_____

			PERCENTAGE
Sales		$828,090	
Less sales returns		42,800	$785,290	(100.0)
Cost of goods sold*			482,695	(61.5)
Gross profit on sales			$302,595	(38.5)
Less expenses				
Administrative expenses	$ 65,700			(8.4)
Selling expenses	210,038			(26.7)
Total expenses			275,738	(35.1)
Net income from sales			$ 26,857	(3.4)

*SUPPORTING SCHEDULE, COST OF GOODS SOLD

Beginning Inventory	$142,280
Purchases	491,435
Merchandise available to sell	$633,715
Ending inventory	151,020
Cost of goods sold	$482,695

Accountants in a large or a small company become involved in many aspects of the business operation. (Courtesy Shell Oil Company.)

DEPRECIATION OF FIXED ASSETS

The Economic Recovery Tax Act of 1981 recognizes five classes of *fixed assets* for depreciation purposes. The assets and the time over which they may be depreciated are:

- Three years for any cars, light trucks, research and development equipment, and other short-lived assets.
- Five years for machinery and equipment. Other tangible personal property not included in another class can also be written off over five years.
- Ten years for public-utility property previously classified with a life of from eighteen to twenty-five years and some heavy equipment and machinery, such as railroad cars.
- Fifteen years for public-utility property with a previously classified life of over twenty-five years.
- Fifteen years for real property, such as land and buildings.

RATIO ANALYSIS The balance sheet shows the total picture of assets, short- and long-term debts, and ownership equity. Management is often interested in a further breakdown of selected items listed on the balance sheet to identify relationships among them. **Many of these relationships are expressed in the form of ratios: current ratio, liquidity ratio, and working-capital ratio, are major ratios used for analysis. A ratio shows the relationship between two numbers.** It is found by dividing one number by the other. Ratios are not revealing when used alone but are significant when compared with other data.

The Current Ratio. One of the most commonly used ratios is the CURRENT RATIO. *It is found by dividing the current assets by the total of current liabilities.* This ratio gives management an indication of the *solvency* of the business and the firm's ability to pay its debts. A company obviously cannot pay its current obligations with fixed assets; buildings are hard to spend.

What constitutes a "good" ratio depends on the nature and type of business. In a business where the turnover of merchandise is slow, such as in a jewelry store, there will be a greater need for cash and a larger current ratio than where the turnover is rapid, as in a supermarket. A department store would have one current ratio, and a motor-vehicle dealer would have quite a different one.

Using the values shown on the balance sheet in Table 17-2, the current ratio for Holbrook Clothiers is 4.05:

$$\frac{\text{Current assets}}{\text{Current liabilities}} = \frac{\$609{,}895}{\$150{,}750} = 4.05$$

This compares favorably with the ratio of 3.86 shown for family clothing stores in Table 17-4.

TABLE 17-4
Current Ratios for Selected Types
of Retail Businesses

TYPE OF BUSINESS	NUMBER OF STORES	CURRENT RATIO
Automobile dealers	92	1.53
Clothing — family	97	3.86
Clothing — men's and boys'	220	2.87
Department stores	333	3.06
Discount stores	98	2.21
Furniture	158	3.70
Hardware	92	3.79
Jewelers	138	1.70
Radio and TV	63	2.20
Shoe stores	102	4.05

The Liquidity Ratio. This is a ratio of cash and its equivalent (such as marketable securities and accounts receivable) divided by current liabilities. It is a supplement to the current ratio. It shows whether a company can meet its current obligations or pay larger dividends. It is sometimes called net quick ratio, or the *acid-test ratio.* The absolute minimum acceptable liquidity ratio would be 1.

The Working-Capital Ratio. WORKING CAPITAL is *the excess (in dollars) of current assets over current liabilities.* It is closely related to the current ratio. It is the same information stated in terms of dollars rather than as a ratio. Working capital indicates a firm's ability to meet its operating expenses and to buy additional goods for resale. If a firm has enough working capital on hand, it can take advantage of attractive buying propositions that it would otherwise have to pass up.

Using the figures appearing in Table 17-2, we see that the working capital for Holbrook Clothiers is $459,145:

Current assets − Current liabilities = Working capital

$609,895 − $150,750 = $459,145

RATIOS THAT MEASURE OPERATING RESULTS

So far, we have discussed ratios used to measure the financial strength of a business. Now let us focus on ratios relating directly to measuring the operating results. Three such ratios discussed here are the inventory turnover, the return on investment, and the return on sales.

Inventory Turnover. The INVENTORY TURNOVER ratio is *the number of times the value of stock on hand (inventory) is sold during the year.* This ratio is found by dividing the cost of goods sold by the average inventory. A high inventory turnover is desirable, for it means the investment in goods is being kept to a minimum. The figure normally used is found by averaging the beginning and the ending inventory. Using the figures from the income statement for Holbrook Clothiers (Table 17-3), we have these calculations:

$$\frac{\text{Beginning inventory} + \text{Ending inventory}}{2} = \text{Average inventory}$$

$$\frac{\$142,280 + \$151,020}{2} = \$146,650 \text{ (average inventory)}$$

$$\frac{\text{Cost of goods sold}}{\text{Average inventory}} = \frac{\$482,695}{\$146,650} = 3.3 \text{ (inventory turnover)}$$

This figure of 3.3 compares favorably with the figure of 3.7 shown for inventory turnover for family clothing stores in Table 17.5.

TABLE 17-5
Inventory Turnover Ratios for Selected Types of Retail Businesses

TYPE OF BUSINESS	NUMBER OF STORES	INVENTORY TURNOVER
Automobile dealers	92	6.7
Clothing — family	97	3.7
Clothing — men's and boys'	220	3.8
Department stores	333	5.5
Discount stores	98	5.2
Furniture	158	4.6
Hardware	92	3.9
Jewelers	138	16.7
Radio and TV	63	5.0
Shoe stores	102	3.7

Inventory storage in the telephone industry. (Photo by Gary Gladstone, The Image Bank.)

Inventory Valuation.   In determining how much inventory is worth, we must consider the time during which the inventory costs are incurred. Two of the generally accepted methods used to determine the time sequence of costs for inventory accounting are *last in, first out* (LIFO) and *first in, first out* (FIFO).

During the inflationary period of the 1970s, many firms switched to the LIFO method of inventory accounting. LIFO is an inventory valuation by which cost of goods sold is based on the most recent materials purchased. By the use of recent prices during an inflationary period, the cost of goods sold reflects a higher cost paid to buy new goods or raw materials. Therefore, using LIFO reduces the profit shown on the income statement because it raises the cost of goods sold. However, those favoring LIFO argue that it provides a more accurate statement of actual profits than does FIFO. During inflationary periods, when LIFO is used, taxes are lowered because profits are reduced.

TABLE 17-6
Comparison of Inventory Pricing

	FIFO	LIFO
Beginning inventory:		
1,000 units @ $10	$10,000	$10,000
Purchases:		
1,100 units @ $12	13,200	13,200
Total available for sale	$23,200	$23,200
Sales:		
900 units at $18	16,200	16,200
Cost of goods sold:		
900 units at $10 each	9,000	
900 units at $12 each		10,800
Profit (before taxes)	$ 7,200	$ 5,400
Federal income tax @ 46 percent	3,312	2,484
Profit (after taxes)	$ 3,888	$ 2,916

WHAT HAPPENS TO CORPORATE PROFITS?

In the late 1970s, most corporations increased the percentage of earnings paid to stockholders as dividends. Continuing into the early 1980s, some corporations paid more in dividends than they earned as profits. In addition to numerous electric-utility companies, Ford Motor Company, International Harvester, and General Motors are examples. In 1982, Caterpillar Tractor had 16,000 laid-off employees. Its earnings for the first half were off by 83 percent. Yet it raised its annual dividend to $2.70, compared to $2.40 for the previous year.

This seems unwise, in view of the fact that dividends are taxed twice. (The corporation pays taxes on its income, then the stockholders pay income taxes on dividends received.) Many accountants hold that, because of double taxation, in the long run both corporation and stockholders would be ahead if smaller dividends were paid. Perhaps some corporations feel a need to placate their stockholders by paying dividends. Sometimes they pay out cash they need for internal financing.

Where corporate profits go is shown in Figure 17-6.

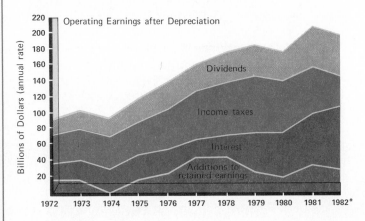

* First quarter

FIGURE 17-6

Where Corporate Profits Go.

Dividends were up in the first quarter of 1982 — to a $55 billion annual rate for nonfinancial corporations. That left very little for capital formation in spite of a tough profits squeeze. The profit total represents reported results less an allowance for inflation-caused inventory gains and inadequate depreciation deductions. (Source: U.S. Department of Commerce; Federal Reserve Board.)

FIFO inventory valuation assumes that the first items bought were the first ones used in production or first sold. Thus, the value of the inventory on hand would be close to current market prices. During times of inflation, the higher inventory value increases profits shown on the income statement. Thus, the amount of income taxes to be paid would also be higher.

Table 17-6 compares the two methods of inventory valuation. Each method can have an effect on profits before taxes. In Table 17-6, FIFO profits are $7,200 and LIFO profits are $5,400. The inventory-valuation method used also makes a difference in the movement of cash in and out of the firm. This movement is called cash flow. For example, in Table 17-7, there is a negative cash flow for FIFO and a positive cash-flow total of $516 under LIFO.

TABLE 17-7
Cash Position at End of Accounting Period

	FIFO	LIFO
Income from sales	$16,200	$16,200
Cost of goods purchased	−13,200	−13,200
	$ 3,000	$ 3,000
Taxes paid	− 3,312	− 2,484
	$ 312[a]	$ 516

[a] Deficit amount.

In Tables 17-6 and 17-7, the accounting figures are the same in each case except for the pricing of inventories. The beginning inventory is 1,000 items carried on the books at $10 each, and the inventory at the end of the accounting period is 1,200 items with a current cost of $12 each. Sales during the period were 900 items at an average price of $18.

Return on Investment. Many company managers consider this ratio the single most important index of overall operating performance. It is obtained by dividing earnings by total capital. For a corporation, total capital would include common and preferred stock, retained earnings, and borrowed capi-

CURRENT ISSUE

SHOULD CORPORATION REPORTS BE MORE REVEALING?

Corporations spend large sums preparing attractive, colorful annual reports for their stockholders. They also give briefer reports quarterly. Some companies have been accused of not giving a true and complete picture of their financial status.

With which of the following statements do you agree, and with which do you disagree?

1. The typical stockholder doesn't know how to interpret the financial statements in corporate annual reports.
2. Stockholders don't pay much attention to annual reports anyway.
3. Management shouldn't give too much information in the annual report, for that tips off competitors.
4. Annual reports should be written more in layman's language.
5. The annual report should be devoted to future plans, not the status quo.
6. Management spends too much money making the report colorful and attractive.

1. Should the typical annual report be enlarged and more detailed, or abbreviated?
2. Should pictures be deleted from annual reports?

tal. **This ratio is considered an indication of how well management has used the total resources available within the business.**

In the case of Holbrook Colthiers, this would be:

$$\frac{\text{Net income}}{\text{Total capital}} = \frac{\$26{,}857}{\$670{,}040} = 4.008 \text{ percent}$$

The national average figure for family clothing stores is 8.3 percent, which would indicate that Holbrook is earning about one-half that of the national average.

Return on Sales. One of the most interesting ratios is earnings as a percentage of sales. This varies greatly by type of business. It is relatively small for grocery stores, motor-vehicle dealers, and discount houses (less than 2 percent), and much higher for jewelry stores, household appliances, and hardware stores. Where this percentage is small, the stock turnover is fairly rapid.

For Holbrook Clothiers, the return on sales is:

$$\frac{\text{Net income}}{\text{Sales}} = \frac{\$26{,}857}{\$785{,}290} = 3.42 \text{ percent}$$

The national average return for family clothing stores is 3.27 percent.

THE FINANCIAL ACCOUNTING STANDARDS BOARD

The national professional organization of practicing CPAs is the American Institute of Certified Public Accountants (AICPA). In 1959, the AICPA created the Accounting Principles Board. The purpose of this board was to set forth accounting principles and policies to be followed by the accounting profession. The board was besieged from all sides during its thirteen-year existence. It came under fire early, being charged with failure to correct alleged abuses. The final result was that on July 1, 1973, it was replaced by the Financial Accounting Standards Board (FASB). The FASB was established as a private, independent board. Whereas its predecessor set forth "principles," the FASB uses the term **financial accounting standards.**

Two of the basic premises of the FASB are that when a standard is established:

1. It should be responsive to the needs and viewpoints of the entire economic community, not just the public accounting profession, and
2. It should operate in full view of the public through a "due-process" system that gives interested persons ample opportunity to make their views known.

One of the most controversial FASB rulings is Standard No. 33, published in September 1979, which relates to inflation accounting. It deals with the valuing of fixed assets and says that fixed assets are to be shown in annual reports at current values rather than historical cost figures.

The board will permit a company to experiment with one of two alternatives. A corporation may present key operating, asset, and market data using current costs to determine whether corporate performance has kept pace with the ravages of inflation. Or a company may disclose essentially the same information in constant dollars by adjusting its numbers with the official consumer price index to show whether its purchasing power has been maintained.

In theory, the standards should help investors analyze, for example, whether a rather handsome earnings increase is due to good company performance or simply the result of inflation.

THE USES OF BUDGETING

We have observed that planning is one of the most important aspects of business management. Much of the financial planning of business is based on budgets. A BUDGET is *a financial plan showing anticipated income and outlays for a given period.* Budgets are usually prepared for both individual departments and the business as a whole. If the expenditures for a department equal the amount appropriated, we say that its budget is **balanced.** When the expenditures exceed the amount budgeted, we say that the department has operated at a **deficit.**

PURPOSES OF BUDGETS

A well-prepared budget helps management in several ways. It serves as a guide in planning financial operations. It also establishes limits for departmental expenditures. Although budgets are at best only estimates, they are usually accepted as the limits within which a department is to operate. If expenses exceed the budget in one area, an attempt must be made to curtail expenses in other areas.

Another important purpose is to encourage administrative officials to make a careful analysis of all existing operations. On the basis of their analysis, present practices may be justified, expanded, eliminated, or restricted.

SEC BANS USE OF DEFEASANCE

The Securities and Exchange Commission, in August 1982, banned the use of "defeasance" by publicly held companies. This action was taken on a temporary basis to give the FASB a chance to take action on the procedure.

Defeasance takes several forms. Under one procedure, a company buys government securities and places them in a trust. It pledges the income from the securities to pay interest on and retire the company's debt as it falls due. Then the company removes the debt from its balance sheet.

Using this technique, Exxon (in July 1982) reduced its balance-sheet debt by $515 million. The Kellogg company management (by using a different variation) said it could add 8 cents a share to its second-quarter earnings.

TYPES OF BUDGETS   Perhaps the most important budget to be prepared—certainly the first one—is the **sales budget.** This is an estimate of the total anticipated sales during the budgetary period. One method of preparation commonly used is for each salesperson to estimate the sales increase he or she can achieve in the territory served. As a rule, these estimates are broken down by principal lines or, in some cases, by individual items.

Another approach is to begin with a line graph of sales for recent years and to project it for the budget period. Any factor or new development that is expected to increase or decrease future sales must be taken into account. This could include such things as changes in equipment or office procedures. In this way, management can make a fairly accurate forecast of total sales and sales by products. It can then determine the expected gross income.

In this same manner, budgets are prepared for production operations, raw materials and supplies, sales expenses, advertising, labor, and plant expansion.

STEPS IN BUDGETING   The first step is to make preliminary plans for the period ahead. All the important phases of the business operation must be studied. The records of past performance are the starting point. Then estimates for the budgeting period are prepared.

The second step is to plan and keep records of expenditures during the budgetary period. These records should be broken down into several budget categories. They must be accurate, up to date, and relatively easy to interpret. Records of this sort enable management to make periodic comparisons to see whether actual expenses are falling into line with the estimates.

The third step is to study any departure from the original estimates. In some cases, management may decide to alter the budget. Such a situation might be created by unusual capital costs, such as building modification that had not been anticipated, or by the replacement of heavy equipment that suddenly becomes obsolete. However, in most cases, management will take steps to bring expenditures into line with the original estimates.

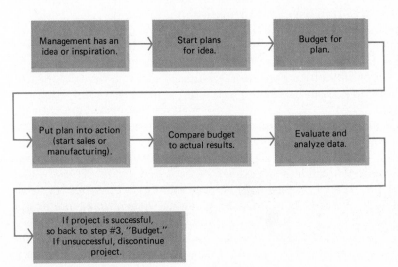

FIGURE 17-7
Budgeting and Control.
This example can be used with the traditional budgeting approach or with zero-base budgeting.

BUDGETS USED FOR CONTROL

If management is to have a fully effective cost-control and/or cost-reduction program, constant review must be applied to costs. Budgets are the tools that management uses for review and control purposes. When they are well prepared and based realistically on past performances, they:

1. Reveal weaknesses in the organization
2. Make it easier to fix responsibility
3. Make possible comparisons that show trends in performance
4. Help maintain balance among the divisions of the organization

Budgetary control helps shape overall plans, set performance standards, and coordinate activities into a unified whole. It is achieved through the use of forms that show at a glance both the budget estimates and up-to-date records based on actual performance. If there should be any deviations from the budgetary plan, they are called to the attention of management. For example, if materials or supplies are being consumed at an abnormal rate, immediate attention is given to improving the materials-control procedures. If sales of a particular product are declining rapidly, or if sales are falling off in a given territory, immediate investigations are held to correct this situation.

Budgetary control includes the development and use of three basic budgets: income, cash, and capital.

The **income budget** includes estimates of both gross and net income. The **gross-income** estimate is based on sales forecasts. The **net-income** estimate results from subtracting anticipated expenses from estimated gross income. Preparing this budget requires perception and analysis of factors outside the business itself. The trends for the industry as a whole and for the regional economy play an important role.

The CASH BUDGET (or forecast) *estimates the amount of cash to be received during a future accounting period and the amount needed to pay for all anticipated disbursements.* (It also shows the amount of cash on hand at the beginning of the period and the amount expected to be on hand at the end of the period.) It represents a combination of the financial position of the business at the beginning of the fiscal period and the expected results during the period. Basically, it shows two things: the estimated cash available for the period, and an itemized list of expected demands for funds.

The **capital budget** indicates how the sums for capital expenditures are to be allocated to the major departments. Like all budgets, these estimates must be kept flexible. Changes in market operations may change plans for expansion. Labor difficulties, even those of suppliers, may force a delay into a future fiscal period. Also, invested surplus funds may earn more than was anticipated.

The income and capital budgets are primarily the responsibility of the operating departments. But the cash budget is solely a financial function. Income and capital budgets are a coordinated plan of action to achieve company objectives. Cash budgets reflect the expected results of those plans.

Budget estimates and performance records draw attention to areas where action is needed. Yet the actual control over funds, materials, expenses, and so on must be exerted by individuals. The budget as a control tool is no better than the knowledge and understanding of the people who prepare it or of those who live with it. Management should create a climate that stimulates interest in budgets and a desire to use them as guides against which to measure actual performance.

ZERO-BASE BUDGETING

Until recently, budget planners started with the current year's expenditures. Then they decided how much more—or less—to propose for the period ahead. Under this method of budgeting, the person preparing the budget was required to justify only the increase in the amount requested.

ZERO-BASE BUDGETING is *a system by which the organization's entire proposed budget must be justified in order to be approved.* Under zero-base budgeting, one starts from scratch and decides first on program requirements. Zero-base budgeting received national recognition when President Carter advocated its use by the government. Since then, much controversy has arisen as to its use by business firms.

Under zero-base budgeting, the budget planners must:

1. Set specific program objectives
2. Define products or services to be required
3. Establish standards to be met
4. In some cases, suggest more than one spending level; the minimum level might very well be below the current spending

Zero-base budgeting has certain advantages. It reveals budget items that cannot be justified and therefore should be dropped. It treats all departments alike, because they are bound by the same standards. It provides increases where they can be justified and involves more people in the decision-making process. It combines planning and budgeting into a single process.

Among its disadvantages are the following: The process may take more time, and therefore it may cost more to prepare the budget. Sometimes reliable cost data are difficult to obtain, and the manager is unable to justify the budget expenditure. More coordination among the departments is necessary. Without complete coordination, managers may be reluctant to use this kind of budget system. Where jobs must be justified, managerial frustration may result if the budget is not approved.

SUMMARY OF KEY CONCEPTS

The accounting department of a business enterprise provides owners and managers with data about finances, sales, operations, and profits.

Reports to stockholders usually go beyond the balance sheet and income statements. They include sales and earnings by product lines, dividends and stock prices, and gains or losses due to currency translations on international sales.

In appraising the results of operations, the financial reports usually show comparisons with previous accounting periods, percentage distribution of the sales dollar among the major expense categories, and ratios that indicate the degree of liquidity enjoyed by the business.

Some of the more commonly used comparisons are of current achievements (1) with past performance, (2) with planned goals, and (3) with the achievement of competing companies.

Commonly used ratios or analyses include the current working-capital, inventory-turnover, and return-on-investment.

Budgeting is an important management function that is dependent upon data prepared by the accounting department.

There are several types of budgets normally prepared by a business enterprise, but budgetary control is centered on the income, cash, and capital budgets.

You should be able to match these business terms with the statements that follow:

a. ACCOUNTING EQUATION   g. CURRENT RATIO
b. ACCOUNTING PERIOD   h. EXPENSES
c. ASSETS   i. INVENTORY TURNOVER
d. BALANCE SHEET   j. LIABILITIES
e. BUDGET   k. NET INCOME
f. CASH BUDGET   l. WORKING CAPITAL

1. The period of time for which profits (or losses) are calculated
2. The formula Assets = Liabilities + Owners' equity
3. The statement of the financial condition of the business
4. Items of value that are owned by the business
5. The debts owed by the business
6. The sum left after subtracting all costs and expenses from gross income
7. Payments for services that reduce owners' equity
8. An amount calculated by dividing current assets by current liabilities
9. The amount by which the current assets exceed the current debts
10. The turnover of the investment in merchandise
11. A financial plan that shows anticipated income and outgo for a period of time
12. An estimate of the amount of cash to be received and spent

1. Explain how accounting data can aid business managers in making business decisions.
2. a. Who has an equity in the assets of a business?
   b. What are the three elements of the basic accounting equation?
3. What does the balance sheet show about a business?
4. What does the income statement show about a business?
5. How is budgeting related to planning?

1. How would a prospective stock purchaser and a union-member employee differ in evaluating a company's financial statements?
2. Which financial statement gives a prospective purchaser of the business the more helpful information?
3. Name three important ratios used in interpreting financial statements, and tell how each is obtained.
4. Select one important ratio and explain how it would be a help to management.
5. a. What is zero-base budgeting?
   b. What are its values?

BUSINESS CASES

17-1

CAPITALIZING ON EXPENDITURE

A national bank with 150 employees and total resources of $50 million purchased four new accounting machines at a cost of $15,000 each. The machines have an estimated useful life of four years and a trade-in value of 12 percent of their cost. The purchase was regarded as an expense and recorded as such on the books. At the end of the month, when the income statement was prepared, the bank was operating at a net loss of $12,480.

In the past, the bank's president has supported the idea of recording fixed assets as an expense. An analysis of the current income statement, however, revealed that this month's loss was the direct result of the purchase of the four machines. Their entire cost was charged as an expense of the month.

The president is recommending that the accounting practice be changed. In the future, fixed assets should be treated as a capital investment. They would then be depreciated over their expected useful life. He has asked you for an argument to support this action.

1. What would you offer?
2. If the four machines are put on the books as fixed assets and depreciated, what would be the monthly depreciation cost?

17-2 ALLOCATION OF PROFITS

A corporation made a profit of $300,000 for the current year. If the entire net income for the year were paid out in dividends, the stockholders would receive a return on their investment of 15 percent for the year.

However, the company must modernize and enlarge its plant facility, at a cost of $2,250,000. The company president recommends that only a 5 percent dividend be declared, and that the remainder be allocated to plant expansion.

Assume that you are a member of the board of directors. What factors would have a bearing on your decision?

Information Management and Computers

study objectives

WHEN YOU HAVE FINISHED READING THIS CHAPTER, YOU SHOULD BE ABLE TO:

1. Describe the parts of an information system

2. Identify the steps involved in processing information

3. Describe how computers serve businesses in processing data and in decision making

4. Name the steps involved in decision making

5. Explain the major user dissatisfaction with computer systems

6. Identify components of an ''automated'' office

"I wouldn't be surprised to find computer science joining algebra as a college entrance requirement within the decade."

Ryal R. Poppa

anagement decisions must be based on up-to-date data, and a business information system must be an effective one. So much information is available that management needs a good system for organizing it.

Business data must be organized and stored systematically so that information can be retrieved quickly. Many companies have installed their own high-speed electronic equipment to do just that. Others contract for computer services or share time with other users through computer service centers. As more micro- and minicomputers come on the market, a company will be able to install its own data-processing equipment, because its cost will be reduced. For example, a versatile microcomputer can be purchased for less than $1,000. It can automate the entire record-keeping process of a small business as well as perform many other chores.

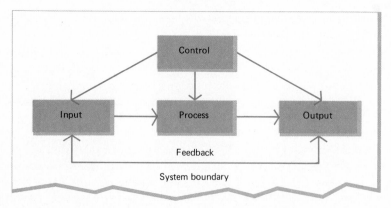

FIGURE 18-1
Basic Components of Any System

Management decision making is an ongoing procedure, not an occasional process. Not only are new decisions being made continually, but earlier ones are being reviewed. One thing that separates managers in high-level positions from those in lower-level positions is their decision-making responsibilities. But sound decisions require adequate and up-to-date information.

In this chapter, we look at the "systems concept" as it is applied to information handling. Then we discuss computers and their role in processing data and examine the decision-making process used in management.

THE SYSTEMS CONCEPT APPLIED TO INFORMATION HANDLING

For the purpose of our discussion here, the word SYSTEM refers to *any series of interrelated items or events that perform an activity*.

Systems is a term used to refer to many different things. Biological "systems" like the human body, educational "systems," and social "systems" are commonly discussed. Each system has several things in common with the others. For example, they all have:

1. Interaction with the environment
2. Purpose
3. Self-adjustment
4. Self-correction
5. Boundaries

Management information systems are under human control, but they are systems nonetheless. For a small business, the information system might consist of information the owner carries around in his or her head, some file cabinets, and a typewriter.

The general model for any system is shown in Figure 18-1. This is, of course, a very simple model; actually, systems may have *many inputs and outputs*. But basically, any system takes an input, processes it, and provides an output. Feedback tells the system whether the output is as it was supposed to be and, if not, allows the system to correct the output. This control provided by feedback can also apply to the inputs or the process itself.

MODERN INFORMATION SYSTEMS **Information systems are collections of people, machines, ideas, and activities that gather and process information. They help managers in accounting, planning, controlling, and day-to-day operations.** Production orders, purchase orders, invoices, payroll reports, and income statements may all be important parts of a management information system.

A good example of the nature of an information system can be presented using product-inventory levels. Many businesses have inventories, and many people are interested in knowing about them. People planning for the future need to know how much inventory is on hand. Purchasing personnel need to know inventory levels so they can reorder. Accountants need inventory-level information in order to prepare the financial statements. Salespeople need to know if the current inventory will support a delivery commitment to their customers. The finance department needs

FIGURE 18-2
A typical computer-based information system. (Courtesy I.T.T.)

inventory information in order to determine short-term cash requirements. It's obvious that accurate and timely information on this one aspect of doing business is critical to many people.

A major tool in information systems is the computer. Computers now process all kinds of business information. At first, computers were used for handling the routine tasks performed by records clerks and calculating-machine operators. Later, they were used for ordering goods and parts, making travel reservations, scheduling production operations, and assisting in the design and control of manufacturing operations. Today, businesses have systems for using computers in processing data that cut across departmental functions and boundaries.

The Diebold Group, Inc., concluded from one of its recent research surveys that approximately 10 percent of new plant and equipment expenditures are for computer systems.

Developing new information systems is a creative activity. The result can be of major benefit to the business. Or it can be a disaster of wasted time and dollars with little payoff. Careful analysis, design, implementation, and evaluation plus experience make the difference.

WHAT IS DATA PROCESSING?

Most people probably think of data processing as the handling of large amounts of numbers by machine at a very rapid rate. However, data processing in its simplest form includes *any kind of information handling:* When a shipping clerk prepares invoices for payment, a records clerk sorts checks, or a typist prepares statements of account to send to customers, this is data processing.

METHODS OF DATA PROCESSING

Data processing is used for two broad purposes:

1. To process transactions
2. To help in decision making

Many routine transactions (such as sales in a retail store) are repeated frequently. Such activities are well suited to computerized processing. Other information is nonroutine and is best handled in other ways. Some data must always be processed by hand in order for them to be in the proper form to be processed later by a machine. Today, we handle most accounting and statistical data by machine. A typical information-management system provides much useful information that was not available to managers a few years ago.

AN EXAMPLE OF DATA PROCESSING

One of the best ways to explain the requirements of business data processing is to examine a typical business transaction involving merchandise. As an example of data processing, let us consider some supplies that must be ordered, received, and paid for.

Computation. Every purchase order describes and states the amount of items wanted and lists the item cost and the total cost of the goods ordered. This latter figure is arrived at by multiplying the price per unit by the number of units. (This figure may, however, differ from the total cost of purchase; other charges may be added.) So **computation** is a necessary operation.

Communication. After the order form is prepared, it is sent to the company from which the goods are to be purchased. This operation can be called **communication.** At a later date, there will be more communicating information — such as when the goods are shipped by the seller, and when a check is issued in payment for the shipment.

Recording and Filing. There are several records to be made in connection with the transaction: a record of the order, of the receipt of merchandise, of the obligation to pay for the goods, and of the payment that is made later. So the process of **recording** is another essential operation in the proper handling of a business transaction. And records do not just float, around; they must be kept together somewhere, so they are usually filed according to some prearranged plan. When records are systematically arranged in specially prepared storage cabinets, we call this **filing.** But when data are recorded by a computer, the term **storage** is commonly used. So the filing or storing of information is another operational function in handling data.

HELP FOR PROGRAMMERS

A Labor Department study says that the computer industry will soon need 164,000 more programmers than are expected to be available. This is partly because today's programmers spend 70 percent of their time redoing old programs rather than working on new ones. To help solve the problem, computer manufacturers are developing "application generators," a standard program module that can be used to simplify software development. Manufacturers estimate that these shortcuts will save programmers much time, but won't eliminate the shortage.

Coding.   Before records are stored, they are usually classified according to the nature of the transaction involved. It is easier and faster to record information by machine if it is stated numerically than if words are used. So the goods to be ordered in our illustration need to be classified — assigned an identification number. This is called **coding,** and it speeds up the operation when large quantities of data are involved.

Sorting.   If you were responsible for paying for merchandise purchased, how would you remind yourself to do this on or before the particular day that the invoice falls due? One way would be to write yourself a note on your desk calendar pad. You might actually make the note on the sixth of the month, but you would put it on the page of the calendar pad that is dated the sixteenth, the date the bill is to be paid.

A better way might be to file the invoice under the date of the sixteenth, and then on the sixteenth issue your check. However, you would at the same time have to prepare checks to pay all the invoices previously filed as being due on that day. So it is clear that when preparing several invoices for filing, you would arrange them in order according to their due dates.

This is called **sorting,** and it is another important function in data processing. (Note that in our illustration we sorted invoices and prepared them for filing by hand; in electronic data processing, the basic data instruments would be sorted rapidly by machine.)

Summarizing.   The final phase of data processing is vital, because it is important to know how many invoices are paid each day and the total amount spent in order to pay them. A list of all invoices paid on a particular date, the amount of each invoice, and the total paid would constitute a summary of this group of business transactions. **Summarizing** is therefore another essential function in handling large quantities of data.

FIGURE 18-3
On-line data entry. (Courtesy IBM.)

INFORMATION MANAGEMENT AND DECISION MAKING

The seven operations we have discussed are:

1. Coding
2. Computing
3. Communicating
4. Recording
5. Sorting
6. Storing
7. Summarizing

These operations together make up the basic elements involved in data processing. We can define DATA PROCESSING, then, as that *group of operations performed in handling units of data from the original entry to the final entry.* A **data-processing system** would be the total method used to carry out the seven basic elements of data processing to accomplish the accounting, statistical, and reporting functions of business management.

THE ELECTRONIC COMPUTER

For centuries, mathematicians sought a machine that would be capable of performing arithmetical calculations rapidly. In about 1880, W. H. Adhner invented the pinset calculator, which could perform arithmetical operations mechanically. And in 1885, William Burroughs developed the first mechanical adding machine for use in business. During the same year, Herman Hollerith introduced the electronic punch-card calculating system. In 1944, Howard Aiken of Harvard University designed the Mark I, which was a mechanical computer. It was operated by a system of telephone relays, mechanized wheels, and tabulating equipment.

In 1946, J. P. Eckert, Jr., and J. W. Mauchly of the University of Pennsylvania developed the first electronic computer. It was called the ENIAC (Electronic Numerical Integrator and Calculator). Five years later, UNIVAC I, the first commercial computer, was built for the U.S. Department of Commerce by Remington Rand (now Sperry Rand). It was used in the office of the Bureau of the Census. Unlike its predecessors, it used binary arithmetic and permitted the storing of instructions in its memory system.

CHARACTERISTICS OF COMPUTERS

Perhaps the computer can best be illustrated by comparing it with an adding or calculating machine. As with these simpler machines, the three basic elements involved are the input, processor, and output units. But the similarity stops there, because in the calculating machine, the keyboard is the only means of putting data into the machine. And the output is achieved through some type of simple printing mechanism.

Figure 18-4 shows the data-processing cycle, using the symbols commonly used in flowcharting systems operations. You can see from Figure 18-4 that the requirements of a data-processing system go well beyond what a simple calculator can provide.

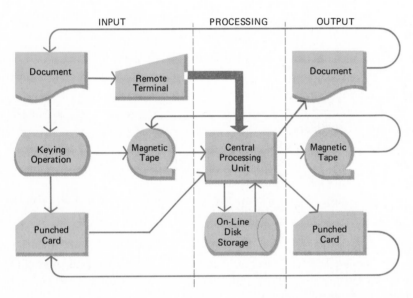

FIGURE 18-4

The Data-Processing Cycle.
(From Alton R. Kindred, *Introduction to Computers,* 1980. Reprinted by permission of Prentice-Hall, Inc., Englewood Cliffs, N.J.)

Modern electronic computers have no moving parts in the central processing unit (CPU)—everything is done electronically. They operate in microseconds and nanoseconds and some in picoseconds.[1] They use "chips" of silicon, each the size of a fingernail, to produce the computing power that required a roomful of equipment to produce just a few years ago. The computer memory (storage unit) serves two purposes: It holds the instructions or program being used, and it contains the data being manipulated. The memories are not volatile; that is, stored information will not automatically

---

[1] A microsecond is one one-millionth of a second; a nanosecond is one one-billionth of a second. A picosecond is one-trillionth of a second. One picosecond is to one second as one second is to 32,000 years.

INFORMATION MANAGEMENT AND DECISION MAKING

be erased by time, by being read, or by having the machine turned off. Memories on some of the smaller micro- and minicomputers, however, *are* volatile.

Computers use the binary number system.

The Binary Number System. Digital computers operate by opening and closing electrical circuits. The circuit is either open, permitting the electrical impulse to go through, or it is closed. So the binary number system is used instead of the more familiar decimal system.

A comparison might be made to an electric light bulb—it is either on or off. Similarly, within the computer, transistors are held in either a conducting or a nonconducting state. And specific voltage potentials are either present or absent. These binary modes of operation are signals to the computer in much the same way that light or the absence of light is a signal to a person. Since an electric current can indicate only an "on" or an "off" situation, only two symbols are registered by the computer—either a 0 (for the "off" position) or a 1 (for the "on" position). In any single position of binary notation, the 0 represents the absence of any assigned value and the 1 represents the presence of an assigned value.

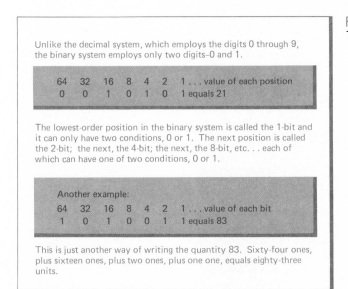

FIGURE 18-5
The Binary Number System

Unlike the decimal system, which employs the digits 0 through 9, the binary system employs only two digits–0 and 1.

64	32	16	8	4	2	1 . . . value of each position
0	0	1	0	1	0	1 equals 21

The lowest-order position in the binary system is called the 1-bit and it can only have two conditions, 0 or 1. The next position is called the 2-bit; the next, the 4-bit; the next, the 8-bit, etc. . . each of which can have one of two conditions, 0 or 1.

Another example:

64	32	16	8	4	2	1 . . . value of each bit
1	0	1	0	0	1	1 equals 83

This is just another way of writing the quantity 83. Sixty-four ones, plus sixteen ones, plus two ones, plus one one, equals eighty-three units.

COMPUTER HARDWARE

HARDWARE is *computer terminology for the machines and equipment that make up a computing center.* There are three components that constitute the computer hardware: the input unit, the processing unit, and the output unit.

THE INPUT UNIT The input unit feeds data into the computer system. Its purpose is to enable the operator to "communicate" with the computer. It performs its function by translating codes from the external form (cards, magnetic tape, or punched paper tape) to the internal form in which data are stored in the memory unit. The data translated might be numbers to be used later in arithmetical calculations, instructions that tell the computer what to do, or numbers and letters to be used in names and addresses.

The **card reader** converts holes in cards into electrical impulses and transmits the information to the memory unit of the computer, ready for processing. Similarly, the **tape reader** performs this function when the input medium is tape instead of cards. The important factor here is that this "reading" of data by the card or tape reader is done independently of human attention.

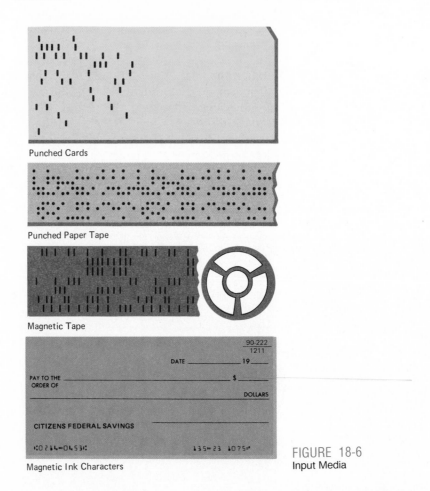

Punched Cards

Punched Paper Tape

Magnetic Tape

Magnetic Ink Characters

FIGURE 18-6
Input Media

Instead of a card reader or tape reader, the **optical scanner** may be used with the input medium. The optical scanner reads each character from some input medium and translates it into electrical impulses that are then transmitted to the computer for processing.

Scanning devices are programmed to read and evaluate certain numerals, characters, and symbols. Rays of light scan a field on a document, form an internal image, and compare it with an image that has been programmed into the scanner's memory component. If the scanner finds the corresponding image, it accepts it and moves on to the next figure. The optical scanner makes possible the use of invoices, journal records, adding-

INFORMATION MANAGEMENT AND DECISION MAKING

machine tapes, and accounting-machine tapes as input media, instead of the usual punched card or punched tape. Ordinary pencils may be used on specially prepared forms for reading by optical scanners.

Information may be put into a computer from a **terminal,** which is a keyboard connected by telephone lines to the computer itself. The many different types of terminals defy precise classification for our purposes. Simply recognize that there are terminals available that will do almost anything. They vary from typewriter devices to cathode-ray tubes (CRTs) that have screens like TV sets and display data.

THE PROCESSING UNIT

The processor (CPU) forms the heart of the computer. It contains the memory or storage and the circuitry that performs the mathematical operations. In the first generation of computers, the circuitry was based on vacuum tubes, like those that were used in radio sets. The speed of operations was approximately 500 additions a minute. These units used a great amount of space, heat, and electricity and were plagued by the problem of tubes burning out.

Later models greatly reduced the size and cost of the computer. They also increased the speed, storage capacity, and reliability. The second-generation computers (1959–65) replaced the vacuum tubes with transistors. The third-generation computers (1965–70) made use of microelectronics (miniature circuits). This increased the packing densities of circuits by a factor of 100. They had the capacity to handle several programs at the same time.

During the 1980s, the fourth-generation computers came on the scene. While increasing the circuitry, they greatly reduced the size of the processor. Minicomputers and microcomputers are now in wide use. Microcomputers are used in homes and can be purchased in consumer retail outlets, such as Radio Shack, and many others.

CPUs vary greatly in operating characteristics, but all have the same basic components. Figure 18-7 shows those components. The control unit executes commands as they are received; the arithmetic-logic unit manipulates data; and the main memory unit stores the information.

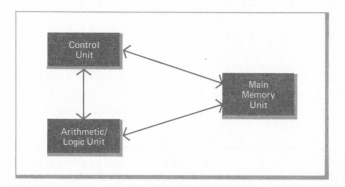

FIGURE 18-7
The Components of the Central Processing Unit

The Computer Memory.   The processor's center of operations is the memory or storage component. All data being processed by the computer pass through it. Immense quantities of data are therefore immediately available to the commands of the computer. The memory holds the input data, the intermediate result of calculations, the program of instructions telling the computer what to do, and the final results to be "read out."

FIGURE 18-8
Fourth Generation Equipment IBM 3033
(Courtesy IBM.)

Several types of memory units are used in computers. One is the **magnetic core,** which is used in most of the high-speed computers. Magnetic cores are made of special magnetic material shaped into circles, or "doughnuts," the size of pinheads. Each core can be magnetized at any time in one of two directions, one standing for the binary 0, and the other for the binary 1. Thousands of these cores are strung on criss-crossed wires, arranged like the strings of a tennis racket, inside a square frame. The frames are stacked one on top of another to make a basic memory unit.

The stacking arrangement places the cores in columns. Each of these columns is assigned an **address,** which is a specific location within the memory unit. Each column of cores can store either one fact or one instruction expressed in binary code. The stored data can instantly be "read out" from any address and used in working a problem. If desired, the data can be erased from any address and replaced with new facts or instructions.

Giants in the data-processing industry, such as IBM and Texas Instruments, are basing much of their future strategy on low-cost storage devices. But it has taken longer to get into production than anyone expected. Bell Laboratories has come up with a new design to speed production.

The "bubble memory" has several advantages over other methods. Probably the greatest is its low cost and high reliability. There are no moving parts, and it is quite small. It is now a U.S.-dominated industry, but the Japanese are pouring money into the bubble memory and will probably provide stiff competition.

There are several types of auxiliary storage: disks, drums, and magnetic tapes. In each case, the data stored must be read into the CPU for the arithemetical operation.

The capacity of a memory unit is measured in words. A **word,** which is a technical term, is defined as a group of binary digits that is treated as a unit and is stored in one location. A **location** is a unit storage position in the main internal storage, in which one computer word may be stored or from which it may be retrieved.

The magnetic disk for storage in computers was introduced in the mid-1950s. Since that time, the disk has been greatly improved. The result is great savings in the cost of storing information. When computer manufacturers refer to the size of their machines, they are referring to their storage capacity. This determines the size of programs and the amount of data available for processing at any one time. Data are represented by binary digits, or "bits." The basic storage unit is eight bits, or a "byte."

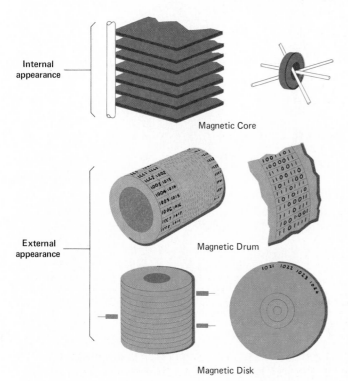

Internal appearance

Magnetic Core

External appearance

Magnetic Drum

Magnetic Disk

FIGURE 18-9

Types of Computer Storage, or Memory

THE OUTPUT UNIT　After information has been processed, it is printed out in the form of a report; this is output. The equipment used is in the form of a high-speed printer, and several printers can be placed on the line with the central processor simultaneously.

In connection with a printed report, the output may take the form of a punched tape or a punched card, magnetic tape, magnetic disk, or cathode-ray tube, depending on the type of output. It is desirable to have a record of the report on magnetic tape when there is a need to process the data further by the use of computers, or to prepare a new copy of the report at a later date.

The output report is the end product of the computer. Some of the types of information that can be produced by a printer are statements of account, journals, trial balances, financial statements, bills, invoices, checks, payroll reports, or just lists of names and addresses.

Figure 18-10 shows the various computer hardware components.

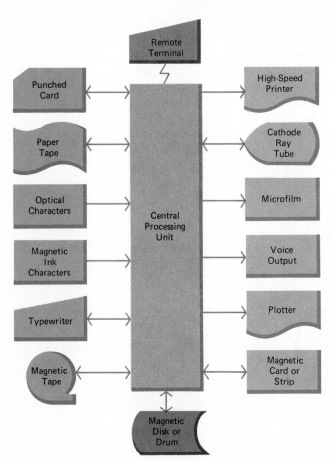

FIGURE 18-10
Computer Hardware Components.
(From Alton R. Kindred, *Introduction to Computers,* 1980. Reprinted by permission of Prentice-Hall, Inc., Englewood Cliffs, N.J.)

COMPUTER SOFTWARE

SOFTWARE is the term used to refer to *the instructions to the computer. The instructions to a computer telling it what to do are in the form of a* PROGRAM. The person who writes these directions is called a **programmer.** A program consists of a set of coded instructions that inform the computer which data are to be picked up to be used, where the data are stored, what mathematical compuations are to be performed, the order in which each operation is to be done, and what is to be done with the output.

PROGRAMS A program is first written out by hand or on a typewriter and is then transferred to cards or tape so that it can be fed into the computer.

There are four basic considerations in the preparation of a program:

1. Defining the problem to be solved
2. Outlining each logical step required to reach the solution
3. Writing the program in machine or symbolic language
4. Translating the program into machine language if the program has been written in symbolic language

A program must be written in a language that the machine "understands." Each step is written out in a carefully prepared sequence. There are several languages used when preparing programs. One common language is called Common Business Oriented Language (COBOL); another is called Formula Translation (FORTRAN); and a third is the Beginner's All Purpose Symbolic Instruction Code (BASIC). COBOL resembles English and can be used by different types of computers. It utilizes the numerals 0 through 9, the twenty-six letters of the alphabet, and a dozen or so special characters, such as the dollar sign, the asterisk, and parentheses.

Computers can be programmed to do many things. An interesting current use is interactive computer modeling in planning or making management decisions.

Sophisticated business systems can be constructed and programmed. Planners can then ask "what if" questions of the computer to see what would happen if the company raised prices, cut inventories, acquired another firm, and so forth.

The computer allows managers to "play games" with their businesses without taking risks. R. J. Reynolds has developed a model to predict cash flow at any given point and predict shortfalls that might occur in any division. The effect of such shortfalls on company goals can be predicted from the model.

The Public Service Gas Company of New Jersey tests its corporate plan once a day against a model incorporating costs and equipment use. A financial decision, such as a cutback in purchases of fuel during an unexpectedly warm winter week, can be tested. As William E. Scott, executive vice-president, said, "Within twenty-four hours we would know the impact of [an oil embargo] and could begin reacting."

OPERATING SYSTEMS Operating systems may be called "executive systems," "control systems," or "system-control software." **A system is a series of integrated programs that make the computer operate in an efficient manner.** A system manages the processing programs and controls the input, output, storage, and retrieval.

BENEFITS OF COMPUTERS IN PROCESSING BUSINESS DATA

There are several benefits to the use of computers in business data processing. We can classify these as direct or indirect benefits.[2]

---

[2] M. J. Cerullo, "Computer Usage in Business and Accounting," *Information and Management*, September 1980, p. 115.

DIRECT BENEFITS   Direct cost savings come from sources such as these:

> Increased accuracy and speed
> Reduced cost of carrying inventory
> Lower clerical costs
> Less manufacturing overhead
> Less supply expense
> Reduced nonclerical labor expense

INDIRECT BENEFITS   Even though the direct benefits may be enough to pay for the expense of a computer, there are intangible or indirect benefits that should be considered too. When trying to decide whether a computer is feasible in their operations, companies should also consider these benefits:

> More accurate and comprehensive information
> Improved customer service
> Improved planning
> Improved control of the business
> Reduced error rates
> Faster availability of information

These indirect benefits may not be considered when the computer decision is to be made. But they are major reasons for using computers.

SOFTWARE GORILLA HIT!!!

Dan Bricklin got an idea while sitting in a college class watching his professor scribble columns of budget figures on the blackboard. From that idea, he developed VisiCalc. VisiCalc (for *visible calculator*) is a computer software package that displays data in charts and graphs. The beauty of it is that whenever a variable changes—say, the level of inventory—VisiCalc recalculates all the other numbers affected by the change and redisplays them. It is the world's first electronic spread sheet. Almost alone, VisiCalc changed the personal computer from a toy for computer buffs to a usable business tool. (It has also made Bricklin rich.)

An Example.   The typical sales-order entry can serve to illustrate this point. As a rule, an order for goods is originated by a salesperson, who writes out a sales order and mails or telegraphs it to the home office. When this order is received, a production order is typed. It repeats the name and address of the purchaser and most of the other information written on the sales order by the salesperson in the field. A copy of much of this information is included in the report that goes to the accounting office, and it is typed out again in the billing and shipping departments.

Actually, less than 10 percent of the information typed on the sales invoice and on the bill of lading is new information—that is, different from that first typed when the production order was prepared. With electronic data-processing equipment, as much as 80 percent of the information on the sales invoice is written automatically from a magnetic or punched tape.

FIGURE 18-11
Retail terminal with direct sensing capability. (Courtesy Federal Express.)

A separate record is prepared on tape for each regular customer, bearing the customer's name and address and all other information needed for any sales invoices issued to him or her. This information is typed only once; then it is reproduced automatically through the use of the tape. New information, such as the purchase-order number, date of order, quantity ordered, unit price, and total amount, is added to the tape by the machine operator.

BUSINESS APPLICATIONS FOR COMPUTERS

The larger the organization, the more likely it is to have its own computer. It has been estimated that there is one computer for every business that has fifty or more employees.

DATA-PROCESSING SERVICE BUREAUS Out of the need for the part-time use of computers, "time sharing" developed. As practiced in computer service centers, time sharing allows many businesses to use the same computer. These service operations (or bureaus) have complete equipment installations and a full staff of specially trained personnel. In addition, they maintain a depository of hundreds of different types of programs—even complete data-processing accounting systems.

Part-time users have only terminals installed in their businesses. These terminals are used for sending and receiving information to and from the center. Through these centers, the advantages of electronic data processing are available to businesses, educational institutions, and hospitals that cannot afford even limited computer installations. This aspect of data processing is expanding rapidly.

CURRENT COMPUTER APPLICATIONS

The uses to which companies put their computers has changed only slightly over the last two decades. They are still used primarily for:

Payroll	Labor and cost figures
Sales analysis	Billing
Accounts payable	Financial statements
Accounts receivable	Mailing lists

In short, the most common use of the computer is as a super-bookkeeping machine. But the potential is there for the machine to provide so much more in the way of service to business. Let's consider some examples.

CRT display of graphic data. (Courtesy Atari.)

EXAMPLES OF COMPUTER USE

It is of course impossible to describe fully the thousands of applications of data processing in business and industry. We can only deal briefly with a few examples.

In Industry. Computers serve General Electric very well at its Appliance Park operation in Louisville Kentucky. Here, in a single location, are grouped several plants that might have been built in several different communities. In one large building, the company manufactures washing machines and dryers; in two other buildings, electric refrigerators and freezers; in still another, ranges. And room air conditioners and dishwashers are fabricated in still two other buildings. In fact, six major operations are carried on, each in a separate building.

In one central office at the park, there is a computer center. Smaller installations of electronic equipment are located in several other buildings serving the different production operations. With all these computer operations located close to each other, all production plants can use the center. A small office crew operates the computers during the night. Thus, an up-to-date inventory can be ready for management the following morning. Here is dramatic proof of what was said earlier: The speed of the computer makes possible the preparation of reports for management that would otherwise be of little value when finally ready to distribute.

Another example of the business use of computers is in controlling energy costs:

> Honeywell sells energy management systems that regulate air conditioning, heating, and lighting in large buildings. On air conditioning alone, Mercy Hospital in Miami estimates that it saved $160,000 per year after installing a $50,000 computer. A large Chicago real estate firm estimates that electricity use has been cut in half since the installation of computers in several Chicago-area office buildings.

In Government. The Internal Revenue Service (IRS) has an automatic data-processing system at the National Computer Center, Martinsburg, West Virginia. The center operates twenty-four hours a day, seven days a week. The computers update, maintain, and analyze a centralized master file of more than 100 million accounts. There is one for every business and individual that files a tax return. Taxpayers file their returns with the ten Regional Service Centers. There the information is transcribed from the returns and documents and then validated, key-verified, and converted to magnetic tape through a direct data entry system.

By having data on all taxpayers in the national file at Martinsburg, the IRS can easily check on those who fail to file returns. It can also tell whether a taxpayer owes anything for an earlier year before paying a refund. If tax credit from past years has been forgotten or overlooked by the taxpayer, the IRS will pick this up. It can also match information on wages, dividends, and interest on taxpayers' returns with information received from employers and financial institutions. In fact, business can now file their tax returns on magnetic tape, provided their tape is compatible with IRS equipment. The IRS is already receiving millions of taped returns a year. Most of these are No. 1099 (dividend-payment) or W-2 (tax-withholding) report forms.

In Banking. Banking operations depend heavily upon computers for processing data. Banks process billions of checks a year. Each check is sorted and cleared many times—first by the bank where it is originally deposited, then by one or more clearinghouses, and finally by the bank where the drawer maintains an account.

As a help in sorting, identification numbers are printed in magnetic ink in the lower left-hand corner of each check. Large banks and the Federal Reserve branch banks electronically sort all the checks they handle.

Branches of many large banks are wired to a central computer for "on-line processing." Deposits or withdrawals are entered on the keyboard console in the branch bank. The branch is connected by a leased telephone line with the computer in the home bank, where each customer's account information is stored in the memory unit. In seconds, the transaction performed at the branch is recorded in the main bank, and its results are reported back to the branch.

Automated teller machines are becoming popular in the large banks. Computers are being used to dispense cash automatically. This frees human tellers from the task of counting cash. Banks are using computers when checks are cashed at teller windows. The customer keeps the original, and the transaction is handled electronically. Truncation is the next step. Here the paper check is held at the first bank it comes to. All other data are handled electronically.

But the real breakthrough is an approach to an almost completely "cashless society." The financial institutions in this country are moving toward a nationwide electronic payment-transfer system. Utility bills and installment payments would be made automatically by the banks for their customers. An automated clearing system would shift funds from one bank to another without checks.

This nationwide payment-transfer system would include all types of financial institutions, not just banks. The stock exchanges are studying a scheme that would give stock purchasers a report of the number and type of stock certificates they own. This would replace the issuing of individual stock certificates for each purchase.

---

[3] J. H. Aulgur, "Computer Information Systems," *Collegiate News and Views*, Winter 1982–83, p. 9.

In Insurance Companies.   Most insurance companies find the electronic computer ideal for keeping policyholder information up to date. Information on premium payments, loans against policies, cash reserves, and dividend payments can be made available at a moment's notice. The data-processing service has made this possible for even the small companies, through shared-time facilities. The minicomputer is also allowing the small company to handle its records electronically.

The loan departments of insurance companies have also found magnetic tape and the automatic typewriter helpful in the study of financial reports. The work is done at speeds much faster than that of the highest-skilled human typist, and the old data in the report need not be proofread for accuracy.

In Retailing.   For several years, retail stores have been using computers to automate the point-of-sale process. Scanning systems are used to record basic information. Thus, mistakes at the register are fewer. Formerly, separate systems were used for inventory control, purchase orders, and so on. These are now being interconnected. Retailers are also placing orders with suppliers by computer.

USER SATISFACTION   Evidence that the great potential of computers in business is not fully realized comes from some recent studies. They show that only a small percentage of companies are satisfied with their computer systems. Fewer

Price scan in Idaho supermarket. (Photo David R. Frazier, Photo Researchers, Inc.)

than one-third have been found to be completely happy with their in-house computer operations. Many managers feel their computer operations are characterized by uncontrolled costs and uncontrolled personnel.

To maximize benefits associated with computer applications to business, companies must do a better job of developing management information systems. Such systems are not being developed well enough in many cases, and the result is dissatisfaction with the computers.

THE CHANGING NATURE OF PROCESSING BUSINESS DATA

As business organizations become more complex they need more information. For a business to compete efficiently, its information must be up to date. This requires fast output and communication of information. Two common approaches to data processing are batch and on-line real-time systems. Each can be fast, but each has its special advantage.

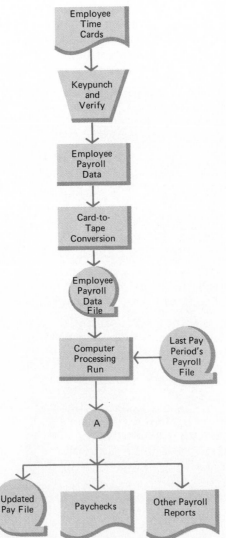

FIGURE 18-12

Simplified Example of Batch Processing of Payroll.

Input into the payroll system is employee time cards, which are keypunched and verified for correctness. Next, the punched card file is converted to a magnetic-tape file, representing the current period's payroll information. As shown here, this file is processed with the previous period's payroll file to generate the outputs—an updated pay file, paychecks, and other payroll reports.

BATCH-PROCESSING SYSTEMS

Many business data-processing applications require a high volume of input. It is often accumulated in batches that are processed at given time intervals or after the batch reaches a certain size. This method of data processing is called **batch processing.**

Figure 18-12 shows an example of batch processing for employee payroll.

ON-LINE REAL-TIME SYSTEMS

Some data processing requires very fast processing and reporting of information. For example, a system that gives a bank teller a customer's account balance must be fast. An airline reservation system has to tell quickly what seats are available on any given flight. In such cases, the processing is said to take place in "real time," because it goes on at the same time the business is being transacted. The output helps control the operation. Real-time systems are often associated with *immediate response.* On-line real-time systems then process individual transactions as they occur and from their point of origin.

Figure 18-13 shows an example of an on-line real-time inventory-processing system.

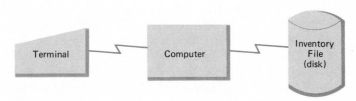

FIGURE 18-13

On-Line Real-Time Processing of Inventory.

This is an OLRT system to process orders of merchandise. An inventory clerk, for example, may receive orders from customers over a telephone. The clerk keys in the appropriate information over a terminal located at his or her desk. The information is immediately transferred to the inventory file maintained on magnetic disk. The system checks to see if the needed amount of merchandise is on hand at the warehouse, and informs the inventory clerk, who immediately informs the waiting customer. The inventory clerk then keys in the order, the inventory records are simultaneously updated, and a sales order is prepared. All these events happen in a matter of seconds, as compared to the batch processing of payroll (Figure 18-12) which may take minutes or hours to complete.

THE NATURE OF TIME SHARING

If a program involves complex calculations, it may tie up the central processing unit for a long time. This would cause other programs and jobs to wait. That presents no problem if processing is being done in a batch method. However, if some of the programs are on-line real-time, this will cause on-line users to have to wait. To avoid this, a form of programming called **time sharing** is used. In this method, a tiny fraction of computer time is allocated to the current program. When that is used up, the system will place the program at the end of its waiting line and go to the next program. The result is that no one program can tie up the CPU too long. The machine works through its line of programs, making each user feel that the system has devoted full time to his or her job.

Time sharing has certain advantages and disadvantages:

Advantages

A small user has equal access to a large computer system.
The response is faster than batch.
Overhead cost is reduced for a large user.
Set can mix interactive and batch modes.

Disadvantages

When the system is down, all users are affected.
The cost is higher than batch.
Response time for everyone can drop with an increased number of users.
Security is lost.

SMALL COMPUTER SYSTEMS

Microcomputers are full computers with CPU, memory, and input/output. Many look like TV sets with a keyboard attached. The keyboard provides input, the cathode ray tube provides the visual display. When a printer and a device for reading tapes or disks are added, a business data-processing system is created. Complete accounting systems for small businesses are available for such machines.

Minicomputers differ from microcomputers in their construction and in their capacity. The large minis allow for more memory and peripheral equipment. But it is becoming increasingly difficult to distinguish between large micro- and small minicomputers.

Combinations of hardware and software are available from a wide variety of firms. These "turnkey systems" are capable of handling a wide variety of business computing needs. They are called turnkey systems because all you need to do is turn them on and they will perform the application for which they were designed. Complete turnkey microcomputer systems range in price from $500 to $30,000. They are usually about half the price of a similar minicomputer system.

THE DECISION PROCESS

For the purposes of this discussion, we use the term DECISION MAKING to mean *the process of choosing a specific course of action from among several possible alternatives.* Decisions can be grouped under two broad categories: policy decisions and operational decisions. **Policy decisions** establish guidelines for action. **Operational decisions** translate company policies into action by determining how they will be carried out. For example, if top management decides to build a new plant to produce a new product, this is a policy decision. Selection of the employees and managers to run the plant is an operational decision.

Management gets information for decisions from many places. Computers can provide only information that has been stored in their memory units. Information comes from people and from the environment outside the business. For information that comes from management information systems to be useful, proper planning for computers and productivity is important.

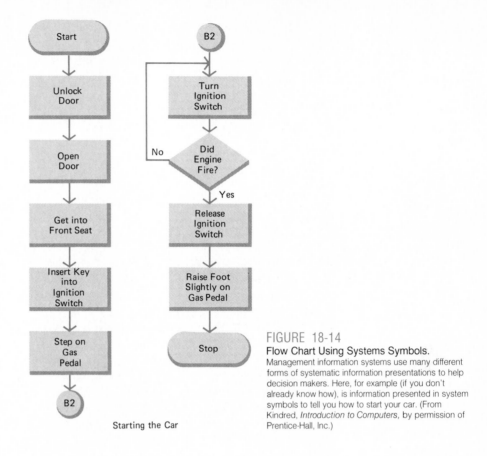

FIGURE 18-14
Flow Chart Using Systems Symbols.
Management information systems use many different forms of systematic information presentations to help decision makers. Here, for example (if you don't already know how), is information presented in system symbols to tell you how to start your car. (From Kindred, *Introduction to Computers*, by permission of Prentice-Hall, Inc.)

PLANNING FOR COMPUTERS AND PRODUCTIVITY

A top priority facing America in the latter half of the current decade is increased productivity, and therefore some important and difficult decisions must be made. Perhaps the lowest productivity is in the area of information management in today's office. The shift from an industrial society to an information society was noted in Chapter 9. David Birch's recent study shows that almost 90 percent of the new jobs created in the 1970s were in information, knowledge, or service jobs.

Louis Harris, in addressing a conference on office management, said:

> Unless employees come to feel truly involved in the decisions that most affect their office environment, this aspect of democracy in the workplace [open planning] might become another "hot" issue over the next ten years rather than a tool for solving a communications problem, with the stakes being productivity in the workplace.

PLANNING FOR COMPUTERS Planning for a computer system takes more than a simple purchase of the hardware and software. Both middle- and lower-level managers who will be working with the input and output must be involved. One device for achieving this is a computer steering committee, which would include management members.

The computer system must be properly secured, controlled, and audited to reduce the likelihood of computer theft. This has become a major problem for some companies where trade secrets or money is available through interaction with the computer system.

THE AUTOMATED OFFICE

Using computer technology to increase the speed and efficiency of office work can include several applications. Here we briefly consider some of them.

Electronic Mail. Electronic or instant mail can be delivered to other computer terminals. Using satellites, such messages can literally be transferred anywhere in the world. Currently, electronic mail is being used for telegrams, memos, and short office messages. Obviously, the recipient must have a compatible computer for the system to work.

Teleconferencing. Teleconferencing can be used to link conference rooms within a large company or between companies. It is much cheaper than flying executives from place to place for meetings. Computer terminals provide displays of prepared materials and serve as an alternative to flip charts. However, many executives prefer live meetings that rely on interpersonal relationships for conducting business.

Electronic Funds Transfer. EFTs are completed by computer and telecommunications. Information on checks is converted to electronic impulses and sent from one financial institution to another. The check itself does not physically move from one place to another.

Word-Processing Machinery.
(Courtesy Wang.)

INFORMATION MANAGEMENT AND DECISION MAKING

The technology for such transfers exists now, and financial institutions certainly spend a lot of money physically moving large amounts of paper around. But EFT has not really caught on, because resistance by individuals and some companies has slowed its progress. Problems include security and loss of privacy.

Word Processing. Word processing is a computerized system of hardware and software for transforming words into printed text. Words are the medium used here, not numbers as in data processing. Computers can compose and format letters, and edit, update, duplicate, and revise all types of text matter. Storage can be in memory, or on disk or microfilm, rather than in a file cabinet.

Word processing will never entirely replace secretaries. Its benefit is primarily for documents that are widely distributed, messages that are repetitive, or documents that must be updated periodically. For such uses, word processing significantly reduces retyping and proofreading time.

SUMMARY OF KEY CONCEPTS

The ever-increasing load of paperwork has made rapid processing of information a necessity.

The computer has made available to management up-to-the-minute information that was not previously available.

The basic components of information handling are coding, computing, communicating, recording, sorting, and summarizing.

Digital computers use the binary number system. In any single position, the current is either *on* or *off*, indicating the presence or absence of an assigned value.

A computer installation would include some type of input unit that feeds data into the system, the memory or storage unit, the calculator, the control panel, and the output (printout) unit.

Almost every aspect of modern business operations utilizes the services of computers —manufacturing, wholesaling, retailing, and finance. In addition, government, hospitals, and schools use computer systems.

Businesses that are too small to have complete computer installations may use the services of data-processing centers.

Decision making is practiced at every level of management—from low-level supervisors to the chief executive.

Automated offices, include the potential for electronic mail, EFT, teleconferencing, and word processing.

BUSINESS TERMS

You should be able to match these business terms with the statements that follow:

a. DATA PROCESSING   f. PROGRAM
b. DECISION MAKING   g. STORAGE
c. HARDWARE   h. SYSTEM
d. OPTICAL SCANNER   i. WORD PROCESSING
e. PROCESSOR

1. A related series of items with interrelationships, organized into a discernible pattern
2. Operations performed in handling information from original entry to final entry
3. Another name for the memory or filing unit
4. The equipment that performs the work in a computing center
5. The instructions to a computer telling it what to do
6. The arithmetical or computing part of a computer installation
7. The choosing of a specific course of action from among several alternatives
8. A device that reads characters and symbols and translates them into electrical impulses
9. A computerized system of hardware and software for transforming words into printed text

REVIEW QUESTIONS

1. What do we mean by the term *system* as applied to the management of records?
2. What are the stages in developing an information system?
3. What are the seven operations in processing information?
4. What types of equipment (hardware) would be found in a typical computer installation?
5. What is a computer program?

DISCUSSION QUESTIONS

1. Besides being faster, what advantages do computers offer over hand and mechanical methods?
2. What contribution does a data-processing center make to our business system?
3. What specifically is involved in making a business decision?
4. In what specific way does a computer aid in making management decisions?
5. What are the major disadvantages of the "automated office"?

BUSINESS CASES

18-1

OPTIMIZE COMPUTER RESOURCES

Two years ago, Uintah Energy Company, a medium-sized gas and oil exploration company, purchased a minicomputer system. The computer can operate in both batch processing and on-line real-time modes. At the time of purchase, the company's bookkeeper, a high school graduate, was sent to a one-week computer training school. She is now manager of the computer department, which includes three other full-time data-processing employees. Since the time of purchase, the manager has used the computer to automate payroll, accounts receivable, accounts payable, the general ledger, and preparation of financial statements.

The president of Uintah wants the data-processing manager to expand the use of the computer into decision-making jobs, but she is uncertain if such applications should be automated. She feels that the company is deriving sufficient dollar benefits from the jobs currently automated.

1. Do you agree with the president?
2. Is Uintah optimizing the computer resource?
3. What types of benefits do you feel the company is receiving from its automated applications?

4. What types of benefits should it be receiving?
5. Assuming that the company expands its computer usage into decision-making jobs, do you feel that it will encounter any problems?

18-2   A COLLEGE COMPUTER PROBLEM

A small college is contemplating the installation of a small computer. You are a member of the committee appointed to recommend whether or not to make the installation. The main problem is that no single aspect of the college program has sufficient need to utilize the equipment full time. The matter of time apportionment is also somewhat of a problem, in that all the departments interested in using the equipment want it sometime between 8 A.M. and 5 P.M.

1. Which aspects of the administrative-office functions might be amenable to using the computer?
2. Which academic departments might need the computer equipment for instructional purposes?
3. How would you schedule all potential users so as to make the maximum use of the equipment and also satisfy everyone's needs?

In The News

An Unusual Bankruptcy

The Manville Corporation filed for bankruptcy in 1982. That is not unusual; certainly, many businesses followed that path in 1982 because of very difficult business conditions. But Manville was different; it was (and is) prosperous. "Our businesses are in good shape," said John H. McKinney, Manville's president.

Manville is using a tactic to try and limit its liability for massive numbers of lawsuits filed against it for health damage from exposure to one product—asbestos. The company concluded that as many as 52,000 suits might eventually be filed, at an expense of over $2 billion. Under accounting rules, once you have an estimate of a liability, you have to set up a reserve for that liability. So Manville's net worth of $1.1 billion would be wiped out.

Manville wrote open letters in major business-media sources to shareholders, employees, customers, suppliers, and creditors. These open letters tried to explain the company's reasoning and explain what each of the affected parties could expect. For example, the ads explained to employees that management expected no workers to lose their jobs, pay, or benefits. In fact, the president said he wanted to try to keep morale high because the employees had done a "bang-up job to keep Manville lean and competitive."

The ad campaign upset some of Manville's creditors because, to them, it said, "Isn't bankruptcy just wonderful!" Manville argued that the ads were necessary to keep customers from deserting to other companies. The giant construction and forest-products company clearly has a fight on its hands, and it will be many years before the final verdict is in. In the meantime, Manville must try to continue to run its business under Chapter 11 of the Federal Bankruptcy Act.

Legal Environment:
Business Law and Ethics

study objectives

WHEN YOU HAVE FINISHED READING THIS CHAPTER, YOU SHOULD BE ABLE TO:

1. Explain the main purposes that law serves in business

2. Discuss the essential elements of a valid contract

3. Name the requirements that an instrument must satisfy if it is to be negotiable

4. Explain when the title to goods passes if they are sold C.O.D., F.O.B., at auction, or under installment contracts

5. Identify an agency relationship

6. Discuss business and ethics

19

Law is the witness and external deposit of our moral life. Its history is the history of the moral development of the race.

Oliver Wendell Holmes, Jr.

The law is important for business. It protects businesses and consumers, but it also provides the framework within which business must operate.

Before we explore the applications of law to business transactions, let us consider the major *kinds* of laws. There are two main kinds of law in the United States: **common law** and **statutory law.**

Common law is *unwritten* law, or case law. It is based on court decisions that become legal precedents. Common law had its origin in England but was later adopted by other English-speaking countries, including the United States. Common law is an attempt to develop equity. EQUITY is defined as *law that grants an adequate or fair remedy.*

The other kind of law is statutory law—*written* law, consisting of formal statutes made by government bodies. The U.S. Constitution, federal treaties, and state constitutions are part of statute law. Much of common law has now been put into statutes, so the two have merged to some extent. If there is a conflict between common law and statutory law, the statutory law prevails.

Statutes having to do with common business transactions have been made uniform among states to eliminate confusion. The Uniform Commercial Code (UCC) is a subject discussed later in this chapter.

THE LEGAL SYSTEM

The American judicial system operates on three levels: federal, state, and local. Figure 19-1 shows the sources of laws at each level and where questions of law are decided.

THE FEDERAL COURT SYSTEM   In the federal system, the U.S. Supreme Court is the court of last resort. It decides constitutional issues, cases to which the states are parties, and matters involving diplomatic staff. Figure 19-2 shows the federal courts and their relationships.

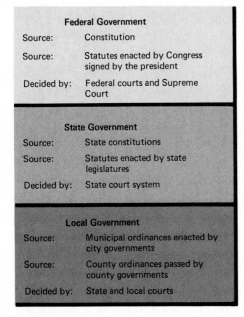

FIGURE 19-1
Levels of Statutory Law in the United States

FIGURE 19-2
Federal Court System

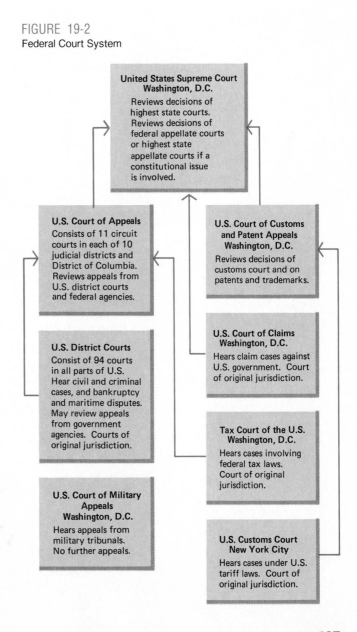

The two main routes for appealing decisions to the U.S. Supreme Court are shown in Figure 19-3. The Supreme Court is the only federal court established by the U.S. Constitution and not by Congress. However, Congress does determine the number of federal justices and their salaries.

The Supreme Court hears a variety of business-related cases. It may either choose to rule on these cases or choose not to rule and let the decision of a lower court stand.

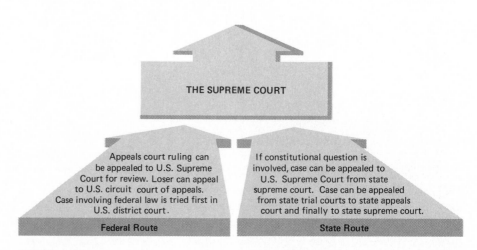

FIGURE 19-3
Two Main Routes for Appealing Decisions to the U.S. Supreme Court.
Other routes include lower court decisions by the U.S. Court of Claims, U.S. Court of Customs and Patent Appeals, and prisoners who contend that their constitutional rights have been violated.

THE STATE COURT SYSTEM

Each state has its own court system. Figure 19-4 shows the organizational structure and composition of the state court system. State courts vary as to what they are called. But common to all states are courts for both civil and criminal matters. Most states have lower courts with specialized or limited jurisdiction. These courts include "small-claims" courts, "probate" courts, and "justice of the peace" courts.

The general trial courts hear both criminal and civil matters. Appeals from the general trial courts are made directly to the state supreme court and through the state appellate courts. State and federal courts operate with a minimum of overlapping jurisdictional authority.

Small-Claims Courts. Small-claims courts are established by state law and vary somewhat from state to state. Their purpose is to hear disputes involving small amounts of money quickly and without formal rules of evidence. Lawyers are not required in most states, and the small amount of money involved often makes it uneconomical to hire them.

The court hears the case and makes a ruling. Suppose you sued someone in small-claims court and won. There remains the issue of collecting the money. The court does not enforce its judgments and collect the money for you. You have to do it yourself.

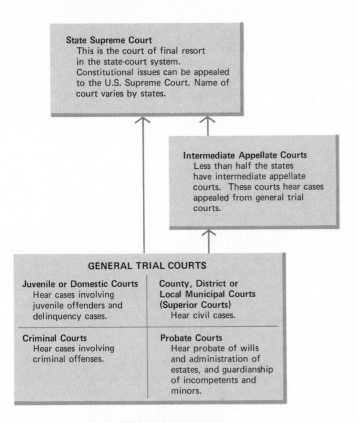

State Supreme Court
This is the court of final resort in the state-court system. Constitutional issues can be appealed to the U.S. Supreme Court. Name of court varies by states.

Intermediate Appellate Courts
Less than half the states have intermediate appellate courts. These courts hear cases appealed from general trial courts.

GENERAL TRIAL COURTS

Juvenile or Domestic Courts
Hear cases involving juvenile offenders and delinquency cases.

County, District or Local Municipal Courts (Superior Courts)
Hear civil cases.

Criminal Courts
Hear cases involving criminal offenses.

Probate Courts
Hear probate of wills and administration of estates, and guardianship of incompetents and minors.

Local Courts
Traffic Courts
Justice of the Peace
Small-Claims Court
Decisions are not normally appealed.

FIGURE 19-4
State Court System.
Each state court system varies as to title and number of courts. Each state has only one supreme court, which is limited to questions of law as opposed to issues of fact.

REMEDIES THROUGH COURT ACTION

Our American legal system provides for a dual system of remedies from the courts: **remedies at law** and **remedies at equity.**

A civil action in which the plaintiff seeks correction of an injustice is known as a suit in **equity.** It is different from a suit in **law,** which is an action to seek monetary damages. A few states require that suits in equity be tried in special equity courts.

A common remedy at equity is a court injunction restraining one party from continuing an injurious action against another. In general, remedies from courts of law can provide (1) the restoring of real or personal property to one from whom it has been unjustly withheld, and (2) the awarding of money damages suffered by the plaintiff.

Either party has the right to have the issues of fact determined by a jury — the fact-finding body. Judges decide the issues of law. But in a court of equity, there is no right to trial by jury.

When someone decides to sue another person, the "attorney for the plaintiff" files a complaint with the court against the defendant. A summons similar to that in Figure 19-5 is issued. *The complaining party in a court action* is the PLAINTIFF. *The party against whom an action is taken* is the DEFENDANT. The purpose of the summons is to notify the defendant that a suit has been started.

If you are ever served with a summons, don't ignore it. A defendant must make some reply to the summons, usually within fifteen days. Failure to respond usually means the plaintiff automatically wins the case by default.

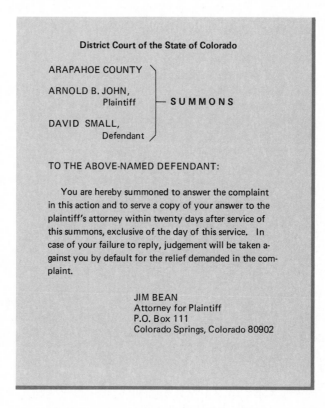

District Court of the State of Colorado

ARAPAHOE COUNTY

ARNOLD B. JOHN,
      Plaintiff — **S U M M O N S**

DAVID SMALL,
      Defendant

TO THE ABOVE-NAMED DEFENDANT:

  You are hereby summoned to answer the complaint in this action and to serve a copy of your answer to the plaintiff's attorney within twenty days after service of this summons, exclusive of the day of this service. In case of your failure to reply, judgement will be taken against you by default for the relief demanded in the complaint.

          JIM BEAN
          Attorney for Plaintiff
          P.O. Box 111
          Colorado Springs, Colorado 80902

FIGURE 19-5
Summons

AREAS OF LAW OF SPECIAL INTEREST TO BUSINESS

In this section, we emphasize some of the major areas of the law that affect business. Torts, product liability, criminal law, and contract law apply here.

TORT LAW A *tort* is a civil wrong—libel, slander, false imprisonment, or fraud, for example. *Slander* consists of defamatory words spoken or gestures. *Libel* is a wrong against an individual in the form of written defamation—in print or picture. *False imprisonment* is unlawful restraint of liberty. *Fraud* is a deliberate act of deceit to deprive one of a right. *Misrepresentation* is misleading another by a misstatement of actual fact.

You can see from the descriptions of the various kinds of torts that the application to business situations is almost endless. Here is a good example of misrepresentation:

Mr. X went to a professional tax preparer that had advertised that its employees were experts in preparing income tax returns. But the tax preparer assigned his case to a new employee who was *not* by any means an expert. Because of the employee's lack of knowledge, Mr. X claimed a tax refund. The government later audited his return and found he did not deserve the refund. In collecting the refund, the government subjected Mr. X to great expense, inconvenience, and embarrassment. He then sued the tax preparer for damages. The jury found for Mr. X and awarded him the sum of all the charges he had paid and an additional $100,000 in punitive damages.

The widest range of tort activity comes from the area of negligence. Negligence exists when a person has not taken the care expected of a reasonable person. If a person is negligent and such negligence causes harm to another person, it may result in a liability for the damage. For example, a grocery store left for several hours cooking oil spilled on its floor. A customer fell and was injured. Would you think it reasonable to allow oil to remain on the floor in a busy store for hours? Most people probably would not.

False imprisonment may occur when a shopper is detained and questioned about shoplifting when there are no grounds for believing the shopper had taken anything.

Many discount stores have guards on duty. (Photo by Donald Dietz, STOCK/Boston.)

Some of the more complex tort cases have to do with slander and libel. We have too little room to explain all the details of libel here, but an interesting variation is **defamation by computer.** When a computer is supplying information to third parties (let's say, credit reports) and someone is damaged by incorrect information, who is liable? If *negligence* or *intent to harm* is involved, then the answer appears to be that the negligent person is indeed liable. Otherwise, it is not clear who would be liable for a person's injury.

Trespass or unpermitted entry onto land is also a tort, as is *conversion*, or keeping personal property from its rightful owner. Tort law is an interesting and imporant area of the law for business.

PRODUCT LIABILITY   The courts have become involved with the question of who is liable when a consumer is injured by a manufacturer's product. The various rules constitute a developing area of law known as **product liability.** Some of these rules are based on tort law, negligence, and warranties law. The current rule of law is much tougher than the former one. Strict liability is the rule now being followed. It, in effect, puts the product, its packaging, and its promotion on trial. The old rule of law was that manufacturers or sellers were liable only when they were negligent or unreasonably careless.

The costs of product liability are estimated at over $3 billion a year. The change in the rule of law has resulted in cases like those in the box below.

To scent a candle, a teen-ager poured perfume made by Faberge, Inc., over a burning wick. The perfume ignited and burned a friend. The friend sued Faberge for failing to warn buyers that the perfume was flammable and won $27,000.

A construction worker riding in a forklift without a roll bar was injured when the truck rolled over on steep terrain. The court ruled that it was up to the manufacturer to demonstrate that the forklift's benefits outweighed its risks. Otherwise the mere fact that there had been an injury showed that it was defectively designed.

A paralyzed high school football player won a $5.3-million judgment against Riddel, Inc., a maker of football helmets. The helmet was never introduced at the trial.

Warranties.   Warranties are important to buyers who purchase goods on the basis of statements made about the products by the seller. Later, the buyers may discover that the goods have defects or are not what they were represented to be.

A WARRANTY is *a promise made by the seller about the goods to induce the buyer to purchase them.* Warranties must be statements of fact and not personal opinions. The UCC recognizes two categories of warranties: express and implied.

An **express warranty** is any statement of material fact, oral or written, by the seller about the characteristics of the goods. Its purpose is to induce the buyer to purchase from the seller. For example, the seller may state to the buyer, "This article is all wool." If the buyer relies on that statement, the buyer has recourse against the seller if the product turns out to be half wool and half polyester.

A warranty that is not specifically stated in certain terms but is implied by law is known as an **implied warranty.** Fitness for a particular purpose is one kind of implied warranty. Boats are usually "implied" to float, for example. Other kinds of implied warranty are that title to the goods is clear and that the merchandise delivered agrees with the sample or description shown the buyer. When a product is sold, there is an implied warranty that it will perform in the conditions under which it is most likely to be used.

> Consider the case of the man who found a human toe in his chewing tobacco. The Supreme Court of Mississippi said, "We can imagine no reason why, with ordinary care, human toes could not be left out of chewing tobacco. . . . It seems to us that someone has been careless." Even without a written guarantee that his tobacco would be free of toes, the court held for the plaintiff. This is an implied warranty.

Magnuson-Moss Warranty Improvement Act of 1975. For the first time, a federal law sets specific standards for sales warranties. This legislation does not compel manufacturers or retailers to use a warranty. *But if they do*, the warranty must be either a "full" or a "limited" warranty. However, the price tag of the goods must be higher than $10.

A limited warranty. (Courtesy of Howard Miller Clock Company.)

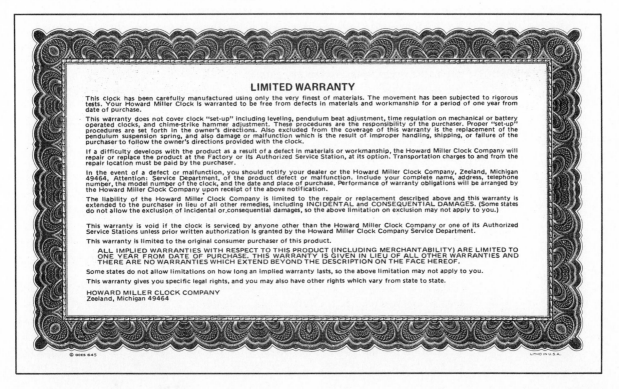

LIMITED WARRANTY

This clock has been carefully manufactured using only the very finest of materials. The movement has been subjected to rigorous tests. Your Howard Miller Clock is warranted to be free from defects in materials and workmanship for a period of one year from date of purchase.

This warranty does not cover clock "set-up" including leveling, pendulum beat adjustment, time regulation on mechanical or battery operated clocks, and chime-strike hammer adjustment. These procedures are the responsibility of the purchaser. Proper "set-up" procedures are set forth in the owner's directions. Also excluded from the coverage of this warranty is the replacement of the pendulum suspension spring, and also damage or malfunction which is the result of improper handling, shipping, or failure of the purchaser to follow the owner's directions provided with the clock.

If a difficulty develops with the product as a result of a defect in materials or workmanship, the Howard Miller Clock Company will repair or replace the product at the Factory or its Authorized Service Station, at its option. Transportation charges to and from the repair location must be paid by the purchaser.

In the event of a defect or malfunction, you should notify your dealer or the Howard Miller Clock Company, Zeeland, Michigan 49464, Attention: Service Department, of the product defect or malfunction. Include your complete name, address, telephone number, the model number of the clock, and the date and place of purchase. Performance of warranty obligations will be arranged by the Howard Miller Clock Company upon receipt of the above notification.

The liability of the Howard Miller Clock Company is limited to the repair or replacement described above and this warranty is extended to the purchaser in lieu of all other remedies, including INCIDENTAL and CONSEQUENTIAL DAMAGES. (Some states do not allow the exclusion of incidental or consequential damages, so the above limitation on exclusion may not apply to you.)

This warranty is void if the clock is serviced by anyone other than the Howard Miller Clock Company or one of its Authorized Service Stations unless prior written authorization is granted by the Howard Miller Clock Company Service Department.

This warranty is limited to the original consumer purchaser of this product.

ALL IMPLIED WARRANTIES WITH RESPECT TO THIS PRODUCT (INCLUDING MERCHANTABILITY) ARE LIMITED TO ONE YEAR FROM DATE OF PURCHASE. THIS WARRANTY IS GIVEN IN LIEU OF ALL OTHER WARRANTIES AND THERE ARE NO WARRANTIES WHICH EXTEND BEYOND THE DESCRIPTION ON THE FACE HEREOF.

Some states do not allow limitations on how long an implied warranty lasts, so the above limitation may not apply to you.

This warranty gives you specific legal rights, and you may also have other rights which vary from state to state.

HOWARD MILLER CLOCK COMPANY
Zeeland, Michigan 49464

© OOES 645   LITHO IN U.S.A.

Specific standards for a full warranty include the following information:

1. The parts of a product that are covered or not covered
2. What recourse buyers have to obtain satisfaction
3. What the warrantor agrees to do if an item is defective or breaks down
4. The period of the warranty

The act also specifies the remedies available to the buyer in case of breach of warranty.

A company may elect to use a limited warranty. This restricts the warrantor's obligation to whatever he or she may elect that is less than the full warranty. The title "limited warranty" must be shown conspicuously.

CRIMINAL LAW

A crime is an act that the government considers harmful to society. Murder and assault are obviously criminal offenses. So are larceny, robbery, arson, embezzlement, and obtaining property by false pretenses. Other business-related crimes include bribery, use of false weights and measures, false labeling, passing of counterfeit money, criminal libel, and use of the mails to defraud.

Crimes are classified according to their seriousness. Treason is the most serious. Then come felonies, crimes for which the penalties are death or imprisonment. Finally come misdemeanors, such as reckless driving, using false measures, and so forth.

A crime consists of (1) an act or omission, and (2) a mental state. In most cases, all that is required for the requisite mental state is that the person committed the act. It does not matter whether or not the person *knew* he or she was violating the law. This is the basis for the statement, "Ignorance of the law is no excuse." However, in other situations, specific intent is necessary. An assault with intent to kill is distinguished from simple assault.

LAW OF CONTRACTS

In business, many transactions involve contracts. A CONTRACT is *an agreement between two competent parties, in the form required by law, that is legally enforceable.* Figure 19-6 shows the five elements that must exist if a contract is to be enforceable:

1. Mutual assent
2. Competent parties
3. Consideration
4. Lawful purpose
5. Required form

Mutual Assent. **The contract must contain an offer and acceptance without any counteroffers.** An advertisement to sell an article at a given price is not a genuine offer; courts have ruled that advertisements only invite offers. There must also be absence of fraud or undue influence (duress).

Competent Parties. To make an enforceable contract, the parties must be legally competent. Not everyone is competent to make a binding contract. Under common law, insane persons, convicts, and people under the age of 21 do not have the right to contract. In Colorado, Mississippi, and the District of Columbia, the age of 21 must be attained before a person can make a binding contract. All other states have set the legal age at either 18 or 19. (Formerly,

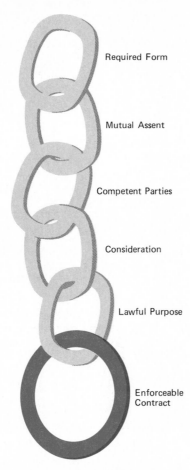

Required Form

Mutual Assent

Competent Parties

Consideration

Lawful Purpose

Enforceable
Contract

FIGURE 19-6
Required Elements for a Valid Contract

most states regarded those under 21 as minors.) People under the legal age may not make enforceable contracts except for necessities. Minors have the right to rescind or avoid contracts. For example, if a 15-year-old boy buys a bicycle and then demolishes it, he can return the wreck to the store and get a refund.

The Twenty-sixth Amendment, adopted in 1971, confers suffrage at age 18. But each state has the right to enact laws to determine the legal status of those between 18 and 21. For instance, the Uniform Minor Student Capacity to Borrow Act, passed by several states, permits minors to borrow money for payment of college education costs. These loans are enforceable under the terms of this legislation.

Consideration. Ordinarily, a promise as part of a contract is not binding unless it is supported by a consideration. CONSIDERATION is *something of value pledged in exchange for a promise.* It may consist of money, goods, services, or even another promise to do or not to do something a person has a legal right to do. For example, Jones agrees to buy an automobile from Bailey for $600 and gives Bailey a $10 down payment. Here the consideration is the $10 exchanged for the automobile. Jones has a legal obligation for $590, and Bailey has an obligation to deliver the automobile.

> An uncle promised to pay his nephew $5,000 if he would refrain from drinking, using tobacco, swearing, and playing cards or pool for money until he was 21 years old. The nephew did this and wrote for the money on his twenty-first birthday.
>
> The uncle replied that he would pay the money; but, "when you are capable of taking care of it." Two years later, the uncle died without having made payment. The administrator of the estate refused to pay the $5,000, and the nephew sued. The court held that a legal contract existed. The nephew had a legal right to use liquor and tobacco, and giving those things up constituted the necessary consideration for a legal contract.

Lawful Purpose. To be binding, a contract must involve a lawful purpose. In states where gambling is illegal, promises to pay gambling debts, even when in writing, are not enforceable. A contract for payment of interest in excess of the legal rate (known as usury) is not binding.

Required Form. Contracts may not need to be written to be enforceable. Oral agreements are enforceable, although there may be some difficulty in trying to prove any disputed facts.

Section 2-201 of the UCC modifies the Statute of Frauds concerning a contract for the sale of goods for $500 or more. This modification provides

FIGURE 19-7
An Agreement or Contract Between Two Parties

FORM 108—NJARB

STANDARD LISTING CONTRACT ADOPTED BY NEW JERSEY ASSOCIATION
OF REALTOR BOARDS FOR USE OF NEW JERSEY REALTORS

To.. Dated...

In consideration of your listing and undertaking to procure a purchaser for the property described on the reverse side hereof, the undersigned hereby authorizes you to sell said property at the price and upon the terms set forth on the reverse side hereof, or at any lesser price or terms the undersigned may agree to accept therefor, and upon your procuring a purchaser during the term of this authorization, the undersigned agrees to pay you a commission of   per cent of the purchase price.

Your authority and rights hereunder shall be for the period of (   ) months from the date hereof.

Signed..

Accepted:
                                             ....
.... Address..
                                                           Owner

that unless otherwise agreed to, a contract for the sale of goods for $500 or more is not enforceable unless the contract is written. The written language must be sufficient to prove that the parties agreed to the sale. The contract shown in Figure 19-7 contains the essential elements that are binding on both parties.

Remedies for Breach of Contract. For various reasons, not all contracts, whether oral or written, are carried out. When a contract is breached (broken), the injured party may decide to pursue legal remedies. For example, the injured party can avoid carrying out part of the agreement, acting in effect as though there had been no contract. The right to cancel a contract is known as the **right of rescission,** *rescission* being a form of the word *rescind.*

Or the injured party may bring an action for actual damages. Even if this person has not had an actual loss from the breach, he or she is still entitled to a judgment for a nominal damage. The term NOMINAL DAMAGE refers to *a trifling sum of money awarded to a person in recognition of a technical infraction by the defendant of the plaintiff's rights.* These awards are often for one dollar.

A third remedy is for the injured party to ask for "specific performance of the contract" by the defendant. A court does not always compel performance if there is some other adequate remedy at law. If a person ordered a one-of-a-kind antique Bentley, specific performance would be an appropriate remedy. Money damages would not be adequate if the seller failed to deliver, because another car could not be purchased. The buyer has the right to specific performance of the contract, to have the car delivered.

As a rule, damages in excess of actual loss (for the purpose of punishing the defendant) cannot be recovered for breach of contract. Such damages are called **punitive damages** (for punishment).

The Statute of Limitations. Each state has a statute-of-limitations act requiring that an action at law be started within a time limit after the infraction. Beyond that time, the remedy is barred. The statute does not have the effect of discharging the contract. It is a defense for breach because no legal action was taken during the prescribed time.

THE UNIFORM COMMERCIAL CODE (UCC)

Since the 1950s, there has been a trend toward the adoption of a uniform code applicable to a variety of recurring business transactions. Originally, business laws varied from state to state. Firms doing business in several states were often confused by the lack of uniformity of statutes regarding business transactions.

To achieve a nationwide uniformity, the National Conference of Commissioners on Uniform State Laws and the American Law Institute agreed on a uniform code. In 1952, the Uniform Commercial Code was published and circulated among the states. The UCC has been enacted as law by the legislatures of every state except Louisiana. The adoption of a uniform code has been recognized as an important step in reducing confusion in interstate trade.

The UCC regulates transactions involving sales, commercial paper, bank deposits, letters of credit, and warehouse receipts. It also includes bills of lading, bulk transfers, securities, and contract rights.

Let us look more closely at what the code says about sales, commercial paper, and secured transactions.

SALES   If you purchase a new stereo system, you have completed an ordinary transaction involving the sale of goods. Goods must be tangible and movable — this covers everything from toothpaste to tractors. Even when you enter a retail store and pay cash for an item, a contract exists.

Generally, the seller's obligation is to deliver conforming goods and the buyer's is to accept and pay for them. Any implied warranties are a part of the seller's obligation. The seller may also have delivery or shipping obligations.

The buyer has the right to inspect the goods before accepting and paying for them. Payment is due when the buyer receives the goods, unless other arrangements have been made.

When the seller fails to deliver goods according to agreement, there are several remedies available to the buyer:

1. The buyer can cancel the contract.
2. The buyer can recover any prepayments.
3. The buyer can "cover" — buy the goods elsewhere and sue for damages for the difference.
4. If the goods fail to conform to the agreement, the buyer can reject the delivery.

When the buyer breaks the sale agreement, the seller may choose from several alternatives as well:

1. The seller can cancel the contract.
2. The seller can withhold delivery.
3. The seller can resell the goods.
4. Sometimes the seller can sue for the purchase price.
5. The seller can retake possession of the goods if the agreement is not kept.

The buyer has the *right* to inspect goods before paying and should have the good sense to become well-informed about the product before making a choice. (Photo by Marc Anderson.)

A LEMON

A man bought a new automobile in December and drove it to Wisconsin in January. The car stood outside overnight and the next day would not run, since there was ice and rust in the transmission. This seemed to confirm a later statement that the car had been in a flood. The dealer offered to repair the car, but the buyer said no, he wanted a new one. He sued the dealer and manufacturer.

The verdict was ultimately rendered for the buyer. The judge said, "We think it is clear that the plaintiff's confidence . . . in his new car was severely undermined. He had bargained for a new car . . . instead he received a product which he understandably feared was what is known in popular parlance as a ''lemon.''

WHEN DOES TITLE PASS?
If goods are damaged or lost, who is responsible for the loss? To answer this, it is necessary to know when title to personal property passes from the seller to the buyer.

The general rule as to the passing of title is that the buyer can ordinarily obtain no better title to goods than the seller had.

Cash Sale.   In a cash transaction, the title to goods usually passes immediately. Generally, the one who holds title must bear the loss.

Goods Sold C.O.D.   In C.O.D. (cash on delivery) sales, title passes to the buyer when the goods are delivered by the seller to the common carrier (transportation company). Generally, the seller designates the carrier as his or her agent to collect the purchase price as part of the condition of delivery.

Goods Sold F.O.B.   The term **F.O.B.** means **free on board.** During the early history of this nation, goods were shipped on canal boats or railroad cars. The shipment was said to be "made on board." Charges for shipping on board were set by either the shipping point or the destination point, known as the F.O.B. point.

When goods are sold "F.O.B. factory," title passes to the buyer when the goods are delivered to the carrier at the shipping point. The buyer pays the shipping charges. Any damages en route are a problem for the buyer, not the manufacturer or seller.

If goods are sold "F.O.B. destination," title passes to the buyer when the goods reach their destination. In this case, the seller is to pay the transportation charges. The seller must bear the risk to point of destination unless the goods are insured.

Goods Sold C.I.F.   Under a C.I.F. contract, the buyer pays the seller the *cost* of the goods, *insurance* on them, and the *freight* to their destination. The C.I.F. obligation of putting the goods in the care of the proper carrier is with the seller. The buyer bears the risk of loss after they have been delivered to the carrier.

Goods Sold at Auction.   In sales by auction, the UCC provides that title passes to the buyer when the auctioneer announces, by the fall of the gavel or in some other manner, that the sale is final.

Sale on Installment Plan. Under the UCC, possession is transferred to the buyer for an installment sale, but title remains with the seller as security until the price is paid. Risk of loss is assumed by the buyer as soon as the goods are delivered.

Sale on Approval. Goods are often sold with the understanding that the buyer has the privilege of returning them. This is known as a sale on approval. The UCC provides that in the absence of a contrary agreement, the title and risk of loss remain with the seller until the sale is agreed upon by the buyer.

For example, if goods are accidentally lost or destroyed on their return following a sale on approval, the loss must be borne by the seller. But if the sale had been on consignment, the loss would have been borne by the buyer.

Sale on Consignment. A consignment sale differs from the ordinary sale in that the title remains in the hands of the shipper, known as the consignor, until such time as the goods are sold by the retailer, known as the consignee. A consignment sale allows the consignor to control the price and to reclaim the goods in case of bankruptcy.

COMMERCIAL PAPER   Commercial paper (or negotiable instruments) is a contractual obligation that can be transferred from person to person by delivery, or by indorsement and delivery. No one knows exactly when commercial paper was first used, but it probably appeared in some form during the Middle Ages.

Kinds of Commercial Paper. Under the UCC, bank drafts, checks, certificates of deposit, bonds, and promissory notes are commercial paper. Although negotiable instruments are contracts, they differ from ordinary contracts in two ways: (1) There is an element of negotiability not found in all other contracts. (2) There is a *presumption of consideration* in all negotiable paper. A negotiable promissory note is shown in Figure 19-8.

$100.00   September 25   19 8X

For value received I promise to pay to ALEX BROWN

or order --- One Hundred and no/100 --- Dollars, in Lawful Money of the United States of America, with interest thereon, in Lawful Money, at the rate of 9 per cent. per ANNUM from date until paid, payable in four installments of not less than $25.00 in any one payment, together with the full amount of interest due on this note at time of payment of each installment. The first payment to be made on the first day of November 19 8X, and a like payment on the first day of each month thereafter, until the whole sum, principal and interest, has been paid; if any of said installments are not so paid, the whole of said principal sum and interest, to become immediately due and collectible at the option of the holder of this note. And in case suit or action is instituted to collect this note or any portion thereof -- I -- promise to pay such additional sum as the Court may adjudge reasonable as attorney's fees in said suit or action.

Due December 1   198X

At FIRST NATIONAL BANK
Portland, Oregon

No. 65

JOY FOX
4200 Main Street
Portland, Oregon
(Maker)

AICO-UTILITY Line Form No. 60-042   Installment Note

FIGURE 19-8
A negotiable installment promissory note.

How Commercial Paper Is Transferred.   Transfer of commercial paper from one person to another is by the simple process of **indorsement,** a signature that should appear on the back of the instrument.[1] The person to whom the instrument is transferred is the **indorsee.** This person is also the **holder in due course,** which means that he or she must either be in possession of the instrument properly indorsed or be the bearer of the instrument, having been named as the payee. A holder in due course is one who acquires the instrument under the following conditions:

1. It must be complete and regular on its face.
2. The holder must have given consideration (value) for the paper.
3. It must be accepted in good faith.
4. The instrument must be accepted without notice of defects in the title or defense against payment.

If you accept a bank check by indorsement under these conditions, you are a holder in due course and the legal owner of the check. You may enforce collection of the instrument against prior parties regardless of their claims or defenses.

If the person who wrote the check has a personal defense, he still has to pay the person who presents the check for payment. For example, if a woman writes a check to pay for fresh lobster but later discovers the lobster is spoiled, she must still pay the person who presents the check for payment. This is true, however, only when the check presentor knew nothing of the spoiled lobster.

SECURED TRANSACTIONS   Most businesses today enter into some kind of debtor/creditor relationship in day-to-day operations. Sometimes that credit can be gained only if the debtor puts up some kind of security or collateral.

When a creditor grants credit, he realizes that the debtor might default. So he wants to retain a specific interest in the debtor's property that can be used to get his money back. For the businessperson to have an enforceable security interest in the collateral, three things must occur:

1. There must be a security agreement describing the collateral signed by the debtor.
2. The secured party must give value (or consideration).
3. The debtor must have rights in the collateral.

When a debtor defaults on a secured transaction, the creditor has a right to the collateral. Usually, the creditor's rights are as stated in the security agreement, unless bankruptcy is involved.

BANKRUPTCY   Bankruptcy is a system whereby an honest but financially overburdened person can be relieved of obligations and start anew. This is usually done when a court takes whatever property a debtor possesses and wipes out his debts. Bankruptcy can be voluntary (debtor files) or involuntary (creditor files).

---

[1] The spelling *indorsement* appears in the Uniform Commercial Code. The spelling *endorsement* is also acceptable.

An involuntary case may be filed only if the debtor is unable to pay debts as they become due; no act or misconduct on the part of the debtor need be shown. The debtor can claim certain exemptions from bankruptcy. These include his or her residence up to $7,500, interest in a car, up to $1,200 of household furnishings, and clothes to a specified amount.

Bankruptcy proceedings are under the control of a federal district judge. The chief officers of the court are the referee and trustee. The referee in bankruptcy is generally in almost complete charge of proceedings. The creditors are brought together, and they elect a trustee who liquidates the assets and distributes them among the creditors. Claims against the bankrupt's assets are paid in the following order:

1. Administration and court costs, including trustee's expenses
2. Wages due employees earned prior to bankruptcy
3. Expenses for disposing of assets
4. Taxes due federal, state, or local districts
5. Debts set by law due persons entitled to priority

Any business or individual can go into voluntary bankruptcy if liabilities exceed assets and total debt is over $1,000. There were more than 35,000 bankruptcies per year during the 1980s. The majority of these were voluntary bankruptcies. Obviously, since creditors usually receive only pennies on the dollar, they do not often initiate involuntary bankruptcy.

A Conference at the Bench in the Courtroom.
(Photo by Bill Bachman, Photo Researchers, Inc.)

INFORMATION MANAGEMENT AND DECISION MAKING

THE LAW OF PROPERTY

The term **property** refers to a right to own something and use it. The law of property not only is an important part of the free-enterprise system but involves your right under the Constitution to own property. This right cannot be denied without due process of law. Daniel Webster said that due process denotes "law which hears before it condemns; which proceeds upon inquiry; and which renders judgment only after trial."

Title to real property is by deed. (Photos by Irene Springer; Erwin W. Cole, Soil Conservation Service, USDA; Margaret Zeaf, Techbuilt.)

The law recognizes different classes of property, generally classified as real and personal. Property is also classified as tangible and intangible.

Real Property. Broadly classified, REAL PROPERTY is *land and anything permanently affixed to it that in a general way is immovable.* Trees and shrubbery, when planted, are real property. Buildings and fences are also considered real property when they are attached to the soil.

The State of Texas,
County of HARRIS

} **Know All Men by These Presents:**

That JAMES GREEN, a widower not since remarried

of the County of   HARRIS   State of   TEXAS   for and in consideration

of the sum of   Ten Thousand ($10,000)--

--- DOLLARS

to be   paid, and secured to be paid, by the grantee

hereinafter named -- **as follows:**

The sum of one thousand ($1,000) dollars to be paid on the delivery of this instru-
ment, the receipt of which is hereby acknowledged, and the further sum of seventy-
five ($75.00) dollars the first day of each and every month thereafter until the
purchase price has been paid in full. All of said sums except the first payment of
one thousand ($1,000) dollars are to be represented by promissory notes in the amount
of seventy-five ($75.00) dollars and to bear interest at the rate of six (6) per cent
per annum from date until paid,

es

have Granted, Sold and Conveyed, and by these presents do/Grant, Sell and Convey, unto the said
WALTER H. JENSEN

of the County of   HARRIS   State of   TEXAS   all that certain

TRACE OR PARCEL OF LAND DESCRIBED AS FOLLOWS, TO-WIT:

     Lot Three (3) Block Six (6) in the OPAL Addition, City of South Houston,
     in the County of Harris and State of Texas.

     TO HAVE AND TO HOLD the above described premises, together with all and singular the rights
and appurtenances thereto in anywise belonging unto the said Grantee, his

es

heirs and assigns forever and he   do/hereby bind

heirs, executors and administrators, to Warrant and Forever Defend, all and singular the said premises
unto the said   grantee, his

heirs and assigns, against every person whomsoever lawfully claiming, or to claim the same, or any
part thereof.

     But it is expressly agreed and stipulated that the Vendor's Lien is retained against the above
described property, premises and improvements, until the above described note , and all interest thereon
are fully paid according to   face and tenor, effect and reading, when this deed shall become
absolute.

     WITNESS this   hand   at, South Houston
this 25th   **day of** November   19

Witness at request of Grantor:

Reeder Greenwood

Coral Griffin

James Green

Walter H. Jensen

FIGURE 19-9
Warranty Deed.
A warranty deed is used to convey title to real property. This type of deed may also contain statements, usually by the grantor, that other things will be done or are true.

Personal Property. *Property that is movable and otherwise not classed as real property* is PERSONAL PROPERTY. **Tangible** personal property includes fixtures, goods, furniture, clothing, jewelry, and so forth. **Intangible** property has no physical existence. It is only the right to property and includes stocks, bonds, accounts receivable, insurance policies, and bank accounts. Mortgages, letters of credit, checks, and money orders are also intangible property.

The WARRANTY DEED is *a written instrument that warrants title to real property without defects.* The warranty deed cannot transfer a better title than the grantor (owner) had. However, the grantor covenants that he or she has valid title to the property and will indemnify the grantee if a loss is sustained owing to a defective title. To become effective, a warranty deed must be recorded by the new owner. A warranty deed is shown in figure 19-9.

REAL PROPERTY

The highest form of ownership one can possess in real property is an ESTATE IN FEE SIMPLE. The owner has absolute and entire interest in the land. The owner can sell it, will it to another, or use it to pay debts. Real property can also be rented or leased or used as security for a loan (mortgage).

Lease. When you own your own business, you may find that it is more satisfactory to lease real or personal property than to own it. Your agreement with the landlord (owner) to use the property is a **lease.** Your landlord is the **lessor** and you are the **lessee.** Under the Statute of Frauds, a lease for longer than a year must be in writing to be enforceable. The ground on which Radio City is located in New York City is leased for ninety-nine years. The more formal written lease, such as that shown in Figure 19-10, usually contains the following:

1. Date of agreement
2. Names of lessor and lessee
3. Property description
4. Duration of lease
5. Manner of paying rent
6. Responsibility for making repairs
7. Liability for injury to third party
8. Right to sublet or assign

Lease agreements have become popular methods for financing both small and large enterprises.

Mortgages. One MORTGAGES *property when it is pledged as security for a loan.* A mortgage against real property is called a real estate mortgage. *A mortgage against personal property* is called a CHATTEL MORTGAGE. When a person who holds a mortgage against property sues to take title to it, this is called a **foreclosure.**

PERSONAL PROPERTY

Personal property (chattels) consists of all property other than real estate. Personal property includes clothing, furniture, food, jewelry, motor vehicles, animals, books, and securities. The basic principles of the law of contracts apply to the law of personal-property sales. Under the UCC, additional rules have been adopted to cover personal-property sales. We discussed these rules, which cover such items as warranties, remedies, and passage of title, when we discussed the Uniform Commercial Code.

The State of Texas,
County of

} **Know All Men by These Presents:**

Made this   2nd   day of   MARCH   , A. D. 19   , by and between

Smithson R. Conway--, known herein as LESSOR,

and   Rollo J. Jenkins-- , known herein as LESSEE,

(The terms "Lessor" and "Lessee" shall be construed in the singular or plural number according as they respectively represent one or more than one person.)

WITNESSETH, That the said Lessor does by these presents Lease and Demise unto the said Lessee the following described property, to-wit: Lying and being situated in the County of   WALLER   , State of Texas, and being A single family dwelling located at 1301 First Street in the town of Hempstead, consix (6) rooms and bath.

for the term of twelve (12) months   beginning the   2nd   day of   MARCH A. D. 19   and ending the   1st   day of   MARCH, 19   , paying therefor the sum of   Twelve hundred ($1200)------------------------------------ DOLLARS, payable   monthly installments the second day of each month in advance.

upon the conditions and covenants following:

First. That Lessee will well and PUNCTUALLY pay said rents in manner and form as hereinbefore specified, and quietly deliver up said premises on the day of the expiration of this lease, in as good condition as the same were in when received, reasonable wear and tear thereof excepted.

Second. That the said premises shall be used for   Family residence by the lessee and his immediate family.

and for no other purpose.

Third. That Lessee will not sub-let said premises, or any part thereof, to any person or persons whatsoever, without the consent of said Lessor, IN WRITING, thereto first obtained.

Fourth. That on failure to pay the rent in advance, as aforesaid, or to comply with any of the foregoing obligations, or in violation of any of the foregoing covenants, the Lessor may declare this lease forfeited at Lessor's discretion and Lessor or Lessor's agent or attorney shall have the power to enter and hold, occupy and repossess the entire premises hereinbefore described, as before the execution of these presents.

IN TESTIMONY WHEREOF, The parties to this agreement have hereunto set their hands in duplicate, the day and year above written.

Smithson R. Conway , LESSOR

Rollo J. Jenkins , LESSEE

FIGURE 19-10
A Lease

A bill of sale is one way to transfer title to tangible personal property, and a deed, as we have noted, is used to transfer title to real property. Some goods are sold on consignment. Bailments are not sales but separate circumstances.

BAILMENTS   **The essence of a bailment contract is that one person (the bailor) places personal property with another (the bailee) for some purpose.** It is understood by the parties that the articles will be returned to the bailor when that purpose has been served. Since there is no passage of title, this means a bailment is not a sale.

The law requires that ordinary and reasonable care be exercised by the bailee while holding the articles. Common carriers, such as airlines and bus companies, have a bailment relationship with those who entrust their baggage to the carrier. Examples of bailment also include borrowing your neighbor's automobile, leaving your watch in a jewelry store for repairs, and storing a trunk in a public warehouse.

THE LAW OF AGENCY

One of the most common legal business relationships is that between a principal and his or her agent. An AGENT is *one who is authorized to represent another person in dealings with a third party. The person for whom the agent acts* is the PRINCIPAL. The usual way of creating an agency is by verbal or written appointment. A formal written appointment is called a **power of attorney.** A proxy form is an example of an agency relationship. When stockholders are notified of a forthcoming corporation meeting, they are given proxy forms. If a stockholder will be unable to attend the annual meeting of stockholders to vote, he or she may appoint another stockholder to be his or her agent to vote the shares.

DUTIES IN AGENCY The principal is obliged to compensate the agent for services according to the contract; to reimburse the agent for necessary expenses unless otherwise agreed; and to pay for losses sustained by the agent. The agent is expected to obey the instructions of the principal; to exercise due skill and loyalty to the principal; and to account for money or property entrusted to the agent.

The principal is liable to the third party for all lawful agreements made by the agent. The principal is also liable for any damages caused by the agent in performing his or her normal duties.

An agency may be created to perform almost any act that the principal could lawfully do. Swearing to the truth of documents, testifying in court, and making a will are exceptions.

Any person who is competent may act through an agent. Groups of people may appoint agents. An agent is usually a person but may be a partnership or corporation. An agency may be ended by one or both parties to the agency agreement.

An **agent** is distinguished from an **employee,** who is not hired to represent the principal, and from an independent **contractor,** whom the principal does not control.

> Sally purchased furniture from a store and found it damaged. The store sent an independent contractor to her home to repair the furniture. He identified himself as being from the store. The lacquer he put on the furniture exploded and hurt Sally. She sued both the store and the contractor. The court held that the contractor was acting as an *agent* for the store, because there was reasonable belief that the contractor was acting in the store's behalf. Both defendants were liable.

GEORGE P. SHULTZ

George P. Shultz was sworn in as the sixtieth U.S. secretary of state on July 16, 1982. He came to that position from the Bechtel Corporation. Prior to this appointment, Mr. Shultz was chairman of President Reagan's Economic Policy Advisory Board.

Shultz graduated from Princeton University in 1942, receiving a B.A. degree in economics. In 1949, he earned a Ph.D. degree in industrial economics from the Massachusetts Institute of Technology. Mr. Shultz was appointed professor of industrial relations at the University of Chicago Graduate School of Business in 1957. He was named dean of that school in 1962.

Mr. Shultz served in the administration of President Nixon as secretary of labor, as director of the Office of Management and Budget, and as secretary of the treasury. He also served as chairman of the Council on Economic Policy.

In 1974, Shultz joined the Bechtel Corporation. Until his appointment as secretary of state, he was president and a director of Bechtel Group, Inc.

Mr. Shultz was born in New York City and spent his childhood in Englewood, New Jersey. He is married to the former Helena M. O'Brien of Nashua, New Hampshire. They have five children.

ETHICS IN BUSINESS

Now that we have examined certain laws pertaining to business transactions, let us turn to the subject of ethics in business. One theme in this discussion is that if business would conduct itself ethically, perhaps fewer laws would be needed.

THE MEANING OF ETHICS

Ethics is a segment of philosophy concerned with values of human conduct. The term ETHICS refers to *a code of conduct that guides a person in dealing with others.* Ethics relates to the social rules that influence people to be honest in their dealings. Ethical rules differ from legal rules. Ethical rules are not enforced by public authority, whereas legal rules are. Society expects businesspeople to act ethically. This responsibility also applies to those not in business. In fact, society expects businesspeople and politicians to maintain even higher standards than others. It is the price they pay for being in the public eye.

Implicit in ethics is the concept of **equity,** a commonplace legal term meaning "justice." The Emperor Justinian I (483 – 565) said that equity means "to live honestly, to harm nobody, and to render every man his due."

Ethics and morals seem to be related. The term **morals** refers to a code of conduct that is often part of our religious beliefs. Most religions have beliefs that say essentially, "Do unto others as you would have them do unto you."

MAKING BUSINESS MORE ETHICAL

Society has a right to expect businesspeople to be ethical. When business fails to meet the expectations set by society, or when business does not comply with the basic social codes of conduct, then society—through the government—often demands that it be required to maintain higher ethical standards.

Many people are cynical about the conduct of business. There are people who believe that business is based only on greed and that profit is the only goal of business. Neither is necessarily true.

Underlying all managerial behavior is each individual manager's personal set of values. These values are not the same for all managers. Certainly businesses do seek profits, but profit is only one value underlying business decisions. Every company exists to make money and would not survive if it did not, but there are ethical constraints on the process.

It has been proposed that industries draw up their own codes of ethics, which members of the industry would accept and apply. One of the heartening signs of our times is that businesspeople are becoming increasingly concerned about the ethical implications of their work.

One attempt to make business more ethical, the Foreign Corrupt Practices Act, has met with mixed reviews. Passed in 1977, the act outlaws the payment of bribes to foreign officials by American businesses. Bribes have never been a major part of American business, but in some countries, they are very much a part of doing business. Some firms argue that the law puts them at a disadvantage in international dealings, but there seems to be little support for changing the law.

CURRENT ISSUE

SHOULD U.S. LAWS RESTRICT AMERICAN COMPANIES FROM INVESTING IN VENTURES IN FOREIGN COUNTRIES THAT VIOLATE HUMAN RIGHTS?

Some Americans feel that U.S. corporations should not be allowed to invest in countries that violate human rights. Others take a contrary position, holding that business is business and that foreign politics is separate from business interests.

With which of the following statements do you agree, and with which do you disagree?

1. The United States has a responsibility to work to improve the welfare of people who live in other countries.
2. Trade restrictions are an effective means of strengthening human rights.
3. Attaining a higher worldwide morality is as important as making profits.
4. The United States should not become involved in the internal affairs of other countries.
5. The idea of free trade among nations should not become entangled with human-rights considerations.
6. If a U.S. company did not do business in those countries where human rights are violated, its participation in international trade would almost cease.
7. We have no accepted criteria by which to judge others when human rights are being violated.

What is your opinion regarding American companies doing business abroad? That is, should they become involved in the politics of the host countries?

CONFLICT-OF-INTEREST ISSUE

One of the most discussed ethical problems is the conflict-of-interest issue involving business executives. In such a situation, an executive makes a decision as president of company A and approves, without regard to competitive bidding, the purchase of a large order from company B. The executive owns stock in company B and, by virtue of this large order, will benefit substantially.

What is wrong with this practice? Is it a violation of any law? In most cases, it is not. But it may be if it can be established that company A acted in restraint of trade by circumventing bidding standards. This practice is, however, a violation of ethics. Another conflict of interest is the use of privileged information obtained by one's official position to acquire personal gain. Businesspeople who accept high government office are expected to sever their financial interests in those firms that have government contracts. This is to avoid a conflict of interest.

SUMMARY OF KEY CONCEPTS

The two main sources of law in the United States are common law and statutory law. Common law is unwritten law, or case law. Statutory law is written law.

Laws concerned with the rights and liabilities of individuals, partnerships, and organizations are private laws. Under the U.S. Constitution, each state has the right to enact its own laws. The Uniform Commercial Code embraces the area of business law.

In the judicial system, federal courts are concerned with cases involving federal jurisdiction, and state courts are concerned with cases involving state laws.

A *contract* is a binding agreement between two or more competent parties. To be binding, it must contain the following elements: mutual assent, competent parties, consideration, and lawful purpose—and required form in some instances.

The law recognizes two kinds of property: real property and personal property. Real property consists of an interest in land. Personal property includes objects that are movable and not attached to the soil.

A warranty deed is used to convey title of property ownership.

A negotiable instrument is a contract that can be transferred by indorsement. Examples of negotiable instruments are checks, notes, and drafts. Under the UCC, an instrument, to be negotiable, must meet certain requirements.

A negotiable instrument may be payable "to bearer" and "to order of." Title passes by indorsement if the instrument is payable to order of a person. If payable to bearer, the instrument is transferred without indorsement, the same as money.

Agency is another legal relationship. The parties to agency are principal and agent.

Each state has a statute of limitations requiring that a legal action be started within a certain time after the infraction. Beyond this date, the remedy sought is barred.

Ethics is broader than law. It involves a violation of a moral standard concerning the difference between right and wrong.

BUSINESS TERMS

You should be able to match these business terms with the statements that follow:

a. ABSTRACT OF TITLE
b. AGENT
c. CHATTEL MORTGAGE
d. CONSIDERATION
e. CONTRACT
f. DEFENDANT
g. EQUITY
h. ETHICS

i. JUDICIAL SYSTEM
j. MORTGAGE
k. PLAINTIFF
l. PUBLIC LAW
m. REAL PROPERTY
n. WARRANTY
o. WARRANTY DEED

1. A branch of unwritten law that grants a more adequate or equitable remedy than is available under common law
2. Law that deals with topics with which the general public is concerned
3. The branch of government authorized to hear controversies between parties and to apply the law to these disputes
4. The party against whom legal action is taken in the courts
5. Something of value pledged in a contract agreement in exchange for a promise or property
6. An agreement between two competent parties that is legally enforceable
7. One who is authorized to act on behalf of another in dealings with third parties
8. The land and anything permanently affixed to it that in a general way is immovable
9. A written instrument that warrants title to real property without defects
10. A written summary of all conveyances, mortgages, and liens affecting the title
11. A pledge of property as security for a loan
12. A mortgage pledging tangible personal property as security
13. An express or implied promise made by the seller about goods to induce the buyer to purchase them
14. A code of conduct that guides a person in dealing with others

REVIEW QUESTIONS

1. What purposes does the Uniform Commercial Code serve?
2. What are the two main routes for appealing decisions to the U.S. Supreme Court?
3. What types of remedies are available to the injured party in the case of a breach of contract?
4. What requirements must an instrument meet if it is to be negotiable?
5. When does the title pass to the buyer under an installment contract?

1. Why do managers of a business need a knowledge of business law?
2. Explain what is meant by the elements required to make a contract binding on both parties.
3. Explain the difference between an *express* and an *implied* warranty.
4. When should a person use a blank endorsement on a check? A full endorsement? A restrictive endorsement?
5. Why is conflict of interest considered a problem in ethics?

BUSINESS CASES

19-1 WEST LUMBER COMPANY VS. H & S CONSTRUCTION COMPANY

Sam Long, owner of the West Lumber Company in Boise, Idaho, brought an action to collect a debt from the H & S Construction Company, a partnership owned by Charles Henderson and Jim Sellers.

The facts show that on June 12, 1981, Henderson introduced Jim Sellers to Sam Long as a partner in the H & S Construction Company. At that time, Long recalled that he had done business with Henderson about five years before, when Henderson was in the construction business by himself. Because Henderson had always paid his bills promptly, Long instructed his cashier to obtain an up-to-date credit rating about the H & S partnership.

On June 16, Henderson bought a small amount of building materials, which he paid for by check. And during the next thirty days, he placed several more small orders, which he also paid for by check.

On October 15, 1981, Henderson placed another order, which totaled $9,800. He paid the full amount of the bill by check ten days later. The following day, the bank informed Long that Henderson's check had been returned owing to insufficient funds. Unable to locate Henderson, Long called Sellers, who stated that he was no longer a partner. He disclaimed liability for this debt. Two months later, Long filed suit against the partnership to recover the debt.

1. Who is liable for the debt? Why?
2. What precaution might Long have taken to avoid this suit?

19-2 A SALE ON APPROVAL

Helen Ray ordered two fur coats from a local department store. Each of the coats was valued at $1,500 and was to be delivered to her home in the same city on approval for three days. When the coats arrived, the ticket clearly showed that this was a sale on approval. Two days later, the coats were destroyed by a fire that started from an unknown origin in Helen's home. The fire occurred on a Saturday night, and since Sunday was the third day of the three-day period, Helen was unable to notify the store because it was not open.

On the following Monday, Helen reported the loss to the store and refused to pay for the coats, claiming that she had no insurance protection and that the title had not actually passed to her because the transaction was a sale on approval.

1. Who is liable for the loss?
2. What is the rule in this case?

PART 6
CAREERS IN ACCOUNTING

FIELDS OF ACCOUNTING

Accounting practice can be divided into three areas: private or industrial, governmental, and public.

Private Accountants. In private businesses, accountants usually start as junior accountants or clerks. Accountants are needed in proprietorships, partnerships, corporations, hospitals, schools, and nonprofit organizations. Private accountants may serve as managers, auditors, cost analysts, tax specialists, and financial managers.

Government Accountants. Government accountants are those employed by local, state, and federal agencies. The accountant in government may take an examination given by the Civil Service Commission or a state merit system. The applicant is then assigned to a separate government agency or bureau. Both the Federal Bureau of Investigation and the Internal Revenue Service employ people with accounting backgrounds. The applicant may be employed as an accountant, cost analyst, auditor, or tax specialist.

Public Accountants. Individuals and independent organizations that specialize in selling their accounting services to businesses and individuals are called PUBLIC ACCOUNTANTS. The public accountant installs accounting systems, audits accounting records, prepares financial statements, and advises clients on taxes and other matters. Public accounting firms are increasing their services to clients to include consultation on problems relating to taxes, management, and corporate strategy.

ACCOUNTING AS A PROFESSIONAL FIELD

The certified public accountant is the top member of his or her profession. The term **certified public accountant** (CPA) is the professional certification for public accountants. The CPA designation is issued by the State Board of Accountancy of each state. About three-fourths of all states require prospective CPAs to be college graduates. Some states require U.S. citizenship; others do not. Most states require at least two years of accounting experience as a prerequisite for taking the examinations. All states require CPA candidates to pass an examination administered by the American Institute of Certified Public Accountants. The examination covers accounting theory, accounting practice, auditing, and business law.

It is not necessary to have a CPA certificate to practice private accounting. But without it, one cannot practice public accounting and certify accounting statements. The CPA does not guarantee the accuracy of the client's financial statements. He or she does, however, certify that the information presented in the financial statements conforms to the generally accepted accounting principles sanctioned by the profession.

Most colleges of business administration offer advanced courses in accounting to prepare the student for the CPA examination. These include accounting systems, accounting theory, auditing, cost accounting, income taxation, and CPA problems.

OTHER CAREER OPPORTUNITIES

In addition to the three main fields of accountancy, there are other specialized areas providing career opportunities, such as:

1. Bank auditing
2. Budget officer
3. Cashier
4. Computer programmer
5. College accounting teacher
6. Systems installer
7. Systems analyst
8. Income tax specialist

CAREER OPPORTUNITIES IN DATA PROCESSING

Decisions are based on information, and that information must be assembled, organized, and interpreted. A person involved in this work might hold any of a number of titles, such as research specialist, economist, statistician, data-processing manager, or systems analyst.

Entry-level positions in data processing may or may not require formal education at the college level. Such positions include:

Keypunch Operator
Data Processing Clerk
Remote Terminal Operator
Computer Operator

Administrative positions in data processing include these:

The *data-processing manager* plans, coordinates, and directs the data-processing activities of the entire organization. He or she must supervise the work of others and should possess high managerial as well as technical skills.

The *manager of computer operations* directs the computer installation, schedules computer time, allocates personnel, maintains the program library, and controls operations within the computer center.

The *systems analyst* creates an ordered system for data collection, processing, and the production of useful information. He or she improves controls and decision making and, at the same time, makes the most efficient use of available data-processing equipment. The largely abstract nature of the work, like that of the computer programmer, requires strong logical and creative abilities.

The *computer programmer* must work closely with the systems analyst to define the problem, analyze data and report requirements, prepare a detailed flow chart of the logical solution, convert this logical diagram to coded instructions for the computer, and test the program to remove errors. Programmers must completely understand the business or scientific problem they are attempting to solve. They must be able to work with a team or alone and be able to communicate with management personnel. They must be sticklers for detail, be logical thinkers, and have no end of patience.

Actually, in data processing, a person's title does not delineate clearly just what the work is. One person with the title of programmer may spend most of the workday writing out specific directions for the computer. Another programmer may spend most of the workday developing problems and even doing systems design.

CAREERS IN BUSINESS LAW

The combination of training in business and a law degree has proved to be a good one. Lawyers have a wide variety of career opportunities available to them. Obviously, the career in private practice is available, and, for some people, very attractive. In addition, when combined with business training and/or experience, many of the following are possibilities, and more as well:

Tax Attorney
Securities Attorney
Corporate Attorney
Real Estate Law
Business-Law Instructor
Equal Employment Lawyer
Labor Lawyer/Arbitrator
Specialist in International Business Law
Corporate-Merger Specialist
Antitrust Lawyer

INFORMATION MANAGEMENT AND DECISION MAKING

GOVERNMENT AND WORLD BUSINESS

The government was not involved in the partnership agreement between Roger and Calvin King. But they did need a permit from the local government to start a business. Also, their building had to meet local building-code standards. And as a factory, the building had to be located in a special area (or zone) within the city.

The corporation charter was issued by the state government. The corporation paid local, state, and federal taxes. And the company managers had to observe many government regulations.

At first King Clothiers used only raw materials produced in the United States and sold all its production in this country. Later, the company started importing some of the fabrics used in production. The managers found it best to use an importer rather than become involved in foreign trade themselves. They soon discovered there was a great demand for work clothes and jeans overseas. To engage in foreign-country operations would add an all-new component to the business. What are some of the problems of engaging in international trade?

PART

7

In The News

Massachusetts State Government to the Rescue

The Commissioner of the Massachusetts Department of Commerce advertised in *Forbes* magazine to explain how government had aided the economy of the state. He pointed out that capital is available, because there are more venture-capital companies in Massachusetts than in any other state except California. In addition, the Massachusetts Industrial Finance Agency had issued over $1 billion in industrial revenue bonds to more than 1,000 companies. The state government created a $6.5-million program (the Bay State Skills Corporation) to train people for entry-level and advanced jobs in business. The legislature had created a $40 million technology industrial park. The ad stated that in four years, 1,325 companies expanded their Massachusetts facilities, contributing an overall employment increase of 150,000 jobs.

The Commissioner claimed these values and benefits:

Massachusetts ranked fourth in the nation in net growth of manufacturing jobs.

The state personal income tax burden had dropped from 17.7 percent to 14.5 percent, saving taxpayers $2.1 billion in 1982 alone.

The state unemployment rate was below the national average.

State tax revenues increased 29 percent in a four-year period.

A surplus was projected in the state's revenue.

It is not unusual to see state governments advertise in top business magazines. In this case, Massachusetts was trying to convince businesses that government–business relations in that state were better than they were perceived to be.

GOVERNMENT'S ROLE
IN BUSINESS

study objectives

1. Describe several ways in which the federal government encourages business

2. Explain why business is dependent upon, and affected by, government monetary policies

3. Identify the types of business that are supervised by governments through the issuance of licenses, franchises, and charters

4. Understand the functions of the chief agencies through which the federal government regulates businesses

5. Define public policy and explain how it relates to business

6. Discuss the ways that taxation affects private businesses

We have a habit . . . of turning our problems over to the government. . . . A dangerous habit. . . . We're hooked. . . . I'm proposing that we all make some tough decisions about who's responsible for what, and then begin placing that responsibility where it belongs.

Gerald J. Thompson

overnment itself is big business. The federal government alone buys more goods and services than any other single business or institution. The combination of the federal government, school districts, and state, county, municipal, and township governments constitutes 80,000 government units with 16 million employees.

Business in the United States has changed greatly since the government first regulated business. The first such law, the Interstate Commerce Act of 1887, was passed to regulate the nation's railroads. Today, business is influenced by government in every area and at every level. At local levels, there are codes and ordinances that regulate business. States, counties, and cities grant licenses to operate various kinds of businesses. Both federal and state laws govern wages, safety standards, and civil rights. There are laws to prohibit monopolies that would restrain trade or prevent competition. There are federal and state controls that regulate energy resources and causes of pollution. Labor laws and consumer legislation affect almost every phase of business.

The mounting costs of government place a heavy burden on businesses and consumers. To maintain the government function requires 28 cents out of every dollar of personal income, and 23 percent of the total U.S. output. As a result, taxation has become a politically sensitive area.

Certainly not all government intervention is designed to curtail and restrict business, for government provides a variety of services to business. In this chapter, we examine the role of government as it relates to the following activities:

1. Authority and functions of government
2. Encouragement and protection of business

The U.S. Capitol, Washington, D.C. (Photo by Stan Wakefield.)

3. Maintenance of a sound monetary system
4. Patents, copyrights, trademarks, and franchises
5. Regulation of business enterprises
6. Regulation of public monopolies
7. Taxation and business
8. Sources of revenue and types of taxes

AUTHORITY AND FUNCTIONS OF GOVERNMENT

The founders of the American government provided for a federal system, with political power divided between the national and state governments. Our basic laws are described in the U.S. Constitution and the constitutions of the fifty states. In enacting federal laws, the federal government derives its authority from the people. The basis of this authority is the Constitution of the United States. Article I, Section 8, of the Constitution gives Congress the power to make all the laws "necessary and proper" to carry out its duties. In addition to the broad powers granted to Congress, the Constitution provides it with certain specific powers, such as the following, that relate to business:

Collect taxes	Establish post offices
Levy duties	Establish systems of courts
Designate roads	Patrol coastal waters
Coin money	Provide for national defense
Grant patents and copyrights	Fix standards of weights and measurements
Regulate trade between the states	
Pay debts of the United States	Make laws to enforce private contracts

WHAT IS GOVERNMENT?

Broadly defined, GOVERNMENT is *the center of political authority having the power to govern those it serves.* Whether at the local, state, or national level, government has the power to regulate and maintain orderly relations. In this role, it is a **protector**. Government maintains an orderly legal and economic system as required by the people. At all levels, government has the right to establish public policy.

Powers of government originate in two ways: (1) through enactment of laws, and (2) through judicial interpretation of laws. The role of government in business has increased because of public demand to protect the people and to provide new services.

In relation to business, government acts to (1) encourage the production of goods and services through private enterprise, and (2) see that the pricing of goods and services is maintained in accord with the public interest. The government attempts to see that competition is maintained in the buying and selling of goods and services. It also encourages economic growth and price stability. Maintaining these powers over the business economy is not always easy, however.

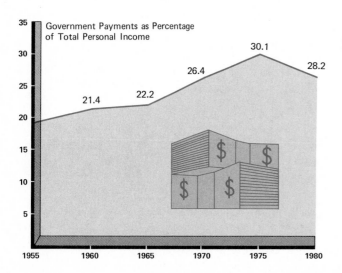

Government Payments as Percentage of Total Personal Income

FIGURE 20-1
For many Americans, government is a source of income. (Source: U.S. Departments of Labor and Commerce.)

In earlier years, the governments of the United States and Canada experimented with controls on prices and/or wages to maintain price stability. Both efforts met with mixed results.

In the United States, wage and price controls led to a rash of price increases before and after the controls. They also caused shortages of supplies in some areas.

When the wage controls expired in Canada, the nation experienced an annual rate of about 7 million lost workdays in strikes as unions rushed to catch up in monetary benefits.

In a "free-enterprise economy," the ideal is a completely free price system in the voluntary exchange of goods and services. In a "modified free economy" such as ours, the government plays an active role. It is expected to prevent practices that restrain trade against the public interest.

Michael Blumenthal, chairman of the Burroughs Corporation and former secretary of the U.S. Treasury, said:

> It is now time for all of us to realize that our present problems have become too big and too complex to be solved by business alone . . . business needs government and government needs business. We must find new ways of organizing into new forms of government–business relationships to solve the problems of the day.

REASONS FOR GOVERNMENT CONTROL OF BUSINESS

The reasons for government control of business can be summarized as follows:

1. To protect the welfare of the individual and to promote higher standards of public health, safety, morals, and general well-being
2. To maintain equality of opportunity for all persons regardless of their sex, national origin, or religion
3. To restrain business from engaging in practices that would be harmful to the public.
4. To protect small firms from unfair competitive abuses by big firms
5. To prevent unfair practices resulting from mergers or other forms of combinations, such as price fixing
6. To conserve our national resources — notably, forests, fuels, and water — and to prevent dangerous pollution of the atmosphere

GOVERNMENT ENCOURAGES AND PROTECTS BUSINESS

The federal government makes many positive contributions to the success of the American business system. It aids and protects business through tariffs, monetary loans, grants, and subsidies. It also sets standards in many areas of business operation.

PROTECTIVE TARIFFS

The federal government's earliest effort to aid business was in the form of protective tariffs. A TARIFF is *a charge or duty levied by government against goods imported from other countries.* The very first tariffs levied by the federal government were largely intended to produce revenue for the government. However, early in the nineteenth century, tariffs were levied to protect some infant industries. Tariffs helped the textile industry during the War of 1812 and the iron industry in the 1840s by protecting them from the competition of foreign goods. Since World War II, the federal government has advocated low tariffs and has favored free trade among nations.

GOVERNMENT LOANS AND GUARANTEES

For many years, the federal government's financial strength has enabled it to provide loans to businesses in one form or another. One of the earliest loans made by the federal government was to the Union Pacific and Central Pacific railroads. These loans helped in the completion of the first transcontinental railroad in 1869. Since 1958, the Interstate Commerce Commission has been authorized to guarantee loans on new equipment purchased by railroads. In the same manner, the Maritime Administration has aided ship construction since 1932. Since 1961, federal funds have been used in the development of urban mass-transportation facilities, including commuter lines. The Chrysler Corporation is operating today because the federal government earlier guaranteed more than a billion dollars of its borrowed funds.

WILLIAM H. MORRIS, JR.

"A new breed of trade booster." That is the label put on William H. Morris, Jr., by *Business Week*. He is responsible for the U.S. Department of Commerce's export promotion programs. He also gives leadership to the managing of international trade issues and policies. He oversees official U.S. participation in international expositions.

Mr. Morris developed policies and procedures to make U.S. export credit financing more competitive. He represents the Department of Commerce as a member of the Commission on Security and Cooperation in Europe. His title is Assistant Secretary of Commerce for Trade Development.

Morris came to the department from a position as president of William Morris and Associates, Nashville, Tennessee, consultants on business management, government relations, and international marketing. Earlier, as deputy commissioner of economic and community development for the state of Tennessee, he helped to open world markets for Tennessee products and sought foreign investment in the state.

Morris began his business career in 1950 in the industrial distribution and wholesale hardware business in Jackson, Tennessee. He is a native of Tennessee and attended the University of Tennessee. He is married and has two children.

Small Business Administration.   One government agency for business is the Small Business Administration. It was created by Congress in 1953 to help small companies meet the rigors of competition. Business and disaster loans are the main type of loans made by the SBA.

FEDERAL GRANTS AND SUBSIDIES   Because transportation has been so vital to the development of this nation, the federal government has made railroads, water carriers, and airlines special objects of support. The westward movement of population encouraged the construction of railroads. Prior to the Civil War, the federal government made huge land grants amounting to 180 million acres to several railroads, mostly in the sparsely populated West. Included among the seventy railroads that shared in the grant program were four western roads — Northern Pacific, Santa Fe, Southern Pacific, and Union Pacific. Together they received almost three-fourths of the total. These railroad land-grant programs ended in the 1870s.

The Subsidy.   Another form of government aid to business is the subsidy. A SUBSIDY is *a government payment or grant to a private enterprise or institution for the good of the public.* Over the years, the federal government has paid subsidies to various groups, such as farmers, railroads, airlines, and shipping companies. For example, in the 1970s, the government boosted the allowable federal subsidy payments to shipbuilding companies on negotiated building contracts from 35 to 50 percent of the total construction costs. These subsidies helped to maintain American shipbuilding facilities in the face of lower costs of foreign ship construction and repair. By subsidizing private enterprise, government acts to improve the economic position of the private group.

In a recent year, 1,250 Americans were contacted in a Louis Harris & Associates poll conducted for *Business Week*. They were asked to respond to the question, "What should government do about companies in important industries that are in severe financial trouble?" Their responses showed that 56 percent favored letting them sink or swim; 30 percent favored bailing them out; 8 percent said, "It depends"; and 4 percent were not sure. When asked if they would favor a bailout if the company's going under would seriously hurt defense production, 59 percent said yes. Most Americans seem to feel that free enterprise includes the "right" to fail as well as succeed.

Farm subsidies have been or are being paid to growers of tobacco, corn, wheat, feed grains, sugar cane, and sugar beets. Farmers producing some specific crop are guaranteed a certain minimum price. If the market price falls below the set minimum, the government makes up the difference as a subsidy payment to the farmer.

LOCKHEED CORPORATION—AN EXAMPLE OF GOVERNMENT AID

In 1971, Congress authorized a guarantee loan program to aid the Lockheed Corporation. The program was justified as protecting the economy of the state of California. (Had Lockheed been forced into bankruptcy, many people would have been thrown out of work.)

Congress established a Guarantee Board and authorized it to guarantee up to $250 million of private bank loans. Lockheed terminated the loan ahead of schedule. During the six years the guarantee was in effect, the federal government supplied no funds as part of the guarantee. It realized more than $31 million in fees and interest on fees, which went into the U.S. Treasury as general-funds revenue.

Farmers and business firms are not the only ones subsidized by the federal government. When workers become unemployed because of the competition from imported goods, they are paid unemployment benefits. Some college students are granted scholarships and low-interest loans, which are subsidies. Hospitals built by nonprofit organizations are given grants and long-term loans at low interest rates.

Parity. The parity concept has dominated farm price-support legislation since the Agricultural Adjustment Act of 1933. PARITY is *government action designed to maintain the purchasing power of farm income at a certain level.* It is supposed to be an expression of economic justice. Parity means

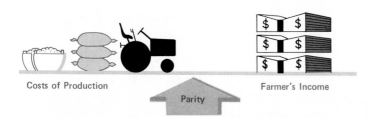

Costs of Production   Parity   Farmer's Income

FIGURE 20-2
The federal government guarantees parity prices to farmers.

placing farmers' income on a par with the cost of producing their crops. It is intended to entitle the farmer to a living standard by the use of two indexes. One is a price index of things farmers buy. The other is a price index of things farmers sell. The base period selected is arbitrarily determined — farm supporters try to get a base that is favorable to farmers. The U.S. Department of Agriculture calculates monthly the price needed to give farmers parity for their crops.

STATE GOVERNMENTS AID BUSINESS AND WORKERS

We naturally think of the larger federal government when the topic of government aid is raised. But state governments aid businesses and workers too. State governments administer the unemployment-compensation programs, and also help finance them. Most state governments have commerce or development departments or bureaus. They may encourage new businesses and industrial plants to locate in their respective states. They can help in finding desirable locations.

An example of state aid is Minnesota's Taconite Relief Fund, designed to aid some of their unemployed workers. The mining of taconite is an important industry in Minnesota. The state legislature, at the governor's request, established a public-works job program. The benefits under this program are limited to residents of an area defined as the Taconite Tax Relief Area. This is an area in Northeastern Minnesota that is largely dependent on the mining industry for its economic well-being. Benefits are made available to unemployed workers whose unemployment-compensation benefits have been exhausted. Priority is given to those who are heads of households, and participation in the program is limited to four weeks per individual.

The source of the funds appropriated by the state legislature for this program is the Economic Protection Fund. This special fund has been accumulated in recent years out of a portion of the tax revenues levied by the state on the mining of taconite. This money is collected from the mining companies in Minnesota rather than local property taxes. Workers employed under this program are paid at a rate which approximates the federal minimum wage for each hour worked.

Connecticut and Indiana are two states that invest taxpayer's money in venture-capital schemes. Since 1975, the Connecticut Private Development Corp. has invested $5.5 million in about 60 promising small companies. The state typically takes a 60 percent share and the entrepreneur holds 40 percent. "If the company is successful, we get back our investment four- or five-fold. If it never makes it, we've lost," says Peter Burns, state deputy commissioner of economic development.

GOVERNMENTS SET STANDARDS

Government standards apply in most industries. The auto manufacturers, for example, are required to meet safety and environmental standards that are set by the federal government. All new automobiles must be equipped with seat belts and shoulder straps. Engines must be equipped with devices that prevent pollution of the air. Businesses and municipalities must meet certain standards relative to water purification and waste disposal. The maintenance of these standards is supervised by the Environmental Protection Agency.

You have undoubtedly heard of OSHA. These letters stand for Occupational Safety and Health Administration, an agency established in 1971. It is responsible for regulating safety and health conditions in all workplaces except those run by government. Stories about OSHA's activities have appeared regularly in business periodicals since it was founded.

State and local governments also inspect hotels, restaurants, barber shops, beauty salons, and so forth, to see that they meet and maintain certain health standards.

GOVERNMENT MAINTAINS A SOUND MONETARY SYSTEM

In the most primitive societies, *one good is traded for another.* This process is called BARTER. In the early history of the American colonies, the fur traders were among the first businesspeople. They bartered furs and grains produced by the colonies for manufactured articles made in England, France, and Spain. But barter has great limitations. For example, how do you trade a pair of shoes for half a cow? Almost immediately, traders needed a **medium of exchange.** When an acceptable medium is developed into a system, it is called **money.** Barter is increasing in importance in this country and in foreign trade.

CURRENT ISSUE

Should the Government Give Financial Aid to Ailing Businesses?

In 1979, the federal government guaranteed loans of $1.2 billion for the Chrysler Corporation. In return, Chrysler's management closed or consolidated twenty obsolete plants and modernized twenty-one others. Chrysler labor settled for $17.50 an hour instead of $20. Executives took a 10 percent pay cut, and the number of white-collar staff was cut in half. The blue-collar workers were reduced by 54,000 to an hourly workforce of 46,000. And Chrysler survived.

Many people do not favor government subsidy of ailing businesses.

With which of the following statements do you agree, and with which do you disagree?

1. It is just as important to subsidize business as it is farming.
2. Subsidies are necessary to help domestic firms compete with foreign companies.
3. Many foreign governments subsidize their new industries, enabling them to compete overseas.
4. A subsidy may be used instead of a tariff—a tariff might encourage foreign governments to retaliate with similar tariffs.
5. Instead of subsidizing one large corporation, it would be better to help several smaller companies.
6. Subsidies encourage marginal firms to stay in business at the taxpayers' expense.
7. Governments should not subsidize businesses—let them sink or swim in the sea of international competition.

In your opinion, should the U.S. government aid ailing businesses?

A MONEY SYSTEM

When money is backed by a government, we have an official national monetary system. **One of the most important functions of government is to provide a sound money system, which is necessary for conducting business transactions.** Here in the United States, the basic monetary unit is the dollar. In Belgium, France, and Switzerland, it is the franc; in Germany, the mark; and in Britain, the pound.

At one time, the U.S. dollar was supported by gold. During this period, the United States, upon demand, redeemed its paper money with gold. Later, paper money issued by the federal government was redeemable in silver. Now our paper money depends only on the credit standing of the government. It is not backed by either gold or silver.

GEORGE WASHINGTON HALF DOLLARS

On July 1, 1982, the U.S. Mint in Denver struck the first George Washington commemorative half dollars. These were the first of 800,000 to be struck during the month of July, recognizing the 250th anniversary of the nation's first president. These coins are 90 percent silver, intended as collectors' items. They were divided equally between uncirculated coins, selling for $8.50 each, and proof specimens, selling for $10.50. The uncirculated coins bear the *D* mint mark of the Denver mint. The proof specimens bear the *S* mint mark of the San Francisco assay office. Ten million is the maximum permitted by law. Donna Pope, director of the mint, said she hoped they would prove so popular that the entire 10 million would be struck.

(Courtesy Bureau of the Mint, U.S. Department of the Treasury.)

THE VALUE OF THE DOLLAR

For a long period in our history, the value of the dollar was "fixed" by the government. This means that the number of dollars that would be exchanged for a British pound was set by the federal government. The number of German marks or Swiss francs per dollar was also fixed. But in 1973, the U.S. dollar was freed to *float* against other currencies. The value of the dollar, as measured in other currencies, is now determined by supply and demand. The number of marks, francs, or yen that one can obtain for a U.S. dollar or a British pound is determined in the international money market.

For many years, the U.S. dollar has been an "international currency." It has been used as a currency of settlement for business transactions outside the United States. The oil-exporting nations, for example, price their products in dollars. This role has led to a large demand by individuals, institutions, and corporations for dollars. Others want dollars for trading purposes and as a storehouse of value as well. Sometimes dollars which are privately

CURRENCY RATES			
	New York Mon	Home Mkt. Mon	New York Fri
(In U.S. dollars)			
British pound	1.5287	1.5270	1.5083
Canadian dollar	0.8118	0.8119	0.8107
(In foreign units to U.S. dollar)			
French franc	7.2650	7.2529	7.2690
Japanese yen	238.10	238.75	239.48
Swiss franc	2.0515	2.0475	2.0540
West German mark ...	2.4265	2.4200	2.4248

Based on average of late buying and selling rates.
Home markets: London, Toronto, Paris, Tokyo, Zurich and Frankfurt.

FIGURE 20-3
Foreign Exchange Rates

held abroad are "dumped" or "hoarded." This then becomes an important element influencing the supply and demand of dollars on the foreign-exchange market. Foreign-exchange rates fluctuate from day to day, and are published in most large daily newspapers.

MONETARY POLICY The rules and regulations relating to the money system constitute our official **monetary policy.** Whether the value of government's money is to be fixed or allowed to float depends on government policy. Whether the amount of money in circulation is to be increased or decreased also depends on government policy. Is credit expansion or contraction to be encouraged? Should interest rates rise or decline? Business is very dependent on the government's monetary policies.

In the United States, the Federal Reserve Board is responsible for setting a monetary policy in relation to money supply and interest rates. This subject is discussed in detail in Chapter 15, "Credit and the Banking System."

PATENTS, COPYRIGHTS, TRADEMARKS, AND FRANCHISES

The government can also grant monopoly power. Laws covering patents, copyrights, and trademarks have the objective of conferring temporary monopoly control on their holders.

PATENTS If you invent a machine or a device, you may apply for a patent. In the United States, a PATENT is *the exclusive right to own, use, and dispose of an invention* and is granted to the owner for seventeen years. After that period,

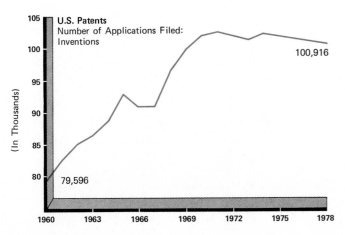

FIGURE 20-4
U.S. Patents Applications.
(Source: U.S. Department of Commerce.)

the patent right expires and is not renewable. More than 1,200 patents are issued every week. Even so, the U.S. Patent Office has a normal backlog of 200,000 applications.

The U.S. Supreme Court has ruled to allow patent rights for biogenic discoveries. These may include creation of organisms such as genes in a laboratory. The full effect of this decision may not be apparent for several years, but it has stimulated an industry in biological engineering.

Congress enacted a law permitting universities and small businesses to keep patent rights to inventions developed with federal research funds. It approved a bill extending the seventeen-year patent life for drugs and chemicals. This is to compensate for the marketing time lost while obtaining FDA approval after the patent is granted.

The expiration of patents can cause problems, as the manufacturers of prescription drugs recently learned:

> In one year eighty-three of this nation's one hundred leading prescription drugs lost their patent protection. The expiration of these patents brought a sudden end to the monopoly that brand-name drug producers have enjoyed for years on popular high-revenue products.

> This moved them into competition with the manufacturers of the so-called generic-equivalent drugs, which cost 15 to 40 percent less. In addition, some forty states now have laws that promote the substitution of generic drugs for brand-name drugs where possible. This is an attempt to cut health-care costs. The difference between the price of a brand-name drug and the price of its generic equivalent may be considerable. For example, *Librium*, a widely prescribed tranquilizer, carried a wholesale cost of $9.06 per one hundred tablets while its generic substitute cost $1.10 per one hundred tablets.

THE $5 MILLION SOCKET WRENCH

Peter Roberts was a clerk in a Sears, Roebuck store in Gardner, Massachusetts, in 1964. He obtained a patent on a socket wrench that has a quick release, which enables the wrench to be operated with only one hand. In May 1964, Roberts sold the rights to the wrench to Sears for $10,000.

Later, Roberts sued Sears to have his contract with the company rescinded. In 1978, a federal jury ruled that Sears had obtained Roberts's patent fraudulently and awarded him $1 million.

Sears appealed this decision to a higher court, and on May 31, 1979, U.S. District Court Judge George Leighton canceled the sales contract and ordered the patent returned to Roberts. Judge Leighton also ruled that Roberts was entitled to all the profits made by Sears on the sale of this wrench.

In April 1982, a jury in Chicago voted Roberts an award of $5 million.[1]

---

[1] Attorneys for Sears said they would ask for a new trial. Roberts's attorney said he would ask U.S. District Judge Nicholas J. Bua to increase the award.

The U.S. Patent Office examines the owner's application to see whether the invention is new and useful as claimed and whether the application conforms to the law. Copies of patent laws can be obtained from the Superintendent of Documents, Government Printing Office, Washington, D.C. 20402.

Large U.S. companies have dominated overall patent approval for years. The General Electric Company, for example, has been assigned more than 50,000 patents. But that dominance is eroding. Smaller companies are coming to the forefront in patent approvals. Also, foreign inventors are receiving an increasing percentage of the U.S. patents issued. Japanese, Germans, and Russians now receive three-fourths of the U.S. patents granted in the fields of TV, photography, photoelectronics, textile machinery, and combustion engines.

THE EUROPEAN PATENT OFFICE

Eleven European nations (Austria, Belgium, Britain, France, Italy, Liechtenstein, Luxembourg, the Netherlands, Sweden, Switzerland, and West Germany) recognize patents issued by the European Patent Office in Munich, which opened in 1978.

An EPO patent is effective in all eleven countries. The 62,000 European applications received since 1978 took the place of some 390,000 applications that would have been necessary in the eleven member countries had there been no European Patent Office.

COPYRIGHTS The word **copyright** literally means "the right to copy." The first American copyright law was passed by Congress in 1790 in keeping with Article I, Section 8, of the U.S. Constitution. A COPYRIGHT *gives an author* (including a designer, a composer, a photographer, a publisher, a sculptor, or an artist) *the exclusive right to publish, print, produce, or copy his or her work.* No one else can do so without the author's permission.

Copyrights, like patents, have an obvious importance to business, since they involve the granting of a government-approved monopoly for a limited time. If your copyright is violated, the copyright law gives you the right to seek redress through the courts. This may include an action for damages, an injunction restraining the continued infringement, and the cost of litigation. Copyrights can be obtained from the U.S. Copyright Office of the Library of Congress upon the payment of a fee and the furnishing of two copies of the material to be copyrighted.

It took Congress more than twenty years to pass the Copyright Act of 1976, which became effective January 1, 1978. Under that act, a copyright covers the lifetime of the owner plus an additional fifty years. According to Barbara A. Ringer, register of copyrights at the Library of Congress, the new copyright law is "a monumental accomplishment compared to the 1909 law that we've been working with." Table 20-1 shows how the copyright law was changed by the 1976 act.

TABLE 20-1
The Federal Copyright Law

PROVISIONS	OLD LAW	NEW LAW
Term	28 years, renewable for another 28 years	Life of author plus 50 years
Photocopying	Not covered	Permits the copying of a limited amount of material for research purposes, but bars "systematic" copying without permission
Cable television	Not covered	Mandates royalty payments on programs and films based on a sliding scale that depends on the TV system's revenues
Phonograph records	Provided flat royalty rate of 2¢ per record	Raises royalty rate to 2.75¢ per record or ½¢ per minute of playing time, whichever is higher. Imposes an $8 annual license fee on every jukebox
Pooled royalty settlements	Not covered	Creates a new, five-person, independent regulatory agency to review license rates periodically and distribute pooled royalties

TRADEMARKS   Many firms use the TRADEMARK—*a distinctive symbol, title, or design that readily identifies the company or its product.* By registering the trademark with the Patent Office, the owner is granted the exclusive right to its use for twenty years. The registration can be renewed once for another twenty years. Once the trademark has been registered, the Patent Office is empowered to deny the registration of infringing trademarks. The owner must initiate legal action to restrain the use by another if the owner feels that the other unlawfully adopted the trademark.

The major benefit of the trademark is that it is *prima facie* ("on first appearance") evidence of the registrant's exclusive right to use the symbol.

Protecting a Trademark Symbol.   Law suits over trademarks may seem frivolous to many consumers, but to companies owning trademarks, protection is no small matter. The legal staffs of corporations scan thousands of articles and advertisements for misuses of brand names and trademark infringements. For example, the Coca-Cola Company retains the services of three lawyers to challenge others who might use the trademark *Coke* in advertising.

In a suit brought before the Court of Customs and Patent Appeals, the Procter & Gamble Company persuaded the judges to reject Certified Chemical & Equipment's claim that involved the use of a stain remover called Mister Stain because it "stimulates the same mental reaction" as P&G's Mr. Clean brand.

Recently, Parker Brothers, Inc., lost its bid for exclusive rights to "Monopoly." The appellate court ruled:

> We hold that, as applied to a board game, the word "monopoly" has become "generic," and the registration of it as a trademark is no longer valid.

A few companies have abandoned efforts to protect their trademark titles by allowing them to be used by the public without prior approval. *Nylon* is now dedicated by du Pont to public use. Some of the most successful

FIGURE 20-5
Many companies use the trademark as a symbol to identify their product or service. When registered with the U.S. Patent Office, trademarks prevent others from using the same name. Some well-known trademarks are shown here. (Courtesy Maytag, Allis-Chalmers, A&P, and RCA.)

trademarks have been lost because of their popularity. They became so firmly entrenched in the language that no single company could legitimately claim ownership. Such casualties have included cellophane, linoleum, mimeograph, and kleenex.

LICENSES AND FRANCHISES

If you wish to establish a new business enterprise in your community, you must obtain a license from the appropriate government agency. Many cities require the licensing of door-to-door salespersons. Professionals such as teachers, physicians, and lawyers are licensed by state governments. Corporations are "chartered" to do business by state governments.

Franchises for Regulated Monopolies. Some business services can be rendered economically only through monopolies. The public utilities (telephone, gas, and electricity) are the best-known examples. Large sums of capital are required to start and maintain a utility system. Local and state governments grant franchises to selected public utilities to provide and distribute these services. A FRANCHISE is *an exclusive right to perform a stated business service in a specified geographical area.* It defines the period of time and the territory within which such services are to be provided.

Every state has some form of commission or state agency that regulates franchised businesses and supervises the rates they charge.

GOVERNMENT AGENCIES THAT REGULATE BUSINESSES

At the federal level, our government has established many agencies to administer federal laws. These agencies are the regulators of business—especially interstate transactions. They determine which firms may enter the field, what rates they may charge, and what rules must be observed. Table 20-2 lists the most important agencies and commissions.

Business's chief complaints against government regulation relate to the confusion and misunderstanding of purposes and guidelines supplied, the time required to prepare reports, the lack of consideration being given to reports, and the duplication of effort required.

Consumer advocate Ralph Nader observes that "our unguided regulatory system undermines competition and entrenches monopoly at the public's expense."

TABLE 20-2
What Are the Federal Regulatory Agencies?

Civil Aeronautics Board	Federal Power Commission
Commission on Civil Rights	Federal Reserve Board
Commodity Futures Trading Commission	Federal Trade Commission
Consumers Product Safety Commission	Food and Drug Administration
Environmental Protection Agency	Interstate Commerce Commission
Equal Employment Opportunity Commission	National Labor Relations Board
Federal Aviation Administration	Nuclear Regulatory Commission
Federal Communications Commission	Occupational Safety and Health Administration
Federal Energy Regulatory Commission	Securities and Exchange Commission
Federal Maritime Commission	

New York Congressman Jack Kemp argues:

> . . . instead of strangling commerce with costly and counterproductive regulations, we must cut out those that do not serve the public interest. . . . We should be reviving the idea of incentives—an idea that we know works, because it is the idea that built this country.

Roy L. Ash, board chairman of AM International, Inc., commented on government in business, "As to business regulation, not only do I as a citizen not know what I'm getting, but I certainly don't know how much it's costing me. I have no way to decide whether I like what I'm getting for my money."

Alfred E. Kahn, while chairman of the Commission on Wage and Price Stability, said, ". . . if we meet the criticisms of regulation that are valid, we

---

A PIZZA WITH THE WORKS
(Including 310 Regulations)

Since New York City restaurants first offered pizza in 1936, pizza has grown into a $6-billion-a-year business. In 1981, Americans consumed more than 1.5 billion pizzas at home, in schools and sporting arenas, and in the more than 20,000 restaurants that serve it. This is about seven pizzas for every man, woman, and child in the United States.

Along with the popularity have come dozens of regulations from the Food and Drug Administration and the Department of Agriculture on the ingredients in what the government describes as "a bread-base meat food product with tomato sauce, cheese and meat topping."

In all, there are some 310 separate regulations, taking up more than forty pages of federal documents, governing what may go on a pizza and how those toppings can be described on labels and menus. For example:

Tomato sauce—Must be of the "red or reddish" varieties and contain at least 24 percent "natural tomato soluble solids."

Onions—Canned onions may be used as long as the onions come from the bulb of the plant and not the stalk.

Crust—Each pound of flour must contain 2.9 milligrams of thiamine, 24 milligrams of niacin, and at least 13—but not more than 16—milligrams of iron.

---

will be in the best possible position to repel the ones that are invalid." As a candidate, Ronald Reagan campaigned for the presidency with "less government in business" as a major plank in the platform of the Republican party.

Here is an example of some of the "plain English" to which business-people dealing with federal regulations object:

> Except as provided in paragraph B of this section, applications, amendments thereto and related statements of fact required by the commission shall be personally signed by the applicant, if the applicant is an individual.

REGULATING MONOPOLIES AND PUBLIC POLICY

The extent to which governments attempt to control business activities is largely determined by what the public seems to want. The doctrine of *laissez faire*, "to let alone," prevailed in the United States from about 1780 to 1890. During this period, the government did not interfere in the conduct of business. The trend toward government regulation of large businesses, starting about 1890, was presumed to be in the interest of public policy. Thomas Edison said:

> There is far more danger in public than in private monopoly, for when Government goes into business it can always shift its losses to the tax-payers. Government never makes ends meet—and that is the first requisite of business.

MEANING OF PUBLIC POLICY

Congress may formulate public policy, which is the result of public hearings, investigation, and debate. Exactly what the public policy means depends mainly on how it is interpreted by government administrators and judges. Public policy also becomes a matter of what those subject to the law interpret it to mean. So public policy is an expression of both public officials and private interests.

A precise definition has not yet been formulated by our courts. As used here, however, PUBLIC POLICY is *a statement or an interpretation of an action that carries the weight of government authority.* It may be used in determining business and political decisions.

CONTROLLING BUSINESS MONOPOLIES

Toward the end of the nineteenth century, stockholders in several large companies were persuaded to turn their shares over to a group of trustees. These trustees were then able to control competition and maximize profits at the public expense. These organizations became known as business trusts. A BUSINESS TRUST is *a combination of businesses operated under trust agreements by trustees for the benefit of the members.* Its purpose is to restrain trade.

In 1882, John D. Rockefeller and his associates organized the first large-scale business trust, the Standard Oil Company. Through a series of trust agreements with some forty different corporations, these corporations were placed in the hands of a few Standard Oil Company trustees, although they did not own the shares. Thus it was possible, through the trustees, to take whatever action was necessary to gain a monopoly in oil. A MONOPOLY *exists when a firm has a large enough segment of a particular industry that it can control prices within that industry.*

Similar trusts were formed to control the source and price of sugar, tobacco, whiskey, cottonseed oil, and machinery for making shoes. By the late 1880s, it became obvious that government regulation to prevent monopolies was in the interest of the public. So in 1890, Congress enacted the Sherman Antitrust Act to control monopolies. This law and its amendments have proved to be milestones in combating trusts and monopolies in the interest of the public.

Sherman Antitrust Act.   Named for U.S. Senator John Sherman (1823–1900), an early sponsor of the act, this legislation became the first to curb monopolies. The act is brief but broad, and its two main provisions are as follows:

> Section 1: Every contract, combination in the form of trust or otherwise, or conspiracy, in restraint of trade or commerce among the several states, or with foreign nations, is hereby declared to be illegal. . . .

> Section 2: Every person who shall monopolize, or attempt to monopolize, or combine or conspire with any other person or persons, to monopolize any part of the trade or commerce among the several states, or with foreign nations, shall be deemed guilty of a misdemeanor. . . .

In the original act, violators could draw a fine of $5,000, a prison term of one year, or both. In 1974, Congress raised the maximum fine to $1 million for corporations and to $100,000 for individuals. A violation became a felony rather than a misdemeanor.

The Sherman Act applies only to firms in interstate commerce (trade between the states), and enforcement is under the Antitrust Division of the

FIGURE 20-6
A Hearing of the Foreign Affairs Committee
(Photo by K. Jewell.)

GOVERNMENT AND WORLD BUSINESS

Department of Justice, in cooperation with the Federal Trade Commission and the courts. The Antitrust Division investigates about 1,200 complaints each year.

Between 1890 and 1914, monopolies still flourished, for the Sherman Act was limited in its scope and some corporations found ways to circumvent the law. Finally the Supreme Court evolved the "rule of reason" concept: A merger may be considered legal as long as the intent to monopolize an industry does not exist.

The Clayton Act. This act was passed in 1914, as an amendment to the Sherman Act. It brings within the antitrust laws some abuses that previously were not covered. **The Clayton Act preserves competition by stating specifically those things that a business cannot do to achieve business growth.** For example, the use of interlocking directorates to bring two companies closer together is illegal, as is price fixing to gain a monopoly. Also, one company cannot acquire stock in a competing company either by amalgamation or acquisition in order to eliminate competition.

The Clayton Act specifically **forbids** the following:

1. The use of interlocking directorates in companies that compete directly with one another
2. The acquisition by one company of more than a limited amount of stock in another company that competes directly with it
3. Contracts that require the purchaser to buy other items in addition to the product desired
4. The practice of charging different prices among various buyers for goods that are equal in quality or quantity, should such action reduce competition or lead to a monopoly

Hundreds of cases have been tried by the Justice Department under the antitrust laws. Probably the most complex case of its kind involved the International Business Machines Corporation. The government had accused IBM of monopolizing what it defined narrowly as the markets for "general-purpose" computers and peripheral products that are compatible with IBM equipment. IBM contended that its early dominance in the industry resulted from superior products and business methods.

More than 200 lawyers were involved, and 2,500 depositions were recorded. More than 66 million pages of documents were made available to the government. Almost 5,000 exhibits were entered as evidence.

Over twelve years after the case was filed, on January 8, 1982, the government dropped the case. U.S. District Judge David N. Edelstein explained that under federal rules of procedure, "when parties agree to drop a case, the approval of the court is not required, nor is there any need to seek it." *United States* v. *IBM* was the longest-running big antitrust case in U.S. history. The suit reportedly cost the government $13.4 million.

REGULATING PRICES AND PRACTICES

The Federal Trade Commission Act. Noting the loopholes that existed in the Clayton Act, Congress in 1914 enacted the Federal Trade Commission Act. This act provides that "unfair methods of competition in commerce are hereby declared unlawful." A five-member commission was established to define and detect unfair trade practices. Included among the unlawful practices are these:

1. Misbranding goods as to quality, origin, composition, durability, and so on
2. Using false or misleading advertising to deceive the public
3. Bribing a customer's employees to obtain orders or to learn their trade secrets
4. Using containers that give a false impression of an item's size
5. Advertising or selling rebuilt or reconditioned goods as new
6. Using business schemes that are based on chance

The commission has a large staff of accountants, lawyers, and economists who investigate allegedly unfair methods of competition and conduct hearings. When necessary, the commission issues cease-and-desist orders. Table 20-3 shows how legislation has added to the powers of the FTC.

TABLE 20-3
Growing Power of the Federal Trade Commission

THE LEGISLATION	ITS PURPOSE
FTC	Originally an antitrust law, passed in 1914 and broadened in 1938 to let the agency attack "unfair or deceptive acts or practices in commerce"
Clayton	The basic antitrust statute, including antimerger provisions and prohibitions on interlocking directorates
Robinson-Patman	1938 amendments to the Clayton Act that require that sellers must offer equal deals to all customers
Truth in Lending	Details the information that must be given to a credit customer
Fair Credit Reporting	Establishes a customer's rights in disputes with credit bureaus
Fair Credit Billing	Protects consumers from unfair and inaccurate billing practices
Equal Credit Opportunity	Bars discrimination by sex, race, religion, or age in loans and credit sales
Fair Packaging	Outlaws deceptive packaging or labeling
Fur Products	Requires accurate branding of fur products
Textile Identification	Requires accurate labeling of fiber content of textile products
Webb-Pomerene	Provides antitrust immunity for U.S. companies that band together in joint export efforts
Magnuson-Moss	Extends the agency's reach to local business dealings and confirms its right to regulate by industrywide rules

The Robinson-Patman Act. This act amended the Clayton Act. Passed in 1936, **its general purpose is "to make it unlawful for any person engaged in interstate commerce to discriminate in price or terms of sale between purchasers of commodities of like grade and quality."**

The FTC conducted investigations showing that large corporate buyers secured discriminatory low prices. These were gained not only on the pretense of quantity discounts but also on getting rebates for brokerage services when no such services were rendered. Large buyers were also using their economic power to extract favorable prices. These were not granted to other, less-powerful buyers and not justified by savings to the seller resulting from differences in cost of manufacture, sales cost, or delivery expenses.

The act prohibits indirect discrimination in price through the use of advertising allowances. It is unlawful to pay brokerage fees to agents under the direct control of the buyer. Brokerage fees may not be paid to the buyer, except for services rendered by the buyer.

The Celler-Kefauver Antimerger Act. In 1950, the Celler-Kefauver Act was passed as an amendment to Section 7 of the Clayton Act. **Its purpose is to forbid mergers that prohibit competition.** Under the Clayton Act of 1914, acquiring the stock of another corporation where the effect might be to reduce competition was prohibited. But later court decisions so weakened this law that it no longer restricted accumulation of assets by merger or acquisition.

Under the antimerger act, corporations that are major competitors cannot merge in any manner. This amendment extends jurisdiction to all corporations subject to the Federal Trade Commission. In formulating the Celler-Kefauver Act, congressional committees stated that this legislation was not intended to stop the merger of two small companies or the sale of a company that was failing.

THE COST OF GOVERNMENT REGULATION

In a televised report to the nation on the economy, President Reagan said that "altogether, regulations . . . add $100 billion or more to the cost of the goods and services we buy."

The calculation of the cost of government regulation originated with Robert DeFina, an economist formerly with the Center for the Study of American Business (at Washington University, St. Louis). DeFina estimated that for every dollar in taxes needed to operate regulatory agencies, it cost business $20 to comply with the regulations. Applying this multiplier of 20 to budgeted data, we can estimate the cost for one year to be $126 billion.

Effectiveness of Antitrust Laws. How effective has the antitrust legislation been in reducing monopolistic business practices? On the positive side, the antitrust laws have contributed enormously toward improving the degree of competition in our system. Those who value free enterprise applaud this kind of government intervention.

Each year, more cases are being investigated and brought to trial and some cases are settled without trial if a consent decree is accepted. American antitrust laws have not been a complete success. But we have only to look at business in certain other countries to realize how much worse off our economy might have been without these laws.

TAXATION AND BUSINESS

Governments can provide essential services only if they collect taxes. The federal government collects about one-sixth of its total revenue through income taxes on private business. In addition, businesses are obliged to pay and collect Social Security and excise taxes.

PURPOSES OF TAXES Taxes have several purposes, the most important of which are to (1) raise revenue, (2) regulate or influence some aspect of the economy, and (3) transfer or redistribute wealth. Most of our taxes serve at least one of these purposes.

PHILOSOPHY OF TAXATION

There are two basic philosophies in this country as to how the tax burden should be apportioned: (1) the benefit principle, and (2) the ability-to-pay principle.

The Benefit Principle.   Advocates of this principle contend that those who benefit from government services should pay for them. No one can argue very loudly that this is illogical. For example, the federal tax on gasoline was passed to provide funds for highways. However, this principle does have its limitations. For example, assume that public-school taxes were levied on the basis of the number of children that parents have in school. In fact, all people derive some benefit from the public-school system, regardless of whether they have children in school. Thus, it would be unsound to tax only those who have children in school.

The Ability-to-Pay Principle.   Taxation based on this principle seems to be preferred to the benefit principle. But how do we measure ability to pay? Net income received during a given year is probably the most widely accepted criterion, though some others prefer to use gross income. But even after a criterion has been agreed upon, there remains the problem of determining the acceptable tax rate.

The income tax is perhaps the best example of applying the ability-to-pay principle. Income taxes are broadly based and are set on the basis of estimates of the people's ability to pay. A person with a $25,000 income is asked to pay more than one who earns $15,000.

During periods of inflation, the government benefits from the income tax, because inflation pushes people into higher tax brackets.

REVENUE SOURCES AND TYPES OF TAXES

Governments obtain their funds from taxes and through borrowing; the money borrowed is paid back with tax money. Local, state, and federal governments together tax away a large part of the income one earns. The expenditures of the federal government are greater than those of all state and local governments combined.

Figure 20-7 shows where the federal government revenue comes from and where it goes. In addition to the proportion paid by business corporations, income taxes paid by business proprietorships and partnerships are included in that portion shown as individual income taxes. Businesses also pay approximately one-half the Social Security taxes.

The Budget Dollar
Fiscal Year 1983 Estimate

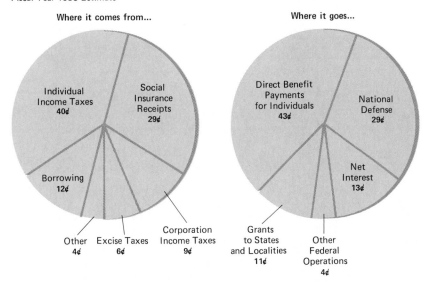

FIGURE 20-7
The U. S. Budget Dollar

TYPES OF TAXES The principal types of taxes levied by all types of government are summarized in Table 20-4. The table also shows where the effect of the tax finally comes to rest.

BUSINESS PAYROLL TAXES Three types of payroll taxes are paid by businesses to provide benefits for their employees: (1) Social Security, (2) unemployment insurance, and (3) workmen's compensation.

Social Security Tax. The Social Security Act of 1935 established a national plan to supplement a person's retirement income. In addition to normal retirement pensions, the act now provides for disability payments and health-care payments (Medicare). To defray the cost of these benefits, both employers and employees pay a monthly tax. For employees, this tax is

TABLE 20-4
Principal Types of Taxes

TYPE OF TAX	DESCRIPTION	PROBABLE INCIDENCE (RESTING PLACE)
Personal income	This is a graduated tax levied directly on individual income. Its rates are progressive, and it is based on the ability-to-pay principle.	On the taxpayer.
Corporate income	This tax is levied on the net earnings of corporations. Because stockholders pay taxes on dividends received, this double taxation is a constant source of complaint to members of Congress.	On the corporation.
Property	Cities, counties, and states levy taxes against both real and personal property.	On the property owner. Taxes on rental property can be shifted to tenants. Taxes on business property can be shifted to consumers.
Sales and excise	States and cities levy retail sales taxes on the buyer or consumer. Excise taxes are levied on the producer or seller. Excise taxes are assessed against such items as jewelry, tobacco, beer, and gasoline.	Shifted to consumers.
Severance	This tax is levied on the owner of minerals taken from beneath the earth's surface — coal, iron ore, oil, etc.	Passed on to ultimate purchaser.
Estate and inheritance	The federal government levies an estate tax on wealth that is passed on to one's heirs. States use inheritance taxes, since they are assessed against the persons who inherit the wealth.	Both are usually paid out of property left by the deceased.
Corporation franchise	This is a tax levied by the state government that grants the corporation a charter for doing business.	Borne by the company as a cost of operation.

deducted from wages; for employers, it is assessed against their payrolls. The rate of the tax and the amount on which it is paid are established periodically by Congress.

Almost everyone who works is covered by the Social Security program including men and women on active duty in the armed forces. Employees of nonprofit organizations may elect to be covered. If the employer and two-thirds or more of the employees vote for coverage, the law will apply to them.

Covered employees who become disabled may qualify for benefits regardless of age. Dependents who are eligible for disability or old-age retirement benefits and who have children under 18 are entitled to monthly payments equal to half the amount of workers' retirement benefits. Benefits stop when the children reach their eighteenth birthday. However, there are two exceptions to this rule. First, a child who becomes totally disabled before age 18 may continue to collect the benefit as long as the disability lasts. Second, a child attending school full time may receive disability payments until age 22.

These payroll taxes have been raised to the point that they constitute a real burden on both businesses and workers. But the additional money is needed to finance the Social Security system.

Unemployment Insurance.   Under the Social Security Act of 1935 and the Employment Security Amendments of 1970, all states and the District of Columbia are encouraged to enact unemployment-insurance laws. Each state now has its own plan approved by the federal government. In every state except Alaska, Alabama, and New Jersey, the cost of the plan is borne by the employer. In these three states, the tax is shared by employer and employee.

The program protects most workers in industry, but few in agriculture. Approximately 80 million jobs in industry, commerce, and government are covered, including those of members of the armed forces. During periods of unusually high unemployment, many state funds become exhausted.

Work Sharing—a State Program.   In 1978, California designed the first work sharing program, and in 1982 Arizona and Oregon began similar programs. Here is how it works.

A company "lays off" workers one day each week. These layoffs are rotated among the work force. The state pays unemployment compensation, about $25, for that one day. Employees retain about 90 percent of their regular take-home pay. In California, in 1982, 100,000 workers, at more than 2,300 companies, collected $18.5 million in work-sharing payments.

The worker, the company, and the union (where there is one) all benefit. More workers keep their jobs, and the company maintains its trained work force. The union keeps a full complement of dues-paying members.

Workers' Compensation.   Another payroll-tax program provides mandatory workers' compensation in most states. It is a form of accident insurance for employees injured on the job. The employer pays the cost of the program and may elect either to buy an insurance policy or to join a state-operated program.

SOME EFFECTS OF TAXATION   Taxes levied by the federal government have a major effect on business. Such business taxes as sales and excise taxes tend to increase the price of goods to consumers. Corporate income taxes, which are levied against earnings, reduce profits that might otherwise be distributed to stockholders. Corporate income taxes also result in the highly controversial problem of double taxation, taxing income once as the corporation earns it, and again when it is received by stockholders as dividends.

FIGURE 20-8
The Cost of Government.
All taxes—federal, state, and local—as a percentage of national income. (Source: U.S. Department of Commerce.)

	Government Spending As % of GNP (a)	Average Investment As % of GNP	Industrial Output	Productivity	Memo: Gov't Spending Excl. Nat'l Defense As % of GNP (a)
			(Avg. Ann.% Increase)		
(1) Japan	9.6%	32.5%	5.3%	6.4%	8.7%
(2) Belgium	16.5	21.8	1.3	5.9	13.8
(3) Netherlands	17.2	21.2	1.6	5.4	14.1
(4) Germany	19.9	22.0	1.7	4.5	17.0
(5) France	14.5	22.7	2.3	4.4	11.1
(6) Italy	15.5	20.1	3.6	3.8	13.5
(7) United Kingdom	20.5	18.7	(2.0)	1.6	15.8
(8) United States	20.4	18.4	1.1	1.3	14.8

(a) Federal, State, and Local Current Spending Excluding Transfer Payments and Capital Spending.

FIGURE 20-9

Economic Performance in Eight Countries, 1973–1980.

(From *Venture, The Magazine for Entrepreneurs*, August 1982, by special permission. © 1982 Venture Magazine, Inc.)

Because of the amount of taxes paid, taxation can have an effect on business policy and decisions. For example, companies with high earnings and taxes may find it advantageous to buy a company that has been losing money. For tax reasons, corporations may decide to engage in debt financing (bonds) rather than sell stock to raise capital. Interest on bonds is part of the cost of doing business, and it is deducted from earnings in computing taxable income. Companies have also been known to move their headquarters from a state with a high property or income tax to one with a low tax.

The cost of government continues to increase as we call upon it for more and more services. Government taxes at all levels—federal, state, and local—now take almost 40 percent of our national income.

Figure 20-9 shows some interesting information regarding the cost of government as a percentage of GNP, including and excluding spending for defense.

THE FLAT-TAX PROPOSAL

Many American taxpayers seem to have lost faith in the progressive income tax. Inflation causes us to climb into higher tax brackets even though we have no increase in purchasing power. Several members of Congress have pushed the flat-rate income tax idea vigorously. One proposal would raise rates progressively from 14 to 28 percent. In addition, it would allow deductions for mortgage interest and charitable contributions. But this is not a true flat tax.

THE FLAT-RATE TAX

In a recent year, Louis Harris and Associates, Inc., conducted a public-opinion poll. The question asked was, "Do you favor a single, 14 percent tax rate for everyone, eliminating nearly all deductions people take so that more of their income is taxable?" Only 25 percent said they opposed it; 62 percent favored it, and 13 percent were not sure.

However, 80 percent said they wanted to keep medical expenses as a deduction; 71 percent wanted to keep interest on home mortgages; 66 percent, charitable contributions; 64 percent, state and local income taxes; and 63 percent wanted to keep casualty and theft losses.

In arguing for the flat-rate tax, Alfred H. Kingon, editor-in-chief of *Financial World*, said, "In one move we can make the taxpayers of the United States honest again; that will do more for the economy than anything else." The fate of the flat-tax idea may not be decided for some time.

SUMMARY OF KEY CONCEPTS

The power and authority of government legislation come from the Constitution and the interpretation of laws.

Government encourages and protects businesses through tariffs, loans, grants, and subsidies.

The exchange of trade requires an acceptable *medium of exchange*. The federal government provides this through a national monetary system.

A business may gain a temporary monopoly of an invention, a writing, or an idea through a patent, a copyright, or a trademark.

The issuing of licenses and franchises provides a simple and direct way to control businesses.

To protect the public interest, government must regulate business.

Government functions and services depend on successful businesses. In order to sustain competition and protect businesses, monopolies must be prevented or controlled.

Revenue to pay for government comes largely from taxes. A variety of taxes are levied against both individuals and businesses.

Some special taxes are levied against businesses, which adds considerably to their cost of operation:

Social Security taxes
Unemployment insurance
Workers' compensation

Taxes have a tremendous impact on business. In fact, intelligent business decisions can be made only within the framework of government rules and public policy.

BUSINESS TERMS

You should be able to match these business terms with the statements that follow:

a. BARTER	g. PARITY
b. COPYRIGHT	h. PATENT
c. ESTATE TAX	i. PUBLIC POLICY
d. FRANCHISE	j. SUBSIDY
e. MONEY	k. TARIFF
f. MONOPOLY	l. TRADEMARK

1. A charge or duty levied by the government against imported goods
2. A government grant to a private enterprise for the good of the public
3. Placing farmers' income on a par with the cost of producing their crops
4. The exclusive right to own, use, and dispose of an invention
5. The right of an author or a publisher to own, sell, or use written material
6. A distinctive symbol, title, or design that readily identifies a company or product
7. The trading of one good for another

A government system establishing a legal medium of exchange as payment for goods or services

The exclusive right to perform a particular type of business service in a specified geographical area

A statement or an interpretation of an action that carries the weight of government authority

A situation where a firm (or a few firms) has a large enough segment of an industry that it can control prices.

A tax levied against wealth passed on to heirs by one deceased

From where does the federal government receive its power and authority?

In what specific ways does the federal government encourage and assist businesses?

In what areas does the government set standards for business?

How do patents, copyrights, and trademarks aid businesses?

What is the chief purpose of a government franchise?

What is the meaning of the term *public policy* as it relates to business?

What is the purpose of parity, and how does it work?

Why is a sound monetary policy important to business?

How do you feel about government regulatory agencies? Do we have enough, or too many?

What in your opinion constitutes a good tax policy?

What specific effects do taxes have on business decisions and consumers?

BUSINESS CASES

20-1 THE NOLAN CORPORATION—A POTENTIAL MONOPOLY

The Nolan Corporation has been one of three companies marketing metal windows and doors in ten western states. Normally, the company sells about 55 percent of the metal windows and doors marketed in the ten-state area. Clark Industries and the Ballard Company account for the remainder of the market. All three companies sell through local retail hardware stores and building and supply companies. The Nolan Corporation has clearly been the leader in this market, and prices quoted by this firm were often adopted by the two competitors. From time to time, the two smaller competitors have complained that Nolan dominates the market through price cutting.

In the early 1980s, Clark Industries began experiencing financial losses, so the directors of Clark offered to sell out to Nolan. The directors of the Nolan Corporation studied their proposal and the market. They concluded that the proposed merger offered some advantages worth considering. For one thing, the merger would enable Nolan to make sufficient economies so that it could cut wholesale prices by 10 percent and still show a satisfactory profit.

Meanwhile, the Ballard Company heard about the proposal, immediately filed a protest with the Antitrust Division in Washington, D.C., and subsequently sent its attorneys to appear at a special hearing. The attorneys argued that this merger would ultimately force the Ballard Company to close its plant, inasmuch as it could not meet the 10 percent price reduction. Moreover, the merger would give Nolan a monopoly that could eventually result in higher prices for its products. Further, competitors operating in the East would find it unprofitable to ship their products to compete with the trade in the western states.

1. Do you think the facts indicate that this merger should be disapproved by the Antitrust Division? Give your reasons.
2. Would this merger be in the best interest of the public in the long run? Explain your answer.

20-2 GOVERNMENT TO THE RESCUE

Hart's Textiles, located in New England, is a small independent operation that employs 180 workers. Hart's Textiles is incorporated, but most of the stock is owned by people who live in the immediate and surrounding area. For the past six years, the company has lost money and has paid no dividends. The two largest stockholders are urging that the company be sold, moved, or liquidated. They have found a suitable location in one of the southeastern states. Labor in this state is plentiful and cheaper than in New England. The city government in this potential location has offered to waive the payment of property taxes for the first five years. It has also offered to build the new plant and lease it to the corporation.

Since hearing this news, the present labor force is urging its local government to buy the plant and forgo the payment of property taxes. A small group has suggested that the workers buy the plant and operate it as a cooperative.

Thus, the alternatives considered so far are:

a. Continue as now organized
b. Move to a southern location
c. Sell out to the local government
d. Sell to the workers and operate as a cooperative

1. Do you see other alternatives?
2. What is the plant's importance to the local government?
3. Assume that the local government has sufficient money to buy the plant. Would it be better off to do so, or should it offer tax concessions for a period of years, thus enabling the company to continue to be privately owned?
4. What would be the determining factors in deciding whether to operate the company as a cooperative?

The General Electric Company has entered a market that is growing 50 percent faster than the U.S. economy — world trade. International trade totaled $2 trillion in 1981 and is expected to reach $5 trillion by 1988.

General Electric ranks third among U.S. exporters, but it is the nation's leading *diversified* exporter. It has sales offices in fifty-five countries, with more than 700 distributors and sales representatives in 140 countries.

GE management established the General Electric Trading Company (GETC). GETC President George J. Stathakis has spent much of his career in international marketing. He says:

> The trading company is an idea whose time has come. It was set up to offer clients one-stop export services, ranging from market identification, to sales and distribution, to financing. . . .

More than 150 years ago, the French writer Alexis de Tocqueville warned the Old World that while its captains stayed close to snug harbors, the Yankee was a trader who pushed his ships out into the stormy seas. With the new General Electric Trading Company, that Yankee trading spirit is alive again.

GE plans to help companies sell products complementary to those GE produces. Examples of such products are small compressors and pumps, gas and diesel engines, and welding equipment.

GE's trading company will concentrate on exports to regions with high growth potential. The Mideast, Africa, Latin America, and Southeast Asia are considered to be such areas.

International Business

study objectives

WHEN YOU HAVE FINISHED READING THIS CHAPTER, YOU SHOULD BE
ABLE TO:

1. Recognize how world trade can benefit those countries that engage in it

2. Name the kinds of products that the United States lacks and must obtain
   from other countries

3. Identify the leading trading partners of the United States, considering both
   imports and exports

4. Explain how one nation gains an advantage over others in production
   through world trade

5. Describe the chief barriers to international trade

6. Define the term *tariff* and summarize the advantages of free trade between
   nations

One of the principal requirements of a strong U.S. economy is the maintenance of open markets both at home and abroad. The United States is more dependent on international trade than at any time in recent history. Exports generate higher real income and new jobs, and imports increase consumer choice and competition in a wide range of goods and services

William E. Brock
U.S. Trade Representative

No nation stands alone; trade with people and businesses in other countries is essential. Almost every nation produces something desired by people in other countries. Money received for these goods and services may be used to purchase items not available at home. Companies large and small make and sell products around the world.

Business abroad merits special study because it is conducted in a different environment. Laws, customs, and currency systems vary from one country to another. Many governments exercise much control over business done in their countries. International trade agreements among countries are common today, and they greatly affect overseas business.

This chapter is based on the idea that trade and investments between nations are a two-way activity. Topics such as tariffs, foreign exchange, marketing practices, and balance of payments are covered. In this discussion, the terms **world business** and **international business** are used interchangeably.

THE DYNAMICS OF WORLD BUSINESS

World business includes services, investments, and monetary transactions as well as goods. A country's balance of payments is affected by all these types of activity. The exchange of goods has, in the past, made up the largest part of trade between nations, but services accounts for an ever-increasing share.

Over the past ten years, the balance in payments for goods has been declining, but the balance for services has been growing. In fact, while the balance for goods has been negative, that for services has been positive.

The unequal distribution of resources — food, wealth, people, and technology — makes world trade vital. As Third-World nations continue to develop economically, the volume of world business will increase. This happens because of the growing demand for goods as countries achieve a higher standard of living. **The shift from a national economy to a world economy represents one of the megatrends in society today.**

It is estimated that by the year 2000, Third World countries will be manufacturing as much as 30 percent of the world's goods. The growth in world trade for two decades is shown in Figure 21-1. The factor of inflation is taken out of the picture, since the graph is in constant dollars.

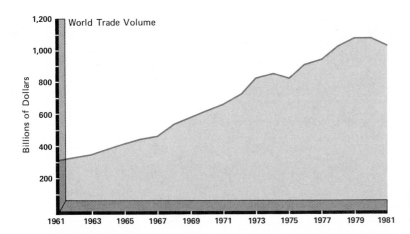

FIGURE 21-1
World Trade Volume.
(Source: International Monetary Fund.)

WHAT IS WORLD BUSINESS?
WORLD BUSINESS may be described as *business transactions between citizens, companies, and governments, conducted on an international scale.* If one country has grain and another has oil, it helps both of them when they exchange these materials. The so-called underdeveloped countries are rapidly increasing their business with other nations. U.S. Senator Charles H. Percy stated:

> Few people realize that the United States currently sells 40 percent of its manufactured exports to developing countries. They form the fastest growing market for U.S. exports, expanding at a rate of 20 percent per year, compared to 15 percent for U.S. exports to developed countries.

Actually, we are becoming "one world of business" as well as one world politically. Donald M. Kendall, chairman of Pepsico, Inc., served as chairman of the U.S. Chamber of Commerce international policy committee in the early 1980s. He said, "Too many people think we are still operating in the Marshall Plan era. But those days are over. . . . Business must prepare for the next decade with a mature view of economic reality. This takes into account such factors as human rights and immigration."

Domestic producers often stand to gain by importing and exporting. Importing crude oil from the Middle East has increased the market there for American goods and services. Imported raw materials are often cheaper and more readily available than the same items supplied by domestic sources. Exporting gives domestic producers a profit on sales from a larger operations base that may result in lower unit costs. (About one job in eight in our production industries depends on exports.) Everyone in the United States is affected by marketing exchanges with other countries. Thus we see that international business is indeed a two-way activity, as illustrated in Figure 21-2.

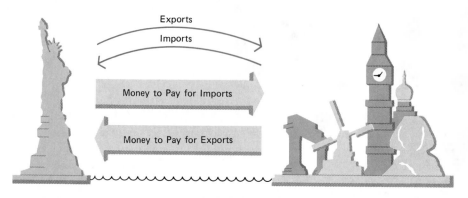

FIGURE 21-2
International trade is a two-way street. The United States is not self-sufficient. Importing goods from other nations encourages them to import goods from us.

COMPOSITION OF INTERNATIONAL TRADE

Despite the versatility of American business, this nation is completely dependent on other countries for supplies of certain commodities. Typical examples are bananas, coffee, tin, natural rubber, and diamonds. Table 21-1 shows the percentage of selected raw materials that we import. Note that for several of these products, we are completely dependent on foreign sources.

TABLE 21-1
Percentage of Selected Minerals the United States Imports

MINERAL	PERCENTAGE IMPORTED
Industrial diamonds	100
Mica	100
Natural rubber	100
Manganese	98
Cobalt	97
Platinum	92
Bauxite	91
Chromium	89
Tin	86
Asbestos	85
Nickel	70
Gold	60

JAPAN'S TRADERS & U.S. GRAIN

Mitsubishi Corporation is Japan's largest general trader; it is probably the *world's* largest trader. Along with other Japanese companies, it has moved in a big way into purchases of U.S. grain.

These companies are buying U.S. corn, wheat, and soybeans to sell to Mexico, Taiwan, and South Korea. Japanese companies hope to handle one-fifth of the grain that the United States sells overseas. Japanese firms own major grain-storage elevators in the grain-producing region of the United States. And they have export facilities at Long Beach, California; Portland, Oregon; and New Orleans, Louisiana.

Goods and services that are produced in this country and sold abroad are called EXPORTS. *Raw materials and manufactured products shipped into this country* are called IMPORTS.

Milton Friedman, formerly of the University of Chicago and a recipient of the Nobel Prize in economics, said this about trade between nations:

Exports are the cost of trade, imports the return from trade. We should be setting a standard for the world by practicing freedom of competition, of trade, and of enterprise.

The United States produces and consumes almost 30 percent of the total world supply of goods and services. American industry exports annually about 6 percent of its production, and it imports about 5 percent of the goods consumed in this country. (These percentages fluctuate somewhat from year to year, depending upon economic conditions here and elsewhere.)

International trade is more important for certain sectors of the American economy than for others. We depend upon foreign markets to absorb about 35 percent of our milled rice and its byproducts, 30 percent of our cotton-farm products, and about 32 percent of our mining, construction, and tractor production. The chemical, machinery, and machine-tool industries also sell significant portions of their output abroad.

OUR TRADING PARTNERS

Who carries on trade with the United States? The largest volume of world trade is among countries with highly industrialized economies. These countries are able to produce a surplus and trade it to other nations. The United States trades mostly with the countries of the Western Hemisphere—Canada, South America, Mexico—and with the European countries and Japan. But American firms also export to the USSR, and to Middle East countries. The developing countries of Africa are now engaging in world trade, for they have products desired by other nations.

Our leading imports from Canada are paper pulp, agricultural products, and lumber. From Germany we buy automobiles, precision instruments, musical instruments, and textiles. Wines, automobiles, and textiles are some of our major imports from Italy. Japan, our largest customer in Asia, ranks second to Canada in export and import trade with the United States. Japan is a leading manufacturer of radios, televisions, automobiles, and steel products. Because of high labor costs in the United States, most American radio

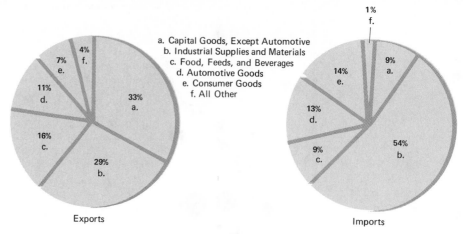

FIGURE 21-3
Composition of U.S. Trade.
(Source: The Conference Board.)

and television parts are made in the Far East. They are manufactured under the trade names of American brands and are returned to this country for assembly. Imports from Japan of automobiles and the parts to keep them running have been a major item.

Spain is not considered to be one of the leading industrial nations. But there are almost 1,000 subsidiaries of U.S. companies in Spain. A comparison of U.S. imports and exports is shown in Figure 21-3.

WHO GAINS FROM INTERNATIONAL TRADE

When we analyze the dependence of the American economy on both imports and exports, it is clear that this nation must continue to promote trade with other countries. Approximately 4.5 million jobs in this country depend directly on import and export trade. Each $1 billion in export trade supports 40,000 jobs in this country. President Ronald Reagan, in his State of the Union address in January 1983, said, "One out of every five jobs in the United States depends upon exports." Because many of the raw materials we need are not available here, we must seek foreign sources. If we are unable to obtain these scarce materials, it becomes necessary to substitute inferior goods or reduce our production. And in the area of exporting, foreign markets often make the difference between profit and loss for some American companies operating in this country.

To remain strong, a country must participate in the international marketplace. American companies must either do business abroad or surrender world markets to foreign competition. Economic isolationism would obviously undermine America's position in the Free World. It would seriously impair our domestic economy and destroy the foundation of our influence in world affairs.

No major nation can take an important step in economic policy without affecting business in other countries. The prosperity of each nation depends upon the well-being of others. International trade is an influence for peace by bringing people together in a common economic purpose.

Multinational companies are major contributors to this nation's strength. They differ greatly in the goods and services they produce and sell,

HONDA OF AMERICA

Honda of America Manufacturing, Inc., invested $250 million to build an auto manufacturing plant in Marysville, Ohio. Honda management said, ". . . by investing in the American economy, we become even more a part of the society we serve." Honda's stamping machines are made in Illinois and its painting system is from Michigan. Forty U.S. companies provide materials for use in the plant.

their sources of raw materials, their capital and labor needs, policies, and practices.

Of the 200 largest American companies, eighty have more than one-fourth of their sales, earnings, and assets abroad. Of Europe's 200 largest companies, approximately eighty also conduct more than one-fourth of their business abroad. During the past decade, transatlantic capital investments have increased about 10 percent per year in each direction.

But a company does not have to be big to be an exporter. In fact, three out of five American exporters have fewer than 100 employees.

A comparison of our exports and imports with those of our major trading partners is shown in Figure 21-4.

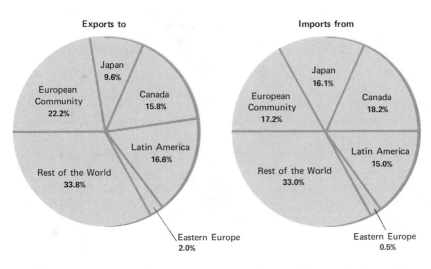

Exports to

- Japan 9.6%
- Canada 15.8%
- Latin America 16.6%
- Eastern Europe 2.0%
- Rest of the World 33.8%
- European Community 22.2%

Imports from

- Japan 16.1%
- Canada 18.2%
- Latin America 15.0%
- Eastern Europe 0.5%
- Rest of the World 33.0%
- European Community 17.2%

FIGURE 21-4
Trading Partners of the United States.
(Source: Data from U.S. Department of Commerce.)

THE INTERNATIONAL BUSINESS ENVIRONMENT

Of the several factors that influence the flow of world business, the restrictions of governments are one of the strongest. Businesses are not free to set up operations wherever they please in another country. The effort of the Canadian government to keep control of Canadian business is well known. But the so-called Third-World nations are also restricting free entry into their countries. "Foreign" businesses are being required to involve local businesses. In some instances, they must employ a certain percentage of local personnel.

JAMES B. SHERWOOD

James B. Sherwood is president and CEO of Sea Containers, Ltd., and SeaCo Inc. These companies and their subsidiaries are known as the Sea Containers Group. Magazine writers have called Sherwood "the wunderkind of the shipping industry" and "the guru of container shipping." Although he has lived in England since 1965, he is actually a citizen of the world. He has a yacht in the Mediterranean and a private jet that takes him around the world for six months of each year.

Mr. Sherwood was born in New Castle, Pennsylvania, in 1933. He was graduated from Yale University in 1955 with a B.A. degree in economics. He served aboard ships and ashore with the Military Sea Transportation Service in the Far East from 1955 to 1958. He was employed by United States Lines, Inc., in 1959. In 1963, he joined Container Transport International, Inc., as general manager. He left that company in 1965 to form Sea Containers.

Today the Sea Containers Group has assets of $850 million, including 250,000 marine cargo containers, 35 container ships, four container factories, and hotels and real estate developments. Its headquarters is in London, England.

Sherwood is a director of several companies engaged in shipping, and of the New England Ice Cream Company, Ltd., the Venice-Simplon-Orient-Express Ltd., and the Through Transport Mutual Insurance Association, Ltd. He is a curator of Transylvania University, Lexington, Kentucky.

Mr. Sherwood and his wife were responsible for bringing back into operation, in May 1982, the Orient Express. This is a luxury train operating between London and Venice by way of Paris. It had been discontinued in May 1977. Five years later, after an expenditure of $20 million, it once again resumed operation. Mr. Sherwood is married to Dr. Shirley A. M. Sherwood, a scientist in the field of drug research, and has two stepsons, Charles and Simon. The family lives in London.

In the area of tariffs and trade quotas, countries are requiring tradeoffs. When limits or duties are relaxed on certain imports, similar treatment on exports is expected.

International finance has become crucial. Nations such as Poland, Mexico, and Argentina are unable to repay their loans on schedule. The seriousness of financing these past-due loans has greatly increased the role of the International Monetary Fund. The leading banks in most industrialized nations have reached the saturation point on overseas financing.

THE LEADING EXPORTERS

The U.S. dollar was especially strong in world markets in the early 1980s; this made selling U.S. products abroad difficult. It has been estimated that each percentage-point rise in the value of the dollar costs the United States $3 billion in net exports.

The Boeing Company of Seattle often heads the list of U.S. exporters. Our ten leading exporters and the products they sell abroad are shown in Table 21-2.

CAPITAL FLOWS

Investment capital, like goods, flows both ways—imports and exports. U.S. investment overseas has been significant for many years, and today, foreign investors are buying into the United States at a rapid clip. Foreign investors are buying established businesses rather than creating new ones.

TABLE 21-2
The Leading U.S. Exporters for 1982

RANK	COMPANY	PRODUCTS	EXPORTS AS PERCENT OF SALES
1	General Motors	Motor vehicles and parts, locomotives	7.79
2	General Electric	Generating equipment, aircraft engines	14.80
3	Boeing	Aircraft	42.93
4	Ford Motor	Motor vehicles and parts	10.07
5	Caterpillar Tractor	Construction equipment, engines	40.49
6	E.I. Du Pont de Nemours	Chemicals, fibers, polymer products, petroleum, coal	7.68
7	United Technologies	Aircraft engines, helicopters	16.73
8	McDonnell Douglas	Aircraft, space systems, missiles	28.32
9	International Business Machines	Information-handling systems, equipment, and parts	5.46
10	Eastman Kodak	Photographic equipment and supplies	17.13

During the 1970s, investments in this country from overseas grew at a compound rate of 16 percent per year. But for the year 1980, they increased 20 percent, and for 1981, 31 percent. This flow of overseas money into the United States is shown in Figure 21-5.

COUNTERTRADE Barter, that ancient method of swapping goods and services, is making a big comeback. An increasing number of countries, strapped for hard currencies, are resorting to barter-type trade agreements. *Barter between or among nations* is called COUNTERTRADE.

Sometimes the only way to make a sale in another country is to accept products from that country. One example was between General Electric and Sweden. To win a $300-million jet-engine order in Sweden, GE developed a countertrade package with twenty-five different elements that helped meet the Swedish government's needs. These included buying Swedish bearings

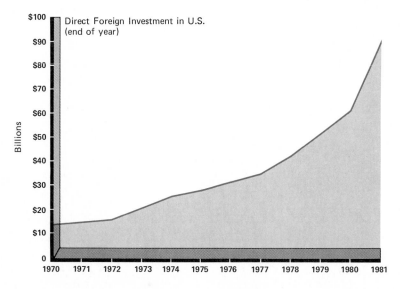

FIGURE 21-5
Direct Foreign Investment in the United States.
(Source: U.S. Department of Commerce.)

for international resale, licensing an electrical generator system from General Electric's aerospace business, and the joint development of a Swedish off-highway vehicle using GE electric wheel technology.

The U.S. Department of Commerce estimates that from 15 to 20 percent of the annual stream of world commerce is in the form of "countertrade."

CONTROL DATA AND THE HERMITAGE MUSEUM

The Control Data Corporation supplied the Hermitage Museum in Leningrad, Russia, with a computer. In return, the museum lent an exhibit of its masterpieces for a two-year tour of the United States. Valued at $110 million, the exhibit is reputed to be the largest Soviet art collection ever scheduled for foreign display. It is also the most comprehensive outside showing of Hermitage treasures ever mounted.

As payment, Control Data received exclusive rights to sell Hermitage reproductions and art books. This right was for the duration of the tour and an undetermined period thereafter.

TARIFFS AND GOVERNMENT TRADE POLICIES

In this country, goods can be shipped from one state to another with little or no government interference. In international trade, however, the same shipment of goods is subject to various controls established by host governments. These controls are in the form of tariffs, quotas, embargoes, and price-fixing agreements. Such controls restrict the free play of economic forces.

DEFINITION OF TARIFF

A TARIFF is *a tax or customs duty levied by a nation on imported goods.* It works both ways. We tax goods entering this country, and other countries tax *their* imports. In the United States, Congress may levy duties only on imports, not on exports, according to Article I of the U.S. Constitution. This nation has had high or low tariffs from the early days of the Republic. Since World War II, the emphasis has been on freer trade among nations, with low tariffs for friendly nations that qualify for "favored-nation" treatment.

WHAT "MOST FAVORED NATION" MEANS

The term *most favored nation* dates back to an agreement signed in Geneva in 1947 by twenty-three of the world's major non-Communist countries. The pact was known as the General Agreement on Tariffs and Trade.

One of its important provisions was the most-favored-nation principle. In essence, the provision states that the signers of the GATT agreement must extend to one another any tariff concession given to any other member country.

U.S. trade law sets tariff rats on thousands of individual products. In general, rates for nations that enjoy MFN status are substantially lower than for nations that do not.

KINDS OF TARIFFS   The two broad categories of tariffs are (1) revenue tariffs, and (2) protective tariffs. The two are designed for different purposes. A REVENUE TARIFF is *a tax on imports to produce revenue.* A PROTECTIVE TARIFF is *a tax on imports to protect domestic producers against competition from foreign producers.*

ARGUMENTS FOR AND AGAINST TARIFFS   The first congressional debate on the tariff issue occurred in 1789. Since then, Congress has taken up the issue periodically. Some people advocate complete "free trade," which would abolish all tariffs. Others argue for "protection" or for quotas. There are sound arguments to support both points of view.

The Infant-Industry Argument.   This is the oldest protariff argument of all. It holds that a new and struggling industry should be protected from foreign competition until the industry has become established. Too often, however, after the infant industry has grown up, new arguments are advanced to retain the high protective tariff.

CURRENT ISSUE

SHOULD AMERICAN INDUSTRY BE PROTECTED THROUGH TARIFFS?

Large proportions of the American textile and radio and TV manufacture have been moved overseas. The steel industries of England, Japan, and Europe have been accused of dumping goods in the American market below their costs of production (through subsidies by their governments). Union leadership argues that we should protect American industry through tariffs.

With which of the following statements do you agree, and with which do you disagree?

1. We should have tariffs in order to keep jobs for our American workers.
2. No country is self-sufficient, and therefore free trade is mutually beneficial to all those concerned.
3. Free trade makes it possible for nations to practice the principle of comparative advantage.
4. When we buy goods abroad, we are exporting jobs that should go to American labor.
5. Nations should have tariffs to protect their basic industries but should sell goods to foreigners through duty-free ports.
6. The U.S. government should maintain tariffs but should encourage U.S. companies to establish subsidiaries overseas.
7. Restrictions against imported goods encourage foreign companies to establish businesses in this country.
8. Instead of having tariffs, the U.S. government should establish import quotas for goods from other countries.

What major criterion should govern whether we establish tariffs, and, if we do, how high they should be?

Arguments for Free Trade.   Free-traders argue that each country should be able to take advantage of its own national specialization and thereby maximize its production. Under free trade, all nations can raise the standard of living of their people. Elimination of trade barriers promotes a free flow of goods between nations.

The Wage Argument.   Labor unions want to maintain high wages. Thus, they often see goods coming from low-wage countries as unfair competition. They argue that tariffs help protect workers' employment. "If we keep out imported goods produced by lower-priced labor, it is possible to sell more American-made goods in America. This maintains a higher level of employment." On the other hand, to keep out foreign competition restricts our volume of exports. If foreign producers are unable to sell to the American market, they will lack the money to buy from us.

FOREIGN-TRADE
LEGISLATION

The Reciprocal Trade Agreements Program.   The present American tariff policies are based on the Reciprocal Trade Agreements Act of 1934 (RTA). Then in 1947, the United States and twenty-two other nations agreed upon a system of procedures and rules for studying tariffs, the General Agreement on Tariffs and Trade (GATT). The basic elements of GATT are to:

1. Provide rules of nondiscrimination in trade relations
2. Negotiate trade concessions
3. Approve prohibitions against quantitative restrictions on exports and imports

The member countries of GATT meet annually to review recommendations, to settle disputes, and to study ways to reduce tariffs.

In 1962, Congress passed the Trade Expansion Act (TEA). This was a completely new approach to world trade for the United States. This legislation gave the president the power to cut tariffs by 50 percent in negotiating new trade pacts during the five years following its inception. The purposes of the TEA, as expressed in the language of the act, were to:

1. Stimulate the economic growth of the United States and maintain and enlarge foreign markets for the products of U.S. agriculture, industry, mining, and commerce
2. Strengthen economic relations with foreign countries through the development of open and nondiscriminatory trading in the free world
3. Prevent Communist economic penetration

U.S. Trade Reform Act (1974).   Under this act, the president is authorized to enter into trade agreements for modifying tariff rates and liberalizing other barriers to international trade. It also gives the president authority to proclaim import measures, for a period of up to 150 days, for balance-of-payments purposes. The antidumping provisions are supposed to help promote fair competition.

In 1977, Congress passed the Foreign Corrupt Practices Act. This act was designed to outlaw bribes and "improper" commissions in international trade. Many corporations, particularly among the multinationals, had been pressing for such help. They charged that its absence was forcing them to forgo dealing with countries where such practices are a way of life.

Tokyo Round of Tariff Negotiations.   New discussions on reducing trade barriers began in Tokyo in 1973. These discussions culminated on April 12, 1979, when representatives of the major trading nations initialed the agreement. Ninety-nine nations participated in these multilateral trade negotiations. The agreement was approved by the U.S. Senate on July 23, 1979.

President Jimmy Carter declared:

> The agreements steer us away from destructive protectionism and into a path of greater export opportunities with the prospects of new jobs, improved productivity and increased industrial and agricultural production.

> U.S. officials estimate that tariff cuts by the Common Market that will benefit American goods average about 35 percent; the average U.S. tariff cut on goods coming from Europe is about 34 percent. Similarly, Japanese tariff cuts on goods exported from the U.S. average 46 percent, while U.S. tariff cuts on imports from Japan average 32 percent.

The agreement took effect on January 1, 1980, lowering tariffs on nonfarm imports an average of 33 percent over eight to ten years. The economic benefits to businesses in this country could be as much as $10 billion per year. Administration foreign experts predict that 130,000 additional jobs for American workers will result from this trade agreement.

THE ECONOMICS OF INTERNATIONAL TRADE AND INVESTMENT

Many textbooks are devoted exclusively to the economics of international trade. Here, we deal mainly with the basic *economic* reasons for having international trade and discuss some of the principles involved.

PRINCIPLE OF ABSOLUTE ADVANTAGE

Specialization in foreign trade is encouraged under the principle of ABSOLUTE ADVANTAGE. The principle recognizes that the costs of producing commodities differ from country to country. According to this principle, *a nation should specialize in an article or service when it enjoys the advantages of low costs on that item.* Such an advantage could be due to a natural monopoly or some unusual technical development. As an illustration, Brazil can produce coffee more cheaply than the United States can. So as a coffee producer, Brazil has an absolute advantage over this country. On the other hand, we have an absolute advantage over Brazil in making jet aircraft. Both countries will gain from the exchange of American jet aircraft for Brazilian coffee.

Let us compare the principle of absolute advantage with comparative advantage. It often benefits a nation to import goods even when that nation can make them for lower labor costs. Although a nation may have a greater absolute advantage, its *comparative advantage* may dictate that it should specialize in the production of another good. It can then use the income from this production to pay for the good bought from another country.

PRINCIPLE OF COMPARATIVE ADVANTAGE

The principle of COMPARATIVE ADVANTAGE implies what we have been stressing in this chapter: (a) *It is to the economic advantage of a country to specialize in goods and services that it can produce more cheaply than can other countries;* (b) nations should refrain from producing those items that they can buy more cheaply elsewhere. Comparative advantage may be due to such factors as a well-trained labor force, an abundance of raw materials, modern and efficient plants, and favorable climatic conditions.

The principle of comparative advantage may be explained further by a hypothetical example. Suppose there were only two countries, the United States and Russia. Each country produced only two commodities of mutual interest, wheat and texiles. And suppose the cost ratios between wheat and textiles differed between the two countries as follows:

UNIT COST (PRICE)	UNITED STATES (DOLLARS)	RUSSIA (RUBLES)
Of wheat	4.00	16.00
Of textiles	2.00	1.00

Disregarding the exchange rate between the two currencies, the cost ratio of wheat to textiles in the United States is 2:1, and in Russia, 16:1. These ratios indicate that the United States would have a comparative cost advantage in the production of wheat and a comparative cost disadvantage in the production of textiles. In Russia, the opposite would be true. **Gainful trade would occur if the United States exported wheat and imported textiles while Russia exported textiles and imported wheat.** The real cost of one unit of wheat in the United States would be half a unit of textiles. In Russia, the opportunity cost of producing one unit of wheat would be five units of textiles. It is obvious that the United States would have a lower opportunity cost of producing wheat and would export it because of the comparative advantage in that commodity.

At this point you might ask, Why shouldn't the United States sell both wheat and textiles to Russia, bringing the dollars home without buying anything from them? The answer is that there would be no dollars in Russia with which to pay for American wheat and textiles, and therefore no dollars to bring home, unless Russians could obtain dollars by selling something to the United States. In other words, we cannot be paid for our goods and services unless we take payment in the form of foreign goods and services. All this reemphasizes that foreign trade travels on a two-way street.

ECONOMIC ADVANTAGES OF INTERNATIONAL TRADE

Aside from these broad aspects of international trade, a high level of commerce with other countries provides individual businesspeople with several specific advantages:

Advantages to Importing.   American business firms import goods because:

1. Foreign prices may be lower than domestic prices on similar goods.
2. Certain goods are not available in this country — or, if they are available, the supply is not sufficient to meet the demand.
3. Ordering goods from foreign firms may encourage them to buy goods from more American firms.
4. Some foreign merchandise is considered to offer more style and prestige than domestic products, and consequently will command higher prices in the United States.

Advantages to Exporting.   Many American firms engage in exporting because:

1. Selling to foreign customers is often less expensive than expanding a new home market.
2. Foreign markets are a way of increasing sales volume and obtaining the economies of large-scale production and lower unit costs.

OVERSEAS INVESTMENT AND JOBS AT HOME

Some people argue that when U.S. companies invest in overseas enterprise, this exports jobs.

The Business International Corporation has undertaken seven special research studies dealing with this question. The most recent study surveyed 124 U.S. firms, covering the period 1970–77. This study reached the same conclusion as the first six: There is a direct correlation between investment abroad and job creation at home.

Specifically, Business International found that those businesses with the most foreign investment increased their U.S. employment by 2.3 percent, while those with the least foreign investment decreased their U.S. employment by 4.1 percent.

DIRECT INVESTMENT OVERSEAS

There are several considerations that enter into a decision of where to manufacture a given product. Labor, transportation costs, the attitude of governments, and the level of technology involved are important factors.

Recently, the General Electric Company decided to close a plant in southern California, where it had been making electric irons from metal. Company management contended that there was no longer sufficient demand for metal irons. Employees contended that the irons were still selling at a profit. In the end, the company officers admitted that the irons could be made from nonmetallic materials overseas at a much lower price. This seems to be a case where the principle of comparative advantage, changes in competition, and scale of operation all played important roles in the decision to move.

EARNINGS ON OVERSEAS INVESTMENT

During the 1950s and 1960s, many U.S. companies expanded their overseas operations. There were outcries about exporting jobs and damage to our balance of payments. The earnings from these plants have become a big plus for the U.S. payments position. The income from direct investment abroad is shown in Figure 21-6.

INTERNATIONAL TRADE COOPERATION

The success of the Marshall Plan in achieving the economic recovery of Europe after World War II is well known. It demonstrated the advantages of closer economic cooperation among European nations. One effective way to promote economic cooperation was for European nations to remove their trade barriers by forming a customs union. A customs union is a geographical region embracing two or more nations within which goods can move freely without being subject to customs duties. Customs unions have been formed in both Europe and Latin America.

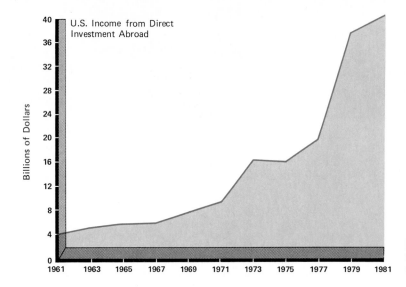

FIGURE 21-6
U.S. Income from Direct Investment Abroad.
(Source: U.S. Department of Commerce.)

The European Economic Community.   One of the most effective and best-known customs unions is the European Economic Community (EEC), referred to as the Common Market. France, Italy, Belgium, West Germany, Luxembourg, and The Netherlands formed the EEC on January 1, 1958. Those six nations worked toward producing a full integration of their economies by 1970. Beyond that, their goal is to achieve political unity. The EEC is also working toward elimination of restrictions in insurance, banking, and labor laws, and toward the enactment of new laws to regulate the marketing of drugs and pharmaceuticals. The ultimate objective of the EEC is to bring about complete political and economic unity.

On October 28, 1971, Great Britain's House of Commons voted to join the Common Market effective January 1, 1973. Denmark and Ireland followed Great Britain in becoming members. Greece joined the EEC in 1980, and Spain in 1981.

The ten nations that make up the Common Market of Western Europe account for about one-third of the world's trade, including trade among themselves. Disputes between the United States and the European countries continually arise over tariff rates for specific commodities.

BARRIERS TO INTERNATIONAL BUSINESS

Certain barriers to foreign trade make selling in an international market a real challenge.

THE LANGUAGE BARRIER   Relatively few Americans are fluent in more than one language, and not all foreign traders speak English. However, English is the second language in many countries, which is helping to lessen the language barrier. Also, an increasing number of American students are learning a second language.

DIFFERENCES IN SOCIAL CUSTOMS   Each nation has its peculiar social customs and business practices, which often serve as a hindrance to international trade. The Latin American *siesta*—the long lunch hour that makes the workday longer—is not com-

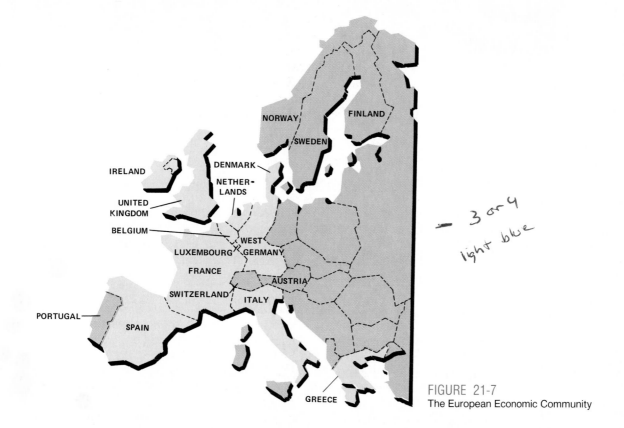

FIGURE 21-7
The European Economic Community

mon to other ethnic groups. Many foreigners working in Latin American countries find this custom difficult to observe. For some, driving an automobile on the left-hand side of the road is confusing. Removing your shoes to enter a residence or a religious building is another unique custom. Strange and exotic foods sometimes create a diet problem for the newcomer abroad. On the other hand, the American practice of one-stop shopping in shopping centers is becoming a common practice in many foreign countries.

One common foreign custom that has caused trouble between American business and the federal government is the "entry fee" or bribe that is often expected when dealing with foreign governments.

Mr. Trilli is president of a large Pittsburgh-based engineering and construction firm. He contends that his company was beaten out of a number of big overseas contracts because competitors paid off government officials. One project was a $40-million brick plant in Iraq. Trilli says, "We had it all wrapped up. All terms had been agreed to, and we were told that the contract would be signed in a month. Then out of the blue, a German firm got the contract." Trilli says the German firm got the contract because it made a big payment to a high Iraqi official.

Midland-Ross Corporation cited two instances of suspected payoffs involving paper-mill equipment for two West African nations. Midland-Ross was favored by the consulting engineer on the project but lost out at the last minute to an Italian firm.

Congressional committees investigated the activities of the Central Intelligence Agency (CIA) and several American firms operating abroad. It was revealed that many cash payments had been made to high government officials in foreign countries. The officials of the American companies testified that such payments were essential in order to secure trade. It was also revealed that such payments were not illegal in many of the countries where they were assessed. All this raises a major issue: If payment to local officials is an accepted practice in a foreign country, is it illegal, immoral, or unethical to make such payments? Or is it just good business for the American firm operating in that country?

In any event, U.S. companies must operate under the provisions of the Foreign Corrupt Practices Act, which makes it an offense to offer a payment to a foreign government official to obtain business. Other industrialized nations do not impose such sanctions on their businesses. Indeed, a treaty proposed by the United States to eliminate bribery in international transactions has received almost no active support in the United Nations. The U.S. brand of morality has not been accepted in most areas.

DIFFERENCES IN LAWS

Another barrier to foreign trade is the differences in laws. For example, the cartel is illegal in the United States, but it is not illegal in most other countries. The Organization of Petroleum and Exporting Countries (OPEC) is a cartel familiar to most of us.

A CARTEL is *an association of individual companies whose purpose is to control prices and/or the conditions of sale.* Cartels are price-fixing monopolies, which are illegal in this country because they violate the Sherman Antitrust Act. Price-fixing by cartels abroad can lead to critical situations in international commerce when an American firm finds it must compete with foreign firms.

Patent laws of various nations differ more widely than do laws relating to other industrial property. Some countries will not grant patents on certain products — for example, chemical compounds. And Russia is not a signatory to the International Patent Agreement. Also, in some countries, **copyright laws** are not complied with as they are in the United States.

DIFFERENCES IN CURRENCIES

Currencies differ throughout the world, which is a barrier to international trade. To illustrate the complications this can create, an American manufacturer who sells goods to a Belgian merchant expects to be paid in dollars. So the Belgian merchant would need to obtain dollars by exchanging Belgian francs on the foreign-exchange market.

There was a period when gold was the common denominator for all currencies. But for several years, it has not been possible to obtain gold when dollars were not available. The fluctuation of these currencies in their exchange values does not simplify the situation.

The United States has $800 million in rupees, kyats, and sylis (pronounced "sillies") in India, Pakistan, Burma, and Guinea. This money is considered "excess U.S.-owned foreign currencies." It resulted largely from payments for U.S. food shipments over several decades. Because inflation makes the money worth less each year, the United States would like to spend

FIGURE 21-8
The busy harbor at Jeddah, Saudi Arabia. (Photo by Robert Azzi, Woodfin Camp & Associates.)

much of these surplus foreign currencies. But there is a catch. The currencies must be spent in their home countries. So while some federal officials have been seeking ways to save government money, others have been trying to find ways to spend it.

The U.S. Agriculture Department's French soil dictionary is an example. The 1,100-page translation cost about $22,000 in U.S.-owned rupees in India. "We got it done there at a fraction of the cost of having it done in France," says the department's Richard Parry. But, he concedes, "it might have been done faster in France." In India, the translation took eight years to complete.

THIRD-WORLD CURRENCIES CAN'T FLY HOME

Airlines lost money in the early 1980s because of the world recession and high fuel costs. In addition, international carriers accumulated piles of "soft" Third-World currencies. They were unable to convert them to U.S. dollars. In Egypt alone in the summer of 1982, eleven airlines were holding $125 million worth of Egyptian pounds.

The International Air Transport Association says the amount of unconverted currencies from ticket sales in Third-World countries reached the equivalent of almost $600 million in 1982. As a result, Germany's Lufthansa closed its office in Zaire in 1978. "We have rather a big sum of money we can't get out, so we closed down," contends Ib Kam, who is the West German airline's area manager in eastern Africa.

International Business

575

Besides the barriers discussed above, other problem areas that serve to make international marketing a real challenge are these:

1. Differences in people's consumption patterns in the various countries
2. Difficulties in obtaining reliable market data
3. Complex and inefficient distribution structures in many countries

EXPORT MARKETING MANAGEMENT

When a U.S. firm decides to sell abroad, certain issues must be resolved by management. These include:

1. Assessing risk and export potential
2. Selecting an appropriate marketing channel (direct or indirect)
3. Choosing an international bank, freight forwarder, and overseas agent
4. Acquiring the necessary in-house expertise to carry out export-related tasks

SELECTING AN APPROPRIATE MARKETING CHANNEL

Management must decide if it will engage in direct selling abroad by using the company's own export division. This is known as a *direct-export marketing channel.* The other method is to sell through independent middlemen located in the United States who specialize in export selling. This is referred to as an *indirect-export marketing channel.*

USING DIRECT-EXPORT MARKETING CHANNELS

Companies that engage in a substantial amount of foreign commerce find that it pays to have their own foreign-distribution facilities. They might also have factories abroad.

Foreign Branches. Foreign branches are divisions of a domestic company located in a foreign country. Their operations range from foreign sales, storage, and warehouse operations to foreign assembly or manufacturing plants.

Foreign Subsidiaries. Foreign subsidiaries resemble foreign branches, but they are in fact virtually separate companies owned and controlled by a parent American company. An advantage of this form is that the subsidiary can handle a complete line of products.

In recent years, the multinational corporation has evolved. The MULTINATIONAL BUSINESS is *a firm with a number of directly controlled operations in different countries and with a worldwide perspective.* American multinational companies include such firms as International Business Machines, John Deere, and Procter & Gamble. Ford Motor Company has plants in twenty countries; National Cash Register and Exxon operate worldwide. Of the 20,000 American companies engaged in international business, about 3,000 have subsidiaries and branches in foreign countries. Among non-American multinational corporations, Nestlé, Volkswagen, and Sony are widely known.

The Built-in Export Department. Aside from the two direct-export methods of marketing abroad, a third method is the built-in export department. Where such a system is in effect, export activities are assigned to certain people in the company. These are usually an export manager and one or two clerks. The export manager does the selling or directs it. The traffic department handles documents and transportation, along with other traffic matters for the company.

The built-in export department is generally small. It is well adapted to the manufacturer whose export volume is small in comparison with the total volume of the business.

USING INDIRECT-EXPORT MARKETING CHANNELS

Indirect exporting uses outside organizations located in the home market. Some of these middlemen take title to goods.

The Export Merchant. The export merchant is an independent middleman who buys and sells abroad on his or her own account. The merchant does both exporting and importing. In exporting, the firm is often known as a trading company, because it buys and sells a large variety of products from many companies.

The Export Agent. The export agent generally represents several noncompeting American firms on a commission basis, without taking title to goods. Sales are made by the export agent for the manufacturer, who finances and ships the product to the buyer.

Buyers for Export. Buyers for export are also independent middlemen. They canvass American markets in search of goods needed by foreign consumers. Buyers for export take orders from foreign clients and are paid a commission by the producer or seller of the goods. The main advantage in selling through export buyers is that there is little marketing expense for the seller.

JOINT VENTURES

Historically, the wholly-owned foreign subsidiary has been the most common way to do business overseas. Along with complete ownership, a company also exercises almost complete control. **Ownership** refers to the supplying of equity capital. **Control** includes operation of the production processes, patent rights, technical knowledge, and marketing procedures. However, in recent years, many government leaders in host countries have decided that foreign ownership does not serve the best economic interests of their countries. As a result, there has been a constant shift toward more joint ventures by multinational businesses.

A JOINT VENTURE OVERSEAS is *an enterprise that is not completely owned or controlled by the parent company.* Participation in the host country may be by private enterprise or by the government. In general, the ratio of joint ventures is higher in developed than in underdeveloped nations.

Advantages to Host Country. The joint venture offers several advantages to the host country. First, it provides investment for local capital. It enables local entrepreneurs to acquire needed technological know-how. It also ensures more local influence over production, thereby preventing domination from outside interests. The government policy in India is that "the major interest in ownership and effective control of an industrial undertaking should, as a rule, be in Indian hands." Mexico and Burma both limit foreign ownership to 40 percent in corporations that engage in a wide variety of economic activities. These activities include mining, coal, petroleum, publishing, advertising, and transportation.

Joint ventures work both ways. U.S. companies operate through joint ventures overseas. And alien corporations have joint ventures in this country.

General Motors in 1982 formed a joint venture with Fujitsu Fanuc Ltd. of Japan. The purpose of this joint venture is to design, build, and market robots in the United States. The new company, headquartered in southeastern Michigan, sold robots initially to General Motors for use in GM plants.

Toyota entered into a joint venture agreement with General Motors in 1983. The undertaking was to produce a small car at a plant in Fremont, California. About half of the car's parts are to be produced in the United States. The remainder of the parts including the engine and transmission are to come from Japan.

Westinghouse Electric Corporation, Mitsubishi Heavy Industries, and five Japanese utilities joined efforts in 1982 to design an advanced nuclear-power plant. The aim of the five-year project is to build a plant in Japan that will be operating by 1990. Total cost of developing the pressurized water reactor design is expected to be $150 million, of which Westinghouse is to provide about $76 million. This arrangement provided Westinghouse with a market so the company could move forward despite depressed demand in the United States.

THE EUROPEAN AIRBUS INDUSTRIE

The European Airbus Industrie consortium is an excellent example of a successful joint venture. It is an alliance of French, German, British, and Spanish aerospace companies. All risk is borne by the partner companies, some of which are government-owned. Government involvement has helped the Airbus Industrie get airborne. Governments put up a large part of the launch costs for a new aircraft. The launch grants for the original A300 Airbus will be repaid in full when the 360th plane is completed in 1985. Meanwhile, aerospace companies in several other countries are seeking to join the consortium.

INTERNATIONAL PRODUCTION AND MARKETING

Management of international business is similar to the management of domestic business. First, there is the matter of organizational strategy and structure. In addition, a global sourcing and logistics strategy must be developed, and suitable personnel employed. There is one significant difference; the two types of business operate within different legal, political, and social environments.

All too often, people think of large enterprises when they think of international business. But small firms are going multinational too. For example, United Industries of Colorado, Inc., has but a single product, auto-battery fluid. The company has only one plant and fewer than a dozen employees. One year after it started exporting its product around the world, one-third of its sales were in overseas markets.

GOVERNMENT AND WORLD BUSINESS

The role of small firms in international business is changing. By the beginning of this decade, there were 21,000 U.S. companies with fewer than 100 employees exporting goods and services. But small companies still lag in export business. Companies with fewer than 250 people account for 17 percent of manufacture, but they contribute only 6 percent of manufacturing exports.

THE BALANCE OF INTERNATIONAL PAYMENTS

The most useful tool to explain the interrelations created by foreign trade is a statistical statement called the **balance of international payments.** It is prepared annually by the U.S. Department of Commerce and is also known as the *balance of payments.* It resembles an income statement rather than a balance sheet, because it shows this nation's sales (exports) and purchases (imports), together with the other forms of receipts and expenditures derived from foreign-trade transactions. An examination of a country's balance of payments shows the country's ability to pay for imported goods. All things considered, a country is either a debtor or a creditor nation.

In addition to the income received by the United States from its exports and the payments made for its imports, the balance-of-payments statement also includes other items. Among these are capital outflow when residents of this country invest abroad, and capital inflow when a foreign resident invests in the United States. Another section shows gold movements, representing gold exports and imports. Still other transactions include money spent by tourists abroad, military-aid payments, dividends, and grants.

Recent trends in the U.S. balance of trade are shown in Figure 21-9. Even though the United States regularly has a record trade deficit, Secretary of Commerce Malcolm Baldridge said:

> . . . we must resist protectionist pressures, which would only damage the world's trading system, and in the end, make matters worse.

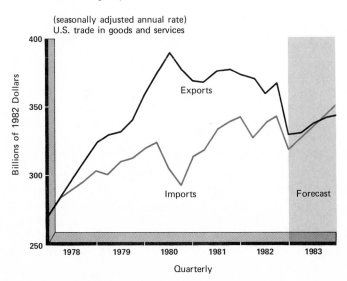

A Vanishing Surplus

(seasonally adjusted annual rate)
U.S. trade in goods and services

FIGURE 21-9
Trends in the U.S. Balance of Trade.
(Source: U.S. Department of Commerce.)

FAVORABLE BALANCE OF TRADE

Balance of trade is a part of the international balance of payments. When a nation's exports exceed the value of its imports, it has a favorable balance of trade. But when its imports exceed the value of its exports, it has an unfavorable balance of trade. The idea conveyed by "favorable" or "unfavorable" is misleading. It implies that a nation should always work to export more than it imports.

The U.S. balance of trade between 1965 and 1975 was generally a favorable one, for this nation's exports exceeded its imports. But although the balance of trade was favorable, there was still an unsatisfactory balance of payments. The exporting of surplus goods was not large enough to offset other expenditures, such as grants, loans, gifts, and military expenses abroad. Persistent deficits would drain American gold reserves to the point of danger to our money system. The balance-of-payments deficits during the 1970s reached major proportions. As a result, the value of the U.S. dollar abroad dropped substantially as compared with other major currencies. Continued deficits can destroy confidence in the American dollar by jeopardizing the stability of our economy. And they serve to create dollar shortages and inflate the economy. But during the early 1980s, the U.S. dollar was strong when measured against the currencies of other nations.

FINANCING INTERNATIONAL BUSINESS

As we have already mentioned, one of the complications of international trade is that the firm selling goods or services expects to be paid in the kind of money it can use in paying debts. But not all nations have the same currency system. English pounds, for instance, must be converted into dollars before an English buyer can pay an American business associate.

Fortunately, buyers and sellers need not meet in order to complete transactions. In this and other countries, there are banks that buy foreign currencies (or claims to them) for use by exporters. Banks also sell foreign currencies to importers who want to make payments in foreign money.

FOREIGN-EXCHANGE MARKET DEALERS

Market values for most of the world's currencies fluctuate almost daily. Foreign-exchange dealers, located in large commercial banks in the major financial centers, buy and sell foreign exchange. American importers who expect to buy a foreign article must keep in mind not only the price they must pay for the item abroad but also the price of the foreign currency they must buy to pay for their import. This price is called the FOREIGN EXCHANGE RATE. *This is the rate at which the currency of one country is exchanged for that of another country.* The foreign-exchange rate is the rate at which a foreign currency can be exchanged for American dollars. This rate changes daily.

Figure 21-10 shows where the countries making the major overseas investments are investing their funds. For instance, Japanese firms make more color television sets in this country than we import from Japan.

Rates of exchange fluctuate in response to the supply and demand of international money transfers. If our total foreign sales are greater than our total foreign purchases, the foreign demand for dollars to make payments rises. But if our imports exceed our exports, the dollar will be at a discount in terms of foreign currencies. This illustrates the effect of the balance of trade.

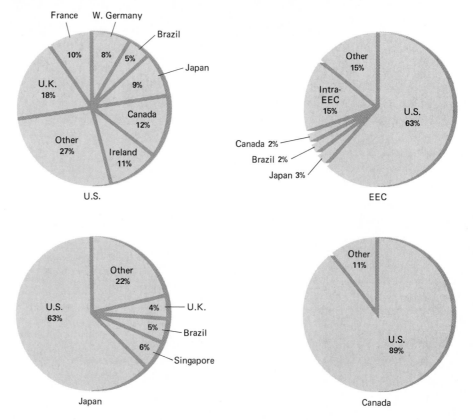

FIGURE 21-10
Where major investors channel their investments. (Source: The Conference Board.)

Actually, money is rarely shipped to another country to settle a debt. Instead, drafts or bills of exchange are used.

FINANCING EXPORTS

Financing is more complicated in international trade than in domestic trade. There is greater risk in extending credit to buyers abroad for the parties are usually unknown to each other. Or the seller may want a down payment with the order, with the balance payable on receipt of the shipment.

As a rule, when an exporter sells goods abroad, he or she takes the initiative in obtaining payment by drawing a draft for the amount of the invoice. This instrument is drawn directly on the buyer (importer), who is the debtor. It may be drawn to become due at sight, on arrival of goods, or at a designated future time. It is customary in such a case to use the services of a commercial bank that offers exporting services. (In most cases, exporters are paid in the currencies of their own countries.)

Export Documents. The export documents that generally accompany drafts are of the following types:

1. Ocean bill of lading, usually endorsed in blank (lists goods shipped and terms of the contract under which goods are shipped by the transportation agency)
2. Commercial invoice (shows quantities, terms, and prices)

3. Marine insurance certificate
4. Special customs invoice (shows weight, value, destination, and class of goods)
5. Inspection certificate
6. Certificate of origin

On receipt of an order from a foreign customer, the American exporter draws a draft (either in dollars or in the foreign currency) against the importer. The exporter takes the draft and the documents listed above to the bank for further handling.

Customer's Draft.   The following example illustrates the steps involved in financing a foreign sale by use of a draft.

The Tejas Manufacturing & Equipment Company of Houston, Texas, sells equipment to Colombiana Importadora, S.A., Bogotá, Colombia.[1] On receipt of an order, the Houston firm (the seller) draws a customer's draft (Figure 21-11) made payable to itself in the amount of $3,500 on Colombiana Importadora. This instrument instructs Colombiana (drawee and buyer) to pay the amount of the draft to the holder at a specified future date. In this case, it is thirty days from the date of the draft.

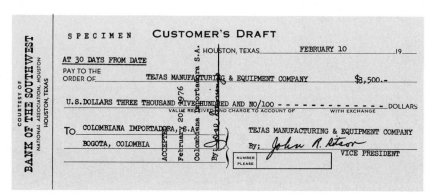

FIGURE 21-11
A customer's draft used in foreign-trade transactions. (Courtesy of The Bank of the Southwest, Houston, Texas.)

INTERNATIONAL BANKS

The Export-Import Bank.   In 1934, the Export-Import Bank of Washington (D.C.) was established as an agency of the U.S. government to finance American exports. The bank tries to supplement, rather than compete with, commercial banks. It lends only to those ventures the ordinary commercial bank is not interested in. It tends to confine its loans to financing productive capital equipment, such as special machinery used in agriculture and industry. It guarantees credit and gives financial counseling. How the Export-Import Bank serves business is shown in Figure 21-12.

The International Monetary Fund.   The International Monetary Fund (IMF) is the world's largest source of quickly available international credit. The purposes of the fund are to:

1. Promote international monetary cooperation
2. Help eliminate restrictions on foreign trade
3. Provide funds to meet temporarily unfavorable trade balances between nations
4. Stabilize exchange rates

---

[1] The abbreviation S.A., used as part of the company title, is derived from the Spanish term *sociedad anónima*, which means "corporation."

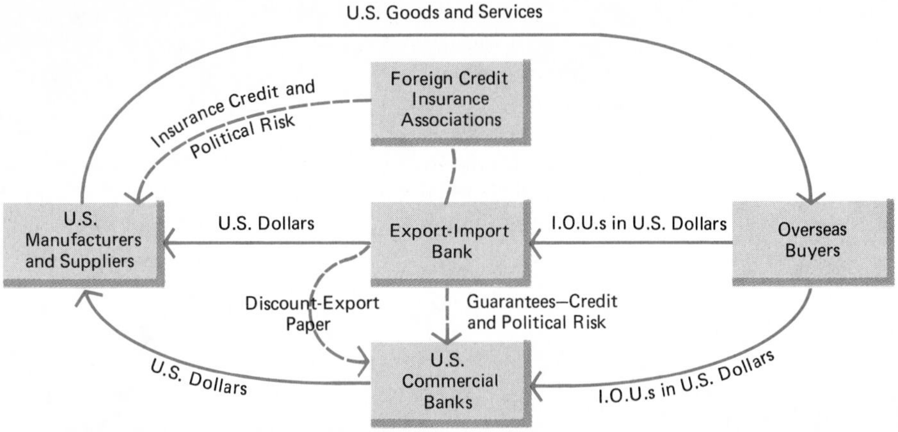

U.S. Goods and Services

FIGURE 21-12
How the export-import bank serves world business. (Source: Export-Import Bank.)

If country A wants to buy goods from country B but lacks the currency to make the purchases, it can borrow the money from the fund in the currency of country B. Country A pays back its debt to the fund in gold or in currency received through transactions with other nations.

The IMF has currency reserves furnished by 125 member countries. Each country's quota is determined by its relative volume of international trade and its national income.

The World Bank. This bank is more properly named the International Bank for Reconstruction and Development (IBRD). It began operating early in 1946 with slightly more than $9 billion of subscribed capital. Since then, the number of countries supporting the bank has grown from 43 to 130.

SUMMARY OF KEY CONCEPTS

The United States is a leading producer of goods and services. Still, it depends heavily on other countries for many raw materials, goods, and services.

Exporting is a means of selling goods in addition to those sold on the domestic market. It thus expands the market for a company's product.

We import because it is impossible to produce some items in this country or because goods may be purchased abroad at lower prices than at home.

The two broad categories of tariffs are revenue tariffs and protective tariffs. A revenue tariff is a tax on imports to produce revenue. A protective tariff is a tax on imports to protect domestic producers against competition from foreign producers.

Reciprocal tariff reductions on a broad scale began in 1947 in Geneva. The result was the General Agreement on Tariffs and Trade.

The Tokyo Round of Tariff Negotiations was concluded in April 1979. In general, this far-reaching agreement reduced tariffs by about one-third. Ninety-nine nations participated in the negotiations.

The principle of comparative advantage states that a nation tends to export those goods that it can produce at relatively low costs. Countries, therefore, specialize in producing certain products.

International trade is far more complex than doing business at home. There are differences in laws, social customs, and language.

Trade barriers in the form of tariffs and quotas restrict the international movement of goods and services.

Some companies that engage in much foreign commerce find that it pays to have their own marketing outlets. These outlets can be foreign branches, factories, or subsidiaries located in other countries.

Other companies find that the most efficient export-marketing channels are the export merchants, export agents, and buyers for exports.

The Export-Import Bank makes loans to foreign countries for mining, agriculture, and industrial ventures to promote foreign trade. The International Monetary Fund helps countries stabilize their currencies and promote trade with other nations.

BUSINESS TERMS

You should be able to match these business terms with the statements that follow:

a. ABSOLUTE ADVANTAGE
b. CARTEL
c. COMPARATIVE ADVANTAGE
d. COUNTERTRADE
e. CUSTOMS UNION
f. EXPORTS
g. FOREIGN EXCHANGE

h. IMPORTS
i. JOINT VENTURE
j. MULTINATIONAL BUSINESS
k. PROTECTIVE TARIFF
l. TARIFF
m. WORLD BUSINESS

1. Business that is conducted between citizens, companies, and governments on an international scale
2. Goods or services produced in a country but sold abroad
3. Barter-type agreements between nations or businesses
4. A tax or customs duty levied by a nation on imported goods
5. Raw materials or goods shipped into a country from a foreign source
6. A tax on imports levied to protect domestic producers
7. The principle by which a country, by specializing in certain goods, can produce them more economically than can other countries
8. A geographical region within which goods move without being subject to customs duties
9. An association of companies working together to control prices
10. A company that conducts operations in several countries and has a worldwide perspective
11. An overseas enterprise that is not completely owned or controlled by the parent company
12. Changing the currency of one nation to that of another country

REVIEW QUESTIONS

1. Why is world trade important to our nation and to American business?
2. What determines the kinds of products that businesses of any nation export to other countries?
3. What is the difference between direct-export and indirect-export marketing channels?
4. Why do governments enact tariffs on imported goods?
5. What is a joint venture overseas?

DISCUSSION QUESTIONS

1. How does international trade promote a higher standard of living?
2. What specific problems make world trade a challenge?
3. What is the chief argument for free trade among nations?
4. What are the main functions of the International Monetary Fund?
5. What causes foreign-exchange rates to fluctuate?

21-1

IMPORT GOODS TO BROADEN SALES?

The Lacy Ceramics Company, located in Ohio, makes wholesale low-price dishes. It sells its product to so-called dishbarns and to discount stores throughout middle America. Last year's sales were $20 million.

The company would like to expand by handling a line of low-priced imported china. The firm's marketing manager is convinced that there is a market for such a line. The company vice-president suggested that goods be bought from Taiwan or Japan. The company treasurer thinks it would be better to buy from English firms.

The company purchasing agent thinks that agents in New York who buy foreign goods should be used. The sales manager wants to send someone to England and Asia on a scouting mission. (In fact, he hopes to make the trip himself.) The company president's only input is that the firm should start on a small scale.

1. How can the management learn about Japanese and English china?
2. What information should the management obtain in order to make a preliminary decision in this situation?
3. Assuming a decision is made to take on a line of imported china, what are some things that must be decided?

21-2

TO BUILD OVERSEAS?

The executive committee of the Newcomb Electronics Company has recommended that the company build an assembly plant in Taiwan. The committee gave as supportive arguments the following:

a. The government in Taiwan will erect the building and lease it back to the company.
b. The company will be given exemption from property taxes on its capital equipment for five years.
c. Labor costs in Taiwan are lower than those in the United States.
d. The company must employ native personnel both in product and in management. But during the first two years, U.S. personnel could be used to train the native workers.

1. Which of these advantages might be available in this country?
2. What arguments can you make for building the new plant in the United States?
3. Which of the arguments made in answering question 2 do you consider to be the most important?

CAREER DEVELOPMENT IN BUSINESS

study objectives

WHEN YOU HAVE FINISHED READING THIS CHAPTER, YOU SHOULD BE ABLE TO:

1. Define *career* and explain what a career is *not*
2. Identify the steps involved in the career-planning process
3. Describe the factors that affect people's choice of a career
4. Indicate the life stages that careers follow
5. Discuss things to be aware of in a job-interview situation
6. Prepare a résumé for use when applying for a position

22

[Alice said] "Would you tell me, please, which way I ought to go from here?"

"That depends a good deal on where you want to get to," said the Cat.

"I don't much care where——" said Alice.

"Then it doesn't matter which way you go," said the Cat.

Lewis Carroll, *Alice in Wonderland*

Like Alice in Wonderland, if you don't much care where your career is going, you can take almost any road. But if you *do* care, then it is important that you take an active role in reaching those goals.

In a recent interview, Douglas M. Reid, Xerox's director of international personnel, pinpointed the change in businesses' approach to career planning:

I think part of the problem is that in the '50s and '60s, most employees expected the company to plan their careers for them. They would work hard, put their heads down and grind away, and if the company said move from Rochester to San Antonio, they packed their bags that weekend and went. Starting in the '70s, however, employees started to speak up. They said, "I don't know if I want to move from this part of the country. I don't know if I agree that this next move makes sense." We spent a lot of time exploring what the issues were, and we have concluded that it's incumbent on us to educate our employees that it's their responsibility to plan their own careers. We can tell them about logical career paths, what the prerequisites for various jobs are, and so on, but each employee is going to have to decide what he or she specifically wants to do and whether to make the investment in training, or whatever it might be to try to enhance his or her chances of success.

The conditions that influence careers today are not new, but it is important that you recognize them. Planning a career requires integrating your work, career, family, and education. It is a continuous process of learning throughout life. Deciding what you want your future career to be like can be difficult but also rewarding. It involves testing the reality of your goals and plans and defining the criteria for career actions and decisions. There are no instant solutions to career-planning choices and problems. However, if we fail to do our homework on careers and on our personal goals, more choices will be made *for us*, and they will not all be to our liking.

WHAT IS A CAREER?

Let us consider a few things about a career.

1. The speed with which your career unfolds does not necessarily suggest success or failure. What happens during the career, rather than the speed with which it happens, is more important. The 35-year-old vice-president is not necessarily more successful than the 45-year-old vice-president.
2. You are the only one who can determine whether your career has been successful. There are *no absolute criteria* for evaluating a career, yet friends, spouse, and society are all too quick to help you determine whether your career has been successful. It is inappropriate for one person to evaluate another person's career. You are the only one who has the right to make your own life choice.
3. A career is not only what you do but how you feel about what you do. People who hate their careers are not successful no matter how much money they make. Your values, attitudes, and motives change as you grow older. Your work is a success or a failure to the degree that it fits your values, attitudes, and motives.
4. A career is a sequence of work experiences, not simply certain jobs. Any work, paid or unpaid, can make up a career. The work you do during your life will constitute your career. It need not be a profession, nor necessarily even paid. It can be volunteer work.

A career includes both your feelings and your activities, and the way in which they are related over the span of your life. A CAREER, therefore, is a lifelong series of work-related experiences.

WHY ARE CAREERS IMPORTANT ENOUGH TO STUDY? Work provides the setting for satisfying many of the needs that people have. The list of human needs identified by Maslow, and discussed earlier in the text, illustrates this well. The whole range of Maslow's hierarchy of needs— physical, safety, social, self-respect, and self-actualization—can be satisfied at work.

What would you do if you suddenly became a multimillionaire? Imagine, for example, that somebody willed you several million dollars and it was no longer necessary for you to work. What would you do with yourself? Most people would probably take a vacation. They might even change jobs and try to find something that they *really wanted to do*. But studies have shown that most people would continue to work rather than sit around for the rest of their lives. Work clearly plays a key role in a person's life. And like other important things in life, you can control it better if you *plan* for it, rather than simply allowing it to happen.

Yet many people do not plan well as far as their careers are concerned.

George Bennett is one of my students and an advisee. A month before graduation last spring, George decided it was time to look for a job. After two weeks of fruitless hunting, he came to my office for a chat and some advice.

I asked what kind of job he was looking for. George's reply was, "I'm not really sure. I kind of liked my marketing courses, so maybe that would be a good field for me. Besides, I had sort of hoped that you could give me some ideas about the functional areas, industries, or companies that would offer the best job opportunities."

Most students are like George. They find that as graduation approaches, they have no job offers, and panic sets in. Unfortunately, an orderly and effective approach to career planning cannot be made in two weeks.

White-collar workers today are willing to change jobs for better opportunities. (Photo by Mark Mangold, U.S. Census Bureau.)

JOB MOBILITY   At one time, people who had changed jobs several times during a career were viewed as unstable. But changing jobs over the course of a career (within reason) is no longer considered a negative factor. It represents a varied experience and often implies a high level of personal drive. Indeed, a person who stays with one organization too long may have difficulty finding and adapting to other work. This is especially true if the technology, economics, or social changes we mentioned earlier force him or her out of the present job.

Studies have shown that the average college graduate changes jobs several times before reaching the age of 30. Such mobility suggests that people are willing to make changes today if it gives them a better opportunity to match job characteristics and personal interests.

But other evidence suggests that people are also less willing today to make job changes that they find unacceptable. Over the last decade, more people have been unwilling to take transfers or promotions when it calls for a move to an unfavorable location. For example, many people are unwilling to move to undesirable metropolitan locations simply because there is a promotion involved. Other people are unwilling to take jobs that they feel do not fit their personal interests or goals, even though they mean a promotion.

CAREER PATHING   Career pathing is an attempt by a business organization to outline a person's possible movement, over time, from a beginning job. It forms a ladder of increasingly more responsible and better-paid positions in a specific area. Figure 22-1 shows a career path for a computer trainee in a large company.

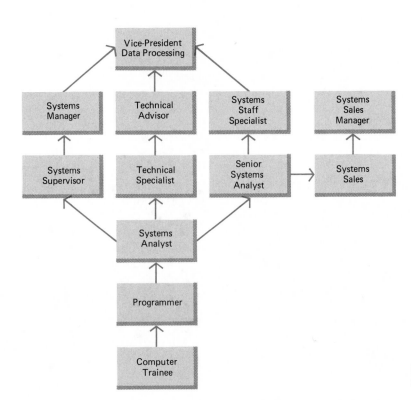

FIGURE 22-1
Career Path for a Computer Trainee

Career paths serve to show employees how they might progress with the company through their careers. Careful analysis and communication of opportunities prevent unrealistic expectations. However, our theme here is that even though a company might help, you career planning is up to *you!*

THE CAREER-PLANNING PROCESS

Career planning is a process that all people must do *themselves*, because each individual is different. But too few people do it. The R.G. Barry Corporation of Columbus, Ohio, has prepared a self-guide for its management group to use in doing career planning. This guide is given to all managers, but those who wish to take it further than the introductory session must do so on their own.

Barry's experience with career planning has been interesting. A spokesperson commented:

> We had about 15 percent of our management people who took the time — and it would have taken perhaps eight to twelve hours to do it thoroughly — to go through the entire exercise and who then came back to the personnel department for additional information or review or who reviewed their results with their bosses. We didn't restrict them; they could go to anyone they wanted for review. The other 85 percent, as far as I know, never took the time to think through these issues regarding their jobs, their career, their profession, their community responsibilities, their family responsibilities, and the other items that are in the guide.

Career planning consists of four phases: (1) finding your personal goals and objectives, (2) evaluating your strengths and weaknesses, (3) analyzing career opportunities, and (4) reviewing and updating the career plan. Let's consider each of these phases.

DETERMINING PERSONAL GOALS AND OBJECTIVES

In setting personal goals and objectives, you should ask yourself the following questions: What kinds of tasks or activities have I enjoyed the most? What kinds have I enjoyed the least? If I could have any job I wanted, what job would it be? The best way to help determine what you really want out of life is to give yourself some honest answers.

Some of the factors that must be considered when answering these questions are **income, geographical location, amount of travel, job security, independence, autonomy,** and **company size.** What price are you willing to pay to get ahead? Are you willing to move whenever and wherever your firm dictates? When you honestly answer those questions, you will have a clearer understanding of your goals, values, and priorities. Goal analysis is a frustrating process and takes a lot of time, but without some idea of where you want to go, it is difficult to plan how to get there. Of course, goals can change with experience, too.

JOB STRESS—THE COST OF SOME CAREERS

We know that some jobs are more physically stressful than others. But some interesting claims on workmen's compensation have been paid because of depression, anxiety, and other *emotional* problems traced to on-the-job pressures.

In California, 4,000 mental-health claims are filed annually, with benefits awarded in about half of them. The average filer of such claims is usually a rank-and-file employee, not an executive. Teachers, secretaries, policemen, and firefighters apply. A stress claim is usually associated with an emotional shock on the job, such as being robbed or witnessing the death of a co-worker. However, stress that builds up over the years can lead to emotional problems, too.

GOVERNMENT AND WORLD BUSINESS

EVALUATING PERSONAL STRENGTHS AND WEAKNESSES

When you have established your goals and objectives, an analysis of your personal strengths and weaknesses is in order. The answers to the following questions can help that analysis:

What are my six strongest skills?
What is my greatest accomplishment in life?
Is it salable?
Why should an employer hire me instead of someone else?

Rate yourself on each of the characteristics listed in the box below. Use the ratings to determine your major strengths and weaknesses. Then go over these strengths and weaknesses with a trusted friend and ask for his or her candid opinion.

Assessing your strengths and weaknesses may be difficult, but the chart can help you identify them. A number of appraisal forms are available to help you identify your interests. The Strong and Kuder interest inventories can help immensely. They are available through college or university counseling groups.

There are informal ways of learning about yourself, too. Ask your instructors or your boss for feedback on your performance. Usually, people

---

MY STRENGTHS AND WEAKNESSES

Academic achievement (grades)	_____
Ingenuity and creativity	_____
Administrative knowledge and ability	_____
Cooperativeness	_____
Ambition and self-motivation	_____
Conscientiousness	_____
Educational credentials	_____
Intelligence	_____
Leadership ability	_____
Maturity and poise	_____
Oral communication skills	_____
Written communication skills	_____
Prior work experience	_____
Sociability	_____
Technical competence (marketing, finance, operations, research, personnel, etc.)	_____

Rate yourself using the following scale:

5 — a major strength
4 — a moderate strength
3 — neither a strength nor a weakness
2 — a moderate weakness
1 — a major weakness

don't get feedback on themselves unless they go out of their way to ask for it. Ask about areas of strength and weakness and what you might do to improve the weak areas. When you have developed a good list of your basic skills, try to develop a number of ways in which your skills can be used. It is important to be honest in your evaluation. You will be suprised at how many different types of careers can be built from a given set of skills and interests.

A growing company in a healthy economy often creates more positions than it can fill. As a result, underqualified managers may be "overpromoted." These "jets" have a number of problems, especially when times get tough. Some can't handle the job; others cannot handle subordinates or company politics. A result is that they usually realize they are in over their heads and become very anxious. The final result can be high turnover and shattered families at home.

ANALYZING CAREER OPPORTUNITIES

Now you can begin to consider paths to reach your goals. Include not only promotion opportunities but additional training and learning experiences that might help you get there.

Take a long, careful look at the industries and jobs that might be appropriate. Table 22-1 lists certain industry, organization, and job characteristics. You should note that jobs change, but company climate and industry health tend to be more permanent. The major criterion for making a choice should be the extent to which the job will help you achieve both your short-term and your long-term career goals.

TABLE 22-1
Industry, Organization, and Job Characteristics

I. Characteristics of the industries you are considering:
   A. Structure (Is it dominated by large companies? Is it geographically centralized?)
   B. Profitability
   C. Growth prospects
   D. Relationship to economic and government-contracts cycle

II. Characteristics of the organizations you are considering:
   A. Profitability and financial strength
   B. Growth potential
   C. Position in the industry
   D. Management style (democratic, autocratic, bureaucratic, etc.)
   E. Company policies regarding career development

III. Characteristics of the job you are considering:
   A. Reputation and importance of the department in which the job is housed
   B. Financial standing and autonomy of the department
   C. Value of the job as a stepping stone to a higher position
   D. Age and characteristics of the people you will be working with (Are the department heads old and due to retire soon, or is the department overstocked with young talent?)
   E. Actual duties and responsibilities you will be assigned

REVIEWING AND UPDATING THE CAREER PLAN

By now, you should have a good picture of your objectives, your assets and liabilities, and the career opportunities available to you. Now commit your career plan to *writing*. This written plan could include a listing of your long-term goals and objectives, intermediate goals for achieving the long-term goals, and schedules to make sure each can be reached in a reasonable length of time.

At this point, you should also note that career planning is an ongoing process. It is not something you can do once and then have a blueprint to follow the rest of your life. It must be continually updated to account for changes in you and your interests. Many people use the technique of reviewing and updating the career plan once a year. Be sure to save old career plans, because they provide a written record of your progression and the changes in your goals and interests.

HOW DO PEOPLE CHOOSE CAREERS?

Recent studies indicate that four general characteristics can affect the career choices that people make:

1. People tend to pursue careers that they think match their interests
2. People choose careers in keeping with their self-images
3. Career choice is usually in keeping with personality
4. Socioeconomic status and the educational and occupational level of a person's parents can influence the person's choice of a career.

All these characteristics are important. People clearly try to match their choice of jobs with how they see themselves.

Social background is indeed an important item in determining the type of job that people are likely to consider. UCLA and Korn/Ferry International surveyed 1,700 senior executives of U.S. businesses. When the executives were asked to classify their fathers' occupations, 22.2 percent said that their fathers had been professional/technical people; 22.8 percent said that they had held managerial positions; and 16.9 percent said that they had been sole proprietors. Thus, 61.9 percent of the sample said that their fathers' occupations had at least been related to an executive career. Only 20.8 percent said that their fathers had been blue-collar workers.

One obvious factor when choosing a specific company is what openings are available when you are looking for work. The amount of information you may have about alternative jobs is important too. Beyond these issues, people seem to pick an organization on the basis of the fit between the climate of that organization (as they perceive it) and their own personal characteristics.

CAREER STAGES

The research on careers generally agrees that a person's career follows four stages. These stages correspond to the person's "life stages"—the steps that one goes through in maturing.

Business offers opportunities for all ages. Young adult; In the 30s. (Photos by Mark Mangold, U.S. Census Bureau.) In the 40s. (Photo by A.T.& T. Co. Photo Center.) The later years. (Photo, ACTION.)

The first stage is **establishing an identity.** This is a period of exploration of alternative careers and of getting into the adult world. It may range from age 10 to age 20 or later. Establishing an identity includes such things as choice of an education, development of a self-image, and a growing need to test one's ability to work and accomplish real-life tasks.

The second stage is **growing and becoming established.** This is a period when people test several different types of work and finally make a commitment to an occupation. During this stage (generally from age 20 to age 40), the person also establishes a home and family life. This early career stage includes major learning periods about what work is, and what kinds of work the person might find satisfying. It also includes some "reality shock" about what the world of work is really like.

The third stage is **maintenance and adjustment to self.** This stage may range from 35 or 40 to age 50 or later. It may include major changes in life plans, such as divorce, changing jobs, or accepting the fact that one's career is at a plateau. This last occurrence may require a reassessment of life objectives and self-concept. If the person is "succeeding," he or she is probably developing special areas of competence. This may be accompanied by the feeling of having "made it" in the organization.

The fourth stage is **decline.** This includes formal preparation for retirement. It is generally a period of diminishing physical and possibly mental activity. This stage is often a result of such socially induced pressures as forced retirement. The person must learn to accept a reduced role or to resist decline.

Within this general career and life-cycle pattern, people make choices that affect their satisfaction with their careers. Now that we have considered how one plans a career and how careers typically progress, let us look at some specific areas that are apt to be good areas for careers in the near future.

ANALYZING THE CAREER ENVIRONMENT

In a view of career opportunities, many different areas should be considered. For example, What is the forecast for long-term economic, social, and political trends that will inevitably influence careers in many fields? Two extensive surveys tried to predict exactly these things recently. One was prepared by the European Common Market Commission, the other by the Organization for Economic Cooperation and Development in Paris.

Both surveys arrived at similar conclusions. They predict a moderate growth of industrial economies through the year 2000, and uneven growth rates in the newly industrialized countries of Asia, the Middle East, and Latin America. The most likely scenario foresees a world that is basically "free-trade"–oriented. The rates of productivity growth will decline in the United States but will increase in other industrialized nations.

SPECIFIC INDUSTRY TRENDS A projection by the U.S. Department of Labor gives the expected growth rate in major industries. Table 22-2 shows that the service industries are expected to have the highest growth rate, and transportation and public utilities will have a low growth rate. Agriculture will actually lose employment through 1985. Within the industries mentioned, certain jobs will have a higher growth rate than others.

TABLE 22-2
Industry Trends in Jobs
Growth, 1976–85

Services	+40%
Mining	+35
Construction	+32
Finance, insurance, real estate	+30
Government	+22
Trade	+20
Manufacturing	+19
Transportation and utilities	+15
Agriculture	−30

SOURCE: Bureau of Labor Statistics.

The Bureau of Labor Statistics also projects the outlook for various career opportunities across industries. A summary of these industries is given in Table 22-3. The outlook for many of the occupations within the business area is quite good. Others will grow more slowly, as the table indicates.

TABLE 22-3
Job Outlook Across Industries to Mid-1980s

OCCUPATION	RATE OF INCREASE
Accountant	Average and faster
Computer programmer	Very rapid
Bank officer	Very rapid
Insurance (general)	Very rapid
Hotel manager	Average
City manager	Rapid
Hospital manager	Rapid
Personnel manager	Rapid
Purchasing agent	Rapid
Industrial designer	Average
Advertising	Moderate
Market researcher	Rapid
Sales	Moderate to slow
Real estate sales	Favorable
Retail buyer	Rapid
Transportation manager	Moderate to slow

SOURCE: Bureau of Labor Statistics.

WHAT PROFESSIONALS WANT FROM THEIR CAREERS

An interesting study of what people with professional training want from their careers was conducted by four magazines in the "professional group": *MBA, Juris Doctor, Medical Dimensions,* and *New Engineer.* The results were reported in *MBA.* The study found that there are differences among members of the "professional groups" in the single most important thing they want from their jobs. The most important items in each professional group were:

	BUSINESS	LAW	ENGINEERING	MEDICINE
Intellectual challenge	1	2	1	3
Money	2	3	3	7
Independence	3	1	4	1
Security	4	4	2	2
Prestige	5	7	6	5
Contribution to society	6	5	5	4
Power	7	8	7	8
Step to another career	8	9	9	9
Social change	9	6	8	6

Notice that business and engineering both ranked intellectual challenge first, whereas law and medicine ranked independence first.

WORKING IN A SMALL BUSINESS

Many people would prefer to work in a small business rather than a large one. The career outlook, however, for small businesses in the United States is somewhat mixed. For certain small businesses, the outlook can be quite good. But for small businesses in general, the overall favorability of the business climate has deteriorated. Small-business owners blame government policies for this situation. Government paperwork is a major complaint. It is estimated that this constitutes a $100-billion added cost of doing business each year. More than half the burden is borne by small businesses.

Unincorporated small businesses may pay a larger percentage of their income in federal taxes than do corporations because of the structure of our tax system. Perhaps the biggest problem for small businesses is their limited ability to raise capital. Financing the small business has always been difficult. But with high interest rates expected to persist through the immediate future, obtaining money has become even more difficult. Small businesses, to be successful in the decade of the 1980s, must adopt more professional and better management techniques than they have in the past.

THE U.S. LABOR FORCE

There have been more than 100 million people in the labor force in this country since 1980, and this number is expected to continue to increase. An ever-increasing number of workers are needed to produce the GNP required to meet the wants of our growing population.

The numbers employed are distributed unevenly between the two sexes and among the various age groups that make up the workforce. Women now make up more than half, and this fraction is increasing. The growth in the number of working women over the past decade has been very rapid. More wives have begun to work to fulfill their own career goals and to bring home an extra paycheck. This has led to a growth in the labor force. In 1965, only 39 percent of women were in the job force. Today, the Labor Department says, the rate is 52 percent and is expected to rise as high as 65 percent by 1995. The distribution by age groups varies according to the birthrate during different decades. Participation in the labor force is shown in Figure 22-2.

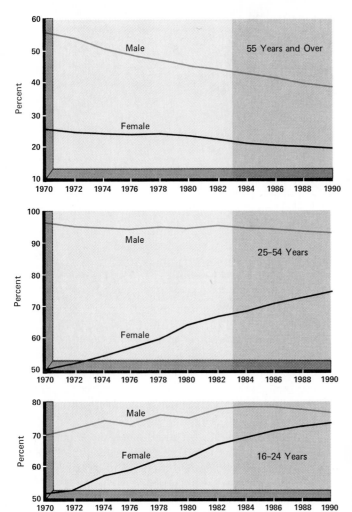

FIGURE 22-2
Labor-Force Participation Rates by Age and Sex.
(Source: Based on data from the U.S. Department of Commerce.)

TRENDS IN THE 1980s White-collar workers (including office employees and those engaged in the professions) outnumbered blue-collar workers (those in the factories and on the farms) for the first time in 1956. During the present decade, there will undoubtedly be a continuation of the rapid growth in white-collar occupations and a slower growth in blue-collar occupations. A faster-than-average growth is expected among service workers, and a further decline is expected among farm workers.

The greater growth of white-collar jobs reflects the continued expansion expected for the information-handling occupations and an increasing demand for research personnel. It also reflects an increasing need for educational and health services and a continuing proliferation of paperwork. A decade from now, electronics will probably be our largest industry. By then we will need a million or more programmers of software in this country alone. Employment by major occupational group is shown in Figure 22-3.

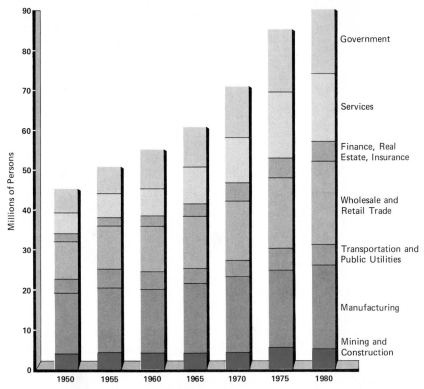

*Nonagricultural Employment by Industry
*Excludes unpaid family, self-employed, and private-household workers

FIGURE 22-3
Employment by Occupational Group

The 1945-to-1965 "baby-boom generation" is shown in Figure 22-4 as the 25–54-year age group. The birthrate began to decline again in the mid-1960s. Yet this big bulge of workers in their prime working years suggests that the economy will need to expand at a rapid rate to provide jobs for people in that group.

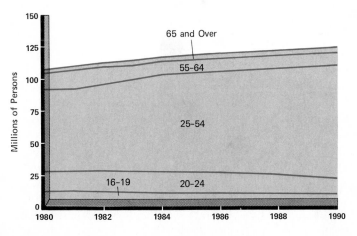

FIGURE 22-4
Labor Force by Age.
(Source: Data from U.S. Department of Commerce.)

Looking for a job is just plain hard work. But the better prepared you are, the better you will be able to cope with the job-hunting challenge. This means preparing yourself through the educational process and doing your "home-work" on the kinds of jobs and companies you might consider. It is advisable to specialize in a major area as part of your college education. You should also develop a second and perhaps a third area of specialization. For example, many students majoring in finance develop a second area of specialization in accounting. Economics majors may find it wise to develop a second area in computer science or one of the business disciplines.

Finding the right position is an active process on your part. There is no substitute for determining the job you want and actively pursuing it. A few students sit back and wait for a job to come to them through the college's placement service or other sources. This may work in some instances, but it is not the best way to go about getting a good job.

PREPARING YOUR RESUMÉ

Some companies will ask you to list your qualifications on a personnel sheet that they have designed. Or the placement office at your college or university may supply a standard data sheet. In either case, it is a good idea to prepare an individual résumé of your experience and education and keep it updated. A good résumé can go a long way toward making a good impression. A really poor one can seriously hurt the chances of an applicant who may be accept-able in every other way.

The content and layout of résumés vary widely, and there is no one "best" format. Some general suggestions do apply in every case, however. You will be on firm footing if you keep it *short* and *simple*. It must be typed, and it must be neat. Spacing can be important, since it can be used to isolate points that you want to emphasize. Crowding too many details too close together results in an untidy appearance as well as a "fine-print" appearance, which can turn a reader off.

Most résumés include the following information:

1. A listing of your academic work to date.
2. A listing of your work and life experience that may be related to the work itself.
3. People to contact if the company would like a recommendation about your work. These may be people who have known you in a professional sense — pro-fessors, employers, and so forth.

Work experience is, of course, the essential ingredient in any résumé. Dates should be given, along with company addresses and a brief description of the work you did. Your job list should ordinarily begin with the last job you held, and other jobs should be listed in reverse order.

Don't overlook your extracurricular activities. Many jobs are especially fitted for the well-rounded. The fact that you have been chosen as a member of an honorary group or elected to professional societies in your field speaks well for your future in that field. If you belong to purely social organizations, list them. A large part of anyone's success in a new job depends on the ability to get along with fellow workers. Figures 22-5 and 22-6 show two different résumé formats.

FIGURE 22-5
A Résumé Format

James E. Doe
10000 University
 Ave.
Minneapolis, Minn.
University 1-4296
(to June 5, 1981)

Home Address:
3414 Nicollet Ave.
Minneapolis, Minn.
742-2001

PERSONAL DATA:

Age: 23	Birth Date: February 27, 1960	Marital Status: Single
Height: 6'1"	Weight: 185	Health: Excellent

OCCUPATIONAL GOAL:

My goal is a job in the field of sales promotion, with the eventual possibility of a management position.

EDUCATION:

University of Minnesota
Degree: Bachelor of Arts, '83
Major: Psychology
Minor: English Literature
Major subjects: Industrial Psychology, General Psychology, English Literature, Economics, Business
 Management and Organization, History
Grades: Good to excellent in major subjects; average to good in others

EXTRACURRICULAR ACTIVITIES:

Secretary, Alpha Pi Zeta, honorary social science fraternity
Member of Student Industrial Relations Society
Vice-president and social chairman of the ABC social club
Swimming team

WORK EXPERIENCE:

Summer, 1980 — Gunderson Manufacturing Co., 1203 Ryan Ave., St. Paul, Minn. Payroll clerk. While working for
 Gunderson Co., I received a cash award for a payroll procedure suggestion that resulted in
 saving time for the company.
Summer, 1979 — Wearever Aluminum Co., door-to-door salesman in Minneapolis.
Summer, 1978 — Lifeguard, Camp Chippewa, Lake Bemidji, Minn.

FIGURE 22-6
Personal Data Sheet

NAME: Jane R. Richards

ADDRESS: 1201 Senator Place, Cincinnati, Ohio (to June 5, 1980)

TELEPHONE: 881-5000

HOME ADDRESS: 12 River St., Portsmouth, Ohio

HOME TELEPHONE: 233-4832

AGE: 22	**HEIGHT:** 5'9"	**WEIGHT:** 159

MARITAL STATUS: Single

EDUCATION: University of Cincinnati
Degree: Bachelor of Science, '81
Major: Chemical Engineering
Class rank: Upper tenth, Dean's Honor List, 1980–81

Major subjects:

Quantitative Analysis	Physical Chemistry	Physics	Geology
Qualitative Analysis	Organic Chemistry	German	Zoology

I received two scholarships to the School of Chemistry, which paid part of my tuition expenses.

EXTRACURRICULAR ACTIVITIES:

Member of American Student Chemical Society
Independent Student Association

WORK EXPERIENCE:

1979–80   General Chemical Laboratories, 3455 Woodburn Ave., Cincinnati, Ohio. As part of my cooperative education program, I have been working full-time, alternate six-week periods as a laboratory
 assistant.
Summer   Ajax Laboratory Supply Co., Portsmouth, Ohio, Inventory Clerk. Promoted from shipping department after first month.

REFERENCES:

Mr. Henry A. Neff	Mr. Walter J. Schapp	Dr. John O. Ryan
General Chemical Lab.	Ajax Lab. Supply Co.	Professor
3455 Woodburn Ave.	Portsmouth, Ohio	School of Chemistry
Cincinnati, Ohio		U. of Cincinnati
		Cincinnati, Ohio

LOCATING JOB OPPORTUNITIES

A number of sources for job leads are available. Private employment agencies may be used, but they usually charge a fee for their services. State employment agencies can sometimes provide job leads, and they do not charge a fee.

A major source is the classified section of your newspaper. Employers usually list their job openings in the Sunday newspapers. Your college professors can be a source of good leads for jobs in your area of specialization. Friends and relatives who are aware of openings in various organizations can be useful too. Many schools and colleges provide placement services for their students. These can be useful sources of initial contacts with companies and organizations.

> The Bureau of Labor Statistics has predicted the industries where the jobs will be in the period through 1990. Leading the pack are the computer industry and communication equipment. Office machines, instruments for scientific measurement, and industrial-control machines (robots) are seen as growing at a significantly faster rate than during the last decade.

PREPARING FOR THE INTERVIEW

An important part of preparing for the interview is to do some research on the company that will be interviewing you. Try to find out when the company was established; where its plants, offices, or stores are located; what its products and services are; what its growth has been; and its future prospects. This will give you something besides yourself to talk about during the interview and will provide a framework for questions you should ask.

Prepare some questions before you go for the interview. There are a number of things that you will want to know about the company. Rather than relying on your memory to supply them, write them down. Most interviewers are favorably impressed by an interviewee who brings in carefully thought-out questions. Appropriate business dress and neatness and cleanliness scarcely need to be mentioned. The importance of the initial impression cannot be overemphasized. To avoid making errors, choose commonly accepted business dress for an interview.

THE INTERVIEW

Be ready for at least one surprise question during an interview, perhaps more. A few interviewers always use one of the following:

> What can I do for you?
> Tell me about yourself!
> Why are you interested in this company?
> What are your weaknesses?
> What are your strengths?
> Why do you want to work for us?

If you think those are easy questions to answer without some previous thought, just try it. You don't have time to flounder around. This is where preparation will count.

A few interviewers like to do most of the talking, and they judge you by your reactions. Others hardly talk at all, and for an amateur, these are the

Make sure that your best points get across to the interviewer. (Photo by Laimute E. Druskis.)

hardest to deal with. Their attitude is that selling yourself is your job. That is where you will have to rely on your knowledge of yourself and your interest in the work and the company.

Make sure that your good points get across to the interviewer. He or she won't know about them unless you talk about them, but try to appear factual and sincere, not conceited or boastful. Be ready to answer the question, "What do you plan to be doing ten years from now?" It is a favorite interview question. A popular alternative is, "How much money do you expect to be earning in ten years?" The purpose of the question is to try to determine your ambition and ability to plan ahead.

> In one study, interviewees rated résumés that showed applicants with *average* grades, *excellent* work experience, and *appropriate* interests lower than they did people with *poor* work experience, *inappropriate* interests, but *high* GPA. In this study, the grades were given so much weight that they overwhelmed the other items. Certain items are obviously more important to interviewers. School grades, even though they are not necessarily good predictors of success on the job, are often weighted heavily by interviewers and employers.

Try to avoid giving the impression that you have come in to look over the possibilities and that you are not sure yet of what you want. Avoid "I'll do *anything* if I'm given the chance to learn," or, "I don't know what I want to do." Wherever possible, apply for a **specific job** or field of work. If there is no opening in the jobs you want, the way you present what you have to offer may well allow the interviewer to suggest another job or department.

If you get the impression that the interview is not going well and that you have already been rejected, don't let your feelings show. You have nothing to lose by continuing to appear confident, and you may gain much. The last few minutes often change things. An interviewer who is genuinely interested in your possibilities may seem to discourage you in order to test your reaction.

What happens if an interviewer offers you a job on the spot? If you are absolutely sure it is the one you want, accept it with a definite "Yes." If you have the slightest doubt, or if you do not want to accept it without some further thought or further interviews, ask for more time to consider the offer. You will not embarrass the person who has made you the offer. Be courteous and tactful and ask him or her for time to think it over. Set a definite date as to when you can give an answer. This will assure the interviewer that you are giving the offer serious consideration. Above all, don't create the impression that you are playing one company off against another to drive up the bidding.

Don't be too discouraged if no definite offer is made. The recruiter may wish to talk with someone else or interview more applicants before making any offer.

FIGURE 22-7
Negative Factors During the Employment Interview That Frequently Lead to Rejection of the Applicant

1. Poor personal appearance	23. Unhappy married life
2. Overbearing—overaggressive—conceited "superiority complex"—"know-it-all"	24. Friction with parents
	25. Sloppy application blank
3. Inability to express himself clearly—poor voice, diction, grammar	26. Merely shopping around
	27. Wants job only for short time
4. Lack of planning for career—no purpose and goals	28. Little sense of humor
	29. Lack of knowledge of field of specialization
5. Lack of interest and enthusiasm—passive, indifferent	30. Parents make decisions for him
	31. No interest in company or in industry
6. Lack of confidence and poise—nervousness —ill-at-ease	32. Emphasis on whom he knows
	33. Unwillingness to go where we send him
7. Failure to participate in activities	34. Cynical
8. Overemphasis on money—interest only in best dollar offer	35. Low moral standards
	36. Lazy
9. Poor scholastic record—just got by	37. Intolerant—strong prejudices
10. Unwilling to start at the bottom—expects too much too soon	38. Narrow interest
	39. Spends much time in movies
11. Makes excuses—evasiveness—hedges on unfavorable factors in record	40. Poor handling of personal finances
	41. No interest in community activities
12. Lack of tact	42. Inability to take criticism
13. Lack of maturity	43. Lack of appreciation of the value of experience
14. Lack of courtesy—ill-mannered	
15. Condemnation of past employers	44. Radical ideas
16. Lack of social understanding	45. Late to interview without good reason
17. Marked dislike for schoolwork	46. Never heard of company
18. Lack of vitality	47. Failure to express appreciation for interviewer's time
19. Fails to look interviewer in the eye	
20. Limp, fishy hand-shake	48. Asks no questions about the job
21. Indecision	49. High-pressure type
22. Loafs during vacations—lakeside pleasures	50. Indefinite response to questions

SOURCE: As reported by 153 companies surveyed by Frank S. Endicott, director of placement, Northwestern University.

Most interviews last between twenty and thirty minutes. A glance at your watch will tell you if your time is almost up. Don't go on talking and talking. Some applicants talk themselves into a job and then right out of it. Be alert for signs from the interviewer that the session is almost at an end.

If you are not successful with your first interview or first several interviews, remember that interviewers, companies, and jobs differ greatly. You will learn much from your first interview, and you will almost certainly do better in succeeding ones. The important thing is to *keep trying*. Figure 22-7 lists the fifty major negative factors that occur during the employment interview. These frequently lead to rejection of the applicant.

WOMEN AND CAREER MANAGEMENT

A career in business, especially in the upper levels of business and management in this country, has typically meant a man. The overwhelming majority of large business firms in the United States are still managed by men. Most women are primarily concentrated in entry-level, supervisory, or trainee positions.

The Wall Street Journal estimates that women hold only 6 percent of all middle-management positions and only 1 percent of all vice-presidential or higher-level positions. However, **changes are occurring.** There are more

Women are now being accepted in and attracted to management positions. (Photo by Irene Springer.)

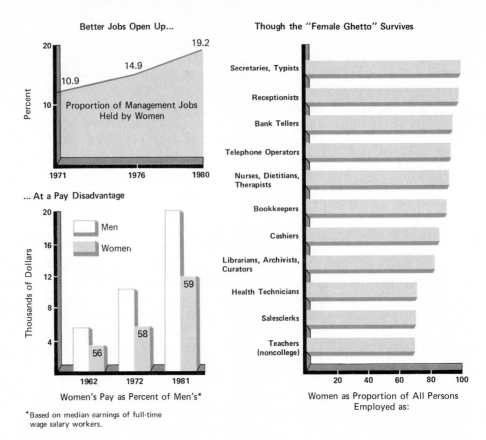

Better Jobs Open Up...

Proportion of Management Jobs Held by Women

20
19.2
14.9
10.9
10
Percent

1971 1976 1980

... At a Pay Disadvantage

Men
Women

20
16
12
8
4
Thousands of Dollars

56
58
59

1962 1972 1981

Women's Pay as Percent of Men's*

*Based on median earnings of full-time wage salary workers.

Though the "Female Ghetto" Survives

Secretaries, Typists
Receptionists
Bank Tellers
Telephone Operators
Nurses, Dietitians, Therapists
Bookkeepers
Cashiers
Librarians, Archivists, Curators
Health Technicians
Salesclerks
Teachers (noncollege)

20 40 60 80 100

Women as Proportion of All Persons Employed as:

FIGURE 22-8

Women at Work. (Source: Data from U.S. Departments of Commerce and Labor, Equal Employment Opportunity Commission.)

women in managerial positions, even if at entry level, than there have been in the past. Figure 22-8 shows the change in the percentage of women in *all* management jobs, and the troublesome pay disadvantage they have faced.

There are more women on corporate boards of directors and more female applicants for professional degrees, including the M.B.A., than ever before. The *New York Times* says that women now constitute over one-third of the law-school graduates and an increasing proportion of the top-flight business-school graduates.

As equal opportunity for women comes somewhat closer to reality, management people in many companies are realizing that some special measures are needed. Some companies provide special training in management to help women move quickly and successfully into the mainstream of managerial action. One study suggests that the development of women as managers seems to require an understanding of their special needs as well as the requirements of the business. Research on women managers leads to the following recommendations for speeding their development:

1. Women need help in raising their self-esteem as managers.
2. Women need training to learn new behaviors for managing interpersonal conflict.

3. Women need training to develop leadership and team-building skills.
4. Women need help with career planning.
5. Training *for women only* is often desirable initially.[1]

Such research will undoubtedly result in better managers, both male and female, and it is hoped that it will also result in a better use of an important resource: **competent human beings.**

SUMMARY OF KEY CONCEPTS

If you don't plan your own career, you are at the mercy of luck and circumstance.

The work you do during your life will constitute a career. It need not be for pay, and you are the only one who can determine whether your career has been "successful."

Job mobility is increasing, *but* people are becoming more particular about changing jobs. If the reasons do not fit their own goals and interests, they often will not change.

A job must fit a person's interests, values, and talents if it is to be a good match.

Career planning consists of a process of determining one's goals, identifying strengths and weaknesses, analyzing career opportunities, and finalizing and updating the career plan.

Career stages follow life stages for most people and include identity, getting established, maintenance, and decline.

Per capita gross national product will remain high in the United States in the foreseeable future, but our rate of productivity will decline.

The service industries will be the fastest-growing industries through the 1980s. Agriculture will actually lose employees.

The outlook for small business is mixed. Many people like to work in small businesses. But getting capital to start or maintain the business is becoming increasingly difficult.

Interviews can be an interesting interchange, but being prepared in advance for likely questions can make the interview pleasant and fruitful. Knowing why interviewers are likely to reject candidates is also helpful.

REVIEW QUESTIONS

1. What is meant by the statement, "Only you can define the success of your career"?
2. Describe the steps involved in the career-planning process.
3. How do personality and self-identity affect career choice?
4. Why do career stages follow life stages?
5. Select the five negative factors that you think occur most often during employment.

DISCUSSION QUESTIONS

1. Why, do you think, do people usually leave their careers to chance instead of planning for them?
2. What is your biggest concern about the job-search process?
3. Given the predictions made by the European Common Market Commission regarding the world economy through 2000, what do you think the "hot" careers might be?
4. Discuss the pros and cons of "proper business attire" as a necessary condition for getting a job.

---

[1] J. Steven Heiner, Dorothy McGlauchlin, Constance Legeros, and Jean Freeman, "Developing the Woman Manager," *Personnel Journal*, May 1975, p. 54.

22-1

DEAD END

Joe Dogeness received a business degree from a well-known university in 1977 and took a job with a large oil company. His career got off to a good start. By 1983, his salary was $28,000 and he was in charge of a five-person analysis team.

Joe was not happy with his career progress, however. Although his salary was satisfactory, his level of responsibility was only slightly greater than it had been during his first year or two with the company. He had been stuck in a staff job at the home office for six years and felt that he would like a change. He requested a transfer to a line-marketing job.

He was told that he was too valuable in his current job to be transferred. He was overpaid for a lower-level line position, and too inexperienced to be promoted to a middle- or upper-level line position.

1. What should Joe do?
2. Why has he gotten into this fix?

22-2

I AM A SUCCESS!!

Roberta Franklin got an M.B.A. in 1973 and went to work for a large New York consulting firm. Within a year, she was in charge of major projects throughout the country, which meant that she was away from home much of the time. Roberta assured her husband that this hectic pace would last only a few years and that she could then settle down to a more normal life.

In 1980, she went to work for a client firm as division personnel manager. But the job had been neglected for some years, and Roberta had to work long hours and weekends to straighten things out. By 1984, she had received two more promotions and was earning over $50,000. She was viewed as a real comer by top management.

Roberta paid a price. Her husband seldom saw her, and he finally asked for a divorce. Roberta has begun to question whether this is the kind of life she really wants. Much of the enjoyment she had had from her work is gone, and she feels that her life is being wasted.

1. Roberta is very successful — what is the problem?
2. Where does she go from here?

ᴘᴀʀᴛ 7

CAREER OPPORTUNITIES IN GOVERNMENT

We have seen that government represents a large number and a wide variety of activities. The result is that almost every career opportunity we have described is available in the business functions of government: accountants of all types; advertising people; computer analysts, operators, and programmers; marketers; inventory-control specialists; managers; personnel administrators; statisticians; and so on.

Since each of these areas is discussed elsewhere in this book, that information will not be repeated here.

CAREER OPPORTUNITIES IN INTERNATIONAL TRADE

Today, an increasing number of American corporations are engaged in international business. As a result, career opportunities in this field are on the increase. Or if you want to work for yourself, you may become an independent importer, exporter, broker commission merchant, or import merchant. There are also opportunities with domestic companies engaged in foreign-freight forwarding.

Generally speaking, there are probably more positions open to the beginner in training programs within domestic companies than for immediate employment abroad.

GENERAL REQUIREMENTS

One of the important skills needed in foreign trade is the ability to speak at least one foreign language. Another is adaptability to a foreign culture, including ways of doing business that are very different from those used in the United States. A college education, preferably with a degree in business administration, is also an important requirement.

EMPLOYMENT IN EXPORTING

The Export Manager.   Experience in business is a necessary prerequisite for this position. The export manager exercises direct supervision over company agents, salespersons, and clerks. He or she must have an understanding of trade documents used in foreign shipments. Such documents include the ocean bill of lading, commercial invoice, marine insurance certificate, and others that we discussed under the subject of financing exports.

The Export Agent.   This is an indirect-exporting position. The export agent is similar to the manufacturer's agent in domestic trade. He or she sells goods in the name of the manufacturer, who finances and ships the goods. The export agent receives a commission. The more successful export agents are those who have lived abroad and know a great deal about foreign-trade operations.

The Freight Forwarder.   There are two types of freight forwarders. One is a domestic-freight forwarder, who consolidates and combines domestic shipments in order to take advantage of the lowest freight rates. The foreign-freight forwarder prepares shipments for foreign countries, usually for companies that ship large amounts abroad and do not require the combining of individual shipments. One of the most important functions of the freight forwarder is to handle documents used in finance and in transportation. Both loading and unloading of shipments can be delayed if the forwarder fails to prepare the documents correctly.

EMPLOYMENT IN IMPORTING

The Import Broker. The broker's function is to bring foreign sellers and American buyers together. This is done in much the same way as it is done by the domestic broker, who finds a buyer and then locates a seller with the article. The import broker rarely takes title but is paid a commission and expenses. Much of the Brazilian coffee trade is carried on by import brokers in the United States who deal with export merchants in Brazil.

The Import Merchant. This person's specialty is buying goods abroad and holding them in either a foreign or an American warehouse until a buyer can be found. The import merchant must take title to the goods until they are sold. On occasion, the merchant sorts, grades, mixes, or blends goods where this must be done for shipment. He or she travels widely in foreign countries to locate goods. Diamonds, rugs, china, liquor, seeds, bulbs, and leather goods are among the many items imported into this country through import merchants.

OPPORTUNITIES IN FOREIGN-TRADE BANKING

As we have seen, commercial banks are important in promoting overseas trade. Many large commercial banks located in harbor cities maintain fully staffed trade departments to handle all the details of preparing, processing, and collecting negotiable instruments used in foreign trade. These departments engage in currency exchange, prepare letters of credit, and handle such negotiable instruments as drafts, checks, and promissory notes. People interested in this area of banking need a broad background in banking and finance.

Selected Readings

PART ONE
BUSINESS AND ITS ENVIRONMENT

Amacher, Ryan C., **Principles of Economics,** 2nd ed. Cincinnati: South-Western Publishing Co., 1983.

————, **Principles of Macroeconomics.** Cincinnati: South-Western Publishing Co., 1983.

————, **Principles of Microeconomics.** Cincinnati: South-Western Publishing Co., 1983.

Bach, George Leland, **Economics: An Introduction to Analysis and Policy,** 10th ed. Englewood Cliffs, N.J.: Prentice-Hall, 1980.

Bowden, Elbert V., **Principles of Economics: Theory, Problems, Policies,** 4th ed. Cincinnati: South-Western Publishing Co., 1983.

Bradley, Michael, **Economics.** Glenview, Ill.: Scott, Foresman, 1980.

Duignan, Peter, and Alvin Rabushka, **The United States in the 1980's.** Stanford, Cal.: Hoover Institution Press, 1980.

Fenn, M., **In The Spotlight: Women Executives in a Changing Environment.** Englewood Cliffs, N.J.: Prentice-Hall, 1980.

Fortune magazine, Vol. 101, No. 3 (Feb. 11, 1980), fiftieth anniversary issue.

Gills, Richard T., **Economics and the Public Interest,** 4th ed. Santa Monica, Cal.: Goodyear, 1980.

Glos, Raymond, et al., **Business: Its Nature and Environment —An Introduction,** 9th ed. Cincinnati: South-Western Publishing Co., 1980.

Hailstones, Thomas J., **Basic Economics,** 5th ed. Cincinnati: South-Western Publishing Co., 1980.

————, and Frank B. Mastrianna, **Contemporary Economic Problems and Issues,** 6th ed. Cincinnati: South-Western Publishing Co., 1982.

Hay, Robert D., and Edmund R. Gray, eds., **Business and Society: Cases and Text.** Cincinnati: South-Western Publishing Co., 1980.

Heilbroner, Robert L., and Lester C. Thurow, **The Economic Problem,** 6th ed. Englewood Cliffs, N.J.: Prentice-Hall, 1981.

Koontz, Harold, and Robert M. Fulmer, **A Practical Introduction to Business,** 3rd ed. Homewood, Ill.: Richard D. Irwin, Inc., 1981.

McKenzie, Richard B., and Gordon Tullock, **The New World of Economics: Explorations into the Human Experience,** 3rd ed. Homewood, Ill.: Richard D. Irwin, 1981.

Naisbitt, John, **Megatrends.** New York: Warner Books, 1982.

Peterson, Willis L., **Principles of Economics: Macro,** and **Micro,** 5th ed. Homewood, Ill.: Richard D. Irwin, 1983.

Pickle, Hal B., and Royce L. Abrahamson, **Introduction to Business,** 4th ed. Santa Monica, Cal.: Goodyear, 1980.

Poe, Jerry B., **An Introduction to the American Business Enterprise,** 5th ed. Homewood, Ill.: Richard D. Irwin, 1983.

PART TWO
OWNERSHIP, ORGANIZATION, AND MANAGEMENT

Beer, M., **Organizational Change and Development: A Systems View.** Santa Monica, Cal.: Goodyear, 1980.

Broom, H. N., and J. G. Longenecker, **Small Business Management,** 6th ed. Cincinnati: South-Western Publishing Co., 1983.

Ford R., and C. Heaton, **Principles of Management: A Decision-Making Approach.** Reston, Va.: Reston Publishing Co., 1980.

Hatten, Mary Louise, **Macroeconomics for Management.** Englewood Cliffs, N.J.: Prentice-Hall, 1981.

Jackson, John H., and Cyril P. Morgan, **Organizational Theory: A Macro Perspective for Management,** 2nd ed. Englewood Cliffs, N.J.: Prentice-Hall, 1982.

Massie, Joseph L., and John Douglas, **Managing: A Contemporary Introduction,** 3rd ed. Englewood Cliffs, N.J.: Prentice-Hall, 1981.

Miles, Robert H., **Macro Organizational Behavior.** Santa Monica, Cal.: Goodyear, 1980.

Mondy, R. Wayne, et al., **Management: Concepts and Practices.** Boston: Allyn & Bacon, 1980.

Ritchie, J. B., and Paul Thompson, **Organization and People: Readings, Cases, and Exercises in Organizational Behavior,** 2nd ed. St. Paul, Minn.: West Publishing Co., 1980.

Scott, William G., et al., **Organization Theory: A Structural and Behavioral Analysis,** 4th ed. Homewood, Ill.: Richard D. Irwin, 1981.

Sisk, Henry L., and J. Clifton Williams, **Management and Organization,** 4th ed. Cincinnati: South-Western Publishing Co., 1981.

Steers, Richard M., **Introduction to Organizational Behavior.** Santa Monica, Cal.: Goodyear, 1981.

Sweeney, Neil R., **The Art of Managing Managers.** Reading, Mass.: Addison-Wesley, 1981.

Szilagyi, Jr., Andrew D., and Marc J. Wallace, Jr., **Organizational Behavior and Performance,** 2nd ed. Santa Monica, Cal.: Goodyear, 1980.

Terry, George R., and Stephen G. Franklin, **Principles of Management,** 8th ed. Homewood, Ill.: Richard D. Irwin, 1982.

Truett, Dale B., and Lila F. Truett, **Managerial Economics: Analysis, Problems, Cases.** Cincinnati: South-Western Publishing Co., 1980.

VanVoorhis, Kenneth R., **Entrepreneurship and Small Business Management.** Boston: Allyn & Bacon, 1980.

Webber, Ross A., **To Be a Manager: Essentials of Management.** Homewood, Ill.: Richard D. Irwin, 1981.

PART THREE
PEOPLE AND PRODUCTION

Chruden, Herbert J., and Arthur W. Sherman, Jr., **Personnel Management: The Utilization of Human Resources,** 6th ed. Cincinnati: South-Western Publishing Co., 1980.

Hendrick, Thomas E., and Franklin G. Moore, **Production/Operations Management.** Homewood, Ill.: Richard D. Irwin, 1981.

Heneman, Herbert G., III, **Personnel/Human Resource Management,** rev. ed. Homewood, Ill.: Richard D. Irwin, 1983.

Herman, E. Edward, and Alfred Kahn, **Collective Bargaining and Labor Relations.** Englewood Cliffs, N.J.: Prentice-Hall, 1981.

Hilgert, Raymond, and Sterling Schoen, **Labor Agreement Negotiations.** Cincinnati: South-Western Publishing Co., 1983.

McClain, John O., and L. Joseph Thomas, **Operations Management: Production of Goods and Services.** Englewood Cliffs, N.J.: Prentice-Hall, 1980.

Marshall, F. Ray, et al., **Labor Economics: Wages, Employment, and Trade Unionism,** 4th ed. Homewood, Ill.: Richard D. Irwin, 1980.

Mathis, Robert L., and John H. Jackson, **Personnel: Contemporary Perspectives and Applications,** 3rd ed. St. Paul, Minn.: West Publishing Co., 1982.

Megginson, Leon C., **Personnel Management: A Human Resources Approach,** 4th ed. Homewood, Ill.: Richard D. Irwin, 1981.

Parham, Christine P., **Basic Psychology for the Work Life.** Cincinnati: South-Western Publishing Co., 1983.

Sayles, Leonard R., and George Strauss, **Managing Human Resources,** 2nd ed. Englewood Cliffs, N.J.: Prentice-Hall, 1981.

Sloane, Arthur A., and Fred Witney, **Labor Relations,** 4th ed. Englewood Cliffs, N.J.: Prentice-Hall, 1981.

Stair, Ralph M., and Barry Render, **Production and Operations Management: A Self-Correcting Approach.** Boston: Allyn & Bacon, 1980.

Stevenson, William J., **Productions/Operations Management.** Homewood, Ill.: Richard D. Irwin, 1982.

Strauss, George, and Leonard R. Sayles, **Personnel: The Human Problems of Management,** 4th ed. Englewood Cliffs, N.J.: Prentice-Hall, 1980.

PART FOUR
MARKETING

Adler, Roy D., et al., **Marketing and Society: Cases and Commentaries.** Englewood Cliffs, N.J.: Prentice-Hall, 1981.

Bellenger, Danny N., and Jack L. Goldstrucker, **Retailing Basics.** Homewood, Ill.: Richard D. Irwin, 1983.

Cravens, David W., **Marketing Decision Making: Concepts and Strategy,** rev. ed. Homewood, Ill.: Richard D. Irwin, 1980.

Cunningham, William H., and Isabella C. M. Cunningham, **Marketing: A Managerial Approach.** Cincinnati: South-Western Publishing Co., 1981.

Diamond, Jay, and Gerald Pintel, **Principles of Marketing,** 2nd ed. Englewood Cliffs, N.J.: Prentice-Hall, 1980.

Enis, E., **Marketing Principles: The Marketing Process.** Santa Monica, Cal.: Goodyear, 1980.

Kerin, Roger A., and Robert A. Peterson, **Perspectives on Strategic Marketing Management.** Boston: Allyn & Bacon, 1980.

Kirkpatrick, C. A., and Frederick A. Ross, **Effective Selling.** Cincinnati: South-Western Publishing Co., 1981.

Kotler, Philip, **Marketing Management: Analysis, Planning, and Control,** 3rd ed. Englewood Cliffs, N.J.: Prentice-Hall, 1980.

————, **Principles of Marketing.** Englewood Cliffs, N.J.: Prentice-Hall, 1980.

Lowry, James, **Retail Management.** Cincinnati: South-Western Publishing Co., 1983.

McCarthy, E. Jerome, **Basic Marketing: A Managerial Approach,** 7th ed. Homewood, Ill.: Richard D. Irwin, 1981.

————, **Essentials of Marketing,** rev. ed. Homewood, Ill.: Richard D. Irwin, 1982.

Mandell, Maurice, **Advertising,** 3rd ed. Englewood Cliffs, N.J.: Prentice-Hall, 1980.

Nylen, David W., **Advertising: Planning, Implementation, and Control.** Cincinnati: South-Western Publishing Co., 1980.

Sandage, C. H., et al., **Advertising Theory and Practice,** 11th ed. Homewood, Ill.: Richard D. Irwin, 1983.

Mehr, Robert I., **Fundamentals of Insurance.** Homewood, Ill.: Richard D. Irwin, 1983.

————, and Emerson Cammack, **Principles of Insurance,** 7th ed. Homewood, Ill.: Richard D. Irwin, 1980.

Neveu, Raymond P., **Fundamentals of Managerial Finance.** Cincinnati: South-Western Publishing Co., 1981.

Ring, Alfred A., and Jerome Dasso, **Real Estate Principles and Practices,** 9th ed. Englewood Cliffs, N.J.: Prentice-Hall, 1981.

Simpson, Thomas D., **Money, Banking, and Economic Analysis,** 2nd ed. Englewood Cliffs, N.J.: Prentice-Hall, 1981.

Solomon, Ezra, and John J. Pringle, **An Introduction to Financial Management,** 2nd ed. Santa Monica, Cal.: Goodyear, 1980.

Unger, M. A., and George R. Karvel, **Real Estate: Principles and Practices,** 7th ed. Cincinnati: South-Western Publishing Co., 1983.

Van Horne, James C., **Financial Management and Policy,** 5th ed. Englewood Cliffs, N.J.: Prentice-Hall, 1980.

Welshans, Merle, and Ronald Melicher, **Finance: An Introduction to Financial Markets and Institutions,** 5th ed. Cincinnati: South-Western Publishing Co., 1980.

PART FIVE
FINANCING AND INSURING THE ENTERPRISE

Bickelhaupt, David L., **General Insurance,** 11th ed. Homewood, Ill.: Richard D. Irwin, 1983.

Blecke, C., and D. Gotthif, **Financial Analysis for Decision Making,** 2nd ed. Englewood Cliffs, N.J.: Prentice-Hall, 1980.

Block, Stanley B., and Geoffrey A. Hirt, **Foundations of Financial Management,** rev. ed. Homewood, Ill.: Richard D. Irwin, 1981.

Brueggeman, William B., and Leo D. Stone, **Real Estate Finance,** 7th ed. Homewood, Ill.: Richard D. Irwin, 1981.

Catheart, Charles D., **Money, Credit, and Economic Activity.** Homewood, Ill.: Richard D. Irwin, 1982.

Francis, Jack C., **Management of Investments.** New York: McGraw-Hill, 1983.

Greene, Mark R., and James S. Trieschmann, **Risk and Insurance,** 5th ed. Cincinnati: South-Western Publishing Co., 1981.

Hirt, Geoffrey A., and Stanley B. Block, **Fundamentals of Investment Management and Strategy.** Homewood, Ill.: Richard D. Irwin, 1983.

Joy, O. Maurice, **Introduction to Financial Management,** 3rd ed. Homewood, Ill.: Richard D. Irwin, 1983.

Kamerschen, David R., **Money and Banking,** 7th ed. Cincinnati: South-Western Publishing Co., 1980.

Keynes, John Maynard, **The General Theory of Employment, Interest, and Money.** New York: Harcourt Brace Jovanovich, 1936.

PART SIX
INFORMATION AND DECISION MAKING

Bodnar, George H., **Accounting Information Systems.** Boston: Allyn & Bacon, 1980.

Calmus, Lawrence, **The Business Guide to Small Computers.** New York: McGraw-Hill, 1983.

Edwards, James D., and Lynn Bergold, **College Accounting Fundamentals,** rev. ed. Homewood, Ill.: Richard D. Irwin, 1981.

Gorsline, G. W., **Computer Organization: Hardware/Software.** Englewood Cliffs, N.J.: Prentice-Hall, 1980.

Horngren, Charles T., **Introduction to Financial Accounting.** Englewood Cliffs, N.J.: Prentice-Hall, 1981.

Moore, Carl L., and Robert K. Jaedicke, **Managerial Accounting,** 5th ed. Cincinnati: South-Western Publishing Co., 1980.

Neeley, L. Paden, and Frank Imke, **Accounting: Principles and Practices,** 2nd ed. Cincinnati: South-Western Publishing Co., 1982.

O'Brien, James A., **Computers and Information Processing in Business.** Homewood, Ill.: Richard D. Irwin, 1983.

————, **Computers in Business Management: An Introduction,** 3rd ed. Homewood, Ill.: Richard D. Irwin, 1982.

Pyle, William W., and Kermit D. Larson, **Financial Accounting,** rev. ed. Homewood, Ill.: Richard D. Irwin, 1983.

————, **Fundamental Accounting Principles,** 9th ed. Homewood Ill.: Richard D. Irwin, 1981.

Rademacher, Robert, and Harry Gibson, **An Introduction to Computers and Information Systems.** Cincinnati: South-Western Publishing Co., 1983.

Salmonson, R. F., et al., **A Survey of Basic Accounting,** 3rd ed. Homewood, Ill.: Richard D. Irwin, 1981.

Sardinas, Joseph L., **Computing Today: An Introduction to Business Data Processing.** Englewood Cliffs, N.J.: Prentice-Hall, 1981.

Taggart, William M., **Information Systems: An Introduction to Computers in Organizations.** Boston: Allyn & Bacon, 1980.

PART SEVEN
GOVERNMENT AND WORLD BUSINESS

Anderson, Ronald A., with Ivan Fox and Donald P. Twomey, **Business Law, Comprehensive Volume: Uniform Commercial Code,** 11th ed. Cincinnati: South-Western Publishing Co., 1980.

Ashcroft, John D., and Janet E. Ashcroft, **College Law for Business,** 9th ed. Cincinnati: South-Western Publishing Co., 1981.

Blackburn, John D., et al., **Legal Environment of Business: Public Law and Regulations.** Homewood, Ill.: Richard D. Irwin, 1982.

Carbaugh, Robert, **International Economics.** Cambridge, Mass.: Winthrop Publishers, 1980.

Cateora, Philip R., and John M. Hess, **International Marketing,** 5th ed. Homewood, Ill.: Richard D. Irwin, 1983.

Donnell, John D., et al., **Law for Business,** rev. ed. Homewood, Ill.: Richard D. Irwin, 1983.

Fritschler, A., and B. Ross, **Business Regulation and Government Decision Making.** Cambridge, Mass.: Winthrop Publishers, 1980.

Kahler, Ruel C., **International Marketing,** 5th ed. Cincinnati: South-Western Publishing Co., 1983.

Keegan, Warren J., **Multinational Marketing Management,** 2nd ed. Englewood Cliffs, N.J.: Prentice-Hall, 1980.

Kramer, Ronald L., and Ruel C. Kahler, **International Marketing,** 5th ed. Cincinnati: South-Western Publishing Co., 1983.

Lindert, Peter H., and Charles P. Kindleberger, **International Economics,** 7th ed. Homewood, Ill.: Richard D. Irwin, 1982.

Lusk, Harold F., et al., **Business Law and the Regulatory Environment: Concepts and Cases,** 5th ed. Homewood, Ill.: Richard D. Irwin, 1982.

Root, Franklin R., **International Trade and Investment,** 5th ed. Cincinnati: South-Western Publishing Co., 1983.

Weidenbaum, Murray L., **Business, Government, and the Public,** 2nd ed. Englewood Cliffs, N.J.: Prentice-Hall, 1981.

Glossary

ABSENTEEISM   Failure of workers to be present at work as scheduled.

ABSOLUTE ADVANTAGE   The advantage to a nation specializing in goods when it enjoys low-cost advantages owing to a natural monopoly or some unusual technical development.

ACCOUNTABILITY   The holding of a subordinate answerable for the responsibility and authority delegated to him or her.

ACCOUNTING   Process of recording and reporting financial information about a business.

ADVERTISING   Any paid form of nonpersonal presentation and promotion of ideas, goods, or services.

AGENT   A person authorized to act for another in transactions with third parties.

ALIEN CORPORATION   A corporation doing business in the United States but chartered by a foreign government.

APPRAISAL   Evaluation of an employee's performance on the job.

APTITUDE   Potential ability to perform satisfactorily a specific type of work.

ARBITRATION   Settlement of a labor–management dispute by a third party, in which both sides agree in advance to abide by the decision rendered.

ARBITRATOR   An impartial labor expert who hears and settles grievances.

ASSET   Any item of value owned by a business.

AUTHORITY   Power to act and make decisions in carrying out assignments.

AUTOCRATIC LEADER   One who makes decisions without consulting others.

BALANCE SHEET   An accounting statement of the financial condition of a business or institution on a specific date.

BANK DISCOUNT   Interest deducted by banks when a loan is made.

BARTER   The trading of one good for another good.

BOND   A certificate of indebtedness indicating debt that is owed the bondholder by the corporation.

BOOK VALUE   The value of stock carried on the company records.

BRAND   A word, phrase, or symbol that gives identity to a product or class of products.

BUDGET   A financial plan that shows the amounts of anticipated revenues and expenditures during a specified period of time.

BUSINESS   Organized efforts of enterprises to supply consumers with goods and services.

CAPITAL   Money, equipment, and machinery used in business and industry.

CAPITALISM   An economic system based upon the right of private ownership and the freedom to make choices.

CARTEL   An association of companies whose purpose is to control prices or the conditions of sale.

CASHIER'S CHECK   A check drawn by a bank against its own funds.

CENTRALIZED MANAGEMENT   A system that delegates authority and control to a central area.

CERTIFIED CHECK   A check that is guaranteed by the bank as to both signature and payment.

CHATTEL MORTGAGE   A mortgage pledging tangible personal property.

617

CLOSE CORPORATION A corporation whose stock is held by a few persons and not available for purchase by the general public.

COALITION BARGAINING The collaboration of different unions within a given industry in bargaining with an employer.

COBOL A computer language—Common Business Oriented Language.

COLLATERAL Property or security deposited with a creditor to warrant payment of a debt.

COLLECTIVE BARGAINING Negotiations between representatives of labor and representatives of management.

COMMON CARRIER A transporter that offers services to the general public.

COMMON MARKET The European Economic Community, a customs union in western Europe.

COMPARATIVE ADVANTAGE A country's ability to produce goods more cheaply than other countries can produce them.

CONGLOMERATE A collection of unrelated companies producing unrelated products.

CONSIDERATION Something of value pledged in exchange for a promise.

CONSUMER CREDIT Credit granted to consumers to promote personal consumption.

CONSUMERISM A movement to inform and protect people who buy goods or services.

CONTRACT An agreement between two competent parties in the form required by law.

CONTRACT CARRIER A transporter that sells services by individual agreements.

CONTROLLING A procedure for measuring performance against objectives.

CONVENIENCE GOODS Low-priced goods that are easily available.

COOPERATIVE A business owned and operated by its user-members.

COORDINATION Synchronization of all individual efforts toward a common objective.

COPYRIGHT The exclusive right to publish, print, produce, or copy one's work (usually granted to an artist, author, composer, designer, publisher, or sculptor).

CORPORATION An association of individuals united for some common purpose; it is permitted by law to use a common name and to change its members without dissolution of the association.

CORRESPONDENT BANK A bank that maintains an account relationship with another bank or engages in exchange of services.

COUNTERTRADE Trading goods or services for goods or services between nations.

CREDIT The ability to secure goods or services in exchange for a promise to pay later.

CREDIT UNION An organization formed by individuals on a cooperative basis to make loans to its members and encourage them to save.

CURRENT ASSET An item of value that will be converted into cash within a relatively short time.

CURRENT RATIO An accounting ratio found by dividing the total current assets by the total current liabilities.

CUSTOMS UNION A geographical region embracing two or more nations within which goods may move freely (without being subject to customs duties).

DATA PROCESSING Any kind of information handling, from original entry to final entry.

DECENTRALIZED MANAGEMENT The delegation to lower levels all authority except that which must be exercised at the highest level.

DEFENDANT The party against whom an action at law is taken.

DELEGATION Giving one person the power and obligation to act for another.

DEMOCRATIC LEADER One who encourages subordinates' participation in decision making that affects them.

DEVELOPMENT The attempt to use new knowledge in the production of useful products.

DIRECTING Achieving organizational objectives by motivating and guiding subordinates.

DISCOUNT RATE The interest rate charged by Federal Reserve district banks on loans to member banks.

DISTRIBUTION CHANNEL The route that goods follow as they move from the producer to the consumer or from the seller to the buyer.

DIVERSIFICATION The making of different kinds of products or engagement in a variety of activities.

DOMESTIC CORPORATION A corporation's designation in the state that granted it a charter.

DORMANT PARTNER A partner who plays no active role and is unknown to the public as a partner.

DRAFT An unconditional written order made by the drawer and addressed to the drawee (second party), ordering the drawee to pay a specific sum to a third party (payee).

ECOLOGY The science of relationships between people and their environments.

ECONOMICS The science that deals with the satisfaction of human wants through the use of scarce productive resources.

ENTREPRENEUR The chief initiator or organizer of a business enterprise. In a proprietorship, the entrepreneur takes the risk.

ENTREPRENEURSHIP The risking of time, money, and effort by investing in and managing a business.

ENVIRONMENT All external forces surrounding and affecting individuals, businesses, and communities.

EQUITY A branch of unwritten law that grants an adequate or fair remedy. Also, the ownership claim to the resources of a business.

EQUITY CAPITAL Money invested in a business by the owners.

ETHICS A code of conduct that guides a person in dealing with others.

EXCLUSIVE DISTRIBUTION Using only one retailer in any given community to handle a product or service.

EXECUTIVE A top-level management person responsible for the work performed by others under his or her supervision.

EXPORTS Goods or services produced in a country and sold abroad.

EXPRESS WARRANTY Any statement of material fact, oral or written, by the seller about the characteristics of the goods.

FACTORS OF PRODUCTION Resources essential to produce goods and services.

FIXED ASSETS Assets whose useful life extends longer than one year.

FOREIGN CORPORATION A corporation's designation in all states other than the state granting its charter.

FOREIGN-EXCHANGE RATE The rate at which the currency of one country is exchanged for that of another country.

FORMAL ORGANIZATION A system of jobs, authority relationships, responsibility, and accountability designed by management.

FRANCHISE A legal licensing agreement between an operating company and a dealer. Also, an exclusive right to perform a stated business service in a specified territory.

FRANCHISEE The dealer in a franchise agreement.

FRANCHISOR The licensing company in a franchise agreement.

FREE-REIN LEADER One who allows subordinates to make decisions with a minimum of direction.

FRINGE BENEFITS Employee benefits or considerations in addition to wages or salary earned.

GENERAL PARTNERSHIP A business with two or more owners, in which each co-owner has unlimited legal liability.

GOVERNMENT A center of political authority having power to govern those it serves.

GRIEVANCE A specific formal dissatisfaction expressed through an identified procedure.

GROSS NATIONAL PRODUCT (GNP) Total value of all finished goods and services produced by an economy in one year.

HARDWARE Machines and equipment that make up a computing center.

HAZARD A condition that leads to an economic loss or makes it more severe.

HEDGING The taking of equal but opposite positions in the cash and futures markets.

IMPLIED WARRANTY A warranty that is not specifically stated in certain terms but is implied by law.

IMPORTS Materials, goods, or services shipped into a country.

INCOME The revenues or earnings resulting from business operations.

INDUSTRIAL GOODS Products, machines, and supplies used by businesses in the manufacture of other goods.

INFLATION An increase in the general level of prices.

INFORMAL ORGANIZATION A network of personal and social relationships that may have nothing to do with formal authority relationships.

INSURABLE INTEREST The possibility of suffering a financial loss to life, health, or property.

INSURANCE A financial arrangement that redistributes the cost of unexpected losses from risk.

INSURANCE PREMIUM The price paid by the insured for insurance protection.

INTENSIVE DISTRIBUTION Saturation of the market by using many wholesalers or retailers.

INVENTORY CONTROL The management of materials, supplies, and finished goods on hand.

INVENTORY TURNOVER The number of times the value of the stock on hand is sold during the year.

INVESTMENT Purchase of securities that offer safety of principal and satisfactory yield equal to the risks.

JOB An organizational unit of work, made up of tasks, duties, and responsibilities.

JOB ANALYSIS Determination, by observation and study, of pertinent information about the nature of a specific job.

JOB DESCRIPTION A written description of what an employee is to do on a specific job.

JOINT VENTURE An association of two or more persons for a limited purpose, without the usual rights and responsibilities of a partnership.

JOINT VENTURE OVERSEAS An enterprise operating overseas that is not completely owned or controlled by the parent company.

JUDICIAL SYSTEM The branch of government authorized to hear controversies between parties and to apply the law to these disputes.

LEADERSHIP The ability to influence others to behave in a certain way.

LIABILITY A debt owed by a business; the equity of some creditor in the business.

LIMITED PARTNER One whose personal liability is limited to the amount invested in the partnership.

LOGISTICS The management process for providing an orderly flow of materials and finished goods.

MANAGEMENT The process of planning, organizing, directing, and controlling activities of an enterprise to achieve certain objectives.

MANUFACTURING The process of using materials, labor, and machinery to create finished goods.

MARKET The exchange of goods or services between buyer and seller at a mutually agreed-upon price.

MARKET ANALYSIS Determination of the supply of, and demand for, a given product.

MARKET COMMUNICATION The flow of information back and forth between buyers and sellers.

MARKET SEGMENTATION Division of the total market into submarkets that have similar characteristics.

MARKET VALUATION Cost-benefit analysis of the marketing exchange.

MARKET VALUE The price of bonds or stock shares on the market.

MARKETING The performance of business activities that direct the flow of goods and services from producer to user.

MARKETING MIX The blending of strategies involving the four ingredients: product, distribution channels, promotion, and price.

MARKUP The difference between the middleman's cost and selling price.

MEDIA Carriers used in advertising to get a message across to intended receivers.

MEDIATION The offering of various suggestions by a third party assisting in labor–management negotiations.

MERCHANT WHOLESALER A wholesaler who provides a wide variety of services to retailers.

MIDDLEMAN One who buys and sells goods as an aid in distributing them from the producer to the user.

MINORITY GROUP A small division of the population, sharing a common historical background and cultural patterns different from those of other segments of society.

MONEY Anything generally accepted in exchange for goods and services.

MONOPOLY Possession of a large enough segment of a particular industry or trade as to be able to control prices within that industry.

MORALE The general attitude and feeling of employees toward their company and their working relationships.

MORTGAGE Property pledged as security for a loan.

MOTIVATION An inner force that moves people toward satisfying a need.

MULTINATIONAL BUSINESS A firm with a number of directly controlled operations in different countries and having a worldwide perspective.

MUTUAL COMPANY An association, owned by policyholders, organized under state law.

NATIONAL BANK A commercial bank chartered by the federal government.

NEW PRODUCT A product that serves an entirely new function or represents a major improvement in an existing one.

OPEN CORPORATION A profit-making corporation that offers its stock to the public on the open market.

OPEN SHOP A business enterprise in which there is no organized union.

ORGANIZATION A structure of relationships to get work done.

ORGANIZATION CHART Blueprint of a company's internal structure, showing key positions by titles, with lines of authority.

ORGANIZING Coordination of human and material resources within the formal structure.

PAR VALUE The value printed on a stock certificate.

PARENT COMPANY A company that owns one or more other companies.

PARITY Government action designed to maintain the purchasing power of farm income.

PARTNERSHIP An association of two or more persons who are co-owners of the business.

PARTNERSHIP AGREEMENT Written or oral provisions agreed to by business partners.

PATENT The exclusive right to own, use, and dispose of an invention.

PENETRATION PRICING Introduction of a product at a price that is low compared to similar products.

PERIL The cause of an economic loss.

PERSONAL PROPERTY Property that is movable and otherwise not classed as real property.

PHYSICAL DISTRIBUTION Movement of goods between producers and users.

PLACE UTILITY Availability of a product or service where it is wanted.

PLAINTIFF The complaining party in a court action.

PLANNING Preparing a plan of action, setting company objectives, determining strategy, and selecting alternative courses of action.

PLURALISTIC SOCIETY The combination of diverse groups that influence the business environment to meet societal expectations.

POLLUTION Deterioration of the natural environment in which we live and work.

PORTFOLIO A collection of investment securities owned by an investor.

PREFERRED STOCK Stock that carries certain preferences over common stock.

PRICE The exchange value of a product or service.

PRICE COMPETITION The strategy of selling goods below the going market price.

PRINCIPAL The person for whom an agent acts.

PRIVATE CORPORATION A business privately operated for profit for the benefit of stockholders.

PRIVATE ENTERPRISE A business system wherein individuals may hold legal title to property and are free to operate their businesses.

PRODUCT An item with a combination of attributes that give it customer appeal, such as style, design, utility, and packaging.

PRODUCT DIFFERENTIATION All the ways that buyers and sellers adjust product offers.

PRODUCT OFFER What the seller perceives a product to be.

PRODUCTION All activities involved in removing natural resources from the earth and processing them into finished goods.

PRODUCTION SHARING Participation of workers in the distribution of profits that result from savings accruing from reducing production costs.

PRODUCTIVITY The efficiency of production—output in terms of input.

PROFIT The net increase in company assets resulting from the operation of an enterprise.

PROFIT SHARING Wage-payment plans that provide remuneration beyond basic pay schedules.

PROGRAM Instructions to a computer—same as *software*.

PROMOTION A position change that increases one's responsibility and pay. Also, advertising efforts to increase the sale of goods.

PROPRIETORSHIP A business owned and operated by an individual entrepreneur—also known as a *sole proprietorship*.

PROTECTIVE TARIFF A tax on imports to protect domestic producers against competition from foreign producers.

PUBLIC CORPORATION A corporation chartered for a public purpose.

PUBLIC POLICY A statement or an interpretation of an action that carries the weight of government authority.

PUBLICITY Information about a firm, a product, or an event, made available to the public without charge.

PURE RISK A risk that involves *only* a chance of loss, not a chance to make a gain.

REAL INCOME The value of wages measured in terms of the goods and services they will buy.

REAL PROPERTY Land and anything permanently affixed to it that in a general way is immovable.

RECRUITING The process of forming a pool of qualified applicants.

RESEARCH Original investigation aimed at discovering new scientific knowledge.

RESPONSIBILITY Accountability for carrying out assigned duties.

RETAILER A business that sells goods or services to consumers.

RETAINED EARNINGS Profits of the firm that have not been paid as dividends to stockholders.

REVENUE TARIFF A tax on imports to produce revenue.

RIGHT-TO-WORK LAW A state law that forbids the forming of compulsory unionism.

RISK Uncertainty associated with an exposure to loss.

RISK MANAGEMENT Plans to deal with potential losses before they occur.

ROBOT A reprogrammable, multifunctional manipulator.

SECRET PARTNER A co-owner of a business whose identity as a partner is not revealed to the public.

SELLING The art of personal persuasion employed to convince others to buy.

SERVICE BUSINESS A business that is basically labor-oriented and provides services rather than goods.

SHOPPING GOODS Items that are bought only after comparison of price, quality, or style.

SIGHT DRAFT A draft payable on demand.

SILENT PARTNER A co-owner of a business who is not active in the management of the firm.

SKIMMING PRICING Setting a high price during a product's introductory stage, then gradually lowering it.

SMALL BUSINESS An independently owned business that is not dominant in its field.

SOFTWARE The instructions to the computer, called a *program*.

SOLE PROPRIETORSHIP A business owned and operated by one person—also called a *proprietorship*.

SPAN OF CONTROL A limit on the number of positions one person should supervise directly.

SPECULATION Assumption of above-average risks for which there is anticipation of higher financial returns.

SPECULATIVE RISK A situation in which there is the possibility of either a loss or a gain.

STANDARD OF LIVING People's living level or quality of life—the degree to which their economic needs can be satisfied by family income.

STATE BANK A commercial bank chartered by a state government.

STOCK COMPANY A profit-making corporation organized to sell certain types of insurance.

STOCK DIVIDEND Distribution of company earnings in the form of stock.

STOCK OPTION A privilege given to executives to purchase company stock under certain conditions of price and time.

STOCKHOLDER A person who owns one or more shares of a corporation.

SUBCHAPTER S BUSINESS A single-owner business organized as a corporation but taxed as a proprietorship.

SUBSIDIARY A company that is owned and controlled by another company, which is known as the holding company.

SUBSIDY A government payment or grant to a business enterprise or institution for the good of the public.

SYSTEM An entity made up of two or more independent parts that interact to form a functioning organism.

TARIFF A tax or customs duty levied by a nation on goods imported from other countries.

TIME DRAFT A draft payable at a fixed future date.

TIME UTILITY Availability of a product or service when it is wanted.

TORT A civil (private) wrong. Torts include libel, slander, and fraud.

TRADE ACCEPTANCE A draft drawn by a seller of merchandise, ordering the buyer to pay the amount of the purchase by a fixed date.

TRADE DISCOUNT A means of adjusting catalog prices to reflect the cost of a service rendered.

TRADEMARK A distinctive symbol, title, or design that readily identifies a company or its product.

TRANSFER A job shift at the same level of employment, without changing the degree of responsibility or rate of pay.

UNION SHOP   A shop in which union membership is required of all employees.

VENTURE CAPITAL   Risk money invested in young businesses that have good growth potential.

WAREHOUSE RECEIPT   A document used as evidence of the deposit of goods in a warehouse and of a contract for storage.

WARRANTY   An express or implied promise made by the seller about goods to induce the buyer to purchase them.

WARRANTY DEED   A written instrument that warrants title to real property without defects.

WHOLESALER   A middleman who buys goods for resale, primarily to other businesses.

WORD PROCESSING   The transformation of words into printed text using computerized hardware and software.

WORK GROUP   A collection of employees who share a common job and view themselves as a group.

WORKING CAPITAL   The excess of current assets over current debts. It is a measure of a firm's ability to pay its expenses and buy new merchandise.

WORLD BUSINESS   Business transactions between citizens, companies, and governments conducted on an international scale.

Index